CAN AMERICA COMPETE?

CAN AMERICA COMPETE?

An Editorials On File Book

Editor: Oliver Trager

Facts On File
New York • Oxford

CAN AMERICA COMPETE?

Published by Facts On File, Inc.
© Copyright 1992 by Facts On File, Inc.

Library of Congress Cataloging-in-Publication Data

Can America compete / editor, Oliver Trager
  p. cm. — (An editorials on file book)
  Includes bibliographical references and index.

  ISBN 0-8160-2704-8
  1. United States--Commerce 2. Competition, International I. Trager, Oliver.
II. Series:
Editorials on File book.
HF3021.C28 1991
  382′.0973--dc20

                                             91-374423
                                                 CIP

                                                     AC

Printed in the United States of America

9 8 7 6 5 4 3 2 1

This book is printed on acid-free paper

Contents

Selected Bibliography

Bluestone, Barry & Harrison, Bennett, *The Deindustrialization of America*, Basic Books, Inc., Publishers, 1982.

Howard, Robert, *Brave New Workplace*, Penguin Books, Viking Penguin, Inc., 1985.

Lall, Betty G. (ed.), *Economic Dislocation and Job Loss*, Cornell University Press, 1985.

Reich, Robert, *Tales of a New America*, Vintage Books, 1988.

CAN AMERICA COMPETE?

Preface

For decades the "Made In America" label was synonymous with craftsmanship, ingenuity and excellence. But in recent years the strength of that claim has weakened. **Can America Compete?** focuses on this alarming and thorny topic.

As the United States finds itself in the middle of a recession, many economic issues and the questions they provoke are at the center of national debate. How is the economic rise of the Pacific rim nations threatening the work force in the U.S.? Has productivity in the domestic labor force slackened? What is the state of the U.S. educational system and what do its deficiencies forebode? How do Japan's economic and business philosophies differ from those of the U.S.? Does the American business management model need reform? Should the U.S. have a national industrial strategy like Japan's and how could such a strategy be implemented? Do current anti-trust laws hinder a unification of American industry? Does a quest for short-term profits govern U.S. economic companies at the expense of long-term investment in research and development? Will foreign acquisition of American high-tech companies weaken the U.S. economy? Did the corporate takeover mania of the 1980s drain resources that could have been used to make American industry strong?

In **Can America Compete?** the country's leading newspaper editorial writers and cartoonists examine the complicated controversies over the U.S. economy raging from the nation's factory floors to its board rooms.

November 1991   Oliver Trager

Part I: The U.S. Economy

An alarm sounded in June 1980 when *Business Week* magazine devoted an entire special issue to detailing a comprehensive plan for revitalizing the U.S. economy. In an uncharacteristic tone of dismay, the editors concluded:

"The U.S. economy must undergo a fundamental change if it is to retain a measure of economic vitality let alone leadership in the remaining 20 years of this century. The goal must be nothing less than the reindustrialization of America. A conscious effort to rebuild America's productive capacity is the only real alternative to the precipitous loss of competitiveness of the last 15 years, of which this year's wave of plant closings across across the continent is only the most vivid manifestation."

The average person did not have to read *Business Week* to know that America was in trouble. Since the early 1970s, every day had brought yet another sign of how bad things were becoming.

One thing is certain: the economy has, for all practical purposes, ceased to grow. During the 1960s, overall real U.S. economic growth averaged 4.1% per year. As a result, the nation's gross national product (GNP) expanded by a hefty 50% over the decade. This permitted the average family to enjoy one third more real, disposable income at the end of the decade than at the beginning. People complained about the Vietnam War and persistent inequality, but – with the notable exception of millions of black, brown, and teenaged workers – few among the great middle class could grumble about the rate at which we were becoming, in Galbraith's words, "the affluent society."

The 1970s were different altogether. GNP grew by only 2.9% per year. By 1979 the typical family with a $20,000 annual income had only 7 percent more real purchasing power than it had a full decade earlier. Ten years had brought a mere $25 more per week in purchasing power for the average family. Moreover, every bit of this growth came between 1970 and 1973, before the first OPEC price shock. Since 1973 there has been virtually *no* real income gain. Thus even before the 1980s began, the American standard of living no longer placed us first among the developed nations of the world. In fact, the best the U.S. could do was tenth, not counting the Middle Eastern oil sheikdoms of Kuwait and Abu Dabai. By 1980 Switzerland, Sweden, Denmark, West Germany, Luxembourg, Iceland, France, the Netherlands and Belgium had all surpassed the U.S. in per capita GNP.

That the average Swiss or Danish family enjoys a higher standard of living than that of the average American family is disturbing to a generation raised on the unchallenged perception of America as Number One. But the U.S. standard of living does not need to be compared to that of the Swiss or the Danish to recognize the depth of the economic crisis.

Adding to the economic despair is America's apparent difficulty competing in the global marketplace. The U.S. share of the world's manufactured exports has fallen from more than 25% to less than 17% in the last 30 years, and relative to the U.S.'s strongest competitors, it could be easily argued that the U.S. is being rapidly pushed to the sidelines. It is disturbing for many American to learn, for example, that the 1990 trade deficit with Japan reached over $50 billion, up more than $40 billion from 1980. Even more shocking is a listing of the two countries' major exports. In terms of dollar value, the number one Japanese product sold to America was passenger motor vehicles, followed by iron and steel plates, truck and tractor chassis, radios, motorbikes, and audio and VCRs. In contrast, America's top seven exports to Japan, in order of dollar value, were soybeans, corn, fir logs, hemlock logs, coal, wheat, and cotton. The trade deficit hides the fact that, at least with respect to our most important competitor, the U.S. has been reduced to an agricultural nation trying desperately to compete with the manufacturer of the world's most sophisticated capital and consumer goods.

Critics of the way in which the U.S. economy is managed contend that underlying the high rates of unemployment and underemployment, the sluggish growth in the domestic economy, and the failure to successfully compete in the international market is the *deindustrialization* of America. By deindustrialization, economists mean a widespread, systematic disinvestment in the nation's basic productive capacity. Controversial as it may be, these critics suggest that the essential problem with the U.S. economy can be traced to the way capital – financial resources and real plant and equipment – has been diverted from investment in the production of actual goods into unproductive speculation, mergers and acquisitions and foreign investment. Left behind are shuttered factories, displaced workers, and a newly emerging group of ghost towns.

The traces of widespread disinvestment show up in aging capital stock at home and in the diversion of investment resources to U.S. corporate subsidies operating abroad. During the 1970s, for example, General Electric expanded its worldwide payroll by 5,000 – cutting its domestic payrolls by 25,000 and adding 30,000 foreign jobs. RCA Corporation followed the same strategy, cutting its U.S. employment by 14,000 and increasing its foreign world force by 19,000.

The movement of capital can take many forms ranging from the virtually invisible to the drastic and dramatic. The most subtle policy consists of the redirection of profits generated from a particular plant's operations without management tampering with the establishment itself. For example, the managers of a multibranch corporation may decide to reallocate profits earned from a particular plant's operations to new facilities or for new product development. Another method of shifting capital involves physically relocating some of the equipment from one facility to another, or selling off some of the establishment's capital to specialized subcontractors. Finally, management can move capital by completely shutting down a plant. It can sell as many of the old facilities assets as possible – sometimes even going so far as loading the machinery onto flatcars or moving vans and setting up the same operation in a location with cheaper labor. This last option earned the epithet "runaway shop" in the 1930s, and again in the 1950s, when industries such as shoes, textiles, and apparel left New England for the lower-wage, non-Unionized South.

The debates that have raged over economic issues since the 1930s are still with us today. Central to the argument are two burning questions: How do we build a stable, humane, equitable community and still have economic growth? And how can we go about the business of constructing a productive economy which produces livlihoods without destroying lives?

Congress Passes Trade Bill

Disregarding a veto threat by President Ronald Reagan, the U.S. House of Representatives April 21, 1988 overwhelmingly passed comprehensive trade legislation aimed at forcing the U.S. to take tougher action to open foreign trade markets and retaliate against unfair trade practices. The bill was then sent to the Senate.

The House cleared the trade bill by a vote of 312 to 107. The three-to-one margin was 24 votes over the two-thirds majority that would be needed to override a veto. President Reagan had repeatedly threatened to veto the legislation. His most recent veto, April 19, was over the bill's inclusion of a provision requiring that workers be given 60 days' advance notice of plant closings or layoffs.

The 1,000-page bill was the most inclusive trade legislation since the Trade Act of 1974. It had gone to the House April 20, after House and Senate conferees had reconciled trade bills passed by the Senate in July 1987 and by the House in April 1987. The conferees had finished their work on the bill by agreeing to drop a provision sponsored by Rep. John D. Bryant (D, Texas) that would have required disclosure by foreign companies of significant direct investments in the U.S.

Only two Democrats, Rep. Richard Gephardt (Mo.) and Rep. Robert Mrazek (N.Y.), voted against the bill. Gephardt had been the sponsor of a provision that would have mandated retaliation against nations running chronic trade surpluses with the U.S., and he had made tough trade policies a keystone of his recently-ended presidential campaign. But after the conferees had discarded his sanctions provision, he voted against the bill because he said it was too weak.

Repeating his veto threat after the House vote, President Reagan said, "If the trade bill comes to me as it is, I will veto it because they've loaded on so many items...If I have to veto it, I'll call on Congress to adopt a trade bill similar to this one without those things that have been added on."

Although singled out by the president, the plant closing measure was only one of several measures included in the bill that displeased the White House. The Reagan administration also had opposed provisions that expanded special assistance to workers displaced because of imports had created a $1 billion retraining program for those workers; sanctions against Toshiba Corp. of Japan, whose Toshiba Machine Co. subsidiary had sold strategic equipment to the Soviet Union, and mandatory retaliation against foreign countries with demonstrably "numerous and pervasive" unfair trade practices unless such nations' "unjustifiable" or "unreasonable" trade barriers were eliminated.

Other measures included in the trade bill would:

■ Allow some protection for companies in industries seriously injured by imports, provided that such companies were willing to make "positive adjustment" to foreign competition.

■ Clarify the Foreign Corrupt Practices Act to specify what kind of knowledge would make U.S. corporate officers liable if their foreign employees or agents were involved in bribery of foreign officials.

■ Repeal the windfall profits tax on oil.

■ Bar foreign firms from serving as primary dealers in U.S. government securities unless U.S. securities firms were granted equivalent status in their nations.

The U.S. Senate April 27 passed comprehensive trade legislation aimed at opening up foreign markets and expanding U.S. trade. But the 63-36 vote left its supporters short of the two-thirds majority that would be needed to override a threatened presidential veto. The vote was seen as a victory for President Reagan, who had said repeatedly that he would veto the bill. The bill would now go to the president, who would have to frame a veto message within 10 days spelling out his objections to the bill.

The Grand Rapids Press
Grand Rapids, Michigan, April 27, 1988

President Reagan's opposition to a plant-closing provision in the omnibus trade bill is unfortunate because it makes the rest of the legislation look harmless. It isn't.

The bill deserves the presidential spike. It is too big, too protectionist, too heavy with special-interest favors and intrudes too much on executive authority.

Of those, the last is the worst. An amendment sponsored by Sen. Donald Riegle, D-Mich., straps the president into a mandatory retaliation against countries perceived to have committed "unjustifiable" foreign trade practices. Another provision mandates sanctions against foreign exporters who violate certain of their own government's trade agreements. These measures are cousins to the attempt of Rep. Richard Gephardt, D-Mo., to force retaliation against nations which enjoy a trade surplus at our expense. The common error is that they strap the president into an inflexible trading policy; the government would have to retaliate in a specified amount and in certain ways. The president would lose important powers of discretion and control, becoming less able to maneuver and use diplomacy in working out differences.

Several times within the past year, President Reagan has shown what can be done with existing trade powers and with freedom of movement. In both the Common Market and in Japan he has opened markets to U.S. goods. He should have applied his options sooner, however tardiness is not an excuse for taking them away.

Another section of the bill transfers from the president to the U.S. trade representative the power to investigate foreign trade practices and to take retaliatory action. The provision dilutes presidential authority and, because appointment of the trade representative is subject to Senate confirmation, creates an opening for legislative intrusion into the executive domain.

The bill, moreover, is a monster — running more than 1,000 pages and containing a diverse bundle of special-interest goods, in much the same manner as the massive omnibus budget bill passed by Congress last December. As an example, oil could not be transported from Alaska to Canada without first passing through one of the lower 48 states — this a concession to the maritime industry. Many of these special gifts will take weeks to unearth. House members decided not to wait even for the bill in final form: They passed it last week on the basis of a synopsis. Among those voting in favor were Reps. Paul Henry, R-Grand Rapids Township; Fred Upton, R-St. Joseph; and Robert Davis, R-Gaylord. Reps. Guy Vander Jagt, R-Luther, and William Schuette, R-Sanford, were opposed.

Mr. Reagan has made opposition to the bill more difficult by focusing attention on the provision requiring employers to give 60-days notice of plant closings or large-scale layoffs. Such notice is not unreasonable and not uncommon in the law or tradition of our trading partners. The president is exaggerating the rule's potential for harm to the economy.

He should be pointing at the protectionist delusions which are at the core of the bill, and at the election-year grandstanding which is behind the congressional majorities for it. The country's trade problems will be best addressed with improvements in manufacturing efficiency and product quality — and with case-by-case sanctions applied by an unfettered executive. This trade bill won't accomplish any of those things.

The Atlanta Journal
AND
THE ATLANTA CONSTITUTION
Atlanta, Georgia, April 26, 1988

It is a crying shame that after all the effort that Congress put into making drastic improvements in the omnibus trade bill, it probably will send it to the president's desk in a form he just can't accept.

So many snake-oil cures were shelved: The Gephardt amendment providing automatic trade reprisals, the Bryant foreign-investment reporting requirement, Band-Aids for this and that industry. But one crucial objectionable provision remains: the mandatory 60-day notice for plant closings for employers of 100 or more workers.

Granted, shifting fortunes of businesses often have left employees stranded and vulnerable. But the practicability of mandating compassion in this way is doubtful. Notices such as these often lead to the drying-up of last-minute loans and the flight of the most marketable skilled workers, virtually ensuring the demise of the affected enterprise.

The experience overseas with comparable laws has been discouraging. It is worrisome that European countries with closing-notice legislation are among the continent's most sluggish economically. The law in France is applicable to companies of 50 workers or more; France now has all too many 49-employee firms, a telling sign of how the law brakes expansion and inspires inefficiency.

The Democrats have picked a bum issue over which to go to the mat with the presi-dent, but he himself has earned part of the blame for not having made his veto intent clearer in the pre-vote haggling.

Now he seems to relish the prospect of a veto, giving his best swaggering, make-my-day impression. Meantime, Senate Majority Leader Robert Byrd (D-W.Va.) is replying in kind, threatening to take the historic Canadian free-trade treaty hostage.

This is no time for childish posturing.

Three options remain to save all or part of the bill, admittedly none of them likely.

• The Senate can send the bill back to conference for removal of the 60-day notice.

• The president can examine the provision for hooks and, possibly, swallow it. After all, one lawmaker, Rep. Augustus Hawkins (D-Calif.) says it has been so revised and watered down it's nearly meaningless.

• If a presidential veto is sustained, the Congress could, at a minimum, vote legislation renewing negotiating authority, now about to expire, on the office of the president for ongoing and vital trade talks, especially the Uruguay round of the General Agreement on Trade and Tariffs.

These are like unto grasping at straws, but any one of them would be an improvement over the backbiting and jockeying for political advantage prevalent on the trade issue now.

Los Angeles Times
Los Angeles, California, April 27, 1988

Congress is about to send a battering ram overseas to do work that Americans once reserved for clipper captains and sharp-trading merchants.

Even if Congress changes its mind about the battering ram—as it should—it still could do great damage to the agreement between the United States and Canada that shows the world how free trade can and should work.

By daring President Reagan to veto the omnibus trade bill and its 1,000 pages of big and little print, Congress may push the calendar to a point where it cannot ratify the U.S.-Canada trade bill. That would be a tragedy perhaps exceeding passage of the omnibus bill itself.

Some parts of the omnibus trade bill now before the Senate have real merit—a program to retrain workers who through no fault of their own lose jobs to foreign competition; a clause that requires companies to give at least 60 days' notice of closing, and presidential authority to negotiate new international trade terms. It is a shame to urge that they be sacrificed.

What is most often written about the bill also is true: It is less protectionist than it was before some of the worst ideas of Rep. Richard Gephardt (D-Mo.) were taken out.

But it still sends wrong signals everywhere—to industrial nations abroad, to industries at home and to American workers who politicians hope will not examine the so-called jobs-protection bill closely enough to see that over the years it will have an opposite effect.

The same goes for manufacturers. The smart ones know that the measure will hurt more than it helps to the extent that it interferes with free and competitive trade. But the smart ones are not the problem for the U.S. trade balance. The rest may get the idea that it is still possible to bully other industrial nations into making America competitive again when in fact the only way to reach that goal is to compete.

For example, presidential authority to use the battering ram against nations that close markets to U.S. products has been watered down, but it remains bad news. Instead of restricting retaliation to specific product lines, everything a competing nation manufactures could be shut out.

A section that increases agricultural subsidies goes directly in the wrong direction for world agriculture.

But the main problem is not the flawed sections of the bill in themselves, it is the emphasis that Congress puts on punishment, as though the United States were in a better position to call the shots on trade than any other industrial nation these days. This country is still very powerful, but it shares that power, particularly in economics, as it has not been forced to do since World War II.

To succeed in international commerce, America must compete with other nations and negotiate rules and regulations that make competition possible. It is not a situation that the United States can change with a law, and it should not even try.

The Oregonian
Portland, Oregon, April 24, 1988

The 1,000-page trade bill is a pudding, three years in the making, that neither the president nor the nation should swallow without a very careful taste test.

Rather, we should learn from the omnibus tax reform bill and the omnibus budget reconciliation act that this latest omnibus legislation, too, is larded with unsavory special-interest provisions.

Many provisions have not been examined. For example, the House debate concentrated on whether workers should be given 60 days' notification before a company closes a manufacturing plant. This question has only the loosest connection to foreign trade and hardly should have shaped debate on this bill.

The real questions are whether the United States needs 1,000 pages of change in its trade policies and, if so, whether this collection comprises the changes that are needed.

When you set aside all the weeping, partisan patter and foreign-devil-seeking, no persuasive case emerges that the U.S. trade deficit requires massive changes in the laws relating to imports and exports. Adjustments, yes; all this, no.

Further, there is no evidence that this bill would make the trade situation better or freer, or that its benefits would flow to the victim of unjust foreign practices rather than to the victim of self-inflicted wounds.

Descriptions of the bill are far from reassuring. Northwest congressmen's pride at having gained special-interest measures to benefit this region presumably is matched by equal smugness around the country — all likely victimizing the U.S. treasury through suspect subsidies.

One piece of trade legislation is truly needed. It is the authority for the president to negotiate changes in the General Agreement on Tariffs and Trade. Beyond that, why tinker with a system that already allows prudent U.S. responses to truly unfair foreign practices?

The doubts that this measure would do more good than harm should put the trade-dependent Pacific Northwest on the side of a presidential veto sustained by Congress. That might spur production of a restrained measure that finally focuses on the real obstacles to free trade rather than catering to the interests seeking to turn the trade issue to their own advantage.

TULSA WORLD
Tulsa, Oklahoma, April 25, 1988

THE legislation overhauling America's trade laws, which was overwhelmingly approved in the House last week and is expected to be approved by the Senate Tuesday, is not perfect.

It contains, however, enough desirable provisions that it should become law. President Reagan should reconsider his announced intention to veto the measure.

Reagan opposes a provision that would require most employers to give 60-day notice of plant closings and large-scale layoffs. Certainly that is objectionable.

But the provision of crucial importance to Oklahoma is one to repeal the windfall profits tax on oil producers.

The windfall profits tax is a major disincentive to domestic oil production. It diverts millions of dollars that otherwise would be invested in exploration and new drilling. It has hurt Oklahoma's economy and also has contributed to the dangerously increasing U.S. reliance on foreign oil.

Except for a brief time last year, the tax hasn't been collected since the oil bust sent prices below the amount at which the tax is triggered. However, the oil industry by one estimate spends $100 million per year just to complete the required paperwork — on a tax that it isn't paying!

Oil state lawmakers have faced an uphill fight to repeal the misguided tax. Industry observers believe the current trade bill is the best — and possibly, only — chance to do it.

Oklahoma's House delegation voted unanimously in favor of the trade bill last week, including the two Republicans who normally would be expected to follow the president's lead.

Sens. David Boren and Don Nickles likewise should put aside their understandable objections to certain provisions and vote with the majority for the measure. And President Reagan should sign it.

The Des Moines Register
Des Moines, Iowa, April 26, 1988

Congress all along has had the ability to cope with the trade deficit. Mainly, coping would require getting the nation's fiscal affairs in order, halting the massive federal borrowing.

But that's too tough. Congress can't bring itself to perform its most basic duties adequately, so instead it postures and pretends it can do something about the trade deficit by passing a trade bill.

At least it's *called* a trade bill, but it's really a Christmas tree. It's one of those massive bills that everyone tries to attach his pet project to. The focus of disagreement between the president and Congress — a requirement that workers be given notice of plant closings — is one example. It would be a lobbying goal of labor with or without a trade bill to attach it to.

Hardly anyone knows everything that is in the 1,000-page bill, but there are scores of provisions tailored for individual industries and companies. The label on the package is trade, but the contents look suspiciously like pork.

That's why it's bound to pass. Even if President Reagan vetoes the current version over the plant-closing provision, the bill will eventually pass in some form. Congress has too much invested — nearly three years and the work of two dozen committees — to let it go for naught. Besides, the bill gives members a chance to assert that they addressed the trade problem, even if they didn't.

Will the bill make a difference on trade? Not much. It would expand the president's power to retaliate for "unfair" foreign trade practices, but the president already has wide latitude on trade, and that wouldn't change much. It would transfer some authority from the president to the U.S. trade representative, but the trade representative is an appointee who serves at the will of the president anyway.

There are some needed provisions, such as the relaxation of export controls that have hampered U.S. firms' ability to sell abroad. There is more assistance for workers displaced by foreign competition. It is perceived as a "tough" trade bill, which may be of some help in trade negotiations.

But the bill is hardly the epic turnaround in U.S. trade policy that its backers claim it to be. It is neither awfully bad nor especially praiseworthy. It is merely something Congress, in its inimitable fashion, has done. If the U.S. trade picture improves, it won't be because of this bill.

...SOME IDIOT IN A FOREIGN CAR!

TRADE BILL

The Honolulu Advertiser

Honolulu, Hawaii, April 23, 1988

Mixed emotions are certainly in order over the trade bill passed overwhelmingly in the House Thursday and expected to get less-enthusiastic approval in the Senate Tuesday.

But President Reagan is threatening to veto it on the wrong grounds. He is centering his objections on a relatively minor provision which would require profit-making employers to give 60-day notice of plant closings or large-scale layoffs.

That requirement would be common decency as practiced in other countries. It would hardly be some kind of blow to America's ability to compete in the world, as Reagan claims.

Still, the debate over plant-closing notice strongly favored by labor does show how the 1,000-page bill is not only a major compromise effort but also something of a grab bag of provisions for various interests.

It is much less protectionist than earlier versions. The Gephardt amendment, for example, is gone in favor of measures aimed more at dumping and export surges of foreign products. U.S. officials would get more flexibility.

As the major target, the Japanese are voicing strong objections, as they would against any such measure. There is something to be said for their argument that too many Americans want to blame Japan for our own economic shortcomings and inability to compete in the world.

But Japan has brought much on itself. A Western diplomat in Tokyo was right when he said: "Is it any wonder Washington passed a trade bill? The Japanese won't budge unless they are pushed and pushed hard."

Whether a Reagan veto could be overridden in the Senate is an open question. The issue could die in a stalemate over the plant closing provision.

But this is an election year, and, wisely or not, voter sentiment favors action on trade tougher than what this bill proposes. So the odds seem to be for a bill, warts and all.

FORT WORTH STAR-TELEGRAM

Fort Worth, Texas, April 26, 1988

After three years of rancorous debate, Congress has fashioned a trade bill that deals responsibly with issues that make the United States' foreign trade position worse than it needs to be.

Now that the bill is free of its most protectionist provisions, such as the Gephardt amendment, the Senate should add its approval to that already given by the House.

President Reagan should resist the temptation to veto the bill, but if he does, Congress should validate its three-year investment of time and effort by overriding his veto.

The opposition of the president and some business organizations is focused on one provision of the trade bill: one that requires large businesses employing more than 100 full-time workers to give employees 60 days' notice of plant closings or large layoffs.

This seems only fair. Combined with the trade bill's provisions extending Trade Adjustment Assistance benefits, such as retraining for workers who have lost jobs to foreign competition, it is a reasonable protection for U.S. workers and their families, too many of whom have suffered from sudden job dislocation in recent years and who lack the "golden parachute" cushion enjoyed by top executives.

The White House and business interests say that the plant-closing notification provision would cause businesses to reduce their hiring and would drive otherwise salvageable enterprises out of business. These are highly conjectural objections. Business enterprises should not be started or expanded — the factors leading to job creation — with the idea that the next step is to close the plant or lay off workers. U.S. businessmen surely have more confidence than that.

In any event, a veto based on the plant-closing provision would be a short-sighted, ill-advised and unjustified overreaction by the president.

The main objective of the trade bill is to strengthen existing free-trade requirements. Its only retaliatory measures — to be employed where fair-trade practices are violated by our trading partners — contain language that protects U.S. national security concerns. The bill relaxes some domestic restrictions on U.S. exports, seeks to bolster agricultural exports and to put U.S. manufacturers in a more competitive posture, forces a harder look at foreign acquisition of American firms and repeals the windfall profits tax on the oil industry.

It is a compromise in many ways. But, shorn of protectionism, it is a reasonable fair-trade approach to our trade problems. Even its opponents admit that. Despite the plant-closing provision, the bill attracted 68 Republican votes in the House and the support of key Republicans in the Senate.

Senators should join their counterparts in the House and pass the bill, and President Reagan should stifle his ideological predisposition to veto it.

The Star-Ledger

Newark, New Jersey, April 26, 1988

The foreign trade bill that has cleared the House and will probably pass the Senate is a far different proposal from the controversial one that congressional leaders agonized over for the past year. In most respects, it is a reasonable document that meets a real need and which a broad-based coalition can rally behind.

Gone is the invidious protectionist Gephardt amendment, which President Reagan claimed would trigger a worldwide trade war that could lead to a global recession. Good riddance to that flawed creation, which would have forced the President to take stern reprisals against trading partners on the flimsiest of provocations.

In its place is a proposal that gives the President powers that he may or may not choose to use. The President has some power now to retaliate when unreasonable trade barriers are erected to keep out American products. The legislation would expand these powers in order to give the chief executive a freer hand.

The measure would repeal the so-called "windfall profits tax" upon the nation's oil producers. This tax was enacted at the time of the energy shortage of the 1970s. It makes no sense today when energy is plentiful and oil-producing areas are experiencing a devastating recession. In most respects, it is a free trade measure that has strong support from American business.

The bill, nevertheless, faces a possible veto from President Reagan because of one provision, a requirement that all but the smallest employers must give 60 days' notice when they close a plant or make substantial layoffs. Mr. Reagan has a point here. Industry needs a free hand to operate efficiently. Notification requirements could prove detrimental to some businesses, particularly when they reach a state in which substantial losses would be sustained during that 60-day period.

The House passed the bill by a 3-1 margin, ignoring the threat of a Reagan veto. The question comes down now to whether there is sufficient support in the Senate to sustain the President's veto. It ought not to come to that. America needs legislation to protect its interests at a time when it is threatened by a persistently large trade deficit. The plant closing requirement in the bill is more reasonable than some earlier proposals, which called for notification six months before plant closings.

Moreover, in an election year, if this bill is vetoed, there is no guarantee that a more acceptable substitute would be found. It thus behooves Mr. Reagan to think twice about using his veto power. On balance, the bill Congress is about to put on his desk will provide a net benefit to the nation.

Senate Passes Revised Trade Bill

The U.S. Senate Aug. 3, 1988 overwhelmingly passed a revised version of comprehensive trade legislation aimed at opening up foreign markets and expanding U.S. trade. The Senate voted 85-11 to pass the revised measure, with 50 Democrats and 35 Republicans voting for the bill. The Senate vote came one month after the House of Representatives had cleared the bill by a vote of 376 to 45.

The revised 1,000-page bill – the most inclusive trade legislation since the trade act of 1974 – was in nearly every aspect identical to its vetoed predecessor. It differed only in discarding two provisions singled out as objectionable by President Reagan in his initial veto of the bill. The discarded provision most objectionable to President Reagan would have required that workers be given 60 days advance notice of plant closings and layoffs. The other provision discarded would have restricted exports of Alaska oil.

Driven by election-year politics, both Republicans and Democrats supported the revised trade legislation. Earlier in the week, Reagan also decided not to veto the plant-closing bill, which had been introduced as a separate measure and cleared by both houses of Congress.

Senate Finance Committee Chairman Lloyd Bentsen (Texas), the Democratic vice presidential candidate and a chief architect of the bill, called its passage "a great victory for the resolution of economic leadership in the United States" that would "open up foreign markets to U.S. products" and "lead the United States into a new era of economic greatness."

Bentsen claimed that lobbyists for foreign governments had spent over $100 million in their attempt to block the legislation. Sen. John C. Danforth (Mo.), one of the principal Republican authors, said the bill constituted "a very real change in U.S. trade policy."

Foreign reaction to the Senate passage of the bill was critical, as governments in Europe and Asia feared that the measure could encourage unilateral U.S. action, including sanctions, to resolve trade disputes.

THE ⬛ SUN

Baltimore, Maryland, August 5, 1988

The omnibus trade bill passed by Congress portends more active, aggressive and unilateralist action by the United States to improve its competitive position in dealing with other countries. Philosophically, the measure represents a step away from the multinational approach promoted by the United States since the end of World War II. But not entirely. Due to Herculean efforts by ardent free traders, mandatory protectionist features that could have triggered trade wars have been stripped away. The bill's main thrust is to force open foreign markets by threat of sanctions rather than close U.S. markets to foreign goods. The next president will retain the powers he needs to implement trade policy in accordance with national rather than narrow interests.

Fortunately for this country (and the world), both George Bush and Michael Dukakis have adopted fairly sensible positions on trade issues. This was easy for the vice president because of Mr. Reagan's *laissez faire* instincts. It was more difficult for Governor Dukakis, who clashed during the early primary season with the most protectionist contender, Rep. Richard Gephardt.

The good news is that trade is largely off the table as a fiercely partisan issue. The bad news is that its popularity with big labor and big business, as well as with both political parties, did not come without a price. As election-year legislation that gradually took on motherhood status, the 1,000-page trade bill emerged loaded with extraneous little payoffs to various economic constituencies. Whether their sum total will be as negative as our trading partners suspect is something the next president can still prevent.

Japan, Korea, and the European Community, which do not come into the arena with clean hands, are objecting to provisions that would have the United States take unilateral actions on matters that are supposedly governed by multinational institutions, especially the General Agreement on Tariffs and Trade. But Mr. Reagan's successor can clear the air on this matter if he uses increased negotiating powers to promote more liberal trading practices during the GATT Uruguay Round, which still has two years to run. While private U.S. industries will find it easier to obtain redress when foreign countries block access to their markets or dump subsidized goods here, the president will have the tools to prevent this from becoming a protectionist avalanche.

In the end, this massive legislation should be judged not only for its effectiveness in reducing U.S. trade deficits but for its effect on world trade. As the world's greatest maritime nation, the United States has to take the lead in maintaining a healthy global economy. The next president needs to elevate trade policy to the status it deserves, but more than that he needs to do so with wisdom and responsibility.

The Register

Santa Ana, California, August 3, 1988

Edward Kennedy keeps asking, "Where was George Bush?" He might as well ask, "Where is Ronald Reagan?" This week, once again, Reagan has sidestepped a fight, this time refusing to veto — or sign, or burn, or feed to the First Dog — the latest version of the plant-closing bill, a version of which he vetoed earlier this year. Reagan's decision means this odious bill will become law, automatically.

Presidential spokesman Marlin Fitzwater cited politics as the reason. Had Reagan vetoed the bill again, it would have created problems for Republican candidates this November, most particularly for Vice President George Bush, running to succeed Reagan. Or so thought top Republicans in Congress and the White House wizards who now run the Reagan administration.

As Senate Majority Leader Bob Dole put it, Reagan is "swallowing something that he doesn't totally like in order to get us off the dime" on another bill, the new trade legislation (itself so bad it should be vetoed). Dole, of course, may be tapped by Bush to run for the vice presidential spot on the Republican national ticket. His wife, former Transportation Secretary Elizabeth Dole, is also talked about for the post.

But this is dumb politics, plain and simple. You don't run on the other side's issues, but create issues of your own. Democrats already are gloating over their victory on the plant-closing bill. Edward Kennedy called Reagan's inaction "a victory for communities across the country, a victory for America's competitive position in the world, and a victory for common sense in the federal budget," blah, blah, blah. It will be easy for Michael Dukakis and Lloyd Bentsen, heading the Democratic ticket, to echo that theme.

A smarter Reagan and Republican strategy would have been to veto the bill, fight a tough battle (again) to sustain the veto in Congress, then have Bush and the other candidates campaign on the wisdom of such a decision. After all, it's not hard to prove that the plant-closing bill will cost American jobs, hurt the very workers it allegedly helps, and destroy America's ability to compete in the fierce world economy.

The plant-closing bill will force any company employing 100 or more workers to give them 60 days' notice before closing a plant or laying off 50 or more workers. This will add production costs to struggling companies that might survive without those costs. Sometimes a company must close a few plants immediately, or risk losing other, more profitable, plants as well, costing even more layoffs.

Given such prospects, many American companies will just build plants overseas. Companies that stick it out in an increasingly anti-business American environment will not be able to close plants quickly; this will add to these companies' overall cost of production. Which in turn will give foreign competitors an edge in price, taking sales from American companies; and that, in the end, means yet more layoffs and plant closings.

Reagan, Bush, and other Republicans should explain this reality to American voters, and contrast it with this new Democratic assault on American jobs. But the Republicans, like Reagan, won't join the fight. Will anyone be surprised if American voters give Democrats the decision in this fall's prize fight, if only because Democrats are the only politicians who showed up in the ring?

Pittsburgh Post-Gazette
Pittsburgh, Pennsylvania, August 5, 1988

The trade bill passed by the Senate and sent to President Reagan for his signature is more notable, on its second passage at least, for what it doesn't contain. Missing from the legislation is a controversial requirement for advance notice of plant closings, a provision that proved to be "veto bait" the first time the trade bill arrived on the president's desk.

Earlier this week, Congress disposed of the plant-closing issue in separate legislation. This time Mr. Reagan declined to veto the measure, allowing it to become law without his signature. That failure to take a stand on an issue that the president judged so critical in the spring thus raised some new and interesting questions.

Are President Reagan's objections to plant-closing legislation stronger than his desire for new trade legislation? Or is his support for change in U.S. trade law more powerful than his belief that a 60-day notification of a plant closing will harm the economy? Over the course of this debate, "yes" has been the correct answer to both questions.

Mr. Reagan's inability to come down decisively on the issue has ended up making him look rather silly. Yet that may be a small price to pay for a goal that this maneuvering has been intended to advance — the election of George Bush as president. The problem, however, is that Mr. Reagan's see-sawing has made the vice president look a little silly, too.

Both men said all too clearly that they didn't like the plant-closing legislation because they thought it was bad for the economy.

Their fears might have been justified by earlier versions of the bill that failed to take into account circumstances in which a required plant-closing announcement could stymie genuine efforts to save the facility in question.

However, the legislation had been steadily improved to the point that it commanded broad support for the reasonable proposition that workers and their families should be given a decent opportunity to prepare for the loss of their livelihood.

Messrs Reagan and Bush didn't keep abreast of the changes in the bill. They did pay attention, however, to the shift of public opinion against them on this issue — and on the threat that posed to Mr. Bush's candidacy.

So the administration's position has evolved to the view that while the legislation still seems to the president to be dangerous, this is no time to offend its supporters — or create an issue for Michael Dukakis.

THE PLAIN DEALER
Cleveland, Ohio, August 6, 1988

After four years of wrangling, Congress has approved a tolerable, if flawed, measure on international trade. When the president signs the watered-down bill into law, it will neither cause irreparable harm to the economy nor provide a quick fix for America's enduring trade problems. But if political pressures made some legislation inevitable, at least this bill isn't as bad as it could have been.

Born of protectionist impulse and anti-foreign prejudice when the U.S. trade deficit was soaring, original versions of the trade measure might have erected the type of import barriers that deepened the Great Depression of the 1930s. In its most noxious form, a proposal by Rep. Richard Gephardt of Missouri—hammered home in the Japan-bashing commercials of his presidential campaign—threatened to start a Democratic stampede to trample fair trade rules.

During the debate, the economy shifted faster than protectionists could keep up with it. The fall in the value of the dollar led to a dramatic increase in U.S. exports, reducing the trade deficit. A series of presidential edicts—limiting Japanese microchips, Canadian lumber and European food products—showed that the United States was not being played for a sucker. As the trade gap narrowed, protectionist arguments weakened, letting free-trade logic sink in.

The final version of the bill—approved 376-45 in the House and 85-11 in the Senate—is imperfect, but many of its objectionable ideas have been softened. In its central provision, Congress has ordered the president to use new powers to retaliate against countries that exclude American products. But there are loopholes that allow a president to avoid retaliation, and only a reckless administration would use its new powers to start a trade war. In any case, Japan and West Germany could appeal any unilateral U.S. move to the General Agreement on Tariffs and Trade, the world's central trade forum.

Parts of the bill expand existing programs, like job retraining for workers in industries hurt by foreign competition. Other provisions call for export enhancement, seeking new markets for U.S. goods. A sensible idea promoted by Rep. Donald J. Pease of Oberlin, who serves on the House Ways and Means subcommittee on trade, directs the Treasury to spell out the federal budget's impact on capital flows and exchange-rate fluctuations. That puts the emphasis where it belongs: American firms' ability to compete has been crippled by the gyrating value of the dollar, due in large part to the Reagan era's mammoth budget deficits.

Inevitably, special-interest favors slipped into the bill: more overseas promotion of U.S. farm goods, repeal of the windfall-profits tax on oil, and special coverage for fur traders, pharmaceutical makers and telecommunications firms. Congress should have shown more self-restraint, but none of the giveaways should doom the bill.

One misguided provision is the weakening of the Foreign Corrupt Practices Act, which has forbidden U.S. firms from giving under-the-table payments to win overseas contracts. In casting the lone Democratic vote in the Senate against the overall bill, Sen. William Proxmire of Wisconsin bravely fought the "bring back bribery" provision, recalling outrages like the Lockheed payoff scandal of the 1970s. Strong anti-bribery statutes should have remained undiluted.

For all its sound and fury, the long debate over the trade bill hasn't produced a great deal; there still is ample reason to believe the broad legislation was not needed at all. Perhaps the exercise was useful if it taught members of Congress that government's chief role in trade policy is to keep the federal budget in reasonable balance, encourage markets to remain open, ease the decline of suffering industries and encourage the training of a versatile work force.

Other corrective action depends on the private sector and its market-based decisions on capital investment, labor productivity and the making and marketing of high-quality goods. Congress may pat itself on the back for tinkering with trade rules, but a stronger economy will be created where it always has been: in America's classrooms, boardrooms, laboratories and factories.

WORCESTER TELEGRAM
Worcester, Massachusetts,
August 8, 1988

Congress has labored for three years to come up with a trade bill that is protectionist enough to please Japan-bashers yet inoffensive enough to a free-trade White House to win President Reagan's signature.

The 1,000-page effort it passed last April ran into a veto. Now Congress has taken out a couple of the provisions Reagan found most distasteful and plunked the bill on his desk again. This time the president has said he'll sign it. He might as well. Any veto would be overridden.

The bill still contains plenty of mischief. It calls for arm-twisting of U.S. trading partners into buying American goods. If a nation refuses, the White House is required to retaliate — or explain to Congress why it isn't doing so.

That seems an unnecessarily negative approach, especially in view of the boom in exports that America is now enjoying. That boom suggests that the Reagan policy of quiet negotiation on tariffs and monetary exchange rates has succeeded. Now is no time for harsh measures that could invite trade wars.

No bill could be as fat as this one, however, and not contain redeeming features. An especially welcome one is the repeal of the so-called "windfall profits" tax on domestic crude oil. This is expected to restore a level playing field to the world oil industry. It may reduce the cost of domestic oil and the need for imports. It is apt to help both the U.S. trade deficit and the depressed Southwest.

This tax was imposed in 1980, when domestic oil prices were decontrolled. Congress thought the American public would not accept decontrol — which ended the shortage of gasoline — without a companion measure that seemed to punish the oil companies. In those days, many people blamed Big Oil for the shortage and for other nations' collusion in jacking up the price of foreign oil.

Ironically, the "windfall profits" tax didn't apply to foreign oil. Nor did it tax any oil company's profits. It just added to the cost of producing American crude, discouraged domestic oil exploration and boosted prices at the pump.

The repeal of this counterproductive tax is a sort of trade-off to the mischievous new trade bill the nation will now be saddled with.

The Kansas City Times
Kansas City, Missouri, August 10, 1988

The massive rewrite of America's basic trade law, shorn of a provision on plant closings, has been passed by the Senate and sent to the president. Some of the bill's most provocative parts have been eliminated and the grossest special-interest giveaways have been deleted. Yet removing a few warts cannot transform a monster; this measure remains one of the most dangerous pieces of legislation to come out of Congress in years.

The Omnibus Trade and Competitiveness Act of 1988 would engineer a fundamental change in our approach to international trade. In the hands of a free-trading administration, its provisions can be sidestepped, but only through determined effort. In the hands of a mediocre president or an administration tied to big business or big labor or both, this would be a mindless instrument that would wreak havoc.

The wide discretion now enjoyed by the president would be replaced by a web of dispute-resolution deadlines and procedures for automatic trade retaliation. Under this bill, retaliation *must* be initiated against any country with an "unjustifiable" trade balance.

A section bearing the Kafkaesque title, "Identification of trade liberalization priorities," orders the administration to single out countries with significant trade barriers, then estimate how much American exports would rise if those barriers were eliminated. This would create an arbitrary standard for judging foreign practices, based on nothing more than a bureaucrat's guess.

Three weeks after submitting these reports, the administration would have to initiate retaliation cases against the offending countries. If the dispute were not settled in six months, Washington would have to impose duties or restrict imports. The price of protection would be paid by consumers faced with higher prices and fewer choices.

Under current law, it is already too easy for U.S. corporations to claim they have been victimized by unfair trade practices. The trade bill would make it even easier. Again, the remedy would be higher tariffs or restrictions on imports. In Congress, "fair trade" means the many must pay to protect the few.

There are escape clauses for many of these rules. But the burden has been shifted to create political pressure in favor of protectionism. One of the most repeated phrases in the bill is "submit a report to Congress"; an administration dedicated to free-flowing commerce will be forced to explain repeatedly why it failed to hit back at whatever nation is considered the villain of the hour.

In the midst of a boom in exports, this bill makes a sad statement — especially since less than 20 percent of the trade deficit is due to overseas commercial barriers. Incredibly, its sponsors deny it is protectionist. It would not directly raise tariffs, they say.

Their argument is disingenuous. By making it easier to bring unfair trade cases and making it harder to avoid retaliation, the result would be the same: Consumers would foot the bill, and the high-handedness of the new procedures would invite retaliation by other countries.

The bill deserves to be vetoed once and for all. But since this version has been enacted without the plant-closings provision to which President Reagan objected, there is a danger he will sign it out of a misguided attempt to aid his party this fall. If he does, he will participate in the diminution of presidential power and threaten future growth in world trade.

THE SAGINAW NEWS
Saginaw, Michigan, August 10, 1988

Amid the sound of boom everywhere, our deaf and all-too-dumb national leaders sometimes act as though the United States economy were crashing.

Eager teen-agers pushed up the July jobless rate a fraction in July. But the real story lay behind the 5.4 percent rate:

The market created 285,000 jobs last month, most of them in retail trade and manufacturing. Factory employment climbed to 19.6 million, 200,000 more than three months ago, and 540,000 more than a year ago. In general, the economy has created an average of more than 300,000 jobs a month over the last year. Are these bad, low-paying jobs? Some perhaps — but in many parts of the country, fast-food type vacancies have gone begging.

So what does Congress do? It passes a plant-closing notification bill, which President Reagan let slip into law without his signature.

The bill will prevent no plant closings, save no jobs and do nothing to help workers who lose their workplace.

At best, a 60-day notification that a factory will close may ease the shock for employees. But at the worst, such a requirement could make employers less willing to take chances with a new product line, an expansion, a new location. If it doesn't work out, the result would be 60 days of enforced losses. Why take the risk in the first place?

What's more, advance notice virtually guarantees that a plant *will* close and its jobs will be lost, because it destroys any chance of rescue. Suppliers and customers alike are certain to disappear. Essential, skilled workers, so much in demand now in many sectors of the economy, will abandon ship without waiting for a bail-out; no one could blame them. In many ways, the notification law actually encourages factories to shut down.

If Michigan Sen. Donald W. Riegle Jr. goes on any more about the virtues of this legislation, he deserves to be called on it during his re-election campaign. If Michael Dukakis keeps defending the bill, he will call into question his ability to dispassionately analyze the economic effects of legislation. Compassion in time of trouble is no substitute for the competence to prevent that trouble in the first place.

The bill did exempt facilities with fewer than 100 employees. And as a practical matter, major firms provide much more than a couple of months' notice. Saginaw, for instance, knew about Nodular for more than a year.

But why, then, with all those exceptions, did support for this proposal gain such popular momentum that, finally, not even Reagan could resist?

Some politicians chose to make it a kind of litmus test of humanity and decency. Never mind whether the bill would do much good for the ordinary worker; never mind that it could do considerable economic harm. (Would a plant with 99 workers ever hire No. 100?) It was a straw-man tactic all the way. But the illusion quickly turned into apparent reality.

Undoubtedly most businesses, given the exemptions, can live with the law. But they must grow in spite of it.

Labor claims to have "won" one, and it matters little that laborers could become the real losers, in terms of risks not taken and jobs not created. Supporters point out that other industrialized nations have similar notification rules. What they failed to mention is that their vote-grubbing has produced a law that could plow under an economic expansion that is the envy of the stagnant rest of the West.

"WELL, YOU **WANTED** ADVANCE NOTIFICATION..."

Rockford Register Star
Rockford, Illinois, August 10, 1988

Washington is agog — it thinks it has produced a great national trade bill.

We don't agree. Neither do some local business leaders actively involved in the day-to-day business of international trade. They range from fearing the bill will hurt to hoping that it won't.

Washington has no such concerns. The trade bill passed the Senate in an 85-11 vote, with Sen. Lloyd Bentsen, the Democratic vice presidential nominee, saying, "What we have seen here is the most important piece of trade legislation in 60 years." President Reagan is excited and immediately promised to sign it.

In Rockford, Ingersoll Milling Machine Co. President Fred Wilson disagrees. He says, "Ingersoll is opposed to it. It is protectionism. It certainly can't help the country as a whole. It cannot work. We ought to get on with our economy."

And Thomas J. DeSeve, senior trade representative here with the U.S. Department of Commerce, said, "I think it is a bad piece of legislation. I think there are too many Band-Aids in it with protectionism written all over them."

For the record, let it be said that this bill is a bad bill. It is not a terrible bill or a disastrous bill. American business and industry will survive, but not as easily.

It is protectionism and invites retaliation against American exports. It is 1,128 pages loaded with special-interest clauses giving pet companies special benefits at the expense of consumers. It repeals the windfall profits tax on oil, to the benefit of Sen. Bentsen's oil-rich friends.

More than anything else, it is government interference in the way American businessmen deal with foreign suppliers and customers. It gives the politicians too much power to meddle.

Norman Estwing, president of Estwing Manufacturing Co. here, says, "We don't think it will hurt us too much. It might help."

But Estwing is a businessman who knows what it takes to be successful. He says the biggest impact has come from the decline in the dollar, which has made American businessmen more competitive in the world market.

That's the key issue. American export business is booming now because it is competitive: not because Congress has produced 1,128 pages of new rules and political interference.

The Houston Post
Houston, Texas, August 14, 1988

The omnibus trade bill passed by Congress with overwhelming bipartisan support isn't perfect. It is too big and contains too many extraneous items. But on balance it has more good points than bad.

The bill, which President Reagan agreed to sign after Congress removed provisions that prompted his initial veto, has a dual thrust: **1)** to toughen U.S. laws against unfair trade practices by other countries, and **2)** to make American industry more competitive.

Most of the measure's blatantly protectionist teeth have been pulled — notably the infamous Gephardt amendment penalizing countries that ran large trade surpluses with us. It still contains such requirements as retaliation against countries engaged in questionable trade practices. But the president can waive these directives.

The bill won't magically cure our $140 billion annual trade deficit, but it embodies a more activist policy on global commerce. As the world's largest debtor nation, we can no longer be casual about exports and imports. A case in point is the windfall profits tax on oil, which the bill repeals. The tax discouraged domestic production, increasing our oil imports and our trade deficit. We're wising up.

Trade Barriers Report Released; OECD Criticizes U.S. Trade Moves

U.S. Trade Representative Carla A. Hills April 28, 1989 released a 214-page annual report on foreign trade barriers to U.S. exports, taking the first step toward retaliation under the so-called Super 301 provision of the 1988 Omnibus Trade Act.

The 1989 National Trade Estimates Report detailed trading barriers in 34 countries and two regional trading groups. It singled out Japan, South Korea, the European Community, Taiwan, Brazil and India for alleged unfair trading practices.

The longest section of the report – 18 pages – focused on Japan, with which the U.S. in 1988 had a trade deficit of $55.4 billion. It listed 34 trade barriers in markets such as telecommunications, supercomputers, semiconductors, construction, agriculture and vehicle parts. The report also charged that "the complexity and rigidity" of the Japanese distribution system reduced access for U.S. exports.

Under Super 301, the U.S. trade representative was instructed to identify "priority practices" that most harmed U.S. exports and "priority countries" with the most extensive trade barriers. The Bush administration by May 30 was required to designate countries with generic or systematic trade barriers for further investigation and negotiations. If protectionist practices were not eliminated within 18 months, U.S. retaliation would follow.

Answering charges that foreign trade barriers were not primarily to blame for persistent U.S. trade deficits, Hills May 1 said, "We know that our $130 billion trade deficit is the product not of any particular trade barrier but rather broader economic factors."

Responding April 29, Japanese Minister of International Trade and Industry Hiroshi Mitsuzuka said the report was based on a "misunderstanding" of Japanese trade policy. He urged the U.S. not to take "unilateral measures" that were inconsistent with the General Agreement on Tariffs and Trade. South Korean Trade Minister Han Seoung Soo May 1 called the charges "incorrect," while a Taiwanese government spokesman complained that it was "unfair to treat [Taiwan] the same as Japan, South Korea and Brazil."

Finance and foreign ministers from the 24 member countries of the Organization for Economic Cooperation and Development June 1 concluded their annual two-day meeting in Paris with a communique indirectly criticizing the U.S. decision to designate Japan, Brazil and India as unfair traders under the Super 301 provision of the 1988 U.S. Omnibus Trade Act.

"Ministers firmly reject the tendency towards unilateralism, bilateralism, sectoralism and managed trade which threatens the multilateral system and undermines the Uruguay Round" of trade liberalization negotiations, the communique said.

The 13-page communique, which was signed by the U.S., followed two days of often sharp criticism of the U.S. move by Japan (the only OECD member-state targeted under the Super 301 provision as an unfair trader) and by the European Community. Both contended that the U.S. decision circumvented the General Agreement on Tariffs and Trade and endangered the multilateral trading system.

U.S. Special Trade Representative Carla A. Hills said U.S. implementation of Super 301 was in accordance with the spirit of the OECD communique because it aimed to strengthen rather than subvert the multilateral trading system.

"If we were a bit smaller nation we could sit back and wait, but we're trying to take a leadership role" in opening markets, she said. Hills added that she would not rule out unilateral U.S. action.

Despite the dispute over U.S. trade policy, and an apparent deadlock over what to do about the rising U.S. dollar, the OECD expressed widespread agreement concerning long-term industrial-country economic policies. It pledged to fight inflationary pressures, called for efforts to reduce the U.S. trade deficit and West German and Japanese trade surpluses and, for the first time, urged greater international environmental cooperation.

The Honolulu Advertiser
Honolulu, Hawaii, May 31, 1989

Has President Bush started a trade war with Japan, Brazil and India under the Super 301 section of the 1988 trade law? It's hoped not, though his actions could still have damaging consequences.

This bad law, passed by congressional Democrats and signed by President Reagan despite his "free trade" rhetoric last election year, abandons quiet negotiation in favor of public accusation and retribution. It imposes a unilateral standard, the U.S. standard, on our trading partners.

There's no denying that our $55-billion-a-year trade deficit with Japan is damaging or that aspects of Japan's economy work against American exports. Still, last year U.S. producers increased sales to Japan by 55 percent.

Nor does the U.S. come to the table with our halo aglow. This country imposes quotas on Japanese cars and steel in a misdirected (and largely wasted) effort to boost our own producers.

U.S. Trade Representative Carla Hills says Super 301 actions against Japan "will not have any dramatic effect on the trade balance." Our problem is the federal deficit, low quality manufactures and unwillingness to adapt to selling abroad.

So it's not surprising that Japan, usually willing to at least talk if not act on trade, says it won't even negotiate under threat of unilateral sanctions, but will challenge the U.S. law before international agencies. Neither can Brazil or India be expected to welcome talks under the stigma of Super 301.

Fortunately for U.S. ties to these three important nations, the Super 301 process has 18 months to run. With any signs of progress, the president may back away from the harshest trade penalties. But the administration, goaded by Congress, is off to a bad start.

THE SUN
Baltimore, Maryland, May 15, 1989

Japan-bashing, a highly developed art form on Capitol Hill, is finding devotees within the Bush administration. What has captured their fancy is the "Super 301" section of the 1988 trade reform act, an election-year creation that reflected popular worry about huge trade deficits. Under Super 301 provisions, Japan may be accused of unfair trading and threatened with retaliation "unless it acts immediately to remedy the practices at issue."

The quoted words are those of Special Trade Representative Carla Hills. She and Commerce Secretary Robert Mosbacher are regarded as administration hardliners with little sympathy for the soft platitudes of the Reagan administration. Mrs. Hills contends she has to uphold the law, which is quite specific in ordering action by the executive branch. Nonetheless, there is sufficient zeal in the Mosbacher-Hills camp to alarm the philosophical free traders in administration ranks.

Michael Boskin, chairman of the president's Council of Economic Advisers, has warned that Japan-bashing and punitive forms of protectionism could cause "worldwide recession" and even "trade wars." His words will be heard in Tokyo, Seoul and Frankfurt, but they may have been aimed at President Bush. By May 30, Mr. Bush has to give Mrs. Hills her marching orders.

New legislation gives Mr. Bush little wiggle room in dealing with Japan's constraints against the import of U.S.-made telecommunication equipment. Motorola, for example, has filed a complaint that Tokyo has failed to live up to an agreement to allow cordless telephone imports on the ostensible grounds that no radio frequencies are available. If Mrs. Hills fails to hit Japan, there will be outrage.

All of this is incompatible with U.S. efforts to place banking, insurance and intellectual property rights (all U.S. powerhouse sectors) under the authority of the General Agreement on Tariffs and Trade, the 144-nation system regulating worldwide commerce. GATT's Uruguay Round of negotiations is at mid-point, with success far from assured. If the U.S. engages in nasty bilateral spats at the very moment it is trying to promote multilateral trade, the GATT talks could be placed at risk.

Such is the classic free-trade argument. But under duress another can be raised — namely, that the best way to preserve the international trading system is to punish the one power, Japan, that has abused its rules more than any other. If Mr. Bush decides to invoke Super 301, sanctions will not go into effect immediately. Japan will have a chance to mend its ways and set an example for other nations, including our own. Only in this way can Super 301 be used not as a protectionist club but as a lever to open world markets.

THE DAILY OKLAHOMAN
Oklahoma City, Oklahoma, May 27, 1989

ACTING under the trade law passed by the last Congress, the Bush administration has placed Japan at the top of a hit list of countries accused of unfair trading practices.

The decision touched off an immediate hostile response from America's second largest trading partner and renewed warnings of a future trade war.

The action was taken to comply with a provision of the 1988 Trade Act known as "Super 301." The act directed the administration to issue a listing of the most flagrant trade barriers against U.S. products.

Japan was cited for its refusal to buy U.S.-made satellites and supercomputers and its barriers on American lumber products.

Two other countries were on the list — Brazil for its import-licensing practices and India for its restrictions on foreign investment — but Japan was singled out as the primary target.

The approving comments from Capitol Hill are not surprising. Democrats pushed hard for a tough trade bill and filled the presidential campaign with soaring rhetoric about the trade deficit. Despite the rejection of their policies last November, President Bush has no choice but to implement "Super 301."

Our allies charge that the unilateral listing of a nation as an unfair trader violates the General Agreement on Tariffs and Trade, the pact that governs world trade.

The president's chief economic adviser, Michael Boskin, said recently that retaliatory measures against U.S. trading partners could lead to a worldwide recession. Time will tell whether his prediction comes true.

Chicago Tribune
Chicago, Illinois, May 24, 1989

Carla Hills, America's chief trade negotiator, is about to wield her crowbar to see if she can pry open foreign markets to expanded trade. By week's end, she must give Congress a list of countries that have erected the stiffest barriers to U.S. products. She wants Japan high on the list, and it should be.

Others in the Bush administration are trying to restrain her, fearing her crowbar may turn into a club. The President's foreign policy advisers, along with Michael Boskin, his economic adviser, and Richard Darman, his budget director, worry that targeting Japan now could weaken an already strained alliance and risk a trade war.

Those are reasonable concerns, particularly when Japan is struggling through a leadership crisis. But the Far East superpower has had many months to keep its name from "going up on the bulletin board," as Hills puts it. The trade bill provision that requires Hills to produce a hit list was passed by Congress last year, and frustrated lawmakers clearly had Japan and its $55 billion trade deficit with America in mind.

Last month Hills released a preliminary list that named Japan, the European Community, South Korea, Taiwan, Brazil and India. Since then, the Western European countries, South Korea and Taiwan have scrambled to narrow their differences with the U.S., and they aren't expected to be cited this week. Hills and Commerce Secretary Robert Mosbacher are still upset with Japan, though, over its refusal to buy American-made satellites and supercomputers.

Japan and the European Community complain that the new trade law sets up America as judge and jury of the world trading system. To her credit, Hills says she will not use the law unilaterally to bully trading partners. But she knows that pressure, especially in the case of Japan, has been an effective tactic. Tough talk and threats have opened Japan to U.S. beef and citrus producers and construction firms.

The law gives Hills three years to negotiate an end to the unfair practices with each offending country. If there is little or no progress, Washington can impose new quotas or tariffs or take other punitive action.

Meantime, it can't hurt to give Japan a whack or two upside the head. That prospect already has Japanese officials hinting at buying more U.S. semiconductors and telecommunications products and a Japanese study group recommending reform of the highly protected rice market. Japan must be on the hit list.

Newsday
New York City, New York, May 25, 1989

U.S. Trade Representative Carla Hills says that, for all the tough talk in the big trade act Congress passed last year, this country isn't going to use the law to bully reluctant nations to open their markets to U.S. goods.

That's OK: By itself, the 1988 law is threatening enough to countries that don't treat U.S. imports fairly. Swashbuckling words from the Bush administration aren't needed. The trade law is a useful tool for persuading nations to open their markets, but if Washington actually starts slapping heavy penalties on imports, it could do far more harm than good.

Besides, there's virtually nothing the trade law can do to significantly improve our trade deficit. Only Americans can do that.

The 1988 trade act requires the administration to identify nations that maintain unfair barriers to trade from the United States, to demand those barriers be eliminated — and to impose restrictions on those countries' shipments to America if they aren't. Sounds fair, right? But it's filled with perils.

Restricting imports would deny U.S. consumers imported goods they prefer. It would curtail competition in the U.S. marketplace. And if Washington actually imposed new limits on goods from Japan or Korea or Germany, those nations might well respond by doing the same thing to our goods. The result: Pyramiding losses on all sides.

So Hills must walk a fine line — growling just enough to get other countries to respond, without actually lowering the boom on them. So far, she seems to be succeeding: Japan, South Korea and Taiwan have come up with various kinds of trade concessions in hopes of forestalling the law's penalties.

That makes for fairer trade, which is fine. But what the trade deficit really means is that Americans consume more than they produce each year — to the tune of tens of billions of dollars. Until Americans restrain their own spending habits, there's no way a trade law can eliminate the trade imbalances.

The Dallas Morning News

Dallas, Texas, June 3, 1989

Looking back from some future vantage point, last week's decision by the United States to cite Japan and other nations for "unfair trade practices" may be seen as a turning point that led to more open world trade. Or it may be seen as the first fatal step toward a world trade war and depression.

The trade showdown is being prompted by the imposition of the "Super 301 section" of the Omnibus Trade and Competitiveness Act of 1988. That act specifies that once a country is put on the list of countries that are unfairly restricting U.S. imports, the U.S. trade representative must begin negotiations to correct the unfair practices. Those negotiations then must be concluded within 18 months. If the listed country has not opened its markets within three years, the United States may close its market to the offending country in retaliation.

The decision by the Bush administration to enforce "Super 301" is a turning point in U.S. policy. Until now, the United States has put its political interests ahead of its economic interests. Important political and military allies, Japan foremost among them, have been granted special privileges in the areas of trade and investment so long as they remained loyal geopolitical allies.

U.S. trade policy also has been a form of foreign aid. The U.S. market was made the purchaser of last resort for products manufactured abroad by political allies. That brought economic progress and a measure of stability in nations such as South Korea. In retrospect, the policy was good, since it allowed the development of producer cultures, not welfare cultures. But the resources of the United States are not infinite. And political goals can become moot as economic power and technological prowess fail.

That U.S. trading partners play by rules different from our own, not even our trading partners deny. What they do often deny is that this is to the United States' disadvantage. In Japan, the entire economic system is rigged against foreign penetration. The Japanese — like the Indians and Brazilians — protest that the tilted system is demanded by their culture and their politics. They warn that any effort to force changes will lead to trade war.

Their warnings may prove valid. The United States must proceed with caution. Nor can the United States use the trade sanctions as an excuse not to address those often painful domestic policies, such as the high deficit and low savings rate, that are at least as much to blame for U.S. failures as are foreign straw men.

The Clarion-Ledger

Biloxi, Mississippi, May 30, 1989

The Bush administration must not flinch in its decision to move against trade barriers in Japan, Brazil and India.

The administration is implementing a controversial provision in the new U.S. trade law that gives the nation more leverage in reacting to barriers most harmful to American producers.

In Japan's case, which is the main concern, the target is that nation's refusal to buy U.S.-made satellites and supercomputers and its restrictions on U.S. lumber products. India is to be cited for its restrictions on foreign investment and foreign insurance companies and Brazil for its import-licensing practices.

While the maneuver could lead to higher tariffs in the short term, it could also have the opposite effect and over the long haul be beneficial. Japan has particularly been a tough trading partner, and failure to respond to its protectionism would encourage an intensification of it.

The administration's strategy will provide for an 18-month period to negotiate the removal of the barriers. If the talks fail, the government could levy tariffs of up to 100 percent against selected imports.

However, the likelihood is that the officials can recognize and negotiate reasonable economic interests. Representatives of the nations involved are not likely to underestimate the possible cost of stubbornly sticking to rigid positions. A fairly recent U.S.-Canada agreement is an example of a successful resolution of trade problems.

While the nation should uphold the goal of free trade, it also must try to make it fair. Nations must see the self-interest in moderating their policies and practices when their trade barriers cause hardship on the other party.

Birmingham Post-Herald

Birmingham, Alabama, May 30, 1989

President Bush's decision to use the nation's new trade law to prod Japan into fairer trade practices should not be viewed as the beginning of a tit-for-tat fight that will lead to less cooperation between our two nations.

The trade law initially calls for an investigative step that can be used to gain agreements with Japan before any actual retaliation is deemed necessary.

The law requires the U.S. trade representative this year and in 1990 to spotlight countries for investigation of unfair trade practices. Those countries are then given 12 to 18 months to negotiate a settlement or face possible retaliation.

Japan has an annual $55.4 billion trade surplus with the United States. It was cited for including government prohibitions against buying U.S.-built supercomputers and space satellites by public agencies, and for blocking imports of U.S. forest goods.

Brazil is to be investigated for unfairly using quotas and licensing requirements to restrict U.S. imports, and for impeding foreign investment. And India was cited for restricting U.S. trade in insurance and impeding foreign investment.

The decision to impose the trade law comes at a particularly bad time. Many in Japan are resentful of the way this nation has argued over the agreement to jointly build the FSX jet fighter. And the resignation of Prime Minister Noboru Takeshita last month leaves a void that will make it more difficult for the U.S. to negotiate a compromise in this latest trade dispute.

Japan is our largest trading partner and closest Pacific ally. We do not wish to alienate the Japanese further. But there is hope that the investigative stage of the new trade law can be used to work out a compromise that would prevent the type of protectionist retaliation that would lead nowhere but to a trade war.

THE CHRISTIAN SCIENCE MONITOR
Boston, Massachusetts, June 1, 1989

THE United States, after speaking softly, loudly, and every other way on trade, last week brandished a big stick. Washington fired shots across the bows of Japan, Brazil, and India by formally designating them unfair traders and beginning a process that could ultimate in retaliatory sanctions against the three countries. Some detractors of the US's tougher trade stance are calling it gunboat diplomacy, but supporters view it as defending national interests.

In an amendment last year to Section 301 of the 1974 trade law, Congress obligated the administration to compile a list of "priority" countries that most run afoul of free-trade principles in their commerce with the US. As part of this "Super 301" Congress further laid out a timetable for negotiations with the offending nations and prescribed retaliatory measures to be taken if satisfactory relief is not achieved.

Now US Trade Representative Carla Hills has presented her most-wanted list to Congress. Japan was cited primarily for alleged unfair practices related to commercial satellites, supercomputers, and forest products; Brazil for restrictive licensing requirements on imports; and India for what an earlier study called a "web" of formidable trade barriers. In most of these cases, the Bush administration has 18 months to negotiate a resolution of the difficulty; if it fails, retaliation will begin.

Super 301 is under attack from several directions. The countries named say they're outraged. Other nations believe that Congress's unilateral procedures violate the rules of the General Agreement on Tariffs and Trade, and they assail the US for going outside the GATT framework. And at home, the process is condemned by free-traders and officials concerned about harmful foreign-policy fallout.

Super 301 does give one pause. The specter of tit-for-tat retaliation leading to a trade war can't be contemplated with a shrug. Washington doesn't want to be a party to raising the level of trade hostilities around the world, especially when it is eager to avoid a Fortress Europe in the wake of the 1992 trade reforms. And if the US does retaliate against the Super 301 scofflaws by raising its own trade barriers, among those to suffer will be American consumers.

Yet there can be no doubt that American producers *are* disadvantaged in many overseas markets, and the laissez faire approach of the Reagan years was not conspicuously successful in opening closed markets. As in the proverb of the mule and the two-by-four, Super 301 has gotten the attention of the US's trading partners. At least one country – South Korea – preemptively lowered agricultural tariffs to avoid being included on Mrs. Hills's hit list.

The test of Super 301 will be whether America's trade negotiators can eliminate the most egregious unfair trade practices without having to unlimber the sanction siege guns. If the law proves its effectiveness as a stern warning, well and good. If it turns out to have been a declaration of war, it will need to be rethought.

The Record
Hackensack, New Jersey, June 4, 1989

In the name of free trade, and in the hope of reducing its trade deficit, the United States has taken direct aim at Japan, and shot itself in the foot.

Under the so-called "Super 301" provision of the 1988 Trade Act, the United States has officially labeled Japan as an unfair trading partner. If negotiations cannot resolve the matter, the law requires sanctions to be imposed against Japan in as little as 12 months.

Brazil and India have also been cited, but merely as window dressing. The clear target is Japan with whom the United States ran a $55 billion trade deficit last year.

In theory, Super 301 is supposed to expand U.S. exports by opening up foreign markets. In reality, Super 301, like all protectionist legislation, will wind up doing more harm than good.

For starters, it won't do what it promises, namely reduce the trade deficit. In the complaint against Japan, Super 301 cites three problem trade areas — supercomputers, satellites, and lumber. But even if all restrictions were taken off these products, the impact on the U.S. trade deficit would be minuscule. It's interesting to note that even such protectionists as Rep. Richard Gephardt have acknowledged that trade barriers are only responsible for 10-15 percent of the U.S. trade deficit.

In return for what amounts to marginal progress, at best, on the trade deficit, Super 301 threatens to chill U.S.-Japanese relations. Strategically and financially, the United States cannot afford such a rift. Japan is the United States' most important ally in Asia. Japan, through its purchase of U.S. Treasury bills, is a major underwriter of the U.S. budget deficit. The dollar would plummet and interest rates would soar if the Japanese, angered by U.S. trade policies, abandoned U.S. financial markets.

The Japanese have been particularly angered by the timing and what they perceive as the hypocritical nature of Super 301. They have a point.

Missing from the Japan-bashing rhetoric so popular on Capitol Hill these days is any recognition of the strides the Japanese have made to open their shores. From 1986 to 1988, U.S. exports to Japan jumped 62 percent to $36 billion a year, according to the International Trade Commission.

This is not to suggest that Japan's borders are completely open to U.S. products. Japan remains highly protective of its agricultural industry as well as of Japanese firms trying to develop new technology. The United States, however, is not immune to protectionist tendencies. Cars, steel, clothing, dairy products, sugar, and bicycle parts are all protected from foreign competition. The United States also subsidizes the export of wheat, poultry, eggs and other agricultural prodcuts.

•

In addition to its inconsistencies, serious doubts have emerged over whether the provisions of Super 301 can be enforced.

What was most notable about the Super 301 "hit list" was its brevity. The administration had identified 13 unfair trading barriers maintained by European countries. But the Europeans short-circuited Super 301 simply by refusing to acknowledge its legitimacy. Facing the prospect of being left alone at the bargaining table, the United States backed down.

Japan picked up on this tactic last week. The result has sent the Bush administration back-pedaling. In a queer bit of logic, Carla Hills, the U.S. trade representative, has told the Japanese that although they have been cited as unfair traders by Super 301, the talks to resolve the dispute need not be officially characterized as Super 301 negotiations.

What's most troubling is that if a settlement is not reached, Super 301 requires the imposition of sanctions against Japan. That would spell disaster. Retaliation soon turns into a costly farce. One needs to look no farther than last June for evidence when the United States tacked a 35 percent tariff on Canadian cedar shingles. The Canadian response was swift. It slapped tariffs of up to 30 percent on U.S. oatmeal, computer parts, tea bags, and Christmas trees. Both sides lost.

Instead of trying to take unilateral actions on trade, the United States would be better served by bringing its grievances under the provisions of the General Agreements on Tariffs and Trade. Though far from perfect, GATT has a solid record on promoting international free trade.

Finally, the answer to the trade deficit is not protectionism, but productivity. U.S. consumers buy Japanese products for their value. To compete, U.S. products must offer equal or better quality. That's the challenge. Not provoking Japan into a trade war with misguided legislation.

Trade Gap Rises Sharply

The U.S. merchandise trade deficit rose in July 1990 to its highest level since January 1990, the Commerce Department reported Sept. 18, 1990.

The $9.33 billion deficit represented a 75% rise from June's $5.34 billion gap. Exports fell to $32.03 billion, down 6.4% from June's record total of $34.22. Imports advanced 4.5%, to $41.36 billion.

One of the major factors in the worsening of the trade figures from the previous month was an increase in oil imports, to 274.5 million barrels from 252 million, an increase that more than offset a decline in the average price of a barrel of crude oil to $14.50 from $14.68 in June. The trade report showed none of the effect on oil prices of the Aug. 2 Iraqi invasion of Kuwait.

The new report was especially disappointing to economists in that it showed a stagnant export picture. Exports had been considered one of the last reserves of strength in the U.S. economy.

July's drop in exports reflected decreased shipments of U.S. aircraft and agricultural products. The rise in imports included such consumer goods as clothing, jewelry and toys.

The data reflected adjustment for seasonal fluctuations.

Before seasonal adjustment, the U.S. registered a $1.33 billion trade deficit with Western Europe in July, following an $810 million surplus in June. The trade deficit with Japan fell slightly, to $2.97 billion. It rose with Canada, however, to $990 million from $710 million in June.

The U.S. trade deficit also widened with the newly industrialized economies of East Asia: Hong Kong, Taiwan, South Korea and Singapore. In July, the U.S. gap with those economies was $2.45 billion. In June, it had been $1.34 billion.

In the first seven months in 1990, the U.S. trade deficit totaled $55.4 billion, or about $95 billion at an annual rate, down from $118 billion for all of 1989.

Herald News

Fall River, Massachusetts, September 19, 1990

About 4,000 textile, garment and footwear workers converged on Washington, D.C., last Wednesday to show their support of the Textile, Apparel and Footwear Trade Act of 1990.

The bill has already been approved by the Senate; and is expected to come up for House action this week. It would create a single quota system to limit the growth of imports of cloth and clothing to one percent annually. Footwear imports would be frozen at the current level — about 80 percent of U.S. sales.

The demonstration was small, as Washington marches go nowadays. Only about 25 workers from Massachusetts took part. Most came from the Carolinas, Tennessee and Pennsylvania.

Ida Cabral, president of Local 178 of the International Ladies Garment Workers Union in this city, has been for many years a champion of workers' rights and dignity. With her comrades, she recognizes the predicament of organized labor today, threatened not only by imports, but by layoffs and factory closings.

The Reagan and Bush administrations have championed the principle of free trade. The plight of garment workers in older New England cities may seem to them just a tiny piece of the international puzzle, not worth worrying about.

In recent years, membership in the ILGWU local has dropped from 12,000 to 3,400; the very future of the apparel industry is doubt.

The Fiber, Fabric and Apparel Coalition for Trade, sponsor of the march, points to a recent study showing the bill could create 41,000 new jobs.

The bill's scope is limited, to protect a small but significant sector of American expertise. In this troubled corner of the northeast, the labor force is developed, and wages are decent. But jobs are sadly declining. Congress should give the region a practical boost, and stem the flood of imports.

Meanwhile, consumers can help by looking for the union label, and buying clothing "made with pride in the USA."

The Washington Post

Washington, D.C., September 20, 1990

WHEN THE House voted for the textile protection bill on Tuesday, it was voting to make consumers pay higher prices for textiles and clothing. It was voting for the worst kind of special-interest legislation—the kind that increases the profits of one favored industry at the expense of everybody else. It was also a vote to violate the trade agreements that the United States has signed with 38 other countries, most of them good friends.

Of the eight people who represent the Washington area in the House of Representatives, there were two principled Republicans who voted against the textile bill—as you would guess, Frank R. Wolf of Virginia and Connie Morella of Maryland. The area's other congressmen all supported it.

Why would a generally well-intentioned legislator like Steny Hoyer vote against the interests of his constituents in Prince George's County to raise prices for the benefit of the textile manufacturers? It's an election year, and voters might want to ask him about that. The answer is, apparently, that he was just going along with the rest of the House Democratic leadership, in which he ranks fourth.

In the Maryland suburbs Beverly Byron, Roy Dyson and Tom McMillen all voted for the bill—which, like a regressive tax, will hit the poor hardest. In northern Virginia Stan Parris, who is usually to be found on the least enlightened side of any issue, did nothing to improve his record here. He was joined by D. French Slaughter—both of them Republicans voting against President Bush.

If you ask why, you will probably hear a lot of claims of dying mill towns, people thrown out of jobs and an industry overwhelmed by an avalanche of imports. The reality is that textiles and clothing are already among the most heavily protected of American industries and are profitable—although they would naturally like to be more so. Regarding the lost jobs, you might ask whether automation didn't have something to do with it. Unlike the old mills a modern textile plant is not labor-intensive—and dozens of new plants have been opened in the past several years. Most of the industry is now highly competitive, and the evidence is its rapidly rising exports—yes, its exports.

In July, incidentally, both Maryland senators and both Virginians voted for this bill. Unfortunately only one of them, John Warner (R-Va.), is running for reelection this year. He's a man with a strong interest in national security, and you might ask him whether he still thinks it's a good idea to enact a bill that would violate American trade agreements with Egypt and Turkey, two of the key countries standing with the United States against Iraq.

This irresponsible bill now goes to President Bush, who has promised to veto it. He will be right to do so.

THE TAMPA TRIBUNE
Tampa, Florida, September 24, 1990

Congress has sent President Bush a bill limiting increased imports of textiles, clothing and shoes to protect the domestic manufacturers of those products. President Reagan vetoed similar legislation in 1985 and 1988, and Mr. Bush says he will veto this one.

He should, and the veto should stick, but there is greater danger of Congress overriding this one than the Reagan vetoes, which were sustained.

This bill is worse both in content and timing than its deservedly unsuccessful predecessors. Unfortunately, that doesn't assure that the Bush veto will be upheld. Proponents of protectionism have undercut some of the previous opposition by providing that textile-exporting nations that increase their imports of U.S. farm products will receive larger quotas.

There are four major reasons why this bill is bad: They are:

■ **Consumer costs.** Economists estimate that the existing protectionist Multifiber Arrangement and quota system on textiles, clothing and shoes costs the average family $238 a year, or $20 billion nationwide. The new measure will increase that by as much as $100 per family.

■ **Economic costs.** Advocates of the bill contend it is necessary to save jobs and to give U.S. manufacturers time to become competitive. Research indicates that protectionism has saved approximately 250,000 jobs in the textile and apparel industries in recent years — but some of the losses it offset were to productivity improvements, not imports.

A study for the Cato Institute by Thomas Grennes, a professor of economics at North Carolina State University (North Carolina has more people working in textile and apparel plants than any other state), found in comparing the costs of jobs lost and price increases that saving $1 in wages costs consumers $7. When other factors, including the average duration of the unemployment (13.3 weeks in textiles and 24.4 weeks in apparel), and losses of jobs in apparel retailing and in other industries subject to trade retaliations engendered by the quotas, each $1 saved costs the economy $25.

There is also the ironic note that major associations of retail trade and of apparel manufacturing oppose the bill. Retailers want access to the widest variety of clothing and shoes possible; manufacturers say that textile quotas make many of the newest fabrics inaccessible or more costly to them in a style-conscious market.

■ **Disastrous timing:** The Uruguay Round of the General Agreement on Tariffs and Trade is nearing its climax. If agreement is not reached by early 1991 the whole worldwide effort toward free trade may collapse. That this is the first round in GATT history in which the United States has agreed to include textiles in the discussions is a major reason for hope there would be a free trade breakthrough. If President Bush's veto is overridden, that hope, and GATT itself, may collapse. That could trigger an international trade war — a war in which the United States, with its huge excess of imports over exports, would enter at considerable disadvantage.

■ **Foreign policy:** For almost a decade, under Presidents Reagan and Bush, the United States has had a declared and logical interest in the economic improvement of the Caribbean Basin — the mainland arc from Mexico through Central America to Venezuela, and the basin's islands. In almost every nation, either textiles or apparel or both are a major export industry. The quota bill would be a huge barrier to our pursuit of the stated policy of "trade, not aid."

Even the U.S. position in the Persian Gulf crisis may be adversely affected by enactment of the bill. Turkey's tremendous contributions both in economic sacrifice and military presence have stimulated in its government officials understandable expectations of more recognition and assistance from the West, particularly from the United States. They echo the slogan, "Trade, not aid." They list as their top economic priority *increased access for their textiles in the American market.*

To the textile industry's plea that it needs "temporary protection" to give it time to respond to competition from lower-cost imports, North Carolina State's Grennes replies: "The United States industry has benefited from extraordinary levels of protection from imports for more than 30 years (since 1957). If 30 years is not enough time to prepare for international competition, will 50 be?"

To protectionists, there is never enough protection. To the rest of us, 33 years of it have been 33 years too much.

President Bush has promised to veto this bill. Florida consumers have a stake in that veto. Florida business, looking to increased trade with the Caribbean Basin, has an even larger stake. It behooves both to urge their senators and representatives to sustain the veto.

ST. LOUIS POST-DISPATCH
St. Louis, Missouri, September 25, 1990

For the third time in five years, the American textile, apparel and footwear industries have persuaded Congress to pass legislation sharply restricting imports — without good reason and at considerable potential cost to both consumers and America's trade relations abroad. Fortunately, Ronald Reagan twice vetoed similar bills and President Bush promises to veto this one.

The makers of sweaters, shirts and other clothing, as well as manufacturers of non-rubber footwear, claim they can't compete with low-wage nations flooding America with much less expensive goods. They have a point. As a result, the apparel industry, for instance, is already highly protected. The so-called Multifiber Arrangement of the General Agreement on Tariffs and Trade — the arrangement governing most international commerce — limits many categories of imports, and under it, America has negotiated more than 1,000 separate quotas with 38 separate countries.

This is more than sufficient protection, established beyond doubt by the fact that domestic shipments are up in recent years, and factories are running at an all-time high. But industry wants more. The bill Congress passed would first freeze for one year and then restrict the growth of imports of textiles and clothing to 1 percent a year thereafter; footwear imports would be frozen at last year's levels. This is unreasonable and dangerous.

The United States is engaged in critical talks to reduce a host of trade barriers worldwide in the so-called Uruguay Round of international trade talks, to be completed this fall. The benefits to be gained by multi-lateral tariff reductions are immense; the cost of not doing so is equally gigantic. If Congress were able to override the president's expected veto, the Uruguay Round would collapse. That would be disastrous, as well as unnecessary.

The Boston Herald
Boston, Massachusetts,
September 23, 1990

Made in the U.S.A. It's the U.S. textile industry's signature. Buy American is what the textile industry is urging every American to do.

This is an admirable, patriotic, and emotionally appealing goal, but one that shouldn't be enforced by restrictive legislation that would curb textile imports, limit consumer choice and force Americans to buy American. The textile industry would like it this way and has so effectively lobbied for restrictions on imports that the U.S. Senate earlier this year and the House of Representatives just last week approved bills that would restrict imports of apparel and shoes. Fortunately, the House approval fell short of the two-thirds needed to override a promised presidential veto.

Proponents of the bill stridently maintain that the U.S. textile industry needs protection from foreign lower-cost imports if it is to thrive. But the fact is that about three-quarters of all textile imports are already under some restrictions and have been for 30 years, and that the U.S. textile industry *is* thriving.

Domestic shipments increased 7 percent and exports were up 27 percent in 1989. Unemployment in most of the major textile-producing states is below the national average. "The textile bill is special-interest legislation with costs that far exceed its benefits," concludes the Cato Institute, an independent public policy research institute, which analyzes and critiques public policy.

Enactment of the textile bill would be devastating. The bill would increase the price of clothing to the American consumer, undermine global trade negotiations, and create ill will among nations with whom we are negotiating to eliminate their trade barriers.

America must not shut its doors to competition. Protectionism is not patriotism. It's up to American consumers, not government, to choose to buy products made in the U.S.A.

The Chattanooga Times

Chattanooga, Tennessee, September 24, 1990

Thousands of textile workers, some of them from Tennessee, showed up in Washington the other day to stage a Capitol Hill demonstration that urged Congress to enact greater protection against competition from the foreign textile industry. The next day the House passed legislation, which had earlier passed the Senate, to do just that. Workers who lose their jobs deserve sympathy, but that's no reason for legislation that will prove counterproductive if it becomes law over President Bush's veto.

The men and women who demonstrated and many of their fellow workers have been told, by their companies and their union representatives, that imported textiles constitute the biggest, if not the only, threat to their jobs. When layoffs are imposed, when mills close or cut back production, it's routine to blame competition from cheap-labor countries, especially Asia.

Obviously the impact of imports on domestic textile production can't be ignored. But if imports were as serious a problem as the backers of this protectionist legislation would have us believe, the entire industry would be comatose. Actually, it's not doing all that badly in Tennessee. According to the state Department of Employment Security, there were 69,400 Tennesseans working in the apparel industry in 1980; nine years later, that figure had declined slightly more than 4,000. The annual average last year was 3,800 fewer workers than in 1980.

The industry is not immune to plant closings and layoffs, but that doesn't mean all of them can be blamed solely on foreign competition. Sometimes a plant closes because it's obsolete — but is replaced by one that is more efficient because it incorporates improved technology.

Proponents of the bill in question, including Rep. Marilyn Lloyd, a prime sponsor, would freeze the level of imports for a year and limit the growth in textile imports to 1 percent a year. That, they say, will "protect" the U.S. textile industry — as if it needed protecting. The protection is likely to be addictive: If the industry doesn't rebound the way the protectionists think it should, will the next Congress be asked to freeze the level for two years and limit import growth to a half-percent a year?

This is nothing but a quota bill to support artificially the market for textile goods priced too high to compete in the free market. If it becomes law, consumers, including textile workers, will pay more for clothing and related goods. Worse, protectionism not only results in higher prices, it invites retaliation by other countries that hurts other U.S. industries.

The Bush administration reported the other day a staggering increase in the U.S. trade deficit. That suggests countries overseas don't want to buy many goods the United States is producing, or that they find them too expensive period. Either way, now is hardly the time to enact legislation that will result in even higher barriers for U.S.-made goods. Protectionist legislation favored by Rep. Lloyd and others is an anachronistic substitute for trade summits and trade negotiations. Mr. Bush should veto this bill, and the veto should be upheld.

The Seattle Times

Seattle, Washington, September 12, 1990

SEN. Jesse Helms wants to make a sweet deal sweeter for North Carolina textile manufacturers at the expense of Washington apples and airplanes.

U.S. Trade Representative Carla Hills made a good case for that parochial view during her Seattle visit this week.

If the 1990 textile bill sweeps through the House of Representatives the way it stormed the Senate, a destructive piece of legislation might have the momentum to survive a presidential veto.

The bill would limit the growth of textile and clothing imports from industrialized and developing countries to 1 percent a year. Most certainly the absence of foreign competition means higher prices for consumers, but an even more bleak prospect is likely.

Hills argues that the first line of retaliation will be against agriculture and high-technology exports from this country, noting that Washington is a major exporter in both areas.

Foreign countries would be drawn to agriculture as a ready weapon precisely at a time the Bush administration is working to knock down barriers to U.S. farm exports.

Passage would likely scuttle the current round of multilateral trade negotiations — the General Agreement on Tariffs and Trade — laboring toward completion in Geneva.

U.S. textiles already enjoy protection under a separate trade agreement that established more than 1,000 quotas covering two-thirds of total textile and apparel imports. Last year, the average tariff rate was 11 percent for textiles and 19 percent for apparel. The average for all other dutiable products was 3 percent.

Enough. The 1990 textile bill is serious trouble. Let Helms find another election-year bouquet for the voters back home.

LAS VEGAS REVIEW-JOURNAL

Las Vegas, Nevada, September 20, 1990

Nevada's delegates to the House of Representatives, to their discredit, threw in their lot with the protectionist forces in the House this week. Reps. Barbara Vucanovich and Jim Bilbray joined 269 others who voted in favor of a bill that would restrict the growth of U.S. textile imports to 1 percent a year and freeze shoe imports at 1989 levels.

President Bush threatened to veto this regrettable measure, and we trust he will, although Congress apparently has the votes to override.

The president called the bill a "threat to the stability of the world trading system and . . . contrary to the economic, commercial and political interests of the United States." He's right.

By limiting imports of textiles and shoes from overseas, congressional protectionists intend to save American jobs and prop up U.S. manufacturers of these essential goods.

But it is more likely to cost American jobs than to save them. Consider that for every American job "saved" in the textile and shoe industries, other American jobs will be lost in the shipping, transport and retailing industries which handle imported goods.

The bill will restrict the import of high-quality, lower cost goods, and American consumers will pay the price. According to policy analyst Charles B. Oliver of the Washington, D.C.-based Citizens for a Sound Economy Foundation, the poorest 20 percent of American households sacrifice an estimated 3.6 percent of their annual income to pay for *existing* quotas and tariffs on textiles and clothing. The bill the House passed this week will, according to House opponents of the measure, raise the cost of clothing to the average American family $100 a year. Lower income families will bear a disproportionate share of the added burden.

The United States, under the Reagan and Bush administrations, has attempted to put itself forward as the world's premier free-trading nation. We are constantly harping on the Japanese to bring down protectionist barriers and allow the free flow of American goods into that country. The protectionist action by Congress turns us into shameless hypocrites. Further, it encourages other nations to retaliate with trade barriers of their own, and, ultimately, this will cost far more American jobs than are "saved" by protecting non-competitive American industries from overseas competition.

THE SACRAMENTO BEE
Sacramento, California, September 23, 1990

Both houses of Congress have passed restrictive trade legislation whose harmful effects would far outweigh the modest number of domestic jobs it would save, if any.

That legislation, HR 4328, would add to the burden of American consumers, who already pay too much for clothing and shoes because of existing import barriers; it would imperil crucial global trade talks in which the United States has much to gain or lose; and it would give further shelter to a domestic industry that's already well protected and making handsome profits. President Bush should make good on his threat to veto the measure.

Fortunately, the House vote last week, 271-149, was short of the two-thirds needed to override a presidential veto. But even if this election-year flimflammery fails, as it has twice before in recent years, the net result will be to strengthen the impression abroad that U.S. trade policy is hypocritical and that the danger of protectionist action by Congress is ever present — this at a time when the United States, in multilateral negotiations now in their most crucial phase, seeks greater access to foreign markets for financial, telecommunications and other service industries in which American firms excel and in which the great majority of new jobs are created.

The bill would limit textile and apparel imports to an increase of 1 percent a year,

freeze non-rubber footwear imports at 1989 levels and bar the president from negotiating any other terms. That would violate an existing international regime, the Multifiber Arrangement, under which the United States has bilateral accords with 38 countries. That agreement in itself amounts to a restraint of trade, but at least it's one to which virtually all trading nations subscribe.

One of the bill's sponsors, Rep. Ed Jenkins of Georgia, defends it on the ground that "we are giving away our entire manufacturing base." Nonsense; thanks to existing import quotas and an average tariff level of 18 percent (compared with 4 percent for manufactures generally), the U.S. textile industry has been able to modernize and to increase profits. In 1989, exports went up by 27 percent; not coincidentally, unemployment in the five major textile-producing states has fallen below the national average.

If further evidence of the hypocrisy of this election-year vote-grabber were necessary, it was provided during the House debate by Rep. David Dreier of California, who pointed out that "there are members on both sides of this issue who are very proud to have their suits made in Seoul." Perhaps he had in mind Sen. Ernest Hollings of South Carolina, a textile-state pol and a principal sponsor of this irresponsible legislation.

The Cincinnati Post
Cincinnati, Ohio, September 1, 1990

The U.S. House soon will consider the Senate-passed Textile, Apparel and Footwear Trade Act of 1990 — a measure that would provide protection from foreign imports to an already strong industry, increase clothing costs to Americans, and very likely wreck historic world-trade negotiations.

This special-interest measure deserves to be taken apart at the seams.

The image of the American textile industry includes hard-working men and women bent over industrial sewing machines in hot factories to provide their families with a decent life — the last people anyone would want to see jobless because of a flood of cheap Asian fabrics.

Though the U.S. textile lords say that just such a scenario looms, their poor-mouthing doesn't square with the facts: a 20.6 percent increase in domestic shipments between 1985 and 1989; greater profits for that period; and, from 1988 to 1989, a 27 percent surge in U.S. cloth exports to Europe and elsewhere.

This robust performance isn't unexpected, because the industry already enjoys huge legislated advantages. Under the 1986 update of the Multifibre Agreement, for example, almost all textile and apparel products made overseas were subjected to import quotas. As a result, foreign-made textiles have not captured one additional percentage-point share of the American market in four years. This choking of supply does, however, inflate consumer prices by depressing competition.

In pushing this bill, the textile industry is shortsighted. After all, its recent and lucrative penetrations of Europe — and Australia, Canada and Saudi Arabia — would be early fatalities in a new cycle of dueling tariffs and quotas. The House should save the weavers from themselves, to say nothing of the general public.

The San Diego Union
San Diego, California, September 14, 1990

Lobbyists for the domestic textile and apparel industries are blanketing Capitol Hill with pleas for additional protection against foreign competition.

There are, already, more than 1,000 quotas covering two-thirds of all textile and apparel imports. The average tariff rate in 1989 was 11 percent for textiles and 19 percent for apparel, compared with a 3 percent average for other products subject to such duties.

Nevertheless, the Textile, Apparel and Footwear Act of 1990 is advancing in Congress.

This bill would apply quotas to new items and make permanent the existing tariffs, thus prompting even steeper prices for consumers. Americans are paying more than $37 billion in inflated clothing prices to protect the domestic industry.

If this new bill becomes law, the average family of four

would spend an additional $2,600 a year on clothing and footwear, according to Carla Hills, the Bush administration's trade representative. The poorest 20 percent of American households would spend an estimated 5 percent of their incomes to protect the textile and apparel industries.

Industry lobbyists plead that additional protection is required to level the playing field with foreign producers. They insist that American companies are being forced to compete against foreign firms that are dumping low-priced goods here.

In fact, sales by the domestic textile industry have increased during six of the last seven years, reaching an all-time high of $63.7 billion in 1989. Although the industry's profits declined somewhat last year because of a weak fourth quarter, net sales were higher.

The domestic industry is also operating more efficiently and creating thousands of new jobs each year. As for alleged dumping, other U.S. trade laws are designed to address that problem, which is clearly outside the purview of the protectionist measure before Congress.

Apart from hurting consumers, added protection for the textile and apparel industry would undermine the Bush administration's goal of promoting free commerce at the upcoming international trade negotiations in Uruguay. It also would compound the economic problems of nations that are standing beside us in the Persian Gulf, notably Egypt and Turkey.

If Congress passes this misguided bill, President Bush should stand by his pledge to veto it.

U.S. Trade Deficit Nears New Levels

The U.S. merchandise trade deficit widened to a seasonally adjusted $12.51 billion in November 1988, the Commerce Department reported Jan. 18, 1989.

The widening of the trade deficit from a revised $10.26 billion in October reflected a rise in imports and a fall in exports. For many economists the report confirmed that a recent improvement in the U.S. balance of trade had come to an end until U.S. economic growth slowed.

The U.S. merchandise trade deficit shrank in 1988 for the first time in eight years to $137.34 billion, the Commerce Department reported Feb. 17, 1989.

The narrowing of the trade deficit from 170.32 billion 1987 reflected a 26.8% surge in exports to tp $322 billion and an 8.3% rise in imports to $459 billion. Most of the improvement occurred in the first half of 1988, with the deficit actually widening in the fourth quarter.

Despite the sizable 1988 reduction, the report confirmed for many economists that long-term improvement in the U.S. balance of trade had stalled. Most believed that any further reduction in the merchandise trade deficit would require a number of conditions including improving the quality of U.S. products, increasing the productivity of U.S. industry, maintaining a weak U.S. dollar and reducing the U.S. budget deficit.

The U.S. merchandise trade deficit shrank to a seasonally adjusted $8.26 billion in April, the Commerce Department June 15, 1989.

The Times-Picayune

New Orleans, Louisiana, January 23, 1989

Apparently many Americans still prefer foreign products to those made in their own country. That, at least, is one of the main reasons the nation's trade deficit popped to a disappointing $12.5 billion in November.

Why do many Americans continue to prefer foreign-made cars, stereos and other goods to those made by themselves or other Americans? Is it mostly habit, or does "Made in America" still connote inferior quality?

Many analysts say it is the latter, that Americans still are not producing goods of equal or better quality than those turned out by their foreign counterparts.

Whatever the answer or answers, the spurt in the November trade deficit is putting new life into the debate over what the nation must do to keep the trade deficit on a downward track.

Some analysts insist that the long-term trend continues downward. They note that the deficit for the first 11 months of 1988 ran at an annual rate of $137.3 billion, almost 20 percent below the record high deficit of $170.3 billion for 1987.

Optimists, including White House spokesman Marlin Fitzwater, suggested that the disconcerting November figure was an aberration. Other administration officials, most notably William Verity, the departing commerce secretary, were not so optimistic.

"All of this means that we have a long way to go," said Mr. Verity. "We must continue to improve our efficiency and quality at home and pursue our efforts to reduce trade barriers abroad."

Some private economists argued that cutting costs and driving the dollar lower will not by themselves keep the trade deficit on a downward track.

The problem clearly is one of rising imports, because the strength in exports that has kept the nation's economy moving along was still evident despite some decline.

November exports slipped by $639 million to $27.2 billion. Imports bounced to $39.7 billion, $1.6 billion more than the October figure.

Despite its recent upward movement, the dollar's long-term trend remains down, many economists say. A declining dollar should help lower the trade deficit further, but it does not appear to be the only answer.

American manufacturers should continue to emphasize not only better product quality but superior quality. Increased productivity is also important to hold down costs and make U.S. products more competitive in price with foreign products.

Meanwhile, the incoming Bush administration should continue to press for fair trade with the nation's chief trading partners. Significantly, the November deficit with Western Europe increased to $2 billion from $1.1 billion in October.

The United States does not want a trade war, but it must insist on trade reciprocity as the European Community moves toward economic unity in 1992.

DESERET NEWS

Salt Lake City, Utah, March 17, 1989

This week the Department of Commerce reported what at first glance may look like a dramatic improvement in one of the nation's most closely watched economic indicators.

As a result, the Bush administration started hailing this development as an encouraging sign of progress in whittling down the huge deficit in the balance of trade between the United States and other countries.

But don't start cheering yet.

At best, the figures reflect an improvement over only one month — and that doesn't make a trend.

Besides, the figures look better than they really are simply because they also reflect a brand-new change in the way the United States keeps track of the business it does with its trading partners.

All that is a shame because a genuine improvement in the trade deficit would take pressure off the Federal Reserve to keep the lid on the American economy with higher interest rates.

In essence, here is what has happened. This week the Commerce Department reported that the U.S. merchandise trade deficit — the new term for what used to be called the international balance of trade deficit — declined 13.7 percent in January to $9.5 billion, the smallest gap since September

But one reason the January figures look good by comparison to December's is that Japan flooded the United States with cars in December to avoid higher tariffs being imposed on certain models starting this year.

Another reason is that 1989 also marked the start of a new U.S. accounting system. The new system counts only the customs value of imports, no longer adding in costs of insurance and shipping as was done the previous nine years.

Is the new accounting method only a trick designed to make the new Bush administration look good by hiding the truth? Though plenty of critics jumped to precisely that conclusion, they acted too fast. The fact is that the new method of keeping track of imports and exports merely brings U.S. practices in line with those of its major trading partners. What's more, though the announcement received little attention, the new accounting method was outlined months ago.

Meanwhile, the bottom line is that despite the apparent improvement in the new trade figures, the United States still needs to do a more vigorous job of competing abroad.

THE ROANOKE TIMES
Roanoke, Virginia, January 6, 1989

THE NATIONAL debt, having reached $3.25 trillion, is nearing a frightening threshold.

You've probably heard about how high a stack of $3.25 trillion in $1 bills would reach, or how many times it would circle the White House and Capitol, and so forth.

Even magnitudes such as light years are becoming easier to comprehend as a result of trying to visualize the national debt. (Going the speed of light, it would take more than 200 days to travel 3.25 trillion miles.)

However interesting and instructive such comparisons may be, here's a different but also startling way to consider our indebtedness:

If you divide the national debt figure by 94 million households in America, the average household's share of the debt comes to $34,574. Using a conservative estimate of $48,840 for the average household income in 1990, the national debt accounts for 71 percent of annual personal income.

If you exclude the 25 percent of households that do not pay income tax, and therefore would not theoretically participate in debt retirement, each remaining household's share of the national debt rises to 95 percent of annual personal income. And the trend is not reassuring.

In other words, if you're an average household, your indebtedness — in terms of your share of the national debt — may pretty soon exceed your annual income.

If that's not a recipe for bankruptcy, what is?

The Washington Post
Washington, D.C., January 11, 1989

THE DEFICIT estimates continue to rise, and with every increase come new calls for Congress to act. What Congress needs to remember is that it has already acted. The deficit reduction agreement of last October was at least as real as it was awkwardly achieved; over time, if adhered to, it will have pretty much the intended effect. In the meantime, it would be as wrong to try to exceed it as to try to undo it.

Official deficit estimates in recent years have mostly been political confections, fiscal cotton candy. The earliest estimates for this year, fiscal 1991, were equally fanciful. The administration gave as its view last January that the deficit would be $100.5 billion, substantially down from the year before. But over the year the politics changed—some would say the reality became harder to evade—and the estimates progressed steadily upward.

By the so-called mid-session review in July the likely figure was said to be $169 billion, and more if you counted the probable cost of the savings and loan bailout. By the time of the budget agreement in October, it was said to be about $250 billion counting the bailout cost, more if you took into account the possibility of recession. Now it is said to be in the range of $300 billion counting the effects of a mild recession, more if you fold in the full cost of Operation Desert Shield. Nor is 1992 predicted to be much better.

A deficit this high at the start of a recession leaves no good policy choices. For structural reasons the deficit needs to come down even as, for cyclical reasons, it needs to be kept up. In terms of fiscal policy, the best thing for both the administration and Congress to do in the circumstances is nothing. To add to the deficit in order to offset the recession's effects would be wrong; $300 billion or $325 billion of deficit is fiscal stimulus enough. If Congress wants to aid the recession's victims—as it should—it must find ways to pay for the aid through offsetting spending cuts or careful tax increases.

Nor can the members afford to do the opposite and in the present circumstances try to *reduce* the deficit much beyond what was agreed last year; they risk deepening the recession. Politicians always want if not not to act at least to look as if they're acting. Now they need instead to wait. In the 1980s the government—in the final analysis both branches and both parties—overspent, undertaxed and lied about the result. Only last year as they were running out of the time and means to do so did they take corrective action. It will take a while for the budgetary effects of the recession, the bailout and Desert Shield to pass and the corrective action to take hold. Meanwhile the moral of the story is to underestimate the deficit no more.

The Gazette
Cedar Rapids, Iowa, January 1, 1989

ECONOMIC ANXIETY, coupled with tension from the Persian Gulf crisis, reportedly has made this holiday season the gloomiest in recent memory. Some signs indeed are worrisome. For example, nearly 270,000 Americans lost their jobs in November. And a "soft ecomony" led to a disappointing Christmas shopping season. Bad weather's onset seems to have heightened the jitters.

Remember, though: Worrying about a bad recession can make the fear come true. As English

When 1992 marches in, we expect to look back and say '91 was far better than most people expected.

cleric W.R. Inge said, "Worry is interest paid on trouble before it comes due."

How can you help make sure a national economic slump isn't a self-fulfilling prophecy?

Two suggestions: Remain aware of the nation's basic strength in world markets. And understand the news media's penchant for exaggeration (more about that later).

Trade deficit notwithstanding, the United States is still the world's No. 1 exporter. Eastern Iowans, among the national leaders in production for export, tend to understand this. But the fact is lost on many Americans. They imagine slippage in overall competitiveness and productivity. The United States' productivity, however, is not declining; it merely is improving at a slower pace. Hence, fewer new jobs. A nationwide recession — not a depression — is under way. It may be relatively short. As stressed here before, though, a recession is not a recession to those left unemployed. To them, it is a depression.

As for the media's role in spreading the news and interpreting it, we are a little embarrassed. Pack journalism is running rampant. One influential journalist shouts "wolf!" and pretty soon most others are in full cry. Look at the weekly news magazines and you will get the picture. It is all the rage to take reversals — the Persian Gulf standoff, the budget mess, the savings and loan debacle, etc. — and build them into a crisis greater, perhaps, than the sum of its parts.

We prefer to remain confident in the nation's underlying economic strength. When 1992 marches in, we expect to look back and say '91 was far better than most people imagined.

Meantime, Happy New Year!

Soon after the start of the race, George began to sense . . .

. . . that his motor was missing.

REMOVED AS COLLATERAL FOR THE BUDGET DEFICIT

TRADE

FREE TRADE

BUSH

TRADE POLICY

©1989 The Courier-Journal

The Dallas Morning News
Dallas, Texas, June 17, 1989

The week brought the announcement that the U.S. merchandise trade deficit had plummeted. It also was announced that the "current accounts" deficit continued to widen. Good news or bad news? More bad than good.

The merchandise figure is the difference between trade in "tangible" goods between the U.S. and trading partners. If purchases of oil, which has been more expensive of late, are deleted, the trade gap in tangibles has shrunk a good bit.

The current accounts figure includes cash flows. Japanese purchases of U.S. Treasury bills increase the deficit. Borrowing to cover the federal deficit from Japan, or anywhere else, widens the trade gap. High interest rates also cause the current accounts trade gap to widen. The higher interest rates go, the more money the U.S. must ship abroad to cover the interest on its debt. High interest rates also create a higher demand for dollars, and that forces up the value of the dollar. That makes goods made in the U.S.A. more expensive abroad, which means fewer export sales.

It is becoming very obvious that the way to cut the *real* trade deficit is to cut the budget deficit, not bashing Japan, or enforcing so-called fair trade laws in an overly tough manner. If the U.S. can get its fiscal house in order, it will have a more solid economic foundation. So far, the president and Congress have largely ignored the deficit. This week's trade figures make clear that they continue to do so at the nation's peril.

The Providence Journal
Providence, Rhode Island, December 23, 1989

The U.S. trade deficit is still with us, as Tuesday's Commerce Department report attests. October's deficit was larger than September's by 25 percent. The October figure could discourage economists encouraged by a report the day before, which said that the deficit declined in the third quarter, and this year's deficit could be 10 percent less than last year's. But many of the same economists are sure it will widen next year.

So what about the trade deficit? Is it good news or bad? Nobody's really certain — but most people don't lose sleep over these numbers, and we can't see why they should.

Of course, this flies in the face of conventional wisdom, which holds that the trade deficit is an unalloyed evil. But assumptions have been changing as five straight years of $100 billion-plus trade deficits have (apparently) had little negative impact on the economy, or on American standards of living. That shift was dramatized by the release last Monday of a report from a panel of experts convened by the Twentieth Century Fund. The majority concluded that the deficit was not worrisome enough to warrant a major change in U.S. policy, which emphasizes free trade. (A minority on the panel disagreed, urging a "managed" trade policy, with Washington doing more to promote exports and restrict imports.)

Inevitably, the trade policy of Japan was mentioned, and there is no denying that Japan is an export powerhouse. But Americans probably would not want to try the Japanese system here if they knew more about it. To the extent that Japan's private sector is managed by Tokyo, it's because Tokyo is the tool of powerful business interests. They don't call it Japan Inc. for nothing. America was preserved from becoming America Inc. by Theodore Roosevelt when he busted the trusts early in this century, and we doubt that most Americans would want to go backwards, even if the reward were a trade surplus. Americans would be appalled at what Japanese consumers pay for domestic goods produced under an export-driven system.

To be sure, in some degree our trade deficit is an indictment of our competitiveness, and to an even lesser degree of other countries' reluctance to play fair. Those are real problems — but managed trade and protectionism will not solve them.

"The notion of turning the United States economy over to a government agency is ludicrous," says Herbert Stein, onetime chairman of the President's Council of Economic Advisers and a member of the Fund's panel. "We are the world's leading exponent of the free-market system whose triumph we are now celebrating."

America's economy is the model, no longer just the envy, of countries around the world. We can help them best by exemplifying, not abandoning, free trade.

MILWAUKEE SENTINEL

Milwaukee, Wisconsin, March 16, 1989

Although the traffic in trade, investment and services continued to flow out of the United States last year in a much greater amount than it came in,

some encouragement can be taken from Commerce Department figures showing a drop of more than 12% in the so-called "current account" deficit for 1988.

End of the year numbers showed that the US imbalance in such exchanges was $135.3 billion as compared to $156.96 billion in 1987.

One conclusion that might be reached from this "progress" is that the successful effort to drive down the value of the dollar against other currencies by Secretary of State James A. Baker III, while he was secretary of the Treasury during the Reagan administration, paid off.

A cheaper dollar does make US exports more salable overseas.

However, the key to making the trade winds blow the other way, most economists say, still is a reduction in the federal budget deficit. That would restrict the relative amount of money that goes to other countries, strengthen the dollar and probably encourage savings.

Good news on that score last week got little notice. Specifically, testimony on Capitol Hill by Congressional Budget Office Director Robert Reischauer revealed that, even using the CBO's pessimistic economic assumptions, President Bush's budget for fiscal 1990 would produce a deficit of only $109 billion.

That's just under the $110 billion which would trigger automatic cuts mandated by the Gramm-Rudman law.

Even Sen. Pete V. Domenici (R-N.M.), the ranking Republican on the Senate Budget Committee, admitted that "those who said the president can't get to the Gramm-Rudman target were wrong."

And this is without raising taxes.

Recognizing that the best-laid plans of budget makers go awry when faced with political realities, it is still apparent that tough budgeting can significantly bring down the deficit.

Trade experts predict that a no-tax-increase budget will exacerbate the deficit in the current account. We shall see. But a budget that shows a $109 billion deficit would be its own reward.

Indeed, it would make Bush's first year in office a rousing success.

The Evening Gazette

Worcester, Massachusetts, May 22, 1989

It's fun to see economists befuddled by a phenomenon that defies their computer models and sets their crystal balls spinning. Of all experts, economists somehow seem the most smug.

So the unexpected sharp rise in the value of the dollar against other currencies in recent weeks is a joy, at least in that regard. It is also welcome on other grounds. Sheer patriotism, for instance. A "high dollar" has a nice ring to it.

From a more practical standpoint, a stronger dollar means Americans can travel or live abroad less expensively. More important, it helps curb inflation here at home, easing the need for the Federal Reserve to keep interest rates high.

But the unexpectedly strong dollar does have serious drawbacks.

The colossal U.S. trade deficit of a year ago has narrowed to a mere $8.86 billion in March, mostly because of a record boom in exports made possible by the decline of the dollar in recent years. But with the dollar now in reverse and soaring, all that could change for the worse.

American goods could become less competitive both at home and abroad. This could lead to a new round of factory layoffs here and perhaps tip the economy into recession.

So it is distressing in this sense that the experts were taken by surprise. The United States and other free-world economic powers had cooperated successfully in recent years to hold the dollar down in order to stabilize the world economy. They thought they had the dollar tamed.

Nobody knows for sure what went wrong, but a complex of factors may have come to bear — high oil prices, the tacit desire of the Fed to curb inflation, an increased flow of capital to the United States because of political instability in Japan and Germany.

While the experts' befuddlement is satisfying, it is also distressing.

Ordinary people do not consider the world value of the dollar a matter of pressing concern, yet price tags and paychecks are at stake. It would be reassuring to know that somebody had the matter in hand.

Let's hope the experts regain their bearings shortly and the free-world powers can bring the dollar back down to a level that bolsters economic stability and prosperity.

The Boston Globe

Boston, Massachusetts, April 5, 1989

Few American problems rank as high as the persistent deficit in trade with the rest of the world. Some gains have been made recently, but much more must be done to bring the deficit down from its current level of $115 billion a year – and there are discouraging signs that both business and government are doing far less than is necessary to promote exports to fertile markets.

The problem is understandable at one level. The American market is so large and easy to reach that manufacturers are often satisfied with devoting their efforts to tapping only the potential of that market. They define success in size of domestic market share. But world markets are enormous and have a huge potential for growth – provided Americans make adequate efforts to reach them.

The American government spends much of its time, effort and resources simply providing information about export opportunities to industries that often pay little attention. Other major industrial countries provide direct assistance to exporters making actual sales. The American Export-Import Bank is involved in only 6 percent of US exports; counterpart agencies in Japan, Britain and West Germany are involved in up to 30 percent, according to the Journal of Commerce.

The difficulties are compounded by the reluctance of Republican administrations to appear to be intervening in the private sector and by a suspicion among many Democrats of any programs that smack of corporate subsidies. The Export-Import Bank is a frequent target of criticism on this ground.

The realities of the times, however, demand more intense direct efforts by federal agencies to stimulate further exports. American industry – including many relatively small corporations – turn out goods for which there is potentially significant demand. Finding international markets for those goods would help improve the lives of other economies and, at the same time, help solve an American problem. There is no need to wait.

Arkansas Gazette
Little Rock, Arkansas, February 24, 1989

After seven years of growth, the United States trade deficit declined last year. Economists, who get their bearings by making comparisons, reported that the 1988 deficit of $137.34 billion was considerably better than the record $170.3 billion posted in 1987, but it was nearly six times as large as the $25.5 billion gap reported in 1980.

International trade is an indicator of economic performance. The country that consistently imports more than it exports obviously is falling short somewhere along the production line. If that yardstick is an indicator, the eight years of the Reagan administration was a bit of a disappointment.

America's international commerce showed uninterrupted surpluses from the First World War until 1971 when it slipped into the red by $2.3 billion. Except for the psychological jolt of realizing the United States had become a net importer, the deficit was not significant. Unfortunately, the joy of buying rather than producing was habit-forming.

President Reagan was shocked by the way his predecessors had mismanaged the economy, but his responsible fiscal policies would correct that little problem quickly. All he had to do was balance the federal budget, implement the Curve of Laffer, and initiate a marvelous cycle of efficient production. Unfortunately, the policies did not seem to work and the trade deficit grew without interruption — until last year.

Frantic efforts to correct the problem reached a crisis in 1985, the second year in which the deficit exceeded $100 billion. James A. Baker III, who was secretary of the Treasury, and Paul A. Volcker, chairman of the Federal Reserve Board, enlisted the aid of the major trading partners in negotiating a weakening of the dollar. The initiative may be working, but economists claim the dollar will have to come down considerably more in order to attain balanced trade.

Further pursuit of the Baker plan could be hazardous. The United States depends heavily on foreign investors to finance borrowing needs. If the dollar declines too far, a thinning of bond buyers could drive up interest rates and slow the growth of the economy.

Exports played a major role in reducing the 1988 deficit. Sales of manufactured goods were up 25 percent and agricultural exports climbed an even stronger 29.3 percent. Before anyone praises the virtues of being a "reliable supplier" of farm products, he should look at the figures. Commodity sales last year were $37 billion, thereby matching the 1984 volume. Exports were below $30 billion in the three years prior to 1988, but nothing was said about "reliability." In 1980, the year that drew heavy criticism of President Jimmy Carter, farm exports totaled $41.2 billion. If this country remains a *reliable* source and other countries experience shortages, commodity sales could regain the pre-Reagan level.

A trade deficit reduction from $170.3 billion to $137.34 billion is a dramatic improvement. Now if the government can trim its budget deficit and if the producing segment of the economy can become more efficient and more competitive, the United States could move back toward the balanced trade it enjoyed prior to 1971.

St. Petersburg Times
St. Petersburg, Florida, March 4, 1989

The U.S. trade deficit for 1988 has just been tabulated, and the news is good — sort of. The deficit is down to $137 billion from 1987's $170 billion, the smallest in three years and the first year-to-year improvement in nine years. The trouble is, it is still extremely high and no one can agree on whether, or by how much, it might shrink further in the year ahead.

One thing is certain: America's trade with the rest of the world continues to grow on an absolute basis, almost without interruption. Rising exports in 1988 have cut the deficit; imports are still rising also — in almost every sector from heavy machinery to canned fruit.

The days are gone when America imported a relatively insignificant percentage of its goods and services while foreign economies lived or died on the strength of their exports to each other. We are all in the same boat now. That truism should instruct us as we seek to settle disputes with our trading partners. There is no substitute for diplomacy in a game where the dependence is truly mutual — as it now surely is.

But trade figures also should be viewed with skepticism. The Commerce Department reported that in December, $368 million in goods were somehow not recorded as imported and that another $800 million a year in electrical power imports from Canada never have been counted, though in the future they will be. The department also will now compute monthly trade figures under a new formula.

So as the trade deficit is recorded in 1989, monthly setbacks shouldn't be taken too seriously; they may not be as great as they appear. The data's quality just isn't good enough to be sure. But make no mistake, 1988's lower trade deficit isn't nearly good enough; further reduction is essential to our economic well-being.

THE BUFFALO NEWS
Buffalo, New York, February 22, 1989

LAST YEAR BROUGHT impressive progress on America's trade front. Figures for the entire year showed the U.S. trade deficit fell to $137.3 billion, a dramatic drop of nearly 20 percent from the record levels run up only a year earlier.

It was the first time since 1980 that the nation's trade deficit, instead of surging higher, declined.

Not only that, but improvement in the balance between the merchandise that America imports and exports resulted from a powerful rise in exports — especially manufactured goods, up 25 percent from the prior year, and agricultural products, up an even more brisk 29 percent.

All of this pumped fresh income and growth into the nation's economy, and serves to rebut the protectionists who contend, falsely, that the United States must build high barriers against foreign goods in order to reduce the trade imbalance.

America must of course fight hard for fair trade conditions with other nations, but this inevitably requires give-and-take compromises between different societies. U.S. trading partners are unlikely to accept blatant protectionist obstacles here against their goods while still welcoming American products sent for sale in their markets.

Despite the cheering news on trade, however, 1988's results should not obscure tenacious problems that persist and could undermine continued future progress.

Some of last year's progress came about because of Washington's policy begun three years earlier, a policy in which our major trading partners cooperated, of lowering the value of the dollar abroad.

As its value fell, U.S. goods became less expensive and, thus, more competitive in these foreign markets.

But there is a limit to how much the dollar can be or should be depreciated. Further steep reductions would not occur without considerable risks. One could be a growing reluctance among foreign creditors to invest in U.S. debt, including that caused by Washington's budget deficits. Another risk is rekindled inflation here at home.

What will contribute meaningfully to improved trade balances is for America to increase its level of saving and its ability, in part through investment of those savings in more efficient plants and equipment, to expand productivity — that is, producing more for the same amount of work time.

After all, even with the heartening gains of last year, the country is still running a huge deficit with our trading partners. As a nation, we are consuming more than we produce. That cannot go on forever without dire economic consequences, including serious decay in our standard of living.

"It would be counterproductive to rely on dollar depreciation alone to restore equilibrium in our international accounts," Bruce K. MacLaury, president of the Brookings Institution, a liberal research and policy organization in Washington, D.C., wrote recently. "Until we reduce domestic consumption — to shift production toward exports — currency depreciation is a prescription for inflation, not equilibrium. We also need strong foreign growth and new markets."

These fundamental needs won't be met overnight. But Washington can help with each of these tasks, and this will bring more enduring progress than quickie expedients, such as deep dollar devaluations.

Few changes would produce a better start by Washington than cutting federal budget deficits, which would cut borrowing needs and free more capital for other investments. As everyone knows, deficit reduction has proved a difficult task. But it is no less essential to continued trade progress and the nation's economic health because of that.

THE ⎯⎯ SUN
Baltimore, Maryland, April 24, 1989

Economists are pleased at the latest export figures, which show American-made goods doing increasingly well in world markets. Instead of the negative growth that greeted the start of the Eighties, U.S. exports are booming, driving a steady upcurve on analysts' charts. What is especially encouraging is the fact that the big growth has come in manufactured goods: aircraft, up 99.4 percent since 1986; electrical machinery, up 133.1 percent; cars and trucks, up 61.4 percent; computers and office machines, up 69.5 percent; and small manufactured goods, up 145.9 percent.

The fall of the dollar's value against other currencies has played a big role, to be sure. Analysts point to an even bigger role for productivity increases on America's shop floors, an improvement many observers gave up on when "trade deficit" joined the lexicon.

U.S. factory productivity grew at an average 3.6 percent a year in the 1980s, making U.S. products cost-effective even as manufacturers struggled to boost quality to match the best imports. In the auto industry, shellacked by Japanese products on one end of the market and European products at the other end, factory efficiency rose about 4 percent a year. Part of that was due to "transplants" assembling Japanese cars, but part of it was due to hard lessons learned in Detroit. Many of those autos being shipped out to foreign ports are American brands, not cars turned out by transplants.

An export boom was predicted by economists studying the specifics of the U.S. status as the world's biggest debtor. What they said during the mid-'80s was that exporting goods was the only way America could pay its bills. That export push would go beyond commodities, for either Americans would reorganize manufacturing to cut costs and boost quality, or others would come in to do it for them, using this country as a low-wage manufacturing center for the world.

American wages have gone down, compared to Europe and Japan. According to the Bureau of Labor Statistics, Americans earn $14.31 an hour in pay and benefits while workers in Germany earn $17.58 and Japanese workers earn $12.63.

Still, the success of the most sophisticated products — aircraft, electrical machinery, cars, computers and office machines — argues for good products, not low wages as the answer. To keep up the strength that produced this surge of exports, now is the time to invest in the kind of educational and job-training reforms urged by the American Society for Training Development in its landmark Labor Department study. Now is the time to implement "Gaining New Ground," the Council on Competitiveness' report and recommendations on industrial strategies. The consensus is in on what works. As a generation of Americans gets ready to retire, it's time to get moving on prepping the replacements for the hard job ahead.

🏛 The Cincinnati Post
Cincinnati, Ohio, April 22, 1989

Take heart, the economy may be snapping out of its coma and showing faint — but unmistakable — signs of life.

The trade deficit is down, claims for unemployment benefits are down and some of the nation's most inventive companies say the recession has bottomed out and recovery may be on the way.

"Our executives are bullish about the spring quarter," says Barry Rogstad, president of the American Business Conference, a coalition of 100 mid-size, fast-growing firms. Sales and profits are up, even though few of the companies are hiring new workers yet.

Consumers will be glad to know that inflation is at its lowest level in nearly five years, interest rates are declining and many bargain buys are available in the cooled-off housing market.

Most of the bad news is on the employment side of the ledger. The jobless rate is at 6.8 percent and still rising

Car sales were dismal in the first three months of the year. That may be partly a reaction to the high jobless rate. New hiring during a recovery could bring buyers into auto showrooms again.

One sign of recovery was the sharp decline in late March and early April in the number of initial claims for unemployment benefits. That's a flimsy reed for optimism, and it may not last, but it's more encouraging than most of the figures we've seen lately.

The stock market, with the Dow Jones average topping 3000 for the first time ever, has been telling us for weeks that better days lie ahead. The market tends to be quirky, but this time it might be right.

When there is a recovery, it will be led by small and mid-size firms, many of them high-tech and service companies. Industries hampered by bureaucratic practices and fusty market strategies are having a tough time competing these days.

Administration Unveils Farm Bill; Senate, House Pass Legislation

Agriculture Secretary Clayton K. Yeutter Feb. 6, 1990 unveiled recommendations for a new farm bill that proposed "flexibility" and "positive incentives" to meet environmental and market concerns. But the bill avoided specifying cuts in farm subsidy programs asked for in the administration's budget proposals.

While requesting $1.5 billion in federal price-support cuts, the administration had deferred to Congress on how to allocate the cuts. Yeutter said the administration did "not intend to make specific recommendations on how to meet budget requirements."

The bill was in many respects similar to the 1985 Reagan farm bill that it was drawn up to replace.

Many of the modifications that were introduced were designed to allow farmers to grow different crops without fear of losing price supports. That flexibility would encourage increased yields of crops such as soybeans, traditionally in short supply, officials said. Yeutter noted that greater crop variety would be better for the environment because it would encourage crop rotation.

Yeutter also proposed expanding a voluntary conservancy program for land that had been subject to soil erosion. The program, which originated with the 1985 farm bill, had thus far set aside 34 million acres.

Yeutter rejected calls from many environmentalists for stricter regulations to reduce problems including soil erosion and groundwater contamination, saying the proposals would unfairly burden farmers.

Congressional Democrats criticized the new bill for failing to adequately address environmental concerns or to specify projected farm subsidies.

"The administration fails to to tell farmers what it thinks target prices should be. American farmers don't know what their incomes will be and Congress does not know how much the administration will be willing to spend on farm programs," said Senate Agriculture Committee Chairman Patrick J. Leahy (D, Vt.).

The Senate July 27 and the House Aug. 1 approved five-year agricultural spending bills that would continue many of the same subsidy programs included in the previous 1985 farm bill. The bills broke new ground, however, in environmental and consumer protection programs.

The Senate bill passed by a vote of 70 to 21, while the House version was approved by a 327-91 margin. The bills were broadly similar, differing mainly in that a House amendment would limit to $200,000 annual federal payments that could go to each farmer. The two bills now faced reconciliation in a House-Senate conference committee.

The cost of the support programs in the bills was estimated at between $53 billion and $55 billion. Farm price supports were set to continue for sugar, milk, wool, peanuts, soybeans and major field crops, including cotton, wheat and corn.

The bills included some programs that would introduce greater flexibility into subsidy programs, allowing farmers to grow a variety of crops. If they grew different crops, however, the farmers would forgo subsidies on them.

New environmental measures added to both bills would eliminate the export of pesticides that had been banned in the U.S. and halt the import of fruits and vegetables on which such pesticides had been used.

The bills would also set up a program of easements to protect U.S. wetlands as preserves and to expand to more than 40 million acres a voluntary conservancy program for terrain that had been subject to soil erosion. In addition, farmers would be offered incentives to curb groundwater contamination.

Under another provision of the legislation, organically grown fruits and vegetables meeting minimum federal organic standards would now have their status certified with a special label. These environmental and consumer measures originated in the Senate, and were added to the House bill as amendments shortly before its passage.

Minneapolis Star and Tribune

Minneapolis, Minnesota, July 22, 1990

This should be a year for a luxurious, yet frugal, farm bill. With the troubles of the mid-1980s behind, Congress could buy good farm policy for much less than the crisis-inflated spending of the past five years. But proposals now under consideration in the House and Senate would spend a lot of money on a little reform. Perhaps lawmakers are less courageous and visionary this year because there is no crisis to force them. But a bad bill could lead to hard times ahead. Farmers, consumers and taxpayers deserve better.

Congress need only build on the sound base laid in the expiring 1985 farm bill. Then, despite the gripping recession, lawmakers had the good sense to lower federal price subsidies. That made U.S. crops competitive again in world markets, with the desired effect: Exports recovered, along with farm incomes and land values.

Much more is needed to position U.S. farmers to prosper in the '90s. This year's farm bill should break the grip federal subsidies have on farmers' planting decisions; make better use of the country's vast agricultural resources to serve growing world markets; reform archaic federal programs for milk, sugar, peanuts and tobacco; and better incorporate environmental and food-safety protections within federal farm policy. With the farm economy healthy again, lawmakers also should abandon the crisis mentality that guided recent farm spending and instead decide what minimum level of taxpayer support is required to protect farmers from extreme market fluctuations and to ensure adequate food supplies.

Don't look for much of that in the bills now before the full House and Senate. Both are better than early versions that attempted to undo the achievements of 1985 by raising federal price subsidies. But both bills would take away some price flexibility and in return provide only a hint of planting flexibility. Sweet treatment continues for crops like sugar. Lawmakers also accept a "baseline" spending level that assumes annual subsidies of about $11 billion a year — less than half the peak reached during the worst of the recession, but more than double spending prior to that.

The Bush administration — too long silent during the farm-bill negotiations — has threatened a veto. Agriculture Secretary Clayton Yeutter objects to the high cost, and is concerned about the effect that regressive domestic farm policy would have on exports and on U.S. efforts to reduce world trade barriers. He has help from a coalition of urban lawmakers who question the fairness of heavily subsidizing farmers while forcing poor consumers to pay more for sugar and peanut butter. Environmentalists and consumer groups, too, are attacking subsidies that encourage poor land stewardship and over-use of chemicals.

There's reason for hope. A proposal to reduce the U.S. sugar price support by 2 cents a pound, for example, is showing more life than have such attempts in the past. The 10 percent cut would be modest — matching reductions in other crop subsidies in the past five years — but would yield some benefits. And if lawmakers dare to reform the sacrosanct sugar program, then they might also dare take on other dragons. The time is right.

THE CHRISTIAN SCIENCE MONITOR
Boston, Massachusetts, August 3, 1990

THIS week the House dealt with a farm bill that pegs the price of corn but fails to address the larger issues of American agriculture policy.

That is unfortunate, because agriculture's larger issues hold lessons for the rest of the US economy. A closer look at farm policy could show the US how to compete – and how not to compete – with Asia and Europe.

The Senate haggled over and last week finally passed a $54 billion farm bill, which continues current farm subsidies and strengthens some environmental provisions of the bill. Any fresh perspectives were quickly lost in the maneuvering over the arcane particulars of marketing loans and target prices.

Yet agriculture is one of this nation's largest industries on the world scene. US farmers face low-wage and highly subsidized foreign competition that would make automakers run screaming from their factories. For 30 years, nonetheless, the US has exported more food and fiber than it imported. Those exports were nice back in 1960, when the nation was running a healthy trade surplus. Today the nation's overall trade balance is billions of dollars in the red, but agriculture is running an $18 billion surplus. Those farm exports are more than nice – they are vital.

Plenty of conservatives say American farmers have suc-ceeded in spite of farm programs. Many liberals would turn their backs on the world market, saying we must preserve the family-run farm at all costs. Neither extreme is correct.

Agriculture is the country's longest, most extensive experiment with a government-managed economy. Sometimes that experiment has worked well; sometimes it has failed miserably. Policymakers ought to take a hard look at those successes and failures and apply their lessons to other key industries. That is especially true now, when the US is casting worried sidelong glances at how Japan and Western Europe use government policy to help industries move forward.

Some claim the US Department of Agriculture is the closest thing the US has to Japan's Ministry of International Trade and Industry. That's a puzzling thought for farmers, most of whom would scrap the USDA if they could force other countries to eliminate their farm programs. Agriculture is no exception to the truism that government is a messy way to direct an economy.

Nevertheless, federal intervention has had its pluses. Land-grant universities have fostered agricultural research. Federally employed extension agents have transferred that research to family farmers. Farmers, in turn, have planted and invested in new technology thanks to steady credit from a quasi-governmental lending system. In the 1980s, the US started subsidizing farm exports, which broke the rules of free trade but helped force the European Community to reconsider its own farm subsidies.

Agriculture's key lesson may be that limited government intervention has its place. In any case, the debate ought to begin.

The Chattanooga Times
Chattanooga, Tennessee, August 15, 1990

Everytime we think Congress is finally getting serious about cutting the federal deficit — and no, the thought doesn't occur very often — along comes legislation that seems designed to ensure that no one should take such deficit-cutting talk seriously. The 1990 farm legislation shows that it's still business as usual on Capitol Hill.

Bills under consideration in the House and Senate contain agricultural programs that are likely to cost American taxpayers an estimated $54 billion over the next five years. But if past performance is a reliable guide, and we're convinced it is, that figure will soon be several billion dollars higher.

At a time when the federal deficit is in the 12-digit range, it's incredible that Congress is unwilling to reduce the soaring cost of farm subsidies. The problem is made worse by the fact that most of the subsidies have long since outlived the usefulness they may have once had.

The direct cost of farm legislation is bad enough, but it's not the only burden that Americans must shoulder as part of federal agricultural policy. The subsidy programs also force up the price of food in the grocery stores by more than $10 billion a year.

Congress may eventually increase taxes as part of a deficit-cutting measure, although we'll believe that when we see it. But until members of the House and Senate try to regain public confidence by cutting unnecessary spending — and farm subsidies are a good starting point — they should not test the public's tolerance for gall by voting to continue outdated, yet seemingly sacrosanct, farm programs.

Chicago Tribune
Chicago, Illinois, August 17, 1990

America's farmers are proud, independent types. When pressed, most will agree they should be making more of their own decisions and assuming more of the risks of business instead of relying on the government.

Yet, if Congress has its way farmers will continue reacting primarily to incentives created by expensive government subsidy programs rather than to market stimulants of supply and demand.

Before they left for their August vacation, members of both the Senate and House rushed to pass versions of a farm bill that will set the course for agriculture for the next five years. Despite a looming deficit of $170 billion and slow, steady progress in reducing farm supports over the last five years, they voted to freeze subsidies at present levels and even create new ones.

Their largess isn't surprising. An election is approaching, so waste and cowardice run amok on Capitol Hill. If the subsidies are not cut in the final version of the bill or by negotiators during the budget summit, the Bush administration will have to veto the 1990 farm bill. In the meantime, though, legislators will be able to campaign at home as champions of the farmer, which is all they cared about in the first place.

Democrats and Republicans in both houses contend they aren't trying to duck a difficult issue or force a showdown with the administration. Instead, they say, they're merely extending current farm policy for another five years.

That would cost the Treasury about $11 billion a year, a far cry from the peak of nearly $26 billion in price supports doled out to farmers in 1986. That $11 billion, though, is only the surface expense. James Bovard, a public policy analyst at the Washington-based Cato Institute, points out that politicians understate the true cost of farm programs by referring only to direct outlays. Add in loan guarantees, subsidized insurance and higher food prices to consumers, and farm programs cost at least $40 billion.

Even that isn't the worst of it. The current system of farm subsidies invites overproduction, inefficient land use and big payments to some farmers who don't need them. Individual farmers aren't supposed to get more than $50,000 a year in income support and $250,000 in total subsidies, outlandish in itself. But many direct their lawyers to subdivide their land into separate trusts or shell corporations to qualify for payments that can exceed $1 million a year.

Despite the obvious abuses and inequities, legislators beat back most attempts to fix the problems. Except for an amendment to kill the tiny $77 million-a-year honey program, they easily defeated proposals to limit payments to wealthy farmers and eliminate specific crop programs. Instead, they created new subsidies for wheat, soybean and feed grain producers.

For now, the lawmakers can't be bothered with correcting even the most outrageous excesses of America's farm policy. They're concerned only with being able to campaign as the farmer's benefactor. If Congress really wanted to do right by farmers, not to mention the rest of the nation stuck with inflated food prices, it would give them what they say they really want—greater autonomy and freedom to compete.

The Oregonian

Portland, Oregon, November 27, 1990

The 1990 farm bill, low wheat prices and changes in farming practices converge to give Oregon its best opportunity yet to plant a major new agricultural product in its economy.

The product is canola, the vegetable oil developed by Canada from rapeseed. It is a favorite of Japanese consumers and gaining favor in the domestic market because it is lowest of all oils in saturated fats.

Rapeseed could become a second crop for wheat farmers of Eastern Oregon. Research by Oregon State University has shown the mustard plant can produce 2,400 pounds an acre dryland, double that irrigated. It also can be grown in enormous quantities in the Willamette Valley.

But right now the importance of a substantial alternative crop is to be found in the wheat lands east of the Cascades. The new farm bill reduces wheat acreage and encourages farmers to experiment with other crops.

Moreover, the low wheat prices caused by a world glut in grain adds incentive to wheat farmers to look for profitable substitutes. Add to that the drive to back away from heavy concentrations of chemicals and switch to more natural methods like crop rotation, and rapeseed looks all the more as though it could have a permanent place in the Oregon agricultural economy

There has to be a marketing structure before farmers can rely on a new crop. It makes little difference that a commodity can be produced in a profitable volume if there is no profitable way to get it to market.

But Japanese interests have pledged themselves to constructing processing plants if enough rapeseed is planted here to support them. Moreover, a market awaits the finished product, both at home and abroad.

So more is at stake than another crop in Oregon's wheat country, important though that is. A whole industry could grow up around it.

As a side benefit, Oregon now imports 120,000 tons of rapeseed mash a year from Canada as livestock feed. The mash is a byproduct of canola, and is particularly valuable for cattle, hogs and poultry.

This state is moving toward finishing more of its beef at home with products grown here. Rapeseed mash might as well be one of them.

CHICAGO Sun-Times

Chicago, Illinois, November 26, 1990

"There is pain here. It is not an easy thing to vote for, when you're dealing with programs that will be cut. For once it's not smoke and mirrors,"—Sen. Patrick J. Leahy (D-Vt.), chairman of the Agriculture Committee, on the 1990 farm bill.

Not quite.

Sure, the $41 billion bill is not the cash cow that farm-state lawmakers wanted. (Curious about what they wanted? Don't ask.)

But it hardly was the jolting hit that most Americans would assume, considering all the austerity talk heard in Washington.

Peanut growers, for example, won price support increases of up to 5 percent annually. Barley growers got an increased subsidy rate that will bring them another $250 million over five years. Oat growers also fared better.

And then there are the wheat growers. As the Wall Street Journal reported, wheat growers will continue receiving their usual subsidies for not growing wheat. While that in itself seems like something hatched by the Mad Hatter, it's now a well-accepted practice.

No, what's amazing about the deal the wheat farmers worked for themselves is this: Normally, when farmers are paid not to farm their fields, they are not allowed to grow anything in the fields. But now, when wheat farmers are paid not to farm their fields, they will also be allowed to grow something on those fields.

That something—as anyone could have guessed—is canola, sunflowers and other oilseed crops. Canola, in case you missed it, is just catching on because it produces canola oil, which is low in saturated fat.

If you're offended, just wait. As the Journal pointed out, the bill is 2,000 pages long; who knows what else might turn up once someone finally gets around to reading the rest of the fine print?

The Miami Herald

Miami, Florida, November 10, 1990

RESTRUCTURING the farm-subsidy formulas in order to save $13.6 billion, the 1990 Farm Bill is a dramatic effort to tie agriculture policy more closely to market economics. The experiment forced by the tandem budget-reconciliation bill is welcome.

Under current law, farmers tend to plant the same subsidized crop year after year and rely on the Government's guaranteed return. Under the new law, farmers of wheat, corn, and other grains may plant whatever they want on 15 percent of their land usually devoted to subsidized crops. That new flexibility is an incentive to rotate crops and to plant the most profitable ones.

The question is, How much flexibility can the Government build into its farm programs without destabilizing farm markets and incomes? The answer remains unclear. The security of the nation's farmers and food supply is at stake. The experiment must be carefully monitored.

Price supports for Florida's dairy and sugar industries technically were maintained at current levels. However, "misery taxes," or service fees and assessments, were imposed on both, thus reducing supports. Dairymen, whose assessments will be triggered and set by production in Wisconsin and California, are at greater risk than sugar growers.

The sugar program still relies on import quotas to stabilize prices. For the first time, imports are guaranteed at no less than 1.25 million short tons. That promises small but welcome relief for Caribbean economies squeezed by falling quotas over the last five years. For the first time, too, the Government is imposing anti-competitive domestic-market limits on crystalline fructose, a break-through corn sweetener.

Corn sweeteners now command 50 percent of the nation's sweetener market. The inclusion of crystalline fructose is worrisome, portending a new program that by design is not tied to market economics.

Although the bill includes important new initiatives to preserve wetlands and control water pollution, Senate Agriculture Chairman Patrick Leahy's initiative to ban the export of pesticides prohibited for use in this country was lost. The ban was intended to halt the "circle of poison" through which prohibited pesticides return as residues on imported fruits and vegetables. It should be revived by the next Congress.

Finally, the bill rightly extends the food-stamp program for five years and streamlines the food-for-peace program to direct commodities to the poorest countries.

Clearly the product of political compromise, the 1990 Farm Bill is more innovative than stifling. The President should sign it.

Wisconsin State Journal

Madison, Wisconsin, October 23, 1990

The 1990 Farm Bill is now complete. Both the House and Senate are set to pass it and President Bush is prepared to sign it. Whether farmers will like it — and whether it proves helpful to the local, county and state economies that depend on farmers as a base industry — remains to be seen.

As everyone who cares about agriculture knows, this could be a watershed year for the farm industry.

The Farm Bill is an experiment. For the first time, farmers will be able to take 15 percent of their land enrolled in farm programs and plant them to any crop they desire.

The traditional purpose of requiring farmers to grow "program crops" on the land they enroll in farm programs is to guarantee that enough feed grains, wheat, cotton and rice are produced to supply the nation's export and domestic demand. The problem has been that the programs encourage overproduction of subsidized crops — and underproduction of other crops such as soybeans and oats.

The new program gives farmers flexibility to plant other crops on land, without forcing the farmers to withdraw that land from potential subsidies in the future. The idea will save taxpayers money and introduce new market forces into agriculture — both of which are positive trends in government policy.

The experiment is not without flaws, however. The major one is that there aren't many "alternative" crops to which farmers can turn. Under the bill, they can't switch to vegetables, fruit or dry edible beans because new production of those crops would destroy markets for farmers already producing those crops. Wheat is already in surplus. And markets for other crops, such as oats or canola, aren't that large.

Still, the 1990 Farm Bill may be the discipline farmers need. It is not a radical bill. It still leaves in place the structure of most programs, including the dairy price-support program. And it comes at time when most farmers have rebounded from the hard times of the 1980s. It is an experiment worth trying.

PORTLAND
EVENING EXPRESS
Portland, Maine, October 24, 1990

To Francis Bacon's observation that crafty men condemn studies; simple men admire them and wise men use them, should be added another category — Congress authorizes them. In fact, so far as agricultural studies are concerned, Congress has run amok.

Make no mistake, studies of such things as composting, gypsy moths and flower sales can be useful. But there is good evidence that many of the studies Congress compels the Agriculture Department to make each year are repetitive, duplicative and unnecessary.

Moreover, they are costly. Senate Minority Leader Robert Dole of Kansas believes that getting Congress out of the agricultural study business could ultimately save taxpayers as much as $100 million over a five-year period.

Here's the situation. Right now Congress dictates what the USDA will study this year, regardless of whether the department sees any need for the inquiries. This year's farm bill, for example, calls for 168 studies, reports and surveys. Many are intended by their sponsors to impress the folks back home or to delay the implementation of legislation a congressman or the farm industry opposes.

Dole's proposal is a sensible one. In brief it would authorize a minimum of a dozen agricultural studies over five years. But, unlike the present system, the USDA would decide what ought to be studied. Then Congress would approve the studies by putting up the money.

Let's hope Dole's proposal, which is a Senate amendment to this year's farm bill, finds it way into law. Taxpayers already spend far too much money subsidizing American agriculture without the added burden of financing expensive studies virtually no one is ever likely to read or use.

THE INDIANAPOLIS NEWS
Indianapolis, Indiana, October 24, 1990

The United States has a federal farm program. And in its farm program it has 128 studies, e-i-e-i-o. With a study here and a study there, here a study, there a study, everywhere. . . .

Sen. Bob Dole, R-Kan., finally rebelled against all the studies required of the United States Department of Agriculture, according to a report by Associate Press farm writer Don Kendall.

Dole proposed and the House-Senate conference committee approved an amendment to the 1990 farm bill that would eliminate a good number of the 168 studies, reports and surveys the farm bill would require of the USDA.

Dole's plan would allow the USDA to pick a minimum of 12 studies to complete over the five-year lifetime of the farm bill. The Senate and House Agriculture Committee chairpersons would have to approve the selections.

Dole's plan is a good one. Not only would the amendment cut the number of studies, but perhaps even the number of employees required by the USDA — a double savings. The savings might even free up resources for additional food inspections for fish and seafood.

Budget savings, however, don't always play well in Washington. Despite the savings the cuts would represent, some legislators are upset because the studies would benefit their constituents. The thought of study losses has signaled some political maneuvering.

House Agriculture Committee Chairman Kika de la Garza, D-Texas, has come to the aid of House Budget Committee Chairman Leon Panetta, who wants to protect a study of how badly the domestic cut flower industry is hurt by imported flowers. Flowers, of course, are a product of Panetta's district in California. Instead of looking for excuses to block foreign flowers from the marketplace, the flower industry would be better off looking for more efficient ways to grow cutflowers in the first place.

Other studies that might be lost include the effects of global warming on rice production, a variety of studies on U.S. export programs, farm safety . . . you name it, the USDA has been ordered to study it.

It's time for agricultural industries to do their own studies, if they are really that important.

The 1990 farm bill must represent a time of belt-tightening. Trimming the federal budget deficit would do more to help farmers compete in the export market than any number of government studies.

San Francisco Chronicle
San Francisco, California, November 30, 1990

THE GOVERNMENT has been encouraging farmers to be inefficient. The 1985 Farm Bill, which fortunately expires this year, kept many farmers from changing crops because they knew they could keep getting a subsidy by planting stuff that wasn't needed.

The new bill, signed by President Bush, cuts acreage subsidies by 25 percent over the next five years. Growers of cotton, wheat, rice and feed grains will find that the amount of land protected by government price supports will decline steadily.

Instead, farmers will be encouraged to grow other crops that have a better chance to be sold on the world market. The result should be a substantial reduction in the nation's trade deficit, along with the savings the reduced subsidies will produce for the nation's taxpayers.

As Bush described the bill, "It lets farmers make more of their decisions based on the market (rather than) the traditional farm program straitjacket."

In addition, the new farm measure provides funds for the creation of wetlands reserves of up to a million acres. It also offers financial incentives for farmers to switch to production methods that protect water supplies from chemical contamination.

"This is the most environmentally sensitive farm bill ever," Bush said.

The bill also renews the food stamp program that has proved its value both in helping the nation's poor and in encouraging agricultural consumption. It serves consumers by setting the first nationwide standards for organic foods.

THE IMPORTANCE of the 1990 Farm Bill may extend well beyond reforms in agriculture. It should prove to be the forerunner of other domestic legislation promoting efficiency in production while, at the same time, reducing dependence on subsidies the government can no longer afford to pay.

Textile Bill
Veto Upheld

The House of Representatives Oct. 10, 1990 failed to override President George Bush's veto of legislation restricting textile, apparel and show imports.

The 275-152 House vote fell 10 votes short of the two-thirds majority needed to override the veto. It was the third time in five years that the House had sustained a presidential veto on textile import curbs.

Sixty-nine Republicans and 206 Democrats voted to override the veto, while 103 Republicans and 49 Democrats voted to sustain it.

The textile bill had been passed by the Senate July 17 by a vote of 68 to 32, more than the two-thirds required to override a presidential veto. The measure cleared the House Sept. 18 by a 271-149 vote.

President Bush vetoed the bill Oct. 5. "This highly protectionist bill would damage the national economy, increase already artificially high costs to consumers of several basic goods and abrogate our international agreements," he said in his veto message.

(According to the White House, it was Bush's 14th veto. All 14 had been upheld.)

Bush said approval of the bill would amount to a subsidy for the textile industry, adding that each job created because of reduced competition from abroad would cost U.S. consumers $70,000. The price hikes resulting from approval of the bill would boost by $2,600 the cost of clothing a family of four over five years, he said.

He said passage would also torpedo the General Agreement on Tariffs and Trade talks aimed at reducing protectionism. Bush predicted that "perhaps half of the 100 nations" participating in the GATT Uruguay Round of trade negotiations would exit the talks immediately if the bill were approved.

House Appropriations Committee Chairman Jamie L. Whitten (D, Miss.) Oct. 10 said before the House vote, "We're headed for a real recession in this because we're letting everyone around the world have our domestic market."

Since the early 1980s, U.S. textile, apparel and shoe manufacturers had sought trade barriers, which they claimed were needed to protect jobs threatened by cheap imports, mostly from Asia.

Omaha World-Herald
Omaha, Nebraska, October, 13, 1990

The 152 House members who voted to uphold a presidential veto this week made an important statement in favor of free trade. Their vote sidetracked a bill that could have hurt the United States in the global marketplace.

Voting to uphold the veto were Nebraska Reps. Virginia Smith and Doug Bereuter, along with Iowa Reps. Fred Grandy and Jim Ross Lightfoot. Casting what amounted to a vote for protectionism was Rep. Peter Hoagland.

The bill, backed by some segments of the textile and clothing industry, would have reduced imports of shoes and other apparel. President Bush said it would "pick the pockets of U.S. consumers," adding $100 a year to the cost of providing clothing for a typical family of four. He noted that the profitability in the clothing industry has been improving.

The bill was designed to protect one industry. But the nature of protectionism is that what happens in one industry can spread. U.S. Trade Representative Carla Hills said the textile restrictions appeared to conflict with various provisions of 38 trade treaties between the United States and other nations.

Some of those nations could be expected to retaliate, perhaps by reducing their purchases of U.S. farm products or high-tech items.

Import restrictions clearly go against the philosophy of free trade toward which more enlightened nations have moved in recent years. During the Uruguay Round of the General Agreement on Tariffs and Trade (GATT) talks, the Bush administration has worked to create clear and enforceable rules to minimize protectionism.

If the textile bill had survived, American credibility in GATT circles would have been damaged. A GATT official said the Uruguay round would have been "finished."

Rep. Dan Rostenkowski, an Illinois Democrat, summarized the case against protectionism succinctly when he said: "We have absolutely no chance to get into foreign markets if we unilaterally close our own markets." Well said, congressman. And, to the 152 House members who stood up for free trade, well done.

The Washington Post
Washington, D.C., October 15, 1990

ECONOMIC isolationism is on the rise again in Congress, as the votes on the outrageously protectionist textile bill show. The House has now failed to override President Bush's veto by 275 votes for the bill to 152 against—not quite the necessary two-thirds, but perilously close to it. So much for the theory that countries' economic interests determine their political attitudes. The United States is a trading nation on a tremendous scale, and to maintain their present standard of living Americans are going to have to increase their exports steadily. But the textile bill is a device to close markets, and the veto is by no means the end of the story.

A long process of worldwide negotiations to open markets and write better trade rules is now coming to its climax. These talks are known collectively as the Uruguay Round, and there are a lot of things on the table there that American exporters urgently want and need—better access to foreign markets, better protection for patents and copyrights, faster and fairer settlement of trade disputes. But it's increasingly probable that this whole gigantic effort is going to collapse.

There are two barriers to agreement, both of them so far intractable. The European Community refuses to give up its disruptive and damaging practice of dumping its hugely subsidized farm surpluses on world markets at prices far below production cost. Equally intransigent, Congress here in the United States continues to insist on protecting textile and clothing manufacturers from imports.

Even though the textile bill has now been vetoed and is dead, it has been extremely useful to the textile producers. It has enabled them to demonstrate that, while they don't have a two-thirds majority, they certainly have much more than a simple majority. That's all they need to block the trade law reforms that the Uruguay Round will—if it's successful—produce.

The override vote was a warning by the friends of the textile industry to the American negotiators not to try to weaken the arrangements that currently protect it. That's an ominous message. If the United States won't give on textiles, and the Europeans won't give on agricultural dumping, there's not much in the deal for the smaller and poorer countries of the world. They will walk out, and the talks will fail.

There's nothing that the textile industry would like better. But limitations on foreign trade are a threat to American growth and economic strength. At a time when the newly freed countries of Eastern Europe are reaching fervently toward open markets, the American Congress is uncertainly shuffling in the opposite direction.

The Salt Lake Tribune
Salt Lake City, Utah, October 1, 1990

When the textile quota bill recently delivered from Congress reaches the White House, President Bush should stick to his promise and veto it. The protectionist measure is no way to conduct this country's foreign trade business.

Once again, states with economies beholden to fabrics, clothing and shoe production have rounded up Senate and House of Representatives majorities for clamping restrictions on textile imports. But the argument for doing so is really no better than it was three times previously, when presidential vetoes wisely rejected such legislation.

The urgency for the domestic textile industry is greater, of course. The current Multi-Fiber Arrangement, a voluntary hold-down on textile imports to this country negotiated with 40 other nations, is due to expire next June. Comfortable with this shield against a more open market, U.S. textile and apparel producers want to roll in the quota law substitute.

As agreed to by Senate and House, the pending law would hold imported textile growth in the United States to 1 percent annually. It can be argued that this is better than having several different multilateral textile restriction agreements with various trading countries.

Except, no one's economy really benefits from this perpetual protection, whether it consists of standard tariffs and quotas or negotiated restraint. Especially when trading partners realize the artificial barriers are becoming permanent and start retaliating.

This country's textile producers have leaned on quotas and other import limits for more than 30 years. The issue is no longer one of helping infant business defend itself against big-boy competition.

Yes, employment in the U.S. textile industry has declined. But it still provides jobs for 1.8 million Americans. Plant and mill capacity is running at 90 percent. Since production has also risen, it's reasonable to assume efficiency, through technological modernization, is occurring at a rate able to make the U.S. competitive without a crutch.

Moreover, it is estimated that protection for the U.S. textile and apparel industry has, as of 1986, cost the American buying public $20.3 billion a year in higher prices for clothing and products containing fabric components.

Dismantling worldwide trade barriers is neither simple nor easy. But careful and patient efforts are being devoted to the task. The textile and apparel issues are being addressed in the current Uruguay Round of General Agreement on Tariffs and Trade (GATT) negotiations. These talks have been joined enthusiastically by the United States but could be wrecked if the textile quota bill succeeds.

This nation's stake in expanding world trade is greater than the narrow concern prompted by textile producers. Access to markets now closed by other countries' tariff and quota barriers can be gained through give and take such as that represented in the GATT Uruguay Round.

President Bush indicates he understands this. He will preserve the opportunities available with a veto of any unilateral enactment of textile quotas.

THE BUFFALO NEWS
Buffalo, New York, October 12, 1990

FOR THE third time in five years, a presidential veto has rightly prevented Congress from doing special favors for the American textile industry at the expense of millions of American consumers. President Reagan invoked the veto twice and President Bush, once.

The House properly sustained the latest veto, by Bush, of this anti-consumer legislation, assisted by the bipartisan votes of Reps. William Paxon, R-Amherst, and John LaFalce, D-Town of Tonawanda.

The bill in dispute is decidedly protectionist. Had it become law, it would have shaved the growth of textile and apparel imports by 1 percent a year and frozen imports of footwear at 1989 levels.

Proponents argued that these special favors, sheltering domestic products from foreign competition, was justified because the textile industry had lost 400,000 jobs (66,000 last year) over the past decade.

It was not a convincing case. Reducing imports also reduces competition among suppliers and limits the choices of consumers. This raises the prices consumers must pay. Had this bill passed, consumers would have shelled out an extra $30 billion over the next five years, according to estimates by the president's Council of Economic Advisers.

In addition, the chairman of the CEA, Michael J. Boskin, estimated that every new job created by such a protectionist bill in the sheltered industry would cost consumers a cool $70,000. Expensive subsidy.

Not only would this bill, had it passed, have clobbered American shoppers. Its adoption would also have violated international trade agreements and damaged the U.S. negotiating position in the current round of international trade talks. Nor would an official, unilateral narrowing of U.S. markets assist American exporters trying to pry their way into foreign markets.

Beyond that, too, is the question of how much help the textile and apparel industry really needed these days. Its profitability has recently improved. In opposing the measure, White House experts stressed that the industry's domestic shipments rose close to 7 percent last year while its exports soared 27 percent.

Clearly, this was a measure, flawed in numerous respects, that did not deserve to pass. It carried political clout on Capitol Hill, where members of the House and Senate appeared eager to do election-year favors.

But the bill would have damaged the country's position in world trade negotiations. It would have discouraged efficiency in an industry already too sheltered from bracing competition.

Worse still, it would have forced consumers — especially those of low and moderate incomes — to pay more than they needed to for essential items of life.

THE KANSAS CITY STAR
Kansas City, Missouri, October 13, 1990

As expected, Congress has failed to override President Bush's veto of a protectionist textile bill. The House vote, however, was only 10 short of the margin needed for override, a result which sends a disturbing message to U.S. trading partners and reveals much about the character of the U.S. Congress.

An attempt to encourage freer trade in clothing and textiles is an integral part of talks being conducted under the General Agreement on Tariffs and Trade. The U.S. position in these discussions calls for a more open market for textiles in exchange for an end to many overseas restrictions in sectors in which the United States is highly competitive, including trade-based investment, services and agriculture.

Success in these talks will create a bull market in international trade, an eventuality that will mean tens of billions in additional exports for U.S. companies.

But success at the negotiating table would only be a first step. Enabling legislation must be enacted by the same Congress that so recently has voted to restrict trade in the very products many Third World nations must sell to maintain economic growth.

For the sake of a profitable industry which already enjoys substantial trade protection, Congress has given the Bronx cheer to the GATT. Since 1985, when the textile industry began clamoring for more favors from Washington, mill employment has risen 3.4 percent. Factories are running at nearly 90 percent capacity.

This is politics as usual in Washington: The scramble to cater to special interests always takes precedence over the national interest, the interest of consumers — and even common sense.

Bieber Backed at UAW Convention

Owen F. Bieber won by acclamation June 21, 1989 a third three-year term as president of the United Auto Workers at the union's triennial convention in Anaheim, Calif.

A union dissident faction was soundly beaten in attempts to challenge the seating of certain convention delegates and in a bid for seats on the ruling executive board.

Dissident leaders Jerry Tucker and Donny Douglas were denied the seats. Tucker's loss came in a re-election bid; he had won a controversial court-ordered election to the board in September 1988 after protesting that the union's hierarchy had unfairly bolstered his opponent's election in a first vote.

The dissidents in general disagreed with Bieber and the current leadership on "jointness" programs undertaken in cooperation with the car companies on plant conditions, everything from day-care programs to choice of equipment. The dissidents protested that the union leadership was getting too cozy with the manufacturers and undermining the interests of union members.

In a keynote address to the convention June 18, Bieber defended the joint programs. "Our participation in joint programs is motivated by only one consideration, and that is the universal desire of workers to have a more satisfying and secure situation at work," he said. "That's not and never has been a response to the corporate agenda or a reflection of a weak union."

The dissidents, known as members of the New Directions movement, provided some lively debate and demonstrations at the convention, but the Bieber forces remained solidly in control.

In addition to Bieber, the delegates elected Bill Casstevens, 61, as secretary-treasurer, the union's number-two post, and, as vice presidents, Stephen P. Yokich, 53, Odessa Komer, 63, Ernest Lofton, 57, and Stan Marshall, 61.

Five of the dissidents had won convention seats in a May 17 vote at the General Motors Corp. plant in Van Nuys, Calif.

Another dissident, Phillip Keeling, was elected president of the UAW local at Mazda Motor Corp.'s only U.S. assembly plant, in Flat Rock, Mich., May 11. The extent of Keeling's militancy, or that of his supporters, was unknown, but up to this point the UAW had attained representation at Japanese auto plants only in return for a pledge to the company to accept Japanese management practices.

Keeling defeated Bill Judson, who had been appointed local president by UAW leaders after the union won bargaining rights.

THE DAILY OKLAHOMAN
Oklahoma City, Oklahoma, July 28, 1989

EMPLOYEES of the Nissan auto plant at Smyrna, Tenn., showed good sense in rejecting, by a 2-1 margin, an organizing effort by the United Auto Workers.

It was a crushing defeat for the UAW, which had hoped to demonstrate at Smyrna that it could win representation rights for workers in the South, where non-union sentiments generally prevail. Moreover, the vote was important for the UAW because it has suffered a 33 percent decline in membership since 1979.

The gamble failed because the workers in the Smyrna plant realize they can get along nicely without a union. As one employee put it, "They (the UAW) can't give us anything we don't already have."

The vote was significant, too, because the UAW had hoped to make Smyrna the first fully Japanese-owned auto factory in the United States to be unionized. The UAW represents workers in three joint Japanese-American auto plants but has yet to organize the major unaffiliated Japanese plants in this country.

Obviously, their workers like the pay, the benefits and the management style. The union claimed the Smyrna plant's assembly line pace led to a high injury rate. The workers didn't buy that.

Union contract working rules at older UAW plants have contributed to high production costs. Thus, U.S. carmakers lost their competitive edge.

By rejecting the union, the Smyrna workers can be expected to keep productivity up.

The Pittsburgh PRESS
Pittsburgh, Pennsylvania, July 30, 1989

The United Auto Workers suffered a stinging defeat at Nissan's Smyrna, Tenn., plant, and the reason was obvious: Workers there thought the union had little to offer them that they didn't already have.

Wages at the Japanese-owned plant are about the same as at other auto factories in this country, benefits are similar and jobs are secure. Not a single worker has been laid off at the Nissan plant since it opened in 1983.

Only 30 percent of those casting ballots voted to unionize the plant. It was further evidence of the declining fortunes of the big union that once claimed the allegiance of nearly every blue-collar worker in U.S. auto plants. For two main reasons — automation and the disappearance of jobs because of competition from foreign automakers — the UAW's membership has fallen by a third in the past 10 years, to slightly under 1 million.

The UAW must bear a significant share of the blame for the loss of jobs at American-owned factories. The union's rigid work rules have put Detroit at a competitive disadvantage against non-union manufacturers, whose managers have more flexibility to move their workers around for maximum advantage.

The UAW has begun to loosen some of its work rules for American manufacturers, but ironically this has led to strong protests by a substantial faction of the union. The dissidents want to get tougher with management, not softer.

Increased militancy would be a mistake. American automakers need to become more competitive with foreign producers in this country and abroad, and that would seem to require more cooperation between the union and management, not less.

Chicago Tribune
Chicago, Illinois, July 31, 1989

There's a certain sense abroad in the land that the Japanese are responsible for whatever economic uncertainties the U.S. faces as it heads toward the last decade of what's been known as the American century.

That may have first arisen because they seemed regularly to beat us at our own games, producing better cars, television sets, video-cassette recorders, stereos, cameras, and you name it, than we did at a reasonable price. But it didn't take long for a lot of smart politicians to seize upon voters' sort of vague concerns and try to pump them up into real fears.

The fact that the phobias grow deeper is tribute to the success of those who see advantage in scapegoating Japan. Which makes all the more ironic the scenes at the Nissan plant in Smyrna, Tenn., last week after employees rejected by a margin of 1,622 to 711 the unionization efforts of the United Auto Workers.

The UAW was wiped out in what earlier had been projected as a close election. And there in front of the Japanese-owned-and-operated truck and auto assembly plant were joyous American workers wearing the company's ubiquitous Nissan T-shirts and waving Old Glory as they danced and thrust their fingers heavenward in the best "We're No. 1!" tradition.

The UAW accused Nissan of "smears and intimidation tactics." Nissan denied the charges, but conceded it spent "all that we needed" to defeat the union. Its president said the union would have hurt quality and productivity. So far, the UAW has never won an elec-tion at a plant in this country owned and operated by the Japanese. However, it has representation at several plants run as joint ventures with U.S. firms.

If the union ever hopes to win at a Japanese-owned plant, it's obviously going to have to figure out why it keeps losing. Some of the answers—at least in Tennessee—seem obvious. Business is increasing. The plant is expanding. Pay and benefits are good, especially for a relatively low-cost area.

None of those conditions will necessarily prevail forever. But Nissan and the other Japanese firms have something more to offer that in the long run may weigh heaviest of all as workers choose. That's a management philosophy that calls for employee participation in production decisions. To encourage that, the shop floor is organized into teams. Tedium is relieved by rotating tasks, even as often as every two hours.

One worker wedded to the teamwork concept said of the union election: "It was like someone was trying to divide our family."

As long as the Japanese management style produces that kind of worker involvement and loyalty, the union will have its organizing work cut out for it. Even if the economy weakens and insecurity makes the nonunion plants more fertile territory, the UAW would do well to come up with ways to assure workers it would not undo the flexibility and input into decisions that has helped relieve the most intolerable disciplines of the assembly lines.

The Chattanooga Times
Chattanooga, Tennessee, July 27, 1989

Within two years, Japanese automobile companies will probably have created enough plant capacity in the United States to produce 2 million cars a year. That's good news for those companies, but bad news for American carmakers who have the capacity to build 2 million more cars than they can sell. In fact, domestic producers are already singing the blues because car sales have declined by as much as 20 percent recently. Yet, paradoxically, executives of those companies predict prices for 1990 models will increase sharply.

Several reasons are behind the increases. All 1990 cars are required by federal law to have passive restraints, either air bags or automatic seat belts, and those features aren't cheap. Other factors driving the price increases are higher prices for raw materials and the almost incomprehensible financing and rebate plans the makers use to lure customers. Finally, there's the companies' desire to protect their profit margins.

The profit motive is a powerful and under-standable incentive, and greatly benefits the companies' stockholders. But it's hard to understand the carmakers' enthusiasm for price increases at a time when the Japanese control 24 percent of the market — even though they are voluntarily restricting their imports into this country. That share of the market will increase when their U.S. plants begin producing cars.

Detroit's problem seems to be its concentration on the short-term solution — hence the price increase to make more on each car, thereby offsetting lower sales overall. Last year the carmakers raised prices by an average 2.8 percent; the increase on the 1990 models could be as high as 8 percent.

That makes little sense when Japanese automakers are cutting prices. Their strategy is clear: Ensure a larger share of the market for long-term advantage instead of focusing on short-term profits — in other words, a lesson from Economics 101. Is Detroit skipping that class?

TULSA WORLD
Tulsa, Oklahoma, July 29, 1989

IN A VOTE that would have been astounding a few years ago, workers at the Honda plant in Smyrna, Tenn., rejected representatation by the United Auto Workers by more than two to one.

The vote is obviously bad news for organized labor. It reflects a trend that has seen UAW membership alone fall by more than a third in 10 years. But there is also a disquieting note here for American management.

Nearly everyone agrees that a major reason for the overwhelming rejection of union representation was workers' general satisfaction with Japanese management. The Honda plant pays good wages, but by union reckoning, somewhat lower than organized auto plants. What the workers like is an overall attitude of Japanese management that makes workers feel good about their jobs. Employees are given a nominal voice in plant operations; the suggestion box is taken very seriously. They are organized in teams, which rotate from one task to another periodically. This cancels much of the boredom that has traditionally made assembly-line work dreary.

The UAW, of course, must take most of the blame for its own failure to win hearts and minds. Its leftist political orientation of the recent past was out of line with the views of many workers. Its excessive demands for slower work and less efficient production methods hurt the industry. And workers realize now that when the industry suffered, workers also suffered.

For American labor and management alike, there is much to learn from the Smyrna election.

GM, Ford, Chrysler Show Losses on U.S. Car Output

The nation's three major auto companies Oct. 26, 1989 all reported reduced operating profits for the third quarter, and all showed losses on U.S. automobile manufacturing.

General Motors Corp. reported profits of $516.9 million, off almost 40% from third quarter 1988. The company did not report specific results for U.S. car operations, but analysts estimated a loss in the hundreds of millions of dollars.

Ford Motor Co. reported profits off 44%, to $477.1 million. U.S. car operations lost $37 million, their first loss since 1982.

Chrysler Corp. Oct. 26 reported profits of $331 million, but that included a $309 million gain on the sale of Mitsubishi Motors Corp. stock. Operating profits of $22 million stemmed from $76 million earned by Chrysler's financing unit.

The auto companies were continuing to have troubles in October, with sales of U.S.-built cars and trucks off 20.5% in the mid-October period from a year earlier. Troubles in the industry had led to lay-offs and some planned factory closings.

General Motors Oct. 16 said it had sent notices to workers the previous week detailing shifts in production that might lead to the closure of several of its North American plants because of declining U.S. market share. The company indicated that factories in Lordstown, Ohio and Scarborough, Ontario could be shut. Company spokesmen said the plants would probably close permanently in 1991.

GM Sept. 14 had announced the permanent closure of its Lakewood, Ga. plant, which employed 3,200 workers.

Ford, which Oct. 12 had announced the sale of the steelmaking operations of its huge Rogue River factory, had earlier reported that it planned to close four of its plants temporarily.

Chrysler had also said it would temporarily close two of its assembly plants, it was reported Sept. 29.

In an effort to avoid layoffs, General Motors and Chrysler Oct. 5 agreed to manufacture jointly certain automobile parts.

The car makers signed a letter of intent to combine the production operations of two plants that made manual transmissions and four-wheel drive components.

Under the agreement, which had no precedent in U.S. automotive history, GM was to assign a Muncie, Ind. plant that manufactured transmissions to the venture with Chrysler. Chrysler assigned the Syracuse, N.Y. plant of its Acustar subsidiary to the agreement. Much of Acustar's four-wheel drive parts production had previously gone to·GM in a sales arrangement.

A total of 4,100 workers were employed at the two plants, and officials of both companies predicted no layoffs as a result of the agreement.

The officials said that the joint venture had the support of Owen Bieber, the president of the United Auto Workers union. They predicted that the arrangement would increase job security at both plants. The companies also said the venture would pass government antitrust scrutiny, because of the previous sales arrangements and because there were no foreseeable "anticompetitive effects."

THE ARIZONA REPUBLIC
Phoenix, Arizona, January 26, 1989

ONCE again the Japanese government, fearing the political clout of the U.S. auto industry and its toadies in Congress, has agreed to extend for a ninth year its "voluntary" quota on vehicles exported to the United States.

Originally adopted in 1981, the import quota (now at 2.3 million vehicles per year) was supposed to last a maximum of three years, just time enough to let Detroit become more "competitive." But in 1985, at the urging of U.S. automakers and the United Auto Workers union, the quota was continued "until the yen and the dollar return to a fair balance."

Since then, the value of the dollar has plummeted by 50 percent, to the point where the U.S. Commerce Department now calculates that it is actually more expensive to build cars in Tokyo than in Detroit. Nevertheless, U.S. automakers and their unions still are clamoring for protection.

This is not difficult to understand. Eight years of protectionism have produced mouth-watering profits. In 1988 the Big Three enjoyed their third-best sales year ever; they expect to tally combined profits of more than $11 billion, a record. Since 1983, General Motors, Ford and Chrysler have put $41 billion in the bank.

The automakers have been cashing in big on the lack of competition, but American car buyers have been taking it on the chin. The average price of a foreign car has increased by 82 percent, and the cost of an American-made car has risen 61 percent. One study estimates that the quota costs consumers an additional $3 billion to $5 billion yearly. Another study found that consumers paid $17 billion more for cars from 1981 to 1984 than they would have without the quota.

Not content with its profits, Detroit now is pitching for an even bigger advantage. The Big Three are pressuring Washington to make the 25 percent tariff on light trucks apply to imported minivans and sports vehicles, raising the price of these popular vehicles by $1,500 to $6,000 each.

The automakers deny any self-serving motive. Wrapping themselves in the flag, they allege that the tariff could help ease the nation's budget deficit. Chrysler's Lee Iacocca, *The Wall Street Journal* reports, wrote Treasury Secretary Nicholas Brady, "I am tired of seeing the U.S. government get flimflammed by people (the Japanese) who want to ... cheat the treasury out of hundreds of millions of dollars."

But in another letter written to Chrysler dealers, a copy of which the *Journal* acquired, Mr. Iacocca's real concern becomes obvious. The expanded tariff, he told the dealers, would mean "a $2,000 per truck cost penalty to your competitors."

If anyone has been flimflammed, it is the American consumers, who have paid dearly for Detroit's profitable protection. Where costly import quotas and tariffs are concerned, it is time to put on the brakes.

ST. LOUIS POST-DISPATCH
St. Louis, Missouri, May 30, 1989

The laws of supply and demand would seem to indicate that when sales turn flat, prices should be cut to increase volume. Presumably this serves the interests of both consumers and manufacturers. But that isn't quite the way much of corporate America sees things today. Consider the behavior of two of this country's supposedly more competitive industries: carmakers and diaper manufacturers.

Ford Motor Co. has just announced it is matching General Motors' recent price hikes on many options on its cars. This is so routine it should shock no one. What is surprising, though, is that prices are going up while car sales are going down — off 8 percent in the first four months of 1989. The industry feels if fewer cars are sold, the price of each must rise to meet corporate profit goals. Ford's public rationalization is that prices are rising to recover increases in

costs, despite Ford's record profits in 1988.

The car companies aren't alone in their reluctance to compete on price. The giants fighting each other in the nation's $3.5 billion disposable-diaper market are competing on frills, not price. Diapers now come in different models for the two sexes, in colors from magenta to lavender, adorned with Walt Disney characters, and so on. But no one wants to win by cutting prices, which are up 15 percent in the last year.

Companies don't like price wars; to win, they must shrink their profit margins. Producers would rather compete on something else. Unfortunately, this attitude allows foreigners to enter the American market as lower-cost producers and clean up. How many times must corporate America make this mistake? Apparently, at least once more; Japan is preparing to sell diapers in the United States.

St. Louis, Missouri, July 7, 1989

Japanese auto companies are on their way to creating enough plant capacity in this country to build 2 million cars a year by 1992 — at a time when American automakers can already build 2 million more cars than they can sell. Indeed, auto sales are already slowing markedly — off some 20 percent in recent days — yet top car-company officials are predicting sharp price increases for 1990. Why?

There are both good and bad reasons. Federal law will require all 1990 cars to have passive restraints — air bags or automatic seat belts — that will cost money; higher costs for raw materials and seemingly endless rebates will also add to expenses. But the more powerful impulse behind another round of price increases is to protect profit margins.

That might be comprehensible if there were little competition in the American auto market. But the Japanese control 24 percent of it — despite voluntary restrictions on automobile imports. As their plants in the United States become operational, they will be able to make and sell still more vehicles.

Yet Detroit still prefers to think of the short run, raising prices precisely because sales are soft, in order to increase revenue per car. Last year's average price hike of 2.5 percent is expected to grow to as much as 8 percent in 1990.

Meanwhile, the Japanese are still cutting prices. They know what the game is about: long-run market share, not short-run profits. That's a simple enough lesson. When will Detroit learn it?

The Miami Herald
Miami, Florida, April 21, 1989

IN 1492, Europeans discovered America; in 1992, Americans will "discover" Europe. That is, 1992's consolidation of the European Economic Community will force Europe's trading partners — especially the United States and Japan — to reassess many of their economic policies.

Moreover, if Washington is to have credibility in pushing for freer trade, it must put its own house in order. Otherwise, EEC and Japanese proponents of managed economies will have the upper hand in any tit-for-tat retaliation on trade.

A good place for the United States to begin? End the costly quotas and lower the exorbitant tariffs placed on imported vehicles.

Instead, Washington is moving the other way. In the latest enlargement in Uncle Sam's subsidies for Detroit, the Feds have decreed that Japanese-made utility vehicles resembling Broncos and Blazers are trucks if they have two doors, though still cars if they have four. The difference? Japanese trucks are subjected to a 25-percent tariff, Japanese cars 2.5 percent.

Meanwhile, the "voluntary" import quotas on Japanese cars — instituted in 1981 as a temporary measure when Detroit's de-

fective gas-guzzlers were losing market share to imports — are still in force.

Those quotas have had several side effects. The Japanese quickly adapted. Given a finite number of cars allowed into the United States, they sent larger, costlier models. Did Detroit take advantage of the opportunity to regain market share? No. it boosted its prices and profits.

Consumers are the big losers. The May issue of *Consumer Reports* cites data indicating that the cost to American consumers runs about $4 billion a year. In one recent year, the average Japanese car cost $1,703 more than it would have without the quotas; the average American car $1,185 more.

When merger mania hit Detroit and the last of the independent manufacturers bit the dust, the surviving Big Three argued that they needed to be large to compete with the giants of Europe and Japan in a new, worldwide marketplace. Now that the consolidation in auto-making has occurred, it is unconscionable for those same companies to argue that they ought to operate as a sheltered cartel in the world's most lucrative car market, the U.S.A. That is why those "temporary" quotas should end now.

The Kansas City Times
Kansas City, Missouri, May 26, 1989

Auto sales figures for the first four months of this year are ominous for domestic producers. Sales for U.S. carmakers fell by 10 percent through April while those of Japanese manufacturers rose by 6 percent.

Part of the reason for the faster-paced Japanese sales is the Japanese lead in engine and transmission technology and fuel economy. But they are also more aggressive. Toyota's prices have been unchanged since last fall, while General Motors and Ford have announced increases. Detroit continues to rely on temporary gimmicks, even as Americans become "incentive proof."

Detroit can no longer complain about being beaten by cheap labor because a growing proportion of Japan's market penetration is from U.S.-based factories. Up to 14 percent of all cars assembled in the U.S. are now built by Americans working in Japanese plants or in joint ventures with U.S. companies.

Detroit bears much of the blame for the presence of these Japanese factories. The Big Three clamored for trade protection and got

it. Then Washington set out to beat down the dollar to make American exports cheaper overseas, and succeeded. Both moves encouraged the Japanese to relocate more production in the U.S. market. This allows them to cut their currency risk and make an end-run around the car quotas.

These developments are good for the nation as a whole. Increased Japanese production in our market not only employs more Americans, but reduces the trade deficit: Many of those cars are built for export.

At the same time, Detroit is being forced to confront the competition it needs to become truly competitive. One can only wonder, however, when the Big Three will start cutting prices, and playing to win.

Big Three Auto Makers Post Record Losses

In its roundup of corporate profits in the 1990 fourth quarter, the *Wall Street Journal* Feb. 19, 1991 found that net income at 617 major corporations it surveyed fell 9% from the year-earlier period. After-tax earnings from continuing operations fell 4%.

In the cyclical products sector, the automobile industry had a year that verged on the disastrous. General Motors Corp. Feb. 14 reported a net loss of almost $2 billion for 1990. The loss in the fourth quarter alone was $1.6 billion, the largest quarterly loss from operations ever for an auto maker. Once again, overseas operations outperformed domestic business.

Ford Motor Co. Feb. 14 reported a 1990 profit of $860.1 million. Overseas operations lost money after helping overall results a year earlier. In the 1990 fourth quarter, Ford had a loss of $519 million, its second-largest loss ever.

Chrysler Corp. Feb. 7 said net income fell to $68 million in 1990 from $359 million in 1989. Fourth-quarter earnings at Chrysler, the smallest of Detroit's Big Three auto makers, were $31 million, after a year-earlier loss of $664 million.

The Big Three U.S. auto makers, battered by the recession and foreign competition, posted combined losses of $1.86 billion in the first quarter of 1991.

Losses from operations totaled $2.3 billion for the quarter, surpassing the record of $2.1 billion set in the fourth quarter of 1990, according to the *Wall Street Journal*.

General Motors Corp., the world's largest car company, April 30 registered a loss of $376.5 million in the first period, while Ford Motor Co. reported a deficit of $884.4 million. Chrysler, the smallest and most vulnerable of the three, May 1 posted a loss of $598 million.

The results at GM were boosted by the sale of its office building in New York City and an accounting change. Without those nonrecurring items, GM would have had a quarterly loss of $1.17 billion. Sales fell 3% to $29.2 billion, despite discounting – now standard among the Big Three – that averaged $1,000 per vehicle.

Nearly every unit at Ford lost money in the quarter. Results were in the red both at its North American operations and at its facilities overseas, which sometimes had cushioned domestic losses. Ford's First Nationwide Corp. savings and loan association posted a deficit of $20.9 million in the first period. In all, revenue at Ford fell 9.7% to $21.3 billion.

Chrysler's loss was exaggerated by a $257 million charge from a sales-incentive accounting change. Excluding the write-off, Chrysler had an operating loss of $341 million. The auto maker said it had no plans to draw on a $1.75 billion line of credit it had recently negotiated with lender institutions. Chrysler's board had reportedly met recently to consider assets that could be sold to raise cash, however. The company's sales plummeted 24% to $5.8 billion the quarter.

The economic downturn in the U.S. had been severe enough in the first period to affect results even at Japanese car companies. But the economic climate had not prevented the Japanese from further increasing their market share in the U.S. at the expense of domestic auto makers.

The Washington Post

Washington, D.C., March 28, 1991

LEE IACOCCA, the irrepressible chairman of Chrysler, is trying to persuade President Bush to limit the number of automobiles imported from Japan. The American economy won't recover strongly from the recession, Mr. Iacocca argues, unless the domestic auto industry is prospering. Mr. Bush certainly should not, and probably will not, interfere with Japanese auto sales here. But Mr. Iacocca's plea raises familiar questions about the future of the American industry.

He is asking for a temporary freeze on the Japanese companies' share of the American market "until the U.S. industry can get back on its feet." You are entitled to ask why the U.S. industry is once again off its feet. Mr. Iacocca attributes it to the recession and the gulf war—meaning the leap in gasoline prices last summer. That kind of explanation was more plausible in the 1970s, after the first oil crisis and the first oil-induced recession, than it is today after the third. It's striking that the Japanese auto industry, like the entire Japanese economy, has succeeded in insulating itself from these repeated eruptions in oil prices far more successfully than the American auto industry or, for that matter, the American economy.

During the last recession, the Japanese companies kept selling cars briskly and emerged with a hugely enlarged share of the market. That's what Mr. Iacocca wants the president to prevent this time. But it's not so simple. Last year 31 percent of the cars sold in this country were made by Japanese companies, but a lot of them were cars made in their American plants by American labor. Some of them were the small cars that Chrysler and General Motors import and sell under their own names.

This country has had a lot of experience with restraints on imports of Japanese cars. They were in force in the early 1980s, and they were harmful not only to consumers but to the American auto industry itself. By cutting down on the supply of Japanese cars, these restraints—in effect, quotas—pushed up the prices. Instead of taking advantage of that to sell more cars, the American companies happily raised their own prices. Unable to ship larger numbers of cars here, the Japanese responded—as many economists had predicted—by shipping more expensive cars and cutting into the highly profitable upper end of the American market. The American companies are weaker now than when the import limits first went into effect. Even if Mr. Bush didn't believe in free trade, that record would argue powerfully against further experimenting with limits on imported cars.

LAS VEGAS REVIEW-JOURNAL
Las Vegas, Nevada, March 29, 1991

Chrysler Corp. Chairman Lee Iacocca has pleaded with President Bush for protectionist measures to limit Japan's share of the American vehicle market.

Iococca wants federal laws limiting Japanese automakers to their current 31 percent of the domestic market. Otherwise, said Iacocca in a letter to Bush, Chrysler and Ford "could be mortally wounded from a competitive standpoint."

So far Bush has been unreceptive to Iacocca's plea. But the Treasury Department did state the president believes the U.S. auto industry would be more sound in the long run if competition from abroad is kept as open as long as possible. That observation is correct.

It is true that U.S. automakers are suffering from a double whammy — recession and war which depressed auto sales, causing thousands of layoffs in the industry, and heightened competition from the Japanese.

Early March figures indicate sales of North American-made autos fell by 16.4 percent compared with last year. Apparently, the auto industry has not yet benefited from the rebounding consumer confidence.

But these dismal figures — bound to improve as the recession ends — are not exclusive to U.S. automakers. While U.S.-made auto sales declined more than 16 percent in February, sales of Honda imports, for example, dropped more than 20 percent and Nissan imports more than 34 percent.

Still, Japan's relative share of the American market is growing, and Iacocca fears that when and if imports account for 40 percent of the U.S. market, even Detroit's Big Three will become endangered.

But Iacocca's call for protectionist measures to freeze Japan's market share is misguided. Protectionism only breeds retaliation-in-kind by other nations. Erecting trade barriers now would only serve to block the inroads American car makers are cutting into the lucrative Asian markets and prompt the booming Pacific Rim nations to erect new barriers of their own.

And it may upset the conventional wisdom, but American car makers — after long neglect of the market — *are* finally making major inroads in Asia. Ford Motor Co., for example, now claims well over 25 percent of the automobile market in Taiwan. General Motors, too, is making a push in Asia and has discovered that its Buick models have suddenly become the rage in Taiwan. Interestingly, Lee Iacocca's Chrysler Corp. is making only token efforts to sell its cars in the robust Asian markets.

Of course, Japan — the economic giant of Asia — remains problematic for U.S. automakers. Part of the problem is relative quality: America must make cars the Japanese want to buy. Part of the problem also is still-extant Japanese trade disincentives and the fact that, until recently, Detroit didn't make a concerted effort to crack the Japanese market. GM has recently expanded its dealership network in Japan and launched a print and TV ad campaign. Surprise, surprise. According to the Wall Street Journal, when the 1991 figures are in, GM sales in Japan are expected to have increased 10-fold from 1986.

Chrysler is the odd man out. Iacocca gripes about Japan and calls for protectionism, but what is Chrysler doing to capture a share of the Japanese market? Not much.

Instead of calling for U.S. trade barriers, Iacocca ought to be drawing up plans to seize bigger shares of the booming markets overseas. He should also study the latest issue of Consumer Reports, which clearly shows that American automakers have, overall, failed to close the quality gap with their Japanese competitors. When Detroit starts turning out cars that can match, in every measure, the quality offered by its Japanese rivals, then the U.S. automakers will begin to recapture lost market share.

The intense competition from Japan has helped improve the quality of American cars. Keeping that competition fierce through free trade will improve it more.

The Duluth News-Tribune
Duluth, Minnesota, March 20, 1991

Cutler-Magner Co. deserves to compete on a price basis with other potential suppliers of road salt to Minnesota government agencies, as it would under a bill given preliminary Minnesota House approval this week.

But the bill to exempt the Duluth firm from the state's "Buy American" law shows the weakness of that kind of law.

If Cutler-Magner ships Canadian salt to Duluth for processing and sale, is it an American or foreign product? What about toys made in Hong Kong but packaged and distributed by an Illinois company? And is a General Motors car made from Japanese parts more domestic than one assembled in Oregon bearing a Japanese auto firm's nameplate?

The Buy American (and Buy Minnesota, Wisconsin, etc.) laws are based on either nationalism or job protection.

If they are based on nationalistic fervor, they are inappropriate in today's world market. If tied to job protection, they likely fail for the same reason — but also because thousands (millions?) of American jobs exist for processing, packaging, distributing and selling foreign-made products.

Instead of having lawmakers grant exemptions from narrow — and often misguided — rules, government agencies should stress paying the least for products and making taxpayers' dollars go farthest.

U.S. Steel Quotas Extended; Steelmakers to End Subsidies

Ending a months-long dispute within his administration, U.S. President George Bush July 25, 1989 said he would extend U.S. steel quotas for another two and a half years. But he stressed that he would seek to negotiate the elimination of all such trade-distorting practices and open world steel markets during that time.

"This program is designed to restore free-market forces to, and end government interference in, global trade in steel," Bush said, adding that his aim was an "international consensus" on lowering trade barriers and eliminating government steel subsidies.

Due to expire Sept. 30, the so-called voluntary restraint agreements (VRAs) limited steel imports to 18.4% of the U.S. market. Under the Bush extension, the ceiling would be raised one percentage point annually, with the increase allotted on a "first-come, first-served" basis to countries committed to steel-market liberalization.

The quotas had been established in 1984 following widespread dumping of low-priced steel in the U.S. by overseas producers. Shortly before election day in 1988, Bush had promised to extend them.

The decision struck a compromise between the interests of U.S. steel producers (who had wanted a five-year extension to allow for major capital-spending projects and further modernization) and U.S. steel consumers (who had pressed for an end to the VRAs).

The extension was regarded as a victory for Treasury Secretary Nicholas Brady and Council of Economic Advisers Chairman Michael Boskin. Commerce Secretary Robert Mosbacher and Labor Secretary Elizabeth Dole had both reportedly favored a five-year extension.

Overseas reaction was critical. The European Community – the largest U.S. foreign steel supplier, with 5.6% of the U.S. steel market and 27% of all U.S. imports – said the American steel industry no longer needed the protection of VRAs.

Japan, which had not been shipping its full 5.8% of the U.S. market under the quotas, echoed the EC but nonetheless said it accepted the decision.

South Korea, having recently expanded into the North American market, condemned the move as "very regrettable...indiscreet, protectionist."

The Bush administration Dec. 12 announced accords with 18 nations to phase out most subsidies to domestic steel industries. At the same time, the U.S. announced new steel quotas for major trading partners.

Quota levels had reportedly been used as leverage to encourage the subsidy accords, known as bilateral consensus agreements. Nations signing the agreements received larger shares of the 19.1% total of the U.S. market allocated to imports under the quotas, which were called voluntary agreements (VRAs).

Shares were also revised according to earlier trade figures. The quota for Japan, which had not shipped all the steel allowed it under earlier VRAs, was cut to 5% from just over 6%.

Such developing nations as Mexico and South Korea, which had sometimes shipped all they were allowed under earlier VRAs, were given slight augmentations.

The U.S. had not yet allocated 6% of the 19.1% total quota. It was reportedly to be reserved as an incentive for nations that had to sign bilateral agreements, such as Austria, Yugoslavia and Finland.

The agreements, which included provisions for arbitration and dispute settlement, were signed by the 12 member nations of the European Community, as well as by Japan, South Korea, Brazil, Mexico, Australia, and Trinidad and Tobago.

Deputy U.S. Trade Representative Linn Williams hailed the accords as a victory for "market-opening goals" and "discipline over trade-distorting subsidies."

The EC Dec. 12 announced that it would end its steel quotas in March 1992, the same time the U.S. planned to terminate its VRAs.

The Courier
-Journal

Louisville, Kentucky,
February 15, 1989

LAST YEAR, America's steelmakers earned $2 billion in profits. Imports, which had badly battered the domestic industry in the early 1980s, fell to under 21 percent of U.S. consumption, from a high of 26 percent in 1984.

But are the steelmakers and their friends in Congress ready to end their demands for import barriers? No way.

The steel industry is lobbying hard for an extension of a five-year-old program of import quotas known as "voluntary restraint agreements," or VRAs. Under these agreements, which are hardly voluntary, foreign countries are forced to limit their steel shipments to U.S. customers.

VRAs protect the profits of domestic steelmakers and the jobs of American steelworkers, but they do so at the expense of other American companies and workers, such as those in the steel-consuming automotive, appliance and construction industries.

Because of the VRAs, these companies are paying more for steel, which puts *them* at a competitive disadvantage. In other words, the steel import quotas may not end up saving American jobs at all. They simply preserve some steel industry jobs while probably costing jobs in other industries.

Bills have been introduced in Congress to extend the VRAs, which expire Sept. 30, for another five years. Unfortunately, President Bush has indicated that he supports an extension. But he should rethink his position. A falling dollar and modernization of domestic mills have given America's steelmakers advantages they didn't enjoy five years ago. They can compete fairly and effectively without government help. They should be encouraged to do so.

Minneapolis Star and Tribune
Minneapolis, Minnesota, February 20, 1989

The U.S. steel industry is a junkie. It's addicted to protection from foreign competition. The industry has grown so dependent that it focuses obsessively on ensuring that its habit will continue to be fed. Another fix is due later this year. Big Steel's dealers — Congress and the White House — seem intent on providing it. That's the way addictions become perpetual — one fix at a time. The solution is to quit cold turkey. Congress and the White House should cut off the supply. If they won't do it, Big Steel's foreign competitors should.

The U.S. steel industry has enjoyed protection from foreign competitors in some form since 1969. Despite the help, the industry failed to modernize, and cost-conscious foreign competitors still captured one-quarter of the U.S. market by the early 1980s. In 1984, with Big Steel apparently on its death bed and with an election-conscious Congress clamoring to impose harsh import controls, President Reagan asked Congress to let him negotiate voluntary restrictions instead. The restrictions would last five years, giving the U.S. steel industry a chance to rebound. Congress agreed, and foreign producers went along for fear that failure to oblige would bring even more severe restrictions on their U.S. sales.

Now the "voluntary" quotas are about to expire. Surprise: Big Steel says it just can't get along without them — even though its profits are extraordinarily healthy, its mills are running at near capacity, and the decline in the dollar has made American steel among the cheapest to produce. U.S. politicians seem determined to keep the industry wrapped in dependency. During last fall's campaign, George Bush pledged his support for a continuation of the controls, and Congress seems similarly inclined.

Steel-using manufacturers are incredulous at this official acquiescence to continued protectionism. They suffer the consequences: highly inflated steel prices and shortages or delayed deliveries of some steel products. Because they must pay more for steel than their foreign counterparts, U.S. manufacturers are at a competitive disadvantage both at home and abroad. Some, like Caterpillar Inc., are fighting back by building new manufacturing plants abroad — at the expense of U.S. communities. All together, steel-users estimate that import restrictions have cost the United States significantly more manufacturing jobs than they have saved in the steel industry.

That's the flaw in protectionism. It helps some Americans but hurts others even more. For five years, steel-using manufacturers and American consumers have carried Big Steel. Now it is time for the industry to compete fairly with foreign producers or get out of the business. Congress should refuse to allow an extension of the voluntary import restrictions and President Bush should decline to negotiate one. If Bush and Congress cave in, as seems likely, foreign producers should refuse to go along.

Los Angeles Times
Los Angeles, California, February 11, 1989

President Bush unfortunately appears determined to make good on his campaign promise to extend import restrictions on steel for another five years when they run out at the end of September. That is bad news for American consumers, bad policy at a time when every effort is being made to free world trade and expand American exports, and bad medicine for American steel producers because it will encourage their bad habits.

When the restrictions were first imposed by President Ronald Reagan, much was made of the need for a few years to allow the U.S. industry to catch up with the rest of the world. The industry has done well in that period. It has eliminated antiquated facilities, reducing capacity since 1982 by 27%. In conformity with the import-restriction legislation, it has reinvested more than $9 billion in plant and equipment. And the industry has turned around from four consecutive years of massive losses to surging profits in the last two years. In the current steel boom, American producers are operating at better than 90% of capacity, and their exports rose 25% in 1988.

Nevertheless, the industry insists that it is still fearful of a flood of cheap foreign steel if the quotas are relaxed. The risk will certainly increase when, true to the cycles that characterize the business, the present boom collapses. In the meantime, however, many foreign producers, notably Japan, are not filling their quotas. Imports have fallen to their lowest tonnage since 1983, less than 21% of the market. And a tougher trade law has been enacted by Congress to add stronger defenses to unfair trading practices, making the demand for special protection less valid than ever.

There may be room for compromise. Bush and his trade representative, Carla A. Hills, have promised to try to negotiate a global agreement ending all subsidies affecting exports and eliminating any excuse for quotas. That, however, is not going to be easy, and would be virtually impossible to negotiate quickly. The steel importers, trying to respond to Bush's campaign commitment, have offered a compromise of their own: If the quotas must be extended, do it for a short period—three years at most—and be selective. One particularly useful suggestion is to remove semi-finished steel from the quotas. Imports of this product, while less than 15% of total imports, are increasing rapidly. Unfinished steel is fed into American integrated steel mills where it is then finished, providing employment both abroad and in the United States.

But the best solution is to let the quotas die. Congress is not bound by Bush's campaign promise, and it is Congress that should refuse an extension. The competitiveness of U.S. manufactured products is an issue of even greater importance than employment in the steel industry. The nation's steel-using industries, many of them major exporters, should not be victimized by import restrictions that can result in price inflation and irregularities in supply. The steel industry is on its feet. It is time for the federal government to let it stand by itself, not leaning on American consumers.

The Oregonian
Portland, Oregon, March 15, 1989

The case history of recent steel import quotas should sober up anyone who still hallucinates that the addiction of trade protection is a victimless crime.

Facing $5.6 billion of losses in 1984, the steel industry pleaded with the Reagan administration and Congress for one more hit in a line of import protections that extends back to 1968. Washington stooped and delivered with import quotas on steel from 29 countries.

Just as these five-year, supposedly voluntary restraints are about to expire in September, the steel industry is roaring back. Mills are operating at 96 percent of capacity; profits have reached $2 billion this year; dividends are on the way to shareholders.

The U.S. steel industry is also roaring back to Washington for import-quota extensions into the mid-1990s. Whoever said the junkie's world makes sense?

The Coalition of American Steel Using Manufacturers is living if imperiled proof that U.S. steel makers' addiction is no victimless crime. The member companies use steel to make everything — ships, planes, washers and dryers, tools and heavy machinery. One member is Gaylord Industries Inc., a Tualatin maker of kitchen exhaust hoods. The users employ more than 5 million workers, as opposed to the makers' 210,000.

Insulating steel makers from foreign competition has hurt steel users and U.S. consumers. According to a study done for the coalition by Paula Stern, former International Trade Commission chairwoman, U.S. steel prices have gone up 15 percent under the quotas between 1986 and 1988; semifinished steel and several stainless products have jumped by more than 40 percent. Along with higher steel prices have come delays and shortages for steel-using manufacturers.

Several studies estimate that voluntary restraint orders have resulted in the loss of 13,000 to 35,000 more jobs in the steel-using sector than the import restrictions have saved in the steel industry.

The voluntary restraint agreements make American products more expensive at home and abroad, promoting inflation and uncompetitive U.S. exports at a time of national worry over both. Artificially high prices for raw steel result in greater imports of manufactured steel products but also in U.S. steel users' search for steel substitutes.

In short, U.S. steel makers' failure to get the monkey of protectionism off their backs could make monkeys of us all.

How hard will it be to shake the U.S. steel industry's deadly habit? During last year's presidential campaign, George Bush weighed in on the side of steel import-quota extension. Drug czar William Bennett, call your office.

THE ARIZONA REPUBLIC
Phoenix, Arizona, June 3, 1989

BY all accounts America's steel industry, once the tarnished symbol of Rust Belt deterioration, has made a shining comeback. Big Steel's profits last year topped $2 billion. Some major U.S. steelmakers recently reported their best first-quarter earnings of the decade.

The industry's impressive turnaround by no means came easy. It took strong medicine indeed to reverse decades of ailing productivity: more than $9 billion was spent on the modernization of aging industrial facilities, thousands of well-paying jobs were eliminated. As a result, it takes 50 percent fewer man-hours to produce a ton of steel today than it did at the beginning of the 1980s.

Big Steel also was helped along toward competitiveness by a network of "voluntary" agreements negotiated in 1984 between the Reagan administration and foreign steel producers. The quota system, applied to 29 different countries, limits the sale of 40 varieties of steel in the United States to no more than 25 percent of the domestic market.

These Voluntary Restraint Agreements are set to expire in September, and with U.S. steel plants operating almost at full tilt, now would seem to be an opportune time to end the market-inhibiting quota system.

It is, after all, difficult to justify protectionism for U.S. steelmakers when their industry is making record profits and when worldwide production is outstripping demand by 100 million tons yearly — especially now that President Bush is campaigning for even freer international trade.

Unsurprisingly, not everyone sees it that way. Content with its profits and guaranteed market share, Big Steel is after more of the same. Hungry for a bigger piece of the protected-profit pie, its unions want a larger slice, too. Both have launched a campaign in Washington to convince Congress and the president to extend for another five years what would amount to a big steal.

Never mind that the quota system now costs America purchasers of automobiles, appliances and other steel products an estimated $7 billion yearly in higher prices. Big Steel argues that it still needs protection because some foreign governments continue to prop up their steel industries, thereby creating unfair price advantages.

If that is the case, what's the problem? The administration has the tools under current U.S. trade law to retaliate on a country-by-country basis to stop the illegal "dumping" of such subsidized foreign steel. Indiscriminate action targeted against all foreign producers, however, only encourages even more market-distorting practices.

When President Reagan negotiated the quota system, the administration said it was intended to be a temporary measure to allow U.S. steel producers a breathing space, to give them some time to get back on their feet. Now that the industry is healthy again, Big Steel should quit bawling, get back to work, and stop leaning on the American consumer for support.

THE SACRAMENTO BEE
Sacramento, California, April 3, 1989

In 1984, the steel industry persuaded the Reagan administration to negotiate "voluntary" import quotas with 29 countries to protect U.S. producers from low-cost competition. Thus sheltered, steel companies spent $9 billion on modernization, slashed employment, increased productivity and — thanks also to a cheaper dollar — turned staggering losses into profits that, in 1988, exceeded $2 billion. So what does Big Steel want now? Five more years of protection that, according to credible estimates, already costs U.S. consumers about $7 billion a year in higher prices.

President Bush must decide shortly what to do when the five-year import restraint program ends Sept. 30. Unfortunately, he committed himself, on the eve of last November's election, to extending the quotas, though without spelling out in what precise form. That gives him room to opt for lowering the barriers behind which the most protected U.S. industry of all has nestled for 20 years. At the same time, such a phase-out must be tied to negotiations to end foreign predatory practices that were the rationale for imposing quotas in the first place and which, under the current regime, Washington simply winks at.

U.S. steelworkers, whose numbers have shrunk from 400,000 in 1980 to about 155,000 today, are now among the world's most productive; U.S. mills are working at more than 90 percent of capacity, and spot shortages have resulted in price hikes of 20 percent or more for some categories of steel. That not only pushes up the cost of domestic products made with steel but imposes a hidden tax on U.S. exporters — Caterpillar is a major example — that are thus rendered less competitive abroad.

Pressed to justify its demand for continued protection, Big Steel says quotas must be kept in place to shield it from the next recession, when, it says, imports of foreign steel at below-cost prices would soar. Even if that's a legitimate fear, it could be dealt with more effectively by relying on truly temporary quotas to combat sudden import surges, or by filing complaints against foreign dumping — a violation of international trading rules and U.S. law — when it occurs. It was the fear of such complaints that induced foreign governments to accept quotas in 1984.

Under the present regime, sporadic shortages — a market-distorting anomaly in a world where steel production outstrips demand by 100 million tons yearly — often force U.S. steel-using firms, including many smaller, innovative ones, to cut production and lay off workers, or pay steep prices, or both.

The worldwide steel glut is the root of the problem. Steel has become a status symbol for many emerging nations, like having a national airline. Clearly only concerted international action can change that. But the Bush administration could take the first step by refusing to sign a blank check for Big Steel. It could extend the quotas for a shorter period, and make them more flexible according to the trading practices of supplier nations. If the White House merely follows the path of least resistance, that path will only lead to greater protectionism and market-sharing agreements that favor producers and gouge consumers — in a word, a cartel, as bad an idea today as it was in the heyday of the robber barons.

The New York Times
New York City, New York, March 27, 1989

Just four days before his election, George Bush promised that he would continue to protect the steel industry against imports. The political motive was clear: He was worried about Rust Belt votes. But the economics were faulty. America's steel industry is healthy again. The Reagan Administration's "temporary" import curbs ought to go.

Steel imports are controlled by a network of so-called "voluntary" agreements that the industry wheedled out of President Reagan during his 1984 re-election campaign. Twenty-nine countries agreed to limit U.S. sales of 40 varieties of steel for five years. In exchange, Washington promised not to challenge their export subsidies or their practice of dumping steel on the U.S. market at allegedly unfair prices.

Mr. Bush wants an international agreement to stop unfair practices. But until that happens, he said last November, the import curbs will stay.

The Government has shielded steel one way or another since 1968 — so long that today's managers have never managed without Federal crutches. In recent years, steel has finally regained its footing by slashing costs and payrolls and slowly adopting modern technology.

Profits last year exceeded $2 billion. Mills today are near capacity. But the industry isn't satisfied. It wants more protection — another five years, covering more countries and more products. Steel spokesmen say they're still not strong enough for open competition when the current expansion winds down, and that foreign mills still compete unfairly. This argument is the well-worn route from "temporary" to just-once-more to forever.

Perversely, continued protection for American producers is continued protection for the foreigners, too. Their supposedly unfair practices remain unchallenged. That makes no sense, but it illustrates the addictive charms of protectionism. Foreign producers, especially inefficient ones, become content with a guaranteed share of the market.

The main victim, as usual, is the American consumer — the many other industries that consume steel, and the people who consume their products. Gary Hufbauer, a Georgetown University professor and trade authority, says it's a reasonable guess that the penalty for limiting imports is $7 billion a year. Paula Stern, International Trade Commission chairman in the Reagan years, points to a 1987 finding that the quotas had saved 17,000 jobs in steel but cost 52,000 jobs in other industries.

Candidate Bush's pledge of protection was not rigid; he acknowledged that quotas offer no permanent solution to the industry's problems. President Bush has an opportunity in the current global round of trade negotiations to start stripping away these pernicious barriers to free and open markets in the most widely used of all metals.

THE BUFFALO NEWS
Buffalo, New York, July 20, 1989

THOSE SKEPTICAL about the steel industry's campaign to persuade the Bush administration to extend limitations on steel imports have received potent support from the General Accounting Office, the investigative arm of Congress.

A GAO report suggests that this is a more appropriate time to end the quotas, imposed in 1985, than to extend them for another five years.

The industry contends that it remains weakened, that it requires the protection of quotas against a surge of cheap foreign imports and that such limitations would be especially essential in the event of a slowdown in the national economy.

But the GAO, which has a respectable record for calling the shots as it sees them, contests the industry case on all points.

The surge of imports, which crested five years ago at 26 percent of the total U.S. market, has since declined, and the GAO study says that the domestic steelmakers have returned to "normal levels of profitability."

Since 1985, it adds, "the industry has regained competitiveness principally as a result of the substantial decline in the value of the dollar, improvements in labor productivity and reductions and slower growth in wages and benefits."

Nor would extension of the quotas provide that much help under current conditions, the study concludes. Most of the 20 separate quotas with 29 nations, it says, "are now going unfilled" and their extension, while possibly affecting a few individual steel products, "would likely have little impact on the market as a whole."

As to the industry's fear of foreign producers dumping their products in the U.S. market at below-cost prices in the event of a recession, the GAO notes that existing trade laws offer alternative remedies.

With the American economy still growing in the longest peacetime expansion on record, steelmakers should test their competitive wings without artificial government restrictions on foreign steel.

By sheltering the domestic industry from full competition, quotas also shelter inefficiency. And they tend to push up the price of steel, and thus the cost of living for customers of the cars and appliances and other goods fashioned from steel. That becomes a factor in inflation.

It would be difficult for Washington to lecture Japan, South Korea, Brazil and Europe one day about unfair trade barriers against American goods — and the next day renew barriers to foreign steel for an American industry that has regained its feet and become profitable.

The evidence is strong that the Bush administration can strengthen its drive for level playing fields for trade by allowing the steel quotas to lapse Sept. 30, as scheduled, or at least significantly cutting them back.

THE SACRAMENTO BEE
Sacramento, California, July 31, 1989

In a bid to win Pennsylvania's 25 electoral votes during last year's campaign, candidate George Bush promised voters that, as president, he would extend five-year import quotas that Ronald Reagan imposed in 1984 to give the unprofitable steel industry time to make itself competitive. Bush won Pennsylvania, but saddled himself with an unwise pledge that he kept this week, though fortunately only in part: Quotas will be extended, but only for 2½ years; in the interim, they can be expanded for countries that reduce subsidies to their own producers.

When Bush made his promise, the U.S. steel industry had already achieved its goal: Protected by quotas that cut the foreign share of the U.S. market to around 18 percent, the industry slashed costs, streamlined processes and increased productivity so much that, by 1987, it was back in the black. In 1988, it was able to undercut many foreign competitors' prices, pay wages well above those in most countries and in most other U.S. industries, and still make more than $2 billion in profits.

But quotas hit hard at U.S. consumers and steel-using domestic industries, costing them about $7 billion annually in higher prices; the few thousand steel jobs saved were far exceeded by those not created in other industries; spot steel shortages forced some firms to turn down orders, or to pay domestic steelmakers exorbitant prices for types of steel in short supply (the latter problem to be alleviated by a speeded-up process of temporary quota suspensions). In these circumstances, the industry's demand for continued protection against the danger that a future recession may bring a flood of cheap imports is tantamount to a plea for permanent shelter that it doesn't need.

Those who sought a five-year extension say the shorter period will provide no incentive for foreign countries to negotiate away subsidies. That may be true in some cases, but existing law gives the president the power to impose temporary quotas against surges of underpriced imports and to seek international remedies against systematic foreign "dumping" of steel at predatory prices.

By linking interim quota increases to curbs in foreign market-distorting practices, and by stressing the need for multilateral action to shrink the worldwide steel glut, Bush puts this country in a stronger bargaining position in the effort to achieve such an accord. That position would be even stronger had he ended quotas altogether; still, the action at least points in the right direction. Congress must resist the temptation to overturn the president's decision, as some protectionist-minded members are already contemplating.

The Globe and Mail
Toronto, Ontario, July 31, 1989

U.S. President George Bush's decision to maintain steel import quotas is a welcome boost for the forces fighting protectionism in the United States.

At first glance that seems impossibly contradictory. Quotas are the first line of defence for protectionists and the antithesis of free trade

In this case, however, it is a clear break from the past. By the way he has extended quotas, the President has signalled that the interests of consumers, not just those of producers, will in future shape trade policy in the Bush administration.

Rather than the five-year extension of current quotas sought by the powerful U.S. steel lobby, the restrictions will remain in effect for only the next 2½ years, as multilateral trade talks continue in Geneva with a goal of eliminating subsidies. During that period, the 29 countries — Canada is excluded from quotas — that voluntarily agree to keep their collective steel shipments to no more than 18.4 per cent of the U.S. market will be allowed to increase their exports by a percentage point per year.

The relaxation of restrictions was made easier by the industry's financial turnaround since quotas began in 1984. Strong demand, the closure of inefficient mills and the rationalization of producers led to an industry profit of $3-billion (U.S.) in 1988.

Mr. Bush's move was a major victory for a national coalition of U.S. steel users that lobbied against the quotas. More encouraging still, the quotas will end in March, 1992, no matter what happens in Geneva. After that date, the United States plans to use only its trade laws on dumping and countervailing duties against subsidized imported steel.

Mind you, those laws can be imposing — as Canadian producers Sydney Steel Corp. and Algoma Steel Corp. discovered last week when the U.S. Commerce Department increased a provisional dumping penalty of 2.72 per cent on their steel rails to 41.5 per cent. (It must still be proved that the 3 per cent of the U.S. market taken by Canadian producers injures the U.S. industry.)

No matter how that dispute is resolved, the steel quota decision suggests fresh trade winds are starting to blow through Washington. The Bush administration may be shifting gears to put its hopes for fair trade on international negotiations rather than selective retaliation against individual countries.

Chicago Tribune

Chicago, Illinois, July 27, 1989

Having promised during a weak moment in his campaign to renew quotas on steel imports, President Bush couldn't very well renege on that pledge by killing the restrictions. But he did the next best thing by outlining a sensible plan to limit their duration and to wean the domestic steel industry from existing protection against foreign competition.

Striking a balance between U.S. steel producers and users, the President extended the quotas two and a half years beyond their Sept. 30 expiration date. U.S. Trade Representative Carla Hills will try during that period to negotiate an end to the trade-distorting subsidies and tariffs common in other countries. But Bush also served notice that regardless of the outcome of those talks, the quotas will end on March 31, 1992.

The quotas were imposed on 29 countries by President Reagan in 1984 to protect domestic steelmakers while they modernized and became more competitive. The breathing space worked. Last year the American steel industry made profits of $2.3 billion and mills are humming at near capacity this year. Even so, steelmakers insist they need another five years of protection, not just the 30 months Bush has given them.

The problem with their argument is that one company's protection is another's burden. A group of U.S. manufacturers, led by Peoria-based Caterpillar, argues that quotas make them less competitive in world markets, forcing them to pay higher prices for steel and at times making it impossible for them to get supplies. Bush responded to their concerns by ordering a streamlined emergency procedure to bypass the quotas and assure adequate supplies of steel.

Meantime, the administration will work to get as many steel-producing nations as possible to play by open-market rules. And despite the steelmakers' skepticism about chances for an international agreement and their threats of thousands of trade suits when the quotas end, there is time for substantial progress to be made. The administration already is involved in formal, multinational talks on liberalizing trade and says it wants them to include a steel agreement.

More important, Hill and her team will use the quotas themselves as a lever in bilateral negotiations with steel-producing nations. Currently, the countries affected by U.S. quotas are limited to 18.4 percent of the U.S. market. That ceiling may be lifted to nearly 21 percent over the two and a half years for countries that step forward on a "first-come, first-served" basis and agree to freer trade in steel.

The Bush plan probably won't end all government ownership and subsidies of steel plants, but it does have the potential to move the world closer to a system where markets, not governments, determine prices and output. That would result in cost savings for consumers, less excess steel capacity and an American steel industry that finally can stand on its own.

The Courier-Journal

Louisville, Kentucky, July 28, 1989

SOMEONE should put a sign on President Bush's desk that says, "There ain't no such thing as a free lunch." Mr. Bush's decision to extend quotas on imported steel for another 30 months is certainly no free lunch. Yes, it will continue to protect domestic steelmakers — though they had hoped for an extension of at least five years.

But the quotas have a price for the rest of the economy. The International Trade Commission, a federal agency, estimates that the quotas — euphemistically called "voluntary restraint agreements" — have cost American industries that use steel $1.7 billion in lost export sales since 1985. The ITC study also claims that the quotas have led to a $2.4 billion increase in imports of products that contain steel, such as automobiles.

In other words, while the quotas were saving steelworkers' jobs, they were eliminating the jobs of other Americans. It has been estimated that, for every steelworker's job saved, three others were either lost or weren't created.

That's a bad trade. And the quotas are also bad for American consumers, who end up paying more for products made of steel.

Meanwhile, the U.S. steel industry is booming, as can be seen in the economic recovery of Indiana communities along Lake Michigan that not long ago were suffering double-digit unemployment.

That's encouraging, and perhaps it wouldn't have happened without import quotas. But Big Steel now looks healthy and profitable enough to stand up to foreign competition. It should be given a chance to do so — quickly.

The Philadelphia Inquirer

Philadelphia, Pennsylvania, July 21, 1989

In the heat of his 1984 campaign, when President Reagan decided to set quotas on imported steel, the U.S. steel industry was halfway through losing $12 billion in five years. But last year, when candidate George Bush said just before the election that he'd extend the quotas, the industry made $2.3 billion. With this year looking similarly good so far, there's no reason to keep limiting foreign producers to 20 percent of the U.S. market.

To hear the steel manufacturers tell it, their condition remains so fragile that the quotas, due to expire this September, should last five more years. Yet the industry also claims to have raised efficiency so much that the quotas aren't hurting consumers by inflating the U.S. price of steel and steel products. As evidence of their ability to compete, domestic producers note that steel imports to the United States last year were nearly four million tons less than the quotas allow.

Clearly, there's a contradiction between the industry's growing competitiveness — which supposedly keeps the quotas from hurting consumers — and the line about how fragile the industry remains. In reality, U.S. steel producers have enormously improved their productivity in the 1980s. Last year they produced 58 percent more steel per employee per hour than in 1981. The dollar's decline also has helped place domestic producers in a position to compete effectively.

The industry bases much of its current plea for protection on unfair practices abroad, including governmental subsidies that allow products to be "dumped" here at below-market prices. But the better approach is for the Bush administration to use existing procedures — which Congress toughened last year — against unfair trade practices. It can also pressure trading partners, such as Italy, to stop underwriting their domestic industries. (It's a fair hunch that the Reagan administration would have made more progress toward free trade in steel if the current cartel-like arrangement weren't pretty comfortable for U.S. companies and most foreign ones — which don't necessarily mind exporting less product at an inflated price.)

The true annual cost of these quotas to U.S. consumers is something less than the $7 billion estimated by one analyst at Georgetown University and something more than the next-to-nothing claimed by the industry. Thus this policy saves jobs in the steel industry, but at the expense of jobs in industries that use steel. (Those industries employ about 30 times as many Americans as work in the steel industry.) By making the economy less efficient, such protectionism tends to cost more jobs than it saves.

Every fight over protecting an industry from foreign competition has a tiresome predictability to it. Lawmakers from Pennsylvania gush that steel must be protected in the national interest. The ones from Arizona talk that way about copper; Floridians shake their fists and their voices against foreign-grown sugar. As a result, U.S. industries don't have to be so competitive, and the average consumer gets to pay the price of the industries' security.

Pittsburgh Post-Gazette

Pittsburgh, Pennsylvania, July 27, 1989

By adopting a shorter extension on steel import quotas than recovering American producers had insisted was necessary to put them firmly on their feet, President Bush has intensified pressure not only on the industry but also on his own administration.

Domestic manufacturers had sought a five-year extension of the voluntary-restraint agreements (or VRAs) in order to finish modernization of their facilities; the president granted them only two and one-half years. In the process he has created a deadline for his trade negotiators to complete arrangements with foreign producers to shed the subsidies that have been so much a part of their industries and prompted the U.S. import limitations to begin with.

As part of his VRA extension package, Mr. Bush has provided his trade experts with an enticing carrot to wave abroad to encourage subsidy reductions — an increase in the import ceiling from 18.4 percent of the U.S. market to 20.2 percent. Allocations will be dispensed, according to U.S. Trade Representative Carla Hills, "on a first-come, first-served basis to countries that commit to removing trade-distorting practices" — namely, subsidies.

The president is caught in a four-way squeeze on the VRA issue. As loudly as steel manufacturers (backed by the United Steelworkers of America) scream for protection, so do American steel users — who feel they are being made to pay the price by being deprived of lower-cost foreign products — cry out against them. Add to that discord the growing unhappiness of foreign trade partners unable to reconcile the Reagan and Bush administrations' basically anti-protectionist posture with the maintenance of rigid steel import quotas

for the last five years.

Eager as he is "to restore free-market forces to, and end government interference in, global trade in steel," the president must be careful not to undermine the restoration of the steel industry now that it has managed to regain, at least in the view of the General Accounting Office, normal levels of profitability.

Steel manufacturers grouse that the two-and-a-half year extension is not enough time to negotiate the type of international consensus necessary to alleviate the need for competitive restraints. What concerns them more is that it is not a long enough period of time for them to be able to count on a controlled marketplace for their capital planning and commitments.

It must be assumed that if there is no dramatic improvement in trade conditions as this extension (which begins Sept. 30) approaches expiration, there is the likelihood that it will be renewed.

But by opting not to go for a lulling, long-term extension at this time, the president has let the steel industry know that he does not want to maintain these restraints a day longer than is necessary and has delivered a more pressing reminder that the time is approaching when the industry must be ready to operate on its own in an open market.

Such a demand, of course, can't really be justified unless Mr. Bush is successful in creating the level playing field necessary for the American steel industry to compete. With this action, both the administration and the steel manufacturers are being placed on a tight, no-time-to-lose schedule.

The Pittsburgh
PRESS

Pittsburgh, Pennsylvania, July 27, 1989

Barely two months before they are due to expire, President Bush has proposed extending quotas on steel imports by 30 months. His plan represents a compromise that has prompted criticism from both sides, but which appears to us to be a reasonable middle ground on this difficult trade issue.

The domestic steel industry had been seeking a five-year extension of the voluntary restraint agreements (VRAs), while critics wanted these trade intrusions — no longer justified, in their view — to die as scheduled on Sept. 30.

Since Mr. Bush had promised, in his campaign for the presidency last fall, to push for a renewal of the VRAs, there was no surprise that he did just that this week. However, the time span that he would propose had been a matter for some speculation.

In Mr. Bush's view, the added 30 months would be enough to accomplish what the VRAs started out to do: To complete fairer long-term understandings with trading partners while steel producers in the United States fully recovered from the difficulties of the early 1980s and became more competitive in the world market.

The VRA program, with an initial five-year life span, went into effect in 1984.

The industry thought it would take another five years to fully accomplish those original goals and intimated that it would not seek additional protection after that; not surprising-

ly, it had the support of the United Steelworkers union for a five-year extension.

But VRA opponents say the import barriers are no longer necessary — a view supported by a recent study by the General Accounting Office — and have contributed to steel-price increases and higher consumer costs in this country.

The VRAs, of course, are only one of many tools used by this country to prevent unfair and harmful competition in the trading markets. For steel, they made it easier to limit imports through specially tailored and separately negotiated agreements that covered 29 countries in the first round.

Without them, the steel industry would not be completely defenseless. But that's not to say the VRAs can, or should, now be dropped. Given their demonstrated effectiveness and the upswing in fortunes of the domestic steel industry, keeping them in place for another 30 months appears to be a reasonable move.

For the moment, we'll take the word of the producers that one more extension is all they'll need, or want, even while acknowledging the risk of temporary government subsidies and protections becoming permanent fixtures.

Once in place, there's always somebody who can find a reason to keep them there. As we may be hearing in 30 months, if Congress approves the VRA extension now sought by President Bush.

The San Diego Union

San Diego, California, July 23, 1989

Protection from foreign competition is a powerful narcotic on which the U.S. steel industry has become increasingly dependent during the last two decades.

In 1984, domestic steel producers persuaded President Reagan to give them another fix in the form of a five-year extension of the Voluntary Restraint Agreements. The deal limited the amount of foreign steel allowed into this country. Now President Bush is being asked for a five-year extension.

Although Mr. Bush promised during the presidential campaign to protect the steel manufacturers, he should also encourage them to kick their habit. This could be done by extending the VRAs for two more years, with the stipulation that the industry will be obliged thereafter to compete in a free market.

That good advice is being offered by Treasury Secretary Nicholas Brady, with support from budget director Richard Darman and Michael Boskin, chairman of the Council of Economic Advisers, all of whom are acutely aware of protectionism's dangers.

From 1969 to 1985, U.S. steel users paid nearly 25 percent more for steel than their competitors in Germany and Japan. This $5 billion subsidy paid to domestic producers by users has added to inflationary pressures, slowed economic growth, and decreased American competitiveness. The long-term implications of continued steel subsidies are lost opportunities abroad and a lower standard of living for millions of Americans who will pay higher prices for automobiles, stoves, refrigerators, and microwave ovens, to name just a few big-ticket items.

Meantime, the domestic steel industry is reaping record profits and operating at 96 percent of capacity, both of which indicate it is capable of surviving without federal assistance.

Apart from phasing out the VRA's, President Bush ought to ensure that U.S. trade laws discourage other countries from subsidizing their steel industries. This, after all, was a prime but futile objective of the steel-import quotas, which have clearly outlived their usefulness.

Kohlberg, Kravis Wins RJR Nabisco with Record $25 Billion Takeover

Kohlberg Kravis Roberts & Co. Nov. 30, 1988 was declared the winner in the contest for RJR Nabisco Inc., agreeing to acquire the food and tobacco giant for a record $25.07 billion. RJR outside directors accepted the sweetened $109-a-share KKR takeover offer following a remarkable all-day bidding session during which RJR directors allowed a supposedly firm bidding deadline to pass for a second time, transforming the final 24 hours into a bizarre spectacle in which all rules and procedures were discarded and competing bids escalated to unprecedented levels.

The KKR victory came despite a higher $25.42 billion offer by an RJR management group backed by Shearson Lehman Hutton Inc. and Salomon Inc. The management group, led by RJR President F. Ross Johnson, had initiated the auction for the 19th-largest U.S. industrial company in late October with a proposed $17 billion leveraged buyout offer.

The KKR-RJR acquisition would be about twice the size of the largest previous merger, the $13.4 billion acquisition of Gulf Oil Corp. by Chevron Corp. in 1984, and over four times the size of the largest previous leveraged buyout, the $6.2 billion acquisition of Beatrice Cos. by KKR in 1986.

While stockholders would reap huge short-term gains from the transaction, the acquisition would burden RJR with $22.8 billion in debt — more than the national debts of Bolivia, Jamaica, Uruguay, Costa Rica and Honduras combined — and force the sale of $5 billion-$6 billion in RJR food assets to finance the deal.

Among the reasons most commonly given for the size of the final price tag were: the supposed inability of the public markets to assess the actual value of corporate assets, especially those of a large and diversified food and tobacco conglomerate such as RJR; the alleged desire by RJR management to acquire the company without regard for the interests of the shareholders whom they were supposed to represent; a perceived ability of management to run RJR more efficiently as a private company than as a public company and thereby enhance its value; and overbidding driven by greed and the egos of the suitors.

THE SUN

Baltimore, Maryland, December 4, 1988

In the biggest, brassiest corporate buy-out Wall Street ever witnessed, RJR Nabisco went on the auction bloc last week for a winning bid of $25.07 billion, a sum equivalent to the gross national product of Portugal. The huge deal will not increase U.S. productivity by as much as one Oreo cookie but it will add mightily to the soaring debt load of U.S. corporations. Since 1982, corporate debt has doubled to more than $1.8 trillion, moving upward at a pace as brisk as the federal debt. Little wonder the national savings rate lags at 2 percent, entrepreneurial investment is too low and the nation is dependent on foreign capital.

Leveraged buy-outs, with RJR Nabisco the most spectacular example, are among the causes of this predicament. The tax laws are rigged for greed. Purchasing stock at inflated prices with borrowed money, LBOs can take companies private, sell off assets to finance their junk bonds and pocket astronomical profits. What is happening is the opposite of the American dream. Instead of spreading industry ownership among millions of shareholders, modern-day robber barons are taking hundreds of companies off the market and constricting the number of outstanding shares. Debt, in other words, is replacing equity as the underpinning of corporate finance, and the implications are disturbing indeed.

The battle for RJR Nabisco should not distract the public from what is really at stake. It may be titillating to watch the company president, F. Ross Johnson, get his comeuppance. But this is not a Punch and Judy Show. It is a Punch and Punch Show. Few cheers need to be reserved for Henry Kravis and the apparent winning team of Kohlberg Kravis Roberts & Company (KKR). They are the kingpins of the LBO business, a firm that has taken over more companies for purposes of financial jugglery than any other. A healthy RJR Nabisco has been transformed into a debt-ridden cripple. There will be jobs lost, companies sold, communities disturbed and blue-chip bonds debased to pay off what is suddenly owed. To be sure, stockholders will get a bonanza, which is why the outcry is unfocused, but the real profiteers are to be found in the financial-legal complex that rules Wall Street.

What's to be done? Nothing that would add up to excessive government control of markets, which by nature are unruly. Congress should make sure that the tax laws do not favor debt financing rather than equity financing in American industry. At present, every penny a company spends on interest payments is deductible from corporate taxes. At the same time, shareholders' profits are taxed twice — once at the corporate level and once at the individual level. Taxation of interest payments on corporate debt incurred for non-productive purposes might be a sensible reform that would discourage Ross Johnson-style excess.

THE DENVER POST

Denver, Colorado, December 2, 1988

RJR NABISCO, which stamps its familiar red triangle on dozens of popular food products, is about to change hands.

Consumers may not notice a difference in Oreos if New York money firm Kohlberg Kravis Roberts completes its purchase. But the $25 billion deal will leave RJR Nabisco with a staggering debt that could be hard to repay out of its $17 billion yearly revenues.

Already, Wall Street is speculating about what pieces of RJR Nabisco might be sold off. Many of its 147,000 employees could find their jobs crumbling like Ritz crackers. Trusty brands like Shredded Wheat could disappear from the shelves.

Regardless of RJR Nabisco's fate, top executives at Kohlberg Kravis Roberts will profit handsomely. Like many large money brokers, KKR rarely holds onto the companies it buys. The firm doesn't have to worry whether the companies it burdens with debt provide good products, services and jobs.

Federal lawmakers have struggled with how to regulate debt-heavy takeovers without strangling free enterprise. It is a difficult problem.

Few businesses want Congress telling them what deals they can make. New restrictions could dry up money sources that business needs to create jobs. Moreover, corporate managers sometimes need a good scare to make them solve difficult business problems.

What is needed is a way to make money brokers more responsible for the long-term health of the companies they acquire and sell at a head-spinning pace.

Congress might consider making these investment firms post a bond proportional to the amount of debt that an acquired company must pay.

If the company stayed healthy for five to 10 years, the obligation would expire. But if the company failed, the bond could be used to pay welfare or other benefits to the unemployed workers. The burden of paying for Wall Street's mistakes would shift from the taxpayers to the financial wizards who profit from such deals.

Free enterprise is an efficient vehicle for creating a strong economy. But the profit motives of a few should not always be the paramount consideration. The consequences for the public simply are too great.

ST. LOUIS POST-DISPATCH
St. Louis, Missouri, December 4, 1988

The leveraged buy-out controversy, which reached new heights with the purchase of RJR Nabisco for nearly $25 billion by Kohlberg Kravis Roberts & Co., raises both an easy and a hard question. The easy one: Is it good for companies to incur so much debt in the process of changing owners that bankruptcy threatens at the first sign of a recession? The obvious answer is no, and the risk is real.

The harder issue is this: Should the government follow the gradually developing conventional wisdom and eliminate the deduction for interest on debt — the device in the tax code that makes the whole takeover and buy-out game possible? Unfortunately, probably not. Yet the alternatives aren't so good either. That's a measure of how hard making economic policy has become in a large, interdependent international economy.

Denying investors a tax deduction for interest on corporate debt above a certain amount, or when incurred for certain purposes such as takeovers above a certain value, is a fairly simple proposition. Indeed, such proposals surfaced in the House Ways and Means Committee as long ago as early 1987. But they carry with them a potentially fatal complication.

If government makes it harder for American companies to use debt, it must make it harder for foreign companies, too. Otherwise, they will buy up our economy at a dizzying pace, with no competition. Their governments don't tax interest paid on debts incurred in the United States to purchase American assets — whether they be U.S. Treasury notes to finance our budget deficit or bonds to buy American companies. And foreign governments aren't about to eliminate an important outlet for surplus capital from their own countries whose earnings in America are making their societies rich.

If our government inhibits foreign investors' freedom in order to solve an internal problem, these same investors may decide to take at least some of their money elsewhere. This would pose an acute problem for the American economy. Government would no longer be able to finance the budget deficit by selling bonds in sufficient amounts to foreigners. To attract the funds necessary to pay for the deficit, interest rates would have to be raised sky high, producing certain recession.

There is another way to discourage debt: Cut the tax on dividends, making stocks more attractive for people to hold than bonds. The problem here is that such a cut would increase already strong pressure on companies to produce short-term profits so they could pay generous dividends to maintain the value of their stock. Vital long-term growth — which often requires some lean years before payoff — would be discouraged even more.

The reality is that there is no easy way to move this or any economy away from reliance on debt. Doing it quickly risks disaster; doing nothing could be equally disastrous. The best course is a modest increase in the tax burden on debt, foreigners' included, and a modest decrease in the tax burden on dividends, adjusted carefully in the general direction of slowly penalizing debt. The lesson of being trapped in the lion's cage applies: No sudden moves are advisable, but don't just stand still, either.

DAYTON DAILY NEWS
Dayton, Ohio, December 15, 1988

If you're wondering what possible good these super-colossal buyouts do, please keep in mind that the bankers' fees — the money paid to the people who arranged the financing — in the RJR Nabisco buyout come to the better part of a billion dollars.

That money will go to the likes of Drexel Burnham Lambert, Merrill Lynch, Morgan Stanley, Chase Manhattan and Citibank.

The average citizen may have some difficulty figuring out why so much money should be changing hands and winding up in the hands of the already super-rich when nothing has been built or created or improved or marketed or distributed or anything.

So does the average — even the exceptional — editorial board.

The people who play these elite games seem to have lost sight of an important truth: that the high-finance sector, like every other important sector of a democracy, must nurture some degree of public tolerance. An aroused public can cause anybody a lot of trouble.

Wall Street would be well-advised to treat whatever public good will it has these days as fragile, as highly leveraged, as borrowed against good times, as a commodity that can disappear with the low unemployment rate.

These leveraged buyouts are nearly as incomprehensible as they are monumental. That's a factor that fuels a potential public backlash. In bad times, the complexity can be portrayed by demagogues as a tactic for confusing the public.

In the 1930s, demagogues developed huge, emotional followings by railing against "the moneychangers." What the high financiers have going for them today with public opinion is the absence of a depression. People are not looking around for a scapegoat.

When bad times come, however, that search always starts. The people who have made billions by participating in the buying and selling of huge corporations — corporations which have, in the process, incurred enormous debts that result in layoffs during recessions — will be likely targets. They seem to be setting themselves up.

THE SACRAMENTO BEE
Sacramento, California, December 6, 1988

Last month's wild bidding war for RJR Nabisco — and the $250 billion reportedly in the hands of leveraged-buy-out moguls on the prowl for other such prizes — have Congress worried, and well they should. But the schemes that have so far been proposed to curb these buy-outs — from tax law changes that would make corporate borrowing more expensive to bans on pension fund participation in leveraged takeovers — could turn out to be worse than the disease they're supposed to cure. By comparison, the plans of several congressional committees to hold hearings early next year may seem a tepid response, but that's exactly what Congress needs to do — proceed with caution.

There is something terribly skewed about an economy that offers its biggest rewards to its most undeserving participants — the investors, lawyers and brokers who can make hundreds of millions of dollars in a matter of weeks on financial maneuvers that add nothing to the long-term wealth or productive capacity of the nation. Yet the same mechanisms these wheelers and dealers use can be just as crucial to those economic activities that the country most wants to encourage. Limiting their availability could prove a serious mistake.

Tax breaks for corporate borrowing, for instance, are still far more widely used by businesses making desirable research and capital investments than in leveraged buyouts. Eliminating them would hurt both kinds of activities. Even a special tax penalty on particularly high interest payments — the kind typical with the junk bonds used in these buy-outs — could hit hardest those new companies, troubled companies and high-risk ventures that also have to borrow at high interest rates for undertakings that could do the broader economy enormous good in the long run.

Similarly, any move to make it more difficult to force ownership or management changes on a company might prevent needed shake-ups of inefficient corporations. And it would be hard to devise a limit on pension fund investment that would apply only to unproductive buy-out schemes, and wouldn't simply prevent the ordinary citizens served by pension funds from earning the same high returns that wealthy investors are able to garner.

If Congress has to move carefully, however, that does not mean that the buy-out moguls should be allowed to proceed complacently in the meantime. Existing securities and antitrust laws, if the administration would only enforce them, could put a damper on deals that mislead ordinary investors or threaten undue concentrations of economic power. And congressional anger and attention, by themselves, could well induce a degree of self-restraint on Wall Street. The one thing already certain, before any hearings are held, is that that is sorely missing.

The News and Observer
Raleigh, North Carolina, December 2, 1988

The takeover war for RJR Nabisco — which seems to have ended with a $24.53 billion offer from buyout king Kohlberg Kravis Roberts and Co. — shows how far the company has come, or gone, from the gentility of its beginnings on the lush lawns of Winston-Salem to the shark-infested sidewalks of Wall Street.

The buyout should not be taken lightly by the American taxpayer as an "over my head" bit of financial maneuvering by the howitzers of big business. That taxpayer could be stung by the buyout, the nation's economy could suffer and an economic slump could mean out-and-out disaster.

Advocates of letting the megamergers fall where they may argue that leveraged buyouts — in which investors buy a company by borrowing money while they use their takeover target as collateral — are all a part of free enterprise capitalism. Going into debt to buy a company forces management to be more efficient, to "trim the fat" both in the high-priced management ranks and in production.

To legislate some controls over the buyouts, those same advocates argue, puts unfair restraints on capitalism. Both arguments have some validity, but they don't address the cost of a laissez-faire policy on massive mergers like that of RJR Nabisco and Kohlberg, or the Philip Morris Inc. plan to buy Kraft Inc. at a price of $11 billion.

First, there's the motivation behind the buyouts themselves. Are they good-hearted efforts to help management? Are they noble attempts to bolster the nation's economy? Are they helping to put better quality products on grocery shelves or in hardware stores? No. They're motivated by out-and-out greed — corporate executives and bankers and lawyers out to turn a monstrous profit.

Second, the leveraged buyout costs the average American in two ways. Because interest on corporate loans is tax deductible, the buyers enjoy a huge tax break, which can amount to billions of dollars in taxes that have to be found elsewhere — mostly in the already-picked pockets of the middle class. And that debt means that a merged corporation can't spend a lot of time and money investing in research and new and improved products because it has to pay off

its loans. That represents a double-edged sword for the ordinary, salaried worker.

Third, just what happens if the national economy — already under huge competitive pressure from Japan and other foreign countries — goes into a bit of a tailspin? The company that's in big debt suddenly doesn't have enough cash to pay that debt — just as the worker who loses his job suddenly can't pay off a big credit card bill. If the worker defaults, he's the only one who's hurt. If a multibillion-dollar corporation defaults, tremors go through the nation's economy.

That seems to show shortsightedness on the part of the corporate executives who started the RJR Nabisco takeover war. F. Ross Johnson, the company's president, lit the fuse by announcing that the executives would try to stage the takeover themselves. But consider that those executives, and the bankers and lawyers involved in the dealing, make millions in profits or "golden parachutes" for

ousted executives no matter what happens.

And stockholders — who nearly doubled their money after the buyout bids started coming in — walk away wealthier as well. That's fine for next week or next month or next year, but what happens if the worst-case scenario — a recession — comes to be? What happens in the long term when American companies are too busy paying off their buyout loans to develop products that can compete with foreign traders?

Congress certainly should not legislate against free enterprise. But lawmakers can take steps to hold the reins on capitalism run wild — for one, by reducing the tax breaks for the billion-dollar borrowers. That would be an injection of caution for the merger maniacs. And it might provide an ordinary parachute for the average American who can be pushed into the economic sky through forces beyond his control.

The Atlanta Journal
THE ATLANTA CONSTITUTION
Atlanta, Georgia, December 4, 1988

The dust will be settling for weeks from the hectic last hours in which the board of Atlanta-based RJR Nabisco Inc. finally chose buyout artist Kohlberg Kravis Roberts & Co. — and $25 billion — over a virtually equivalent bid by the company's own management group headed by President F. Ross Johnson.

In the circumstances, it would appear the board chose responsibly, preferring the KKR offer because it provides a stronger position in the reconstituted company for shareholders and perhaps for employees than the management group's proposal. The board earlier had put RJR Nabisco up for auction, easing ethical questions created by management's closeness to the board and its opportunity to run the company to benefit its own effort to take the firm private and score personal fortunes. In choosing KKR, the board again avoided any charge its decision was compromised by coziness with the buyer.

Still, there is little to be said on behalf of this corporate feeding frenzy, in which stock only recently selling for $55 a share was bid up to $109, "greed" became the word by which just about everyone characterized the affair and financial communities that had become accustomed to huge leveraged buyouts questioned the propriety of one this large.

Yes, shareholders obviously will take a big short-term profit as KKR buys them out. But bondholders are left with paper whose value is diminished by the new debt; two firms are suing. Key parts of the company will be sold off to help pay the debt. Layoffs, lower wages and higher consumer prices are likely for the same reason. Any gains in efficiency forced by the need to pay down the debt are speculative at this point, and even if they occur, what does that say about management's ability to dis-

cipline itself without such prodding?

Parochially, if you will, Atlanta has reason to feel had. RJR Nabisco, which moved here a year and a half ago with great fanfare, reportedly will be returned to North Carolina. You have to wonder: Did management, already calculating its own takeover ploy, make the costly and disruptive relocation in the first place just to free itself of the clamors that could be expected in the company's hometown?

The economy has nothing new to show for all of this — no new product, no technological breakthrough, no new marketing network — all the things that American-style capitalism needs if it is to succeed in international competition.

Key members of Congress are planning hearings next year on leveraged buyouts. That's precisely one of the consequences the business community feared from the excesses of the RJR Nabisco game, but there are basic policy issues that clearly demand ventilation.

Can bondholders be protected from the devaluation of their notes in such cases? Shouldn't a Bush Justice Department be prodded to police mergers and acquisitions, as the Reagan Justice Department has not? Should taxpayers continue to subsidize these buyouts by providing unlimited tax deductions for the borrowing? What is the propriety, and what should be the legality, of managers arranging fail-safe fortunes for themselves if they flop while trying to enrich themselves further by buying the company?

This exercise in capitalism amok has pushed the dubious business of debt-fueled buyouts to an extreme that raises urgent questions of how this society is using, and how it should use, its economic resources.

AKRON BEACON JOURNAL

Akron, Ohio, December 5, 1988

THE DIZZY race of leveraged buyouts and hostile takeovers continues. The numbers boggle the mind as corporate heavyweights topple and eager sharks swallow whole huge American enterprises.

The $25 billion takeover that will have Kolberg, Kravis, Roberts & Company engorge tobacco/food giant RJR Nabisco is but the biggest and latest of these deals. The country reels as it watches the feeding frenzies in the turbulent waters of the financial markets. As Akron well knows, communities and longtime employees quake as the junk-bond artists and the leveraged buyout experts ply their trade of raiding, dismemberment and fast profit.

The complex issue arising from all this is whether these feeding frenzies are really good for the country. Are they good for the free enterprise system? Are they good for the development of new products, markets and competition?

What is it about the free market system that is causing a company's stock — its market value — to be worth $55 one day, in the case of RJR Nabisco, and worth $109 a share only six weeks later?

A national debate rages on the value or the dangers of such deals. One view is that they must be curbed, for the good of American business; that selling off strong companies and slicing them into pieces for the benefit of a few buyout artists is not healthy. A counter argument is that this is simply the marketplace sorting out the business structure, and that a free market, unfettered by restraints, is best for business and the country in the long run.

The latter view is usually true, all other things being equal. They are not in these cases; leveraged buyouts are encouraged by the tax laws, through allowing tax deductions for debt interest. Thus, all of us as taxpayers are helping to subsidize the purchase and potential split-up of the RJR Nabiscos.

Congress, which loves to tinker with the economy, but does not always do so wisely, is already eyeballing the era of LBOs, and considering either prohibiting them or restricting the tax advantages involved.

Other possibilities include eliminating the double taxation of dividends, to help end the incentives for buyouts, or even eliminating the corporate income tax. The latter would not be as radical a step as some might think, since business always passes on the cost of taxes to customers and consumers anyway.

There are legitimate and useful mergers and even purchases and sales of companies in the world of business. The modern form of such activity, however, seems largely propelled by the lure of high, fast profits. Unless curbed voluntarily or by some non-Draconian change in the tax law, the time is fast approaching when Congress may have to consider radical surgery to keep American corporations from being torn apart and discarded solely for the benefit of a few skilled practitioners of the new art of takeovers.

The Record

Hackensack, New Jersey, December 2, 1988

To the victor the spoils . . . and the headaches.

The small but powerful investment house of Kohlberg, Kravis, Roberts & Company has won Wall Street's mega-dealmaker crown with its victory in the takeover sweepstakes for RJR Nabisco. KKR edged out a group led by RJR Nabisco's management by bidding almost $25 billion for the food and tobacco company.

Waiting to see what it will mean are RJR Nabisco's employees, 4,500 of whom work in New Jersey. Those lucky enough to own significant amounts of stock will make small fortunes. But some employees may lose their jobs.

If the deal goes through, the $25 billion price tag will be the largest ever paid for a corporation. The KKR offer almost doubles the previous takeover record of $13.4 billion, paid for Gulf Oil in 1984.

The RJR Nabisco deal is also four times larger than any previous leveraged buyout. Leveraged buyouts or LBOs are takeovers financed with large amounts of borrowed money, backed by company assets, and repaid through the sale of assets and company cash flow.

The structure of LBO financing brings us to KKR's first headache. Debt. The deal will saddle the company with more than $20 billion of debt. That's more than the combined national debt of Bolivia, Jamaica, Uruguay, Costa Rica, and Honduras.

If KKR is as shrewd as it thinks, it will be able to pay shareholders their cash and securities package worth $109 a share and still turn a profit. To do this, KKR will most likely sell off all or part of the company's food businesses, which make such familiar products as Ritz crackers, Fig Newtons and Life Savers, and keep its cigarette business, which generates enormous profits with brands such as Winston, Salem, and Camel.

Market conditions could sour the deal. The high price means KKR will have to get premium prices for any assets it sells. A downturn in the economy or increases in interest rates would reduce that likelihood. Wall Street analysts also worry that lawsuits tied to the dangers of cigarettes could cut tobacco profits.

KKR's second major headache is that it is entering uncharted waters. In the past, KKR only undertook friendly LBOs, deals struck with the blessing of management. The RJR Nabisco deal has given new meaning to the term hostile takeover, as the brash egos of key players like Henry R. Kravis and George R. Roberts of KKR and F. Ross Johnson, the chairman of RJR Nabisco and leader of the competing buyout group, have repeatedly clashed. The tone was set back on Oct. 25 when both sides met in an attempt to fashion a joint venture. The meeting began with Mr. Roberts asking members of the RJR Nabisco team not to smoke and ended with RJR Nabisco telling KKR to get lost.

What's problematic for KKR is that once the deal goes through, it will be charged with managing the nation's 19th largest industrial concern without the help of the company's top management. Finance, not management, is the strength of KKR.

Finally, there is the matter of people. Nabisco employees are no strangers to the takeover game. Nabisco merged with Standard Brands in 1981 and with RJR in 1985. In both cases, layoffs were kept to a minimum.

Workers may not be so lucky this time. The jobs of most production workers are probably safe. Someone has to bake the cookies, or so the logic goes. But other jobs are clearly in jeopardy. If, as expected, Nabisco's operations are sold in small pieces and folded into larger food companies, jobs in research and administration are likely to be eliminated.

The layoffs will be easier to accept for Nabisco employees who own stock. Before the bidding war began, RJR Nabisco was at $55 a share.

But all employees are entitled to a fair shake from their new boss, whoever that eventually turns out to be. The new owners should not lose sight of the fact that people, not paper deals, are responsible for profits.

Greenspan Optimistic on Economy; Fed Sees Economic Bottoming

The U.S. government's index of leading economic indicators climbed 0.8% in December 1989, the Commerce Department reported January 31, 1990.

The indicator data lent support to Jan. 30 testimony by Federal Reserve Chairman Alan Greenspan that the economy would avoid a recession. Greenspan told the Joint Economic Committee of Congress that "such imbalances and dislocations as we see in the economy today probably do not suggest anything more than a temporary hesitation in the continuing expansion of the economy."

On June 18, 1991, Fed Chairman Greenspan and another key member of the Federal Reserve Board told Congress recent statistics indicated that the U.S. economy was on the rebound. While barriers remained to a robust recovery, a gradual upturn was likely to begin by the third quarter of 1991, they said.

Fed Chairman Alan C. Greenspan told the House Ways and Means Committee that statistical evidence overwhelmingly suggested "that the [economy's] bottoming is somewhere in the second quarter." Recent favorable indicators had included rising corporate payrolls and industrial output coupled with continuing declines in inventories.

Despite his assertion that the downturn had ended, Greenspan said he was uncertain about how soon an expansion would be seen. He predicted that factors including a credit crunch and a glut in commercial real estate would impede any robustness in the economy in the short term.

Separately, Fed governor David W. Mullins Jr., who had been nominated to be the Fed's vice-chairman, echoed Greenspan's conclusions at his confirmation hearing before the Senate Banking Committee. He said the third period should be "squarely in the plus column," and that growth in the first year of the recovery would be between 2% and 4%.

Democrats on the panel, pointing to the previous month's upswing in the unemployment rate, urged further cuts in short-term interest rates. Mullins, however, argued that further such cuts could actually stall an economic recovery by causing bond traders to drive up longer-term interest rates as a hedge against inflation. Financial markets viewed both officials' comments as signs that additional rate decreases were unlikely, and stock and bond prices June 18 fell in reaction.

The nation's unemployment rate in May increased to 6.9% from 6.6%, the Labor Department reported June 7. A measure of the jobless rate that included military personnel rose to 6.8% from 6.5%.

The unemployment rate was based on a telephone survey of households. That survey counted each jobholder once, while the payroll data, based on a survey of employers, counted the number of jobs held. The survey of households showed a drop in civilian employment of 800,000 jobs in May.

Analysts said that unemployment as measured by the household survey, which excluded from its jobless figures unemployed workers who had given up looking for work, often continued to rise during the first months of an economic recovery. Rumors of increased hiring often drew unemployed workers back into the labor market, thus increasing the overall pool of "jobless" workers. Economists generally watched the payroll survey as a better indicator of he direction the economy was taking.

According to the telephone survey, the unemployment rate for adult men rose to 6.5% from 6.2%. Unemployment among adult women rose to 5.8% from 5.5%. The jobless rate rose in other categories, including whites (to 6.1% from 5.8%), Hispanics (to 9.7% from 9%) and teen-agers (to 19.1% from 18.1%).

Unemployment among blacks rose to 13.0% from 12.6%, while joblessness among black teenagers fell to 33.5%% from 37.1%.

THE PLAIN DEALER
Cleveland, Ohio, December 3, 1990

If it feels like a recession, it probably *is* a recession. There is little point in economists' prolonged sparring over semantics, even though relentless optimists are struggling to find a soothing euphemism: President Bush last week called it a "serious slowdown," White House economist Michael Boskin termed it a momentary "lull," and Federal Reserve Chairman Alan Greenspan dubbed it a "meaningful downturn."

Discard the textbook definitions and survey the latest data. The trend is clear: A general recession — the first since the excruciating downturn of 1981-82 — has begun or is about to begin.

It is tempting, but not entirely accurate, to blame the recession on the oil shock triggered by Iraq's invasion of Kuwait, since higher energy prices have reduced the money available for business investment and household purchasing power. But energy-price increases were just another drag on an economy that already had been slowed by many factors, some of them unavoidable: tight interest rates (amid the Fed's sensible campaign against inflation), banks' tougher lending standards (as bankers and regulators rightly tightened oversight and capital requirements after the savings-and-loan disaster) and consumer credit exhaustion (after a decade-long buying binge).

Thus far, the Great Lakes states have not suffered the worst of the region-by-region doldrums. Instead, the worst effects are being felt in the areas that saw the greatest excesses in the 1980s: New England, where the real-estate bubble was bound to burst; the Northeast Corridor, where layoffs in the financial industry have shrunk payrolls; and California, where the post-Cold War "peace dividend" is forcing cuts in high-tech defense plants. But those regions' white-collar woes will reduce demand for manufactured goods, boding ill for heavily industrialized areas like Northeast Ohio.

The Cleveland area is feeling the first recessionary effects. Some building plans are being reevaluated; the apparent delay of the new Ameritrust tower on Public Square shows that anxiety is running high in the hard-hit banking sector. Federal budget cuts are worrying employees at NASA and related high-tech firms in Brook Park. The nationwide slowdown in automobile sales has provoked General Motors to cut back its auto production for the rest of the year; if that trend spreads among other Big Three automakers, it will hit many Northeast Ohio autoworkers and parts suppliers. City, state and federal finances will suffer, too, as less tax revenue comes in and more money goes out for unemployment and welfare benefits.

Modest-sized recessions aren't a calamity; occasional downturns are an all-but-inevitable part of the business cycle. But policymakers will have fewer weapons to combat a recession in the 1990s, since mammoth federal budget deficits — thoughtlessly amassed during the boom times of the 1980s — reduce Washington's capacity for stimulative, "countercyclical" spending. Perhaps that's why the Bush administration hesitates to admit that the recession has arrived. Having missed the chance for a "soft landing," it won't be easy to prevent the hard landing from ending with a nasty jolt.

The Miami Herald
Miami, Florida, December 8, 1990

THE FOURTH branch of American Government — not the three you learned about in school, but the independent Federal Reserve System — took another step this week to avert recession. Despite anxious words from legislative and executive corridors, the responsibility for fighting recession has rested almost exclusively lately with the often-mysterious Fed, an agency controlled by none of the Government's traditional branches.

After Fed Chairman Alan Greenspan predicted a "meaningful downturn" in the national economy, the Bush Administration and others hoped that he would respond with an equally meaningful new stimulus. Instead, the Fed wisely chose a tactic more psychological than economic.

By lowering the reserve requirements on certain foreign and corporate deposits, the Federal Reserve Board provided a small increase in available funds. In the end, however, the effect on interest rates and large-scale lending could be neutralized by other forces. Overall, the net economic effect on the money supply will be marginal at best.

But the symbolic effect of the Fed's action may far outweigh the technical eco-nomics. This signal to the embattled financial industry that the Fed is encouraging more lending, that it will maintain the liquidity needed to expand credit, appears to have had an encouraging effect on bank management. By taking an uncommon action — reserve requirements haven't been lowered since 1983 — the Fed clearly is willing to use dramatic means if needed.

This cautious-but-rational approach to an uncertain economy relegates the President and Congress largely to the sidelines. There isn't much that they could do anyway. The budget deficit has all but neutralized the main economic weapons that they control, taxing and spending. If the "meaningful downturn" is to be abbreviated, only the Federal Reserve — which is under no public, elective control — has the broad means to do it. This isn't how your high-school texts said that the Government was supposed to work, but at least it is working with a clear and reasonable strategy.

Meanwhile, if the Executive and Legislative Branches want to regain an important role in economic policy, they will first have to solve their budget woes. Until then, keep your textbook on governing on the shelf — and your eye on the Federal Reserve.

The Times-Picayune
New Orleans, Louisiana, December 1, 1990

An indispensable qualification of Federal Reserve Board chairmen is that they be able to speak in ambiguities, the more convoluted and seemingly contradictory the better. The idea is to keep Wall Street constantly off balance as to the central bank's likely tilt on interest rates.

Paul Volcker, appointed by President Jimmy Carter and Fed chairman during the Reagan presidency, demonstrated this essential quality to a high degree. Yet the present chairman, Alan Greenspan, might be the Fed's most artful dodger ever.

Mr. Greenspan was at his ambiguous best during his recent appearance before the House Banking Committee.

Perhaps the two most important economic questions before the nation are these: Is the national economy in a recession? If so, can the nation expect the Federal Reserve Board to cut interest rates soon and substantially?

In the best Fed tradition, Chairman Greenspan provided no unequivocal answers. He stopped just a gnat's hair short of declaring a recession, but he stopped short all the same.

"A meaningful downturn in aggregate output occurred" in October and November, the chairman conceded in the sonorous yet almost somnolent tones that have become his trademark. Furthermore, he said, the downturn probably means that the nation's gross national product, which measures the total output of goods and services, will shrink in this year's last quarter.

The government reported 1.7 percent GNP growth in the third quarter. The stan-dard definition of a recession is two consecutive quarters of negative GNP growth.

But lest the world get the notion that Mr. Greenspan is convinced a recession is at hand, he abruptly changed course in his testimony before the House committee.

"We won't know whether it is the beginning of a recession, or just some aberration, for quite a while, " he said. What's more, he went on, the economy is not as weak as people think it is.

With a million Wall Street ears waiting eagerly to hear an interest-rate pin drop, he drove home his basic equivocation: "The world out there, when you look at the hard data, is not in as bad shape as it feels."

So does that mean the Fed will be lowering interest rates or not? The answer is that it probably means it will.

For all the storied and studied ambiguity associated with Fed chairmen, it is highly unlikely that the present occupant will openly acknowledge a "downturn," if not a recession, and not encourage lower interest rates.

Perhaps the most relevant question is whether the Fed is too late with too little. Under Chairman Greenspan, it has gradually lowered interest rates by manipulating the federal funds rate that banks charge each other on overnight loans.

A "downturn" should be enough to warrant a clear signal from the Fed that a recession, or the distinct possibility of one, will shortly bring a substantial reduction in the key discount rate.

Of course, Mr. Greenspan did not rule that out, either. Or did he?

The Salt Lake Tribune
Salt Lake City, Utah, December 23, 1990

Now if the White House could only be as persuasive with Saddam Hussein as it evidently was with Federal Reserve Board Chairman Alan Greenspan. In fact, the Fed's cooperation makes avoiding a Persian Gulf war all the more crucial.

Finally convinced that looming national recession required action, Fed Chairman Greenspan loosened the country's money supply. Lowering interest rates on funds major banks borrow from the U.S. Treasury, Mr. Greenspan gave the economy a chance to absorb more consumer and industrial spending, deflecting current trends away from job loss and financial contraction.

But, in present international circumstances, risks from this sort of manipulation are greater than normal. The Persian Gulf crisis broods over the economy like a gathering typhoon.

Bush administration officials have been suggesting Fed relief work for several weeks, since economic indicators clearly confirmed that the country, especially New England and the East Coast, had entered recession. Moderate inflation made it feasible to cause the kind of interest rate declines which can stimulate more borrowing, spending and investment — usually effective recession antidotes.

However, nothing fuels inflation like a war, and war in the Persian Gulf could be wildly inflationary, as oil prices rocket through the ceiling. In such an event, the Fed will have contributed to economic battering rather than strengthening.

The White House would be due its share of the blame, too. Conversely, if Iraq's Saddam Hussein becomes as convinced by the military prospects facing him as Mr. Greenspan was by the economic conditions he contemplated, the Baghdad bully will evacuate his troops from occupied Kuwait and the emerging peril will subside.

The United States and the world will not only be spared a terrible and unpredictable war, but a steep, potentially ruinous economic decline as well. The Bush administration, on both counts and in the aggregate, can emerge covered with glory or festooned with abject failure.

DESERET NEWS
Salt Lake City, Utah, January 6, 1991

Re-ces-sion.

There. They said it. President Bush and his advisers have used the word that everybody else has been whispering for months.

It's no longer a question of whether there is a recession, but how long it will last and how bad it will be. The consensus of crystal-ball gazers seems to be that it will be short and mild. That's based on favorable factors such as a low rate of inflation, no great backlog of unsold inventory, and a declining dollar, which stimulates exports.

Doomsayers, on the other hand, point to factors such as a shaky banking industry, mountains of debt and weak consumer confidence as the stuff of a real downer.

Your guess is as good as the experts'. In truth, nobody knows the future. No mortal can predict the course of the recession.

Another truth is that the government can't do much about it. Except for the action the Federal Reserve Board already has taken to lower interest rates, the nation can do little but ride out the downturn — unless it turns into a depression that would require public-works programs and other measures to prime the pump.

Barring that extreme, the recession probably will be curing itself before anything that Congress and the president might do in response could take effect.

All of which suggests that what Congress and the president should be doing in response to this recession is to start worrying about the *next* recession. Their job is to build an economy that is stronger at its foundations, so that the next recession and every one after that finds Americans less vulnerable.

Their job is to try to build the kind of economy that steadily improves the prosperity and security of ordinary Americans — something that hasn't happened much lately despite the much-bragged-about Reagan-Bush "record economic expansion." That debt-fueled binge may have left America weaker, not stronger.

Building a stronger economic foundation requires, above all, improving the reservoir of knowledge, skills and talents among the American people. It means a national commitment to education that goes beyond lip service. The appalling ignorance and lack of skills among too many young Americans is a clear and present danger to national security.

Particular attention needs to be given to training more engineers, scientists, designers, inventors, builders, doers. A strong future economy will depend on the ability of Americans to make things, not merely make money.

Then, too, an economy functions no better than its infrastructure. The need for better highways, rail systems, airports, water and sewage systems, telecommunications networks, mass transit can't be put off much longer.

And an economy is no more productive than its people. People are more productive when they face fewer hassles in life — hassles such as a lack of decent child care, discrimination or harassment in the workplace, inept management,

worry over health care or job security or retirement or affording college or a hundred other things.

If President Bush and Congress want to respond to the recession in a constructive way, there's no shortage of things to be done.

The Times-Picayune
New Orleans, Louisiana, February 1, 1991

Half of the conventional definition of a recession has now been delivered by the federal government. To use the goofy but widely accepted term, the conventional, statistical definition of a recession is two consecutive quarters of "negative GNP growth."

The government reported Friday that 1990's fourth quarter had, as was generally expected, produced negative GNP growth. The nation's economy declined at an annual rate of 2.1 percent.

That figure, of course, is subject to revision, and the revised figure could be somewhat better or worse.

Many economists expect that the fourth-quarter decline was not the first and probably will not be the last. But it is the first official declaration of negative GNP in the current downturn. Indeed, the Bush administration and the Congressional Budget Office are predicting that the current quarter also will show negative or minus growth.

The official designator of recessions, the National Bureau of Economic Research, has already declared a recession. Bureau officials have said they probably will determine that the recession began during the third quarter of 1990, although overall GNP, the sum of the nation's goods and services, registered a positive 1.4 percent rate during that quarter.

For all of 1990, the GNP rose an anemic 0.9 percent, the Commerce Department reported Friday. That was about one-third of the 1989 increase of 2.5 percent and the economy's

poorest performance since a 2.5 percent annual decline in 1982.

The 2.1 percent decline in last year's final quarter revealed weakness throughout the economy, economists said. The decline was led, they said, by a $21 billion decrease in consumer spending, with Americans cutting back purchases on everything from autos to clothing and even food.

Since consumer spending accounts for two-thirds of the GNP, the importance of consumer psychology cannot be overestimated. Should consumers turn more optimistic, the economy could lurch out of recession rather abruptly.

And there are those, including members of the Bush administration, the Congressional Budget office and many private economists, who expect the economy to begin a recovery phase as early as the next quarter. Other economists are predicting the recession will end by the fourth quarter. Even pessimists expect recovery to start in the first or second quarter of 1992.

If the "short and shallow" recession theory held by such optimists as Federal Reserve Chairman Alan Greenspan proves correct, the worst of the recession is already behind us.

Thus, in a paradoxical sense, the arrival of the first official quarter of negative GNP can be interpreted as good news, the darkest hour before the dawn.

The Hartford Courant
Hartford, Connecticut, January 12, 1991

President Bush has uttered the "R" word, recession. "We're in a slowdown economically in this country, if not recession," he said in a recent Public Broadcasting Service interview. "In some areas we're clearly in a recession, and this concerns me because people are hurting."

The president went on to say, "I happen to believe and I think that most economists believe, that the recession will be mild and that the whole country will come out of it, in not too many months from now."

Mr. Bush is right in finally uttering the word. Now that he is facing reality, it should be easier to resolve to do something about the weak economy.

Is the president right in predicting the recession will pass away? No one really knows, but in case the economy gets worse, the president ought to have a contingency plan. There is no evidence that he does.

Mr. Bush seems to talk about recession as if it were a blight on apples, something everyone needs to endure with Norman Rockwell-like courage and solidarity. But the action that counts from a president is to stimulate, control and otherwise manipulate the economy for the social good.

Not that every Keynesian approach to economics contains all the answers. There may be no permanent solutions in public policy, but there are usually mitigating steps worth taking. A president cannot afford to remain passive in the face of economic assault.

Mr. Bush said, in the PBS interview, that he wants to run again in 1992. He ought to remember what Harry S Truman said. When your neighbor is out of work, it's a recession; when you're out of work, it's a depression. If this nation slips into a deep recession, Mr. Bush could be out of work.

382
can
Can America Compete?

McCLELLAN MEDIA CENTER
9417 GEYER SPRINGS RD.
LITTLE ROCK, AR

326061

RECESSION — 51

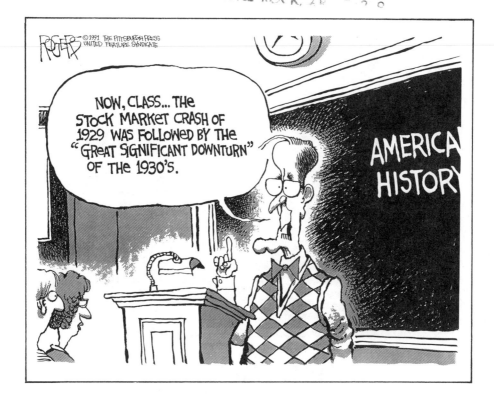

ST. LOUIS POST-DISPATCH
St. Louis, Missouri, January 6, 1991

The debate over whether the recession has finally arrived has concluded. The debate about how long it will last is about to begin. No longer able to deny the obvious, the administration wants to put forth an optimistic prediction of the severity of the storm. It is probably wrong.

Michael J. Boskin, chairman of the Council of Economic Advisers, acknowledged the other day that the economy almost certainly contracted this fall and will again this winter. But by spring, he believes, it should resume growing, though slowly. That rosiest of scenarios let President Bush proclaim there is no need to create jobs or take special measures to pump up the economy. After all, the recession is supposed to be half over already.

But not everyone agrees — with good reason. Manufacturing output fell in December to its lowest level in eight years; so did car and truck sales. Construction spending is at a two-year low. The consensus judgment is that the economy shrank this fall at more than 4 percent on an annual basis, only a little less than the rate of contraction in the worst months of the 1982 recession, which was the severest since the 1930s.

Weak bank balance sheets, unusually high levels of corporate and consumer debt, sharply higher oil prices and uncertainty stemming from the prospect of war in the Persian Gulf add up to powerful restraints on economic activity — and consumer and investor confidence. These will probably take longer than a mere six months to reverse. The average length of recent recessions is twice that.

The administration is trying to put a pretty face on things, no doubt to encourage business confidence. A more helpful confidence-building measure would be to promise just those job-creation programs it now forswears if the recession runs longer than the administration hopes it will. That would give the public a welcome sense that its government is ready to stay on top of the problem.

The Gazette

Cedar Rapids, Iowa, January 4, 1991

FINALLY THEY have said it. After weeks of calling the economic slump a "downturn" or "slowdown," people from the White House have indicated that the nation is in a recession.

Spokesman Marlin Fitzwater told reporters Wednesday, "We're in a recessionary kind of period." (At least he didn't say "recessionary mode.") And in a TV interview Michael Boskin, chairman of the President's Council of Economic Advisers, said, "It does appear that after the longest economic expansion in the peacetime history of the United States, the country probably has entered a recession."

President Bush himself, in a Dec. 16 interview taped for broadcast Thursday night on the Public Broadcasting Service, said some regions were definitely in a recession but that he was not prepared to declare one nationwide. "I happen to believe, and I think that most economists believe, that the recession will be mild and that the whole country will come out of it in not too many months from now."

If Bush and his aides hadn't acknowledged the recession, they would have looked ridiculous. Regional recession, especially in the Northeast, has been a fact for months. And recent interest-rate cuts by the Federal Reserve underscore an urgency to jump-start the economy.

Recession's arrival, however, does not mean the sky is falling. A "recession," according to Webster's New World Dictionary, is "a temporary falling off of business activity during a period when such activity has been generally increasing."

That's what is happening in the United States today. So there's no need to search for euphemisms — "economic softening," "periodic adjustment," "lull."

"YOU'RE RAINING ON MY PARADE, GREENSPAN!"

ST. LOUIS POST-DISPATCH
St. Louis, Missouri, June 30, 1991

The White House has announced that the recession is over. The numbers suggest it may be, or at least that the economy is no longer contracting. But that doesn't mean a genuine recovery has begun — and that's what counts to unemployed workers and struggling businesses. An economy growing only modestly is effectively still in recession for most people.

While consumer spending rose 1.1 percent in May and personal incomes edged up 0.5 percent, bank earnings remain depressed, credit is tight and unemployment is still rising. Indeed, since employment growth usually lags behind consumer spending, it is likely to rise higher than May's 6.9 percent — a considerable number — before starting down.

Moreover, a national recovery could still leave many regions in recession for months. St. Louis, for instance, is burdened by layoffs in the defense and auto industries. The residential and commercial real estate markets remain weak both here and else-

where as a result of substantial overbuilding. This could extend economic weakness for millions of people for perhaps years to come.

In short, the need for the government to ease the plight of those suffering from the recession has not evaporated. Unfortunately, the Federal Reserve refuses to lower interest rates further for fear of re-igniting inflation. But the Fed is debating its money supply targets for next year, which fuel growth every bit as much as loan rates. Given that money has been tighter in the last five years than at any time in the last 30 and that inflation is under control, the time has come for easier money. Failure to adopt this policy could choke off the recovery before it starts.

Congress should also increase transportation spending to create public works jobs and should extend unemployment insurance. These are minimal and perhaps inadequate steps. But they are the least that should be done. The recession isn't over.

DIARIO LAS AMERICAS
Miami, Florida, March 21, 1991

Aside from the fact that all the problems of the Near and Middle East have not been solved, though a resounding military victory was achieved, President George Bush has to insist in finding a solution to the grave financial situation that is afflicting the United States of America and that, in the opinion of experts, is the most serious since the great 1929 crisis.

President Bush not only because of his well-known patriotism, but also because it is politically good for his reelection, must be perfecting a plan with the help of his top financial advisors to restore normality to the American economy. This economy is in a critical condition that hurts everyone, not necessarily all alike, but it can be said that —in general terms— no one escapes from the consequences of what is taking place.

In Florida, particularly in the Greater Miami metropolitan area, the crisis has been felt in a significant way. To compound matters we had the disaster caused by the Eastern Airlines bankruptcy and the loss of jobs of many thousands of individuals whose families were left without their main means of support with the same thing happening to other families that in some way depended from the first. Whatever might have been the

mistakes made by management in Eastern Airlines, the truth is that the whims of the union leaders caused this disastrous outcome that has been so detrimental for the many thousands of families who worked for the airline, and for South Florida in general. Of course, this applies not only to South Florida, but also to other states, particularly Georgia, that had, in Atlanta, an operations hub for that airline with an important labor force.

There are signs that President Bush is taking the necessary measures to vitalize the nation's economy. But it is important that those measures be taken swiftly before more harm —perhaps irreparable— be done to companies all over the nation that are closing their doors or considerably curtailing their operations. All this causes unemployment and greatly discourages any new ventures.

As psychological factors play an important part in economic development, though this not be the fundamental, just knowing that there exists a serious plan to reactivate the economy is enough to bring about improvement and to promote the cautious development of small or large concerns.

The Times-Picayune

New Orleans. Louisiana, April 24, 1991

Few things have been predicted as often as an end to the 1990-91 national recession. Some economists were predicting its demise almost before there was statistical evidence (two successive quarters of negative gross national product growth) that it in fact existed.

"Short and shallow" has been the consensus phrase attached to the recession. A few brave economists have dared to demur, seeing a recession neither so short nor so shallow.

A surprising drop in the number of people filing initial claims for unemployment benefits in the week ending April 6 has provided new grist for the mills of "short and shallow" seers.

A decline of 22,000 in unemployment claims filers came after a drop of 70,000 a week earlier. The U.S. Labor Department noted that the two weekly declines pressed the total for initial claims downward to a seasonally adjusted 451,000 for the first week in April.

These figures were wildly cheered on Wall Street and in other economic circles because initial claims had been above 500,000 for three consecutive weeks in March. That was the highest level since the 1981-92 recession was bottoming out.

The reversal in initial unemployment claims is not to be dismissed lightly even if it was only for two weeks. Unemployment tends to peak when recessions are approaching their end.

If successive weeks establish the reversal as a trend, there will be good reason to think that the worst of the recession could be behind us. But will it mean that the recession is over and the "short and shallow" crowd is right?

For our part, we would like to see considerable confirmation in other areas. The continuing shrinkage in the trade deficit is encouraging, indicating strength in manufacturing and exporting. But a strengthening dollar, making U.S. goods more expensive abroad, could slow that trend.

Because consumer spending typically accounts for two-thirds of the nation's gross national product, we need to see solid evidence that consumer confidence is rebounding. The best evidence of course is consumer spending.

When consumers start putting their money where their mouths are by stepping up to the plate for the big-ticket items (cars, washing machines, etc.) we will be satisfied that the national recession is indeed behind us.

Meanwhile, some economists are cautioning that the recovery, too, could be shallow, lacking vigor and therefore vulnerable to a reversal. In addition, the recovery, like the recession, is expected to be uneven, with some regions experiencing a stronger rebound than others.

As part of the statistical Southwest, Louisiana is expected to be among the beneficiaries of a better-than-average rebound. We can look forward to that while we wait for the facts to catch up with the short-and-shallow seers.

LAS VEGAS REVIEW-JOURNAL

Las Vegas, Nevada, March 26, 1991

The 1980s were the "decade of greed," an era of heartless economic policies, the time when the "rich got richer and the poor got poorer." And it was all the fault of Ronald Reagan.

That's the standard line of liberals who retain a visceral hatred for Ronald Reagan and everything he stood for.

But did the richer get richer at the expense of the poor during the Reagan years? Was Reaganomics — the policy of lowering taxes and loosening the fetters on the free market — really a heartless approach that fed the fat cats and bled the poor?

Republican Sens. Pete Domenici of New Mexico and Phil Gramm of Texas set out to answer those queries in a recent report to Congress called "Another Look at the 1980's: A Decade of Growth and Prosperity."

Drawing on wide-ranging sources — from the Bureau of Labor Statistics and the Department of Commerce's Bureau of Economic Analysis, to the Congressional Budget Office — the senators, as the title of their study indicates, found much to praise in the Reagan years.

During the 1980s, the senators concede, the rich did get richer — but so did the poor and the middle class.

Among the senators' findings:

— Between 1983, the first full year of the Reagan economic expansion, and 1989, real (inflation adjusted) family income for the lowest 20 percent of families on the income scale rose 12 percent.

— Between 1982 and 1989, real median family income for all income groups rose 13.6 percent.

— From 1983 to 1989, the national poverty rate fell from 13.7 percent to 11.4 percent.

— Between 1982 and 1989, the share of families classified as low-income (under $15,000 in constant 1989 dollars) declined from 20.7 percent to 18 percent, while the share of high-income families (more than $50,000) increased sharply (from 21.2 percent to 29 percent). The middle class declined (from 57.8 percent to 52.9 percent) *because more of its members moved above the $50,000 threshold into the high income group.*

— The notion that black Americans fared ill under Reagan is also wrong, the senators say. The employment-to-population ratio for black American adults rose to 56.9 percent by 1989 — the highest recorded level since the Bureau of Labor Statistics started keeping such records 18 years ago.

— The seven-year economic expansion initiated under Reagan created more than 20 million jobs, 93 percent of them full-time jobs, and 82 percent of them in the managerial, precision-production and professional fields. Only 12 percent of the new jobs were created in low-skilled service operations.

— During the Reagan years, inflation, which climbed about 12 percent during Jimmy Carter's last year in office, averaged 3.6 percent. By 1989, the civilian unemployment rate dropped to a 16-year low of 5.3 percent.

So these were the heartless Reagan years?

Diehard Reagan haters and liberal Democrats who distrust the free market will not like the message contained in the Domenici-Gramm report. But it's hard to ignore the facts presented therein: that the Reagan economic expansion helped all demographic groups in this country and the strong free-market approach was indeed a rising tide that lifted all ships. As the senators said: "A job remains the best anti-poverty program." Indeed.

Los Angeles Times
Los Angeles, California, December 6, 1990

With all the talk of recession, it's time to turn aggressively, but prudently, to stimulating the economy. The Federal Reserve Board seems headed in that direction but it needs to do more. The numbers indicate a slowing national economy, with the Northeast hit the hardest. Decisive action now by the Fed could help other regions of the country help offset the worsening downturn.

The Fed sent a clear signal to banks on Tuesday to loosen up their lending to ease the credit crunch and stimulate the economy. In a highly unusual and symbolic move, the Fed cut reserve requirements on certain deposits for the first time in seven years. That will give the strapped banking industry about $14 billion more to lend, which should improve its profits.

What's needed now for the economy is an extra kick by the Fed to nudge interest rates down. In normal times, banks cut interest rates if the Fed reduces either the federal funds rate that banks pay on overnight borrowing from each other or the discount rate that banks pay for loans direct from the Fed. That has not been the case this time despite three cuts in the federal funds rate since July.

Banks have been reluctant to reduce interest rates and lend money because of the uncertain economy. That's been a big disincentive to borrowing by both consumers and business, which only adds to the credit crunch. Economists believe another interest rate cut by the Fed, even by a minimal one-quarter percent, would trigger a round of bank interest rate cuts. That's why the Fed should reduce interest rates when it meets next week.

It would reinforce the Fed's unusual cut in reserve requirements and pump even more cash into the economy to relieve the credit crunch. Fed Chairman Alan Greenspan has been exceedingly cautious. But the unusual dynamics of the downturn call for aggressive actions that might not be textbook economics. Caution hasn't stopped the recession, so erring on the side of pumping up the economy is worth a try.

The Star-Ledger
Newark, New Jersey, December 7, 1990

The recession talk we have been hearing with increasing frequency from the nation's private economists now has taken on official substance in a bleak economic assessment by Federal Reserve Board Chairman Alan Greenspan.

While Mr. Greenspan did not go so far as to say that the nation's economy is in a recessionary stage, he was the first top government official to publicly admit that the economy has slipped into "a meaningful downturn."

But one congressman, Rep. Charles Schumer (D-N.Y.), noted that the Greenspan assessment was "a nice way of saying that we've entered a recession." And even if we have not dipped into that unhappy economic stage, it is apparent that it has become imminent, evident in the latest indicator that the economy has been shrinking in the last couple of months.

A major contributing factor for the current economic downspin is the Persian Gulf crisis, which precipitated a surge in oil prices. Another concern is the continued tightening of credit by banks. Still another unsettling sign of progressive economic weakening was the latest Commerce Department report which showed a lackluster 1.7 percent annual growth in the July-September quarter.

The official definition of a recession is a decline in the gross national product for two consecutive months. Still, there is a growing consensus among private economists that the recession already has begun.

A contracting economy means reduced business activity, a higher rate of unemployment, and a significantly larger federal budget deficit as a result of declining tax revenues and increased government spending for unemployment and welfare programs. An encouraging aspect is that the threat of inflation appears to have declined in recent weeks after the initial impact of the sharp escalation of imported oil prices on energy costs.

While Mr. Greenspan, in reporting to Congress on the state of the economy, did not make any commitment to lowering interest rates to spur a lagging economy, this is something the Federal Reserve would have to do if the economy continues to worsen. And that dim prospect continues to loom larger in the final quarter of the year—possibly a final countdown before the nation moves into a recessionary stage.

The Seattle Times
Seattle, Washington, December 3, 1990

WHEN Alan Greenspan announces the nation is experiencing an economic downturn, things are likely to become far worse than they are now.

Most businesses, workers and local governments have been anxiously watching sales figures, salaries and tax revenues shrink. Consumer confidence is nearly as low as housing starts. People are bracing themselves for hard times, hoping the slump is more momentary than long-term.

Now the chairman of the Federal Reserve Board confirms a decline in the gross national product in October and November. A few more months of a downturn, and the nation will be in the middle of a full-blown recession.

The R-word has been avoided carefully by federal budget writers who were hoping a strong economy would bail out the federal budget deficit. The budget plan passed this October was premised on growth in the economy, not a decline. All the tax increases and spending cuts (and the bruising fights in Congress required to achieve them) become meaningless as the economy drifts away from growth projections made this summer.

Congress acquiesced to overly optimistic growth assumptions because that made the budget-cutting process easier. Economic reality now is beginning to hit home: The budget deficit will be far bigger than expected. The tax increases will bring in lower revenues. Worse, the government will have to spend more for higher welfare and unemployment caseloads.

Greenspan attributes the economic contraction to rising oil prices, uncertainty about the Persian Gulf crisis and tighter bank credit. Greenspan does not indicate whether and when he will lower interest rates. And a resolution to the Persian Gulf crisis may not come for many months.

The message for the winter of 1991 is batten down the hatches and wait.

The Philadelphia Inquirer

Philadelphia, Pennsylvania, December 11, 1990

Some 7.4 million Americans are now unemployed — an increase of nearly one million since June. Behind those cold numbers are real people whose pocketbooks and pride are taking a beating. There's the factory worker whose company tightened *her* belt. There's the lawyer who was gunning to make partner, but got laid off. And as the recession hurts a lot of people used to working, it makes things even more hopeless for the hard-core unemployed.

To a frustrating degree, people's ability to land a new job depends on something that nobody knows: the future course of the economy. Predictions of a mild, short recession have now been undercut by a surprisingly big jump in unemployment last month. That not only reduces some people's ability to spend money — it will probably push consumer confidence even lower, which means that the typical worker would save more and spend less. And these factors will be reverberating against built-in negatives such as the weakness of many banks and S&L's.

In other words, this recession may get a lot uglier. But at the risk of sounding like a Pollyanna, let's review some major forces that could well moderate the recession and hasten a recovery.

One powerful factor is the confidence of consumers, whose actions account for about two-thirds of the gross national product. Right now, after the longest peacetime recovery ever, consumers may be even gloomier than the situation warrants. Their confidence plummeted at summer's end, but it might rebound just as sharply if the Mideast crisis is brought to a peaceful conclusion.

There are more dependable factors as well. U.S. exports have been expanding at roughly twice the pace of U.S. imports. In the near term, the recession will further reduce imports (by lowering consumer spending) and probably help exports (by making European currencies and the yen stronger against the dollar). Another plus: U.S. businesses have gotten better at controlling inventories, so that they're adequate but not excessive. Thus the slowed purchasing is less likely to wreak havoc among suppliers and manufacturers.

What's more, the folks who control the money supply — the members of the Federal Reserve Board — have gotten better at it in recent years. Remember, over the last eight years, with the economy growing and the government running up big deficits, inflation did not fly out of control. That was due to the Fed's skill in handling the money supply. If its record holds, it should thus be able to respond to the current barrage of negatives and help bring about the eventual recovery.

Of course, nobody knows what impact these countervailing forces will have against this recession. The economy's unpredictable — that's why rookie economists are advised: "If you've got to predict, forecast often." Meanwhile, the unemployed will be hurting ... and hoping that the optimists are right.

The TENNESSEAN

Nashville, Tennessee,
December 3, 1990

MR. Alan Greenspan, chairman of the Federal Reserve Board, has put the official government stamp on the conclusion that the nation's economy is in decline.

Still, he has not said that the nation is in a recession. And that puts him in disagreement with most of the nation's economists.

Mr. Greenspan told the House Banking Committee last week that economic activity is in a downturn. He said the downturn began in earnest last month. But he said it is too early to tell if a recession is at hand.

Technically, a recession is defined as two consecutive quarters of decline in the gross national product. Data for the third term showed an increase of 1.7%, but that increase came primarily from growth just before the Persian Gulf crisis.

And on Friday, another economic barometer, the Commerce Department's Index of Leading Indicators, showed a 1.2% drop in October. That was the fourth consecutive monthly drop in the index.

Now, it will not be Mr. Greenspan's words but his actions that will be closely watched. The Federal Reserve has the power to lower interest rates to give the economy a boost. There is wide speculation that the board will do just that. Mr. Greenspan has not discussed what he will do. He has expressed some optimism, concluding that some data may show that things are not as bad a many people feel.

President Bush has reluctantly uttered the "R" word, recession, admitting that he is worried about its possibility. To this point, Mr. Greenspan has not been inclined to use the word. A report last week indicates that three out of four of the country's top business economists believe recession is here.

It is true that Mr. Greenspan has a great deal more information at his discretion than many economists on which to draw his conclusions. But it is significant that he has officially acknowledged that the economy is sliding — a revelation reached much earlier and quite often by other close observers.

Mr. Greenspan can join the club. ▪

'Why yes! A recession! I believe a recession is indeed a possibility!'

Bennett Attacks Trade School Fraud

Secretary of Education William J. Bennett Feb. 9, 1988 sent Congress a report harshly criticizing the nation's for-profit trade schools. Bennett asserted that such institutions, known as proprietary schools, were guilty of "exploitative and deceitful practices" that defrauded students.

The education secretary sent the report to Sen. Edward M. Kennedy (D, Mass.), chairman of the Senate Labor and Human Resources Committee. In an accompanying letter, Bennett urged Congress to impose tougher standards on proprietary schools to cut down a "pattern of abuse...that is tragic and shameful."

Describing his report, Bennett wrote: "You will find accounts of semiliterate high school dropouts lured to enroll in expensive training programs with false promises of lucrative jobs, only to have their hopes for a better future cruelly dashed. You will read of falsified scores on entrance exams, poor quality training and harsh refund policies."

Although the report acknowledged that a "majority of private career schools seem to produce well-trained students," Bennett asserted that "many" proprietary schools were doing a poor job of teaching and in some cases were guilty of fraud.

One of the biggest problems was the high rate of loan defaults among trade school students, Bennett said. He noted that more than 600 of the nation's nearly 7,000 trade schools had student loan default rates of more than 50% in fiscal 1985. Only 33 four-year colleges and universities had similar default rates over the same period.

(The Education Department had announced in November 1987 that it would restrict from participation in federal financial aid programs any school that had a loan default of more than 20% in the year 1990.)

Other abuses cited in the report included deceptive recruiting, admissions and financial aid practices, as well as the failure of some schools to provide students with adequate or truthful information about their programs.

In response to the report, trade school representatives argued that the Education Department had not accurately depicted the majority of such schools. "There are a lot of people out there doing a great job," said Christopher Davis, a spokesman for the National Association of Trade and Technical Schools. "It's unfair for the image of those schools to be tainted because of the few."

However, Sen. Kennedy, who earlier had disputed Bennett's allegations concerning proprietary schools, acknowledged that the Education Department's report documented "serious abuses in federal student-aid programs." He added, "The situation requires urgent action by both Congress and the Department of Education to end the abuses while preserving the essential role of these programs in helping needy students."

Secretary Bennett, in his letter accompanying the report, urged Congress to impose new accrediting standards on proprietary schools that would "emphasize student learning and truth in advertising."

Bennett suggested that Congress should: require students to have a high school or equivalency diploma before they would qualify for federal aid; require lenders to pay part of the cost of defaulted loans; and permit the Education Department to create a comprehensive computer file that would list all students who held outstanding federal loans.

The Atlanta Journal AND THE ATLANTA CONSTITUTION
Atlanta, Georgia, May 24, 1989

Dan Quayle used it as a brag in the campaign, but that mustn't keep the administration from taking a sharp pencil to his Job Training Partnership Act (JTPA) now that the election is behind it. The law does indeed need to be rewritten to direct more spending to teenagers and the poor, as its critics have charged and Labor Secretary Elizabeth H. Dole has come to agree.

"Funds do not always reach the individuals and areas who need help the most," she said recently.

That is not conjecture, but fact. Studies show the act has shortchanged the hard-core unemployed, under federal policies stressing cost-effectiveness in placements. In practice, that has meant funneling the "job-ready" into dead-end jobs with no prospect of advancement.

In one Atlanta project, federal funds were used to "train" large numbers of young black women, who probably could have found menial work on their own, to be hotel maids.

Intensive remediation for high-school dropouts or skills training for the underemployed — intervention that could have made a qualitative difference — would have been too costly and would not have resulted in as many initial placements.

That could change under suggestions recommended by a federal panel appointed by Ann D. McLaughlin, labor secretary under President Reagan, and lately advanced by Mrs. Dole.

Though touted by Vice President Quayle, its principal sponsor, as more "efficient" than the jobs program it replaced, the JTPA has emphasized private-sector (rather than public) employment, made little effort to direct inner-city youths to the suburbs where job opportunities were being created and proved downright inhospitable to the long-term unemployed.

Mrs. Dole would separate youth-training efforts from adult programs and require more coordination with education, counseling and other government services — changes she says are suggested more by the changing nature of the work force than by major flaws in the program.

However it is framed, JTPA is ripe for an overhaul, as Mrs. Dole has the good sense to affirm.

THE ~~SUN~~

Baltimore, Maryland, May 26, 1989

This nation's continuing quest for a sound and suitable jobs policy took a new turn with the Bush administration's recent proposal to focus more money and attention on disadvantaged teen-agers. It would mark another fundamental shift in the government's approach, and at this point it looks like a good one.

The last big jobs policy review resulted in enactment of the 1982 Job Training Partnership Act, designed to get more bang for every buck spent on jobs programs. JTPA replaced the giant CETA program, which, despite improvements and revisions, never shook its reputation as a huge, wasteful, inefficient maze of make-work, dead-end jobs. At its peak in the mid-1970s, CETA provided 750,000 jobs at a cost of $10 billion a year. The Job Training Partnership Act, on the other hand, cost the federal government $2.4 billion last year, and was responsible for job training and placement for 1.9 million beneficiaries.

On the positive side, the new program achieved the desired effect of a higher success rate in placing unemployed people in jobs, and it did so with greater involvement of the business community than CETA had ever achieved. But there was a negative side, too, in this more-bang-for-bucks approach: the emphasis on high placement rates, combined with its limited resources, led to a phenomenon known as "creaming" — concentrating on applicants who needed little assistance while ignoring hard-to-place applicants who would require costly training and remedial help.

The Bush proposals, which are similar to changes being pushed by congressional Democrats, aim to direct the program away from the "cream" of the unemployed crop and concentrate more heavily on "the least skilled and most disadvantaged," as Labor Secretary Elizabeth Dole put it. This would be more expensive. It would be worth the extra money, though, if the new program is carefully focused to produce results, and jobs, for those who need help the most.

The State

Columbia, South Carolina, March 22, 1989

BACK when the Job Training Partnership Act was created in 1982, the U.S. unemployment rate was in double-digit figures and there was a desperate need to get people back to work. But a national study panel has now recommended changes in the program to reflect the needs of today's workforce in a revived economy.

The 38-member JTPA advisory committee suggested major revisions to target the money more effectively, set long-term funding commitments and help adults and youths find meaningful work.

Perry Gaines, chairman of the Governor's Job Training Council and a member of the national panel, said the changes, if adopted by Congress, "will benefit South Carolina and all states."

As the report pointed out, JTPA was a recession-spawned program that encouraged quick job placement over career-track training. In many cases, jobs were short-term and workers were returned to the ranks of the unemployed without the necessary skills to find other jobs.

Therefore, the panel recommended changing the formula used to allocate JTPA money so that a majority of funding would go to train economically disadvantaged people who either have serious skills deficiencies or are welfare dependent. Currently, two-thirds of JTPA funds for adults are spent on the basis of an area's unemployment rate rather than on the individuals' need for skills training.

The study group also said long-range planning in the JTPA system "has been rendered virtually impossible by the short-term, year-to-year orientation of the program.... The adoption of a longer-term perspective must become a priority."

Training programs for youths should be separated from those for adults, it said, and beefed up with an additional $500 million, most of which would be spent on dropouts and other unskilled youths no longer in school. The report also suggested restructuring youth-training programs with a year-round focus instead of separate school-year and summer programs.

Harry Miley, who oversees economic development in Gov. Carroll Campbell's office, said South Carolina already has adopted some of the panel's recommendations.

For instance, contractors who provide job training are now given more incentive money for targeting the hard-core unemployed and welfare recipients and for providing longer-term skills training. "Two years ago, about 16 percent of JTPA participants were on welfare," Mr. Miley said. "Now, 25 percent of adults and 30 percent of youths in the program are welfare recipients or from welfare families."

Mr. Gaines said he plans to testify in favor of the panel's recommendations before the Senate Labor and Human Resources Committee. "I am extremely optimistic that the changes will be adopted," he added.

Certainly, if JTPA is to continue as a meaningful program, it must change direction and effectively target those most in need by providing comprehensive training for jobs available in today's marketplace.

The Star-Ledger

Newark, New Jersey, June 17, 1989

Fortunately, few Americans remember CETA, the hapless federal job training program. This was the well-intentioned social experiment that made the government an employer of final resort in an effort to help the nation's disenfranchised become employable, productive citizens.

But somewhere, this noble initiative became badly skewed. It deteriorated into a sprawling, excessively costly bureaucratic boondoggle. Instead of achieving its job training objective, it became, for the most part, a make-work patronage conduit for politicians at the local and state levels.

CETA, the acronym for the Comprehensive Employment and Training Act, was one of the first Great Society programs to be killed by President Reagan. Given its huge costs and meager returns, there were few mourners over its demise.

But with unemployment hovering at a 10 percent level, there was an obvious need when CETA was phased out to fill the void. It was replaced in 1982 by the Job Training Partnership Act, a program that involved private industry in job training, replacing the local governments that were a key part of the defunct CETA.

As a less costly clone of CETA, its successor was aided by a recovering economy. Nevertheless, the results have been mixed; there have been shortcomings—federal funds did not always reach individuals and regions that needed the aid most. And there was an inclination among some local councils to give a premium status to the easy job training cases, a process known as "creaming"—taking cases where persons might have found work on their own rather than the hardship cases.

At a recent Senate committee hearing, Labor Secretary Elizabeth Dole conceded that the Job Training Partnership program can be improved. An emphasis will be given to young people with problems that make it difficult for them to succeed in the job sector on their own. Under proposed revisions, youth training efforts would be separated from various adult programs.

Most federal spending under the changes will be concentrated on teenagers and the poor—the disadvantaged groups that need it the most. This is the right way to go. A smaller, more effective program would be an improvement over the fragmented approach that has marked past job training efforts.

Labor Day Celebrated Throughout the U.S.

Aside from marking the traditional end of summer, Labor Day is the time when workers and newspaper editorial writers alike reflect on the state of American labor. In 1990, the Labor Day parade up New York City's Fifth Avenue returned after a one year hiatus.

THE BUFFALO NEWS
Buffalo, New York, September 3, 1990

THIS IS a Labor Day that workers celebrate with a disquieting sense of unease. While downing hot dogs and beer, tossing frisbees in the park or touching up the house with late-summer paint, everyone keeps one eye on the volatile Middle East and the other on a slowing economy.

In the last year, to be sure, workers have won deserved victories. For one thing, a multi-year stalemate blocking increases in the national minimum wage ended last fall. Washington enacted improvements that will put the wage floor for adult workers at $4.25 an hour next April 1.

Until recently, too, employment boomed. Along the Niagara Frontier, non-farm jobs hit a record 559,000 in June and the national unemployment rate has hovered around 5 percent.

So people have been working and earning money.

But moods of the moment often depend not on what has happened but on what we expect to happen, and recently employment has turned down and jobless rates up. Inflation is growing stronger, not weaker. Major national indexes of consumer confidence reflect less of it.

Worse yet, of course, is the threat of a punishing war in the Middle East. But 70,000 or so American service men and women, plus tons of equipment, are already in Saudi Arabia to counter Iraqi aggression.

It is worth remembering that for these men and women, there is no holiday on this Labor Day. Even in the shaky peace, working conditions on the Saudi sands aren't the best. The service people sweat under the baking sun and wrestle with the most daunting risks and uncertainties of life.

They are doing the heavy lifting to protect America's security.

As we at home sit on the patio, occasionally tempted to grouse as much as celebrate on this traditional holiday for workers, that's a contribution of working Americans for which we must all be grateful.

The economy may turn down temporarily and the cost of living up, although thankfully neither problem is guaranteed. But even if they do materialize, resourceful workers will weather the storm — in part because of the vital, practical freedoms that they enjoy and that their sisters and brothers in that hottest of all work places, the Arabian desert, labor to protect.

It is, then, an uneasy Labor Day. But as always, one not without reasons to celebrate hopes and confidence at work.

The Houston Post
Houston, Texas, September 3, 1990

LABOR DAY MEANS different things to different people. To some, it still means that hard-working men and women are worthy of praise and celebration. To others, it means a day off from work and the Muscular Dystrophy Telethon. And to a whole lot of others, it means that summer is at an end and the crisp coolness of fall isn't too far away.

Labor Day always falls on the first Monday in September. It starts the month that traditionally has signaled a return to the rigors of school, the month of the first high school and college football games, and the month with a holiday set aside to pay tribute to the many contributions labor has made to our country.

Because of laborers, Americans have a standard of living and a way of life envied by most of the world.

When Labor Day was first started in the United States, the word "labor" was most often used to describe those workers who engaged in manual work — lifting, pulling, bending, or reaching. It meant working with one's muscles. But in today's industry, labor is almost always viewed as any type of work. It's basically performing a task for pay. That has changed because there aren't very many muscle-man jobs left in industry.

The holiday was originally tied to the militancy of the labor movement. The celebration of the day was started by the Knights of Labor, who held parades in New York City from 1882 until 1884. One report says that in the last year of those parades, one of the Knights, George R. Lloyd, proposed a resolution that future parades be held on a day called Labor Day. That resolution passed without any trouble.

But having the day fall on the first Monday in September is of no historical significance. Some records indicate that in 1882, American labor leader Peter J. McGuire suggested the day because it was midway between the Fourth of July and Thanksgiving. McGuire was just hoping to fill the more than four-month gap between two distant legal holidays.

Oregon was the first state to pass legislation for the general observance of Labor Day as a legal holiday. This law, enacted Feb. 21, 1887, specified the first Saturday in June as Labor Day, but in 1893, the day was changed to the first Monday in September.

Although this holiday has somehow turned into a day that merely signals the last chance to hold that big end-of-the-summer bash, it is a perfect time for all of us to take a moment to reflect on — and to bring into focus — the achievements of the American workers of the past.

At the same time, it is a good day for us to look ahead and consider our own direction for the future.

The Honolulu Advertiser
Honolulu, Hawaii, September 3, 1990

Some decades ago, Labor Day was a celebration of the role of labor unions in bringing democracy to the work place and dignity to those who toil for an hourly wage.

Now in many minds it just marks the end of summer and the beginning of a new year of school. It is a time when we come back to cold reality, and this year deeper into the election campaigns.

But as the 1990s dawn there are predictions by the experts that labor issues will be making a comeback. If the 1980s seemed to belong to yuppies of the "me" generation, they say, this is a decade likely to see the flowering of worker unrest.

One of the main reasons is a backlash against the economic squeeze of the middle and lower classes in the 1980s, a subject covered in a Richard Reeves column on this page.

Union leaders hope this growing dissatisfaction will help revive the labor movement, which has been in decline nationally in recent years. Only about 16 percent of U.S. labor force is unionized now. (Hawaii has about 25 percent of workers in unions, including virtually all of the people who write, edit, print and distribute this newspaper, but organized labor is not the force here it used to be.)

Still, the 1960s showed us that periods of national turmoil do not necessarily mean a better climate for labor unions. In the 1980s many union members supported a "Reagan revolution" that worked against their interests.

So the 1990s and their economic problems may seem ripe for the labor movement, here and nationally. But much will depend on whether unions can, in a time of low unemployment, again show attractive leadership and dramatize the value of collective action.

Herald News

Fall River, Massachusetts, September 3, 1990

Labor Day was initiated in 1882 by the Knights of Labor, followed by the approval of several states (Massachusetts was the third to endorse it). In 1894, the first Monday in September was confirmed by Congress as a national legal holiday.

Much progress has been made in labor-management relations over the century. All workers of today, in and out of unions, owe a debt to the pioneer trade unionists whose militant dedication gained a deserved dignity for working men and women, and protected children from the exploitation so vividly documentd at the turn of the century by the photographer-reformer Lewis Hine. They also led the demonstrations, marches and protests that showed the nation's workforce was not a mere machine, but a human power to be reckoned with. The paintings of Ralph Fasanella capture these days of struggle and solidarity, and rank among the greatest social statements of the century.

Fall River was a center of the 19th century industrial revolution, and had its share of labor unrest. For a vivid composite view of the lives of immigrants who made this city one of the textile centers of the world, see "The Fabric of Fall River," a regular feature at Heritage State Park. It's an compressed educational experience, worth more than one viewing.

All Americans can be proud of enlightened legislation that regulated minimum wages and hours, protected workers from industrial hazards, and entitled them to benefits — paid vacations, disability, social security, and old age.

In recent decades, federal and state labor laws have made strides in forbidding discrimination on the basis of age, race or sex, and assured the right of free association in unions, collective bargaining, the filing of grievances, and, except in situations where the public trust would be violated, the right to strike.

In modern times, mutual respect has fostered more cooperation between unions and management, based on the realization that neither group can flourish and realize its goals without the help of the other. The current recession puts an extra strain on both sides.

Since the mid-1980s the power of organized labor has declined, largely because the U.S. manufacturing base was supplanted by service occupations, oriented to people rather than products. Workers in these fields tend to resist organization.

As a prelude to Labor Day, *The Wall Street Journal* (Aug. 28) forecast "more confrontation in labor relations in the year ahead."

It's a time of budget deficits on the national scene, and also, throughout the New England states. Layoffs are held mainly responsible for the rising jobless rate in Massachusetts, which soared to 6.1 percent in July. Moreover, Greater Fall River had the highest unemployment rate among the state's major labor areas, 8.6 percent.

The recession in Massachusetts is proving to be worse than expected. In the past year, *The Boston Globe* reported, 93,100 jobs have been lost, primarily in manufacturing and construction, but also in the retail sector (25,000) and government (10,000 jobs).

The high-tech manufacturing sector was hard hit. Thousands of people have been cut from the payrolls of computer companies. Health and social services showed some growth, but these depend largely on federal funding, also in jeopardy.

These grim figures were abulated before the Persian Gulf crisis, which, as the *Wall Street-Journal* News Roundup indicated, caught many employers off-guard. Some 40,000 military reservists were called to active duty. This raised a hornet's nest of diverse and unanswered questions about job continuity, pay, medical insurance, and other problems.

The IRS will decide whether employers must continue health coverage for dependents of reservists. The military has a plan that picks up some dependent costs.

The United Auto Workers's three-year contract with the Big Three — General Motors, Ford and Chrysler Corp., — expires Sept. 14, signalling a period of heavy bargaining and mutual distrust, despite the fact that encroaching Japanese auto companies threaten both the American car makers and the UAW. Economists forecast that no creative solutions will be reached. Gregory A. Patterson comments, "The union will get a more comfortable safety net for displaced workers, and the companies will get a little more flexibility. The Japanese will keep their huge advantages in costs and efficiency."

With an international crisis impinging on a serious home recession, managers and workers alike are faced with anxious decisions. Military contracts, however, are bound to step up.

THE DAILY OKLAHOMAN

Oklahoma City, Oklahoma, September 3, 1990

THIS Labor Day, thousands of U.S. workers face the prospect of future layoffs because the government can't manage its finances.

The federal budget mess gets worse all the time. Private industry would not tolerate the disgraceful way public funds are handled, nor would the average American family.

Once again, with less than a month to go, Congress and the administration have failed to complete work on a budget for the new fiscal year. In the absence of an agreement, the White House has ordered an across-the-board cut of federal spending beginning Oct. 15, as required by law.

Agencies have begun to send furlough notices to employees. The nation's 2.4 million federal workers are being told they may have to take up to 22 days of unpaid leave during the coming year. The immediate outlook is for workers to forfeit pay one day a week through December.

The threatened layoffs could not come at a worse time. The Federal Aviation Administration would have to operate short-handed during a period when travel is heavier than normal. The Social Security Administration is under the gun to process a cost-of-living adjustment to be included in January benefit checks. And the Defense Department faces increased demands as a result of the Persian Gulf military buildup.

All of this because politicians in Washington cannot or will not learn to practice fiscal responsibility.

Whether or not the furloughs become a reality, federal workers are being subjected unfairly to conditions of great uncertainty about their financial future. They are, in effect, being held hostage to a budget process that is a miserable failure.

For all of its flaws, the federal government has many capable and dedicated men and women serving the public. They deserve better treatment than to be used as pawns in a game of budget politics.

The Star-Ledger

Newark, New Jersey, September 3, 1990

American holidays are serious commemorative events, but they are also fun days. The serious purpose of every holiday is to some degree obscured by the desire to have fun. But on no holiday is this quite so true as it is on Labor Day.

Labor Day was, as the name suggests, founded to mark the role that the labor movement plays in American life. There are formal observances—parades, bands, speeches—marking the history and the spirit of the holiday. But it is also a holiday for millions of Americans who couldn't care less about labor—whose only concern about labor on this day is to avoid it.

It is possible to be a right-wing, pro-business, anti-labor millionaire and have a fine old time on Labor Day, taking it easy or playing hard, depending on the mood and the weather.

Labor Day has several other distinctions, none of which has anything to do with labor. It is the traditional beginning of political campaigns, when the oratory starts to grow loud and the handshaking comes fast and furious. And, for younger Americans, it is a last day of freedom. For many, school starts immediately thereafter.

For traditionalists, it's the end of summer, and never mind that the calendar says there's still almost three weeks left. For merchants, it's the start of a new selling season. And for shrewd vacationers, it's the beginning of a wonderful holiday season, when the temperatures are still pleasant but the crowds thin out and the prices go down.

Those who do use the day to reflect on the role of labor in American life will have few happy moments. It's been a difficult decade indeed. There have been major setbacks, both in the auto industry and elsewhere, in its attempt to sign up new union members. The days of the ever-increasing inflationary pay settlements have long since passed. And a weakening economy only compounds the problems.

There is another factor that makes this Labor Day grimmer than those in the past—the threat of war that overhangs the Persian Gulf and the fact that tens of thousands of our troops are spending the holiday in a most unfestive way, in a state of readiness in the hot desert sands.

But despite these somber notes, for most New Jerseyans—indeed, for most of the nation—it is simply a chance for one more three-day weekend. If the ocean is clean, the temperature warm and the skies blue, it will be a good Labor Day indeed.

The Gazette

Cedar Rapids, Iowa, September 3, 1990

WHILE WE ALL greet it as the last holiday of summer, it's a safe bet few of us will give much thought to the significance of this Labor Day. We should. All of us. Today provides the annual reminder of the contributions made to our country by anyone who now, or ever has, drawn a paycheck.

Like our nation's Thanksgiving, Labor Day is a universal holiday — no religious, ethnic, cultural or other qualifications necessary to join the celebration.

And it should be a celebration for us. Those who doubt it might spend just a few moments contrasting the opportunities available to us in the United States with those being sought in other nations.

Since most of us are preoccupied with conditions in the Middle East, consider the consequences of the Iraqi invasion of Kuwait on surrounding Arab nations. Economies are struggling mightily to absorb the flood of refugees from Iraq. Indeed, a reported 1.6 million Egyptians fled their jobs in Iraq and returned home, creating widespread unemployment and serious economic troubles for Egypt. The two Germanies similarily must confront the realities of unity for the first time in almost a half-century. The challenges and changes will be enormous.

This Labor Day should remind all of us again of the wonderful advantages that have been won and opportunities created for Americans by generations of laboring men and women who dared to invest themselves wholly into developing the country — their sweat, toil, muscle, minds, money.

The job they started isn't done, of course. Let's hope it never is.

THE INDIANAPOLIS STAR

Indianapolis, Indiana, September 3, 1990

Enjoy summer's final holiday, but take a little time to realize that American labor is what makes it enjoyable.

A million genies from a million magic lamps would have had to work overtime to build this land and fill it with cities, parks, houses, pavilions, cars, boats, planes, bikes, roads, paths, beaches, delicious food and all of the other things that go together to make holidays enjoyable.

Even for a million genies, or 10 times that number, the job might have been too big.

What built it and filled the land with the goods and necessities of life was American labor. That is what Labor Day has been celebrating for 108 years, ever since the idea first cropped up at a labor parade and picnic in New York.

Its workers have made this nation the world's magnet.

Life for laborers was hard then. Most unskilled workers made under $10 a week, and most skilled laborers under $20 a week. Child labor, unsafe and unsanitary conditions, work weeks of up to 60 hours and more, and a widespread lack of collective bargaining and benefits now taken for granted all contributed to the growth of unions which, in the years that followed, brought fantastic improvements in the rewards and conditions of labor.

American brains and brawn made this nation No. 1 in the industrial world — a supremacy that is now under challenge by the peoples of other lands, while the nature and patterns of work are undergoing vast changes brought about by revolutionary technology and shifting habits, wants and customs.

But U.S. labor is facing the challenges constructively, and its power and creativity are strikingly evident in the sights and sounds of a great country both on its workdays and its holidays — the bustling superhighways, boulevards, skyscrapers, jets, airports, trains, harbors, ships, industries, farms, offices, metropolises, towns and villages.

American workers have made, and continue to make, this nation strong and wonderful, the envy, model and magnet of the world.

So on this day, *The Indianapolis Star* joins in the national salute to American labor. It is an honor that is deserved.

The Hutchinson News

Hutchinson, Kansas, September 3, 1990

Kansas in 1990 remains a fine state in which to live and to raise children, but it is a state that does not offer enough decent jobs.

We need more and better-paying jobs.

In the last primary contest, John Carlin may have lost the nomination of his party, but his words cannot be denied.

He said that while unemployment in Kansas remains low, the number of jobs being created remains below the national average. Rural areas, especially, offer limited opportunities for work.

"U.S. Bureau of Economic Analysis statistics also show that too many jobs being created are not good jobs," Carlin said. "We need to concentrate our efforts on developing the kind of jobs that pay an adequate wage and provide the kind of benefits that allow workers to provide for their families."

Unfortunately, Carlin's awareness is not echoed by the surviving candidates for governor.

While abortions and puppy mills may evoke emotional responses from special-interest groups, resolution of either issue won't put food on a family's table.

The celebration of Labor Day allows us to put priorities in perspective.

One of the failures of the Hayden administration is the governor's inattentiveness in continuing the ground-breaking work begun by Carlin in pursuing overseas business. While the Department of Commerce continues to make strides in this endeavor, it appears to lack the same enthusiasm from Hayden that it got from Carlin.

The next governor will have to do better.

Kansas needs a more diversified economy, and it needs to import industry. Jobs will follow, better schools will follow, and Kansans can then have the luxury of spending their time and taxes on such non-economic concerns as puppy mill inspectors.

The two gubernatorial candidates, Mike Hayden and Joan Finney, are now attempting to appeal to rural emotionalism by suggesting that voters should have more say in government. That's touching, but it doesn't create jobs.

This Labor Day we are reminded that the existence of jobs is the beginning of any economic success. Kansas doesn't have enough adequate employment. That ought to concern residents, employers, and government officials. Especially candidates who themselves are looking for good jobs in government.

SYRACUSE
HERALD-JOURNAL

Syracuse, New York, September 3, 1990

The World Book describes Labor Day "as the holiday honoring working people . . . but for most people it is a day of rest and recreation." It is true. Gone are the days when Labor Day paid homage to the labor unions. The holiday no longer is a day to honor labor, but to refrain from it.

In the minds of many, labor unions are passe, caricatures of themselves. Names like the AFL-CIO, United Auto Workers and Teamsters once sent shivers through politicians, who knew its leadership had control over millions of dollars and voting members. But Ronald Reagan proved union members no longer vote for the same people their dues support. Ironically, it was Reagan who cut into the Democratic stronghold of union votes in 1980. And, it was Reagan who destroyed the air traffic controllers union, a move which dealt labor one of its harshest blows.

On this day and every day, all of us owe a debt to unions. Without them, many employees would be risking their lives in unsafe conditions. Others would be working inhumane hours for inhumane wages. Health benefits would be non-existent. Without unions, many businesses would still operate as sweatshops, with no regard for their labor force.

Unfortunately, some unions got too full of themselves and used their influence to make demands with no accountability. Salaries got fatter, but the work didn't get any better — a fact that explains much of America's preoccupation with foreign-made goods. Unions have been linked to organized crime, which hasn't helped their image. They also have been perceived as greedy. Now, many are considered just plain ineffective — especially since union-busting became popular in the '80s. Had airline czar Frank Lorenzo taken on the Eastern and other airlines' unions in the '70s, it's doubtful he would have been as successful.

Unions were created for the worker, not vice versa. If they are to be the voice of the voiceless again, then they will have to convince members of their worth. Otherwise, unions will disappear, and that will be a sad thing. Unions keep many companies honest, and honest companies respect their workers, not abuse them.

The Washington Post

Washington, D.C., September 3, 1990

THE NEWS OF this Labor Day is that it's not such a good time to be a working man or woman in America. The eight straight years of economic expansion that are the pride of Republican policy have had an uneven effect. A new analysis of mostly government data by the Economic Policy Institute here shows that income from capital has risen much more than income from labor, and income from labor—average hourly earnings—has risen much more in the upper reaches of the economy than in the middle and below.

The typical worker earns *less* today, in terms of purchasing power, than did the typical worker 10 years ago, the study indicates. Families are keeping up only by having fewer children and working more hours. Even so, some basic costs—of a first home, shelter generally, health insurance—have risen faster than ability to pay. Either these things are less affordable or there is less left over when they have been bought.

The broadest indicator of economic well-being, real per capita income, continues to rise. But this is a deceptive average. It has risen largely because of enormous increases in the incomes of the richest fifth, in particular the richest 5 percent, of Americans. The middle fifth, by contrast, has by most measures gained only slightly, while the bottom two-fifths have lost ground—and ground that the poorest especially could not afford.

Income inequality is up. At roughly an eighth of the population, the poverty rate for this point in the business cycle is also high. It remains particularly high for children—nearly 20 percent. The poverty gap—the distance between the average poor person and the poverty line—has also increased.

Government policies haven't so much caused as they have exacerbated these trends, many of which predate the 1980s. The causes are deeper, from such sources as increased vulnerability to competition from abroad. The role of government should be to lean against such polarizing trends in the society. Instead in the 1970s and 1980s the tax structure became much less progressive, while in the early Reagan years means-tested federal benefits were cut. The government now does less than it used to or it should to moderate the distribution of income.

All these are points to remember not just on Labor Day but as the budget negotiations between the president and Congress resume this week. The result of these negotiations needs to be fair as well as forceful. The big winners in the past 20 years have been the people at the top of the society. This time the middle and bottom deserve the help.

The Chattanooga Times

Chattanooga, Tennessee, September 3, 1990

This is Labor Day. It's celebrated the first Monday in September, year after year. So what's so special about it?

Labor Day doesn't have the flags and pageantry of the patriotic holidays, such as Memorial Day or Independence Day, nor does it conjure up in the mind's eye any particular symbols, such as tinseled trees or turkeys. Yet, next to Christmas, Thanksgiving and the Fourth of July, it is probably the American holiday most vigorously celebrated by the widest assortment of our citizens. And why is that?

Because it is a day shared by all who work. It is a day which pays homage to the work which, bit by bit, built this great nation and holds it together, the work which has allowed us to enjoy such great freedom and such a high quality of life. And it is a day which honors not only work, but the workers themselves — their ability to work and his right to work and the results of their work.

Even beyond recognizing the individual workers who are the backbone of our economy, however, Labor Day was conceived and established to pay tribute to the many contributions organized labor has made to the development of this society. The American labor movement, dedicated to protecting the dignity and expanding the rights of working men and women, is surely deserving of this annual recognition.

In Australia the holiday which honors labor is called the Eight-Hour Day. The name itself serves as a reminder of the debt owed those who struggled and sacrificed to achieve humane limits on the length of the workday and an abundance of other improvements in the lives of working people.

In the days of the sweatshops, organized labor arose as the needed brake on the tendency of unfettered capitalism to exploit the human workers essential to its success. And today, the gains initially secured by the efforts of organized labor are enjoyed by countless American working men and women who have never belonged to a union and may never give a thought to the positive effect the labor movement has had on their lives.

Today is a good time to consider that effect, and to give honor where it's due.

These are hardly the glory days of the American labor movement; union membership has dwindled steadily in recent years. Yet the Labor Day holiday stands as an annual reminder of how much this society has benefited from the presence and power of organized labor. And it is right that we should remember.

The Salt Lake Tribune

Salt Lake City, Utah, September 3, 1990

If the 40-year-old Cold War has ended, with the United States prominently triumphant, then the nation's working men and women are entitled to appropriately share the credit. In the evident success of free enterprise capitalism reside the availing efforts of all its adherents, not the least being countless salaried employees and wage-earners.

According to astonishing events of recent months, market-driven economics have been acknowledged as preferable by those who previously paid homage to collectivist theories applied through central government planning. This following a prolonged, sustained struggle during which the laboring multitudes on both sides were required to make profoundly important contributions.

To a significant degree, fundamental changes affecting human relations have always been affected by rank and file workers, groups and individuals called upon to solemnly validate or actively reject conditions in which they and theirs were obliged to either prosper or merely subsist. History teaches that while there may be probabilities, there are no guarantees animating this consequential arrangement.

It was always so, then, that a solidly heaving shift in allegiance was necessary to determine the outcome of socialism's 20th century challenge to capitalism. That the shift is toward capitalism speaks for a worker steadfastness which should not be taken for granted.

Whatever its station now, the U.S. economy was the mighty engine responsible for returning the Western Alliance of nations to free market prominence following World War II. Workers essential to this achievement deserve as much recognition for unwavering devotion to the task as prominently maneuvering politicians, government policy-makers and resourceful diplomats.

Labor Day, 1990, is a suitable occasion for doing precisely that. Unfulfilled expectations, often articulated through shrill demands, still incite the country's labor movement, and in varying degrees probably always will.

But on this ceremonial day, when the ascendancy of free market principles can be justifiably hailed, a salute belongs to those workers, men and women, who through four exacting decades helped establish the productivity, the profitability, the equity and, ultimately, the superiority of the economic system in which they distinctively toiled.

The Miami Herald

Miami, Florida, September 4, 1990

LABOR DAY 1990 no doubt will be celebrated quite traditionally with parades, picnics, softball games, and — in Florida — flag-waving politicking. Today's labor force, however, is anything but traditional blue-collar, white male. Nationwide, the industrial economy is yielding to a service economy. Nearly one-third of all the jobs in Florida now are service-related, and service wages are low.

Indeed, most Florida families find that it takes two wage earners to make ends meet. Almost half the state's work force is female. According to the Florida Chamber of Commerce, 57 percent of these working women have children under age 6 who require day care. Two-thirds are either the sole support of their families or married to men earning less than $15,000 a year. Only 7 percent of American households fit the 1950s stereotype of breadwinner husband and stay-at-home wife with two kids. That's about the same number as don't have telephones.

Statewide, African-American workers represent 15 percent of the labor force; Hispanics 11 percent. But in Dade County, where trends are made, not followed, 22 percent of the work force is black and 45 percent Hispanic. Between now and the year 2000, minorities will constitute 29 percent of all new U.S. workers.

A new phrase, "the sandwich generation," is also rapidly gaining acceptance. It refers to workers who are trying to provide both for children and for aging, frail parents. It has a special significance in Florida, where about 18 percent of the population is 65 or older.

Is there any wonder, then, that on a holiday one day before a primary election, Florida politicians are called to account for their votes on such issues as day care, family leave, job discrimination, minimum wages, and health insurance? Time and need are overtaking the placating expressions of concern, promises to "study it," and exhortations to voluntary management compliance. A changing work force is bringing new perspectives to the work place, and changing realities are bringing new demands.

On this Labor Day, day care is as strong a rallying cry as the 40-hour week was 60 years ago. The 40-hour week also took an act of Congress to achieve. This Congress must not rest until child care and family leave have been woven into the fabric of American labor law in spite of the Bush Administration's anachronistic objections.

President Grover Cleveland in 1894 signed the bill that made Labor Day a national holiday. It was both a recognition of the dignity of workers and a commitment from Government that henceforth it would act to ensure that basic human needs were met. The 1990s require a renewed energy to that commitment.

The TENNESSEAN
Nashville, Tennessee, September 3, 1990

LABOR Day, somewhat misnamed since it is a traditional day of rest, gives Americans a chance to look at the progress of working men and women over the past year.

Tennesseans can celebrate the day with jobs. The state's uunemployment figures for July showed a 5% unemployment rate, nearly half a point better than the previous month and a half point better than the national average. Nashville showed a 3.7% unemployment rate.

For both the state and nation, the unemployment rates are encouraging.

While the unemployment figures remain low across the country, the quality of jobs is increasingly becoming a major issue, one that is likely to be played out in congressional campaigns this fall. While old legislative battles focused on wages and job conditions, the concerns today are about quality.

One old labor matter — discrimination — and one new one — family leave — were behind two hard-fought congressional battles this year with President Bush.

With women entering the work force in larger numbers than ever, the family leave bill started out anticipating the needs of working mothers. But it became a more inclusive bill, recognizing the needs of both men and women to fulfill family health obligations or needs without the threat of losing their jobs.

The civil rights legislation attempted to recover gains for minorities lost by a series of U.S. Supreme Court decisions last year.

President Bush vetoed family leave and has threatened the same with the civil rights legislation. Senators have vowed to keep bringing up family leave again.

Another major concern of working parents — affordable day care — is still on the agenda. President Bush favors credits for families while Democrats want more direct benefits.

American voters observing this Labor Day should note that the news on jobs is mixed. There is reason to be dismayed that hard-won gains in fighting discrimination in the workplace could be lost. But there is also room for optimism when Congress talks not just about the worker and his or her job, but about jobs and families. ∎

The Hartford Courant
Hartford, Connecticut, September 3, 1990

Labor Day has become less a day for honoring labor than an occasion for a long weekend, or a day for picnics and kicking off election campaigns. Politicians have come to believe that they can probably make no fatal mistake until after Labor Day. Voters have come to believe that they need not really pay attention until then.

This is not a bad use of Labor Day, but neither is the original one: to honor the dignity of work.

Curiously, at a time when work seems to be the dominant force in many of our lives — never mind the lip service we pay to church, family and community — there is little serious thought given to why work is important.

Few people doubt the importance of work as an economic activity. Most need it to eat, to pay the bills, to educate children, to provide shelter. But we seldom stop to contemplate the social, intellectual and even psychic importance of work.

Socially, work gives the individual standing in the community. Sometimes it is the only thing that does, so much has civic life and duty been reduced. It also provides fraternity, a feeling of being involved in an enterprise larger than oneself, which is a feeling hard to find in modern, atomized society. Most people spend roughly as many waking hours with work mates as with families. Few people work alone.

Intellectually, work gives most people a chance to create or to organize. These are inherent drives in human nature, even though few of us are lucky enough to have creative jobs. Karl Marx was correct in seeing that factory work leaves little possibility for the creative or ordering impulse. But he did not anticipate that a Marxist economy would aggravate the problem. Marx might have approved of some modern Japanese factory practices because they promote shared responsibility for the product. The worker is a partner, not a cog in a machine. To be relevant only as a producer is the ultimate exploitation. Even though he may work longer hours than the mere producer, the middle manager or the foreman feels he or she is a player, not a pawn.

Psychologically, work offers the possibility of virtuosity — the chance to do well, to shine, even if only in one's own eyes. Work allows individuals to be craftsmen in their chosen fields, and it is a satisfying thing to be a craftsman. To make well, to do well, is what is nowadays called self-actualizing. Only the brain-dead do not wish for this.

Whether the job is parking cars, writing sonnets or selling boots, if one can do it well, and with flair, there is immense satisfaction.

Work does not always provide social, intellectual and psychic rewards. In fact, it seldom provides all this. But it can — that's the point. And these are the things that most of us seek from work, other than pay. These are the things that give work its deepest value.

Drudgery is not work at all, but waste. Leisure is the opposite of work, but it is necessary for good work. May the leisure of Labor Day give rest from all drudgery, hope for its end where it predominates and — where there is work to be done — energy for the tasks ahead.

Portland Press Herald
Portland, Maine, September 3, 1990

While Labor Day is still a day in which to honor the working men and women of America — as it has been since the first one was celebrated back in 1882 — it has also come to mean a lot more than that.

Here in Maine, it is more or less the official end of the tourist season (a time to reclaim our state for ourselves) and the official beginning of the election campaign season (a time to wake up and begin taking notice of candidates and issues).

For most youngsters it marks the start of back-to-school week. For all motorists it means remembering that kids on the way back to school are capable of movements that are impulsive, heedless, totally unexpected and faster than a speeding bullet.

For some, this Labor Day will mark the beginning of a season of uncertainty — over oil deliveries, a sluggish economy, unemployment, a housing market still in the doldrums — conditions always made more worrisome as we enter the colder months.

For many, Labor Day is just one more long holiday weekend, something more to be enjoyed than celebrated. The old-style observances, marked by speeches, parades and picnics, are pretty much gone these days.

Still, it is a good day to remind ourselves that the labor movement has been — and in many ways still is — a political and economic force of tremendous influence on the lives and well-being of ordinary working people.

If it weren't for organized labor, most of us would not be enjoying the standard of living we are today.

We would not be assured of decent working conditions or of the availability of between-jobs benefits or any of a thousand accommodations we have come to take for granted.

That's something worth taking a few minutes off today to remember — and to celebrate.

Part II: Japan & The Pacific Rim

Ever since World War II, when the United States defeated and subsequently occupied Japan, the relationship between the two countries has been an uneasy one. No doubt the strains of the occupation, which lasted from 1945 until 1952, and the paternalism that accompanied it, explain some of the uneasiness. But other factors have divided the two nations as well. These have included dramatic differences in culture, politics, history, geography and language.

The primary tie that has bound the two countries for the past 45 years has been opposition to Soviet expansion in the Pacific. But as this threat, which resulted in the basing of U.S. military forces in Japan, has receded in recent years other tensions between the two nations have increased.

The most notable irritant in relations between the two countries in recent years has been Japan's large trade surplus with the United States. One reason for that trade imbalance many U.S. critics say, is that the Japanese have had an unfair economic advantage because the island nation has enjoyed the benefit of the American defense umbrella while only having to devote a fraction of its own national wealth to defense. This accusation has been heard even more vociferously since the war in the Persian Gulf. Japan's slow response to U.S. entreaties for financial support for Operation Desert Storm – and its failure to send any personnel – didn't sit well with many Americans, who felt Japan, which is dependent on the Middle East for nearly 70% of its oil, was taking another free ride on America's back.

It was Japan's bad luck that the gulf conflict came just as the United States was entering a recession. With unemployment growing, profits falling, and Japan's trade surplus with the U.S. remaining high, another U.S. complaint has escalated: the conviction on the part of many Americans that Japan's huge trade surplus with the U.S. – $41.71 billion in 1990 – is the result of unfair trade practices on the part of the Japanese.

In March 1991, for example, many U.S. newspapers ran front-page stories about Japanese threats to arrest U.S. farmers who were displaying American rise at an international trade show in Tokyo. Japanese rice growers claimed the display was a violation of Japan's law prohibiting rice imports.

Congress has responded to the controversy with a rash of bills aimed at punishing Japan. Most recently U.S. President George Bush initiated the first trade retaliation against Japan since 1987. On April 27, 1991, the administration announced that because of insufficient progress in talks aimed at opening the Japanese construction market to U.S. firms, it was taking steps to ban Japanese companies from U.S. government contracting. But Japanese officials quickly responded to criticism of their ban on rice imports by saying that it is different only in degree from the strict quotas the U.S. places on imports of sugar and textiles. In addition, Japanese officials point out that official trade barriers – tariffs, quotas and outright exclusion of products – are lower in Japan than in many industrial countries. In fact, Japan's average tariffs of 2% are among the world's lowest.

U.S. officials, while not denying the importance to U.S. trade of bringing down federal deficits, have alleged that Japan is, indeed, an unfair trader. Despite Japan's relatively low official trade barriers, Japan's entry in the U.S. trade representative's annual report on foreign trade barriers is the longest in the book. According to U.S. trade experts, that is in large part because the remaining Japanese tariffs and quotas are concentrated in product areas where the U.S. is most competitive, including supercomputers, telecommunications equipment, semiconductors, intellectual property matters, paper products and a variety of agricultural products.

U.S. and European trade experts have long complained that non-traditional barriers to trade are systematically entrenched in Japan's manufacturing and distribution sectors.

The best-known example of Japan's informal trade barriers is the way Japanese companies are combined within closely knit groups called *keiretsu*, which finance each other's projects, use each other as suppliers and so forth. Japanese officials have long maintained that *keiretsu* only work to maximize efficiency and do not unfairly exclude foreign products. And Western economists have not had access to the kind of data needed to prove that *keiretsu* are a trade barrier.

As for why Asian and European countries have managed to significantly increase their exports to Japan in recent years, while U.S. companies have not, some U.S. experts argue that there are explanations besides lack of U.S. competitiveness. In the case of Asia, they say the increase in imports is due in large part to imports from Japanese companies that have responded to rising wages in Japan by moving to nearby Asian countries such as Malaysia and Thailand. The rise in imports from Europe is accounted for mostly by luxury items, such as Gucci leather goods and high-priced German cars – product sectors in which Japan has not yet attempted to compete.

Many Western analysts from both government and acedemia seem to agree that outside pressure is required to open up Japanese markets. But disagreement comes over how much and what type of pressure is needed.

In recent years, the Bush administration has argued against taking drastic steps against Japan. Despite the great number of outstanding trade complaints, U.S. Trade Representative Carla A. Hills announced in April 1990 that the administration had decided against naming Japan as an unfair trader. She said cooperation, not confrontation, was what was needed to bring about change.

But while the administration tends to measure progress by agreements reached, business interests tend to look at the bottom line. And the bottom lines hasn't changed much.

Over the past couple of years, there have been increasing calls for harsher measures against Japan. Among the suggestions are that the U.S. abandon the idea of negotiating away barriers with Japan and simply set an appropriate trade balance and let Japan meet the goal however it chooses. A variant of that idea would hold that any year in which the U.S. doesn't increase its exports to Japan by, say 15%, the U.S. would automatically impose a tariff on Japanese products.

Finally, some analysts have proposed that the U.S. emulate at least parts of Japan's strategy by encouraging closer cooperation among U.S. companies, and between those companies and the government. One proposal that keeps cropping up in Congress is for suspension of U.S. antitrust laws to allow high-tech companies to cooperate not only on the research and design of products, but on production and marketing as well.

Many economists warn, however, that putting the government in the position of picking winners and losers is not a strategy that will work over the long haul.

U.S.-Japan Beef, Citrus Pact Signed

Japan's agriculture minister, Takashi Sato, and U.S. Trade Representative Clayton K. Yeutter June 20, 1988 signed a trade pact in Tokyo that would gradually remove Japanese quotas on imports of U.S. beef and citrus products.

The accord, reached after months of negotiations, ended the latest confrontation in a series of disputes between the two countries over trade relations.

Yeutter hailed the pact as "a landmark agreement in U.S.-Japan economic relations." He estimated that American beef and citrus exports to Japan, which in 1987 were valued at about US$600 million, would double to more than US$1 billion a year by the time Japanese quotas were completely removed.

Under the terms of the agreement, Japan's quotas on the import of U.S. beef, currently limited to 214,000 metric tons (236,000 tons) a year, would be increased by 60,000 metric tons, annually for three years.

THE INDIANAPOLIS NEWS
Indianapolis, Indiana, May 24, 1988

A pound of sirloin beef costs $3.99 in Indianapolis. In Japan, a pound of sirloin costs $28.80 — 3,700 yen.

Japanese consumers, of course, would rather pay less for their meat. The problem is that the powerful farm lobby in Japan has a chokehold on government trade policy. The result is a highly regulated and protected beef market that keeps competitors out and prices jacked up to four and five times what people in other countries pay.

All of this has not escaped the attention of American farmers, who have succeeded in making access to Japan's beef market a top U.S.-Japanese trade issue.

The dispute has taken on greater significance than the numbers might suggest. In 1987, U.S. beef exports to Japan totaled $800 million. Compared with the $58 billion trade deficit the United States has with Japan, beef is a relatively minor item.

But Japanese farmers and officials worry that if protection for domestic beef goes, so will protection for a whole range of other agricultural products. The result, they fear, may be the end of agricultural production in Japan.

The Japanese farmers have a point. They do have a lot to lose if the government takes away their free ride, which the Japanese consumer pays for so dearly. The average herd of a beef producer in Japan is six cattle. The average rice field in Japan is about the size of a football field. Japanese farmers, unlike so many other Japanese businesses, seem to have little idea of what it takes to survive in the face of international competition.

"Japanese agriculture has dug a deep hole for itself and is up to its neck in subsidies, price-fixing boards and quotas . . ." writes The Chicago Tribune's Ronald Yates. "Japanese producers insist that when cheaper American and Australian beef begins to flow across its borders in greater volume than the current 214,000 tons a year (out of a domestic market of some 600,000 tons), they will be driven into extinction."

"How can we take the chance now that we can ever compete?" Yates quotes Japanese cattle producer Mitsumasa Okano as saying. "We have become used to things the way they are."

Okano and his fellow farmers have pitted themselves against U.S. officials, who want American farmers to be able to freely sell their products in Japan the way so many Japanese businesses freely sell their products here.

The battle is likely to become more fierce, especially given the political clout of Japanese farmers, who control 200 of the 445 ruling-party seats in parliament. "The most bountiful and efficient crop produced by Japanese farmers," says one Japanese political science professor, "is votes."

New Prime Minister Noboru Takeshita has quite a chore ahead, balancing the interests of one of his party's core constituencies against the good of the nation as a whole.

Takeshita should keep in mind that other countries are getting fed up with Japan's mercantilist "we sell, you buy" policies. Japan's success has come from free trade. Doors must open there or they will close here, to the detriment of all involved.

The Star-Ledger
Newark, New Jersey, July 14, 1988

Most people who had been carefully following the scenario had given up hope that a happy ending could ever be achieved. Japan was a tough customer to do business with, and officials in Tokyo showed no inclination toward compromise.

At issue was a determined effort by American negotiators to get Japan to loosen up and buy more U.S. beef and citrus products. The stubborn refusal of the Japanese to give on the matter has been straining relations between the two countries.

Quite unexpectedly, however, the diplomatic stalemate has been amicably resolved. U.S. Trade Representative Clayton Yeutter, in announcing that an agreement had been signed, called the development "a great day for American agriculture, a great day for Japanese consumers."

Under the pact, annual beef shipments from the U.S. to Japan could nearly double, from the present $550 million to approximately $1 billion. Exports of oranges and juice, now less than $100 million, could increase to $150 million. In addition, there will be tariff reductions on lemons, grapefruits and other U.S. agricultural products.

Japan had been stonewalling for years, resisting all efforts by the U.S. to ease its unfair restrictions on the commodities. But patience, persistence and persuasiveness by Mr. Yeutter, fully supported by President Reagan and reinforced by pressure from Congress and private groups, finally produced the desired—and desirable—breakthrough.

Not included in the agreement were some concessions sought on the exporting of U.S. rice to Japan. But this issue will be resolved during trade talks under way in Uruguay, where representatives of the member nations are reviewing the General Agreement on Tariffs and Trade, the international trade agreement.

The beef and citrus concord almost certainly will prove beneficial to both countries. But beyond the promised gains, the agreement indicates that Japan has come of age as a first-rank trading nation while, most importantly, eliminating a bone of contention between the U.S. and Japan.

The Hartford Courant
Hartford, Connecticut. December 29, 1988

If they aren't careful, the United States and the European Economic Community could soon find themselves engaged in large-scale trade combat.

On Sunday the Common Market is expected to start refusing imports of American meat containing hormones fed to cattle to promote their growth. The Reagan administration has vowed to retaliate by slapping 100 percent duties on a variety of European food products, which would dramatically raise their retail prices in U.S. stores. Do that, say the Europeans, and we'll fight back.

The impending conflict isn't inevitable. The resolution could take the form of a compromise that would postpone the ban on meat imports and form an independent scientific panel to study if hormone-fed beef affects the consumers' health.

U.S. officials say there's no scientific evidence that the hormones threaten human health. Indeed, most beef-producing countries use growth-inducing substances on cattle. West Germany, the leader of the hormone boycott, permits German farmers to use other, untested growth-promoting substances.

Perhaps the chemicals are indeed harmless to humans. But perhaps they aren't. One growth hormone, known as DES, has been associated with human health problems, and its use has been banned in this country. It isn't far-fetched to suppose that other hormones also pose risks. It isn't also far-fetched to supposed that the Common Market countries, which have a surplus of meat, do not look forward to beef imports from the United States.

If the Reagan administration and the Common Market won't agree on a compromise, they should at least find some third party to settle this dispute before it gets out of hand. A trade war is expensive, hurts international relations and settles nothing.

Minneapolis Star and Tribune
Minneapolis, Minnesota, December 30, 1988

With disheartening predictability, the United States and the European Community are poised to go to war over beef hormones. The impending trade battle was foreshadowed earlier this month when both sides "agreed to disagree" at world trade-reform talks in Montreal. They could not agree then on broad measures to remove subsidies and barriers that interfere with global agricultural trade. They cannot agree now on specific remedies to their hormone dispute. But the world does not need another macho trade showdown. If consumers and farmers are ever to benefit from freer global commerce, these two economic powers must recognize it is in their best interests to agree.

The beef hormone dispute is clearcut, making the impending exchange of trade counterpunches all the more disappointing. The European Community has banned the use of hormones in beef raised within its 12 member countries, and on Jan. 1 will ban imports of beef containing growth hormones. The United States, which will retaliate against several European products the same day, correctly insists that the hormones used to fatten beef meet international health standards.

Although it has been shunted aside in this showdown, the General Agreement on Tariffs and Trade (GATT) provides alternatives to a trade war; the reforms now being discussed promise even better solutions. A key part of the proposed farm-trade reforms deals with setting international health and quality standards for agricultural products, which would smooth a common source of trade friction. Another part would strengthen GATT procedures to give it a stronger hand in mediating disputes.

Those reforms are needed. Yet as long as it remains committed to protecting domestic farmers behind a wall of subsidies and barriers, the community will find compromise unpalatable. And if U.S. belligerence produces a long-running trade war rather than forthcoming concessions, it will hurt American farmers who depend on export sales. The $100 million showdown over beef hormones should remind the $150 billion trading partners why they need each other, why they need farm-trade reform and why they need a strong international mediator to help keep trade moving. As the E.C. ban and U.S. retaliation take effect, both sides should get back to the negotiating table.

Chicago Tribune
Chicago, Illinois, December 29, 1988

The opening battles in the imminent trade war between the United States and Western Europe over groceries probably can't be prevented, so it's high time to start working toward a truce.

Beginning at midnight Saturday, the 12 nations of the European Community will ban imported meat treated with growth hormones. Argentina, Australia and New Zealand, big exporters of beef, have decided to ship only hormone-free meat to the 12 nations. The United States, which sells the European Community about $100 million annually in meat treated with the banned hormone, is responding instead by slapping a 100 percent tariff—doubling the price—on many imported European foods, including Danish hams, Italian tomato sauce and pork products.

The European nations threaten to retaliate with more bans and tariffs, which would force re-retaliation in Washington. On both sides of the Atlantic, consumers and farmers will be the casualties if the trade war continues. Both sides should ask for truce talks under the General Agreement on Tariffs and Trade, an ongoing process to promote freer trade.

The United States has a strong bargaining chip: We buy $450 million in meat annually from the European Community, much of it—according to U.S. officials—treated with hormones banned in this country as well as in the Community's member nations. The growth hormone that will be prohibited in the European Community beginning Jan. 1, though, is not considered dangerous here. If the European Community does not agree to crack down on its farmers who use illegal hormones and postpone its ban in favor of truce talks, the United States should respond with a ban on all the meats it imports from the 12 member nations.

The truce talks should try to determine whether the growth hormone is as harmful as the Europeans contend. If the answer is no, the ban should be dropped. If it's yes, U.S. farmers should adjust as their counterparts in Argentina, Australia and New Zealand are doing. And we shouldn't have to eat it here, either.

The Oregonian
Portland, Oregon, December 16, 1988

Cattle ranchers ride a wild and woolly economic cycle as tough to stick with as any bronco. The difference is that the horse eventually is broken. Historically, the cycle has never been tamed.

Beef production now is at a low point, signaling an end to the present cycle. Beef prices are relatively high. Expansion of the nation's herd has already begun with ranchers keeping more of their heifers for brood stock.

If the new cycle follows the pattern, expansion will continue until beef prices are too low to be profitable. Then will come the gradual paring of the herd.

Government has not involved itself in price supports and production controls of beef to buffer the harsh cycle. While the size of individual ranches has grown in recent years, they are still so numerous and small that ranchers making their personal business decisions cannot balance supply and demand, as industries dominated by a few large corporations may.

The Oregon Department of Agriculture doubts the cycle can be conquered, but does predict some mitigating factors that may ease its impact, at least in this state. Essentially, they boil down to expanding markets to make use of increased production.

Japan's agreement to reduce its rigid quota system opens one of the brightest prospects for Oregon beef. That market obviously should be vigorously pursued, with every effort to tailor the product to the tastes of the Japanese consumer.

A number of Oregon ranchers have joined the movement to grow natural beef. By staying away from artificial fatteners and turning out lean meat, they are responding to the health concerns of their customers.

Boom or bust, beef is the No. 1 agricultural commodity in Oregon. Its yearly value currently is listed at $240 million, and it has approached $300 million. With the ripple effect of so large a financial pool, the cattleman's chance to sell the product at profitable levels translates into profits and jobs throughout the state. The rancher does not ride the economic cycle by himself.

The Atlanta Journal
THE ATLANTA CONSTITUTION
Atlanta, Georgia, January 29, 1989

If it will just listen to Texas Agriculture Commissioner Jim Hightower, Washington might be able to un-pick the dangerous trade war it has picked with Western Europe. Oddly, however, Washington, with the support of at least one major farm group, seems keener for the war than for trade peace.

The United States in December raised its tariffs on $100 million worth of various European Common Market goods, just retaliation, Washington said, for Europe's ban on U.S. beef, fattened by growth hormones the Europeans consider a health hazard. Americans say no hazard exists, but it doesn't really matter. Nations must be allowed to set reasonable criteria. After all, the United States requires more anti-pollution control equipment on imported cars than Europeans think necessary.

It has always seemed that the relatively small trade disadvantage posed by the beef ban could be made up by a simple free-enterprise adjustment in the United States, and Mr. Hightower agrees. He says Texas farmers would be willing to contract with the Europeans to raise enough hormone-free beef to take up the slack.

Yet the U.S. Department of Agriculture is dithering, saying it would have trouble figuring out how to verify that beef is free of hormones, and the American Farm Bureau Federation is uneasy with the idea, fearing the accommodation would weaken the United States in other trade negotiations with Europe.

Texas has found a way to keep the European money coming into the United States, and the Europeans, at least tentatively, like the idea and want to pursue it. You would think the new U.S. administration would be delighted at even the possibility of avoiding a trade war that could escalate dangerously through a series of tit-for-tats.

Unless it finds some unmendable flaw in Mr. Hightower's plan, Washington is being confronted with an easy out from an unnecessary bind. The administration should dive for it.

The Seattle Times
Seattle, Washington, January 12, 1989

TWENTY years ago, French academics marveled at the great machinery of U.S. commerce. Poor, lethargic Europe, they lamented, was no match for American business savvy and technical genius.

In the next two decades, while this country fretted over quarterly dividends and takeovers, its Atlantic competition organized. By 1993 the European Community, a 12-nation trading bloc, plans to convert itself from a dozen feuding economies into one unified market.

For trade and business purposes, the EC has patiently worked to become a mini-U.S., with limited barriers to the movement of goods and services across borders.

The U.S. would not be competing against Spain, Italy or West Germany for world or European sales, but a united EC committed to doing business with itself.

This is the broader picture behind the EC's ban on U.S. beef treated with growth hormones used to fatten cattle. Our side claims there is nothing unhealthy about such beef. The EC, which has its own beef surplus, says it's a matter of public preference, not trade warfare.

The Reagan administration retaliated with sanctions against Danish hams, canned Italian tomatoes and other products to match the $100-million loss to U.S. exporters.

In a second round of diplomatic shoving, the EC said it would strike back against dried fruit and walnuts from the U.S.

Who is right? International trade rules allow countries to ban products if similar restrictions are applied at home. The U.S. does not allow the import of cheese made with non-pasteurized milk. Presumably, the Europeans can set their own meat standards.

The lesson is that world trade is pitting continents against continents. America's best defense, our most logical protection, is improved trade with our own neighbors. Canada is our largest trading partner, Mexico our fourth.

U.S. trading markets are just developing in Asia, but the ties that bind those countries will be difficult to overcome.

Meantime, nurturing our own trade with Mexico and its fragile economy and warmly embracing new opportunities with the Canadian free-trade agreement may be the best remedy to European obstinacy.

The Miami Herald
Miami, Florida, January 2, 1989

GET READY for a showdown at the EC Corral. The Reagan Administration this week warned that it will impose $100 million in new import fees on European foodstuffs if the European Community (EC) persists in banning U.S. beef raised on growth-producing hormones. The deadline is midnight tomorrow.

The Administration's strong defense of free trade is to be welcomed. What's at stake is not just a $120-million market for U.S. beef. It's whether Western Europe, which hopes to consolidate its market by 1992, will follow Japan's lead and impose a host of exclusionary trade barriers.

Virtually no one acquainted with the roots of this dispute believes that it is a public-health issue. Years ago the United States and the EC barred hormones linked to health problems. There is no scientific evidence that the five growth hormones still allowed in feed for U.S. beef — testosterone, estradiol, progesterone, zeranol, and trenbolone — pose any health threat whatsoever. Moreover, half of U.S.-raised cattle are never fed hormones. That beef could be certified hormone-free, but, absent legitimate concern, why should any nation bear such expense?

The EC simply seized on the opposition of German consumer groups to camouflage protectionist farm policies, which the United States rightly seeks to dismantle under the General Agreement on Tariffs and Trade (GATT). EC members also are wary of the implications of the recent U.S.-Canadian trade pact and a U.S. ban on imported cheese made from unpasteurized milk.

So, tit-for-tat, the EC has warned the United States that if it doubles tariffs on Danish hams, Italian canned tomatoes, and other such products, the EC will respond by raising fees on U.S. honey, dried fruit, shelled walnuts, and canned corn. This imminent food fight could become a ruinous trade war. Yet given the right incentives, there are ample ways to settle this dispute. Among them: arbitration and compensation under GATT, country-of-origin labeling permitting consumers a choice, and bargaining to open other avenues of trade.

Regrettably, it still seems to take a flash of steel in a showdown to force serious negotiations to open world markets — even the markets of friends. Since the EC drew first, let Washington not blink now.

LEXINGTON HERALD-LEADER
Lexington, Kentucky, February 8, 1989

While the rest of the meat-eating public has been complaining about the European ban on hormone-soaked beef, Texans have figured out how to make a buck on the deal.

Texas Agriculture Commissioner Jim Hightower has concluded that if you can't beef with the Europeans and win, then it's best to join 'em. Hightower has told Europe that Texas will supply the continent with all the hormone-free beef it can stomach.

Hightower, the author of this free-market approach, is a liberal Democrat. The conservative Republicans in the Bush administration are intent on solving this problem through government intervention. Do you need more proof that old political labels don't have a lot of meaning anymore?

THE ASHEVILLE CITIZEN
Asheville, North Carolina, February 5, 1989

Europeans are learning what free trade is all about. They also are experiencing a taste of some of their own medicine, or in this case, wurst.

Now, if they only would apply these lessons to the matter of hormone-fed beef from the United States ....

The European Economic Community is taking down most of the remaining trade barriers between its member countries. By 1992, goods will flow across Europe's internal borders almost as freely as they move across state borders in the United States.

Countries have ceded authority on trade matters to the EEC, which decides which restrictions are justified and which are not. Most do not stand up to EEC scrutiny. When it comes to their own trade laws at least, Europeans have a keen eye for self-serving restrictions — for protectionist barriers that go under the guise of something else.

Rulings by the EEC have been educational. German beer makers were stunned two years ago to learn that the country's purity laws for beer were not essential to the health of the German people. If Germany wants to limit its own beer makers to nothing but barley, water, hops and natural yeast, that's fine, said the EEC, but Germany cannot use those restrictions to forbid the import of beers that contains other ingredients.

This time it is wurst. No country in Europe has laws as stringent as Germany on what may go into sausage. Other countries permit wurst to be made with a wider range of meat products, and most allow additives such as soybean meal, milk proteins and artificial coloring. Because of German requirements, wurst makers in other countries effectively were cut off from the German market.

The German government argued that its requirements were health-based. All-meat wursts are more nutritious than those containing plant proteins, it said.

The EEC's Court of Justice decided otherwise. It ruled that German meat laws were aimed mostly at protecting German producers, not at protecting public health.

Other European countries hailed the decision. Meanwhile, they are happy to see the same subterfuge used against the United States. The EEC imposed a ban Jan. 1 on imported beef that contains growth hormones. European beef producers do not use such hormones, by EEC law. Most U.S. producers do.

Until the ban, U.S. cattle growers were selling about $100 million of beef a year in Europe. The United States retaliated by placing steep tariffs on $100 million of European farm products. The issue is still under negotiation.

Cattle that are fed hormones grow faster and produce beef that is leaner and more tender. Exhaustive research has found no harm to human health from such beef, yet the EEC invokes health concerns as the basis for prohibiting it. The United States says Europeans simply want to protect their producers from superior U.S. beef.

Actually there's more to it than that. Europe has an influential animal-welfare movement, which seeks to do away with "factory animal farms." Animal-rights activists believe it immoral to confine animals in feedlots, to manipulate the conditions under which they are raised, or otherwise to use "inhumane" (meaning non-natural) methods for intensive production.

This excessive and anthropocentric concern for the feelings of animals reached its greatest silliness yet in a Swedish law, enacted last summer, that extended habeas corpus to chickens (no more coops), granted "grazing rights" to cattle, and liberated pigs from their pens.

Hormones and other drugs make intensive production possible, so animal-rights activists want to outlaw drugs for animals. Alleged health concerns merely offer a more acceptable way to express this desire.

European meat producers, understandably, don't want to compete with cattle raisers who are not under such restrictions, and they welcome protectionism in any case. They have gone along with the health ruse for the sake of keeping out imports.

All of this violates the concept of fair trade. Perhaps one day, we will have an international organization with the authority to impose the same discipline as the EEC does on its own members.

The Washington Post
Washington, D.C., February 15, 1989

SMALL TRADE quarrels have a remarkable power to sour relations among big countries. The dispute between the United States and the European Common Market about hormone-treated beef has taken on an importance all out of proportion to the amount of meat and money involved. Both sides are going to try again this week to find a way around it.

It's a dangerous case because each side sees in it the shadow of tendencies that it fears in the other. It began when the Europeans, in response to public concerns, banned all beef treated with hormones. American cattle growers, who argue that hormone treatment produces healthier beef, were outraged. Objecting that the Europeans had no right to impose restrictions that were not based on scientific evidence of a threat to health, the United States imposed punitive tariffs on a range of European goods coming into this country. The Europeans have replied that under international law they have every right to reflect public attitudes and if the United States does not yield, they will retaliate with tariffs on American exports.

The Europeans see, in the American position, an overbearing insistence that the American standard must prevail worldwide. The Americans see a European agriculture policy that has become so deeply entangled with the domestic politics of the Common Market's 12 member countries that it has become immovable and that its complexity is making negotiation impossible.

In truth, neither side is on entirely solid ground when it talks about the principles allegedly at stake. When Congress first imposed restrictions on automobile exhaust emissions, for example, the scientific evidence of the threat to health was far from conclusive. Conversely, the Common Market has not hesitated to strike down health standards that it considered to be spurious and merely a restraint on competition—like the famous purity law that Germany had been using to keep Dutch and Danish beer out of its market.

Most of the world's governments are currently trying to work out international rules for agricultural trade, a process in which both the United States and the Common Market have enormous interests. But progress there is blocked by a deadlock between them over subsidies, that deadlock in turn being exacerbated by the much narrower dispute about the hormone-treated beef. No doubt the beef case is, in political terms, difficult. But it's the kind of difficulty that politicians are paid to solve.

U.S.-Japan Sign Semiconductor Accord, Reach Computer Pact

In a precedent-setting legal victory for Intel Corp. over NEC Corp. of Japan, Arizona U.S. District Judge William Gray Feb. 6, 1989 ruled that the internal design of computer chips was protected by federal copyright law. But the judge also ruled that Intel had failed to demonstrate that NEC had illegally copied the microcode of Intel's 8086 and 8088 chips. The microprocessors acted as the "brains" of personal computers, office machines and other electronic equipment. Intel had hailed the intellectual-property aspect of the ruling as a "landmark."

Trade representatives from the U.S. and Japan June 4, 1991 came to terms on an agreement covering trade in computer chips. The intent of an earlier agreement to boost the U.S. share of the Japanese market in semiconductors was renewed, but under less stringent terms. That agreement, signed in 1986, was due to expire in July.

The pact would last for a guaranteed three years, with an option to extend it for a further two years. It included an understanding that the private sectors of both nations would cooperate to allow U.S. microchip makers to increase their share of the $23-billion-a-year Japanese market to more than 20% by the end of 1992, from about 15% currently.

In return for Japan's agreement to renew the pact, the U.S. made concessions, including lifting the remaining sanctions imposed during the Reagan administration. The sanctions, import duties on products including Japanese color televisions and laptop computers, had been instituted in retaliation for Japan's perceived failure to comply with the 1986 microchip pact. The new treaty also barred the U.S. from retaliating through sanctions for any future perceived Japanese shortcomings.

The negotiators were unable to agree on a common measure for calculating U.S. market share in Japan, so they agreed to use both of their preferred measures. The Japanese measure included purchases of American microchips by U.S. companies' subsidiaries in Japan.

The new treaty was received favorably in Japan because it relied less on government regulation and more on market forces to bring about its goals. U.S. computer and semiconductor companies generally lauded the pact, set to take effect Aug. 1, as the most favorable that Japan could be expected to sign.

Trade negotiators for the U.S. and Japan March 23, 1990 announced a new pact that would make Japanese markets more open to U.S.-made supercomputers.

The agreement was aimed at winning increased supercomputer purchases by the Japanese public institutions.

In order to reach the agreement, Japanese negotiators made a number of major concessions. They included commitments to:

■ Use performance, as well as the previously emphasized question of price, as a prime criterion in selecting supercomputers.

■ Use criteria other than that of "theoretical peak performance" in computer selection. Peak performance measured a computer's ability to solve certain theoretical problems at high speeds in a fraction of a second. The test was said to discriminate against U.S.-made supercomputers, which emphasized more realistic types of problem solving.

■ Follow the lead of the private market in negotiating purchase prices in order to avoid the deep discounts – sometimes amounting to 80% – frequently offered by Japanese companies seeking prestige sales.

■ Publicly brand as "unfair traders" companies setting unfairly low prices.

U.S. corporate and congressional leaders commended the new pact, but said they were eager to see concrete results. Some noted that a previous pact, completed in 1987, had not led to a single sale of a U.S.-made supercomputer to a Japanese public institution. U.S. supercomputer manufacturers reportedly had little trouble selling their products to Japanese corporations.

Some analysts said Japanese negotiators had been under mounting pressure from their superiors to reach an agreement on at least one of the trade areas currently under negotiation. In addition to supercomputers, the areas included satellites and wood products.

DESERET·NEWS
*Salt Lake City, Utah,
January 17, 1988*

Why do Japanese companies consistently beat their American competitors in the technology marketplace? The reasons are several, but one major difference is that the Japanese simply are more aggressive.

A recent U.S. industry report on the computer market for 1988 showed that the Japanese had captured half the world's $50 billion semiconductor market, an increase of 2 percent, while the U.S. share fell 2 points to 37 percent. That $50 billion market total was a third higher than the year before.

One reason for the Japanese success in this expanding market is that they apparently put major emphasis on the fastest growing segments of the computer industry, while American companies did not take advantage of the high-growth areas to the same extent.

That seems to say that the difference is not superior technology or lower costs, but rather, alert business practices, a keen sense of technological frontiers, and a superb selling job.

All of those characteristics used to be hallmarks of aggressive American business. Somehow, U.S. firms must recapture a better sense of awareness of where the action is going to be, and do a better job of planning to get there first.

This especially applies to the exciting new field of superconductors, the ultra-cold materials that carry electricity without any loss of energy. New research has shown that extremely cold temperatures may not be necessary, after all.

Both the U.S. and Japan are considered "neck and neck" in the research, but the Japanese are seen as better structured to develop new materials and get them into the marketplace.

The U.S. should learn from its past mistakes and not let Japan grab the lead in this new technology as it has done with semiconductors.

The Star-Ledger

Newark, New Jersey, February 6, 1990

Chalk up another victory for the booming Japanese computer business. Without so much as a whimper, a U.S. initiative intended to recapture control of computer chip-making from Japan has collapsed.

The ignominious failure sheds light on the important difference between the two nations in the scramble for superiority in the world markets. What makes the failure doubly regrettable is that it was a good strategy and deserved a better fate.

This was a billion-dollar venture that brought together some of the biggest names in the U.S. computer industry—International Business Machines, Digital Equipment, Hewlett Packard, Intel, Advanced Micro Devices, National Semiconductor and LSI Logic. They advanced the money to form U.S. Memories, a corporation that would manufacture computer memory chips called DRAMs, an acronym for dynamic random access memories—the basic element of modern computers.

After seven months, not a single chip had been made. The founding companies were unable to attract other firms to join the venture, and more important, to provide capital that was essential to provide the financing for the ambitious project.

In the meantime, tne shortage of DRAMs which had prompted the joint venture had been overcome —at least temporarily—by stepped up production by companies in Japan, South Korea, West Germany and one U.S. maker, Motorola. The bottom line is that the U.S. computer makers are still at the mercy of foreign competitors because Motorola's output does not begin to satisfy domestic demand.

There is still some hope, however, that fresh investment dollars can be attracted and the joint venture salvaged, although this is only a remote possibility at the moment.

Two observations are in order. In other countries, an undertaking of this nature would have received the active support of the government, and measures would have been adopted to aid the project and insure its success. In the United States, companies are motivated by short-term considerations and have, for the most part, abandoned long-range planning and development to their more aggressive competitors abroad.

So long as these factors dominate business and government attitudes, the U.S. will continue to slip from leadership in the international marketplace.

The Washington Post

Washington, D.C., July 21, 1989

BY RELAXING export controls on personal computers, the Commerce Department is only acknowledging that the technology is now familiar worldwide. The Defense Department's angry dissent was not surprising. The struggle between the two departments over exports of technology has been a fixture of bureaucratic politics in Washington for years. But the fears at Defense are overdrawn to a point at which they undercut its case.

This decision by the secretary of commerce, Robert Mosbacher, serves the national interest in two ways. Obviously, it encourages exports by one of this country's most competitive industries, and it's essential to get American exports up. Less obviously, it also strengthens the export control system by relieving it of requirements that most sensible people regard as futile and foolish.

The Western alliance maintains a list of equipment of strategic importance that all the member countries agree not to sell to the Soviet bloc. When the United States insists on including technology that is readily available throughout the world, it generates exasperation among its partners and a tendency to take the whole effort less than seriously.

Mr. Mosbacher's ruling affects only the middle range of personal computers. The most advanced, the internal workings of which have not yet become common knowledge in Taiwan, India and Singapore, will remain under control. But the engineering of the midlevel machines has been disseminated beyond recapture. Last year American companies alone sold 6 million personal computers of the class covered by this decision, and nearly half of them went overseas. Similar machines are now being produced in many countries outside the alliance, including some in the Third World with no export restrictions whatever.

When President Bush was in Poland and Hungary last week, he gave his blessing to the reforms under way there and to wider trade with the West. Among other things, the message was that the United States would not carry on the kind of harassment of trade with the Soviet bloc that had characterized the early Reagan years. To maintain that pledge, the White House is going to have to see to it that the Defense Department and its friends in Congress do not succeed in challenging this decision.

It's true that personal computers have a political significance, and it reaches far beyond the military applications that the Defense Department has in mind. Computer and communications technology is deeply subversive to the kind of central control under which Eastern Europe has lived for 40 years. As computers become more common there, they will hasten the end of the old style of politics and work in behalf of the reformers. That's not the least of the reasons to encourage Eastern Europe to experiment with them.

The Atlanta Journal AND THE ATLANTA CONSTITUTION

Atlanta, Georgia, July 22, 1989

Defense Secretary Dick Cheney's objection to the Commerce Department ruling making it easier to sell PCs to Soviet-bloc countries just doesn't compute.

The personal computers in question — specifically some models of Apple Macintosh Plus and IBM PS-2 lines — are classed as middle-level technology. Computers of this type can be of sufficient sophistication to be used, as the Apple II is, for targeting U.S. tactical nuclear weapons in Europe.

The point is, however, these computers are readily available worldwide since they are manufactured in 10 other countries besides the United States including, notably, Hungary and Czechoslovakia.

It doesn't make sense, if the Soviets are going to get access to this technology anyway, for Washington to penalize U.S. computer makers by denying them a market.

Another factor to consider is that whatever marginal military benefit the Soviet Union might derive from more personal computers is likely to be outweighed by the security risks to the state with these devices in the hands of Soviet hackers of a curious, skeptical or even hostile frame of mind. As startling as the revelations of glasnost have been, the unearthing of buried Soviet secrets might get really out of hand with the stroking of a few carefully selected keys.

The fuss that Mr. Cheney raised over the computer decision may have as much to do with observing bureaucratic niceties as with national-security considerations. He is reported to have been piqued by what he considered the peremptory way in which Commerce Secretary Robert A. Mosbacher handled the matter.

Be that as it may, Mr. Mosbacher's call was the right one.

'Big Three' Allege Minivan Dumping

Responding to foreign pressure, the U.S. Treasury Feb. 16, 1989 ruled that most imported minivans and sports utility vehicles would continue to be classified as cars rather than trucks.

The decision reversed a Jan. 4 Customs Service ruling that all imported vans and sports vehicles previously classified as cars and subject to a 2.5% tariff would henceforth be regarded as trucks and face a 25% duty.

The new Treasury rules would base the classification on such design factors as number of doors, seating arrangement and window location. Although considered as cars for tariff purposes, the vehicles would continue to be considered as trucks for safety purposes by the U.S. Transportation Department.

The ruling was regarded as a victory for foreign makers of the popular vehicles – particularly those from West Germany, Japan and Great Britain – and a defeat for U.S. auto makers, who had argued that the U.S. Treasury would lose about $500 million in additional revenue if the tariff were not raised.

About 280,000 of the vans and sports vehicles had entered the U.S. as imports in 1988, giving them about 2% of the U.S. auto market. A 25% duty would raise their price by $1,500-$3,000.

The Big Three U.S. auto companies May 31, 1991 filed a complaint with the U.S. Commerce Department and the International Trade Commission alleging that their Japanese competitors were unfairly dumping minivans in the U.S. market.

The action came amid slumping sales by the U.S. auto makers and steadily increasing Japanese market share in the U.S. in all automobile categories. The complaint alleged that Japanese auto makers, and especially Toyota Motor Corp. and Mazda Motor Co., had engaged in predatory pricing, selling their minivans to dealers for less than was charged to dealers in Japan.

The New York Times

New York City, New York, January 24, 1989

Is a sporty van a car or a truck? That's a megadollar question. The Bush Administration's answer, which could come as early as this week, will be its first major test on trade policy. If the answer is truck, Detroit's prospering auto makers will have wrested yet another unwarranted shield against imports.

For years, most imported minivans and sport/utility vehicles have been classified as cars, with a 2.5 percent tariff. The Customs Bureau proposes to reclassify them as trucks, with a tariff of 25 percent — a staggering increase that would add between $1,500 and $6,000 to each vehicle's cost. Sensing a storm, the Treasury has taken the customs ruling under review.

Minivans and sports/utility models are hot commodities. They currently constitute about 10 percent of total car and light truck sales, with Detroit dominating the market.

Which is the car?   Which is the truck?

At the current volume of imports, roughly 200,000 a year, the higher duty would add an estimated $500 million. Costs to the consumer would be still greater, since increased import prices would let Detroit raise its prices, too.

The 25 percent truck tariff is the unhappy legacy of an earlier trade war — the so-called "chicken war" of 1963 ignited by the European Common Market's levies on poultry imports. The tariff hit all truck imports.

The question now is whether the tariff applies to vans and sports vehicles. Both have adaptable versions, for either passengers or cargo. Heretofore, the answer turned on whether the rear space was open (it's a truck) or fitted out with a seat and carpet (it's a car). The new ruling calls most of them trucks.

Representative John Dingell of Michigan, chairman of the House Commerce Committee, has given his support to Detroit's quest for such a finding. The industry finally won after the new trade law ordered all tariffs reclassified, to harmonize America's descriptions with other countries'.

The harmonization prompted an inquiry by Suzuki, which makes the sporty Samurai. The Japanese auto maker has intentionally shipped some Samurais as trucks — no rear seat — to get around Tokyo's so-called "voluntary" quotas on car exports to the United States. Suzuki, a relative newcomer to the American market, has a small quota. When seatless Samurais evaded the quota, Detroit was understandably angry.

But every car buyer has a right to be even angrier at the quotas that prompted Suzuki's evasion. Theoretically temporary, the quotas are now in their ninth year. Prices, and Detroit's profits, are higher because imports are limited.

This is a classic case of how protectionism can spread, starting with Europe's farm policy, followed by a punitive truck tariff, "voluntary" car quotas and bad-faith evasion. Tariff harmonization is not a simple matter, but neither is it supposed to create major new distortions. The Treasury's review can start the new Administration's trade policy off on the right foot (it's a car) or the wrong one (it's a truck). copyright © The New York Times 1989

The Register

Santa Ana, California, January 27, 1989

One of the best steps President Bush could take is to dismantle the tariffs and quotas now imposed against foreign-car imports. These include the "voluntary" and "temporary" auto quotas imposed by President Reagan in 1981, which were really mandatory and perpetual. Every time Tokyo hinted it might "voluntarily" end the quotas, the heavily protectionist Reagan administration came down on the Japanese with the weight of a three-ton 1974 Cadillac Fleetwood.

According to a study by the Brookings Institution, the quotas have boosted Japanese car prices by $2,500 and domestic car prices by $1,000. That comes to about $15 billion a year out of consumers' pockets.

The quotas also have given the Japanese an excuse to enter the mid-level and luxury car niches, traditional Detroit territory, with such new models as Honda's Acura line. The small-car market the Japanese are leaving is being filled with Korean marques. As always, government economic controls backfire against the industry they're supposed to help. Bush can easily end this folly by slipping the Japanese the word that, if they discard the "voluntary" quotas, he won't say a word.

He should also act to ward off another attack on the auto market. The trade bill passed by Congress last summer included a requirement that the Customs Service look into reclassifying some types of imports. As you might expect, the Customs bureaucracy has ruled in a way that increases government power. In particular, it ruled that minivans and sports-utility vehicles are "trucks," subject to a 25 percent import tax, instead of the 2.5 percent tax when they were classified as "cars." Only a bureaucrat could tell you how a vehicle can be a "car" one minute and a "truck" the next.

Bush should stop the Customs Service flim-flam by reversing the reclassification. If not, you could pay from $2,000 to $2,500 more for one of these vehicles. Some Japanese firms say they will just stop selling such models. The increased prices will also boost, to a lesser degree, the prices you pay for sedans and other models not directly affected. Many former van buyers will switch to sedans, reducing supply, and so driving up prices.

Many US auto-industry executives love the idea, since it will boost sales of domestic autos. The major cheerleader is Chrysler Chairman Lee Iacocca, always ready to use government power to take money from your pocketbook to slip into his own. He has come up with that all-purpose phony argument of the late 1980s: The federal deficit will be reduced by the $500 million seized by the tariff. Wrong. That money will be taken from other sectors of the private economy, hurting other businesses, and thus actually reducing economic output.

Iacocca also ignores the fact that the tariff, and the Reagan "voluntary" quotas, remove the all-out competition Detroit needs to reform itself. Does President Bush understand that reality?

THE TAMPA TRIBUNE

Tampa, Florida, January 28, 1989

America's Big Three auto makers were in terrible shape just eight years ago. Chrysler was effectively bankrupt, Ford appeared to be on the verge, and General Motors sustained its worst loss — almost $800 million — in company history. My, how times change.

The Big Three in 1988 chalked up a combined profit of $11 billion, making last year the best by far the domestic auto industry has ever known. It accomplished this feat by building better cars, by slashing bloated corporate bureaucracies, by jacking up prices willy-nilly, and by cadging special favors from the federal government.

The most famous favor, of course, was the arrangement of federal loan guarantees for Chrysler. But the most important favor was Washington's decision to control the importation of foreign vehicles, especially Japanese vehicles. The move was designed to "give Detroit time" to modernize antiquated factories, and to figure out how to build quality cars. Detroit has done that.

But the Big Three aren't satisfied with astronomical earnings and the continuation of Japan's "voluntary" limit on the number of vehicles shipped to the American market. They are now demanding still more protection from foreign competition. They want the Treasury Department to impose a 25 percent tariff on imported minivans and sports-utility vehicles, both of which are enormously popular with U.S. buyers.

Although G.M., Ford, and Chrysler are arguing that the extraordinarily high tariff is necessary because of America's trade deficit, they are not motivated solely by patriotism. Chrysler Chairman Lee Iacocca, for instance, has attempted to enlist the support of Chrysler dealers by noting in a letter to them that the 25 percent tariff would mean "a $2,000 per truck cost penalty to your competitors."

The deal is this: Imported cars rate a 2.5 percent tariff. But the tariff on imported trucks is 10 times as much — 25 percent. The Big Three want foreign-made vans and sports-utility vehicles to be considered trucks and not cars. If the Treasury Department agrees, of course, the American consumer would be the loser. Indeed, it's well to remember that when imported vehicles go up in price, so do domestic vehicles. That's not a casual supposition. That's the straight skinny from Frank McCarthy, executive vice president of the National Automobile Dealers Association, as reported in the Wall Street Journal.

The Journal story goes on: "... the National Automobile Dealers Association, which represents more than 20,000 car dealers, is opposing the tariff, though that isn't too surprising. Times have changed since dealers carried a single line of cars, all of which were made in Detroit. Now more than half the association's members hawk imports right along with their Chevys and Plymouths, and would therefore be hurt by a new import tariff.

"'I really can't see who benefits in this equation,' says Ron Tonkin, an Oregon dealer who is about to become the association's president. 'Certainly not the consumer, not the dealers. And when it's all sorted out, I don't think it will really benefit any of the manufacturers.'"

We agree. It's time for the Big Three to stop thinking of Washington as a wet-nurse. And it's time for President Bush, who was elected on an anti-protectionist platform, to remind Detroit that it's unseemly, to say no more, for an industry making fantastic profits to conjure up new ways to bash the consumer.

ST. LOUIS POST-DISPATCH

St. Louis, Missouri, February 1, 1989

A car is a car is a car — or is it a truck? It depends on whom you ask and for what purpose. The U.S. government levies a 25 percent tariff on imported trucks but only a 2.5 percent tariff on imported cars. The government recently ruled that mini-vans and sport-utility vehicles are trucks to help Detroit avoid competition in what is fast becoming the hottest segment of the American market. This blatant form of protectionism should be reversed.

The Big Three automakers argue disingenuously that under a new, so-called harmonized tariff system that went into effect on Jan. 1, the government is required to define trucks by the nature of their design, not by how such vehicles are used. In response, the U.S. Customs Service, on Jan. 4, began classifying sport-utility vehicles and mini-vans as trucks, hiking the tariff from 2.5 percent to 25 percent. This will make it virtually impossible for foreign imports to compete, leaving Detroit free to raise prices, costing consumers plenty.

Worse, two of the Big Three automakers have long been classifying as cars some of their own sport-utility vehicles assembled in Mexico to avoid the 25 percent tariff they want imposed on Japan and Europe. To be sure, Japanese automakers themselves indulge in fancy tricks — calling their vans and utility vehicles cars until their annual voluntary import quota is reached, then reclassifying them as trucks in order to exceed their own self-imposed limit.

But consistency isn't the point. The real issue is competition in the American auto market. Detroit wants it limited and has pressured the government into helping out. Fortunately, the Treasury Department has suspended the new rule while it reviews the issue. It should promptly overrule the Customs Service and restore competition in the American automobile market.

The Record

Hackensack, New Jersey, January 26, 1989

Detroit's Big Three auto makers have asked the Treasury Department to slap a 25 percent tariff on imported minivans and sport-utility vehicles. Although the request is cloaked in patriotism, it is little more than a grab for profits at the expense of consumers.

General Motors, Ford, and Chrysler say they need the tariff to protect them against foreign competition. But the facts speak otherwise. The Big Three will report record profits of $11 billion for 1988.

U.S. auto makers say the tariff will improve the nation's trade deficit. That may be true, but the improvements won't be enough to justify the estimated $500-million a year that the tariff would cost consumers.

In addition, the tariff might also push up domestic prices. Toyota and Volkswagen say they're considering halting shipments of these vehicles to the United States, if the tariff is approved. With the threat of foreign competition removed, the Big Three would have a freer hand to raise prices.

Besides angering consumer groups and importers, the proposed tariff has raised opposition from the 20,000 member National Automobile Dealers Association. The 25 percent tariff would add between $1,500 to $6,000 to the cost each vehicle.

But the most troubling aspect of the Big Three proposal is that it confuses need with greed. The days when the U.S. auto industry was in trouble have passed, and the threat of foreign competition has diminished. General Motors, Ford and Chrysler control 90 percent of the van and sport-utility market in the United States.

Instead of looking to Washington for tariffs, the three auto manufacturers should find ways to compete with foreign automakers on price and product. Customers respond not to unnecessary surcharges, but to design, reliability, and price.

Conditions now allow Detroit to build and market the car of the future. Existing import restrictions and a weaker dollar have given domestic automakers a considerable price advantage over foreign competitors. Detroit should use that price advantage to win back customers, not ask for tariffs to box out competition.

President Bush campaigned on a pledge of free trade. He should live up to the pledge and instruct the Treasury Department to reject the tariff request.

The Washington Post

Washington, D.C., February 22, 1989

SEEN FROM ONE ANGLE, imported vans and utility vehicles look like cars. Seen from another, they look like trucks. The difference is that imported cars pay a tariff of 2.5 percent, while trucks pay 25 percent.

The Customs Service used to classify most of them as cars, which drew shrieks of protest from the domestic manufacturers. Then at the beginning of this year it changed its mind and said that they were trucks, drawing shrieks of protest from the importers. Now the Treasury Department has overruled Customs with a decision that has a positively Solomonic beauty to it.

Vehicles that are designed primarily to transport people are deemed to be cars, the Treasury says, and those designed to haul goods are to be known as trucks. Back seats, rear windows, access and so forth are evidence that the designer had passengers in mind. That's how the Treasury arrived at its ruling that a four-door van is a car but a two-door van is a truck.

Absurd, you say? True, but in a rough sort of way it's a fair compromise. The real absurdity here is an American tariff on trucks that is 10 times greater than the tariff on the cars that are produced by the same industry using the same labor.

The American auto companies wanted the higher tariff because it would have enabled them to raise their prices on their own vans and sporty little utility vehicles, the fastest growing part of their business and one of the most profitable. The Treasury's ruling may turn out to be the most important single action that the Bush administration takes this winter to hold down inflation.

But there's more to it. Many of these vehicles will continue to come in as trucks regardless of the tariff, because trucks aren't counted in the import quotas on Japanese cars. Each of the Japanese companies will now balance the mathematics of the tariffs and the quotas to its own greatest advantage.

Those quotas deserve your attention. They were first imposed eight years ago, when the American companies were struggling to cope with high gasoline prices and the swing to smaller cars. They needed time to get their breath, they panted—and they got it. By the time they had caught their breath, they complained that they were being killed by the high exchange rate of the dollar. But now both the dollar and the price of gasoline are down—and the automobile industry's profits are way, way up. A question for the Bush administration: Why continue to protect this profitable industry from its foreign competitors, at the customers' expense, when the reasons for protection have long since vanished?

Newsday

New York City, New York, January 25, 1989

On its way out the door, the Reagan administration quietly arranged to inflate the cost of passenger vans to U.S. buyers by $2,000 per vehicle or more. The U.S. Customs Service proposes raising the duty on imported vans and sport / utility vehicles by 1,000 percent, giving Detroit room to raise prices on comparable machines.

That's highway robbery. The Bush administration should bring it to a screeching halt.

Customs is reclassifying utility vehicles and passenger vans, formerly categorized as cars, as light-duty trucks. It says it is reclassifying vans because they can be used as trucks.

They can. But, by international convention, the U.S. and other industrial countries all have taxed vehicles set up to carry passengers — with plush seats, carpeting and such — as cars for years. Why the sudden change?

Dealers of foreign-made vans think it's a favor to domestic car makers. The switch would make the imports — already hurting from the drop in the dollar's value — even less competitive. The tariff on cars is 2.5 percent; the tariff on trucks is 25 percent. That translates into a

price boost of $1,500 to $6,000 per vehicle, the importers say. They cite a telegram that Chrysler chairman Lee Iacocca sent to his dealers, asking them to lobby for the new duty, saying that it "translates into a $2,000 per truck cost penalty to your competitors."

It's not hard to read between those lines: Domestic van prices will rise if this decision isn't reversed. The cost to consumers of the higher tariff and the higher Detroit prices could top $1 billion a year, opponents say.

Treasury Secretary Nicholas Brady is reviewing the new duties; he's expected to decide the issue this week. The customs decision is arbitrary and extraordinarily costly — and bears a distinctly protectionist stamp. One of the Bush administration's first official acts should be to stop it in its tracks.

New York City, New York, February 20, 1989

King Solomon, in his wisdom, is believed to have discovered which of two women claiming to be the parent of a baby was the true mother by proposing, absurdly enough, to divide the child in two. Horrified, the real mother instantly offered to give up the child rather than see it torn asunder. As a result, she got the kid.

Now the Treasury Department has come up with a comparably absurd plan for deciding whether an imported van or utility vehicle is a truck or a car — but without the redeeming virtues of Solomon's scheme.

For the purposes of levying tariffs, the Treasury has figuratively split those imports through the middle: If only the front half of a vehicle has passenger doors, it's a truck. If the rear half has passenger doors too, it's a car.

But this time, it is profit — not justice — that's being served. The tariff on car imports — which until now included all multi-purpose vehicles — is 2.5 percent; the tariff on trucks is 25 percent. By changing the definition of a two-door Suzuki Sidekick or Mitsubishi Montero to "truck," the Treasury has imposed huge price increases on car buyers — and has given Detroit automakers an opportunity to

raise their prices on similar vehicles.

Washington should have left the tariffs as they were. If something is equipped with seats like a car, it should be taxed as a car. But the real question here is: Why in the world should trucks be tariffed at 10 times as much as cars in the first place?

No good reason, it turns out. The tariffs were jacked up years ago to punish Europe for some trade restrictions it had placed on goods from this country. And who's going to pay for Europe's past sins now? You got it: Good old American consumers.

The Seattle Times

Seattle, Washington, March 5, 1989

LET'S hear it for this guy named Fred Molnar, who for 15 years has run a cocktail joint in a little Wyoming town called Alpine. When Fred was a kid, his dad nicknamed him "Jeep," after a cartoon figure in the Popeye strip. The name stuck and Molnar naturally named his place in Alpine "Jeep's Bar and Lounge."

Lately, according to the Newhouse News Service, the big guys at Chrysler Corp. have been pressuring Molnar to sign a document promising he won't expand his business or use the Jeep logo in his advertising. Chrysler says it's worried about infringement on the trade name.

After a visit to corporate headquarters, Molnar said "I told 'em I sell whiskey, not cars. I can't believe it. A billion-dollar corporation and it's coming down on me."

Molnar, obviously a courageous character, said he has no intention of signing. "If Lee Iacocca wants to drive the 1,700 miles down to Alpine," he said, "I'll more than glad to sit down and have a meeting."

In Jeep's bar, of course.

The Hartford Courant

Hartford, Connecticut, February 3, 1989

The official line from Detroit has been that they aren't afraid of imports. Heck no. We are making more dependable, more efficient and safer cars than ever.

In fact to hear the auto industry moguls talk, the Japanese did them a favor. The U.S. automakers say they have learned a lot about management and engineering and are ready, willing and able to compete.

So it is a surprise to learn that some from the Motor City and its environs still want to sneak through a little protection when they get the chance.

U.S. Rep. Jonn D. Dingell of Michigan is backing a U.S. Customs Bureau proposal to reclassify imported minivans as trucks instead of cars. The difference is a 25 percent tariff vs. a 2.5 percent tariff, which would add between $1,500 and $6,000 to the cost of each vehicle.

Mr. Dingell is a man who once said that he wasn't all that sure he was happy to have a Mazda plant in his congressional district, because some of the profit would still go to Japan. Never mind that those dreaded Japanese have been financing the federal debt created in Washington.

Detroit's motives are not hard to figure. U.S. automakers long ago cornered the minivan market. Plymouth and Dodge made the best selling and most highly regarded ones. This was one area where the Japanese were late. Now they are getting into minivans in a big way, and based on their past record, one might reasonably assume they're getting in the market in a pretty effective way.

If the protectionist proposal succeeds, it will mean that Detroit is still afraid to compete, and that is bad for everyone — U.S. manufacturers, autoworkers and consumers. It is bad for the the economy.

The Bush administration is reviewing the Customs Bureau ruling. We hope the decision will be in favor of competition.

The Des Moines Register

Des Moines, Iowa, March 10, 1989

The most popular cars in America are trucks.

People are trading off the family sedan and switching to pickup trucks, utility vehicles and vans. In the auto business, it's called the "crossover factor."

Reuters news service reports that last year 23 percent of all truck buyers — nearly a million people — got rid of a car and switched to a truck as their primary vehicle.

The most popular vehicles in America last year were two trucks — the standard Ford and Chevrolet pickups. More than half a million of each were sold.

The crossover factor is somewhat of a surprise to automakers, says Reuters. Previously it was thought that the boom in truck sales was because people were buying them as second or third vehicles in addition to their car.

As it turns out, lots of people are getting rid of their cars and driving trucks instead.

A glance at rush-hour traffic confirms the trend.

Why the trend? Maybe it's just common sense among consumers. Cars have become so expensive that it makes sense to switch to a durable, practical vehicle that's going to last a few years and won't go out of style before it's paid for.

Too bad Detroit doesn't make cars like that, too.

THE BLADE

Toledo, Ohio, April 3, 1989

IT HAS been known for some time that Chrysler Corp. would eventually run into stiff competition for the Jeep Cherokee produced in Toledo, and now it is happening.

The popularity of this sports-utility model is undeniable. Last year Chrysler sold nearly 140,000 of the four-wheel-drive, four-door vehicles, and the company expects to do better this year. Its importance to this community — with some 6,000 workers producing vehicles at the company's North Cove Boulevard and Stickney Avenue plants — is obvious.

It is not surprising, therefore, that at least three Japanese auto firms, as well as Ford and General Motors, are entering the competition with similar models. Jeep may hold its own against these intrusions, but the fact is Chrysler's eggs in this segment of the market are in one basket, and that basket is in Toledo.

The implications are clear enough. At some point the company will face a decision as to whether to diversify its Jeep production here, consider the possibility of new facilities, or simply phase out its operations in the Toledo area.

The decision, of course, will be made in the Chrysler corporate boardroom; that, after all, is management's responsibility. At the same time, however, the decisions cannot be made in a vacuum; an industrial operation that employs thousands of Toledo citizens and has a major economic impact on the community necessarily involves the public interest.

Cherokee sales may well continue to increase despite the competition now on the horizon; in fact, they may grow to the extent of outgrowing the aging production facilities currently use. That in turn implies a need for input by local and state governments and economic-development agencies in providing the best possible incentives for Chrysler to keep producing vehicles in this area.

Cooperation between management and unions is not a one-way street. A company generates the revenue, true, but workers and the community as a whole each have much to offer an employer in terms of services, educational facilities, work skills, and cooperation in general.

In spite of pervasive doomsday talk and the departure of some firms from the local business scene, these are some of the strengths of Toledo that point to future growth and the ability to meet the toughest competition. They should not be ignored by management, government, unions, or residents.

U.S. Fighter Deal Set

The U.S. and Japan reached a formal agreement Nov. 29, 1988 on the production of a new jet fighter for the Japanese military.

Under the accord, signed by Japanese Foreign Minister Sosuke Uno and U.S. Ambassador Mike Mansfield, the main contractor for the new aircraft would be Mitsubishi Heavy Industries Ltd. The subcontractors were to be U.S.-based General Dynamics Corp., Kawasaki Heavy Industries Ltd. and Fuji Heavy Industries Ltd.

The plane, dubbed the FSX, was to be based on General Dynamics's F-16. It was to be designed and built in Japan but was expected to incorporate an American-designed engine.

Japanese officials estimated that the cost per plane for an initial order of as many as 130 aircraft would be 5.15 billion yen (US$42 million).

DAYTON DAILY NEWS
Dayton, Ohio, January 25, 1988

The American complaint that the Japanese should spend more on defense has had an ironic ring, since it was the United States, at the end of World War II, that got the Japanese to remain pacifist and agree not to develop an offensive force.

In recent decades, the Japanese have been dumped on for not putting enough (less than 1 percent) of their gross national product into defense, while the United States throws 6.2 percent of its gross national product into defense. The U.S. military provides, among other things, a nuclear umbrella that protects Japan so it can do its business thing.

The United States, which is running up a dollar-eating trade debt with Japan, has been within its rights to pressure the Japanese to help offset the costs of superpower defense and some policing of the Persian Gulf through which oil leaves for Japan. Japan is responding by increasing by 11 percent its defense budget to share more of the costs of supporting the 47,600 U.S. troops stationed in Japan.

And the Japanese have agreed to buy more U.S. defensive weapons (anti-submarine helicopters, for example).

The United States has to keep the lines of its policy straight, though. For example, after being urged to build up its defensive capability, the Japanese decided to build a new jet fighter. The U.S. aerospace industry rang its alarm bells at the prospect of the competition this could bring.

So the Japanese decided to ease American anxieties by agreeing to build 130 F-16 aircraft under license from the General Dynamics Corp.

The Japanese-American military relationship seems smooth and on the right track as it is. Americans should be careful, though, about requiring a lot more of the Japanese in building up their forces. Americans in 1945 also encouraged the Japanese to put their energy into capitalist production, and look what happened: The Japanese did it.

The Houston Post
Houston, Texas, March 15, 1988

Japan's sale of "quiet submarine propellers" to the Soviet Union last year has the Reagan administration going around in circles.

When news of Toshiba Machine's controversial deal was disclosed, U.S. officials screamed loud and long, saying it would now cost Western allies billions of dollars upgrading equipment to track the improved Soviet subs. Toshiba Machine was barred from receiving any Defense Department contracts, and Japan also took corrective measures. Still, there has been talk in Congress of imposing further sanctions, even banning virtually *all* Toshiba imports.

Last month, however, the assistant secretary of defense — hoping to ease strained trade relations between Japan and the U.S. — told Congress the Soviets had the quiet propellers three years *before* the sale. The actual damage was "difficult to assess," suggesting the administration's original complaints were overwrought. *Now* the Defense Department has repudiated that repudiation and claims the Toshiba sale *did* substantially improve the Soviets' submarines.

Well, which is it? Trade considerations shouldn't alter national security concerns. But were the Reagan administration's objections just so much rhetorical growling? Watching this propeller issue go round and round is making us dizzy.

The Honolulu Advertiser
Honolulu, Hawaii, March 3, 1988

With little fanfare, Japan has agreed to pay a greater share of the cost of American military bases there. Amid complaints about trade, this essential bilateral strategic tie is often ignored.

Japan contributes $2 billion to support 60,000 U.S. troops and homeporting of the 7th Fleet, our only aircraft carrier group based overseas. These forces enable this country to maintain our regional defense capabilities.

And, though Japan is often criticized for not spending more on defense, its $30-billion budget is the world's fifth largest and the second largest among non-nuclear powers. Japan's defense spending has grown faster over the last decade than NATO's.

Economically, Japan *is* an aggressive exporter. Its domestic markets *have* been hard to crack due to their intransigence and our ineptitude. This country's $60-billion trade deficit is cause for concern across the Pacific.

So far, the yen's strength against the dollar has not been as effective as hoped in starting to balance trade. And electioneering here is feeding protectionism and encouraging irrational, nationalistic and perhaps racist "Japan-bashing."

Anti-Japan sentiment has led to strange contradictions. Last month, a group of congressmen tried to block the Japanese government's purchase of a sophisticated U.S. Navy air defense system. Concerns were raised about keeping the technology secret — the Pentagon says it's not worried — but also about trade and military practices.

The sale would be a $500-million contribution to reducing our trade imbalance and help fulfill Japan's promise (at American urging) to be able to defend its sea lanes out 1,000 miles, giving this country more military flexibility in the Pacific.

Not all criticism of Japan is "bashing," to be sure. But Japan's critics can't have it both ways: complaining that Japan doesn't buy U.S. goods and doesn't shoulder its share of the defense burden, then blocking Japan's attempts to do so.

The Honolulu Advertiser
Honolulu, Hawaii, May 19, 1988

The forced resignation of a Japanese Cabinet member for saying Japan was not the aggressor in World War II but was fighting Asian colonization by the "white race" may quiet matters for the moment.

Several times in recent years such injudicious remarks, or textbooks whitewashing Japanese atrocities in the war, have raised outcries in countries that were targets of Japanese attack. Even after 45 years, the specter of Japanese militarism causes justified protest in Asia.

Americans can hardly complain of renewed militarism, since this country has led in demanding that Japan increase military spending, despite a "no-war" constitution we imposed. But such outspoken remarks may be symptoms of other U.S.-Japanese troubles.

Japan drew much of its ancient culture (including its writing) from China, sometimes by way of Korea. But Japanese rationalized their country's invasion of China in the 1930s as a case of a vigorous younger brother "helping" a decadent older brother regain purity and righteousness.

Granted, China was troubled and divided in the 1930s, but Japan's arrogance cost millions of Chinese (and many Japanese) lives plus loss of fortune and, ultimately, Japan's defeat.

These days, Americans detect a dangerous new Japanese arrogance, perhaps that of a younger brother which has mastered the art of industrial competitiveness and proposes to preach to an older brother it sees as fallen on hard times.

As Gerald L. Curtis, director of Columbia University's East Asian Institute wrote recently, "It is arrogance for Japan to believe that its success gives it the right to think the rest of the world is simply not as competent, that for others to make demands upon Japan is a sign of their weakness."

The Houston Post
Houston, Texas, April 30, 1988

A Japanese Cabinet minister has proclaimed that his country was not an aggressor in World War II, perhaps overlooking the events of Dec. 7, 1941. Several Asian neighbors who experienced that non-aggression have taken him to task for his perversion of history.

So, thankfully, have Japanese opposition parties. Members called for an emergency parliamentary debate on the comments, and said the minister should recant or resign. The issues of guilt and responsibility are sensitive ones in Japan. But revision of history won't help the Japanese or anyone else deal with them.

ST. LOUIS POST-DISPATCH
St. Louis, Missouri, April 25, 1988

Congress has only a few days to act to stop what may turn out to be one of the most harmful and irreversible actions of the Reagan administration. An agreement it signed last fall with Japan, giving Japan permission to ship, by air, 400 metric tons of plutonium over the next 30 years, will take effect unless both the House and the Senate object by the end of this month.

The pro-industry Reagan administration favors the agreement as a means of ensuring foreign markets for U.S. uranium. The uranium industry, of course, favors the agreement.

But why anyone else should is a puzzle. The casks in which the plutonium is to be shipped from European reprocessing sites back to Japan have not been tested. An accident could easily result in contamination of hundreds of square miles of the Arctic icecap, an area where life is so fragile the least disruption can take years to restore, if it can be restored at all.

The Nuclear Regulatory Commission — by any standard a conservative agency weighted toward favoring industry wishes — warns that it will be impossible to keep tabs on what happens to the plutonium in Japan. When only a few pounds is needed to make a bomb, the least slippage in accounting systems can be devastating.

In short, if the agreement takes effect, the United States will have given up its ability to have any control over plutonium that results from the reprocessing of nuclear fuel provided by U.S. firms to Japan. In an administration as concerned with national security as this one purports to be, that could represent an inexplicable and irresponsible abrogation of public trust.

Americans still have a lot to learn about accepting Japan as an equal economic power. Little is to be gained from Japan-bashing, even over troublesome trade disputes. But America-bashing by Japan — or simple indifference to legitimate U.S. trade concerns — is not acceptable either.

Some of the narrowly nationalistic Japanese revisions of the wartime history raise danger signals — not about military aggression, but about attitudes to other countries.

The Pittsburgh PRESS
Pittsburgh, Pennsylvania, April 5, 1988

In a speech that deserves far more attention than it has received, Japan's Prime Minister Noboru Takeshita recently said his country should build "defense capabilities commensurate with our national power."

That formulation amounts to a call for Japan to become a military superpower. Americans — even those old enough to remember Pearl Harbor — should welcome it.

The Japanese have the mightiest economy in Asia, but they spend only about 1 percent of gross national product on defense. We Americans spend more than 6 percent; our major allies in Europe spend about 5 percent, and we rightly rebuke them for not spending enough.

Like the Europeans, the Japanese are under the guns of the Soviet empire. Also like the Europeans, they are guarded by a U.S. military presence never interrupted since 1945.

When Europe and Japan were struggling to rebuild from the ashes of World War II, only the United States could bear the burden of protecting them — but now they can share that cost as mature allies.

Japan is now the most stable, peaceful and prosperous democracy in Asia. If Tokyo builds the military strength to match its economic clout, the world will be a safer place.

The Houston Post

Houston, Texas, November 30, 1988

A RECENT SERIES OF INCIDENTS threatens to further irritate an old sore spot in U.S.-Japanese relations — defense burden-sharing. Washington and Tokyo should move quickly to reduce the friction before it strains an alliance critical to both countries' security as the Soviet Union expands its Pacific presence.

Earlier this month, a U.S. Navy ship inadvertently fired shells near a Japanese coast guard vessel at the entrance to Tokyo Bay. On the Japanese island of Okinawa, where 35,000 U.S. troops are based, residents complained that bullets hit houses during recent maneuvers, and two tear-gas canisters went off in a crowded nightclub.

These are but the latest in a long list of acts involving American military forces that have sparked official and public protests as well as critical editorials in the Japanese press. But as long as Japan relies heavily for its defense on the 65,000 U.S. military personnel stationed there, such problems cannot be totally avoided.

That doesn't mean we should turn a deaf ear to Japanese complaints — nor do we. The captain of the U.S. ship that fired the practice rounds near the Japanese vessel was promptly transferred, and an apology was issued. And an investigation was swiftly ordered into the tear-gas incident. Our forces, after all, are there to serve our security interests, too.

The obvious alternative to having a large contingent of foreign troops manning an extensive network of air, naval and ground-force bases on their soil is for the Japanese to assume a larger share of their own defense. It is a role we have urged upon them for years.

The Japanese spend about 1 percent of their gross national product — $30 billion annually — on defense compared to our 6 percent or $300 billion. As an economic superpower second only to the United States, Japan can afford to contribute more to protecting itself. And it should, considering our huge budget and trade deficits.

Japan could ease our burden by expanding its self-defense force, or by picking up more of the cost of maintaining U.S. forces in the region, or both. This could be done without launching Japan on a major military buildup, which nobody wants.

U.S. and Japanese armed forces, bitter foes in World War II, now engage in joint training exercises and express high regard for each other's capabilities. That spirit of cooperation at the grass-roots military level should be reinforced at the highest diplomatic level.

𝒯𝒽𝑒 LeaderPost

Regina, Saskatchewan,
September 29, 1988

Kichiro Tazawa, 70, a former Japanese agriculture minister, was flagged to take over as defence minister following the resignation on Wednesday of Tsutomu Kawara.

Kawara resigned as a gesture of moral responsibility for the July collision between a submarine and a pleasure craft in which 30 people died. The submarine crew was criticized for slowness in helping to rescue people after the collision at the entrance to Tokyo Bay.

The choice of Tazawa would preserve the balance among factions making up the Liberal Democratic party.

The Japan Defence Agency has just finished issuing its budget statement, which is being submitted this week to the Finance Ministry. The defence statement dwells on the continuing Soviet military buildup in the Far East and, under U.S. pressure to take more defence responsibility upon itself, says Japan must continue its five-year defence expansion. The budget for the next fiscal year is $35.5 billion Cdn, over one per cent of the gross national product.

The statement spoke of a Soviet deployment of "enormous forces" on the Soviet-Chinese border, positioning of SS-24 intercontinental missiles, commissioning of a fourth Kiev-class aircraft carrier, and deployment of a fourth-generation fighter plane.

Japan, with 270,000 defence personnel, is developing a surface-to-ship missile and anti-submarine deck helicopter, and seeks to add 16 F-15 jet fighters, two new warships and a submarine to its arsenal.

In choosing the former farm minister for defence, though, is it a case of beating an old plowshare into a sword?

The New York Times

New York City, New York, December 17, 1988

An American negotiating team trying to sell F-16 fighters to Japan was defeated last month and is now in Tokyo to receive its second humiliation.

Japan wants to buy 140 new fighter planes. General Dynamics makes the world's best fighter, the F-16, in numbers that assure unmatchable economy. Furthermore, by buying American Japan could reduce the trade surplus that so aggravates its major trading partner and help alleviate the burden America bears in defending, among other countries, Japan.

Surely in this case, Japan will buy American, no? No. Japan prefers to develop the FSX, loosely patterned on the F-16, at more than twice the cost. In an agreement signed last month in Tokyo by the retiring Ambassador, Mike Mansfield, General Dynamics has been designated a subcontractor, with a promise of 35 to 45 percent of the development work. In gratitude, the company will hand over all the necessary F-16 technology.

Has the Defense Department given away the store? Its negotiators worked harder than it looks. At first the Japanese insisted on developing a wholly new fighter. The Pentagon finally induced Japan to base the plane on the F-16. New technology developed for the FSX will be made available to the U.S., for military though not commercial use.

Still, the deal is one-sided and unfair. Japan shuts out American companies when it wishes to develop a new industry. Japan's insistence on developing the FSX may not relate to its effort to build up its aviation industry. Even so, the rejection of a superior American product seems familiar, and unfair.

Japan argues that defense is in a special category, and it is quite true that many countries like to build their own major weapons systems. But Japan and America have a special relationship. They are major trading partners; America shoulders the heavier part of their mutual defense, spending 6.5 percent of its gross national product on defense compared with Japan's 1 percent. The resources America diverts to defense have a lot to do with the trade imbalance that so benefits Japan.

The Defense Department, having agreed that Japan will develop most of the FSX, has now sent a team to Tokyo to plead for a share of the production contract. Agreeing to that seems the least Japan could do.

In the case of the F-16, the United States had every reason to expect that Japan would want to buy American, and every reason to be disappointed at the grudging concessions Japan has made to the two countries' common interests.

The Houston Post

Houston, Texas, June 17, 1988

It is not good news to hear that a group of Japanese companies led by Mitsubishi Heavy Industries is "virtually certain" of winning a $3 million U.S. contract to work on the Strategic Defense Initiative.

Japan and the United States agreed last year to allow Japanese participation in the development of the Star Wars program — an agreement that opened the door for the Mitsubishi group to become Japan's first full-fledged participant in SDI.

Some U.S. officials are certainly correct in voicing their reluctance to include Japan in the development of strategic U.S. technologies — especially in view of a Japanese court's ruling that Japan's Toshiba Machine Co., a subsidiary of Toshiba Corp., had illegally sold high technology to the Soviet Union.

Making matters worse, news of the SDI contract follows closely on the heels of a much-hindered proposal that would allow U.S. companies to bid on Japanese government construction projects. The Japanese, who have come up with several areas of disagreement over the proposed accord, have been accused by a U.S. official of "dickering" and trying to give as little as they can.

In one of the disputes, the Japanese told the United States that the agreement does not allow U.S. firms to bid on new radar units to be installed during the expansion of Tokyo and Hiroshima airports. This came after they seemingly agreed to allow U.S. participation.

In addition, the Japanese say U.S. companies that incorporate in Japan will be treated as domestic companies — not foreign companies — and will have to show a proven track record in Japan before they can bid on government projects. Since U.S. firms have not been allowed to bid in the past, they *have* no track record.

With the Japanese making it so difficult for U.S. firms to bid on Japanese government projects, the United States should do likewise and institute equally tough standards. Let's go tit for tat.

ST. LOUIS POST-DISPATCH

St. Louis, Missouri, June 21, 1988

Japan's gross national product has surpassed that of the Soviet Union, making it the No. 2 economic superpower. This development has many foreign observers — and more than a few Japanese — worried that Japan may decide to become a military superpower as well. That would be a radical change and a potentially dangerous one.

Technically, under Article 9 of Japan's postwar constitution (a document written by Gen. Douglas MacArthur and his staff during the occupation) Tokyo is not even allowed to have a military. But under American pressure in the wake of the Korean War, Japan did establish a "Self-Defense Force" and since the 1950s it has slowly grown in both size and capability. With some 246,000 men under arms, Japan's military ranks far behind that of the United States and the Soviet Union. But it is a modern, highly capable force, particularly the naval and air units. More important, Japan's defense spending has been on a steady rise and has broken the symbolically important 1 percent of GNP that many earlier Japanese governments had set as a ceiling on arms spending.

Washington has been a driving force behind the Japanese arms buildup as a way of countering Soviet military power in Asia. And this pressure is likely to grow, given the U.S. deficit. However, for the United States, this is a shortsighted policy. While Japan should pay for its own defense, greatly expanding the Japanese military would send political shock waves through Asia. Not only the Soviets, but both Koreas, China and the nations of Southeast Asia would feel threatened. The result would be heightened tensions and new arms races. American policy, therefore, should encourage Japan to keep its arms spending at a moderate level.

Pittsburgh Post-Gazette

Pittsburgh, Pennsylvania, July 26, 1988

The politicians this year are talking about the need for Japan to carry more of the financial weight of its own defense.

But what many may not realize is that quietly but steadily Japan has built its Self-Defense Forces to the point where at $48 billion a year, Japan's defense spending now is the third-highest in the world, surpassed only by the two superpowers. It has the world's fourth-largest navy in terms of tonnage, and by 1990, Japan will have more tactical aircraft than the United States has defending its shores.

An article by Peter Hartcher in The Sydney Morning Herald also points out that in two years Japan will have three times as many destroyers and five times as many anti-submarine aircraft as the U.S. Pacific fleet. All this has been accomplished by the Liberal Democratic party since 1955 by being "exceptionally adept at circumventing even the constitution's most explicit prohibitions, ignoring public opinion," the Australian writes. The Japanese constitution, pushed on the vanquished country by Gen. Douglas MacArthur's occupation government, specifically states that "land, sea and air forces as well as other war potential, will never be maintained." The Self-Defense Forces were envisioned only as a sort of reserve.

No one seems to be particularly concerned about Japan's rising military strength. But it is well to be aware of what has happened, if for no other reason than to keep in better perspective repeated calls from American politicians for more military spending by that island nation. It is also noteworthy that Japan is so well off that it has been able to accomplish this buildup by spending only 1.6 percent of its total economic output on defense. That is far below the United States' 6 percent or the Soviet Union's 12-15 percent. "Even placid Australia spends 3 percent," Mr. Hartcher notes.

Newsday

New York City, New York, May 23, 1988

It's not hard to understand why Japan's Asian neighbors are upset. Just imagine the outcry in Washington if a member of Japanese Prime Minister Noboru Takeshita's cabinet said that the Imperial Navy attacked Pearl Harbor in self-defense, or really gave the United States exactly what it deserved.

That's why Japanese Land Minister Seisuke Okuno, under fire from the Japanese media and opposition parties, was forced to resign after claiming last month that Japan's invasion of China during the 1930s was not an act

of aggression but a move to fight Asian colonization by the white race. Shrugging off his country's responsibility for millions of casualties, Okuno opined that the judgments reached at the Tokyo war-crimes tribunal, convened by the allies after the war, were simply "punishment of the losers by the winners."

There has been no real apology, nor even a clear public statement from either Takeshita or Japan's ruling Liberal Democratic Party that Okuno, director of the secret military police during the war, was wrong. The best

the prime minister seemed able to do was to acknowledge that Japan's wartime action was under "severe international criticism."

It will take something a lot more forthright to dispel suspicion that the mood of an economically resurgent Japan is to rewrite its World War II record of invasion, occupation and atrocities. Asahi Shimbun, the country's leading liberal daily, said that Japan "cannot leave things vague over the Okuno remarks" and must "accurately recognize the facts of history." Exactly so.

Takeshita Urges Larger World Role in Open Markets

Japanese Premier Noboru Takeshita, in one of his first major policy speeches, Jan. 25, 1988 told the Diet (parliament) that Japan needed to open its economic markets and take a broader role in global affairs.

"It is essential that we make Japan a country contributing to the international community," Takeshita asserted. "It is extremely important in terms of our global contribution that, maintaining free-trade arrangements, Japan ensure that its markets are open and that other countries have access to these markets."

Despite his calls for an increased international role for Japan, the premier pledged that his country would not become "a military power such as might threaten other countries."

Earlier, Great Britain's Prime Minister Margaret Thatcher Jan. 19 had called on Japan to open its markets to foreign trade and to reduce its trade surplus with Britain. Thatcher had made the remarks in London during a meeting with Trade Minister Hajime Tamura.

THE KANSAS CITY STAR
Kansas City, Missouri, September 29, 1988

C. William Verity is singing a different tune and the change is welcome. On his first trip to Japan as commerce secretary, he was aggressive and bellicose. He offered the strange argument that the Japanese failure to raise prices in line with the soaring yen constituted dumping. He hinted at retaliatory duties.

But on his most recent trip the mood was entirely different. Perhaps Verity has been disarmed by the sheer inertia of U.S. companies in key industries. Despite a new agreement providing more access to the Japanese construction market, for example, few American operators have submitted bids. This is a sorry statement, since every difficult negotiation with Japan takes its toll on the overall relationship.

In fact, many of our attempts to "protect" American industry over the last few years have only weakened this country and strengthened the leading Asian economies. Voluntary auto import quotas raised prices for U.S. consumers and pushed the Japanese into the high-end market; Japanese manufacturers decided that if they must import fewer cars, they might as well send the more profitable luxury models.

The misguided agreement on semiconductors, by establishing price floors in the U.S., only reduced the losses of Japanese producers facing a production glut. Memory chips, and virtually every product using them, are costlier today, thanks to Washington's "help."

The Japanese market may still be a tough place to sell, but access can be gained if exporters are willing to make the same kind of effort to serve it that the Japanese make in serving our own. IBM, McDonald's, TRW and American Express are examples of companies that made the effort and found success.

For the last eight years, Washington has pressured our trading partners for more access to their markets and, grudgingly, many have opened their doors wider. Now some are waking up to discover it has been a blessing in disguise.

Irving Ho, who leads Taiwan's efforts in computers and information technology, told *The New York Times* that the years of trade friction with the United States have "forced all of us to learn how to respond more flexibly. We're stronger for it."

There's a lesson in this for Washington. With the coming change in administrations, we hope at least some of it has been absorbed.

Chicago Tribune
Chicago, Illinois, September 15, 1988

The Japanese, as most American trade negotiators will tell you, don't make decisions without trying to reconcile conflicting interests within their society. So though their commitment to open up the world's second largest economy appears genuine, progress toward that goal is often piecemeal, painfully slow and not achieved without outside pressure.

Last week, for example, the Japanese agreed to allow a little more foreign competition in their financial markets. Specifically, the finance minister announced that foreign firms can participate to a greater degree next year in the Japanese government bond market, second in size only to our own government securities market. The announcement, although largely symbolic for now, was balm to irritated Treasury officials in Washington and bankers in New York.

In recent years, Japan has limited foreign firms to only a tiny share of its government bond sales. But in our hospitable U.S.A., six Japanese firms act as primary dealers of government securities and often buy more than a third of new Treasury notes and bonds sold through competitive auction. This has long been a sore point with U.S. officials. A provision in the recently passed trade bill denies primary-dealer status to foreign firms whose countries don't offer similar competitive opportunities.

Despite that threat, Japan still isn't willing to embrace a full auction system. Instead, beginning next April, it will sell 40 percent of each 10-year bond issue through open, competitive bids. The other 60 percent will be reserved for the Japanese underwriting syndicate. Many small Japanese banks and investment houses will continue to get their share of any offering and be protected from foreign competition.

This concession may seem paltry, but along with recent Japanese agreements to accept more foreign shipments of beef and oranges and to allow foreign participation in public works projects, it is significant evidence of Japan's commitment to open its markets.

Lately, American officials have been turning up the pressure on Japan to reform its arcane distribution system, where goods may change hands as many as a dozen times and small shopkeepers can, by law, prevent larger stores from opening nearby. This protects jobs but results in exorbitant consumer prices and prevents many foreign goods from reaching the Japanese people.

At the Toronto economic summit earlier this year, Prime Minister Noboru Takeshita pledged to begin deregulating his country's retailing system. In this, as in the opening of its securities market, change in Tokyo won't come easy. Washington will have to lean heavily on its ally to keep it on track. Progress may be slow, but nudging Japan to open its markets will produce more jobs and other economic benefits for this country. The alternative, narrowing our markets through protectionism, bashes our economy just as much as it bashes the Japanese.

THE ARIZONA REPUBLIC
Phoenix, Arizona, August 20, 1988

THE changing economic times have been traumatic. Its traditional manufacturing base is being assaulted by lower-cost imports. An influx of illegal immigrants, willing to work for lower wages, threatens native job holders. Societal mores — frugality, the work ethic, family values — are noticeably eroding.

If the problems seem familiar, they should. U.S. policy-makers are still debating solutions to such issues. But for Japan, the experience of factory closings, illegal immigration and lifestyle changes is something new. Prosperity, it seems, is exacting a price. Many Japanese already consider it much too high.

But Japan and its people have little choice. No matter how uncomfortable the Japanese are with their newfound role, their booming economy has transformed the Asian nation into a world power again, with all the opportunities and headaches associated with lofty international status.

As London's *Economist* puts it: "The country is being thrown headlong into the outside world — which in turn is fast forcing its way into Japan." The economic revolution is rapidly changing Japan's society, its politics and its foreign policy. The traditional, closed, homogeneous society is being quickly destroyed by the modern-day reality of expanding and interrelated international relations.

Today Japan boasts the world's second-largest economy and perhaps is the pre-eminent financial power on the globe. Its gross national product last year amounted to $19,200 per person, compared with $18,200 for each American. Its defense spending, while constitutionally limited to about 1 percent of its GNP, falls behind only the U.S. and the Soviet Union in total cash expended.

Even though its total economy is about half the size of America's, Japan this year is expected to surpass the United States as the world's largest donor of economic assistance to developing nations. Its military forces are participating for the first time in the United Nations monitoring of the Soviet troop withdrawal from Afghanistan.

Everywhere one looks in the world, especially in the rapidly developing Pacific region, Japan's presence and influence are growing. Following the path set by his predecessor, Prime Minister Noboru Takeshita has made 13 trips to 10 countries since he took office last November and has sent high-level emissaries to talks on such sensitive issues as Cambodia's reunification and the ongoing Israeli-Palestinian conflict.

Japan's emergence as a powerful force, no matter how involuntary, is troubling to many of its Asian neighbors and to many older Japanese who remember all too well the country's imperialistic past. Others, however, recognize that Japan, by virtue of its economic prowess, can no longer remain, in policy or politics, merely an isolated island in the Pacific.

Without military might and the will to use it, Japan falls short of superpower status. But its economic power and influence provide the opportunity for Japan to play a leading part on the international stage. The sooner Japan defines its role and makes peace with its decision, the better off the world will be.

Pittsburgh Post-Gazette
Pittsburgh, Pennsylvania, September 12, 1988

Japan's management methods have been so universally praised that it is a surprise to hear them questioned from an unlikely source inside Japan.

The Japan Committee for Economic Development (Keizai Doyukai) in its annual policy statement has declared that Japan is headed for disaster unless it jettisons traditional employment practices. According to the newspaper *Asahi Shimbun* of Tokyo, "The influential business organization recommends that such bulwarks of the Japanese work ethic as guaranteed lifetime employment and the seniority system be abandoned."

In the past, Japanese big business tailored management strategy to quantitative growth, expanding plant and equipment and increasing market share. That formula no longer works, the JCED report said. American managers who have been lambasted for failing to emulate the Japanese example will be startled to read that "the transition from an export-dependent economy to one based on internal demand, a new emphasis on profitability, and a need for products with high value added call for a U.S.-style management methods."

However, the report won't be all that comforting to old-line American managers, either. *Asahi Shimbun* quotes Ken Moroi, chairman of Chichibu Cement and one of the authors of the JCED report, as contending that Japanese companies are failing to adapt to the changing business environment "because management clings to the myth of mass production. But you can't run a service or high-technology business on assembly-line principles." Mr. Moroi adds that "corporations no longer need to hire large numbers of think-alike [management] recruits each year. . . . We need self-starters, individuals who can thnk for themselves."

Asahi Shimbun also cites Nippon Kokan, the steel company, as having changed approaches. "The firm used to penalize employees for even minor mistakes by delaying promotion. Now it emphasizes outstanding achievement instead. The company has established monetary awards for personal initiative and plans to shift to a wage system based on merit."

Finally, in another break with tradition that American management would do well to heed, "Nippon Kokan organizes brainstorming sessions, where employees from different divisions can swap ideas informally. Last year, it began allowing workers to take suggestions directly to the top."

The salient point from the *Asahi Shimbun* article is that the far-sighted in Japan industry are seeing the need to shift away from the winning "Japan No. 1" strategies of the past and to more American methods — but with an emphasis on cooperative methods that has meaning on both sides of the Pacific.

The Honolulu Advertiser
Honolulu, Hawaii, September 21, 1988

Japan-U.S. economic relations have been relatively calm lately. The trade imbalance has even slowed its meteoric rise.

But there has been a flurry of Japanese activity on other parts of the world stage. This is a surprise since many expected Prime Minister Noboru Takeshita to be less active than his more-outgoing predecessor, Yasuhiro Nakasone.

In the 10 months since taking office, Takeshita has made eight trips to 13 countries, including two to Europe and a very productive visit to China. Among Japanese diplomacy's recent string of firsts:

● A Japanese civilian was appointed an observer with the United Nations team monitoring the Soviet withdrawal from Afghanistan. Others are to join the Iran-Iraq peacekeeping effort.

● Japan's defense agency director visited Southeast Asia to promise that militarism will not rise again, a routine assurance as easily made in Tokyo.

● Japan's foreign minister visited Israel. Since Japan is completely dependent on imported oil and 70 percent of it comes from the Middle East, that was a daring move.

The Japanese people are trying to come to grips with their new status based upon economic power not intertwined with military and political might. "Internationalization," though ill-defined, is all the rage in Japan now and for the first time its diplomacy seems to have not just commercial but political and strategic purposes.

Considering the distrust of Japanese overseas initiatives that still exists in Asia (and among some Japanese as well), these overtures will remain cautious and tentative.

In its own interests, if not the interest of world peace, Japan has a role to play beyond that of "electronic appliance salesman to the world."

And in the many cases where Japan and U.S. interests coincide — as in Japan's support for the Sihanouk-led resistance in Cambodia or its urging the Philippines to make a reasonable agreement on U.S. bases — Japan's new assertiveness on the world stage will be in the United States' best interests as well.

Japan's '87 Foreign Investments Reported

Direct overseas investments by Japanese companies increased by 49.5% during fiscal 1987, to a record US$33.36 billion from US$22.32 billion the previous year, the finance minister reported May 31, 1988.

Japanese investments in the U.S. increased by 45% during the year, to US$14.7 billion, or about 44% of the total.

At the same time, the finance ministry reported that foreign investment in Japan had more than doubled during fiscal 1987, to US$2.21 billion from US$940 million the previous year.

U.S. companies were the largest investors, accounting for US$938 million 42.4% of the total.

In a related development, Japanese investment in U.S. real estate continued to soar in the first eight months of 1988, it was reported Oct. 9, 1988. According to a study by Los Angeles-based accounting and consulting firm Kenneth Leventhal & Co., Japanese investors spent a record $8.96 billion on U.S. property from Jan. 1 to Aug. 31. The study found that the Japanese, once considered strictly buyers of prestigious office towers and first-rate commercial property in New York, Los Angeles and San Francisco, now owned virtually all kinds of U.S. real estate, expanding their holdings of so-called mixed use properties (which usually combined condominiums, offices and stores) by about $1 billion in the first eight months of 1988 and their investment in warehouses and industrial properties by $270 million during the same period.

Japanese investors now owned $35.2 billion in U.S. real estate, an amount greater than 1% of the $2.5 trillion total.

The value of publicly reported Japanese corporate acquisitions in the U.S. had increased 8% to a record $13.7 billion in 1989, it was reported Jan. 16, 1990.

THE CHRISTIAN SCIENCE MONITOR
Boston, Massachusetts, July 1, 1988

IF there were one main theme to Japanese history, it might be described as the challenge a small island nation faces to maintain its distinctive identity while still borrowing and adapting endlessly – words, political ideas, technologies – from neighbors around the world.

The Japanese have a marked introspective concern with what it means to be Japanese even as they wonder how to define their "place in the world." Their commendable willingness to learn from others, despite a strong sense of national identity, sets the Japanese apart from the Chinese, for instance, whose sense of being at the center of the universe has left them largely uninterested in other countries.

But Japan has come only slowly to a more active role on the international stage – not without reason. In the aftermath of World War II there was every desire to prevent the rearmament of Japan. Now that the concerns of Western allies have shifted to the Soviet bloc instead, they might wish to have Japan assume more of the costs of defending itself and its Pacific neighbors. But the Japanese politely say, no, thank you, and continue quietly along with military spending at only a hair above 1 percent of their gross national product – a fraction of the proportion of GNP other nations devote to defense.

More recently the Japanese have moved into a new role as foreign-aid superpower. Last week the Cabinet in Tokyo approved a five-year, $50 billion aid program expected to make Japan the world's leading foreign-aid donor. It's not a role that Japan has come to without some nudging, however. For one thing, Japanese foreign aid has seemed intended to benefit Japanese business interests – construction companies, for instance – more than needy people abroad.

And Japanese tend to be braced for not being liked. The rice subsidy and other programs intended to keep Japan self-sufficient in food production are maintained in part because of concern that in another war, Japan would have no allies willing to sell it food.

But curiously, Japan often seems unwilling to requite affection. The annals of Japanology are strewn with Westerners who have broken their picks trying to be truly accepted by the Japanese, from Lafcadio Hearn, the turn-of-the-century interpreter of Japan to the West, to a more recent writer, Alan Booth. His "The Roads to Sata," an account of his walk from one end of the country to the other, ends with someone's telling him bluntly, "You can't understand Japan."

Meanwhile, the Japanese go on making their selective borrowings and continuing their study of English – taking care not to learn so much that their Japanese-ness is endangered. But a distinctive identity, like happiness, is better achieved as a byproduct than as a principal goal in itself: This may be the lesson the Japanese must learn.

Last in a series.

THE BUFFALO NEWS
Buffalo, New York, June 26, 1988

JAPAN HAS long been rightly accused of enjoying a free ride in defense spending, basking under the American defense umbrella and thereby increasing its economic competitiveness in world markets.

In response, Japan has made modest increases in its defense budgets, and now it is showing its world responsibilities in another area by boosting its outlays for foreign aid.

The Japanese government has just approved the expenditure of a massive $50 billion over a five-year period. The plan would put Japan slightly ahead of the United States in outlays for foreign aid and make it the leading donor nation in the world.

As a percentage of gross national product, Japan is already ahead of the United States, spending 0.31 percent of GNP on foreign aid, compared with 0.23 percent by the United States. However, this is below the average expenditure of 0.35 percent by Western European countries.

As the second economic power in the non-communist world, Japan has a responsibility in world affairs, but the memory of Hiroshima and Nagasaki has made military spending unpopular. Japan has officially renounced the use of war but maintains a small "self-defense" force. No one wants to see a revival of Japanese militarism, but Japan could do more to share the defense burden in the Pacific.

After much prodding, it has now brought its defense spending above the previous ceiling of 1 percent of GNP. This compares with a 6 percent outlay by the United States. Japan now sees the most important component of its foreign policy in the field of foreign aid, which has been exempted from budgetary cutbacks in recent years.

The planned $50 billion outlay is double the amount authorized in the previous five-year period ending in 1987. A large part of the increase, however, is attributable to the sharp rise of the Japanese yen in relation to the U.S. dollar.

Japan also plans to improve the quality of its foreign aid, which has been sometimes criticized for being tied to projects that brought big contracts for Japanese businessmen. There will be greater emphasis on grants rather than loans, and the money will be distributed both bilaterally and through international organizations such as the World Bank.

While Japan's defense contributions still remain small, the Japanese foreign aid plan is a welcome indication of an increasing readiness to share in the economic burdens of the free world.

The Augusta Chronicle
Augusta, Georgia, July 11, 1988

Why is it the United States can't sell what it invents?

In recent decades, U.S. scientists pioneered the technologies that gave the world color televisions, videocasette recorders and semiconductors. But despite this headstart in three major consumer product areas, it was mostly the Japanese who got rich off the opportunities.

And, according to the Congressional Office of Technology Assessment, they are about to do it again — in superconductivity.

In 1986 two IBM scientists won the Nobel Prize for discovering the magic ceramics that become superconductive. The discovery could lead to countless new electronic wonders, including magnetically elevated 300-mph trains and computers that work 100 times faster than today's models.

The OTA study notes Uncle Sam is spending $95 million on superconductive research, but nearly half of that is for defense. Japanese firms, with government help, are pouring $70 million into developing superconductive products for commercial purposes.

This points up a central difference between the U.S. and Japan regarding the marketplace. Most U.S. firms, under pressure to show short term profits and getting little help from their government, take a wait-and-see approach to innovative product development.

But not the Japanese — they jump right in. And they don't worry about profits until after they carve out market share. Unless there's a monumental change of attitude among U.S. executives, American firms will once again be left eating Japan's dust, the OTA reports.

The OTA's solutions, championed by Sen. John Glenn, D-Ohio, a top vice presidential prospect, is to loosen antitrust laws to allow more joint ventures among industrial companies and to increase government funds for commercial research and development.

It will be interesting to see how Glenn's party, which perceives "Big Business" as a Republican conspiracy to rip off consumers and avoid paying taxes, responds to these very "pro-Big Business," but imminently sensible, proposals.

Finally, there's one question the OTA didn't address. Why shouldn't the Japanese, who spend only $30 billion annually on defense compared to the U.S.' $300 billion, contribute to superconductivity defense research? They will benefit from it as much as we do. Surely they should pick up part of the tab.

The Dallas Morning News
Dallas, Texas, July 17, 1988

A recent *Business Week* cover story dealt with one of the more volatile and sensitive subjects in modern U.S. politics: the vast Japanese investment in the United States, especially in the nation's lobbying, universities, museums and community philanthropy. To date, the Japanese have poured $310 million into such enterprises.

There is nothing illegal about the Japanese investment, but questions are being raised about just who will be the ultimate beneficiary of this largess. Some contend that Americans are being subtly seduced by Japanese yen, and that we will wake up one day to find the U.S. a mere subsidiary of Japan Inc.

Critics of Japanese philanthropy and lobbying argue that a U.S. elite is being bribed to ignore broader national interests. Still, others see smiling Japanese faces at cultural exhibitions as a way of humanizing what is in reality an economic juggernaut bent on incorporating the U.S. into a Pacific co-prosperity sphere similar to the East Asian model that the U.S. fought World War II to break up.

There are dangers. The Japanese are no more likely to invest in ideas, institutions and people speaking against their interests than are Americans, and that can tilt the national dialogue in their favor.

But on whole, the Japanese investment in the U.S. is positive. Supporting U.S. philanthropical endeavors and universities and museums does help compensate for the cost of the U.S. defense shield around Japan. And unlike Japanese investment in Treasury bonds, there is no interest to be paid on gifts to libraries.

The fact is the U.S. and Japan are becoming bound in new and unique ways. The Japanese are investing here because they consider the U.S. a superior investment and a reliable long-term market. Their investments require a follow-up effort to see that the U.S. remains a good growing market.

The U.S. should benefit from Japanese influence just as it has from the influence of others who have invested so heavily in the United States.

The Honolulu Advertiser
Honolulu, Hawaii, October 15, 1988

A cooling of the fevered pace of Japanese buying in the Islands was predicted. So it should be no surprise that California, New York and Illinois have passed us as magnets for Japanese real estate purchases so far this year.

What changed? With $3.3 billion in Japanese purchases last year and $1.2 billion in the first eight months of 1988, much prime real estate has been snapped up.

And public outcry — most vocally by Mayor Fasi raising the alarm over Japanese residential purchases — has led prudent investors to slow down and look elsewhere.

As we've noted, Japanese commercial purchases have by and large been good for Hawaii, especially when new owners create new jobs and become good corporate citizens through respect for community needs and charitable contributions. (Japanese tourism is also extremely beneficial here, but that's another story.)

But Japanese purchases of homes (not just in pricey neighborhoods but across Oahu) and purchases and development of golf courses are far more worrisome and controversial.

Local golfers justifiably fear being denied access to courses because the price is too high or tee times too rare. Home owners justifiably worry that big-ticket home purchases will boost property taxes and change neighborhood ambiance.

But it's worth recalling that for every Japanese or other foreign buyer, there's an American seller. Many companies, home owners and real estate brokers here have done quite well by the strength of the yen.

So it's possible to say that foreign investment can generally be a very good thing in capital-short Hawaii, but the present slowdown can also be a good thing.

Sudden, massive purchases are felt more sharply here than in places like California or New York that are bigger and economically more diverse.

We want the best kind of foreign investment in Hawaii, at a pace and level that the community can absorb without a negative reaction.

Kaifu Sees Bush in U.S.; Trade Imbalances Discussed

Premier Kaifu March 2-3, 1990 met with President Bush in Palm Springs, Calif. and promised action to remedy the long-standing trade imbalance between the two countries. He returned home to face a storm of protest.

The hastily arranged meeting, announced Feb. 24, focused on the increasing economic tension between the U.S. and Japan. Bush told Kaifu that the U.S. Congress was in a "very tough mood" because of the U.S. trade deficit with Japan. He warned that Congress was ready to enact trade barriers in an attempt to close the deficit. The U.S. had measured its 1989 trade deficit with Japan at $49 billion.

Kaifu March 3 pledged that Japan would take action by basing future Japanese growth less on exports and more on domestic demand for consumer goods and services. The premier said that he was "determined to firmly tackle structural reform...with a view to improving the quality of Japanese life."

Kaifu did not promise any specific programs to make such changes.

Opposition leaders were quick to attack Premier Kaifu upon his return to Japan March 4. Tsuruo Yamaguchi, secretary general of the Japan Socialist Party, said that Kaifu had too readily accepted Bush's proposals for structural change in Japan. Other opposition leaders asserted that Kaifu seemed to have no agenda of his own at the talks.

Pittsburgh Post-Gazette
Pittsburgh, Pennsylvania, March 3, 1990

As President Bush meets this weekend with Japanese Prime Minister Toshiki Kaifu in Palm Springs, trade relations will be high on the agenda. A helpful background for that touchy subject was recently given to the America-Japan Society of Pittsburgh by an American expert on Japan, who suggested that Americans wont to complain about Japanese barriers to imports would be wise to take another look at the statistics.

James C. Abegglen, president of the Asia Advisory Service K.K., Tokyo, said that since new Japanese trade policies went into effect in March 1985, Japanese imports of manufactured goods have gone up 2½ times. In fact, manufactured goods now constitute more than half of all Japanese imports.

But if that's the good news, Mr. Abegglen went on, the bad news is that the American share fell to 25 percent from 35 percent in that period, despite the advantages that came from the fall of the dollar's value against the yen. Of that U.S. loss, the nations of East and Southeast Asia picked up six points and Europe — Germany, France and Italy in particular — the other four. The high growth rate in East Asia is not coming so much from the familiar NICs (newly industrialized countries) — Taiwan, Korea, Hong Kong and Singapore — but, rather, from Thailand and Indonesia. The potential of that total region equals that of all the European Community or of all North America, Mr. Abegglen said.

As to Europe, Germany's BMW alone has sales of $1 billion a year in Japan, and Daimler-Benz is busy purchasing Japanese gasoline stations to expand its market share.

"We have a competitive problem," Mr. Abegglen declared, that no longer can be blamed solely on Japanese trade barriers. He noted that in that same period, Japanese exports to the United States doubled — a major reason for the current $49 billion trade imbalance in Japan's favor.

Japan's capital investment per capita now is more than twice that of the United States. Its research and development per capita is equal to that of the United States, but in terms of non-military research and development Japan's is twice as large.

Mr. Abegglen said that it is true that the Japanese have some problems ahead, such as a labor shortage (1.2 million job vacancies) with inflationary implications. Recent government scandals have created a psychological crisis for the Japanese people, who have felt they had a system where all were treated fairly but now are not so sure.

But, he went on, in the U.S.-Japan trade situation, it is the United States that has the problem. "We still are not prepared to treat the matter as a priority issue — that it is *our* problem rather than the inadequacies of our trading partners," Mr. Abegglen told his Pittsburgh audience.

The American problems Mr. Abegglen outlined are familiar — low savings, low investment, deficiencies in our educational systems, management's short-time horizons and the high cost of capital, attributable in part to our federal deficits. The Japanese can afford lower profits and yet have more plant investment at the same time, he explained, because of 5 percent interest rates compared to the 10 percent rates American corporations face.

The Post-Gazette believes that the United States needs to keep pushing for a greater entree into the Japanese market. But Mr. Abegglen's outline should make it clear that blaming it all on the Japanese no longer will get the job done. We have plenty of work to do on this side of the water to stay in the race.

The Houston Post
Houston, Texas, March 7, 1990

THE FAILURE of President Bush and Prime Minister Toshiki Kaifu to break the stalemate in U.S.-Japanese trade negotiations over the weekend raises the specter of protectionist skirmishing between the two economic superpowers. In the interests of both countries, that should be averted.

At issue for U.S. negotiators are Japan's laws and regulations restricting other countries' access to its markets. Relaxing those barriers, we argue, would help reduce our trade deficit with Japan, which ran $39 billion last year. That is nearly half of the annual U.S. trade deficit.

The Bush administration is sending somewhat mixed signals on this prickly problem. During his two-day meeting with Kaifu in Palm Springs, Calif., the president declared that the United States should not try to correct the U.S.-Japanese trade imbalance by "restricting our markets or by managing trade." He struck a conciliatory tone, noting that Japan is our second-largest trading partner (after Canada) and that the talks were "a two-way street."

But the president's special trade representative, Carla Hills, warned Monday that the Japanese "risk having our markets closed or at least gravely limited" if they do not open their markets more.

Similar sentiments have been expressed by influential members of Congress, including House Democratic leader Richard Gephardt of Missouri. As a candidate for his party's presidential nomination in 1988, Gephardt called repeatedly for tariffs against Japan and other Asian countries with which the United States ran persistent deficits.

Furthermore, new trade legislation passed by Congress in 1988 narrows the president's discretion in applying sanctions against countries that engage in what the law defines as unfair trade practices.

Aware of growing U.S. impatience after a succession of Japanese leaders failed to comply fully with pledges to lower their country's trade barriers, Kaifu promised to move Japan toward a more consumer-oriented society. That's the direction we want it to go, contending that it would be beneficial for both nations.

At the same time, the Japanese criticize what they regard as U.S. fiscal and economic policy shortcomings. These include the huge federal budget deficit; U.S. corporations' grasping for short-term profits and not investing enough in research and development; poor education and job-training standards; and low personal-saving rates compared to Japan and most of the world's other major industrial nations.

The U.S. economy would undoubtedly be sounder and more competitive if these problems were solved — and they should be. But this does not alter the fact that Japan has been reluctant to open its doors wider to the United States and other countries' goods while it pursues aggressive export policies.

The situation feeds frustration and resentment among Japan's trading partners that can only be dispelled by a more forthcoming attitude on the part of Tokyo.

MILWAUKEE SENTINEL
Milwaukee, Wisconsin, March 7, 1990

President Bush reportedly got his dander up a little bit more than is usual in weekend trade talks with Japan's Prime Minister Toshiki Kaifu, and with good reason.

Kaifu showed up at the meeting without his new trade minister, a clear indication that he wasn't giving high priority to the biggest issue, from the American perspective, in US-Japan relations.

Bush, quite properly, put trade on the front burner, anyway. And he left, at least, the inference that retaliatory action might be taken if progress is not made soon in bilateral talks on such items as supercomputers, semiconductors, satellites and lumber products.

Deadlines from negotiators dealing with this matter fall next month, and time is short.

Kaifu promised to tackle structural reforms, which would tear down some Japanese trade barriers and improve the lot of Japanese consumers, too. He also talked about "a global partnership."

The US, of course, has heard this kind of talk before without results. But it looks like Kaifu, whose ruling Liberal Democratic Party survived a strong challenge last month, cannot rely on the president to be as good-natured as Bush's predecessors were about these stalling tactics.

The US trade imbalance with Japan was a hot issue in the presidential campaign. And the Democratic opposition in Congress would like to stir it up again. More importantly, American consumers are well aware that Japan's restrictive trade policies are hurting their pocketbooks.

If the president can accomplish a turnaround in that situation, the Democratic assault will be blunted. And if he is forced to do so with trade war tactics, the voters will see Bush as the first American to get the best of Japan since Gen. Douglas MacArthur.

That's a big incentive for the president to prevail, but he already has a hero's medal from one war with Japan, and obviously doesn't want to go that route again.

Kaifu's incentive should be to dispel feelings of economic enmity, from a country that is its best trade customer, by taking down Japan's trade barriers voluntarily.

That would be a good start toward an overdue resolution of trade differences between the two countries. It also would be a good foundation for that "global" partnership Kaifu says he wants.

AKRON BEACON JOURNAL
Akron, Ohio, March 13, 1990

CARLA HILLS, the U.S. representative, puts the circumstances of international trade succinctly.

"There's no question that Japan has gained its economic well-being from worldwide trade and worldwide investment," she said. "If it fails to open its markets to the same extent to our entrepreneurs, they risk having our market closed or at least gravely limited and therein risk killing the goose that laid their golden eggs as well as ours."

U.S. negotiators are telling the Japanese that they must reform their distribution system to allow sale of more imports and tighten enforcement of anti-monopoly laws to prevent Japanese companies from keeping foreign business out.

President Bush has added his weight to the discussion. He said trade barriers threaten U.S. industry and free world trade. Talks have become heated since they started between the two nations eight months ago, especially in light of the $49 billion U.S. trade deficit with Japan.

The Japanese have complaints also. They say the U.S. saving rate is too low; that business is intent on short-term profit rather than long-term competitiveness; that research funds are too limited; and that workers have insufficient training.

There are common-sense elements in the positions of both countries. Unfortunately, the logic expressed seems to be largely limited to comments on what the other is doing, not in addressing problems at home.

Prime Minister Toshiki Kaifu of Japan already has promised that his nation's future economic growth would be based more on domestic demand and less on exports, a strategy that would lower Japan's trade surplus. But no details of that strategy have been offered and previous promises of similar fundamental changes have not been kept.

Obviously, U.S. and Japanese business want a stronger bottom line. But negotiators have not reached a common understanding. They are not talking the same language. Until they do, there cannot be a significant improvement in the trade imbalance.

San Francisco Chronicle
San Francisco, California, March 6, 1990

THE JAPAN-U.S. trade summit held over the weekend in Palm Springs accomplished about all that could be expected under the circumstances. It was arranged pretty much at the last minute by George Bush — so specific action was not anticipated. The point was to emphasize the great importance of U.S.-Japan trade relations and to demonstrate that both sides are working hard to moderate a complex and thorny problem. That was done.

Symbolic progress must be followed by real steps

Now comes the hard part. Prime Minister Toshiki Kaifu of Japan was pinned to the wall of parliament on return with the question: "What promises did you make to President Bush?" This kind of "why-did-you-give-away-the-store?" query puts a man on the defensive.

So Kaifu made a quite reasonable rejoinder: "The United States is willing to have a dialogue with us. Do you really believe that a dialogue is bad?"

George Bush is in a similarly delicate position when it comes to Congress. He can talk all he wants to about "good will" and the sense of new "cooperation," but unless specific steps are taken, that destructive call for trade barriers will rise.

Bush has already said he wants to help cut the trade imbalance by reducing the U.S. deficit and increasing savings and investment. Still, the ball is in the Japanese court. Kaifu has got to show some progress on promises to reform his country's distribution system and ease other trade impediments, or else the sound of Japan-bashing will rise on the Potomac.

THE PALM SPRINGS meeting emphasized good will. Now that good will needs to be implemented. The U.S.-Japan relationship is too vital to be scarred in a trade war that would injure both nations.

St. Paul Pioneer Press & Dispatch
St. Paul, Minnesota, March 2, 1990

No sooner had Prime Minister Toshiki Kaifu learned that his leaky Japanese political boat hadn't been capsized than President Bush called him urgently to a summit that begins today in California.

While the president's action lacks decorum, it shows initiative in trying to get at a festering problem between two interdependent economic powers.

The United States is on a tight legal deadline to get Japan to make it easier for U.S. products to enter its markets, cutting down a whopping $49 billion Japanese trade surplus. If there isn't progress by April 30, U.S. law says this country must impose politically and economically tough trade sanctions on Japan that aren't in either country's genuine interests.

That seems to be the motivation for a midnight call Mr. Bush made just a week ago to Mr. Kaifu. Amid waves of political upheaval in Japan during the last year, the Structural Impediments Initiative talks have bogged down at the bureaucrat level.

Optimism about Japan's willingness to move quickly to change its economic infrastructure would be misplaced. Mr. Kaifu comes to the Palm Springs summit on short notice and with only the barest of job security. He is viewed as a government caretaker, and his Liberal Democratic Party just fended off the most serious challenge to its rule by winning elections last month for Japan's upper legislative chamber. The jitters in international financial markets during the last week show just how big a case of nerves has built up over Japan's internal situation.

Mr. Bush is right to push on the trade situation. Let's hope things move in the right direction — away from forced choices.

DESERET NEWS
Salt Lake City, Utah, March 6, 1990

Back home after their cheerful and optimistic summit meeting in California, President Bush and Japanese Prime Minister Toshiki Kaifu this week found much more critical audiences demanding to know what they had really accomplished — if anything.

The key to the summit in Palm Springs was economics, specifically the $49 billion a year trade deficit the United States suffers in its business dealings with Japan. American firms are increasingly frustrated over their inability to penetrate the tightly-protected markets in Japan while the United States is largely wide-open to Japanese products.

As Japanese success and the trade deficit get more and more public attention, there is an unfortunate anti-Japanese feeling growing in America, including in the U.S. Congress. At the same time, there is increasing and aggressive resistance by the Japanese public to giving in to American "demands."

While the meeting was friendly and full of familiar promises of cooperation, it lacked specifics for dealing with the trade deficit. The meeting was more like a public relations encounter designed to smooth feelings on both sides. Kaifu promised to "firmly tackle" the obstacles that tend to shut U.S. goods out of the Japanese market.

Yet when Bush and Kaifu returned home, their language altered to some degree. Bush claimed that he talked tough to Kaifu in language "just as clear as any congressman would have liked." For his part, Kaifu told party leaders in his own country that he had not yielded to U.S. pressure.

If nothing comes of the summit promises — including reviving the stalled Structural Impediment Initiative negotiators designed to reform Japanese practices that obstruct sale of U.S. exports to Japan — Congress may take matters into its own hands. That could be a disaster of significant proportions.

Congressional leaders say they will wait until summer to see if the trade issue improves. If it does not, Congress will come crashing in with its own remedies. They could be drastic — like calls already circulating for tariffs up to 100 percent on some Japanese goods.

That could lead to a form of economic warfare. While the Japanese undoubtedly would be hurt, they are not exactly powerless, since so much of America heavily uses Japanese products, including basic computer chips. There would be economic casualties on both sides. Any such conflict should be avoided.

Certainly, the United States cannot stand idly by with its own markets open to Japanese goods and Tokyo keeping its own markets closed to America. There must be equal access and fairness. But let's not panic into "Japan bashing" and tariff wars.

After all, America's trade deficit problems are not all due to a closed-door Japanese policy. Even if Japan were wide open, there would still be a U.S. trade deficit.

Most of the $49 billion deficit is there because American consumers frequently prefer Japanese products, which they see as being superior in quality and performance.

Until U.S. manufacturers can successfully compete for the business of their own fellow Americans, the trade deficit will remain.

Chicago Tribune
Chicago, Illinois, March 2, 1990

Celebrating the end of one cold war, President Bush doesn't want to get embroiled in another. So he'll sit down Friday and Saturday in Palm Springs with Japanese Prime Minister Toshiki Kaifu and try to ease the growing tension between the world's largest economies.

Officials on both sides of the Pacific stress that this is not an emergency session, but clearly it's of some urgency. Bush called the newly re-elected Kaifu late one night last week to ask for the meeting after two days of trade talks in Tokyo ended in bitter frustration, anger and more finger-pointing.

With much of the world undergoing profound economic and political change, the two statesmen must find some way to defuse the hostility and distrust between the United States and Japan. With emerging democracies in Eastern Europe and Latin America seeking help to rebuild their stagnant economies, demand and competition for capital will require close cooperation between the two economic superpowers. And with so much instability elsewhere, the Pacific Basin needs the continuation of a sound political, military and economic relationship between the two allies.

The complex partnership is increasingly strained by a stubborn trade imbalance—the Japanese sold nearly $50 billion more in goods to this country last year than they bought from us—and by rising nationalism in both countries. In America, highly visible Japanese investments have intensified Japan-bashing and given some intellectual and political respectability to the idea of Washington getting more involved in managing trade between the two nations. In Japan, politicians and business executives are fed up with the United States, which they see as a demanding bully incapable of putting its own economic house in order and training its people to be productive workers.

The situation worsened last week when trade talks that the U.S. hoped would further open Japanese markets to foreign investment and trade produced only a "defense of the status quo," according to one American negotiator.

There will be another round of talks before a progress report is issued in April, and both Bush and Kaifu have a critical political stake in assuring some breakthroughs. If not, Bush may find that trade policy with Japan has slipped into the hands of a frustrated Congress. The lawmakers, egged on by anti-Japanese sentiment, may push for a new regime of tariffs and quotas that will force up prices for U.S. consumers and eventually kill more jobs here than it will create. For Kaifu, failure to ease bilateral tensions could lead to an early ouster as prime minister because of rivalries within his ruling Liberal Democratic Party.

On the eve of the hastily called summit, Kaifu is saying the right things: He'll work to strengthen Japanese-U.S. relations, take steps to open agricultural markets to our products and encourage more consumption by Japanese families. That's fine, but Kaifu should also assure Bush that Japan will contribute more to Third World development, share technology with America and contribute more to its own defense.

President Bush should urge Kaifu to deliver on his pledges and work for the further lowering of trade barriers and restrictive regulations. But he should acknowledge, too, that despite our unhappiness at the pace of change, Japan is slowly becoming a more democratic, consumer-oriented, outward society.

Foremost, however, Bush must try to cool the rhetoric and cure America's irrational Japan-phobia. Despite the recent surge in foreign investments, they comprise only 5 to 6 percent of total U.S. assets; about 80 percent of that is financial—bank deposits, corporate stocks, U.S. treasury notes. We sorely need this foreign capital to cover our federal budget deficits, make up for our low personal savings rates and stimulate economic growth.

The president should encourage Japan to become a full participant in the world's free trading system and in its financial institutions for aiding developing countries. He should also assure Americans that no other nation is about to walk off with our riches, that vigorous competition and open trade is still the best route to a better standard of living, and that the only sound alternative to more foreign investment here is more savings and a smaller budget deficit.

Chicago, Illinois, March 7, 1990

Only a few days after President Bush and Japanese Prime Minister Toshiki Kaifu met to defuse rising tension between their countries, some U.S. officials were warning of a possible trade war and some of Kaifu's foes in Tokyo were delivering harangues about his "spineless diplomacy."

The hot rhetoric is unjustified. Kaifu has pledged to open more markets to U.S. exports and initiate economic and regulatory reforms—not because Bush pressured him, but because the changes would raise Japan's standard of living.

That couldn't have been easy for a new leader still trying to solidify his political base, but it wasn't good enough for protectionist demagogues like House Majority Leader Richard Gephardt of Missouri. "Nothing has changed," he huffed on national television.

Some frustration and impatience is understandable. America's trade deficit with Japan seems stuck at $50 billion a year despite the sharp devaluation of the dollar. Meantime, our trade imbalances with West Germany and Korea have declined substantially.

Japan could help itself in the United States, and elsewhere for that matter, by lifting more barriers to exports of satellites, supercomputers, wood products and telecommunications equipment, open its retail distribution system and end anti-competitive contract practices. Still, the country is shifting from an economy driven by exports to one more reliant on domestic demand. Its exports have held steady over the last three years while imports jumped by about 40 percent a year. But even if the Japanese were to remove all trade barriers, economists estimate our trade deficit with Japan would improve by only $10 billion a year—a mere 20 percent reduction.

That's not insignificant, of course. Yet it's evidence that Americans have a hearty appetite for the goods made in Japan. The way to cope with that is not to deny Americans things they want to buy, but to produce higher-quality goods in this country—to sell here and to market aggressively around the world.

THE INDIANAPOLIS NEWS
Indianapolis, Indiana, March 12, 1990

The mini trade summit between President Bush and Japan's Prime Minister Toshiki Kaifu several days ago did not get good reviews. In fact, the meeting, which served as a preview of coming attractions scheduled for April in Washington, set the stage for talk of trade wars between the United States and Japan.

Richard Gephardt, Democratic majority leader in the House of Representatives, quickly took advantage of the less than eventful summit. He barely waited for the curtain to close in Palm Springs before beginning his protectionist monologue on sanctions. And U.S. Trade Representative Carla Hills picked up on Gephardt's cue to add her own version of trade retaliation. In essence, Hills said that if the Japanese don't open their markets, ours will begin to close, thus killing the goose that laid Japan's golden egg — and ours. The "ours" is the key word in her trade tale. Trade wars hurt everyone, not just the targeted country.

Certainly, putting pressure on other countries to trade more freely may be necessary from time to time, but such action cannot erase substantial trade imbalances such as the one between the United States and Japan. Even if these two countries dismantled every barrier that hinders trade, the change would do little more than scratch the surface of the trade imbalance.

What would begin to tip the scale, however, is a good whack at the U.S. budget deficit, something President Bush has promised to work on. He also told the Japanese prime minister that he would work to increase savings and investment.

The first priority should be cutting the budget deficit, because no matter how much businesses and individuals save, if the government is borrowing to pay for its spending habits and thus running a huge budget deficit, that habit will eat up the savings, which in turn will not be available for investment. Granted, some government spending is investment, though it is not counted as such in the budget. For instance, building roads and paying for education should be considered investments, but not all spending falls into those kinds of categories.

Further, since budget deficits are inflationary, they drive up the prices of our goods and services and discourage consumers, both U.S. and foreign, from buying U.S. products.

Bringing down the federal budget deficit, of course, is only one factor in the formula that would even up the balance of trade between the United States and Japan. For example, the value of the dollar in relation to the yen must be considered, too.

Nonetheless, bringing down the budget deficit should be a top priority for legislators, even though it would involve spending cuts and/or tax hikes, two effective but politically unpopular tools.

To take the budget deficit in hand, rather than drawing up new trade barriers, would be the best way to make our products so attractive that even the Japanese couldn't resist "buying American."

The New York Times
New York City, New York, March 6, 1990

President Bush's weekend talks with Prime Minister Toshiki Kaifu produced yet another Japanese pledge of economic reforms that could ease the two nations' tension over trade. Previous Prime Ministers have been unable to deliver as much as they seemed to promise but Mr. Kaifu introduced a welcome new element. His aim, he said, is to improve the quality of life in Japan — that is, to make changes because Japan needs them, not because America demands them.

The bilateral friction turns on Japan's huge and seemingly intractable $50 billion surplus in trade with the United States. Removing Japanese barriers to imports won't remove the surplus but should reduce it.

It is unrealistic for Washington to demand a revolution in Japan's consensus-bound society. But Japan's friends in America and Europe grow increasingly impatient with a supposed "partner" who exports aggressively while limiting imports.

Mr. Bush proposed the meetings on the spur of the moment after Mr. Kaifu's re-election last month. If the President meant to convey frustration over the lack of progress in current trade negotiations between Washington and Tokyo, he surely made his point. If he sought an immediate breakthrough, he pounced too soon.

Mr. Kaifu had barely patched together his Cabinet before he was off to California to discuss fundamental issues he hasn't yet resolved at home. As Prime Minister, he has much less governmental power than a U.S. President. And Mr. Kaifu is further handicapped by the lack of a political following.

He was a compromise choice of the long-dominant Liberal Democratic Party when its leaders were disgraced by scandal. To make matters worse from the American perspective, all the major candidates took tough positions on trade issues.

•

There are two negotiations under way, both forced on Japan by last year's U.S. trade legislation. In one, on specific products, Washington is pressing the Japanese to open their markets for supercomputers, communications satellites and wood products. In the other, broader talks, both governments seek basic changes. The U.S. wants Japan to open up its retail distribution system, to crack down harder on antitrust violations and to encourage consumption. Japan says America should reduce its budget deficit, raise its savings rate and improve education.

In terms of pure economics, both sides are talking good sense — about the other side. America could improve its competitiveness by doing what Tokyo urges; even President Bush agrees, but offers half-measures. Japan, in its turn, could improve the lot of the Japanese, and its acceptance as a world power, by opening up. Its hostility to foreign commerce and investment serves neither its own interests nor anyone else's.

No one should expect miracles from the new Prime Minister, still struggling to establish his grip. But his willingness to meet on short notice and his positive response to the President's arm-twisting demonstrate a welcome tilt toward comity.

THE 🚂 SUN
Baltimore, Maryland, March 1, 1990

Prime Minister Toshiki Kaifu had better bring authority to institute reforms in Japan's economy when he visits President Bush in Palm Springs, Calif., tomorrow and Saturday. Otherwise, the United States will initiate new trade barriers this spring, against its own better judgment and to the detriment of both nations. Yet the likelihood is that Mr. Kaifu is coming ill-equipped.

With Japan's election out of the way, Mr. Bush invited Mr. Kaifu to join a high-level political push to the "structural impediments initiative" (SII) talks, which are stalled at the technocrat level. The U.S. urgently seeks reform of the Japanese distribution industry to give U.S. products a chance at redressing the $49 billion Japanese trade surplus. Washington seeks other Japanese reforms, including wider land ownership and higher Japanese consumption. Japan reasonably urges U.S. deficit reduction and increased savings and investment in return.

The deadline for progress is embedded in the U.S. 1988 trade act, which requires the administration to impose retaliatory sanctions by April 30 if Japan fails to open its markets to specified products by then, and to issue a report the last day of March on trade barriers maintained by all trading partners. Mr. Kaifu comes strengthened politically by his Liberal Democratic Party's survival in the election. He has named a 21-member cabinet with new faces and none prominently tainted by scandal. His victory over party bosses in this, however, left him little further clout with which to impose economic reforms.

The Palm Springs meeting comes after two weeks of turmoil in Japanese stock and money markets that illustrate the interdependence of the two economies. Early this week the Federal Reserve Board bought yen in hopes of stabilizing Japanese currency. The Tokyo stock market slide apparently responded to economic forces outside Japan, including the large presence in the world's largest stock market of Western financial institutions and their computerized trading.

The rise of West German interest rates, as Bonn sucks in money to pay for absorbing East Germany, attracts mobile money that had been parked in Japan, which accounts for the fall of the yen. The higher Japanese interest rates in response, and predictions of still higher rates to come, dampen the otherwise rosy prospects of Japanese industry, bringing the Tokyo stock market down from abnormal highs.

So far, the Tokyo market slide has not hurt business. Failure of President Bush and Prime Minister Kaifu to bring Japanese trade concessions sufficient to head off U.S. sanctions, however, would. The structural impediments to trade really do need to be reduced.

U.S. and Japan Pledge New Trade Openings

The U.S. and Japan April 5, 1990 pledged to move to eliminate some major structural barriers to free trade.

Under heavy pressure from the U.S. to reduce a U.S. trade deficit that measured $49 billion in 1989, Japan promised to seek changes in corporate spending policies aimed at boosting domestic consumer demand and curtailing monopolistic practices.

U.S. commitments to reform domestic impediments to free trade were somewhat less sweeping. Much of what the U.S. pledged, such as reducing national and individual debt, improving education and research and development, liberalizing imports of steel and machine tools and promoting exports, had already been articulated as policy goals in President George Bush's State of the Union address and elsewhere.

The pledges from the two trading partners came at the end of the fourth round of talks known as the Structural Impediments Initiative (SII). The pledges were listed in a scheduled interim report, which was to be followed by a final report in June.

Although trade negotiators from the U.S. and Japan hailed the agreement as a substantial step forward, many in the U.S. Congress were skeptical. The said they would be satisfied only by measurable increases in trade resulting from the agreement.

Such increases could be slow in coming, according to many analysts. The Japanese government would face opposition from some powerful interest groups if it tried to change many of the targeted laws, the analysts said.

Much of the U.S. legislation that aimed to enact the pledges made in the SII agreement, such as an administrative plan to encourage personal savings, appeared to have become bogged down in Congress for lack of funding enthusiasm.

The specific Japanese pledges included commitments to:

■ Open the nation's retail system. Currently, the system provided unusual protection to "mom and pop" retailers by requiring government approval of plans for large-scale stores. Under the agreement, the licensing time for such stores would eventually be reduced to 12 months from the current indefinite period. In addition, any retailer devoting more than 1,000 square feet to foreign-made goods would be granted an immediate license.

■ Boost public works spending, speeding up completion of projects including airports and highways. Such projects would provide potential markets for U.S. goods and services. The increase in such spending would amount to some unspecified percentage less than the 10% that U.S. negotiators had originally requested.

■ Loosen Japan's exclusionary business practices, which some American economists had accused of being monopolistic. Japan promised to strengthen antimonopoly laws, as well as its Fair Trade Commission. In addition it required greater disclosure of *keiretsus* (secretive links between some Japanese corporations).

■ Strengthen patent protection.

■ Relax restrictions on land-use policies. The pledge was aimed primarily at encouraging Japanese real estate development, a step that would most likely increase Japanese consumption of foreign goods and services.

■ Relax rules restricting foreign investment.

■ Recognize a recent survey that determined Japanese consumers paid on average 70% more for products than did U.S. purchasers, and generally target policies found to exacerbate the discrepancy.

In addition to its generalized pledges, which reiterated commitments already made, the U.S. agreed to export Alaskan crude oil to Japan for the first time. U.S. oil companies had opposed the move, preferring to sell only the refined Alaskan product.

Omaha World-Herald

Omaha, Nebraska, April 10, 1990

The progress made by U.S. and Japanese negotiators toward a trade agreement could help the two countries achieve a more reasonable trading relationship. We hope that skeptics in Congress will give the agreement a chance to win acceptance here and abroad.

The agreement was reached after four days of bargaining in Washington. The talks, known as the Structural Impediments Initiative, were devised by the Bush administration last July to address the underlying cultural reasons for America's $49 billion trade deficit with Japan.

This effort differed from other negotiations. For the first time, representatives reviewed each other's economic failings and made suggestions for changes. From the lengthy lists supplied, both governments drafted a set of commitments that they would be willing to make.

The Japanese proposals have strong backing from Prime Minister Toshiki Kaifu. But Kaifu is not trying to downplay the potential pain the changes could inflict on his nation's economy. In announcing the agreement, he promised that the changes would lead to an improved quality of life for the Japanese people.

Among the concessions announced by Kaifu: adopting measures to make it easier for foreign companies to compete in Japan's market; regulating Japan's complex distribution system, which makes it difficult for foreigners to get products into the country; increasing spending for construction of airports and harbors where foreign goods arrive; and reducing the amount of time it takes to approve the opening of large retail stores.

Some skeptics seemed eager to torpedo the agreement. Sen. Lloyd Bentsen, D-Texas, said, "Put me down as a skeptic who has seen too many (Japanese) agreements in which the results didn't match the rhetoric."

Historically, Japan has had protectionist trade barriers. It is easy to understand the frustration that some members of congress feel about the trade situation. Unfortunately, negative comments from political leaders give unneeded ammunition to Japan-bashers.

The credibility of the latest concessions is enhanced because of accords that were reached recently to increase access to the Japanese market for American supercomputers, communications satellites and telecommunications equipment. Carla A. Hills, the U.S. trade representative, said the new agreement should "facilitate capital flows" and "walk the two countries toward greater parity."

With a little patience from Congress, maybe the country can move closer to President Bush's goal of making it as easy for Americans to do business in Japan as for the Japanese to do business in America.

The Philadelphia Inquirer
Philadelphia, Pennsylvania, April 8, 1990

Michael Jackson, whose presence made President Bush's summit news on Thursday so picturesque, would have been perfect for the trade deal announced a few hours later. Picture Mr. Jackson moonwalking in honor of all the times that U.S. and Japanese negotiators have *seemed* to be moving forward, but weren't.

This agreement looks promising for the same reason that these talks did all along: The two sides avoided individual grievances and focused instead on the fundamentals that make one nation a low-consumption exporter and the other a high-consumption importer.

For its part, Japan promises to emulate the United States by raising government spending, breaking down anti-competitive arrangements among Japanese companies and letting U.S. retailers open stores there without ridiculous delay. But despite the benefits of freer trade to Japanese consumers, these promises must overcome powerful forces for the status quo.

While worrying if Japan will keep its end of the bargain, Americans should be even more concerned about what the U.S. government does. That's because the trade deficit is made inevitable by chronic budget deficits, along with too little saving by individuals and businesses. The U.S. is promising yet again to attack the budget deficit, and no other step has as much power to shift the nation away binging on deficit-financed consumption. But how to make this transition happen? Uh, oh.

Instead of taking Japanese suggestions such as raising the gasoline tax and discouraging consumer borrowing, the agreement reads like a cut-and-paste job from the 1988 GOP platform: lower taxes on capital gains, new tax breaks for small savers and big business, no new taxes for anybody, etc.

Even in the week when the national debt hit $3 trillion, why should the Japanese object to the White House's economic illusions? After all, it hurts Americans far more than it hurts them.

The Phoenix Gazette
Phoenix, Arizona, April 9, 1990

"Politics, as hopeful men practice it in the world, consists mainly of the delusion that a change in form is a change in substance."

H L. Mencken's observation is an appropriate description of the so-called "landmark trade accord" signed by the United States and Japan.

However, given the nature of Japanese and American political realities, the agreement is probably the best that could be expected.

Prime Minister Toshiki Kaifu faces tremendous political difficulties in translating the agreement's positive rhetoric into practical policy. His government is divided, with the lower house led by Kaifu's ruling Liberal Democratic Party and the upper house controlled by the opposition.

Opponents doubtless will attempt to frame the agreement as Kaifu's caving in to U.S. efforts to dictate Japanese domestic policies. The Japanese no more can be blamed for resenting the U.S. insistence that the Japanese "substantially" increase spending for public works projects than Americans can be faulted for bristling at the Japanese criticism that the United States contributes to the trade imbalance with its large budget deficit, low savings rate, short-term corporate planning and weak education system.

U.S. promises to remedy these shortcomings are worth at least as much as Japanese promises to persuade the Japanese government bureaucracy, which has great leeway in how it enforces and implements policies, to open the Japanese market to American construction firms.

As Professor John Mathis suggested in a telephone interview with *The Gazette,* instead of Japan-bashing, the U.S. ought to be setting its own house in order. Congress needs to reduce the budget deficit and to tailor domestic policies that encourage investment and growth.

Mathis, who is professor of International Management and Banking at the American Graduate School of International Management, also pointed out that the important thing to remember is that the economic pie is not a fixed size. The objective should be to make the pie grow for everyone, not to haggle over the size of the pieces.

Economic policies do not change overnight. It takes time and commitment. Mencken notwithstanding, the trade accord is encouraging because it indicates a mutual commitment to avert a trade war and work on those areas that have elevated tensions between the two nations.

THE PLAIN DEALER
Cleveland, Ohio, April 5, 1990

T he dangerous rise of global trade tensions is leading the United States to practice some diplomatic brinkmanship with its commercial competitors. Washington last week published a 216-page volume of its rivals' unfair trade tactics, increasing the pressure on 35 countries and commercial blocs that have failed to open their markets to international goods and services. Japan remains at the top of the list of nations that may soon be slapped with sanctions under the so-called "Super 301" provision of the 1988 U.S. trade law.

Any trade negotiation involves some risk for countries (like the United States) that believe in free trade. Although free-trade advocates may threaten to close their markets to punish unfair competitors, they hope that their bluff won't be called: Everyone realizes that no industrialized, trade-dependent nation can prosper by closing its markets and thus causing the contraction of commerce. Yet free-traders are unlikely to force any concessions from their rivals without at least threatening the use of trade sanctions.

The Bush administration recently has been playing a skillful game of "good cop, bad cop" with Japan, which enjoys the world's largest trade surplus. Like its predecessors, the Bush administration has achieved only limited progress in narrow sectors of the high-technology market. But by letting the "bad cops" at the Commerce Department and the Office of the Trade Representative absorb the blame for hinting at protectionism, the "good cops" at the White House and Treasury have been able to uphold the principle of free trade and thus avoid disrupting U.S.-Japanese relations.

Insulating the presidency from any accusation of Japan-bashing — a charge that might poison the bilateral relationship — Bush apparently cajoled Prime Minister Toshiki Kaifu at their meeting in California last month to prod his trade negotiators toward faster action. Treasury Secretary Nicholas Brady, whose department must cooperate with Tokyo in taming the volatile fluctuations of the dollar and the yen, reinforced that message last week in his talks with Finance Minister Ryutaro Hashimoto.

While Bush and Brady have been prodding the Japanese, Commerce Secretary Robert Mosbacher and trade envoy Carla Hills have been steadily hammering them — apparently with good effect. Last week's talks brought Japanese concessions on supercomputers and telecommunications; negotiations continue on satellites and wood products. The hard-driving Hills expects further Japanese concessions but has pointedly said that Washington is "prepared to review all of our options" if progress is not made by the June 16 Super 301 deadline.

Progress will never come fast enough to satisfy populists in Congress (especially those Democrats who have unwisely abandoned their party's historic free-trade position), yet the Bush administration's "good cop, bad cop" routine is producing results. It may not conform to pure free-trade ideology, but the tactic is a clever way to play hardball in trade policy.

AKRON
BEACON JOURNAL
Akron, Ohio, April 9, 1990

THE NEW agreement between the United States and Japan to reduce barriers to trade is an extremely positive step. Making it easier for others to do business in Japan would give American business the opportunity it has been seeking for decades.

Some skepticism on what the agreement means is warranted. Other agreements have been bypassed in the past and made meaningless.

However, it is appropriate to withhold judgment because such an accord has the potential to provide the climate for higher American profits and increased employment. It also could provide the vehicle needed to reduce the U.S. trade deficit, which was $49 billion last year, although it is unlikely that the agreement will change much overnight.

Little short-term impact on the trade deficit with Japan can be expected because some of the steps will require years to implement. Carla Hills, the U.S. trade representative, did say that the move should have some impact on the flow of capital and "walk the two countries toward greater parity."

As a preliminary to the trade agreement, more limited accord was reached to allow American business to sell supercomputers, communications satellites and telecommunications equipment. The stage seems to have been set in a meeting a month ago by President Bush and Japanese Prime Minister Toshiki Kaifu.

Japan will amend its anti-monopoly law to raise fines and name those who violate the law. It also promises to bring criminal charges in antitrust cases in the same way that such matters are handled in the United States.

The Japanese distribution system has frustrated the efforts of U.S. business. A special stumbling block has been the approval system required to open big retail operations.

In another development, Japan has said it wants to set up a study group to boost sales of foreign microchips to Japanese auto makers. In the past, few foreign manufacturers have been able to sell microchips in Japan.

Some skepticism has been voiced in Washington following the trade agreement. Sen. John C. Danforth of Missouri, the ranking Republican on the subcommittee for trade, said the talks had been worthwhile, but he added that "seeing is believing" in any trade agreement with Japan.

Sen. Max Baucus of Montana, a Democrat, said he was encouraged, but felt that much work remains to be done. And Sen. Lloyd Bentsen of Texas, a Democrat, called himself a skeptic.

Obviously, we have not heard the last word or seen the last volley on the trade agreement with Japan. But the accord is a necessary first step. Americans will be watching to see what happens next.

The Washington Post
Washington, D.C., April 8, 1990

JAPAN AND the United States have now made a series of remarkable promises to each other. It's a change of direction in their long quarrel about trade. Each has pledged broad reforms in its internal economy and even social policy. Each would serve its own people well, as well as its trading partners, by carrying out these promises. On the whole, the Japanese promises look more plausible than the American promises.

For years Americans have been complaining about Japanese protectionism, and with reason. But both governments knew that the real reasons for the huge trade imbalances between them lay much deeper, embedded in the ways that they choose to run their economies. A couple of years ago, they decided to begin talking about that.

Japan tolerates an extreme shortage of housing, pouring its capital instead into industry. It protects a traditional, highly inefficient system of retail distribution, which, with its cozy networks of suppliers and dealers, makes it extremely difficult for a foreigner to break into the market. On their part, Americans notoriously refuse to save enough money to provide adequate investment for modern industry. Their federal government aggravates that shortage of savings with its own vast deficits. The United States runs a slack school system, putting American companies at a competitive disadvantage. The litany is familiar. The extraordinary thing is that each government has now said that it intends to do something about it all.

Japan, of the two, seems more serious. Japanese consumers are well aware that their standard of living has been sacrificed to other national purposes. There's a pattern in Japanese politics of using foreign pressure as a lever to accomplish necessary changes at home. The American response, in contrast, is merely a repetition of the administration's goals for balancing budgets, improving schools and so forth.

For Americans, the key point is that their trade deficit has little to do with Japanese behavior or misbehavior. Any country's trade deficit balances the amount of capital that it imports from abroad. As long as this country chooses to keep living on money borrowed overseas, it will have a trade deficit precisely equal to those borrowings. The fastest and surest way to get the trade deficit down is to get the federal budget deficit down. When and if the United States gets its trade in balance, with exports equaling imports, its disputes with Japan will become more manageable. This time American trade interests depend less on Japan than on how well the United States government carries out its own promises.

THE SACRAMENTO BEE
Sacramento, California, April 7, 1990

Logically, this week's agreement between U.S. and Japanese negotiators to remove structural impediments to expanded trade — in particular, expanded U.S. exports to Japan — ought to defuse mounting bilateral tension. Yet it may not, first because the changes promised are too fundamental to produce an early shrinkage of the $49 billion U.S. trade deficit with Japan; second because reforms promised by Japan's negotiators must win approval in the Diet, the national legislature; third because key figures in Congress are spoiling for a trade fight with Japan and refuse to be satisfied until they see a lower trade deficit. Fourth, this is an election year.

Fortunately the Bush administration is less agitated. Trade Representative Carla Hills implies that Japan will not be on an annual "hit list," required by Congress, of foreign countries engaging in trade practices deemed unfair. Congress is right to be skeptical about a new set of Japanese promises, given the stubbornly high level of the trade deficit despite previous concessions dating back several years. Yet the sweep of the changes agreed to now is such that it's worth giving Japanese Prime Minister Toshiki Kaifu the benefit of the doubt. If he delivers, U.S. access to Japan's markets could expand dramatically.

Japan responded to a surprising number of U.S. demands that any self-respecting people might resent. Tokyo promised to crack down on corporate collusion against foreign firms, to streamline an antiquated retail licensing process that allows small "Mom and Pop" stores to block new department stores (which carry more foreign goods) for up to 10 years, to stimulate construction and allow foreign companies to bid competitively for projects and to speed up patent approvals and import clearance procedures.

In return, Washington offered little, mostly repeating past promises by President Bush to strengthen education and training, increase savings and to tackle the federal budget deficit. U.S. negotiators rejected more specific demands, such as increasing gasoline taxes, limiting executive bonuses, restricting credit card accessibility and eliminating the tax deductibility of mortgage interest.

If these and others among 80 specific proposals by Tokyo about how Americans can better run their economy seem insulting, they're no more so than the 240 items submitted by Washington to the Japanese, including one that would have major Japanese corporations publish the minutes of their board meetings. Too much of such gratuitous nitpicking only adds friction to an already troubled bilateral relationship. Congress succeeded in forcing the administration to pressure the Japanese to the negotiating table, and so far the results seem positive. Now it must at least be patient enough to allow the difficult process to work.

PORTLAND
EVENING EXPRESS
Portland, Maine, April 9, 1990

For Maine businesses, like others throughout the United States, there's promise in the lowering of Japanese trade barriers heralded last week.

But in matters of U.S.-Japanese trade, it's wise to be cautious. Despite other agreements, U.S. businesses trying to compete there — from retail toy store chains to public works contractors — have found themselves persistently frozen out.

Will this latest agreement, one U.S. Trade Representative Carla A. Hills calls a "good blueprint" for ongoing negotiations, change that? Only time — and ratification of the proposals by the Japanese parliament — will tell. As Sen. John C. Danforth, R-Mo., says, in any trade agreement with Japan,"seeing is believing."

If implemented, the proposals would open more of Japan's economy to U.S. competition. Changes could invite retail competition in Japan, where U.S. goods and large U.S. stores are not free to compete. And they could erode the notorious Japanese "tea house" system, through which public works projects are divided among major Japanese contractors in bidding effectively closed to foreigners.

President Bush has his own vision of what U.S.-Japan trade should be. He wants a two-way street in which U.S. companies and goods are free to compete in Japan and Japanese goods and companies are equally free here.

But the economic system which has brought Japan great prosperity since World War II is built on a different model. It is a system in which Japanese business interests are protected by stiff trade barriers while heavily exporting themselves. One result is a $49 billion U.S. trade deficit with Japan last year.

Bush has indicated that won't be allowed to go on. Failure to open Japanese markets will result in new trade restrictions here. As a result, progress has been made in areas such as computers and semiconductors. More is promised by last week's agreement.

It's essential. Japan can no longer be largely a closed market, selling but not buying in an open world economy.

THE INDIANAPOLIS NEWS
Indianapolis, Indiana, April 13, 1990

Getting beef into Japan will require more than the dismantling of trade barriers. The 1988 pact between the United States and Japan that tears down import quotas on beef, replacing them with gradually diminishing tariffs, won't guarantee an instant market for U.S. ranchers.

While the Japanese government slowly dismantles its beef barriers, Japanese cattle growers are working hard to find ways to raise cows that can compete with U.S. bovines. Among the strategies of the Japanese cattle growers is a feeding program that gets a cow from birth to the market faster and yields high-quality meat. Their experiments look promising.

U.S. cattle ranchers should take note of these efforts and not expect to automatically dominate the Japanese beef market when all the barriers fall. Now is also the time to be looking for innovative ways to sell beef, and that may take some extra work, including some research into the lifestyles and eating habits of the Japanese.

One U.S. meat packer, Hamilton Meat Co., based in San Diego, already has a marketing plan. It has hooked up with a Japanese beef importing outfit to form a joint venture. The U.S. company will process packages of seasoned beef for steak and sukiyaki and ship them off to Japan, where the other company will market the frozen meat from vending machines located near railway stations and convenience stores. That way consumers can pick up a package of U.S. beef on the way home. Not a bad idea.

That's the kind of thinking all U.S. businesses need to do if they expect to sell their products in Japan or in the other countries that are opening their borders to outside trade.

Now is the time to be aggressive. U.S. businesses cannot not sit back and wait for trade barriers to come down. Instead, they must constantly strive to better their products and find news ways to market them at home and abroad.

St. Petersburg Times
St. Petersburg, Florida, April 7, 1990

The truism that trade is a two-way street does not necessarily apply to the remarkable promises that Japan and the United States exchanged this week. If Japan keeps its part of the bargain, it will give more than it will get. Japan will become a different society than it ever was — not quite so hard-working, more consumer-oriented. The United States will save more, borrow less and invest in the future, which merely describes Americans as they used to be before Ronald Reagan ushered in the Age of Indulgence.

For their part, the Japanese pledged a long list of specific and controversial political initiatives, such as severe penalties for anti-trust violations, tax reforms to make more land available for residential and commercial construction, a 40-hour, five-day week, a limit of a year and a half (down from 10 years) on the time it takes to open large retail stores, 24-hour import clearance for foreign goods, and improvements to airports and harbors where those goods arrive. The Bush administration promised nothing of substance that it had not already promised Americans in one form or another: savings incentives, better education and progress toward a balanced budget.

Cynical members of Congress question how many of their promises the Japanese will keep. The same skepticism ought to be directed toward the Bush administration's purported concessions, which reportedly include even his 1988 campaign promise to cut the capital gains tax. There is no agreement in Washington that this would achieve the intended result of stimulating savings; much evidence suggests otherwise. The only certain outcome would be an iniquitous windfall for the rich, and if Prime Minister Toshiki Kaifu is counting on the U.S. Congress to rubber-stamp that, he should not hold his breath.

Neither should Americans expect the Japanese parliament to ratify everything Kaifu promised. Though Japanese living standards unquestionably would improve, the influence of many vested interests would decline. Kaifu will have a hard fight on his hands. That he is willing to undertake it speaks volumes about how highly the Japanese value their access to the American marketplace and how much they fear a protectionist Congress will shut them out. That the Japanese addressed their complaints about the United States to the debt-ridden materialism of recent years was a timely and true reminder of the real causes of last year's $109-billion worldwide trade deficit.

ST. LOUIS POST-DISPATCH
St. Louis, Missouri, April 11, 1990

One of the more elaborate international charades came to an end last week with the announcement of an accord between the United States and Japan to undertake some broad measures to make each other's markets more open to foreign trade. The agreement will do little to reduce the massive U.S. trade deficit with Japan in the near term.

This doesn't mean the pact has no value. If all of its provisions are actually implemented — a doubtful proposition — the Japanese market might eventually be somewhat easier for foreign manufacturers to penetrate, and American products might be a little more attractive to Japanese consumers.

The United States promised to foster savings and investment, reduce the cost of capital and improve education. These are very general goals that relate only loosely to the nation's specific export performance. The Japanese pledges were of similar character: to open its retailing system to make it easier for Americans to establish stores, to boost public works spending to give American companies a larger share of the contracts and to strengthen antitrust enforcement to give Americans a better chance to compete against domestic giants.

The value of these steps in reducing the trade deficit in the short term is impeached by the very fact that the two nations reached quite separate accords on expanding access to Japan's markets for supercomputers, satellites and telecommunications. These are areas where the United States demanded immediate reduction in barriers that effectively limit sales to Japan. Such agreements should be hailed; they are the meat of the effort to open Japanese markets.

As to whether the administration should now certify that Japan has made sufficient progress in opening its markets to avoid mandatory retaliation under American trade law: of course it should. Retaliation rarely makes sense, and the specific agreements are worth something. But more talks about specific markets, not more general pledges, are what is wanted — and needed.

The Atlanta Journal
AND
THE ATLANTA CONSTITUTION
Atlanta, Georgia, April 11, 1990

As the old saying goes in Japan, the nail that sticks out is the first one hammered.

What extrudes most irritatingly in the U.S.-Japanese relationship, from this side of the Pacific anyway, is the trade surplus Japan keeps ringing up — $49 billion in 1989.

U.S. officials did some heavy pounding on that point during four days of extraordinary bargaining in Washington last week — extraordinary in the sense that what was at stake was the basic restructuring of each nation's economy to reach an equilibrium.

Diplomats, as a rule, are more apt to make disparaging remarks about their counterparts' mothers than they are to mess in the other side's domestic policies. However, restraint no longer applies in the Tokyo-Washington dialogue. Each side insists the nagging imbalances can be corrected if only the other will change its ways. The Japanese want us to get serious and become a little more like them; we want them to loosen up and become a little more like us.

From a bargaining standpoint, our negotiators got the better of the deal last week. In exchange for commitments on U.S. budgetary discipline and tax policy that President Bush had made already in his State of the Union address, the Japanese promised drastic changes in the way they do business.

Hopefully, last week's compromise by Japan signals a widening recognition that (1) for its export-driven economy to continue to function smoothly, it has to be more sensitive to its trading partners and (2) the policies that have fueled its breathtaking growth have shortchanged its own people.

Indeed, the chance at a much-improved standard of living is Prime Minister Toshiki Kaifu's strongest selling point for winning widespread support for reform. Without popular backing, he will be at the mercy of political rivals and entrenched interests like farm and small-merchant groups.

Be warned. Many of the promised changes could be laboriously reviewed and possibly held up by a bureaucracy skilled in the arts of frustration. Some alterations also require legislative action that might take a year's time under the best circumstances.

Still, there are substantive reforms here, well worth investing U.S. patience in: accelerated Japanese processing of import shipments and of patent applications, vigorous enforcement of anti-monopoly laws, easing of foreign investment regulations, increased public-works spending, with an implied opening to U.S. construction firms.

Happily, Japan has at last in Mr. Kaifu a leader committed to carrying out these and the other promised steps, not just because they repair the U.S.-Japanese relationship but because they enrich the economic and social well-being of Japan itself.

Indeed, the general thrust of Japan's recommendations to America would, undeniably, be good medicine for what ails us, too, especially the emphasis on balancing our books, promoting private savings and increasing public investment in education and infrastructure to spur U.S. competitiveness.

Mr. Bush's standing is far firmer than that of his newfound friend in Tokyo, Mr. Kaifu, so there's no reason the president should be any less bold at taking political risks and guiding his countrymen to make similarly hard decisions for their own good.

THE INDIANAPOLIS STAR

Indianapolis, Indiana, April 12, 1990

In his speech to the Indianapolis Economic Club Monday, Tommy Koh, Singapore's ambassador to the United States, noted that the Japanese are the successful beneficiaries of American generosity, technology and markets. More should be made of that point.

When Prime Minister Toshiki Kaifu, waving the new U.S.-Japanese trade agreement, said the Japanese people must show understanding and cooperation in making sweeping changes in their business practices, the response of his country's retail lords was not enthusiastic.

There are signs that the hard-nosed economic samurais running the retail system may resist discarding the porcupine-like defenses that exclude Americans from their multibillion dollar monopoly.

If so, the trade agreement will be just a scrap of paper, the nearly $50 billion trade deficit will continue to erode the U.S. economy and American tempers will get hotter.

There is a lot of admiration for Japan in the United States. One measure is the number of Japanese practices hailed by Americans as models for business success. Another is the study and admiration of Japanese culture, sports and language in America.

But the tempo of Japan-bashing also is rising. And while the U.S. image and pop culture still have tremendous appeal in Japan, especially among the young, polls there suggest that Japanese respect for America is falling.

Japanese look at the United States and see problems: drug and alcohol addiction, lazy workers, too many racial and ethnic groups, greedy workers and bosses and not enough long-term investment.

They see "overwrought crybabies, grousing about trade problems primarily of their own making — product of a flaccid fiscal policy, an inability to make goods anyone would want to buy . . . Japan is tired of the whining about the difficulty of penetrating its market," according to an April 2 *Newsweek* cover story that analyzes Japanese-American discord in considerable detail.

Some Japanese intellectuals believe that America, like ancient Rome, "can bear neither its ills nor the cures for them."

Chrysler Corp. chairman Lee Iacocca says some of the criticisms are right on target. He adds: "We've got to address our mistakes, but they've got so many that never get addressed by themselves or the American press."

Iacocca derides talk of "too fat" management from a Japanese industrialist — Sony chairman Akio Morita — "who's making billions of dollars a year." He disagrees "violently" with the criticisms of American heterogeneity. He says we have more arguments, litigation and problems. "But never underestimate the heterogeneous nature of Americans and what really makes them great."

As for economic conflict, if the trade imbalances are not corrected, "there is going to be one hell of a train wreck" some time ahead, says Iacocca.

Japanese consumers, he says, would greatly benefit from increased U.S. imports. As for getting tough with Japan, he says a president who is determined to reduce the trade balance can do it.

The bottom line is that both the Americans and Japanese have far more to gain by being friends than by being enemies.

But President Bush must impress on the Japanese that it takes two to tango — and perhaps remind them, as Ambassador Koh suggested here Monday, that they got to the top with the help of a benevolent United States.

Houston Chronicle

Houston, Texas, April 7, 1990

Have the Japanese really made unprecedented trade concessions? Or have the Japanese shunted the United States off on a siding to wait and wait?

The negotiators on both sides are hailing great progress. President Bush, however, said the American public won't be convinced until concrete results are seen. He's absolutely right.

When American goods hit the shelves of big discount stores in Tokyo, the public will be convinced. When the U.S. trade deficit with Japan drops way below last year's $40 billion, the public will be convinced.

The Japanese promised to increase taxes on farm land, raise prices to Japanese consumers and deregulate their distribution system. The U.S. negotiators promised to balance the budget, encourage savings and improve basic education.

We don't know how difficult it will be to win approval in the Japanese parliament for tax hikes, deregulation and prices increases. If it is as long as it will take for the U.S. Congress to balance the budget, these trade negotiations won't have any impact any time soon.

Expect $40 billion trade deficits with Japan to continue for many more years.

ALBUQUERQUE JOURNAL

Albuquerque, New Mexico, April 8, 1990

It seems like much ado over a "first step."

The United States and Japan unveiled their trade accord with optimistic predictions it would begin opening the Japanese market to foreign goods.

But while U.S. Trade Representative Carla Hills praised the agreement as "substantive," she predicted it would probably have very little immediate impact in reducing this country's $49 billion trade deficit with Japan.

Despite the fanfare, the accord itself is only an "interim report," with a final agreement scheduled for sometime in July.

The hoopla suggests, however, that both Washington and Tokyo recognize that something must be done or the political pressure in the United States for punitive trade barriers against Japan will become overwhelming.

In Europe, in North America, the trend is to eliminate trade barriers, to recognize that unfettered economic activity is in the best interests of world peace and prosperity. The success of U.S.-Japanese efforts to bring parity to trade relations is a crucial element in maintaining this healthy global trend.

The New York Times

New York City, New York, April 7, 1990

The new trade agreement between Japan and the United States is promising. Japan pledges to reduce its barriers to imports and foreign investment. America says it will become more competitive. Neither will happen overnight, and some undertakings won't be fulfilled. But the fact of a broad understanding may help calm the two nations' increasingly contentious relations.

The agreement is an "interim report" on lengthy talks over deep-rooted practices that hamper trade, such as Japan's law that limits department stores and the U.S. law that won't let the Japanese buy Alaskan crude oil. A final report is due in July. The proof will be in the follow-up. Politically difficult legislation is required of both countries — and, even more difficult, new attitudes among bureaucrats and businesses.

•

Japan's commitments are substantially broader than any it has made before. Previous agreements have dealt with disputes over specific products or trade restrictions. Indeed, Washington proposed the broader talks in hopes of reducing item-by-item bickering.

Parts of the new agreement do relate directly to trade, such as speedier customs clearance for imports to Japan. New ground is broken by Japan's pledges to bear down on antitrust violations and price-fixing, speed approval for new department stores, stem the land price spiral with new taxes and spend more on public works. These measures should stimulate Japanese consumption and, it is hoped, boost imports. Likewise, in side agreements Japan said it would increase imports of U.S. supercomputers, telecommunications equipment and satellites.

The United States, for its part, has agreed to little more than existing Administration policy, including better education, increased private savings, reducing the cost of capital and putting out a welcome mat for foreign investment.

How likely is it that either Government will deliver? Prime Minister Toshiki Kaifu admits that some Japanese interests will find the proposals "painful." But he rightly points out that Japanese consumers would gain from such things as the wider variety offered by department stores, and moderated prices for land and thus housing. How much he can push through the Diet is unknown; his party controls only one chamber. Also, there's no telling what Congress will approve. In both capitals, some proposals will be rejected.

How much will America's trade deficit with Japan be reduced? That's impossible to quantify. The changes would help, but not right away. The important point is that the Japanese economy will be more open to foreign competition from all quarters. And the whole world benefits from expanded trade.

The Miami Herald

Miami, Florida, April 8, 1990

THE NEW U.S.-Japan trade agreement embodies one of judo's essential principles. Judo, which in Japanese means "the gentle art," uses an adversary's force to one's advantage. Thus, instead of resisting American demands for changes in Japan's "structural impediments" to U.S. imports — impediments that could have set off a trade war — Japan has apparently "given in" to the United States.

Both sides are rightly touting the agreement as a landmark approach to redressing the trade imbalance, now $49 billion a year in Japan's favor. But protectionists in Congress will be far more mollified than some of Japanese Prime Minister's Toshiki Kaifu's troubled colleagues in the Japanese Diet.

Some of these politicians will no doubt be perturbed by an accord that is a curious example of mutual meddling in the internal affairs of another country. The nature of the "meddling," varies, however. The United States, for example, has managed to wrest concessions that would impose changes on Japan's restrictive distribution system and land-use practices, increase its spending on public works, and lower trade barriers that have excluded some high-technology U.S. products. If carried out, these concessions would bring about immense transformations in Japan. Japanese consumers would benefit.

Similarly, the United States has agreed to take steps to redress some of the self-evident problems afflicting its economy. In the short term, however, these "concessions" cannot really be implemented. The Bush Administration agreed to increase the national savings rate, reduce the budget deficit, intensify Federal commitments to education and research, and to increase exports. These grandiose goals are all so desirable that hardly anyone would oppose them. But it is hard to imagine that by themselves, Japanese demands are going to achieve reforms that the Federal Government has not had the courage to undertake.

Yet even if Mr. Kaifu is stymied by several powerful Japanese constituencies, his government's decision not to resist American demands has averted a destructive trade war. That is an exemplary way to begin righting trade imbalances.

THE BUFFALO NEWS

Buffalo, New York, April 7, 1990

THE MAMMOTH U.S. trade deficit with Japan is the target of a sweeping new agreement with Japan designed to reduce the barriers to trade. Many previous plans to cut the deficit have not had notable success — except perhaps to prevent further rises in the trade deficit, which totaled a huge $49 billion last year.

Previous programs have sought to increase exports of specific U.S. products, but this one is unprecedented in that it seeks to attack the underlying causes of the deficit in Japanese society. Basically, Japan has agreed to try to persuade its people to work less and buy more — partially reversing the process by which Japan has built its economic might.

For example, Japan will seek a 40-hour week for public and private jobs, a limit now far exceeded in many positions. It will reduce curbs on big retail stores so that American retailers will be able to open outlets in Japan, thus improving competition and spurring sales.

At present, Japanese consumers sometimes pay 50 percent more than Americans for products that are made in Japan. Japan has pledged to curb the many anti-competitive practices that fix prices and limit distribution of products.

For its part, the United States has promised actions on its own to reduce its overall trade deficit, including proposals already made by the Bush administration to improve education and encourage savings and investment.

Japanese critics of the program complain that the United States is trying to remake Japan in its own image, but the Japanese government appears to be pressing the program in good faith as a means of improving Japanese quality of life.

The proposed changes are basic ones that will obviously take years to show any results. Many in Congress are skeptical. Sen. John Danforth, the ranking Republican on a key trade subcommittee, said that with Japanese commercial agreements, "seeing is believing." Appropriately, he's from Missouri.

Such skepticism is understandable, but perhaps unwarranted in this case. Hopefully, the new approach taken in this latest round of negotiations will begin to make basic change in Japanese lifestyle and buying habits.

The Orlando Sentinel

Orlando, Florida, April 9, 1990

As U.S. and Japanese negotiators wind up talks on removing structural barriers to trade, there is plenty of evidence that the two governments are quite friendly. After all, only friends presume to meddle so much in each other's internal affairs.

U.S. negotiators want Japan to revise its land-use policies and streamline its retail distribution — for example, switch to big stores and malls rather than have a jillion mom and pop operations. The Japanese suggest that we quit letting consumers borrow so much on credit cards, improve our schools and get the federal deficit under control.

Compare this frank exchange to the guarded communications between, say, the United States and the Soviet Union, and you can see that being allies means never having to say, "Mind your own business."

Rockford Register Star
Rockford, Illinois, April 11, 1990

The United States and Japan have been poised on the brink of economic tragedy for months. Last week they agreed to take a giant step back toward safety. That should be cause for rejoicing in both nations. For both Americans and Japanese, it can help assure continued prosperity.

The two nations, split by deep cultural and economic differences, have seemed to be moving inexorably on a collision course toward a bitter trade war that neither country wants and the world's economy could not tolerate.

That situation was eased greatly last week by an unprecedented trade agreement aimed at tearing down broad barriers and producing a significant new trade understanding.

For Americans, it could mean some relief from the crushing $50 billion annual trade deficit. It could mean expanded markets abroad for American products. It surely means easing of the threat of a trade war that would increase the cost of many consumer products and cut deeply into our standard of living.

This is not the end of trade problems between the two nations, nor is it the end of trade negotiations. Japan has not yet, of course, actually implemented any of the promised changes. And the tentative accord reached last week is to be expanded during further talks this summer.

But last week's agreement does promise to tear down many of the artificial barriers to trade across the Pacific.

Crucial to the new agreement was a brutally frank discussion of economic shortcomings within each nation. U.S. negotiators pointed out the need to deregulate Japan's cumbersome system for distribution of all products. The Japanese cited the economic damage done by America's huge budget deficit, low savings rate, short-term planning and credit-card economy.

Some of those problems are firmly rooted in the differing cultures of the two nations and thus are not apt to change. But, by recognizing and accepting them, the new trade pact could focus on those artificial trade barriers the two governments can control and eliminate.

That's a major move toward greater trade understanding, acceptance and improvement. It was the major step necessary for an agreement that promises to reduce trade fiction and to deliver broad-based reforms in the economies of both countries.

THE WALL STREET JOURNAL
New York City, New York, April 10, 1990

Trade negotiators from Washington and Tokyo have completed a pact that even Democratic Senate trade hardliner Max Baucus of Montana has lauded. Among other things, the Japanese would agree to loosen the restrictions on creating large retail outlets, increase government public works spending, deregulate the nation's distribution system and stiffen antitrust enforcement.

The Japanese concessions, which would benefit European Community traders as well as the two principal nations, is a continuation of Japanese efforts to lighten up on its economy. The bureaucratic elites at MITI made a show of noting the limitations of the agreement, and some U.S. interests spoke of the need for "monitoring" and "enforcement" procedures, evoking the world of nuclear first-strikes and arms-control treaties. At the more sensible level of the voting public, though, there is strong evidence that what Americans and Japanese want most is to receive the full benefits of a free trading system.

The Japanese electorate has demonstrated a desire for an open economy that more clearly favors consumers. Overall, Japanese imports shot up 40% between 1985 and 1988. The Japanese current account surplus between April 1989 and January 1990 was down 36.8% from a year earlier. This past weekend's agreement comes on the heels of Japanese concessions on the import of supercomputers and satellites.

Those who want to claim that the recent concessions are a victory for the Super 301 bludgeon should remember that none of the other nations named as part of the act have been so forthcoming. The Japanese have demonstrated how much they want good relations with the U.S., so much in fact that the leaders of the Liberal Democratic Party were willing to set aside their power squabbles to unify behind this deal.

But as the trade agreements go to the politicians in the respective legislatures, this progress could be undone. Some congressional Democrats have apparently decided that the party can establish its macho credentials by being Ramboesque on trade.

If the coming months see a revival of congressional Japan-bashing in the United States, the Japanese may decide that concessions don't produce long-term improvements in relations. They'll conclude, correctly, that Japan-bashing by U.S. politicians exists mainly to serve domestic political needs and is unconnected to Japanese behavior. More bashing or more Super 301 activity would strengthen protectionists in the Japanese Diet. Japan has its own domestic politics, where for instance the operators of mom-and-pop stores oppose opening the kinds of large department stores that will provide Japanese consumers the imported goods they've been calling for.

More than domestic demagoguery threatens the accord. In the past, U.S. protectionists have been mesmerized by the trade deficit figures. It seems silly, but it is an article of faith among many protectionists that any trade surplus is proof of unfair trade barriers. Congressional leaders have already declared that this pact will be deemed a failure if the trade figures worsen in coming months. The figures have dropped from their highs, mainly because of lessened U.S. demand. But in the course of normal fluctuations in U.S. consumption, they could widen again, through no fault of the Japanese.

For their part, U.S. negotiators made concessions in several broad or vague areas, such as the savings rate, budget deficit and the quality of U.S. education. Of these, getting the education system back on track would probably make the strongest contribution to ensuring the competitiveness of U.S. exporters.

For now, the important goal is to avoid letting relations between the U.S. and Japan deteriorate over trade frictions. With the post-Cold War world evolving and with the political economy of Europe being transformed daily, this is hardly the time for the U.S. and Japan to go off in a corner for a round of trade retaliation. The weekend's agreement suggests that these two important governments are trying to stay out of that corner and remain in the business of building a new world order.

San Francisco Chronicle
San Francisco, California, April 6, 1990

THE JAPAN-U.S. trade relationship is one that veers back and forth between near-crisis and almost-relief. Such volatility will doubtless continue as long as the trade disparity between the two countries remains at its present high level. So it is encouraging to see that three days of intensive trade talks have ended with compromise that should usher in a period of relative calm.

Japan has made what are seen as meaningful concessions toward reducing what are referred to in economic circles as "structural impediments," and opening up its market to more imports. If all goes well, there should be significant deregulation of Japan's intricate goods-distribution system.

Achieving structural adjustments won't be easy

That difficulty in penetrating the system has been one of the most sensitive chafing points for Americans. And many Japanese, as Chronicle Asia Bureau Chief Michael Berger revealed in a recent special report, have reason to be self-critical. One Tokyo office worker told him: "It is almost shameful that we have to be forced by the Americans to make policy reforms, which, in the end, are going to help us most of all."

AMERICANS SHOULD BE self-critical, too. Japan-bashing and thundering about raising trade barriers do nothing to help resolve a complex situation with emotional overtones.

The Japan-U.S. relationship is too important to be allowed to founder because of closed minds and failure of communication. Achievement of structural adjustments won't be easy, but this agreement surely points in the right direction.

U.S. and Japan Reach Final SII Pact

The U.S. and Japan June 28, 1990 signed a final agreement that committed both nations to reforming their domestic economies with the aim of reducing the U.S. trade deficit with Japan.

The 57-page agreement concluded the second stage of talks formally known as the Strategic Impediments Initiative (SII). The SII talks, unlike most trade negotiations that the two nations had pursued before, were dedicated to making fundamental structural changes in their economies. In general, the reforms were aimed at making the U.S. economy more productive and at promoting consumption in the Japanese economy.

The trading partners in April had signed an interim agreement tentatively pledging reforms. The final agreement committed the two nations, and especially Japan, to more concrete measures.

In one of the largest commitments made, Japan agreed to spend a sum of 430 trillion yen ($2.78 trillion at current exchange rates) over the next 10 years on public works programs, ultimately increasing annual public-works spending to 63% above the current level. The U.S. negotiators contended that the spending increase would heighten Japanese demand for foreign goods. The Japanese finance ministry had resisted out of fears that it would spur inflation.

Japan also agreed to try to increase public and private antitrust actions; reduce the time that it took to obtain a patent to 24 months from 37 months; loosen traditional protection of small stores (which tended to stock primarily Japanese products); break up the close business alliances known as *keiretsus*; boost foreign investment; introduce measures designed to reduce the price of Japanese real estate, and create an import advisory board under the prime minister.

THE SACRAMENTO BEE
Sacramento, California, July 4, 1990

The trade agreement reached by the United States and Japan last week — the latest phase in what's formally called the Structural Impediments Initiative — addresses problems in each nation that should have been confronted even if there had been no complaints from the other country.

In Japan, those problems include economic policies that sharply favor producers over consumers and that tolerate anti-competitive agreements among businesses; a restrictive domestic marketing system; and antiquated public infrastructure. In the United States, they include an excessive budget deficit and public borrowing; lagging savings and investment and profligate consumption; and an educational system that, despite a decade of reform, still trails much of the world in academic standards and achievement.

Under the agreement, each nation commits itself to address those problems; it's reported that President Bush's much-discussed change of position on tax increases resulted in part from the discussions in Tokyo that led to the agreement. Thus, as part of a pledge to increase the volume of imported goods, the Japanese have agreed to sharply raise public works spending, to enforce laws against bid-rigging and other anti-competitive practices and to reduce the time it takes to issue patents.

Similarly, this country agreed to increase spending for scientific research and development, to reduce the budget deficit and to improve education for the U.S. work force.

There are widespread doubts on both sides

of the Pacific about how vigorously each country will pursue its commitments. In many respects, the agreement is unprecedented, touching on matters that had always been regarded as part of the domestic political prerogatives of sovereign nations. Equally important, a number of the commitments made by each side — among them, the U.S. agreement to change its antitrust laws to allow companies to enter joint ventures and to allow the export (to Japan) of California heavy crude oil — are not likely to be domestically popular.

While those changes may well be in this country's best interests, like the implicit agreement to raise taxes, they involve political decisions on what most Americans would regard as issues that are no other nation's business. As such, the agreement is a declaration of interdependence.

With the growth of rival economies and with the end of the Cold War, the United States' ability to call the shots for the rest of the world would have declined anyway. But the pressure to make this kind of commitment would not have been half as acute had the country pursued more disciplined and farsighted economic policies in the past decade — if it hadn't been living on hundreds of billions of dollars of borrowed money. At the Houston economic summit next week, the the United States is likely to get another strong indication of how much its global influence has declined. Until it gets its economic house in order and learns to discipline itself, that decline will continue.

The Phoenix Gazette
Phoenix, Arizona, July 2, 1990

The unusual trade agreement reached by negotiators from the United States and Japan appears to wrap up the major issues separating the two industrial giants. Each side pledges to do its part to reduce the trade problems between the nations, so that's that. Or is it?

On closer inspection, the agreement might be more like each country's New Year's resolutions than signed-in-blood commitments.

For example, Japan pledges to transform its economy, making it easier for foreigners to do business there. It specifically pledged to increase its public works spending over the next 10 years by 63 percent, reduce the time it takes to issue patents from 37 months to 24 months, drastically reduce protection of small businesses and embark on zealous enforcement of price-fixing and other anti-competitive actions that have been accepted business practice in Japan.

In return for Japanese concessions, the United States pledged to move toward eliminating the federal budget deficit, to reform anti-trust laws to allow companies to enter joint production ventures and to provide more education for the American work force.

We hope everything is done just as the negotiators pledged. Perhaps Japan can deliver; we shall see. As for the United States, however, forgive us for thinking these resolutions sound like the country pledging to stop eating fattening food, to lose 50 pounds and to run three miles a day. It's possible, but it's unlikely they will be accomplished.

We are intrigued at the American promise of significant new spending for education coupled with the pledge of eliminating the federal budget deficit. This is a neat trick, one that has been attempted often in the past, and which has had no small part in getting us to the bloated federal deficit we have. It is difficult to see how we can deliver, at least not without major philosophical change in Congress and, presumably, major changes in how congressional elections are won and lost.

We wish the agreement luck. If its major provisions come to pass they will greatly minimize the trade friction between two superpowers of the economic world. And Americans would benefit also if the government ever got serious about eliminating the deficit.

THE BUFFALO NEWS
Buffalo, New York, July 4, 1990

HOW MUCH is Japan willing to change to make America happy? And can the United States bring itself to change at all where its freewheeling economic ways are concerned?

In a historic agreement, both are pledging to try. They should carry through. The goal is to reduce the American trade deficit with Japan, now holding at about $50 billion a year despite previous joint efforts to get it down. If it is successfully reduced, growing American resentment of Japanese economic power should go down with it.

The new trade agreement has been reached after a year of talks on what the governments are calling "structural impediments." In other words, the negotiators have been getting at the basic economic arrangements in the two countries that may be feeding the trade imbalance.

What the parties have agreed to do shows a lot about where they stand in the world economic order.

The Japanese concessions are those of a thrifty, hardworking and self-protective country to one trying to woo some of its tightly guarded wealth away.

Many of the American concessions — embarrassingly — largely involve basic reforms the United States should be making for its own good, Japan or no Japan.

American businesses frequently complain of being squeezed out of the Japanese market without being given a chance to compete. Several concessions are offered in response.

Japan will take away much of the protection of the small shops that dominate Japanese retailing, a switch that should help Americans crack the market and also get lower prices for Japanese consumers.

The Japanese will also reduce the time it takes to issue patents and will change the laws that keep tiny farm plots going in the heart of densely populated parts of Japan.

Laws against bid-rigging and price-fixing that already exist are to be more rigorously enforced, and the Japanese equivalent of the Federal Trade Commission is to be strengthened. And the government will try to attack the Japanese habit of tight relationships of companies, something so basic to the Japanese way of doing things that it may be hard to budge.

Tokyo has also agreed to a massive increase in public works spending. American negotiators feel this investment in better housing, roads and services for the ordinary Japanese will not only eat up some of the capital that otherwise would be plowed into export businesses but also might help raise the expectations of the Japanese people, making them more avid consumers and less assiduous savers.

In return, the United States has promised to work to reduce its federal budget deficit, which the Japanese all too accurately identify as the chief cause of the American trade problems.

Washington also agreed to provide more education for its work force and more federal money for scientific research — two obvious investments in a better future.

And it agreed to relax some antitrust laws to help companies cooperate in joint ventures, a change that must be handled carefully to protect consumers but may be inevitable as the nation faces global competition.

For both countries, the concessions asked by the other side are, in a way, intrusive. The negotiations have covered areas that nations usually consider their own domestic business and no one else's. On both sides, there could be resentment.

"Structural" change is not easy, but in this case, it is in both countries' interest to try for it.

The Honolulu Advertiser
Honolulu, Hawaii, July 2, 1990

Administration officials are saying pressure from Tokyo gets at least part of the credit for convincing President Bush to agree to raise taxes to reduce the federal deficit.

One Japanese demand in the just-ended Structural Impediments Initiative talks was for this country to clean up its financial act in exchange for Japan's promise to remove obstacles to trade and investment.

Japan's role in rewriting the message on Bush's lips may outrage those worried about the alleged "pernicious" influence of Japanese economic muscle on U.S. politics. But that attitude ignores that Japan is only insisting that America do what sensible Americans believe we should do for our own good — balance the budget, increase savings, educate workers and retool the industrial economy.

Likewise, what this country insists Japan do would benefit most Japanese, particularly middle-class consumers, through more public works spending, lowering land prices and increased housing.

Whether the accord indeed improves the quality of life in both countries remains to be seen. There have been many past measures promised, but the annual U.S. trade deficit is still near $50 billion and Japanese consumers still pay exorbitant prices for imported, and even preferred domestic, goods.

On both sides, the agreement requires legislative action, economic changes and cultural concessions that face considerable resistance.

Sadly, anti-Japanese sentiment has never been higher here. And Japan's new anti-American mood is a response to the feeling it has kowtowed too long to complaints about its hard-won success.

Despite the seeming success of the trade talks, little hopeful is on the bilateral agenda of the world's most powerful allies. That's dangerous for two nations so interdependent.

ST. LOUIS POST-DISPATCH
St. Louis, Missouri, July 8, 1990

The United States and Japan have just signed yet another trade agreement to facilitate commerce between the two nations. Unlike others before it, this one pledges both sides to undertake fundamental reforms to increase the openness and competitiveness of their economies. But the promises are so broad and ambitious that one is tempted to dismiss them as meaningless. That may not be right.

The agreement, known as the Structural Impediments Initiative, contains a surprisingly detailed list of commitments. Japan promised to increase spending on its infrastructure by 63 percent in the next decade, agreeing to the specific figure of $2.8 trillion. It also committed itself to vigorously enforce laws against bid-rigging, price-fixing and other anti-competitive behavior that has long sharply limited American imports. It will also reform zoning and land-use policies that retard development of residential real estate and the consumption boom that should accompany it.

The United States for its part promised deficit reduction, more assistance to education, worker retraining and relaxation of antitrust restrictions to permit more joint ventures. The agreement also contains a host of still more specific, though less sweeping, commitments to internal domestic economic reforms never before the subject of international agreement. To be sure, the pact lacks an enforcement mechanism. But the two nations have agreed to meet five times in the next two years and to issue annual reports on progress toward implementing its provisions.

The agreement may in the end amount to no more than a gigantic effort at moral suasion — but even that would be important. For the first time, both governments have taken joint, public aim at powerful forces on each side that stand in the way of freer trade. Moral suasion has proved itself important on issues from race to the environment. Why not on economic policy?

THE BLADE

Toledo, Ohio, July 3, 1990

JAPAN and the United States have finally agreed to a trade deal ending their contentious, year-long "structural impediment talks." One ventures that neither will try it again, because each country is asking the other to make changes that will be wrenching and painful.

As one Japanese newspaperman wrote, "We are one of the wealthiest countries in the world, yet we fall silent before U.S. criticism. 'You haven't got enough sewers, you need more roads,' the Americans say. 'Land prices are too high. Your distribution system shuts out U.S. products. And the exclusionary practices of your business groups are scandalous.' U.S. trade negotiators never stop. 'Abolish your large retail store law. Strengthen the anti-monopoly law.' Washington has a list of more than 200 items for discussion and action."

The Japanese editor, Tsuyoshi Sato of the Tokyo Shimbun, commented that the American list angered him, and he likened it to the third U.S. intervention in Japanese internal affairs, the first being Commodore Perry's forcing the closed Japanese society open in the 1850s and the second being the reforms made during the American occupation of Japan after World War II.

Yet, as Mr. Sato points out, these proposed reforms, if they are actually carried out, could bring major benefits to Japanese consumers. The huge trade surpluses fuel real estate speculation in Japan and abroad. "This wonderful bonanza doesn't do the average person here any good," Mr. Sato wrote.

Japan has promised to raise public works spending by $1 trillion — to a total of $2.77 trillion in the coming decade. It will try to make housing more accessible and affordable, ease import restrictions, impose stronger penalties on unfair business practices, and encourage more direct foreign investment.

In return, the United States will try to raise taxes to reduce the federal budget deficit, encourage higher savings, promote better education of the work force, promote exports including California oil, and relax certain anti-trust provisions involving joint ventures. Two of these — promoting savings and improving education — are very difficult, and depend upon basic changes in our society which the government cannot guarantee.

The agreement was reached because President Bush and Japanese Prime Minister Toshiki Kaifu want a harmonious climate for the upcoming economic summit in Houston. Basically, the agreement makes sense, and, as Mr. Sato pointed out, will help Japanese consumers as well as American workers. But it would be well to withhold applause until we see how it is implemented.

RAPID CITY JOURNAL—

Rapid City, South Dakota, July 2, 1990

Last week leaders from Japan and the United States agreed there was a connection between curbs and gutters in Kyoto and savings accounts in Spearfish. That could mean a quantum leap in the way nations relate to each other.

Of course, forecasting such a leap depends on the assumption that the Soviet Union and Eastern Europe will continue staggering towards democracy and market-based economies. There are dangers in assuming that, but for the sake of argument let's do it.

Seen in that light, last week's trade accord between the United States and Japan is startling. Both countries agreed to pursue specific — and possibly painful — domestic policies in order to prevent an economic war. Negotiators haggled over taxes and trade barriers instead of bombs and barbed wire.

For example, the Japanese agreed to spend more on public works in order to increase imports. The U.S. agreed to increase tax revenues and save more. The immediate goal is to reduce the U.S. trade deficit with Japan, but the larger goal is to preserve and expand trade between the two nations. It turns out, we need each other.

Along the same lines, the U.S. is negotiating a free trade deal with Mexico. Again, it involves pain. Some U.S. unions and industries fear the competition and oppose the deal, and the administration is moving slowly.

But the plain fact is, we need Mexico, too — an economically healthy Mexico. And if the U.S. is going to lose some jobs to developing countries any — and it is — then better a neighbor should get them.

Europe already recognizes the power of lowering barriers. In 1992 those nations will become one economic entity. To compete, the U.S. will have to fashion more deals like the one made with Japan and the one proposed with Mexico.

It's a different way of doing business, but this is a different world. And Rapid City and Mexico City are in it together.

The Seattle Times

Seattle, Washington, July 2, 1990

PRESIDENT Bush tried to muffle his bombshell about tax revenues by making the announcement on the day Nelson Mandela addressed Congress, and Cabinet secretaries talked about offshore oil drilling and spotted owls.

One key audience thousands of miles away was not distracted. What Bush did not want U.S. voters to notice came through loud and clear in Tokyo.

A presidential concession on raising taxes to offset federal budget deficits and outstanding debt was a key Japanese demand at the year-long Structural Impediments Initiative talks.

The negotiations with the stilted name were more akin to truce talks between combatants in an undeclared economic war. Each side accused the other having deep-seated societal problems that aggravated their economic differences.

In a rude shorthand, the Japanese said the United States suffered massive trade deficits because it squandered money, and because U.S. schools and industrial training produced workers who made shoddy goods no one wanted to buy.

The United States portrayed the Japanese as tightwad protectionists. Washington could not be as nasty because Japan has been buying the U.S. Treasury paper that bankrolls government operations.

After Bush moved his lips last Tuesday about new taxes, the talks quickly moved toward a conclusion. Prime Minister Toshiki Kaifu promised to increase spending for public works over the next 10 years to $2.76 trillion, and to make $162 billion in capital investments in the Nippon Telegraph & Telephone Corp. and Japan Railways.

These were key points for U.S. negotiators because they represent major opportunities for American electronic sales and construction contractors.

Japan promised to untangle its import and patent processes, and allow the kind of large retail stores that might carry U.S. goods. Bush pledged to improve American education and worker training, which must have been galling. It is one thing to campaign as the education president; it is quite another to admit failure in order to keep qualifying for loans.

Moreover, what Bush could not be cajoled into doing by Democrats, or restrained from doing by Republicans, the Japanese were able to finesse: They moved his lips on taxes.

Newsday

New York City, New York, July 8, 1990

The idea behind the U.S.-Japanese trade agreement last week is simple enough:

The United States has a trade deficit with Japan because Japanese spend too little (and so don't buy many U.S. goods) while Americans spend too much (buying too much of everything, including Japanese imports). Now we're going to change that.

It's not nearly that simple, of course, nor is the outcome at all sure. But at the moment, it's the best game in town.

The analysis behind the trade pact is just fine: The Japanese are famous savers and Americans (and their federal government) have borrowed ravenously and consumed more than they've produced. That is indeed one of the roots of the U.S. trade problem.

To say that changing all that will be difficult is a gross understatement. It will require shifting deep-seated governmental, commercial and consumer habits in Japan and entrenched political practices here. Although all the U.S. policy shifts are desirable, we haven't had the will to do them before. Will we now?

Still, it's worth a try: Chipping away at Japanese markets piecemeal, as our trade officials have done in the past, may win a few contracts for a few big U.S. companies, but it won't correct imbalances between the two economies. Besides, some observers think Japanese consumers are eager to consume more anyway.

The trade agreement requires that the Japanese increase public-works spending to sop up excess savings; discourage high-cost farms that require trade protection; free up the retail distribution system to let outsiders in; crack down on corporate monopolies that dominate some markets, and speed up patent awards to better protect U.S. inventions.

It demands that America cut federal deficits, the biggest drag on U.S. savings; educate workers better; increase research spending; loosen antitrust law to allow internationally competitive business consortiums, and permit sales of Alaskan oil to Japan.

Not one bad idea there. Still, some skeptics argue that those changes just won't come about or, if they do, they won't be enough or will take too long. But perhaps the biggest problem is the risk of exacting new concessions from Japan just as the Japanese are coming to realize their country's strength. Some Japanese even argue that maintaining a trade surplus is a good policy goal.

So the potential for a serious new conflict between the two major Pacific allies is there. That means leaders on both sides must walk a delicate diplomatic line, pushing the other to act without lighting any fuses. Failure — and a resurgence of extreme U.S. protectionism — would be too damaging to be thinkable.

San Francisco Chronicle

San Francisco, California, July 2, 1990

SOME MAJOR STEPS were taken by both Japan and the United States in their recent agreement aimed at reducing the current trade imbalance. These were steps meant to address underlying causes of the trade disparity, and, as a result, they tended to address broad issues generally — without the tough specificity some may have wished.

The question must be raised: is this another well-intentioned exercise in futility? Will this supposedly surefire way to reduce the huge U.S. trade deficit turn into a trap?

Addressing 'structural' reasons for the imbalance

If anything, as a news analysis by financial writer John Eckhouse so cogently points out, the Structural Impediments Initiative signed last week with Tokyo may have as little impact on the $1 billion-a-week deficit with Japan as have all the other past agreements between the two countries.

Indeed, the SII may wind up strengthening the Japanese economy by prompting Tokyo to spend $2 trillion in the next decade on public works improvements. That could lead to a Japan that is even stronger financially.

BEARING ALL THIS in mind, it would still behoove politicians in both countries to hold off the standard sniping. An effort has been made. Let's see how the figures fall.

The Courier-Journal

Louisville, Kentucky, July 5, 1990

IT SHOULDN'T require trade friction with Japan to prompt America to live within its means and to invest more in research and development and in education. And it shouldn't take U.S. bullying to force political leaders in Tokyo to give Japanese consumers a break and to build more badly needed housing, roads and sewers.

Things shouldn't work this way, but they do. U.S. and Japanese trade negotiators reached an agreement last week under which both countries would make far-reaching changes in their economic policies in an effort to reduce Japan's $50 billion surplus in trade with America.

The agreement on removing "structural impediments" to more balanced trade between the two would require Americans, and their government,

> 'The important thing is for politicians . . . not to add to popular fears and resentments. In a recent series of articles on U.S.-Japanese relations, *The Wall Street Journal* found that these feelings are growing, especially among the young.'

to behave more like the Japanese — meaning they'd start spending less and saving more. The Japanese would do just the opposite. They'd start spending more — and so would their government.

How do you get people to change their spending and saving habits? The agreement calls on the respective governments to take the lead. The U.S. government would reduce its budget deficit and provide more incentives for individual saving. The Japanese government would break up business cartels that keep consumer prices high and would spend more on the basic infrastructure.

Frankly, we're skeptical that either government will live up to this agreement — or that the Japanese and American people will change their economic behavior in the unlikely event that their governments make basic policy changes.

But if this whole exercise is necessary to head off a protectionist orgy in Congress, so be it.

We just wish everyone in Washington would look at the benefits of current U.S.-Japanese trade relations. Americans get a chance to buy products they want at prices they're willing to pay. Yes, that means billions of dollars get shipped to Japan each year. Eventually, however, these dollars end up back in the United States in the form of private, job-creating investment or financing of our government debt. And the average American family gets to live better than the average Japanese. If either side is getting cheated in this exchange, surely it's not the U.S.

This isn't to suggest that Americans can afford to be complacent. Our over-all trade deficit, as opposed to our bilateral deficit with Japan, is worrisome because it suggests we are becoming less competitive in the world market. Some of the steps in the agreement with Japan — especially a bigger investment in education — would address that problem.

The important thing is for politicians in Tokyo and Washington not to add to popular fears and resentments. In a recent series of articles on U.S.-Japanese relations, *The Wall Street Journal* found that these feelings are growing, especially among the young. As the Cold War with the Soviet Union comes to an end, do we really want to risk a mutually destructive trade war with Japan?

Debate Rages Over High-Tech Products

International Business Machines Corp. (IBM) April 1, 1988 confirmed that for over two years it had secretly supplied several of its U.S. and European competitors with state-of-the-art computer chips.

The IBM statement followed claims made by former Commerce Department chief trade negotiator Clyde Prestowitz. In his book *Trading Places: How We Allowed Japan to Take the Lead*, Prestowitz had revealed that IBM had offered to supply chips, the core technology in advanced computers, to Digital Equipment Corp. (DEC).

According to Prestowitz, IBM had made the unprecedented offer in order to prevent DEC, its greatest competitor, from becoming increasingly dependent on Japanese suppliers. Previously, IBM had refused to sell its semiconductors to competitors, and had used them only in its own equipment.

IBM denied that its aim had been to prevent its competitors from becoming dependent on Japanese chips. It claimed instead that it had sought to sharpen its own competitiveness by allowing its competitors to choose freely between its chips and those of Japanese suppliers, such as Fujitsu Ltd. and Hitachi Ltd. IBM also refused to identify which competitors had been offered the choice, confirming only that fewer than a dozen had.

IBM denied that it had acted in response to U.S. Government pressure, stating that it had sold only the chips themselves, not the underlying designs or process technology. On numerous occasions, the U.S. government had made clear its wish that IBM sell chips to U.S. companies to keep them independent of Japanese suppliers.

The Japanese government April 4, 1988 charged two Tokyo-based trading companies with illegally selling sophisticated electronic measuring equipment to China. The sales violated regulations of the international Coordinating Committee for Multilateral Export Controls (Cocom), which barred the transfer of certain types of high-technology products to communist countries, officials of Japan's ministry for trade and industry said.

One of the companies, Kyokuto Shokai Co., a chemical and equipment trader, was believed to have shipped five digital memory devices, a signal analyzer and a sample oscilloscope to China between June 1985 and June 1986. The equipment, used for computer manufacturing, was worth about 34 million yen (U.S.$273,000). The other firm, Shinsei Koeki Co., a textile and electronics trader, allegedly shipped two sets of digital memory devices to China between August 1986 and November 1986. The devices were worth a total of about 14 million yen (US$112,000).

Japanese police April 5 raided the trading companies' headquarters in search of evidence to support the charges.

Police sources April 6 claimed that executives of the two companies had admitted under questioning that their firms had sold the equipment to China and had been aware that such sales violated Cocom restrictions, the *Journal of Commerce* reported.

The Japanese government had begun investigating the companies after receiving a tip from U.S. authorities in August 1987, news reports said.

In July 1987, in the wake of revelations that Toshiba Machine Co. had been engaged in illegal dealings with the Soviet Union, Tokyo had promised the Reagan administration that it would crack down on companies violating high-technology export restrictions.

THE BLADE

Toledo, Ohio, March 31, 1991

DESPITE the literally smashing success of U.S. weapons in the Gulf war — which has led to a wave of "we can do it" thinking in this country — technology experts warn that the country's lead has been slipping or already lost in some vital areas.

According to a study by the Council on Competitiveness, a group of corporate, university, and labor leaders, the United States leads or is holding its own in 61 of 94 technologies regarded as important to economic prosperity, including such areas as rocket engines, computer software, biotechnology, advanced welding techniques, and environmental cleanup technology. It is competitive in fiber optics, superconductors, and alternative fuel engines.

However, the United States is slipping behind in fuel-efficient engines, liquid-crystal displays for computers, computer memory chips, and new materials, all of which must be regarded as being at the forefront of modern technology. In too many areas the United States has been coasting or living off the technological achievements of earlier years.

Unfortunately, it is easier to diagnose the problems than to solve them. American universities are the best in the world, considered across the board, and these are still the major centers of research in many fields. However, in many cases foreign students are taking the place of American researchers because there are not enough of the latter to go around.

While there are many structural changes that can be made to improve the flow of research to the industries and laboratories that can perfect and apply the knowledge to products, the major problem is that too many young Americans are avoiding the tougher disciplines in science, advanced mathematics, and engineering.

In recent years our society has made it quite clear that a knowledge of how to use junk bonds to leverage buyouts of large companies is a far more remunerative line of work than the hard sciences.

That may be changing now. Despite this country's undoubted lead in military matters, the landing from the giddy flights of Reaganomics has been a hard one. It is difficult to fly without wings. We should be grateful that the country is still doing as well as it is in many major fields of technology. However, the world is changing rapidly, and this country has yet to shake itself free from its Cold War mentality. All the flag-waving in the world won't restore leadership in an industrial field where we quail at the thought of competing.

The Courier-Journal

Louisville, Kentucky, March 9, 1991

NATIONAL security depends on more than weapons — it depends on economic strength as well. The technical skills that helped develop the Patriot and cruise missiles are part of what makes this country strong. Another part, however, is our ability to create and produce non-military products for the world market.

Americans invented video, but the Japanese are building all our VCRs. An American came up with the concept of high-speed magnetic levitation trains, but the Germans and Japanese actually built them. Innovations in cars, television sets, computer chips and machine tools often come from countries other than our own. In fact, an increasing number of the components of those high-tech weapons we're so proud of come from foreign suppliers.

This "technology gap" between military and commercial industries is causing concern. Senate Majority Leader George Mitchell asked in the Democratic response to the State of the Union message, "If we can make the best smart bomb, why can't we make the best VCR?" Of course we could, if we cared to. But this year, of the $71 billion the U.S. government will spend on research and development, only 2 percent is for R&D with commercial applications.

There's evidence of a connection between our superior technology in weaponry and our lagging technology in commercial production. According to Lloyd Dumas, a political economist at the University of Texas, 30 percent of our engineering and scientific talent is working on military technology. And, although Japan's top engi-

neering graduates go to work for companies like Sony, almost all of ours go to work for government contractors. After all, government contractors don't have to be competitive; they can pay higher salaries and provide better laboratories. And design — not the need to get to the market quickly and hold down costs — is paramount.

Further, universities — because of their large R&D grants from the Defense Department — are less of a resource for commercial industry. Over time, their engineering courses have come to emphasize rockets, for example, over cars.

Concern over these issues has grown. Manufacturers, think tanks and business groups are asking Congress to set commercial research goals, too. "Electronics is the crude oil of the information age," warns Intel's lobbyist. Even President Bush — who has refused to interfere with the free

ILLUSTRATION BY GEORGE JOSEPH

market — is acknowledging the need for government help.

There's talk in Congress of looking at all new legislation in terms of how it affects competitiveness. Bills have been introduced to help convert defense industries to commercial ones, so politicians won't vote for even dumb weapons in order to protect jobs.

Dr. Dumas believes, "Prohibiting Japan and Germany from being military powers was the biggest favor we ever did them. They've become powers through economics instead." To revitalize our own commercial industries will take time, money and technical talent. It won't require backing away from military research. It will require the same enthusiasm for the products of peacetime as for the weapons of war.

The Orlando Sentinel

Orlando, Florida, March 31, 1991

Japan may have become synonymous with technology and it may have cornered the computer chip market, but guess what? Personal computers don't sell in Japan. Only 4 percent of the population is estimated to use them.

There is a reason, and it's a lulu. Rather than 26 characters like the Roman alphabet, the Japanese language has more than 7,000 characters. Consequently, the keyboard of a Japanese computer looks like a

cathedral organ. Too many keys for just eight fingers and two thumbs.

In the land of rising tech, the pencil and paper remain the word-processing and number-crunching tools of choice.

So we seem to be a step ahead of the Japanese on this.

Now if we could only figure out how to use that new software . . .

The Atlanta Journal and THE ATLANTA CONSTITUTION

Atlanta, Georgia, March 17, 1991

American and Japanese officials are meeting in Tokyo to reconsider a 7-year-old accord that limits the sale of supercomputers. The mega-machines can be used for peaceful purposes, such as weather forecasting and scientific research. But they also can serve as powerful tools in making nuclear weapons and advanced missiles.

So far, the United States and Japan have been able to contain the spread of supercomputer technology to Third-World countries and Eastern Europe, but several Western countries are on the verge of making their own supercomputers. Once Britain, Germany, France and others develop the technology, it may not be long before supercomputers end up in countries that have not signed the Nuclear Non-proliferation Treaty.

The United States hopes to get Japan to go along with a plan to invite several other nations to join in a new agreement to limit the export of such high technology.

But the supercomputer problem goes beyond just trying to find the right words to control the transfer of a specific product. The problem is technology can be a lot tougher to control than traditional exports such as wheat and textiles. No matter what governments say, scientists often can find ways to get around restrictions.

For example, in recent years, researchers have developed a new class of computers, known as parallel computers, that can do the same kind of work as a supercomputer. The inventors don't need the specialized components that go into a supercomputer because they can get almost the same results by chaining together several conventional microprocessors to work simultaneously.

How can governments control the export of knowledge that is carried around in people's heads? How can governments limit the creativity of scientists all over the world who can think up ways to outfox legal accords?

More than ever, peace depends upon the willingness of all industrialized countries to cooperate in defining and controlling emerging technologies. A "new world order" is needed for machines as well as nations.

The Courier-Journal

Louisville, Kentucky, April 23, 1991

TO HEAR some politicians tell it, America is the industrial equivalent of George Foreman: over-weight and over-the-hill. The only way to save our vital industries and to protect jobs, they say, is by sharply limiting imports.

Luckily, that gloomy vision doesn't jibe with the facts. Since 1986, U. S. exports of manufactured goods have soared by 76 percent. The dollar's fall from its unre-alistic heights in the mid '80s was a big factor, of course, but it's not the whole story.

As *The New York Times* reported Sunday, U. S. manufac-turers have become leaner and more cost-efficient. What's more, made-in-America is once again a sign of pride and quality.

Best of all, this renewed Ameri-can competitiveness isn't limited, as it was a few years ago, to air-craft and a few other high-tech products. The resurgence is broad. U. S. factories are exporting more cars and trucks, machine tools and computer chips. Even America's steel and textile industries, which are forever complaining about cheap imports, are shipping more abroad. Steel exports have nearly tripled since 1985.

Thanks to the surge in exports, the U. S. trade deficit has been falling. In February it hit its lowest point in seven years.

Exports are also becoming an increasingly important source of economic growth in this country.

But the growth in ex-ports won't continue if the U. S. re-treats from its traditional leadership role in pro-moting free trade. Some lawmakers — most of them Democrats — want to erect new barriers to im-ports. But that's a sure way to pro-voke other countries to retaliate by barring U. S. exports.

And President Bush's push for authority to negotiate a free trade agreement with Mexico is under attack from some of these same protectionists — even though ex-panded U. S.-Mexican trade is the best way to generate jobs and growth in both countries.

If the protectionists win, we'll all be the poorer.

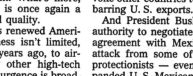
ASSOCIATED PRESS
U. S. manufacturers are exporting everything from computer chips, like those shown here, to steel and textiles.

The Hartford Courant

Hartford, Connecticut, April 13, 1991

What's this? The Japanese are inviting repre-sentatives from U.S. and European companies and universities to work with them on computers for the 21st century. Do do we dare work together on what's called the Sixth Generation Project?

U.S. business leaders and political strategists are debating whether to go it alone or join the Japanese. The potential risks and rewards of an exclusive effort are huge. Sharing Japanese re-search funds and technology would be safer, but it would mean sharing the results as well.

Rather than build a fortress and refuse to cre-ate research consortiums, the United States should join Japan in this project, which appears to be beyond the capability of any one nation.

At stake is the design of a super-supercom-puter made up of as many as a million smaller machines. To greatly increase computing speed, lasers and other light beams will replace the wires inside the hardware. Even harder to de-sign than the equipment will be the software to run it all.

Japan has long used government-sponsored consortiums to pursue research and development. The Bush administration views such cooperation as interference with the marketplace.

Some U.S. and European researchers bar Jap-anese nationals from their projects, while others are developing joint ventures with Japan. To en-courage more cooperation, Japan has said it soon will allow foreign participants in research projects to control up to 50 percent of the inven-tions from them. Currently, Japan retains control of everything that arises from research it sponsors

Japanese officials hope that promoting co-operative research will ease the criticism in Wash-ington of Tokyo's limited support of the military coalition's effort in the Persian Gulf. The West should at least be willing to take a serious look at the invitation to join the hunt for the next genera-tion of computers.

DESERET NEWS

Salt Lake City, Utah, April 2, 1991

It's no secret that the United States has been falling behind in industrial technology for years. Computers, electronics, engineering and the oth-er research and development fields that contribute to a modern industri-al-based economy are dominated by foreign competitors.

A study, however, documents just how far the United States has fallen behind. The Council on Competitive-ness study says that in a majority of 94 critical technologies, the United States is no longer a key player.

This doesn't just mean a factory in some other country can turn out cheaper and more efficient electronic toys. These technologies are vital, not only for our economic well being, but to our security and national defense as well.

Part of our problem is the continu-ing reliance on private industry to ei-ther fund its own research or, using research from government or univer-sity laboratories, to fund its develop-ment. This is becoming too expensive for the private sector.

But companies are prevented from sharing research or development ef-forts by anti-trust laws.

As an example, a proposed joint venture by American firms for re-search on high resolution television technology, supported by the Penta-gon as vital for defense systems, was killed because it was seen as violating U.S. anti-trust laws.

The result is that Japan is now leading the field in that research. Japanese companies and their gov-ernment have a closer working rela-tionship that moves basic research into usable products much faster than U.S. industry can.

The council, made up of executives from industry, labor, and education, has worthwhile recommendations:

— Establish technological leader-ship as a national priority with a stronger leadership role assigned to the existing federal Office of Science and Technology.

— Increase federal research funds.

— More emphasis on research and development in universities with re-sults transferred more quickly to the commercial sector.

— Revamp anti-trust laws to allow sharing of information on emerging technology.

The United States cannot afford to sit passively while other industrial-ized nations seize technological con-trol of the future.

The Honolulu Advertiser
Honolulu, Hawaii, February 25, 1991

The Wall Street Journal recently confirmed a trend noted here — that while Japan's economy remains resilient, it is feeling a financial squeeze.

Higher interest rates, a stock price collapse and real estate jitters are the cause. Said the Journal: "Japanese investors are selling U.S. Treasury securities and New York office towers. The wave of foreign takeovers by Japanese companies is subsiding. And even Japanese banks have become tightfisted."

The ripples have been felt locally with some Japanese subsidiaries and joint ventures facing problems or slowdowns. Some Japan-owned properties are said to be on the block.

New investments in U.S. real estate peaked in 1988 at $16.5 billion, fell 11 percent to $14.8 billion in 1989 and may have been only $10 billion last year, according to the Kenneth Leventhal accounting firm.

Wouldn't it be strange to find Hawaii wishing for more of that good old-time Japanese investment that looked like such a threat a few years ago.

©1991 INTERNATIONAL COPYRIGHT BY CARTOONEWS INC., N.Y.C., USA

EIICHI NAKAO, Japan's Chief of the Ministry of International Trade & Industry (Miti)

THE KANSAS CITY STAR
Kansas City, Missouri, June 9, 1991

The new semiconductor agreement between Japan and the United States could have been worse. Some provisions are worth a cheer or two, notably those that eliminate $165 million in punitive tariffs on Japanese laptop computers, power tools and other imports with certain kinds of computer chips.

The touchiest aspect of the agreement concerned market share. As a goal, Tokyo agreed to a 20 percent share for American chip makers but made no guarantees. This contrasts with the pact of 1986, which included secret protocols that Washington said amounted to a market-share pledge, later disputed by Tokyo.

The 1986 agreement has been Washington's most notorious experiment in "managed trade" and a case study in why such concepts cannot work.

In the mid-1980s, U.S. semiconductor makers complained about low Japanese prices. Eager to "help," the bureaucrats stepped in and imposed price floors right before an upturn in the chip market. Severe shortages developed, and a black market in chips sprang up. Prices of some semiconductors quadrupled. In an embarrassing turnabout, some U.S. chip producers actually urged Japanese companies to lower their prices to help revive demand for computers.

Because of the 1986 agreement, Japanese manufacturers never paid the penalty for over-investment in chip factories. Through artificially high prices granted by the U.S. government, they made windfall profits and re-invested the proceeds to enhance their competitiveness.

In the new agreement, price controls are not scrapped entirely. The pact requires Japanese companies to quickly surrender price and cost data to the U.S. government if any American manufacturer complains of dumping. In practice this could prove more disruptive because it is less predictable.

The spectacle of bureaucrats sitting down to decide how much of one country's market should be captured by companies in another country is ridiculous on its face. Why 20 percent? Why not 25? Why not 50?

Whoever observed that virtually all numerical mandates by government are arbitrary was absolutely correct. Still, by rolling back punitive tariffs and transforming the 20 percent market share from a perceived guarantee to a mere goal, this agreement is better than expected.

U.S. Targets India for Trade Retaliation

U.S. President George Bush April 27, 1990 decided against identifying Brazil and Japan as unfair trading partners under the so-called Super 301 provision of the 1988 Omnibus Trade Act.

But the president did designate India as an unfair trader for the second year in a row. Bush cited what he said were Indian barriers in insurance and investment.

All three nations had been named as unfair traders in the first use of the Super 301 provision in 1989. At the time, they had been granted from 12 to 18 months to eliminate trading practices specifically cited.

Japan and the U.S. had negotiated intensively during the months preceding the April 30 deadline for the second Super 301 report. The trading partners had completed agreements in areas that included super-computers, satellites, wood products and structural impediments to free trade.

"Perhaps Japan had farthest to go [of the countries initially designated unfair traders in 1989], but it moved farther and faster than any of our other trading partners in the past 12 months," said Carla A. Hills, the U.S. special trade representative.

In talks with India, however, "we have made no progress whatsoever," she said. Since it was the second year that India had been assigned unfair trader status, the nation could be targeted for retaliation if it showed no changes from current policy before a July 15 deadline.

The critical issue in the Super 301 debate had been whether to target Japan, with which the U.S. ran its largest bilateral trade deficit. The U.S. was Japan's largest export market, while Japan was the U.S.'s second-largest export market after Canada.

Some accounts said India was targeted in part to appease congressional critics who wished to see the Super 301 provision used actively in U.S. trade policy. While Japan's yearly trade surplus with the U.S. had stood at $49 billion in 1989, India's amounted to just $851 million.

Although India's trade policies were not considered exceptionally protectionist by standards of developing countries, the U.S. had long complained about trade barriers there. The U.S. also was said to be angry at India's lack of cooperation with the efforts at the General Agreement on Tariffs and Trade (GATT) Uruguay Round to protect intellectual property rights and liberalize trade in services.

The Atlanta Journal
AND
THE ATLANTA CONSTITUTION
Atlanta, Georgia, May 1, 1990

Thanks to adroit manuevering by President Bush and Prime Minister Toshiki Kaifu, the United States and Japan have confronted each other on divisive economic issues without causing any serious cracks in the foundation of our relationship.

Japan was able to offer enough concessions so that Mr. Bush could resist protectionist sentiment in Congress to name Japan for a second straight year as an unfair trader. That could have triggered a round-robin of hurtful, self-defeating sanctions.

Capitol Hill's Japan-bashers are suspicious of what they see as Tokyo's tactical retreat. Just the same, some of them boast U.S. pressure is finally budging the Pacific colossus. They delude themselves, though, if they think they can go to the well indefinitely without coming up dry.

They fail to appreciate that citing Japan a second consecutive year under the "Super 301" provision of the Omnibus Trade Act of 1988 would have dealt a blow to the political stock of Mr. Kaifu, a strong advocate of consumerism and a more open Japanese economy. It also would have run the risk of undoing recent compromises on wood products, supercomputers and space satellites, so prickly are some Japanese over what they perceive as unceasing U.S. harassment.

Messrs. Bush and Kaifu did well to communicate cordially but frankly with each other well before the Super 301 mechanism shifted into automatic. Making high-level trade talks a regular routine, as the Japanese trade minister urges, is a good idea.

Bilateral contacts, however, have their limitations. America and Japan have opened up a few trade sectors and tentatively agreed to some basic alterations in our economies in the Structural Impediments Initiative. Those are real accomplishments for the first half of 1990, but our focus for the rest of the year has to be on the global trade talks of the Uruguay Round, where we stand to gain far more — in terms of intellectual property rights and our service industries and agricultural exports — than in all our haggling with Tokyo.

THE COMMERCIAL APPEAL
Memphis, Tennessee, May 1, 1990

BY refusing to place Japan on this year's "hit list" of unfair trading partners, the Bush administration has struck a blow for flexible and realistic trade policy.

Some powerful critics on Capitol Hill show little inclination toward either flexibility or realism. Sen. Lloyd Bentsen of Texas, chairman of the Finance Committee, accuses the administration of gutting the 1988 Trade Act. As punishment, he threatens to block badly needed legislation liberalizing trade with Eastern Europe.

Bentsen and his allies want Bush to invoke the "Super 301" provision of the Trade Act, which would set in motion a series of actions designed to retaliate against Japan for our $49 billion trade deficit. No Capitol Hill sport is more popular than Japan-bashing — or more dangerous for consumers and the American economy.

The President should be commended for refusing to play. When the administration labeled Japan an unfair trader last year, it pledged to restore the country's status if the Japanese made progress in opening their markets to American products. Though Bentsen might not like to admit it, the plan worked as designed.

In trade matters, said U.S. Trade Representative Carla Hills, "I think Japan has moved further this year than any other country." As a percentage of total U.S.-Japanese trade, the deficit has steadily declined. Punishing so crucial a partner in the face of this progress could set off a retaliatory spiral with disastrous consequences.

Even the progress recently made could be reversed. Over the past several months, Japan has expanded its markets for American supercomputers, telecommunications equipment and communications satellites. On the day Bentsen made his threat against the administration, it announced an agreement encouraging U.S. lumber sales in Japan. The extra sales could amount to $1 billion, creating 15,000 American jobs.

Give the Japan-bashers this much credit: Without the Super 301 threat, Japan would have been less likely to open its markets this way. But the tough talk has done its job.

In trade relations, the carrot-and-stick strategy works only if you know when to put away the stick.

THE ARIZONA REPUBLIC
Phoenix, Arizona, May 3, 1990

PROTECTIONISTS in Congress are flustered over President Bush's decision to delete Japan from the "hit list" of countries singled out for unfair trading practices. Japan-bashing, after all, has become a hobby among the Democratic leadership.

But even casual observers of the strange goings-on in Washington must wonder just what it is the Democrats really want.

Last year the Bush administration cited Japan under the so-called "Super 301" provision of the 1988 trade law for its import restrictions on U.S.-made computers, telecommunications equipment, space technology and lumber products. Under that provision, the U.S. trade representative could retaliate with restrictions on Japanese products.

What happened? Tokyo entered into negotiations with Washington. It agreed earlier this year to open its markets to those U.S.-made goods and to enact other structural trade reforms as well. And, just before the administration announced its decision last week to remove Japan from the Super 301 list, Tokyo unveiled an agreement on lumber sales that could pump as much as $1 billion into the U.S. economy and create thousands of new jobs.

Unsatisfied, Texas Sen. Lloyd Bentsen called the administration's Super 301 decision "a serious mistake." The leading Japan basher in Congress, Rep. Richard Gephardt of Missouri, said the U.S. had given Japan "a free-trade furlough." They and other Democrats claim the administration is not serious about enforcing Congress's trade law.

They could be right, which reflects well upon President Bush's determination to seek more liberal trade practices worldwide. By any measure, the 1988 trade law, cobbled together by the Democrats to appease big labor and some uncompetitive American industries, is anti-free trade in intent and anti-consumer in practice.

Moreover, its unilateral and restrictive approach to resolving trade issues runs directly counter to on-going negotiations at the General Agreement on Tariffs and Trade talks designed to increase the global free exchange of goods and services.

To be sure, the U.S. and Japan have had their differences over trade and other policies, and no doubt will to continue to have them. But the U.S., with its 8,753 tariff rates, quotas and restrictions on imported goods from footwear to foodstuffs is hardly in a position to do much finger-pointing at Japan.

It is hoped, as reflected by the sensible U.S. position at the GATT talks, that the days of restrictive trading practices are numbered, that unilateralism and bilateralism soon will give way to a multilateral system encouraging free trade worldwide. Ironically, political barriers to free trade here at home, not foreign obstacles, may prove to be the most difficult to overcome.

The Dallas Morning News
Dallas, Texas, May 2, 1990

The Bush administration is rewarding Japan for recent trade agreements by not citing Japan for unfair trade practices under the "Super 301" provision of the Omnibus Trade Act of 1988. Last year, Japan was one of several nations on the bad conduct list. This year, only India remains.

The president has made the correct decision. The recently concluded, arduous negotiations with Japan have produced several important openings in categories such as wood products and supercomputers. Moreover, Japan seems ready to move toward a significant restructuring of its social and economic system that would encourage greater Japanese consumer spending, bring down the absurdly high price of land, and open the Japanese agricultural market to greater U.S. imports of rice and beef.

Positive results from all these steps will take time. Japanese politicians must deal with public opinion just like American politicians do. However, it is encouraging to note that Japanese public opinion seems very much in favor of breaking up the many monopolies that keep foreign goods out and Japanese consumer prices sky high.

President Bush knows that there is a danger of overplaying his hand and forcing a backlash among the Japanese people. Removing Japan from the blacklist turns down the heat and allows Japan to make progress.

What the president also knows is that Super 301, with the higher tariff requirement, is almost certainly illegal under the General Agreement on Tariffs and Trade, and that punishing Japan under this provision could jeopardize the organization's negotiations now under way in Mexico.

Only last week, General Agreement on Tariffs and Trade members were waxing outraged that the U.S. continues to protect its sugar industry, costing U.S. consumers $15 billion a year, while demanding that other nations cut their agricultural subsidies. Japan is well entitled to ask why it should open itself to U.S. rice imports when the U.S. shuts out sugar imports.

The president knows how much the U.S. has to lose from pushing Japan too far. Japan is this nation's primary lender, and as long as the budget deficit yawns wide, the U.S. cannot afford to aggravate its banker to the point the loan window gets shut.

Japanese trade policies are just one factor of many causing this nation's massive trade deficit. The budget deficit is another. And the continued inability of U.S. industry to match the quality and price of foreign goods cannot be blamed on foreign competition.

The Japanese have taken some important steps to cutting their trade deficit with the U.S. Now the U.S. must take some steps to get its own dilapidated house in order.

The Honolulu Advertiser

Honolulu, Hawaii, April 30, 1990

President George Bush deserves praise for courage in refusing to place Japan on the unfair traders "hit list." That would have required sanctions that might have done as much damage here as there.

Congress passed the "Super 301" section of the 1988 trade bill as a two-by-four to batter Japan, so some lawmakers are in an uproar. But too many, in Congress and out, are blindly blaming Japan for our own economic shortcomings.

Under "Super 301" pressure, Japan has already agreed to open its market to U.S.-made supercomputers, satellites and wood products and to make it easier for American department stores to open there.

It's true there have been many such concessions in the past, some of them more show than substance, with disappointing results in trimming our $49 billion annual trade deficit.

But Japan is also sure to be denied its "demands": that this country reduce our federal budget deficit, encourage savings and improve industrial output through efficiency and a long-range viewpoint.

Despite our differences, Japan and the United States are irretrievably intertwined.

Americans insist on Japanese consumer goods and Japan depends on American raw materials. Japan needs us as its major export market and we need Japan — temporarily, let's hope — to finance the national debt and economic expansion. And our military cooperation guarantees peace in Asia.

Bush has bravely confirmed his commitment to free trade and a healthier U.S.-Japan relationship. Trade sanctions such as those envisioned by "Super 301" proponents would hurt chances for success in the multilateral negotiations. And that would ultimately have been to our great disadvantage.

The Record

Hackensack, New Jersey, May 3, 1990

The Bush administration was right to drop Japan from the list of countries that maintain unfair trade barriers. Citing Japan — as the United States did last year — would have scored easy political points. Protectionism, like Japan-bashing, is popular, and Japanese trade practices are often infuriating. But targeting Japan as an unfair trader, which carries the threat of retaliatory sanctions, would have done little to close America's trade deficit. It also would have made productive negotiations with the Japanese even harder.

The Bush administration announced last week that it will drop Japan from the list of countries that, the United States believes, use high tariffs and other anti-competitive practices to keep out foreign goods.

What would be wrong with including Japan on this list? Plenty. It risks a trade war that would leave consumers the loser by making foreign goods more expensive. Along the way, it pretends that America's trade problems are all Japan's fault and never our own. One by-product of recent Japanese-American trade talks, for instance, was a promise that the Japanese government would limit its work hours, and encourage the Japanese private sector to do the same. Even hard work is portrayed as a vice, when it is Japanese who are working hard.

Japan is certainly guilty of unfair practices that make it hard for American construction companies to win bids there, or for American companies to export wood products, automobile parts, and other items to Japan. The Japanese once argued that American skis couldn't be sold in Japan because Japanese snow was different, for example. Add a network of alliances that link Japanese businesses, and tie those businesses closely to government, and the result can be a closed, monopolistic market that is difficult to penetrate. Many American companies, from IBM Corp. to McDonald's, have succeeded in Japan. Many others have found doing business there to be impossibly difficult.

The government of Prime Minister Toshiki Kaifu, under pressure from the United States, has recently negotiated no less than eight new trade agreements. The Japanese have agreed to drop some of the barriers to U.S. business, to increase public works spending to create more of a market for goods and services, and to make other fundamental changes. The United States should keep applying the pressure for further improvements. The best way to do that is through long-established, multinational negotiations. Anti-competitive policies affect all countries, not just the United States. They all must work together for improvement.

The improved relationship won't make much of a dent in a U.S. trade deficit with Japan that hit $49 billion last year. American consumers will continue to appreciate the quality of Japanese goods. Many Japanese consumers will continue to reject American goods that are ill-suited for the Japanese market because of poor workmanship or because they're not appealing to the Japanese consumer.

For all its genuine strength, the Japanese economy is still buttressed by protectionism. That should change. But the way to change is through steady, quiet negotiation, not the threat of sanctions and trade wars. In the meantime, the United States will have to recognize that many of its trade problems have their origin not in Japan, but right here at home.

Detroit Free Press

Detroit, Michigan, May 1, 1990

Members of Michigan's congressional delegation, Democratic and Republican, are firing predictable election-year criticism at President George Bush's refusal to cite Japan this year for engaging in unfair trade practices — a declaration that could have led to further U.S. trade sanctions. For once, though, Mr. Bush's lack of action seems the correct policy to pursue.

Protectionist lawmakers and their allies sought to invoke a 2-year-old trade law and keep Japan on a list of countries that maintain excessive market barriers to U.S. import penetration; Japan was so named last year under the "Super 301" section of the law. That designation could have allowed Congress to retaliate with higher tariffs and other restrictions on Japanese exports to the U.S. if the barriers were not bargained away. That likely would have resulted in further Japanese reprisals.

Japan still accounts for half of the $100-billion-a-year U.S. trade deficit. Yet as U.S. Trade Representative Carla Hills notes, Japan has "moved farther and faster than any of our other trading partners" in making concessions since it found itself on the "Super 301" hit list last year. U.S. and Japanese negotiators have reached agreements on supercomputers, satellites, telecommunications and wood products.

Those concessions prove that the get-tough trade law is working, its advocates argue. But the moves also have generated attacks on Japanese Prime Minister Toshiki Kaifu by protectionists in his own government, who complain that Washington is bullying Tokyo and want to respond in kind. Enhancing trade tensions now might only harden positions on both sides, jeopardizing the progress that already has been made.

If Washington really wants to dismantle unfair trade barriers, it might start with some of the ones it erects. The U.S. Commerce Department, for example, has denied a request by a money-losing candy maker in Chicago to skirt federal import quotas and buy sugar more cheaply on the world market. Without that cost-saving measure, the Chicago plant is likely to close, throwing its 3,500 employees out of work.

Genuinely free and fair trade is more likely to be arrived at by global negotiations and compromise under the General Agreement on Tariffs and Trade — however maddeningly slow that process often appears — than by unilateral threats and chest-thumping attempts at confrontation. America has plenty to do to better its own competitive position, such as reducing its budget deficit and improving its schools, before it seeks external scapegoats. That's where the attention of Congress and the White House needs to be directed.

The Providence Journal

Providence, Rhode Island, May 3, 1990

Officials in Tokyo are relieved at the decision by President Bush to take Japan off Washington's list of official trade villains. So are we. Another year on that list and the gears of retaliation would have started to turn at the Commerce Department. We're pleased that the prospect of a trade war with Japan has been thwarted — at least for now.

Let's say it again and again: The United States cannot solve its trade problems with a trade war, and recourse to such a strategy can only create losers, especially among American consumers. A trade war cannot be won, and it should not be fought.

It has been suggested by some of the trade hawks on Capitol Hill that dropping Japan from the list will signal Tokyo that it may relax its efforts to import more goods from the United States. That's doubtful. Sens. Carl Levin (D-Mich) and Arlen Specter (R-Pa.) are already proposing legislation to force the White House to kick Japan, proving that bad policy on trade is a bipartisan concern. This being so, Japanese officials are not likely to turn suddenly complacent.

Indeed, pressure on Japan to change is coming not just from Washington, but from another large interest group: Japanese consumers themselves. Largely as an offshoot of the trade debate in America, which is followed closely in Japan, consumers there are beginning to recognize that their mammoth economy is no longer doing much to improve their standard of living. Eventually, the collective interests of consumers in a democracy will outweigh the business interests that keep prices sky high in Japan.

But that could take time. Meanwhile, Japanese leaders have signed several agreements with the United States in recent months. Tokyo has pledged to import more American satellites, supercomputers and wood products. It has also promised to restructure the Japanese economy to promote consumption. And yesterday came news that the Japanese trade surplus declined 30 percent last year, pushed down by growing imports from America and other nations.

This progress is encouraging. So is President Bush's wise decision not to punish Japan for taking the very steps that Washington has recommended.

The Chattanooga Times

Chattanooga, Tennessee, May 3, 1990

The latest U.S. trade accord with the Japanese, President Bush affirmed last weekend, will keep Japan off Washington's list of unfair trading nations and clear of retaliatory U.S. sanctions. Japan's concrete concessions — to open a few market niches and spend more money — were, in fact, modest. The admissions implicit in *our* demands were much more noteworthy.

Essentially, we extracted promises from the Japanese that they would work less and spend more to help ease our staggering trade imbalance. The idea seemed to be that if we can't be as competitive as they are, let's get them to ease up to our less disciplined standard before they buy us out.

This amounted to an astonishing — and embarrassing — role reversal for the self-professed international champion of capitalism and free trade. Nevertheless, having swallowed our pride and asked for such favors, the Japanese concessions are unlikely to matter until Washington imposes financial discipline and shows leadership on core issues.

Coerced Japanese sloth — as if we could arrogantly dictate a change in the Japanese national character — will not solve such domestic problems as: the federal budget deficit and debt service cost; our low and sinking savings rate; the comparatively poor standing of our K-12 schools and entering labor pool; a deteriorating infrastructure; and diminishing investment by government and industry in research, development and plant capacity.

Most of these are directly traceable to our huge budget deficit. It starves funding of roads and schools. It soaks up national savings that otherwise would be available — and at a lower interest rate — for investment in plant capacity and product development. Economists, in fact, call the federal borrowing to finance deficit spending *dissavings* because it competes in financial markets for investment funds and offsets the positive savings rate.

The Reagan and Bush administrations have gotten appreciable, but unearned, mileage out of their no-tax, but-borrow-and-spend policies. Unfortunately, the spending has been in the wrong place: Military spending has gotten the lion's share at the expense of productive investment. The true cost of the administration's fiscal policy is, however, becoming clearer all the time: a lower U.S. standard of living as better-funded, better-educated economic competitors race ahead in industries the United States used to dominate.

Coercing unfair concessions from Japan and other trading partners, moreover, is likely to be counterproductive. The Japanese save six times more per person than do we, and that investment will go someplace. Total capital investments in Japan already exceed ours in percentage terms (24 percent to 10 percent of gross national product) and in absolute dollar terms ($750 billion to $500 billion). Forcing the Japanese government and industry to spend more has already fueled research and retooling, for example, that has made Japan's steel industry more competitive than Korea's. And in a labor-short Japanese society, more spending is expected to be translated to more robotics and higher efficiency in other sectors of the economy.

In fact, Washington may be further solidifying Tokyo's future supremacy. Washington should re-examine its strategy on the "strategic impediments initiatives" that led to the Japanese "concessions." Our leaders may find they've outsmarted themselves. The United States is more likely to continue to lose economic ground until the president and Congress deal with the real problems in their own backyard — the deficit of their own making.

Chicago Tribune

Chicago, Illinois, May 4, 1990

From playing baseball at Yale to chasing tennis balls on the White House court, George Bush knows the psychology of competition. He recognizes when to apply pressure on a rival and when to let up.

After leaning hard on Tokyo for a year to remove trade barriers, President Bush wisely decided to relax a bit. Despite demands from protectionists in Congress to continue the press, he took Japan off his official list of unfair players in world trade and removed—for now—the threat of retaliatory tariffs.

A year ago, the White House named Japan, Brazil and India as the worst discriminators against U.S. imports. Under the "Super 301" section of the 1988 federal trade act, the administration must publish this hit list annually, negotiate with the culprits and retaliate if trade agreements aren't reached. This year, Bush targeted only India for possible reprisal.

It was time to ease up on Japan, a strong economic competitor and valued ally. After Bush got personally involved in talks aimed at removing some basic causes of America's stubborn $50 billion-a-year trade deficit with Japan, Tokyo hurriedly promised to open its markets to foreign-made supercomputers, telecommunications equipment, satellites and wood products.

Brazil, which is undergoing sweeping economic reform under a new president, had agreed to lower trade barriers and also deserved to be removed from the hit list. But India, which refused to negotiate and continues to restrict foreign investment and deny access to its $3 billion-a-year insurance market, did not.

Predictably, the trade hawks in Congress condemned the administration's action. House Majority Leader Richard Gephardt whined that Bush had given Japan a "free trade furlough." Some said the president had set himself up for a political fall because Japan would surely return to its old, trade-distorting ways once the heat from Washington was off.

But Bush was smart to back off. For one thing, the constant badgering by Washington was threatening political stability in Japan. Also, rather than heighten tension and pick new spats with other trading partners, it makes sense to concentrate on bringing a successful end to the current Uruguay Round of international trade liberalization talks. Those talks, scheduled to be completed this year, are aimed at committing nearly 100 nations to open markets and freer trade.

To his credit, Bush didn't make more out of his trade amity than was justified. He cautioned that the recent agreements with Japan alone won't have a big, quick impact on the trade deficit. Work to open markets must continue.

But, for now, it's better to reward Japan for cooperating in a game where everyone will be a winner through expanded trade than to resort to punitive barriers that will hurt Americans every bit as much as Japanese. And as the veteran competitor in the White House knows, the heavy pressure can always be reapplied when that's what it takes to score more points.

Los Angeles Times

Los Angeles, California, April 28, 1990

Japan-bashers in Congress, led by House majority leader Richard Gephardt (D-Mo.), have been noisily calling on the Bush Administration to again this year label Japan an unfair trading partner, arguing that not to do so would be to waffle at the very time that a policy of hard negotiating backed by congressionally threatened punitive tariffs is starting to pay off. President Bush, taking the advice of Carla A. Hills, the tough-minded U.S. trade representative, has rejected that demand. He was right to do so, and congressional trade hawks would be right to back off and give the recent progress made in U.S.-Japan trade talks a chance to show results.

The last few weeks have seen an impressive list of agreements reached on a number of enduring and irritating trade disputes. The latest came in Tokyo the other day when Japan agreed to remove barriers on imports of wood products, long a protected area in the Japanese economy. Earlier, after much foot-dragging, Japan agreed to open its markets to supercomputers and satellites, two low-volume but high-cost products in which the United States excels.

Additionally, Japan has promised to take steps to ease so-called structural impediments, informal but often potent barriers to foreign goods seeking to enter the domestic market. For instance, steps are to be taken to reform Japan's near-feudal product distribution system, to overhaul its archaic pricing methods and to enforce laws against connivance by businesses to perpetuate monopoly practices.

None of this, admittedly, will make much of an immediate dent in the $49-billion trade surplus Japan still runs with the United States. But it does represent an important shift in attitudes and in official policy. Congressional critics of Japan's trade practices would be doing a key ally as well as their own government an injustice if they fail to recognize the political and economic significance of the changes that Tokyo has pledged to make.

U.S.-Japan in Auto Debate

U.S. President George Bush March 21, 1991 met with the chairman of General Motors Corp., Chrysler Corp. and Ford Motor Co., the three largest U.S. car makers, to hear their concerns about the current economic climate. But he rejected Chrysler Chairman Lee Iacocca's suggestion that the U.S. help the industry by restricting Japanese auto imports. Japanese companies had for years limited exports to the U.S. under a so-called voluntary agreement, but Japan's U.S. market share continued to grow with the increased sales of Japanese models manufactured in the U.S.

In a related development, the Ministry of International Trade and Industry announced Jan. 10, 1989 that it would continue to impose a quota of 2.3 million units on auto exports to the U.S. in the fiscal year beginning April 1.

The so-called voluntary restrictions had first been imposed by the Japanese government in 1981. Since 1985, the quota had remained set at 2.3 million vehicles a year.

In fiscal 1987, Japanese manufacturers had exported a total of 2,214,000 cars to the U.S., marking the first year the quotas were not met.

In previous developments:

■ In an unusual move, the U.S. subsidiary of Toyota Motor Corp. Sept. 13, 1988 announced that it would sell $200 million of three-year notes in the U.S. The offering, by Toyota Motor Sales U.S.A. Inc. unit Toyota Motor Credit Corp., would be one of the few instances of a nongovernment-controlled Japanese industrial corporation issuing straight debt in the market. According to U.S. investment bankers, the Japanese had previously hesitated to raise funds in the U.S. because of the detailed disclosure requirements of the Securities and Exchange Commission. The last such offering by a Japanese industrial corporation that was not government controlled had been in 1978.

■ Chrysler Corp. Feb. 1, 1989 said it had signed a marketing agreement with Hyundai Motor Co. of South Korea. Under the terms, Chrysler would sell low-cost Korean cars while Hyundai would gain access to the U.S. auto maker's distribution network and move one step closer to its aim of becoming a global car manufacturer.

THE PLAIN DEALER
Cleveland, Ohio, January 16, 1989

When is an import quota not an import quota? When it's disguised as a "voluntary restraint agreement," a market-rigging device that allows an industry to sweeten its profits by driving up the costs paid by the consumer. This insidious form of protectionism afflicts the U.S. market for Japanese cars.

To the chagrin of American consumers, the Japanese government last week decided to continue limiting the number of Japanese-made cars shipped to the United States. It's no wonder that Detroit rushed to applaud the quota. By restricting consumers' range of choices among higher-priced goods, the deal allows Japanese firms to pad their profits and provides cover for U.S. automakers to inflate their sticker prices.

Auto-import restraints began in 1981, when Detroit was being battered by recession. In truth, there wasn't too much "voluntary" about it: Unless Japan had found a way to pre-empt Congress, protectionist fervor might have led to mandatory U.S. import controls. From a ceiling of 1.68 million vehicles in 1981, Japanese shipments have gradually risen to 2.3 million units in 1988. The same limit will apply for 1989.

Numerical quotas didn't inhibit Tokyo very long. Instead of shipping their low-cost models to the United States, Japanese automakers concentrated on exporting option-laden units with higher price tags and higher profits. American car-buyers had no trouble finding Toyotas or Hondas weighed down with automatic transmissions or air conditioning or sun roofs, but bottom-of-the-line units became scarce.

This suited Detroit's Big Three fine: As long as their Japanese competitors had raised their prices, there was nothing preventing U.S. firms from jacking up their prices, too. The consumer was stuck with the tab.

As if higher prices weren't bad enough in the short run, the myopia of U.S. automakers has left the industry vulnerable to longer-range crisis. If American auto firms had been looking toward the future, they would have used their mid-1980s breathing space to retool their assembly lines to produce fuel-efficient models to suit the coming era of scarce oil supplies. Instead, Detroit took the easy way out: It ceded the small-car segment of the market to the Japanese, preferring the higher short-term profits of large cars.

This should have been the year to end the auto-import restraints: Detroit needs no further coddling and Tokyo is vexed by a strong currency that makes it difficult to sell their goods overseas. Instead of insisting that the quotas be ended, the Reagan administration was silent on the issue for fear of arousing another round of Japan-bashing in Congress. Thus the counter-productive quotas persist: helpful for Japan, profitable for Detroit, expensive for consumers. Alas, having chosen to ride the tiger of protectionism, Tokyo and Washington now find it hard to dismount.

THE SPOKESMAN-REVIEW
Spokane, Washington, January 25, 1989

George Bush campaigned for the White House as an advocate of free trade, of requiring U.S. industry to modernize and compete rather than giving it government protections against the rigors of the global market.

A request from the Big Three automakers soon will put Bush's rhetoric to the test.

The choice his administration makes will have direct consequences for American auto buyers — but even more important, it will send a signal about whether Bush will maintain his predecessor's hard line against protectionism.

Chrysler, General Motors and Ford want the U.S. Treasury Department to impose a 25 percent tariff on imported vans and sport-utility vehicles.

This highly popular category of vehicles is, oddly enough, one in which U.S.-made entries are beating the Japanese and European competition.

Indeed, the Big Three are raking in their highest profits ever. During the past decade, they have fought back in fine competitive style, slashing overhead, closing obsolete factories and building modern ones, holding down labor costs, designing competitive vehicles and implementing better quality control. It has been a comeback of huge significance to the country's economic well-being.

The Big Three are making two remarkably different arguments for the proposed tariff.

To the Treasury Department, they characterize the tariff as a way to generate more revenue for the deficit-ridden federal budget and as a way to discourage sales of imported vehicles and thus reduce the nation's high trade deficit.

Heartwarming as such concern for the economy might be, it conceals a motive that is anything but selfless. In a letter to auto dealers, Chrysler Corp. Chairman Lee Iacocca said the tariff would create "a $2,000-per-truck cost penalty to your competitors."

What would the Big Three do after such a tariff had boosted the price of foreign-made vehicles?

If history is a guide, they would raise their prices, too. When currency-exchange rates of the last few years caused a substantial increase in the price of all imported vehicles, U.S. automakers imposed parallel price increases even though their costs had not gone up, opting for higher profits instead of a dramatic price differential that might have enabled them to win back some of the market share that foreign autos had seized in the 1970s.

Competition did help save the U.S. auto industry, and the national interest requires Bush to force the industry to stay competitive — the hard way.

Protectionism is a dangerous tactic under any circumstances, but it is an odious one when it would give a recently reformed and recovered industry an unearned windfall.

Los Angeles Times

Los Angeles, California, January 20, 1990

The '80s were pretty horrid for Detroit's Big Three. Japanese auto makers control 40% of the California market, and all the Hondas and Toyotas and Nissans on the freeways often make it seem like more than that. "It scares the hell out of me to drive around Los Angeles," one General Motors marketing executive told Times writer James Risen recently.

But 1990 could be even worse than the '80s, because the Japanese keep coming at you. They are competitive tigers, they offer quality products, they never stop innovating. When Japanese managers set up production plants in the Midwest, they hire the very same American workers once blamed for the shoddy quality of American cars, and produce autos of a superior quality that was seemingly impossible under American management. But was it impossible?

Until recently, Detroit seemed not to have a clue to the reasons for the Japanese ascendancy; now the industry has stopped blaming everything on Japanese cultural and economic advantages and discovered that to be competitive you have to *really* compete. They're finding that you have to have very good products on line and terrific new ones down the road. Detroit has met the enemy and found that, in part at least, it's Detroit.

So it can only be a good sign that the Big Three domestic auto makers have set up their own think-tank-type design labs in Southern California. These labs have deliberately been located far away from the monster auto bureaucracies in Michigan and purposely planted in a section of the country noted for its atmosphere of innovation and daring. Will anything of value come out of them?

Well, the GM lab in a remote section of Ventura County recently unveiled a startling, and promising, prototype. It's an electric car that can outrace some gas-powered cars, an 870-pound vehicle that can get to 75 m.p.h. in 8 seconds, and travel up to 124 miles on one overnight charge of its 32 10-volt batteries.

Is it practical? Will it ever go into production? There are no sure answers yet but no doubt many people are hoping that will happen, if only to avoid ecological meltdown. The market potential for electric-powered cars will depend on many factors, most importantly its impact on electric power capacity and, of course, sticker price. But proposed federal and local clean-air laws are increasingly demanding, and may tilt the market scales toward a new, almost pollution-free product line.

It has been true that Detroit reacts to new realities with all the speed of a backlash of taffy. The industry still has many problems and not enough answers. But the Japanese challenge, despite its devastation of U.S. industry, has had the unintended effect of finally waking the sleeping giant in Detroit.

The San Diego Union

San Diego, California, November 7, 1990

General Motors Corp.'s staggering $2 billion loss during the third quarter is both a storm warning and an opportunity.

There is no denying that the nation's largest auto maker has slipped badly during the last two decades. It now is responsible for just 36 percent of domestic car sales, compared with more than half of the American market in the 1960s.

It must be noted, however, that most of GM's quarterly loss is attributable to the cost of closing unproductive plants. Over the long term, this action will make the company more competitive at home and abroad. GM is gradually coming to understand, along with Ford and Chrysler, that it must adapt to changing market conditions in order to survive.

For far too long, American auto makers have wasted valuable time deluding themselves.

First they dismissed foreign competitors as opportunists who got lucky during the oil shocks of the 1970s. Then they persuaded Washington to strong-arm Japanese manufacturers into limiting their U.S. sales. When that failed to shore up the domestic producers' sagging market share, the Big Three complained that foreign firms should make more of their cars in the United States. Seizing upon this invitation, Japanese makers are continuing to expand their sizable market share while building more cars in this country.

Even so, there is still a reluctance among American auto makers to acknowledge the possibility that foreign competitors are building better cars. This thinking persists despite the fact that the Japanese market share has reached a record high of 33 percent. Moreover, only one American firm, Buick, made the top 10 in a recent consumer survey.

But there are a few signs of life among the Big Three, as illustrated by Ford's relatively strong showing during the last few years. GM could be poised for a similar comeback now that Robert Stempel has replaced Roger Smith as chairman. Stempel is widely viewed as a "car guy," someone who not only understands the importance of increased productivity but also knows how to go about achieving it.

Stempel should take a long look at GM's European operation, the company's sole success story in the 1980s. While GM's domestic plants were being micromanaged from Detroit, GM Europe was allowed to run its own show for the most part. The upshot of its decentralized, back-to-basics philosophy has been streamlined plants that produce appealing, technologically sophisticated cars which sell at reasonable prices.

Meantime, GM's domestic operations have produced slight variations on the same old products, but at higher and higher prices. No wonder GM's European operation is responsible for such a significant share of the corporation's profits.

Stempel's challenge is to marshal the creative talents of a new breed of leaders who began their careers when imports were already threatening the company. They know that a global marketplace is unforgiving of companies that fail to adapt and diversify.

GM, like Ford and Chrysler, cannot afford to lose more ground. Otherwise, the Big Three in this country may ultimately consist of Honda, Toyota and Nissan.

The Oregonian

Portland, Oregon, January 26, 1989

Big Three automakers again have the pedal to the metal for trade protectionism, and U.S. consumers may pay between $2,500 and $5,000 per vehicle for Detroit's latest joyride.

How's that for sticker shock?

Chrysler, Ford and General Motors are lobbying the Treasury Department to press ahead with a decision to slap a 25 percent tariff on imported minivans and sports utility vehicles. The Customs Service moved in early January to redefine these multipurpose vehicles as light trucks — a designation that triggers an additional tariff on imports such as Volkswagen Vanagons, Isuzu Trooper IIs, and Toyota 4Runners.

Foreign automakers and their U.S. dealers have won a temporary suspension of the Customs Service's ruling that should give consumers the opportunity to see what kind of ride they're about to be taken on by the Big Three. The Customs Service should take the opportunity to make this suspension permanent.

The ruling overturned long-established policy without so much as a public hearing or comment period, and it runs common sense right into the ground. These minivans and sports vehicles may have trucklike bodies and chassis, but they are chiefly used to haul passengers and not cargo. Ask any owner or potential owner. The ruling could affect 250,000 new vehicles annually.

U.S. automakers have trumpeted the 25 percent tariff as a tremendous boon to the deficit-plagued U.S. Treasury. How patriotic. But even this transparently self-serving rationale is hardly sufficient justification for a nation committed to free trade. This is protectionism pure and simple.

The rule would be a tremendous bane to U.S. consumers. The price of new Mazda MPVs and the like would be driven up. Some models could disappear altogether. Reduced competition would allow domestic manufacturers to hike prices on their own multipurpose vehicles.

There is ample precedent for this scenario under the "voluntary" quotas on Japanese auto exports to the United States. The Reagan administration muscled Japan into these limits beginning in 1981. The reason was to give the faltering American industry time to retool. Eight years later, a revolutionized industry is about to announce record profits. The quotas are still in place.

An International Monetary Fund study estimates that U.S. consumers spent more than $17 billion more for cars between 1981 and 1984 because of the quotas, and those same U.S. consumers may now pay for a trade ruling that has a direct connection to the quotas: Japanese automakers have previously brought in sport utility vehicles as both light trucks and passenger cars in order to avoid exceeding their car quotas. This is yet another illustration of protectionism's perversions.

A true free-trade policy would end the reclassification, end the truck tariff and end the quotas.

Japanese Ownership of Yosemite Causes Stir

Interior Secretary Manual Lujan Jr. Dec. 31, 1990 said he would try to prevent Japan's Matsushita Electric Industrial Co. from retaining control over the concession service in Yosemite National Park. Matsushita had acquired control over the service, Yosemite Park & Curry Co., when it bought the concession's parent company, MCA Inc. Curry Co. operated hotels, restaurants, grocery stores and campgrounds within Yosemite park. Although Lujan had previously suggested that Matsushita donate the park concessions to the National Park Service, MCA officials had rejected that proposal, saying they would seek an American buyer for the Curry Co. service within 12 months.

MCA, Inc. agreed "in principle" Jan. 8, 1991 to sell its concession facilities in Yosemite National Park to a private, non-profit group, the National Park Foundation, for $49.5 million. The price was well under the $100 million at which MCA had valued the concession service, Yosemite Park and Curry Co., which operated hotels, restaurants and shops in the park. After MCA was sold in December 1990 to Japan's Matsushita Electric Industrial Co., Interior Secretary Manuel Lujan Jr. had mounted a campaign against Japanese ownership of the concession service. He had asked MCA to donate Curry Co. to the U.S. government, but MCA had refused.

Los Angeles Times
Los Angeles, California, January 3, 1991

Interior Secretary Manuel Lujan Jr. only wants the best deal he can get on a concessionaire's holdings at Yosemite National Park. And that's OK. But the way he is going about it sometimes sounds suspiciously like Japan-bashing.

The fuss involves the sale of MCA Inc., an entertainment giant, to Matsushita Electric Industrial Co., an electronics giant.

With MCA go the hotels, restaurants and other enterprises operated by Yosemite Park & Curry Co., whose contract with the Park Service expires in 1993.

Matsushita recognized that foreign ownership of property at Yosemite, as much a national monument as a park, might not look good. So it decided to try to sell Curry Co. to an American buyer and put interim profits in escrow for a park foundation.

Lujan's office has not approved the plan, apparently still hoping that Matsushita will donate Curry properties that may be worth $300 million, something no publicly held company wants to do. Legally, the Curry sale probably can go through, but a sale to an American firm would go more smoothly if Matsushita and the Interior Department worked side by side.

It could be that the longer Lujan holds out, the stronger the chance that Curry will remain in foreign hands. That would be an ironic outcome of his campaign. But the Interior secretary must be careful. It's smart to take a public negotiating position designed to drive a price down. And a lot of Americans would feel uncomfortable with the Yosemite concession in foreign hands. Just don't go overboard.

The Providence Journal
Providence, Rhode Island, January 14, 1991

Some Americans seem to have the idea that when US corporations are bought by foreigners, something irretrievable is lost to the nation. For example, many were upset when Japanese investors bought a stake in the company that owns Rockefeller Center. Well, the last time we strolled down Fifth Avenue, Rockefeller Center was still there, casting its long shadows. The ice-skating rink had not been shipped off to Tokyo. Indeed, everything was as exhilarating as ever.

Nor do we expect that following its purchase of the entertainment giant MCA, the Japanese electronics giant Matsushita will replace American actors with Japanese, or stage Hollywood chase scenes exclusively with Hondas and Toyotas. American movies will retain their American flavor. Neither tourists nor bears at Yosemite National Park will be eating sushi anytime soon.

But Interior Secretary Manuel Lujan is worried. When Matsushita bought MCA, it acquired the firm that holds the US contract to sell lodging, snacks and souvenirs at Yosemite. That's not quite up Matsushita's alley, and so it wanted to find a buyer at a reasonable price. But Mr. Lujan wanted Matsushita to give the concession to Interior gratis — or, at the most, sell it at a bargain-basement price. This week he got his wish: Interior got the concession for half of its value. What was the secretary so worried about?

The park would have remained here. So would the employees. Nor would tourists have had to visit Japan to patronize the concession. Matsushita has no more desire to wreck the business than its American owner had, and its earnings in dollars would — perhaps without even a stopover at Japanese banks — have ended up in American hands in return for US goods, or as investments in American businesses.

Secretary Lujan should keep these facts in mind. And so should US trade officials, who will visit Tokyo next week to follow up on Japanese commitments under the trade agreement signed last year between the two nations. Tough trade signals have been sent recently by Washington to Japan regarding other areas of the bilateral trade relationship. Some are based on valid complaints, and some are not. In any event, the goal of encouraging a serious Japanese response won't be served by American officials flogging spurious issues such as MCA and the Yosemite National Park.

The San Diego Union

San Diego, California, January 4, 1991

Like a Third World strong-man threatening to expropriate properties owned by foreigners, Interior Secretary Manuel Lujan is trying to force a Japanese firm to relinquish a subsidiary that operates concessions in Yosemite National Park.

You would think, judging from Lujan's crass appeal to Americans' resentment over Japanese ownership of U.S. assets, that Matsushita Electrical Industrial Co. had acquired the park itself. But that is hardly the case.

Rather, the Japanese industrial giant has acquired the Yosemite Park Curry Co., which has exclusive rights to provide food and lodging to tourists in the California park. Curry is a subsidiary of MCA Inc., the entertainment conglomerate which Matsushita recently purchased for $6.6 billion.

Lujan is determined to ban from America's national parks any commerce that is controlled, directly or indirectly, by Japanese interests. His nationalistic sensibilities apparently are not offended by McDonald's selling hamburgers in Tokyo, but only by the Japanese selling hamburgers in Yosemite.

Interior Department officials have been quoted as saying they hope to pressure Matsushita into turning over free to the National Park Service the assets of the Curry Co. — an investment worth $300 million. Lujan's strategy seems to be to generate a public backlash against the Japanese firm's ownership of the park concessions. He has been urging MCA to donate Curry to the government or sell it under value, suggesting the firm could earn public good will through such a magnanimous gesture. Such tactics smack of political extortion.

Curry's 30-year contract at Yosemite expires in 1993. But Lujan has threatened to cancel the contract immediately because of Matsushita's acquisition of the firm. The legality of such an action by Lujan would be highly questionable.

Over the years, Curry has reaped windfall profits from its cozy relationship with the park, paying only 75 cents to the government for every $100 in revenues. But the legal way to rectify this is by opening the Yosemite concession to competitive bids when the current contract expires.

At that time, the Yosemite service contract should be awarded to the firm offering the best proposal — regardless of whether it is headquartered in New York or London or Tokyo.

The Washington Times

Washington, D.C., January 9, 1991

The mergers-and-acquisitions department over at Lujan Inc. (a k a the U.S. Department of the Interior) is in the midst of a decidedly unfriendly takeover attempt these days. It wants control of more than $100 million worth of Yosemite Park facilities held by a subsidiary of the MCA Corp. (now owned by the Japanese Matsushita conglomerate), and it wants them now. If that means arranging for the National Park Service to renege on its park concessions contract with the subsidiary, the Curry Co., well, so be it.

Today Rep. Bruce Vento intends to open hearings on the takeover attempt, and both parties, as well as assorted conservation and environmental groups, are expected to testify. As we noted earlier, there is a property-rights issue here that deserves a hearing.

But beyond the question of property rights, there is the matter of protecting a scenic area that lots of people like to visit. The Interior Department says the takeover is designed to preserve our national treasures. That's a nice goal, but there are two little problems with Interior's solution. First, scientific research has yet to demonstrate a link between Japan-bashing and the preservation of our environment. Second, the historical record suggests that the federal government is as adept at preserving our wilderness as it has been at shoring up savings and loan institutions.

Mr. Lujan doesn't like the fact that MCA pays a ridiculously low fee to the government for monopoly concession rights in Yosemite, about 0.75 percent of its annual park revenues. He is right, of course. It's a stupid policy, and the feds ought to put the concessions up for bid.

But who negotiated that fee, which must be renegotiated every five years? Uncle Sam. Who encouraged a monopoly on concession rights in Yosemite? Uncle Sam. Who charges a ridiculously low $5 weekly admission fee to the park overall, which means it has more visitors than its resources can stand? Uncle Sam. Who spent $2 million upgrading safety around a $75-a-night Curry Co. hotel with pool, golf course and tennis courts, and subsequently approved $1.2 million for water, sewer and power for a new Curry Co. employee dorm? Guess.

Yosemite, alas, is not an isolated example of inefficiency. Our entire Park Service is a testimony to the impotence of good intentions. Remember when some mavens within the Park Service decided that we ought to preserve Yellowstone National Park by letting it burn down "naturally"? They contributed to a conflagration that turned some parts of the park into a moonscape.

Author Alston Chase has pointed out that Park Service hands-off management made a mess of Yellowstone's flora and fauna. The Political Economy Research Center has cited a few of the problems caused by other agencies under the Department of the Interior: "The Bureau of Land Management, which supervises vast stretches of grazing land in the Southwest, 'chained' thousands of acres of land each year — using giant crawler-tactors pulling anchor chains between them to uproot pinyon and juniper trees — so that more grass would grow. The Forest Service cuts down trees in the Rocky Mountains that will take many decades to replace, although cutting them and hauling them out often costs more than they are worth. The Bureau of Reclamation builds dams and canals that destroy canyons, river beds and farmland, even when these dams produce benefits far smaller than the costs." And so on.

In this context, Mr. Lujan's brief foray into Japan-bashing is small potatoes. If Mr. Vento really wants to help the park system, he ought to open things up. Why not invite naturalists, such as Mr. Chase or the economists at the Political Economy Research Center, who argue persuasively that "free market" parks make sense from an environmental, economic and constitutional point of view? These people may offer clues about how to avoid not only small embarrassments, such as the tacky Battle of the Yosemite Concessionaires, but also big ones, like the way in which our parks policies have nearly destroyed our parks.

The Boston Herald

Boston, Massachusetts, January 9, 1991

For 65 years, the United States government has granted the firm of Yosemite Park and Curry sole rights to operate concessions within Yosemite National Park. In 1989, the concession took in $78 million from tourists who spent their money on lodging, food, and gifts. This netted Yosemite Park and Curry a $17 million profit. In turn, it paid the government a mere $580,000 in fees. It has been a sweet deal for Yosemite Park and Curry, and not an unusual one.

All the companies — and there are more than 500 — that operate concessions within America's 355 national parks have sweet deals. For decades, the government has awarded these contracts without competitive bidding. Interior Secretary Manuel Lujan has for the past year been criticizing this practice. Rightly so. Last summer, he raised fees and established a new policy which does away with the awarding of contracts. The contract with Yosemite Park and Curry, however, doesn't expire until 1993.

All this wheeling and dealing, interesting as it may be, would never have been headline news if Matsushita Electric Industrial Co. of Japan hadn't acquired Yosemite Park and Curry with its recent purchase of MCA, Inc. The fact that the Japanese will soon be reaping profits from an American national park has Lujan fuming.

"The whole question is foreign ownership of a part of our heritage," he has said, adding warnings about the Japanese "buying up" our country.

But Yosemite Sam is not about to become Yosemite Samurai. The Japanese did not purchase Yosemite National Park. They bought a service business within the park. Late yesterday, Matsushita agreed to sell Yosemite Park and Curry to the National Park Foundation, a non-profit group, for $49.5 million when its contract with the government expires. In light of the agreement, for Lujan to react to the company's good business sense — which the U.S. government obviously lacks — by slinging anti-Japanese rhetoric is unnecessary and unfounded sour grapes.

The Courier -Journal

Louisville, Kentucky,
January 11, 1991

INTERIOR Secretary Manuel Lujan can take credit for successful negotiations on behalf of the American people and Yosemite National Park. Unfortunately, he must also take blame for some Japan-bashing along the way.

"Happy New Year! A Japanese company now owns exclusive rights to do business in Yosemite!" he proclaimed after Matsushita Electric Industrial Co. bought MCA. Besides making movies, MCA holds the exclusive rights to operate the concessions at Yosemite National Park.

What Mr. Lujan had really wanted was for MCA to donate its concessions business "to the American people." Its value is between $100 million and $200 million. Not surprisingly, MCA said no.

But Matsushita and MCA were sensitive to the politics of the Japanese making money on a U. S. national park, and they were willing to deal. In the end, Matsushita was allowed to keep the concessions business until the contract expires in 1993. At that time, it will be sold for $49.5 million to the non-profit National Park Foundation, which will turn over all buildings and rights to the National Park Service. The park service will take bids and choose a new concessioner, who will lease the buildings and repay the $49.5 million.

The Park Service is thrilled: At no cost, it gets ownership of Yosemite's historic buildings. Preservationists are, too: For years, they have objected to the way MCA ran the business at Yosemite. The company added so many accommodations, restaurants and shops that it was accused of destroying the park to make more money for stockholders. The current park director recently remarked, "Due to the bus roar in Yosemite, my home in Yosemite Valley is noisier than it was in the Miami suburbs."

With MCA out of the picture, it's possible that in 1993, Yosemite's concessions will be run by preservationists. The National Park Foundation may bid for the contract; last fall another preservation group, the Yosemite Restoration Trust, said it definitely will. Its members would return all profits to the park.

In his negotiations, Mr. Lujan won riches for the American people. Too bad he felt he had to take cheap shots at the Japanese.

The Record

Hackensack, New Jersey, January 10, 1991

The decision by a Japanese-owned company to sell its Yosemite concessions is being hailed as a victory by supporters of U.S. Secretary of the Interior Manuel Lujan. Victory for whom? And at what price?

The National Park Foundation certainly won. It will be able to buy the hotels, restaurants, and stores at Yosemite National Park for a fire-sale price. The price tag will be $49.5 million — roughly half of what the company, MCA, says the properties are worth. The decision to sell followed a relentless lobbying campaign by Mr. Lujan, who argued that the hotels and soft-drink stands at one of America's most scenic national parks should be owned by Americans. A Japanese firm, Matsushita Electric Industrial Co., acquired the concessions last month, when it bought MCA, a giant entertainment conglomerate.

What taints this victory is the less than subtle note of Japan-bashing in Mr. Lujan's attacks. He grumbled at one point that the concessions should remain in American hands. He pointed to a widely held "impression that the Japanese were buying up the whole United States." And he volunteered that he doesn't drive a Japanese car.

This is xenophobia, pure and simple. At a time when the United States is, quite properly, pressuring Japan to open its markets, it is dismaying to see a member of Mr. Bush's Cabinet practicing such bias and applying protectionist policies of his own.

Nor is Mr. Lujan's position supported by logic. Does he believe that the Japanese are somehow less capable than Americans of appreciating the wonders of Yosemite? Is he suggesting that a Japanese company is unqualified to run hotels and restaurants?

Mr. Lujan's remarks have played well with the public, and with some members of Congress. On a recent visit to Capitol Hill, he was reportedly praised for having the courage to speak out against Japan.

Paul Pritchard, president of an environmental group called the National Parks and Conservation Association, even invoked the specter of Pearl Harbor. "If you allow a Japanese firm to do business in Yosemite, you're saying it's OK for a Japanese firm to own the USS Arizona, which is a national monument, or for a British firm to have the concession at Bunker Hill," he said recently. This is the kind of hysteria that Mr. Lujan has encouraged.

Mr. Lujan is right on one point. The Interior Department's contract with MCA's Yosemite Park & Curry Co., which returns only 75 cents on every $100 in gross receipts to the Park Service, was ridiculously low. The way to deal with that was to renegotiate the contract, not to badger MCA into disposing of its property for far less than its real price. Mr. Lujan has won something of a victory, all right. But it's the kind of victory we don't need.

THE SACRAMENTO BEE
Sacramento, California, January 10, 1991

No matter how well-intentioned his objectives have been, Interior Secretary Manuel Lujan's involvement in the controversy over who should run the hotels and other concessions in Yosemite National Park has been stained by an ugly element of Japan-bashing as well as an unmistakable tinge of racial antipathy. But Lujan also recognized that there's an underlying need to overhaul the entire system of concessions in the national parks, and on that more basic level, the deal he's negotiated in Yosemite must unquestionably be counted as a big success.

The Yosemite concessions — hotels, stores and other services — are currently run by MCA, an American company whose recent acquisition by the Matsushita Electric Industrial Co. stirred Lujan's ire. Under the deal that the secretary has worked out with the Japanese conglomerate, Matsushita will restore to public ownership all of MCA's current holdings in the park for $49.5 million, which is a lot less than experts say the company could have demanded. What matters more than the bargain price, however, is that the deal opens the way for the more orderly and equitable management of Yosemite in the future, and it may set a precedent for related reforms throughout the park system.

The agreement calls for Matsushita to continue operating the concessions until MCA's current contract expires in 1993, which is a lot better than trying to find someone to step in on short notice for that two-year interim. That will give the National Park Service plenty of time to conduct its first-ever completely open competition for the next contract. Potential bidders won't face the financial burden of having to buy the hotels and other park facilities that MCA owns because they'll now belong to the public, which is just as it should be. And the park service will be able to pick the concessionaire that offers the best deal for the park and the public interest, without being hamstrung by the preferential rights that MCA was granted many years ago.

Who'll qualify to bid for that next contract in 1993, what kind of terms they'll have to meet and whether there should be any preference given to bidders who propose to operate on a non-profit basis are all questions that Lujan and the park service will have to resolve in the months ahead. It should be clear to all from the outset, however, that protection of the park's resources and implementation of the management plan for its long-term preservation have to be the primary goals of the contracting process. Fortunately, Lujan's success in restoring all of the park's facilities to public ownership is a big step toward ensuring that that's what will happen.

The Register-Guard
Eugene, Oregon, January 4, 1991

American paranoia over Japanese ownership of things formerly American has a new and curious manifestation. The government, in the person of Interior Secretary Manuel Lujan, is taking a strong stand against Japanese ownership of the food, lodging and commercial service concession at Yosemite National Park.

Why would the Japanese want this anyway? They don't necessarily. But one of their larger firms, Matsushita Electrical Industrial Co., just bought MCA Inc., an American entertainment conglomerate that also owned the Yosemite and Curry Co., which has the park concession.

MCA had agreed not to let Yosemite and Curry come under foreign control. But the Matsushita buyout has gone through, the Japanese are temporarily in control and they and Lujan do not agree about how Yosemite and Curry should be transferred, or to whom.

The business details are convoluted, but the public policy point is plain: Secretary Lujan does not want the profits from the commercial side of a major national park flowing overseas.

The question is: Why?

Foreign ownership of commercial operations in the United States has become common. Many well-known American brand names are owned by businesses that are subsidiaries of foreign corporations. And foreign firms own outright a lot of American real estate, from the Pebble Beach golf complex in California to Rockefeller Center in Manhattan.

With this degree of intrusion, as critics would describe it, why suddenly draw the line at the food and lodging concession of a national park? There is no potential threat to national security. It is not in any sense a fundamental industry on which the nation's welfare depends. Nor is it engaged in the kind of cultural/communications production in which there is legitimate sensitivity to foreign control.

Granted, the park itself is a national treasure. It would be a travesty for it to be transferred from government to private hands, foreign or domestic — although some of the more extreme advocates of "privatization" would applaud.

But the services offered to park visitors by the Yosemite and Curry Co. constitute a strictly for-profit private business. It doesn't make any difference to the customers whether the owner of that business is MCA or General Motors or Matsushita. In this day of global corporate interchangeability, it shouldn't make any difference to Manuel Lujan, either.

THE SPOKESMAN-REVIEW
Spokane, Washington, January 7, 1991

The stakes have gone up again in the poker game played by Japanese investors on American soil. Never mind the Rockefeller Center.

Yosemite National Park is involved.

Secretary of the Interior Manuel Lujan Jr. has declared it unacceptable for the Japanese giant Matsushita Electrical Industrial Co. to own the concessions in Yosemite.

Lujan also has a larger goal: to keep more of the profits from hotels and restaurants in national parks across the country. Yosemite is fast becoming a test case in this cause. While this goal is understandable given the financial pressure on the federal government, Lujan is making a mess of this deal.

The hotels and restaurants in Yosemite are owned and run by the Curry Co., which in turn is owned by MCA Inc., an entertainment conglomerate. Matsushita has just bought MCA. Hence all the fuss.

Lujan has been negotiating with MCA and Matsushita for several weeks, trying one approach or another to prevent Curry Co. from going into foreign ownership. He initially urged that profits from the concession firm be placed into an escrow account, with an agreement that MCA would sell the firm to another U.S. owner within a year. MCA said yes. But days later, he changed tactics, suggesting that MCA donate the company to Uncle Sam.

Hell, no, the answer is reported to have been. And with good reason. There are various estimates of the company's worth, but the lowest figure is $50 million.

It's anyone's guess how long that appraisal will be good, however. If the contract for concessions in national parks is rewritten as planned to skinny down the profit margins for operators, the Curry Co. and its brethren across the country could be worth far less.

Now that the MCA-Matsushita deal has gone through, Lujan complains that MCA has been arrogant with him. He has asked his staff to check the concession contract to see if the sale is legal without his approval. Why he didn't request this research months ago, possibly avoiding the whole mess, is anyone's guess.

Many Americans are uneasy about foreign investment. Particularly when it is Japanese. But this time around, it sounds as though Lujan has been the problem child.

If he hopes to revamp the entire concession system, he ought first to address the question of whether *anyone*, even the feds, ought to tuck away fat profits stemming from our national parks.

In the meantime, the so-called "Japan bashers" ought to think before they yipe. After all, we haven't whined about Japanese investors propping up our deficit with their purchases of government bonds.

The Washington Post
Washington, D.C., January 5, 1991

MANUEL LUJAN JR., the secretary of the interior, doesn't think that a Japanese company ought to be allowed to run the concessions in Yosemite Park. The concessions—the restaurants, hotels, camping grounds and so forth—belong to a subsidiary of MCA Inc., and now MCA has been bought by Matsushita Electric Industrial Co. Several separate issues are tangled together here, and the secretary's scarcely veiled appeal to prejudice does little to straighten them out.

The Bush administration, and the Reagan administration before it, have been working with great energy to open up international markets in investment and services. Those are primary goals for the United States in the Uruguay Round of world trade negotiations, which will either succeed or finally fail within the next few weeks. When Japan tries to do to American companies what Mr. Lujan wants to do to Matsushita, President Bush's trade negotiators object sharply—and rightly.

For some time Mr. Lujan and the Interior Department have been trying to change relations between the parks and the concessionaires in general. The department thinks that some of the concessionaires have become too influential in the management of the parks and are returning too little of their profits to the public. That's a legitimate objection, and it involves all the concessionaires regardless of nationality.

The department also argues that Matsushita itself offered to sell the Yosemite concessions to another operator, and the only question is the terms. Officials further suggest that MCA may already have breached its contract with the government by being taken over—in effect, changing the concessions' ownership without the required approval of the government. Those issues can be left to the lawyers.

But beyond all the other objections there is Mr. Lujan's assertion that a Japanese company, for purely symbolic reasons, shouldn't be allowed to run the concessions in a great American park. In his words you can hear all kinds of unpleasant echoes, including those of the Japanese politicians who explain that their market can't possibly be opened to foreign rice sales because of the deep and mystical significance of rice for Japanese culture.

In every country, a lot of people have endless reasons for keeping foreigners out of this activity or that one. Among their other objectionable features, these reasons add up to a world economy in decline. Fortunately, Mr. Bush's trade policy and we would hope his instincts generally are aimed in the opposite direction.

The Gazette

Cedar Rapids, Iowa, January 8, 1991

INTERIOR SECRETARY Manuel Lujan Jr. should stop nagging Matsushita Electric Industrial Co. about what it plans to do with its newly acquired hotel, grocery, campground and restaurant concessions at Yosemite National Park.

Lujan has been giving the Japanese conglomerate a bad time ever since last year when it bought MCA and, as part of the deal, the MCA subsidiary that owns and operates the Yosemite concessions. The interior secretary is concerned about the "impression that the Japanese were buying up the whole United States" and he has called upon Matsushita to donate its newly acquired concessions to the National Park Service.

We agree with Lujan up to a point. Things would be ideal if Matsushita gave up its part of Americana and donated the concessions to the Park Service. But we don't think nagging the company or trying to bully it into making the donation does anything to dignify the office of secretary of the interior — or the United States government, for that matter. We suggest that Lujan lay off and let nature take its course.

Nature is already working relatively well. Matsushita officials are fully aware of how their ownership of the Yosemite concessions tends to depress the American national morale. The Japanese firm is doing everything it can to alleviate the hard feelings — everything, that is, short of donating the concessions to the Park Service. The company has promised to put the Yosemite operation into escrow for 12 months, until an American buyer can be found. In the meantime, profits generated by the concessions will be donated to the National Park Foundation, a private, nonprofit group that channels money to the parks.

Initially, the escrow agreement pleased the Department of Interior. It issued a press release thanking the Japanese "for working so hard to find a mechanism whereby the interest of our great national park will be served." Since then, however, the pleasure has faded. Lujan's department failed to approve the escrow deal and has reiterated its demand that the concessions be given to the Park Service.

That's too bad. Although we, too, would rather see Matsushita make the donation, the escrow plan is still a fine arrangement. With it, no one can sensibly argue that the Japanese exercise undue control over Yosemite. American morale is intact.

It's time to quit nagging and go with the escrow deal.

The Seattle Times

Seattle, Washington, January 5, 1991

INTERIOR Secretary Manual Lujan's Japan-bashing is inappropriate and embarrassing. Lujan, in an unseemly show of xenophobia, rants against the acquisition of hotel and restaurant concessions in Yosemite National Park by the Matsushita Electric Industrial Corp.

The concession rights were owned by a subsidiary of MCA, the entertainment conglomerate recently purchased by Matsushita. Lujan had hoped MCA would donate its Yosemite subsidiary to the federal government prior to the corporate buyout. MCA refused to make the gift, and efforts to sell the subsidiary to an American purchaser fell through.

Lujan says MCA and Matsushita's failure to get his approval for the ownership transfer may allow him to cancel the concession contract. Whether he's right on that legal point remains to be seen.

The disturbing truth is that Lujan opposes Matsushita solely because it is a foreign corporation. Yet foreign or American ownership has absolutely no bearing on whether a company is competent to manage hospitality services.

His comment, "I do think it's inappropriate for a Japanese company to come over and run an American concession when an American company can't run one in a Japanese shrine," is preposterous. He seems to forget that the National Park Service eagerly sought commercialization of Yosemite and willingly sold exclusive concession rights

The federal government makes 75 cents for every $100 spent by visitors in Yosemite. Many of those visitors are foreign tourists. It's ironic that Lujan should protest Matsushita's ownership when a big portion of the park's revenues comes out of foreign wallets.

Lujan's job is to get fair payment for concession rights and to ensure that the needs of park visitors are served. Mindless Japan-bashing is not in his job description.

The New York Times

New York City, New York, January 12, 1991

Interior Secretary Manuel Lujan proclaims that he wouldn't buy a Japanese car. In fact, he wouldn't buy any foreign car. "I don't think it does any good to siphon our money overseas," he said recently. To Mr. Lujan, it would seem, to buy American is to be all-American.

But how so? If Americans buy fewer Japanese, German or British cars, then the Japanese, Germans and British will earn fewer dollars with which to buy American soybeans. Or American computers, airplanes, pharmaceuticals and chemicals and graduate school educations.

To put the point another way, by persuading Americans to buy less from foreigners, Mr. Lujan would cause the dollar to rise in value, making it harder for American exporters to sell abroad.

The logic of trade compels the following question: If it's all-American for Mr. Lujan to help preserve jobs of Detroit auto workers, is it also all-American for him to obliterate the jobs of American farmers, chemical workers and aeronautical engineers? And if the Japanese sell fewer cars here, what happens to the jobs of thousands of Americans who now work for companies like Honda, Nissan and Toyota in the U.S.?

Perhaps the Interior Secretary should redirect his all-American attention to matters of the interior, leaving matters of external trade to officials who know the difference between facile xenophobia and hard-won foreign earnings.

San Francisco Chronicle

San Francisco, California, January 7, 1991

MANUEL LUJAN should recognize that he is no longer an obscure congressman but a member of the president's cabinet. The interior secretary may gain some political points among the yahoos when he gives way to Japan-bashing in negotiations over the concessions in Yosemite National Park, but he embarrasses the nation he purports to represent.

"Happy New Year!" Lujan said the other day. "A Japanese company now owns exclusive rights to do business in Yosemite."

Paying a ridiculously low fee of 75 cents per $100

When Matsushita Electric Industrial Co. bought MCA Inc. for $7.5 billion, it announced it had no plans to retain MCA's Yosemite Park and Curry Co. subsidiary. But Lujan and officials of the American entertainment giant have not agreed on how much the company should receive when it surrenders its investment in the Curry concessions, which include the Hotel Ahwahnee and other commercial enterprises whose value probably exceeds $100 million.

WHEN POLITE negotiations broke down, Lujan resorted to crude appeals to prejudice.

In the process, he damaged a good case. The Curry Co. has been permitted to operate its valuable concessions while paying the government a ridiculously low fee of 75 cents for every $100 it collects in sales. Because even Curry officials describe their contract as unfair, Lujan is correct in asking MCA's new owners to let the nation acquire Yosemite's commercial properties at well below their market value.

IT IS UNLIKELY that he can succeed in getting the new owners to make a generous deal if he keeps calling them nasty names. And it is equally unreasonable to expect them to sell the property at a bargain rate until Lujan agrees that the Yosemite concession will go to a nonprofit venture whose profits will be used for the benefit of the nation's national parks.

After all, MCA should hardly be called on to make a gift whose fruits might be enjoyed by a firm like the Walt Disney Co., Great America or some other competitor in the entertainment business.

ALBUQUERQUE JOURNAL

Albuquerque, New Mexico, January 3, 1991

If there is a tourist concession at Japan's Mt. Fuji, it is hard to imagine a Yankee concessionaire making the sales and raking in the profits. It is not the Japanese way.

Should the United States indulge in the sincerest form of flattery and bar Japanese ownership of the concession in one of America's natural jewels? Is that the American Way?

When Matsushita Electric Industrial Co. laid out $7.5 billion for the entertainment-leisure conglomerate MCA Inc., one of the assets acquired was Yosemite Park Curry Co.

The concessionaire holds exclusive rights in Yosemite National Park under a 30-year contract up for renewal in 1993. Given xenophobic attitudes about Japanese control of U.S. business and real estate, the contract may not survive until 1993.

"Everywhere I go, people are not happy with foreign ownership of these . . . resources," says Interior Secretary Manuel Lujan Jr. Lujan is happy to use that sentiment for leverage to pry the Yosemite hotels, campgrounds, restaurants and stores away from Matsushita.

Lujan has proposed that Matsushita simply "give" facilities valued at $300 million to the park service. Maybe the IRS would allow the Japanese company to write that off as a public relations expense — that would take some of the sting out of what Mineral Belt Republicans like Lujan used to call "nationalization" when it happened to U.S.-owned copper mines in Chile. Certainly public relations is closer to the American Way than nationalization of business assets.

Another undeniable aspect of the American Way is maximizing profit, particularly when that involves taking Uncle Sam to the cleaners. People might not be happy with the current American concessionaire, either, if everywhere he went Lujan pointed out that Curry Co. gives the government a measly 75 cents of every $100 it grosses.

A deal's a deal, even one as bad as the Interior Department made nearly 30 years. Instead of trying to weasel out of it, Lujan should bring Matsushita to the table with the carrot of gaining face, then renegotiate a deal, for a change, that's at least as good for the park and the taxpayers as it is for the concessionaire.

Matsushita Sets MCA Deal

Matsushita Electric Industrial Co., Japan's largest electronics company, Nov. 26, 1990 agreed to buy MCA Inc. of the U.S. for about $6.59 billion. It was the biggest U.S. acquisition to date by any Japanese company.

Matsushita and MCA concluded terms for a $66 per share offer. The deal included a stake in MCA's WWOR-TV television station in New York City, valued at an additional $5 per share. MCA, one of the largest entertainment companies in the U.S., comprised Universal Pictures, the MCA and Geffen record labels, Putnam Publishing Group, a 49% stake in Cineplex Odeon Corp., two theme parks and other real estate.

Matsushita, which manufactured consumer electronics under the Panasonic, Quasar and Technics brandnames, was said to have pursued the acquisition because of competitive pressures. Matsushita's major Japanese rival, Sony Corp., had purchased Columbia Pictures Entertainment Inc. in 1989.

With the completion of the MCA deal, which was expected to take place in early 1991, foreign companies would own four of seven major U.S. film studios. MGM/UA Communications Co. had been purchased by Italian-owned Pathe Communications Corp., and 20th Century Fox was owned by News Corp. Ltd. of Australia.

As part of the deal, MCA would transfer a majority stake in WWOR-TV to current MCA stockholders, in compliance with the federal regulations that prohibited foreign ownership of U.S. television stations. MCA would also sell its Yosemite Park and Curry Co. concession in California to an as yet undetermined U.S. company.

The Atlanta Journal AND THE ATLANTA CONSTITUTION
Atlanta, Georgia, December 2, 1990

If there is cause for concern in the purchase of entertainment conglomerate MCA Inc. by a huge Japanese firm, it is not the buyer's nationality. To suggest that the MCA purchase by Matsushita is any more dangerous than recent sales of other major Hollywood companies to Australian, Italian or German interests is both racist and absurd.

Still, the question is asked: Will the new owners impose Japanese sensibilities on MCA's film, television and music production? Hardly. The people running Matsushita are good businessmen. They are spending almost $7 billion to buy an American movie, TV and music conglomerate because Americans know how to produce entertainment better than anyone in the world. For Matsushita to force MCA to adopt Japanese methods and values would be as stupid as buying Toyota and forcing it to act like Detroit.

The real issue involves a trend in the entertainment industry called "vertical integration." It would work something like this:

Tom Clancy signs a contract to write a new techno-thriller for his publisher, Putnam. After months on the best-seller lists as a hardback, it is published in paperback by Berkley and movie rights are sold to Universal. A soundtrack to the movie is put out by MCA Records to people who take it home and play it on a Panasonic CD player. Universal puts the movie out on video and sells it to people who take it home and play it on a Technics VCR. Finally, a few months later, the movie that began its life cycle as a Clancy novel ends by being shown on the USA cable network, where people watch it on a Quasar TV.

Every company mentioned above, including Tom Clancy's publisher, is a Matsushita subsidiary or will be if the MCA purchase is approved as expected. Matsushita will then be able to control every aspect of an entertainment product, from its inception as a creative thought through every technology in which it can be expressed.

That is cause for concern, at least in theory. But in an international economy, the U.S. government has little ability or, to be honest, interest in blocking vertical integration. If it tried to bar U.S. companies from the continuing round of international mergers, it would accomplish little except to put domestic companies at a competitive disadvantage in world markets. Instead, it will probably remove restrictions that have forbidden U.S. companies such as General Electric from buying Hollywood movie and TV studios.

Not that it mattered in this instance. Matsushita will reportedly pay most of the $7 billion price tag for MCA out of cash reserves, something no U.S. company could have done. That is the real cause of our anxiety.

THE TENNESSEAN
Nashville, Tennessee, December 3, 1990

THE lights of Tinseltown flickered a bit last week with the announcement that a Japanese electronics firm will acquire MCA/Universal.

After weeks of negotiating, Matsushita Electric Industrial, the world's largest consumer electronics manufacturer, sealed a deal to buy MCA, one of the world's largest producers of films and television shows. MCA/Universal includes Universal Studios, Universal Pictures, Geffen Records, as well as MCA Records and MCA Music, both of which have Nashville offices. The conglomerate has given the world films such as *E.T.* and *Born on the Fourth of July* and television programs such as *Murder, She Wrote.*

The selling price of $6.59 billion makes this the largest purchase ever of a U.S. company by a Japanese firm.

No doubt, it's a smart purchase for Matsushita, which has a reputation for caution. Matsushita already manufactures TVs and video equipment through its Panasonic and Quasar brands. It also makes the new high-definition television, or HDTV equipment, and has been pushing Hollywood to switch over to the new technology to produce films. Obviously, if Matsushita companies are producing films and videos using high-definition technology, American consumers are much more likely to purchase HDTV equipment.

The purchase was also smart for MCA. It takes big bucks to compete in film and television production and MCA was competing with deep-pocketed production firms like Columbia, which is owned by Sony, and Time Warner Inc.

It was perfectly clear that for a creative production company in that league, MCA needed a parent that could afford a generous allowance. In Matsushita, it has found one.

MCA Chairman Lew Wasserman drove a tough bargain. Chief executives at MCA properties were given management contracts, assurances of autonomy, and the guarantee that all divisions will operate independently.

Any MCA officials who might still be nervous about their new owners should make a trip to Middle Tennessee. Here they could find several established Japanese-owned firms, including Nissan, Bridgestone, and Toshiba, that have been great corporate citizens, bringing jobs to area residents and revenue to local economies. In fact, Matsushita is already in Tennessee, with Matsushita Electronic Components Corp. in Knoxville and Matsushita Refrigeration in Lenoir City.

Film and television are powerful media. They play a special role because they reflect as well as influence this nation's culture. But the best way to keep American films and American television programs strong, creative, and competitive is with solid financial backing. And on that score, MCA made a very smart deal. ■

THE COMMERCIAL APPEAL
Memphis, Tennessee, December 5, 1990

MANY Americans wrung their hands when Matsushita bought MCA, seeing in the purchase yet another sign that the Japanese are turning the United States into a bargain basement.

Look at the bright side. At least we don't work for the Soviet space program.

When the manned Soyuz TM11 rocket blew into space the other day, a Japanese television reporter was aboard. His network had paid handsomely for his berth (ratings war with rival network).

The rocket was Soviet, but you couldn't tell. On its side was the Japanese rising sun. Along its barrel were logos for a Japanese pharmaceutical company and a Japanese maker of sanitary napkins.

The Soviet cosmonauts wore T-shirts sporting the logos of other Japanese companies. The launchpad was covered with billboards advertising Minolta cameras and electronic audio equipment — Japanese equipment.

A day earlier, our shuttle Columbia lifted off, gleaming white, with only the stars and stripes for decoration.

So dry those eyes, Japan-bashers. Things could be worse.

THE INDIANAPOLIS NEWS
Indianapolis, Indiana, November 28, 1990

Takeovers of nations can be aggressive and direct. They can be slow and subtle. The method is not so important as is the end result — control.

He who controls a nation's resources has effected a takeover. Ancient Japanese proverb.

Here are some of the largest acquisitions and interest purchases, with the most recently consummated transactions listed first, of U.S. companies by Japanese businesses over the last three years. Information was compiled by IDD Information Services and the Associated Press:

● MCA Inc., for $6.6 billion by Matsushita Electric Industrial Co. Ltd., announced Nov. 26, 1990. The deal includes $66 per share in cash and $5 per share in stock of an MCA television station.

● Aristech Chemical Corp., for $859 million by Mitsubishi Corp., announced Jan. 16, 1990.

● Rockefeller Group Inc., for $846 million by Mitsubishi Estate Co., announced Oct. 30, 1989.

● Columbia Pictures Entertainment Inc., for $5 billion by Sony Corp., announced Sept. 27, 1989.

● CIT Group, for $1.28 billion by Dai-Ichi Kangyo, announced Sept. 18, 1989.

● Inter Continental Hotels, for $2.27 billion by Seibu Saison, announced Sept. 30, 1988.

● Gould Inc., for $1.05 billion by Nippon Mining Co. Ltd., announced Aug. 30, 1988.

● Firestone Tire & Rubber Co., for $2.65 billion by Bridgestone Corp., announced Feb. 16, 1988.

● CBS Records, for $2 billion by Sony Corp., announced Nov. 18, 1987.

● Westin Hotels and Resorts, for $1.53 billion by Aoki Corp. with the Robert M. Bass Group, announced Oct. 27, 1987.

Japanese ownership of U.S. property was at about $5 billion in 1980. Now it's over $70 billion.

The Japanese are also opening laboratories to do research in the United States, luring American computer scientists to work for them. NEC Corp. has opened a research laboratory in Princeton. Matsushita, new owner of MCA, is planning to open a lab near San Francisco next year. Canon is starting one in Stanford, Calif. Mitsubishi is talking about starting a lab near one of the top technical schools in the nation, the Massachusetts Institute of Technology in Cambridge, sometime next year.

You see, equity isn't just real and personal property. Equity also is personnel property.

It also means purchasing American debt. It means loaning money to American businesses which will become Japan's if those loans are defaulted upon.

The Japanese are well aware of what it takes to exert power — money. Whether for a U.S. conglomerate or an experienced Ph.D. in electrical engineering, the Japanese know that the top dollar will win the bidding game.

They have the money to bid. MIT computer scientist Thomas Leighton, who has had "informal talks" with Mitsubishi, confirmed that Mitsubishi salaries are 20 to 30 percent higher than the best offers U.S. scientists could get from universities or American labs.

So what is the nature of Japan's economic incursion? Is it aggressive and direct? Or slow and subtle? Has it been revengeful these past 45 years — buying up and dividing America's economic prizes? Or is Japan's ownership of such American bastions as CBS Records, the Rockefeller Group and Firestone merely an unavoidable facet of world trade to which Americans can only shrug their shoulders?

These are interesting philosophical questions. Should Americans continue to philosophize upon the finer points of Japanese methods and motives, gee-whizzing about the next U.S. conglomerate Japan just purchased or, instead, put the brakes on Japan's unimpeded economic takeover?

The debate should begin now.

The Hartford Courant
Hartford, Connecticut, November 28, 1990

Quick quiz: Who are Hollywood's newest movie moguls?

Akio Tanii and Norio Ohga, of course.

Such names cause discomfort among those who believe that the ultimate expression of America's culture should remain in the hands of Americans.

Mr. Ohga is president of the Sony Corp., which owns Columbia Pictures and CBS Records. Mr. Tanni is president of Matsushita Electric Industrial Co., which has agreed to pay $6.13 billion for MCA Inc., owner of Universal Studios as well as one of America's biggest record labels, a publishing house and theme parks.

Japan's business barons have been doing what their American counterparts had done for decades: buying companies here, there and everywhere — giving meaning to such terms as the global corporation and international conglomerates.

Before joining the call for rebuilding a fortress America, consider that the acquisition of MCA would put roughly one-quarter of the American movie-making market into the hands of Japanese-based companies. That is scarcely domination of the market.

Consider also that the huge price Matsushita is paying for MCA indicates that America's economy is still strong and that this nation remains a crucial player in the global economy.

What about the Nipponization of Tinseltown? That won't happen. Japanese firms that have already bought into entertainment businesses in the United States have not influenced the "software" side of things — the films, television programs, music. The Japanese do best with the hardware.

Rather than fearing the foreign takeover of the entertainment industry, Americans should be glad that a concern is willing to pump in the billions of dollars that Hollywood needs to continue taking risks. MCA chairman Lew Wasserman acknowledges that his firm has not had the needed financial resources to keep up in the emerging global production and distribution system.

The Matsushita-MCA deal may benefit America's three major television networks indirectly. The networks, unlike the foreign investors, cannot own a film studio or buy an interest in a show made by Hollywood. Outdated protectionist regulations, imposed to keep the TV moguls from taking over Hollywood, should be repealed.

In addition to capital, the Japanese may bring some discipline to the entertainment industry. Matsushita officials say they expect to leave most of MCA's management intact but will impose budgetary restrictions on the company's farflung operations. Japanese competition has "encouraged" America's auto makers and their unions to be more efficient and make better-quality cars. Hollywood and its celebrities should take note.

THE PLAIN DEALER

Cleveland, Ohio, November 29, 1990

Many Americans understandably feel uneasy about increased foreign ownership of U.S. assets. Those fears have been further inflamed by this week's $6.59 billion purchase of a giant U.S. communications and entertainment firm, MCA Inc., by a Japanese conglomerate, Matsushita Electric Industrial Co. The MCA purchase — the largest ever by a Japanese company in the United States — surpasses recent deals for other high-profile U.S. properties, including Columbia Pictures, Firestone tires and New York City's Rockefeller Center.

Similarly, this week's announcement that Toyota, the giant Japanese automaker, would expand its plant capacity in Kentucky has stirred considerable U.S. resentment. Even though mountains of economic data show that foreign-owned auto plants in the United States have higher productivity than plants owned by Detroit's Big Three — and are, on balance, a positive addition to the U.S. manufacturing base — Toyota's announcement grated on many Americans' feelings, coming as it did when domestic automakers are under severe stress.

Each transaction provokes an outcry that newly rich foreigners are buying up the nation's wealth. Ironically, the United States is now on the receiving end of the capital flow it once dominated: For most of the years since World War II, aggressive American purchases overseas fed foreigners' resentment of U.S. arrogance.

Are Americans' economic anxieties justified? Yes, in part. Something is indeed out of balance in the international economy: The United States surrendered its global economic pre-eminence during the 1980s, falling from the world's largest creditor nation to become the world's largest debtor. But blind bashing of foreign investors diverts attention from the genuine cause of the U.S. economy's woes.

Home-grown errors, not foreign-made conspiracies, weakened America's stature in the 1980s. Throughout the decade, the United States pumped a vast amount of dollars overseas — through the federal budget deficit and the consumer-driven trade deficit — effectively mortgaging part of its future to foreign creditors. It is no surprise that those dollars, which helped pay for the consumption binge of the 1980s, are now coming back in different forms: as purchases of financial assets, direct investment in plant and equipment, and ownership of U.S. Treasury bonds.

Foreign investment is not an economic disease; it is only a symptom of a deeper malaise. The overextended U.S. economy, like any enterprise that has taken on too much debt, has lost some of its flexibility. Rather than bemoan their lost economic stature, American consumers, corporations and government leaders must take the steps that will be essential in working off the debt: balancing the books, reducing consumption, reaping slimmer short-term profits and investing toward greater long-term rewards.

Stepped-up foreign investment is sending a signal to Americans for the 1990s: After a decade of self-indulgence, the United States must brace itself for a decade of self-discipline.

The Des Moines Register

Des Moines, Iowa, November 30, 1990

Yet another American fish has been swallowed by yet another overseas whale.

There's already been a loss of national pride with the previous sales of such national symbols as Rockefeller Center and the original Standard Oil (Sohio), sold to deep-pocketed foreign bidders. But with Matsushita Electric's purchase of the MCA entertainment conglomerate (MCA brought us JAWS, E.T., and Conway Twitty), there's growing concern about the imposition of foreign values on American culture.

Will MCA's new owners interfere with the selection of scripts and movie topics, Matsushita's president was asked? According to a New York Times report, he declined to answer.

Was he thinking what many people in other countries might be expected to think? That after decades of Americans unloading everything from Ronald McDonald to "Dallas" on them, it's about time they do a little unloading on us?

Perhaps. But if MCA's new owners are as shrewd as they appear, they won't do anything to offend American buyers of their products, which now range from home electronic gear to movies, records and tapes.

Of more concern to Americans ought to be the economic conditions that have resulted in the United States rapidly becoming a debtor nation — a lack of savings, the high federal deficit that has fed a huge trade imbalance and a loss of competitiveness.

Foreign investment in America is not necessarily negative. The United States is attractive because it is politically stable and because investments here are relatively secure. And foreign owners have upgraded many of their purchases, making them more competitive.

For their part, Americans continue to want to invest abroad and to trade on the growing world market. That's precisely why Gov. Terry Branstad, as you read this, is in Southeast Asia promoting Iowa products and encouraging investment in the state.

America increasingly must operate in a world economy. It can't be successful by rejecting foreign investment. It can be successful only by addressing the underlying economic problems that continue to eat away at its ability to compete.

The Miami Herald

Miami, Florida, December 1, 1990

AMERICANS HAVE a knack for fantasy, a knack perfected in the postwar years when the U.S. economy briefly became an Emerald City, seemingly Great and Powerful beyond measure, surrounded by munchkins. The movie imagery is no mere figure of speech: Nothing typified and entertained America's heroic self-image like Hollywood, the garish but oh-so-bountiful curator of the American soul.

Well, so much for that. Much of Hollywood is part of Japan now, as is much of that other American icon, the auto industry. In the last few days, two giant Japanese companies dropped a couple more ice cubes into America's Big Chill. Matsushita bought the Hollywood conglomerate MCA, and Toyota announced a new Kentucky plant, its second, that could make it one of the Big Three auto makers, outpacing Chrysler.

One common reaction: fury and handwringing. "Japan is buying America on the cheap; we need protection, barriers to investment; we must thwart the invader." This, too, is a reaction out of Hollywood (John Wayne comes to mind), but it is the wrong reaction. Japan earned the pre-eminence that it now enjoys. Besides, America *needs* Japanese investment, having too little of its own to feed its consumer appetite.

During that fantastic postwar period, investors and Wall Street money managers gradually replaced the engineers and entrepreneurs who created America's industrial strength. It wasn't long before American ingenuity was devoted more to quick financial gain than to the long-range manufacturing and product development on which Japan has built its empire.

Admittedly, much of Japan's empire also rests on fierce, unfair protectionism, industrial oligopoly, and a government control intolerable to Americans. But it has produced unprecedented private savings, long-range planning and development, and consumer products that Americans can neither disparage nor do without.

America is not defeated, merely challenged. Hollywood would know how to handle this scenario: an epic of long, patient struggle with a cast of endearing young toughs showing pluck and mettle, rediscovering their ancestors' values, and finally reemerging to oust the foe. In Hollywood, it would take about two hours. For American industry, the trial will be much longer.

The Washington Post

Washington, D.C., November 28, 1990

ANOTHER tremor of uneasiness will run through this country as a gigantic American entertainment company, MCA Inc., is taken over by an even more gigantic Japanese conglomerate. The buyer, Matsushita Electric Industrial Co., is the second Japanese firm to buy a major American movie maker; Sony Corp. took over Columbia Pictures last year. How much uneasiness is justified?

The first concern is foreign influence over American popular culture. A movie studio is arguably very different from a tire manufacturing company or a hotel chain—other recent Japanese acquisitions. Movies are powerful conveyors of attitudes and impressions, and there's always a possibility that a foreign owner might try to use the studio for national advantage.

But as possibilities go, that's pretty remote. The United States has had a lot of experience with foreign investment in sensitive areas, and it's hard to think of examples of a foreign owner exercising that kind of influence successfully. Any attempt to try it would risk wrecking the American subsidiary's reputation—and profitability.

That raises another concern: Can a Japanese parent, imbued with an utterly different view of the world, successfully run any operation as freewheeling and un-Japanese as a Hollywood studio? That's not entirely a private matter for the stockholders. The entertainment industry is an important part of the American economy.

Beyond those questions lies a range of anxieties about foreign ownership in general. It's a lot easier for Japanese investors to buy a company here than for Americans to reciprocate. But a lot of the doubts here are visceral. Americans are more accustomed to owning companies abroad than to having foreigners own them here. The balance swung last year, and now foreigners have more dollars directly invested in companies in the United States than Americans have abroad.

In one crucial respect, anyway, that's excellent. Foreigners have earned hundreds of billions of dollars through the enormous American trade deficits of the past nine years, and it's good for the economy that they are investing them here in productive enterprises. Having lived well through the 1980s on money borrowed from abroad, Americans are in a poor position to complain when some of the lenders cash in those debts for eye-catching assets like Rockefeller Center, or Columbia Pictures or MCA.

But if Americans think that the surge of foreign ownership has gone far enough, they have a remedy at hand. It requires them to spend a little less, save a little more and eliminate that foreign trade deficit. As the world becomes more closely knit together, companies will continue to buy and sell each other across national boundaries. But with the trade deficit eliminated, foreign ownership here would no longer grow faster than American ownership abroad.

The Philadelphia Inquirer

Philadelphia, Pennsylvania,
November 28, 1990

Our thoughts about Japan's Matsushita Electric Industrial Co. buying the parent company of Hollywood's Universal Pictures *(Jaws, E.T., Born on the Fourth of July)* are akin to our thoughts last year about the Mitsubishi conglomerate purchasing Rockefeller Center: It's all legal and proper, but it serves to remind us of the price the country pays for running humongous trade deficits with Japan.

Last year, we proposed renaming the New York City landmark Mitsubishi Center to help people understand what it means when America loses its competitive edge. By the same token, we would hope that Universal Pictures becomes Matsushita Pictures — perhaps using Mount Fuji in its logo.

One could argue, and even take comfort in these times of self-doubt, that the Japanese are actually paying tribute to America. They're acknowledging that making movies is one thing that Americans still do better than anyone else. Go to any world capital, including Tokyo, and you'll find that American movies dominate. But now that four of the seven principal Hollywood studios are about to be foreign-owned, you have to wonder who's dominating whom.

Bush, Kaifu Confer
on Trade Frictions

U.S. President George Bush April 4, 1991 conferred with Japanese Premier Toshiki Kaifu in an effort to smooth frictions over world trade and funding for the Persian Gulf war.

The meeting, in Newport Beach, Calif., appeared to be largely symbolic. Both leaders were apparently seeking to present a united front in the face of widespread charges in the U.S. that Japan was an unreliable ally.

Following their 90-minute meeting, held over lunch, Kaifu said his nation's efforts to to help in the Persian Gulf war had "not been fully understood and appreciated" in the U.S. Some American lawmakers had complained that Japan had made no human commitment in the gulf and that its pledge of financial aid to the war had been made reluctantly.

Bush said he hoped "most Americans understand the constitutional constraints on Japan in terms of human forces." Japan's so-called peace constitution, drafted by the U.S. after World War II, forbade the use of the military for non-defensive purposes.

Of $13 billion pledged to help fund the war, $7.8 billion had so far been paid by Japan. An installment of aid pledged by Japan in February had been donated in yen. Because the dollar had risen against the Japanese currency, the contribution's value had fallen to $8.6 billion from $9 billion. Some lawmakers had said the original dollar amount of the pledge should have been honored.

The leaders said they had discussed recent disputes on trade but reached no substantive agreement. Bush reiterated his belief that the General Agreement on Tariffs and Trade multilateral trade talks were the best forum in which to resolve such disputes.

Chicago Tribune

Chicago, Illinois, April 2, 1991

Japan seems to be going out of its way these days to disappoint, if not anger, its friends. Its halting response to the Persian Gulf war was annoying, even if it ultimately was generous.

But its recent refusal to allow American growers to display 10 pounds of rice at a food exhibition in Tokyo was a needless provocation, and it drew a justified rebuke from Washington.

Japanese farmers complained that the display violated the country's ban on imported rice. That a few small bags of rice posed a threat to an industry that sells 10 million tons a year is patently absurd. That government officials would act—some say threaten—to have the rice removed is outrageous.

The incident shows why free trade and the multinational trading system are in jeopardy. Four years of talks to liberalize and expand the rules of trade collapsed last December when Germany and France led a European effort to protect their farmers and block open agricultural trade. Instead of siding with the United States and other food-exporting nations against the Europeans, Japan remained silent.

The trade talks have resumed, and Washington wants Japan to open its rice market—if only a crack—as a symbol of support for the world trading system and for a successful end to the latest round of negotiations. But Tokyo doesn't want to upset Japan's 3 million farmers, many of whom are more efficient at political influence than at growing rice on their tiny paddies. As a result, the government coddles them with subsidies and protection, and the Japanese pay more than twice what Americans do for rice.

Meantime, the Japanese are said to be worried that the U.S., fresh from its victory in the Middle East, is itching for another fight—this time over trade. Certainly, many in Congress and in U.S. industry are unhappy with Japan. The National Association of Manufacturers recently asked the Bush administration to reassess the nation's alliance with Japan. In a report last month, the White House singled out Japan as the worst offender in trade barriers.

Some lawmakers want the White House to step up pressure on the Japanese to open markets and further reduce the trade deficit with the U.S. It has been declining in recent years, dropping to $41 billion last year from $49 billion in 1989.

The United States shouldn't throw its weight around unilaterally and insensitively, ignoring cultural differences. But when President Bush meets with Japanese Prime Minister Toshiki Kaifu later this week in California, he should continue to push for open markets and free commerce, while working to strengthen the critical alliance with Japan.

As for Japan, it's time to wake up. It must become more assertive in the post-Cold War world. That means accepting the responsibilities of leadership as well as the benefits of the orderly environment created by others. It means that, instead of sending police to check out exhibitions of foreign rice, it must relax its own offensive ban on rice imports and become a more responsible partner in the system of free trade that has made it so wealthy.

THE CHRISTIAN
SCIENCE MONITOR
Boston, Massachusetts,
April 10, 1991

THE brief Newport Beach summit between President Bush and Japanese Prime Minister Toshiki Kaifu last week produced soothing words about stopping the "bashing" on both sides of the Pacific. These words were needed, since the emotions between Tokyo and Washington have been rising of late, stoked by ongoing trade frictions and controversy over Japan's contribution to the war.

Such fuming can tend to blur the critical importance of Japan to the US, and vice versa. The leaders were right to refocus attention on the need to work cooperatively.

President Bush gave the prime minister a political boost by affirming the US was satisfied, overall, with Japan's war contribution. The actual payment to Washington from Tokyo came up a little short of the $9 billion promised because of shifting exchange rates. But if Japan makes up the last few hundred million in aid to refugees in the Middle East, that ought to be fine by the US, given current pressures to address the region's humanitarian crisis.

The trade issues will be harder to lay to rest. Mr. Bush raised the touchiest of these: US rice exports. An opened Japanese market would not amount to much economically, except to a few US farmers. Japan already imports over $8 billion in US farm goods, 20 percent of total US agricultural exports.

With rice, it's the symbolism that counts. Sales to Japan would demonstrate that the Japanese had agreed to take down their most venerable trade barrier. They would also indicate that Japan was ready to join the US in breaking through the farm-subsidies logjam that brought critical international talks on the General Agreement on Tariffs and Trade to a halt last year.

Kaifu has hinted that Japan may be ready to give a little on rice, opening perhaps 10 percent of the market to US growers. Such hints have been heard before. This time, we hope, they'll be followed by action.

Other issues are queued up along with rice – Japanese government procurement policies that exclude foreign suppliers and barriers to US service companies, to name two. But many of the "barriers" to US penetration of Japanese markets have more to do with understanding the Japanese business environment than with legal restriction.

Recognition of interdependence – many US companies and employees now rely on Japanese goods, after all – should stop any emotional drift toward "bashing" and punitive trade practices.

The Cincinnati Post
Cincinnati, Ohio, April 5, 1991

Japan's Prime Minister Toshiki Kaifu says U.S. criticism of his country's record on trade makes him gnash his teeth. His discomfort evokes limited sympathy here, since the critics are mostly justified.

As President Bush properly emphasized at the two men's mini-summit in California Thursday, progress has been made; Japan has dropped some tariffs and complied with numerous commitments to lower import barriers to U.S. goods. Those efforts are appreciated.

But Japan without question must do much more. Trade is too central to the health of the world economy today for so mighty a commercial nation to resist the rules.

The overall international rules are those of GATT, the General Agreement on Tariffs and Trade. GATT's future is in the balance, partly because of Japan's tepid support for including services and agricultural products in the free-trade system.

Kaifu insists he is firmly committed to the Uruguay Round of talks on expanding GATT. Yet Japan's tariffs on agricultural products, for example, average an unduly high 12.1 percent. Quotas limit imports of wheat and flour, and foreign rice is altogether banned, in violation of the "minimum access" principle.

Partly for political reasons, Japan's ruling party is loath to discomfit the country's three million farmers who grow rice. But production costs are six times as high in Japan as in the United States. Even with government subsidies, Japanese consumers pay two and a half times as much for rice as Americans do.

The picture is not uniformly bleak. The U.S. trade deficit with Japan is shrinking. And far-reaching talks on fundamental cultural and economic structures impeding trade between the two countries are under way. All the same, the case of rice illustrates the reasons for Americans' frustration.

The San Diego Union
San Diego, California, April 4, 1991

The recession is intensifying protectionist fever on Capitol Hill. And no target looms larger than Japan, which is widely seen by Americans as having shirked its responsibility in the Persian Gulf while persisting in unfair trade practices.

President Bush needs to convey this mood to Prime Minister Toshiki Kaifu when the two meet today in Newport Beach. Tokyo must understand that its lack of token participation in the gulf coalition, combined with doubts about whether it will provide financial assistance, threatens to further hamper U.S.-Japanese relations.

During last year's meeting in Palm Springs, Kaifu assured the President that many of Japan's trade barriers would be lowered, allowing U.S. goods greater access to its growing domestic market. Although a few barriers were lowered last year, a Bush administration report confirms that Japan remains one of the most protectionist of America's leading trading partners.

Japanese tariffs still keep out petrochemicals, paper products and aluminum. Many types of farm imports are barred from Japan, even though the country cannot produce enough food to feed its population. Another sore point is Japanese barriers against rice imports. If these barriers were removed, American rice exporters could increase their sales by $656 million annually.

Japan has made a few trade concessions by opening its markets to beef, citrus, satellites, supercomputers and wood products. But Kaifu has not fulfilled his promise to make it easier for foreigners to invest and do business in Japan. Similarly, Japan's procurement policies routinely exclude many kinds of U.S. goods and services.

U.S. Trade Representative Carla Hills has been prodding Japan to liberalize its rigid import policies. Meanwhile, Commerce Secretary Robert Mosbacher and a delegation of American businessmen are in Tokyo, trying to pry open the Japanese market.

By taking a tougher line with Japan, the Bush administration helped bring about a $7 billion reduction in the U.S.-Japanese trade deficit last year. Nevertheless, the remaining $41 billion deficit with Japan is this country's largest.

President Bush should tell Prime Minister Kaifu that the surest way to blunt the protectionist momentum in Congress is for Tokyo to lower its trade barriers. Otherwise, the protectionists will exploit fully the surge of anti-Japanese sentiment which the gulf war has helped to create.

THE SUN
Baltimore, Maryland, April 8, 1991

It will take more than a sunny meeting between President Bush and Prime Minister Toshiki Kaifu to smooth over the troubled American-Japanese relationship. While the two government chiefs dutifully put their emphasis on blandness rather than bashing during their short summit in California last week, they could not wish some very real irritants out of existence.

At the top of the list is trade friction, emphasized only recently by Japanese threats to arrest American rice exporters trying to display their wares in Tokyo and by Japan's perch at the top of a U.S. list of unfair trading nations. Add to that U.S. criticism of Japan's refusal to send military personnel to the gulf war, and you get an unhappy situation that the summiteers tried to mitigate.

For Mr. Bush, the session helped him accumulate IOUs that, presumably, he will cash if and when Tokyo's support (rather than its past sabotage) is needed to rescue the General Agreement on Tariffs and Trade. Mr. Kaifu's objectives were more immediate. The Japanese prime minister could lose his hold on office if his candidate for the governorship of Tokyo does poorly in next weekend's election. Equally important, he needed a show of trans-Pacific solidarity before facing Soviet President Mikhail S. Gorbachev April 16, date of the first visit ever of a Kremlin boss to Japan.

On the Kaifu-Gorbachev agenda is the perennial question of the return of four islands north of Hokkaido that the Russians occupied at the end of World War II. If Mr. Gorbachev pulls one of his surprises by giving back the islands, he might be able to attract Japanese investment in the exploitation of Siberian resources, much to the advantage of the foundering Soviet economy. Such a development could deflect some Japanese capital needed to finance the U.S. budget deficit and set up a new triangular relationship in which the U.S. inevitably would lose some leverage.

In our view, Mr. Kaifu's continuation in office would be helpful. While he could not overcome opposition in the Diet to Japanese participation in the gulf war, he risked his political neck in pushing through an $11 billion contribution that Mr. Bush rightly labeled as generous. He also could be instrumental in overcoming the $41 billion U.S. trade deficit with Japan if his position is strengthened at the polls and through lengthening incumbency.

"Toshiki Kaifu and I are committed to see that bashing doesn't go forward and that this relationship goes on," Mr. Bush said after the summit. Fair enough, but the relationship had better change substantively for the better — and soon.

Los Angeles Times
Los Angeles, California, April 4, 1991

California seems to provide a rejuvenating setting for U.S.-Japan relations. For the second year in a row, President Bush will venture from the Beltway—and Prime Minister Toshiki Kaifu will travel across the Pacific—for a West Coast tete-a-tete aimed at calming down roiling U.S.-Japanese relations.

The two leaders will meet in Newport Beach today to make up for a spring trip to Tokyo that the President postponed in order to meet with the Persian Gulf allies. The Japanese prime minister is eager to reaffirm the U.S.-Japan global partnership, strained anew by Tokyo's disappointing response to the Gulf crisis.

Tokyo hopes to recoup lost respect and status at a time when Washington is short on patience and long on criticism. Polls reveal that grass-roots America feels let down by Tokyo's checkbook diplomacy in the Gulf; in Congress, Tokyo sometimes seems to have replaced Moscow as everyone's candidate for knocking. Despite a hefty $11-billion contribution to the multinational forces in the Gulf, the perception is that an unsure and reluctant Tokyo didn't carry its fair share. For its part, Tokyo cries foul, noting that it did as much as possible considering its constitutional ban on sending troops overseas. It's getting very tired of what it sees as unrelenting Japan-bashing.

Such emotions are damaging to U.S.-Japan relations at a time when the two nations need to work more closely than ever on the mutual concerns of trade, the Mideast and Tokyo's upcoming talks with the Soviet Union. The big challenge for Bush and Kaifu is to break an unsettling push-pull dynamic that is distorting the relationship. Washington finds itself doing a whole lot of pushing—playing hard ball with Tokyo to secure changes in trade policy. In response Tokyo does a whole lot of pulling—relying and even encouraging foreign pressure—*gaiatsu*—before mustering the political will to instigate changes within Japan. The fallout from such a dynamic engenders a sometimes hegemonic attitude on the part of Washington that results in bullying consensus-driven Tokyo into making promises public before it can secure the political clout to deliver them.

Ironically enough, U.S.-Japan relations are turning frosty precisely when the fundamentals of their trading relationship are improving—albeit slightly. The U.S. trade deficit with Japan has been less terrible each year for the past four years, narrowing to $41.1 billion in 1990—the lowest level since 1984. Japan is the largest importer of U.S. agriculture. Meanwhile, Tokyo and Washington have resolved many major trade issues. Washington, to be fair, has not been particularly speedy in delivering on its promises to cut the U.S. budget deficit, shore up savings and improve the education system.

Still, with $40-plus billion still to go on the trade deficit account, and with U.S. exports a driving force in the nation's recovery from recession, trade is important to the Bush Administration. Unfortunately, the United States still does not have the trade opportunities in Japan that Japan has here. Tokyo erects too many barriers to trade.

Tokyo's continuing ban on rice imports has been a particularly divisive issue. The Administration was disappointed by Tokyo's lack of support on agricultural issues at multilateral trade talks last December. A recent threat by Japanese agricultural officials to take legal actions against the USA Rice Council for displaying American-grown rice in Japan did little to relax the relationship. Perhaps Tokyo will address the rice issue after Japan gets through its local elections Sunday.

The image of Bush and Kaifu as pals makes for a wonderful photo, but it oversimplifies the realities of the U.S.-Japan connection, complicated by differences in cultures, political systems and priorities. Still, the mutual and proper priority is in improving U.S.-Japan relations. The best way to achieve that is to work at it constantly, step by step. Today's summit meeting won't accomplish a great deal, perhaps, but it is hard to believe that it can hurt.

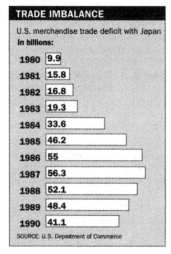

TRADE IMBALANCE

U.S. merchandise trade deficit with Japan

In billions:

Year	Deficit
1980	9.9
1981	15.8
1982	16.8
1983	19.3
1984	33.6
1985	46.2
1986	55
1987	56.3
1988	52.1
1989	48.4
1990	41.1

SOURCE: U.S. Department of Commerce

The Seattle Times
Seattle, Washington, April 7, 1991

WHEN George Bush met his friend Toshiki Kaifu in Newport Beach, Calif., a few days ago, he was too polite to offer the Japanese prime minister some American rice and a ripe Washington apple. Yet those and other trade barriers continue to rub raw a unique marriage of economies that has linked Japan indelibly to America, and especially to this region.

Every time a president meets a Japanese prime minister, the interests of Washington state are not far away. Sales to Japan from Washington companies total over $4 billion a year, or 21.5 percent of all exports from the state.

Japan leads all countries in buying Washington saw logs, lumber, fish, aluminum and wheat. About 18 percent of all Japanese imports entering the United States come through Washington — $16.5 billion worth of goods.

These are crucial ingredients to the vitality of the Northwest. Over four decades, the United States and Japan have merged their economies in useful, irrevocable ways, often to the benefit of the people of Washington.

But sometimes, even in the best of marriages, things can go sour in a hurry.

The Gulf War was hugely unpopular in Tokyo, especially when Japanese families learned that their high cost of living would rise to help pay for the war. Japanese complain that the United States will not live within its means and will spend itself into the poorhouse. Irritatingly, they then paid $13 billion of war contributions in yen instead of dollars, causing a $400 million shortfall.

In America, manufacturers see a new assault on the domestic market in auto and truck parts, matched with Japanese bullheadedness over opening their own rice and produce markets, always at higher prices to Japanese consumers. Many Americans feel a war has just been fought so that Japan could continue to prosper at our expense.

It's enough to give any marriage counselor a headache.

Bush and Kaifu smoothed over these differences and pledged once again to work toward mutual cooperation, but the hardest months may be just ahead. A presidential campaign in which Democrats are looking for a solid bread-and-butter issue leaves Japanese trade policies vulnerable to some tough sloganeering.

Unless Japan opens its markets to more U.S. — and Washington state — exports, Japan could find itself as the Willie Horton of the next campaign.

Rising Friendship

The Honolulu Advertiser

Honolulu, Hawaii, April 5, 1991

The mini-summit between President Bush and Japanese Prime Minister Toshiki Kaifu yesterday was an effort to put a happier face on a partnership neither side can escape. It was a mixed success — at best.

Bush thanked Kaifu for Japan's contribution to the Gulf War. That's appropriate, though many still feel it came too slowly and grudgingly.

Japan's constitution prevented sending combat troops, but the failure to make even a symbolic non-monetary commitment rankles those already angry over the latest trade differences, like rice. On these issues Bush said it's time "to move ahead." When was it not?

Japan's first post-Cold War attempt to answer the question,

Kaifu

"What do we stand for in a changing world?" was frustrating all around. Talk now of reconstruction and environmental clean-up aid, while useful, somehow rings hollow.

On the horizon is Soviet President Mikhail Gorbachev's visit to Tokyo in 10 days, the first by a Soviet leader.

With U.S.-Japan ties still so rocky, some see a stronger Soviet-Japan relationship as a new equation in the emerging "new world order."

The Japanese and American economies are now intertwined so tightly it's hard to imagine a more remote relationship. But some positive, future-looking joint project is still badly needed to revitalize this often difficult but enormously beneficial alliance.

THE KANSAS CITY STAR

Kansas City, Missouri, April 4, 1991

President Bush meets today in California with Japanese Prime Minister Toshiki Kaifu, and the White House has been receiving a good deal of advice about which issue should receive the greatest emphasis. Some say Bush should press Kaifu for an end to Japan's rice-import ban. Others call for Tokyo to augment its Gulf War contribution to cover the value lost caused by the declining yen.

Japanese-American relations are at a low point, and certainly the two leaders will have much to talk about. But most of the differences are minor next to the importance of success in talks under the General Agreement on Tariffs and Trade. The current GATT round of negotiations, the eighth since World War II, is attempting to broaden world trading rules to cover a number of new sectors, such as intellectual property, trade-related investment and services. The most contentious area is agriculture, and here Japan's role is crucial.

If these talks are to succeed, Tokyo must put aside its impulse to cringe in the background. Japan must play an active and positive role. In December, when the negotiations collapsed over how, when and how much to roll back farm subsidies, Japan actually helped in the scuttling; it sided with the Europeans in rejecting a Swedish-proposed compromise.

It is a sad statement on the quality of Japanese leadership, but Bush must remind Kaifu of Japan's real interest. Certainly, success in the GATT would be a huge boost for the U.S. economy, but for a nation such as Japan — which lives and dies by commerce — the stakes are even larger.

It is true that on the issue of agricultural subsidies, Kaifu and the ruling Liberal Democratic Party are in a tough spot. The farm sector is one of the LDP's main props, and any government that agrees to roll back subsidies and allow the import of foreign rice will pay a heavy price.

Yet failure to do otherwise will exact a greater toll in lost opportunity — a loss that will be borne for generations not only in Japan but throughout the world. For Tokyo, the choice is inescapable. Bush must make his case forcefully.

Japanese Rice Issue
Causes Friction with U.S.

Officials of Japan's agriculture ministry March 26, 1991 said they would send a delegation to Washington, D.C. to try to reduce trade frictions that had been heightened by Japanese authorities' threat to arrest U.S. rice producers who were exhibiting their wares at a show in Tokyo. The threat drew a sharply worded letter to Japan's minister of agriculture, forestry and fisheries from U.S. Agriculture Secretary Edward Madigan. Japan currently barred all rice imports. Its stand had been a stumbling block in the General Agreement on Trade and Tariffs multilateral trade talks.

Los Angeles Times
Los Angeles, California, June 5, 1991

Will the summer of 1991 be the season for a new bloom in U.S.-Japan trade relations? Long, difficult negotiations have finally yielded two agreements that will give American and other foreign companies greater access to Japanese construction and semiconductor markets. Now if Tokyo would only accept a similar agreement for rice.

The actual economic benefits of these market-opening measures may be minimal initially, but they are powerful symbols of the trade issues causing discord in the U.S.-Japan partnership.

Washington and Tokyo reached a tentative agreement Saturday to open up 17 more public-works construction projects to U.S. and other foreign firms. The number is less than the United States wanted, but it spares Tokyo sanctions that Washington had threatened to impose.

On Tuesday the two nations agreed to extend a 1986 semiconductor agreement that will increase foreign companies' share of the Japanese chip market over five years. In exchange, $165 million in U.S. sanctions imposed on Japanese electronics imports in 1987 will be lifted.

Despite this progress, Tokyo's ban on foreign rice continues, much to U.S. irritation. Japanese politicians, beholden to farmers, defend the policy on grounds of food security and the sanctity of rice. But if Washington had played by such a rule, the United States would never have tolerated Japanese auto imports. The almighty automobile, after all, has been at the heart of American life and industry. The lesson of openness is one facet of U.S. business that Tokyo has yet to master.

The State
Columbia, South Carolina, April 6, 1991

THE JAPANESE protect their markets more than any of the world's modern economies, particularly the relatively small and inefficient agricultural segment. How fiercely protective are they?

When Americans displayed 10 pounds of rice at a food exhibition recently in Tokyo, the reaction couldn't have been more pronounced if the United States had announced intentions to open an Uncle Ben's plant with free introductory samples for all. The Japanese farmers called it a flagrant violation of the Japanese law banning imported rice. They threatened the exhibitors, first with a turn-off of electricity and then with arrest, before the Americans retreated upon advice of the U.S. Embassy.

Japanese rice costs six times as much to produce as American rice. This would suggest trade opportunities, and Washington is suggesting to Japan a modest opening of its rice market: 3 percent of its total annual production of 10 million tons, or 300,000 tons. The chief beneficiaries wouldn't be American growers, but large Southeast Asian producers like Thailand.

But establishing this modest trade goal will be difficult to achieve with intransigent attitudes as those held by the Japanese farmers.

THE SACRAMENTO BEE
Sacramento, California, March 22, 1991

As top-level U.S. and Japanese officials work to smooth over testy feelings about trade issues and Japan's reluctant role in the Persian Gulf War, those down in the trenches show a real knack for triggering new skirmishes. Consider last week's Rice Offensive.

At a food fair in Tokyo, U.S. rice producers put on display 10 pounds — 10 pounds! — of American-grown rice: No sales, no free samples, just a few small bags of rice. Officials at Japan's Food Agency, which distributes heavily subsidized homegrown rice at high fixed prices and enforces the ban on the sale of foreign rice in the country, were not amused. This is sales promotion! they complained, and after the U.S. exhibitors ignored a demand that the rice be removed, the food police threatened to arrest everyone connected with the exhibit. The rice was then removed.

In Japan, rice is so sacrosanct that the protection of the industry is even justified on national security grounds. In response, U.S. members of Congress have made such a fuss that it's caused needless friction — needless because if Japan stopped growing rice tomorrow and bought only American rice forever, the resultant decline in the U.S. trade deficit would be almost too small to notice.

So why are Americans so shrill about rice? Because it's easier than explaining the much more subtle trade barriers that Japan erects — a complex distribution system, for example, or a de facto "buy Japan" public procurement policy. It also diverts attention from our own failure to produce more competitive products.

Yet overall, U.S. exports, including farm exports, to Japan are huge and rising. The trouble is that Japanese exports to this country are even greater, although in fact the gap is narrowing rapidly. Both countries are guilty of a variety of trade sins, solutions to which are complex and long-term. Public squabbling over 10 pounds of unsalable rice is a wonderfully stupid way to make the task even more difficult.

The Gazette

Cedar Rapids, Iowa, June 9, 1991

FOR IOWANS, the accomplishment may not offer much in the way of personal reward. But it could. The apparent readiness of Japan to relax its rigid refusal to import American rice is an important crack in Japan's armor. Iowa cattle farmers have made modest inroads recently, of course, but the rice-import issue marks perhaps a more significant step toward removing some of the impediments to equitable trade created by Japan.

While it's not an accomplished fact at this time, there is strong evidence that barriers soon will be lowered, if not eliminated. Japanese leaders, long adamantly against an import policy that might challenge the domestic rice monopoly, are taking a more realistic approach. A partial gap in the trade barrier, they say. Others hint that Japan may be ready for a compromise.

It may not mean much in terms of paring the United States trade deficit — although last month brought good news on that front, as well. The smallest trade imbalance in years. Acceptance of imported rice speaks of far more than the immediate monetary gain to American rice-growers.

It whispers of potential field-leveling opportunities in other areas of trade where Japan has imposed tight restrictions on its import policy while ringing up huge trade surpluses abroad. That the gap between exports and imports was narrowed last month is less a result of Americans buying less Japanese merchandise, than a monetary rate that made U.S.-made goods more attractive overseas.

Given the chance, there's no doubt that American goods can compete anywhere, under any conditions.

Rice may not mean much to a factory worker in Iowa, but the fact that Japan might be ready to put American rice on its store shelves is cause to hope more of our products may follow. Soon, we hope.

Newsday

New York City, New York,
March 23, 1991

It was only 10 pounds of U.S.-grown rice, on display at a trade fair in Tokyo. You'd think it was Godzilla or something, the way the Japanese government moved to banish it.

No, the rice was no threat to health or safety; by law it couldn't even be sold in Japan. It's offense was that it was *cheap*. It sells in America for less than half the price of rice in Japan.

But for Tokyo, cheap is a gargantuan problem. It's a threat to Japan's trade policy, which bars rice imports entirely even as Japan swamps the globe with cars and TV sets, and to farm policy, which rewards inefficient rice growers at the expense of consumers.

With the world's major nations engaged in fierce negotiations at Geneva to lower barriers to agricultural trade, Tokyo is rightfully worried that it will get some of the blame if the trade talks fail because of its trade barriers.

So fearsome were those 10 pounds of U.S.-grown rice that Japan's Ministry of Agriculture actually threatened to arrest the Americans staffing the display of the U.S. Rice Council if they didn't hide the grain.

If the prospect of a few bags of cheap rice being on public display is *that* scary to the Japanese government, maybe — just maybe — it is doing something wrong. And knows it.

The Phoenix Gazette

Phoenix, Arizona, June 4, 1991

Extraordinary. Historic.

There is no other way to describe what is happening in Japan. First, the Japanese agreed to send four minesweepers to the Persian Gulf to help in the mopping up of Iraqi mines, the first overseas mission by Japanese military personnel since World War II.

Then, following deft diplomatic pressure applied by Vice President Dan Quayle, Japanese Prime Minister Toshiki Kaifu and Eiichi Nakao, minister of international trade and Trade, agreed to address the imbalance in automobile trade between the two countries.

Finally, the last sacred vestige of Japanese trade barriers is about to succumbed to diplomacy and political reality: Japan will soon allow foreign rice into its long-locked doors.

The change has international consequences because agricultural trade issues dominated December's General Agreement on Tariffs and Trade — and caused that "Uruguay Round" to fail.

Those GATT talks focused on trade in services and agricultural goods as the United States, Australia and Canada argued for expanded global agricultural trade. But the European Community resisted. European farmers, heavily subsidized, fear that liberalized agricultural trade will mean American products will come pouring into Europe.

As the EC and the United States battled over the issue, American diplomats understood that if Japan announced it would open its own restrictive markets to rice imports, however modest, that sea change would encourage the European Community to be more flexible about opening its own agricultural market to foreign products.

Though he received little credit when he was in Japan in November for Emperor Akihito's enthronement, Vice President Quayle raised the issue of rice imports with the Japanese and encouraged the Japanese to relax their restrictions on rice imports and help in pressuring the EC to be equally flexible.

The longer they delayed, Quayle reminded them, the less credit they would be given by the U.S. government for saving the GATT talks.

In Japan, rice has always been am emotional issue, a part of the culture. For a Japanese politician to suggest Japan should open its rice markets is as if a U.S. Congressman would argue that Social Security benefits should be cut 40 percent to help balance the budget. But, such arguments are now being heard in Japan, indicating that the closed door is about to open, indicating that such change can be both profound in Japan and helpful to the United States.

THE INDIANAPOLIS STAR

Indianapolis, Indiana, June 5, 1991

Vice President Dan Quayle and Canadian Prime Minister Brian Mulroney may have budged Japan from its long time ban on rice imports.

In recent visits to Japan they strongly urged it to break the deadlock in international trade talks sponsored under the General Agreement on Tariffs and Trade (GATT), the world's main free trade authority. The talks stalled in December over agricultural supports and trade barriers.

Japan may be bowing to pressure on the issue. On May 28, *Yomiuri Shimbun*, its largest circulation paper, said Japan would allow entry of foreign rice, but limited to 5 to 10 percent of its $23.5 billion rice market. Foreign rice is currently limited to only 0.5 percent, which means the market is effectively closed.

The Federation of Economic Organizations, Japan's largest business group, now supports opening the rice market. It fears that if the trade talks remain stalled, it may face tough U.S. sanctions, probably on automobiles and other manufactured goods.

But Japan also faces heavy domestic pressure from the Central Union of Agricultural Cooperatives, a powerful group representing farmers, which is intensifying its lobbying efforts against imports.

The Japanese, heavy rice consumers, have ambivalent feelings about that staple. They pay more for it because of the import ban. Others back the ban, expressing concern over insecticides and a desire for rice self-sufficiency. Probably rice growers, fearful of cheaper foreign competition, support the ban more than do rice consumers.

Sources say Prime Minister Toshiki Kaifu's decision to allow rice imports will be announced in late June shortly before a summit of leading industrial nations in London.

If so, Quayle and Mulroney will deserve points for winning that small victory for freer world trade.

Bush Backs Special Trade Status

President Bush May 15, 1991 said he favored extending China's most favored nation (MFN) trading status for another year. Bush's statement provoked criticism in Congress and appeared to have caught members of his own staff off-guard. MFN granted the most favorable rates possible on U.S. quotas and import tariffs.

"I look at the big picture," said Bush, explaining his position. He announced his stance to the press in an unscheduled question-and-answer session after a luncheon with Senate Republicans at which he said he made a "big pitch" for renewing MFN for China.

A decision on MFN had not been due until June, the deadline for the administration to formally notify Congress of its intentions on the issue. Bush had revealed his stance before receiving the normal option papers from government agencies. Following the president's remarks, White House spokesman Marlin Fitzwater claimed that Bush had not made a formal decision on the question.

In his remarks, Bush cited China's lack of opposition in the United Nations to the U.S.-led war against Iraq. "I look at the support we got from China back in Desert Storm, the importance of China as a country. And I don't want to see us isolate them," he said. He conceded, however, that "there are major problems in China."

The president had headed the U.S. mission in China in 1974–75. He generally took decisions on China in consultation with only one or two advisors.

A series of recent events had heightened tensions with China and fueled opposition to extending its MFN status. China had been accused of sending missiles to Pakistan and of helping Algeria construct a nuclear facility that could be used to make atomic weapons. The Commerce Department had listed China as an unfair trader. And a visit to Washington, D.C. by the Dalai Lama, Tibet's spiritual leader, had served as a reminder of China's uneven human rights record.

Many lawmakers had criticized Bush administration policy toward China as too soft since the crackdown on pro-democracy demonstrators in Beijing in 1989. They said Bush had failed to condemn the crackdown strongly enough and that he had been too eager to ease diplomatic and economic pressures in the following years.

Bush's most recent remarks on China's trade status came as legislation was being prepared in Congress to either amend or end that status. A bill that had been introduced in the House favored granting MFN status to China for another year while specifying that it would expire in 1992 if no progress was made on human-rights and trade issues in the meantime.

U.S. President Bush May 27 said he would renew most-favored-nation trade status for China. In an apparent effort to mollify domestic critics of the renewal, the White House May 27 announced sanctions aimed at punishing China for recent weapons sales in the Third World.

At a May 27 Yale University commencement address, Bush argued that continued trade with China would provide the best leverage for reforms there. He derided foes of MFN for China as advocates of a U.S. policy of "righteous isolation." Such an approach would amount to a disengagement from China's problems, he said. Many Democrats had opposed continued MFN status because of China's human rights record.

In the sanctions announcement, made separately, the Bush administration banned exports of certain sensitive high-technology equipment to China. China was rumored to have been selling ballistic missiles to Pakistan that were capable of carrying nuclear warheads. The items barred from export included high-speed computers, satellites and missile technologies.

Bush's decision on most-favored-nation status could be blocked by a resolution supported by majorities in both houses of Congress. But if Bush vetoed the resolution, a two-thirds vote of both houses would be required to override the veto.

THE DENVER POST

Denver, Colorado, May 17, 1991

GEORGE BUSH is poised to renew special trade benefits for China, despite his claims that he hasn't formally made up his mind.

That means China will continue to export its goods to the United States and pay only the lowest tariffs possible, despite the fact that many of those goods are produced by imprisoned political dissidents working in slave-labor conditions.

China also will continue to enjoy trade benefits America supposedly extends to friendly and cooperative nations, even though the People's Republic exports nuclear arms and long-range missile technology to such unpredictable Third-World governments as Syria and Algeria.

What's more, Bush will continue to pretend that America profits from commerce with China, even though the imbalance of trade between the United States and China is exceeded only by our import-export deficit with Japan.

If the United States plans to use its trade barriers as a diplomatic tool to encourage other nations to respect human rights and behave honorably in global matters, then we should do so consistently. But by continually granting most-favored-nation trade status to China, when that country has made almost no progress in those crucial areas, America shows itself to be egregiously hypocritical.

An unlikely political alliance is forming in Congress to nix Bush's decision. But even with disparate players such as Republican arch-conservative Jesse Helms and Democratic pragmatist Daniel Patrick Moynihan as part of this nascent alliance, it may be difficult to rally the two-thirds vote needed to overturn the president's decision.

A more practical move may be to suspend China's most-favored-nation status for a year. If China stops enslaving political prisoners, and if it stops exporting the tools of Armageddon, then the United States could restore the trade benefits.

At this point, because of China's poor record of responding to America's pleas for better behavior, it seems the United States has little to lose by playing hardball.

THE SACRAMENTO BEE
Sacramento, California, May 17, 1991

THE CHINA issue has moved to the center of post-Cold War American foreign-policy debate. The immediate question is the technical one of whether and on what terms to renew most-favored-nation (normal) trading status for China. The larger, political question is how the United States ought to weigh "soft" factors such as human rights in the new circumstances of fading strategic urgency. That the White House and Congress are in the different parties' hands adds an aspect of institutional and partisan conflict to the brew.

President Bush has not wavered in his determination to offer China another annual extension of MFN. Over the weekend, speaking at Yale, he polished up his principal argument—that it is dangerous and false to think the United States can influence China more by snubbing it than by "engaging" it. His is a more "moral" approach, he protested, than that of his critics. Further to dull their edge, he announced some new sanctions, which penalize China but keep an executive hand on the tap. These suspend sales of further high-speed and super computers, halt exports to a Chinese arms corporation on grounds that Beijing has transferred ballistic missile technology to Pakistan and restrict approval of new satellite licenses until China "satisfies" U.S. "missile technology concerns."

Congressional Democrats are loading for bear. They contend with much merit that the Bush approach is not only immoral but foolish in that it practically invites China to ignore American strictures on human rights, trading practices and weapons proliferation. They have in mind extending MFN for only six months or revoking it altogether, and they are drafting tougher sanctions and setting out to write them into law.

Mr. Bush is right on the broad requirement to avoid an all-or-nothing showdown that might spin out of control and cost Washington the links it uses for contacts with the outward-looking, export-oriented elements of Chinese society and for leverage on the Chinese authorities. By his own past insensitivity to official human rights violations, however, he has conveyed indulgence for the aging rulers in Beijing and lost much of his claim to congressional deference. Congress may have trouble mustering the two-thirds majority needed to override the expected presidential veto of heavily conditioned sanctions legislation, but it can make sure the Chinese hear a loud and unequivocal American protest about their errant ways.

The Washington Post
Washington, D.C., May 29, 1991

President Bush has ended speculation about whether he will recommend continued favorable trading status for China by saying emphatically that he will. "I look at the big picture," he says.

That's hardly surprising from a president who sees himself as an Old China Hand, and whose response to the bloody crackdown against pro-democracy dissidents in Beijing two years ago was restrained, to say the least. Persuasively, Bush says it's important not to isolate a major Asian power and the holder of a veto in the United Nations Security Council. Less persuasively, he argues that things are "an awful lot better" in China than when he served as U.S. envoy there during the mid-1970s.

Up to a point, Bush is right: When he was in Beijing, the Great Proletarian Cultural Revolution, in which countless acts of official brutality were committed in the name of Communist purity, was not quite over; it was followed by a springtime of hope as Deng Xiaoping introduced economic reforms, including an opening of the country to foreign business, and, by Chinese standards, a measure of personal freedom.

More recently, China has retrogressed. Hundreds of dissidents have been given long prison sentences — an unknown number are believed to have been executed — for no more than advocating democracy; the repression of Tibet continues, mostly hidden from Western eyes; human rights groups accuse China of using forced labor to produce exports, in violation of international conventions; Beijing's soaring trade surplus with this country is abetted by tightening restrictions on access to China's market; intelligence reports tell of Chinese sales of missile launchers, nuclear weapons-making know-now and other artifacts of modern warfare to several Middle Eastern countries.

All of this helps to fill out Bush's "big picture" of Chinese reality, one that has stirred many in Congress to support revocation of China's privileged trading status when it expires July 3. At the very least, there ought to be an extensive debate in which Beijing's behavior can be fully aired; at the very least, Congress ought to tie continued trading privileges to specific improvements in China's human rights, arms sales and trading practices.

Rep. Nancy Pelosi of San Francisco has reintroduced a bill to make such a link. It deserves support, both from those who, like Bush, can see the "big picture" and those who are simply outraged by the behavior of a regime that violates so many civilized norms and, when criticized, ominously threatens "serious repercussions" against anyone who dares to impose sanctions.

Americans should not flinch from such threats. China may have supported the U.S. position on crucial Security Council votes against Iraq, but beyond that it has hardly been cooperative. Its support of the Khmer Rouge guerrillas in Cambodia's civil war remains an obstacle to ending that conflict. Indeed, its behavior abroad is much worse than that of the Soviet Union, which is still waiting for the favorable trading status with Washington that Beijing has enjoyed for more than a decade. Congress must put China on short notice that that status is very much at risk.

The Union Leader
Manchester, New Hampshire, May 19, 1991

President Bush's bid to extend most-favored-nation status with Red China is politically stupid and morally repugnant.

The man who went to war to liberate tiny Kuwait ignores the monsters who terrorize the single largest population on earth.

New Hampshire Congressman William Zeliff backs Bush, which is very disappointing and may come back to haunt the freshman congressman.

"My biggest concern would have been back around Tianamen Square," Zeliff told The Union Leader last week. "We've made some progress and they've made some progress . . . To disrupt it now would be ridiculous."

It is Zeliff who sounds ridiculous.

Why the U.S. should have to make progress is beyond understanding. It is the Chinese butchers who massacred their own children at Tianamen Square. And the progress they have made has been to buy their way into the President's good graces by donating to the Gulf War effort.

Since the war, however, evidence has mounted that the Chinese are back to supplying Iraq with illegal weapons.

The day after Rep. Zeliff's remarks, the Chinese made even more "progress" by shutting down a demonstration in Tibet, the tiny nation it seized years ago.

Zeliff should listen to his colleague, Sen. Bob Smith.

The Chinese "must stop exporting products manufactured by forced labor and demonstrate good faith in controlling the proliferation of chemical and biological technology and weapons," Smith said.

Indeed, much of China's export products are made by prison labor — a fact Senate Democrats like Pat Moynihan were quick to point out last week.

The Bush administration is giving the Democrats a free ball with this issue. It will deserve all the bashing it gets in return.

THE TAMPA TRIBUNE
Tampa, Florida, May 28, 1991

Freedom demands sacrifice. And the battle for freedom draws upon people's most heroic instincts and abilities.

I call on Prime Minister Li Peng to free political prisoners in China and allow the United Nations Commission on Human Rights to investigate possible human rights violations in China. I challenge Mr. Li Peng to let China live in peace with its neighbors. And I challenge Mr. Li Peng to follow the examples of countries like Nicaragua, Panama, Paraguay and Chile in their achievement of new democracies.

Put democracy to a test — permit political parties to organize and a free press to thrive. Hold free and fair elections under international supervision.

Our goals for the Chinese nation, shared by Chinese everywhere, are plain and clear. Freedom and democracy, Mr. Li Peng — not sometime, not someday, but now. If China holds fully free and fair elections under international supervision, respects human rights and stops subverting its neighbors, we can expect relations between our two countries to improve significantly.

Thank you, and may God bless the freedom-loving people of China and the United States.

* President Bush never has directed words such as these at China. These words are precise excerpts from Mr. Bush's broadcast appeal to Cuba on May 20. The only changes are that when the name Fidel Castro appears we substituted Li Peng and for Cuba we substituted China, the hardline Communist nation for which Mr. Bush announced Monday that he will seek unconditional renewal of most-favored-nation trade privileges.

THE TENNESSEAN
Nashville, Tennessee, May 17, 1991

A nation that tortures people, imprisons political activists, trades arms with outlaw nations, ignores international law and enslaves human beings deserves no favors from the United States.

China is guilty of all of those charges. Although other world events have pushed China off the front pages, its record on human rights has not improved in the last 12 months.

And, sad to say, neither has President Bush's judgment in regard to China.

President Bush suddenly declared this week that he wants to extend most-favored nation trading status to China. That status means that goods exported from China to the U.S. would have the lowest possible tariffs.

No foreign policy issue has divided the Bush administration and Congress more than that of this nation's relationship with China. In 1975, Bush served as envoy to China, and he has revisited China several times since then.

Clearly, on this one nation, Bush feels that he is his own best adviser. This week, he announced his decision to extend China's favored trading status even before the required reports on China were delivered to the White House.

The granting of most-favored nation status is solely within the authority of the White House. Bush officially has until by June 3 — which is, by the way, one day before the second anniversary of the Tiananmen Square massacre — to recommend the extension.

Congress can vote to reject the favored nation status for China, as it did last year. But since that vote would surely be vetoed by Bush, Congress would need to muster two-thirds of its members behind such a resolution in order to make it stick.

This year, Bush contends that China deserves special consideration because it was an ally of the U.S. during the tense preamble to the Persian Gulf War.

He is right that China voted with the U.S. against Iraq in the U.N. Security Council. But so did the Soviet Union. And that nation doesn't enjoy most-favored nation status.

Congress is already positioning itself to mitigate any favoritism Bush demonstrates to China. Senate Majority Leader George Mitchell introduced legislation yesterday that would grant favored status to China, but six months later would require Bush to certify that China had made radical progress on human rights, trade, weapons sales and forced labor.

The people of the United States were appalled at the actions of China against its own people two years ago. Rarely in modern times has a peaceful movement toward democracy been so brutally crushed.

Bush has a soft spot both in his heart and in his head about China. He has a special relationship with China's leadership. But he should ask himself what good that relationship does if the U.S. continues to make all the concessions and China continues its brutal repression. ∎

Post-Tribune
Gary, Indiana, May 23, 1991

President Bush finds himself the target of well-founded criticism after his abrupt announcement that he wants special trade status for China continued.

The president should rethink the extent to which the United States will support China's hard-line Communist leaders and the repression they brought to the country after its flirtation two years ago with democracy.

The designation would allow Chinese exports to enter the United States at a favorable tariff rate.

> **Our opinion**
>
> The president should rethink the extent to which the United States will support the repression in China after its flirtation two years ago with democracy.

Senate Majority Leader George Mitchell, D-Maine, accused Bush of having a blind eye for China. Bush served as ambassador to China during the Ford Administration. Bush is not blind. It's his heart that is in the wrong place.

The massacre at Tiananmen Square two summers ago was more cold-blooded than the invasion of Kuwait by Iraq. Saddam Hussein at least had an economic goal in mind — control of Kuwaiti oil fields. The violent crackdown in China and the subsequent squelching of dissident voices seeks to break the human spirit.

Nor have Chinese leaders kept their end of the bargain they agreed to when special trade status was renewed last year. China promised to stop selling weapons to the Middle East; it didn't. American trade officials also accuse the Chinese of exporting goods to the United States that are made by prisoner labor, which violates treaties China signed. This is not the kind of economic activity that the United States should foster.

Continued most-favored-nation status would send a message to the world that the United States will tolerate oppression, if it comes from the right quarter.

The special trade status is automatic unless Congress votes it down. Such a vote should be forthcoming.

Rockford Register Star
Rockford, Illinois, May 19, 1991

It is only right that many members of Congress, conservative Republicans as well as liberal Democrats, are raising a fuss over President Bush's announcement that he wants to extend China's favorable trading status with the United States for another year. Beijing's dubious record on human rights hardly merits such deference.

Those trading privileges, known as most-favored-nation status, are set to expire on July 3. The president has until June 3 to formally recommend the extension, which will take effect 90 days thereafter — unless Congress rejects it. Congress should do just that, or at least include stiff conditions for maintaining the status, as would be the case with a bill introduced last week and sponsored by 37 members of the Senate.

The Bush adminstration's attitude toward China is passing strange, especially as compared to its policies in the Middle East. The president boldly sends a half-million U.S. troops to war in the Persian Gulf in defense of oil-rich dictatorships, but he only winks at Beijing's brutal suppression of pro-democracy demonstrators in Tiananmen Square.

The problem would seem to be Bush's assessment of himself as a genuine expert on China, stemming from his days as envoy to Beijing in 1975. He seems unduly reluctant to strain or sever his ties with the Beijing regime. But what kind of expertise is it that advocates granting extraordinary trading privileges to a regime that stubbornly clings to its brutal, communistic ways? What kind of "new world order" does Bush advance with this hypocrisy?

Better that Bush — or Congress, if need be — force China to make a choice between having relatively free access to American markets or continuing its abysmal policies regarding basic human rights.

Newsday
New York City, New York, May 17, 1991

President George Bush's decision to renew most-favored-nation status for China was unfortunate and clumsy — not in substance, but in timing. By announcing it at this time, Bush has tossed away his chance to use the lure of favorable trading terms to persuade China to side with the United States in the coming vote at the United Nations to establish a security force for Kurdish refugees in Iraq.

China had already indicated it might veto the UN resolution, fearing it would set a dangerous precedent for intervention in domestic ethnic disputes. A Chinese veto would mean that U.S. troops would remain deployed in Iraq much longer than expected.

Granted, the decision to grant MFN status just before the UN vote may dispose China

more favorably toward the United States. But maybe not. Keeping China guessing may have exerted more effective pressure, combined with skillful behind-the-scene maneuvers.

The president, however, should not be faulted for the merits of his decision. True, Beijing has yet to clean up its act on human rights violations. But taking away the MFN designation, which allows China to export goods with the least restrictive tariffs, should have been done immediately after the Tiananmen Square massacre, not years later.

Bush fears that taking away MFN now would further isolate China and strengthen the hand of hard-liners who could then claim they had nothing left to lose in perpetuating human rights abuses. Distasteful as the cur-

rent Chinese government practices are, Bush has a valid point.

But the announcement of his intent was premature. Perhaps in belated recognition of this haste, Bush later said he would consider attaching some unspecified conditions to MFN status for China. Bush need not have precipitated a pitched battle with Congress over this issue at this time. And he should have at least taken time to consult with his own staff experts on the MFN issue, rather than making a seemingly high-handed decision based largely on his own gut instinct as a former ambassador to China.

For someone who prides himself on his skill at diplomacy, Bush proved himself remarkably maladroit.

Hong Kong Port Plans Unveiled; China, Britain Discuss Troop Issue

The Hong Kong government Oct. 11, 1989 announced plans to build a major new international airport and a harbor for container shipping in the territory during the next two decades.

The HK$127 billion (US$16 billion) project, reported to be the largest civil engineering venture in Hong Kong's history, was unveiled by Gov. Sir David Wilson in a speech to the British colony's legislature. The announcement was considered by many observers to be aimed at boosting confidence in Hong Kong amid the uncertainty surrounding the territory's future under Chinese rule. Hong Kong was to be returned to China in 1997.

The centerpiece of the project was to be a huge, two-runway airport constructed on Chek Lap Kok, a small piece of Lantau Island, about 15 miles from downtown Hong Kong.

Scheduled to be opened in early 1997, the airport would be able to operate 24 hours a day and would have the capacity to handle 80 million passengers a year. Hong Kong's existing airport, Kai Tak, located in the densely populated Kowloon peninsula, currently handled about 15 million passengers a year. When the new facility was fully operational, Kai Tak would be closed, officials said.

The complex would be connected to the rest of Hong Kong by a new high-speed rail system, a new bridge and tunnel and a six-lane highway.

In addition, a container port would be constructed on landfill along the western coast of Hong Kong, near Chek Lap Kok. The port, scheduled for completion in the year 2006, would increase by five times the territory's capacity for container shipping.

Chinese and British negotiators met for three days in London Sept. 27-29, 1989 to discuss the transfer of Hong Kong's sovereignty to China in 1997.

The meetings reportedly were dominated by debate over China's professed right to station regular army troops in Hong Kong once it regained control over the British colony.

THE PLAIN DEALER
Cleveland, Ohio, June 8, 1989

No wonder anger and panic have gripped Hong Kong. Already fearful of what lies in store when China takes back the colony from Britain in 1997, Hong Kong's capitalist-minded masses, like most other people, have been outraged by events in Beijing. With more reason than most, they also have been alarmed by the Chinese government's ruthless suppression of popular expression in favor of democracy. While Hong Kong itself is not a democracy, its people today enjoy a greater measure of freedom than their mainland compatriots; they must wonder how long that privilege will continue once China annexes the territory.

Unfortunately, the British government, led by Prime Minister Margaret Thatcher, this week offered little to encourage Hong Kong residents who are worried about their future. There was no tough talk, as some newspapers had demanded, of breaking off negotiations with the Chinese, of unilaterally introducing democracy in Hong Kong, or of reviewing the colony's status. Instead, Thatcher spoke vaguely of seeing "what can be done" to strengthen legal and constitutional rights for Hong Kong's 5.6 million people, of whom 3.5 million are Chinese holding British passports.

Ultimately, however, Britain will honor its bargain with China. Perhaps, in the long term, given China's massive presence adjacent to the tiny colony, the British have no alternative. Yet not all her compatriots are convinced the Thatcher government is powerless to secure more guarantees for Hong Kong's population.

Particularly vexatious is the fact that Chinese holders of British passports are not automatically eligible for immigration to Britain, even though other Western countries have offered hospitality to Hong Kong residents who are prepared to bring capital with them. This week, the government confirmed its resistance to accepting Chinese refugees en masse, citing existing difficulties in absorbing smaller numbers of immigrants from other former British possessions. Officials evidently were not moved by the plea of a leading Hong Kong resident who said: "I sometimes wonder what the British people feel when they read about Hong Kong British subjects scurrying about the world to find somewhere else to take them in."

Of course, by 1997, a new, more enlightened regime might be in power in Beijing and the students' sacrifices might not have been in vain. It is easy to understand, however, why Hong Kong's people are not optimistic and why many of them believe that, in one way or another, a British government too eager to ingratiate itself with China has betrayed them.

ST. LOUIS POST-DISPATCH
St. Louis, Missouri, February 18, 1989

In 1997, a 99-year lease between the English and Chinese governments will end, and the crown colony of Hong Kong is to pass from British to Chinese control. This event in the making already is having a noticeable impact throughout Asia.

Last year, 45,000 people moved out of this crown jewel of capitalism because they fear the conditions that will prevail when the Chinese communist government in Beijing takes over. The exodus is expected to grow, particularly if details of an agreement for the future political structure of Hong Kong are not resolved to ensure full democracy. Banks and other commercial enterprises have begun to relocate in such Asian cities as Singapore and Bangkok, where the economies, if not the politics, are freer than Hong Kong's may be in a decade.

Whenever they have left former colonies, the British have tried with varying degrees of success to leave a democratic government in place. Hong Kong may be the exception. The Chinese have agreed to maintain Hong Kong as an autonomous region for 50 years after 1997, but they are hanging tough in preventing the spread of very much political democracy among the 5.5 million residents. In an apparent concession to its own future commercial interests in China, Britain is not driving a hard bargain for more democratic institutions.

London has known for years that China would invoke the end of the lease, which was forced on the Chinese emperor during the height of British imperialism. Yet the British have done little to instill full democratic traditions in its colony. It has kept the fixture of an appointed governor, which is advised by an unelected executive council. Such representatives are allowed mainly as advisers. Had the British really intended to leave behind their proven political system of democracy, they should have started decades ago. Now, the possibility of reform has been delayed.

The Globe and Mail

Toronto, Ontario, July 5, 1989

If the Chinese government pursues its self-interest in a sensible, rational way, it will leave Hong Kong alone. Hong Kong is a major investor in new mainland businesses, and the Chinese government has substantial interests in established colony corporations. Above all, Hong Kong can provide the mainland regime with foreign currency to buy the technology it desperately needs.

That's the line of argument that sold the British in the early 1980s when they negotiated the terms of the return of Hong Kong to China in 1997. The Chinese would never be so rash as to kill the goose that lays the golden egg, British Foreign Office types said confidently.

The view was not confined to the British. Until a few months ago, Hong Kong businessmen were praying that paramount Chinese leader Deng Xiaoping enjoy good health and a long, long life. They were convinced that if Mr. Deng could assure a smooth succession in Chinese leadership, and perpetuate his policies, their interests would be protected.

But can the Chinese government be expected to exercise enlightened self-interest? And will it abide by the treaty with Britain that guarantees no interference in Hong Kong's social and economic life for at least 50 years? This week, British Foreign Minister Sir Geoffrey Howe was in Hong Kong trying to convince citizens of the colony that both questions can be answered affirmatively. However, he does not exude the confidence of old.

China's past offers no comfort in the matter of enlightened self-interest. The history of twentieth-century China is an unrelenting chronicle of convulsion and national mutilation. These days, it is difficult to believe that any country operating along the lines advocated by Marx and Lenin is enlightened or even vaguely aware of where its best interests lie. When Maoist innovations such as the Cultural Revolution are added to the mix, the picture turns grisly.

On the issue of whether Chinese leaders can be expected to honor their promises, it is necessary only to remember Li Peng's vow never to use violence against the students of Tiananmen Square. The Chinese government's media campaign to deny the slaughter of students and other citizens of Beijing provides a neat insight into its respect for truth. Moreover, China never accepted the legitimacy of Great Britain's 150-year-old administration in Hong Kong. It is hard to imagine that the Chinese government, once it has taken possession, will feel under any continuing obligation to its treaty with Britain.

Although more than three million citizens of Hong Kong hold British papers, the documents have not been adequate to win entrance to the mother country for decades. Besides, for most of the people of Hong Kong, China, not Britain, is the motherland. A recent poll indicates that less than 6 per cent of citizens would go to Britain even if they were offered the choice.

It is probably unrealistic to hope that a more enlightened Chinese leadership will succeed the one now in place and recognize the virtues of an unreformed Hong Kong. However, it is certain that the politics of China will shift again when Mr. Deng dies, and it is hard to imagine that the new regime will be less enlightened.

The best that can be hoped is that the international community will receive those citizens of Hong Kong who want to leave and will provide them with an opportunity to pursue a life of freedom and prosperity. Having forsaken its obligation to offer citizens of Hong Kong haven in Great Britain, Margaret Thatcher's government should at least help organize relief elsewhere.

Joe Clark could usefully raise this matter at the upcoming Commonwealth Conference in Kuala Lumpur. There is much to be done.

The London Free Press

London, Ontario, July 8, 1989

The British find themselves somewhere between the proverbial rock and a hard place in responding to demands that they open their doors to an estimated 3.7 million Hong Kong Chinese eligible for British passports. That would be a compassionate response, but it's also socially and economically impractical.

Foreign Secretary Geoffrey Howe dealt with that troubling reality this week in a forthright speech in the soon-to-be former British colony. He was no doubt dispatched by Prime Minister Margaret Thatcher to dispel any hopes that Hong Kong residents, fearful of losing their freedom when China takes over in eight years, would be welcome in Britain.

Under a 1984 British-Chinese agreement negotiated by Thatcher, China is to resume political control over Hong Kong in 1997. Under the agreement, China guarantees that Hong Kong can keep its capitalist economic and political system for 50 years after the turnover and enjoy a "high degree of autonomy."

Following the brutal suppression of reform in China last month, residents of the British outpost have become increasingly apprehensive about their future. Billions of dollars of capital are flowing out of Hong Kong, much of it destined for Canada, particularly British Columbia.

Britain, of course, bears primary responsibility for the plight of its colonial subjects, but immigration of such potentially massive proportions could create havoc in an environment already plagued with social upheaval caused by earlier open immigration from Commonwealth countries. Granted, a recent poll indicated that only six per cent would move to Britain if given the opportunity — but how reliable is a poll based purely on hypothesis in a situation like Hong Kong's?

So Howe had legitimate cause to tell his audience, which was angrily unreceptive, that there was no way the British government could invite several million people to immigrate. He said it would impose unbearable strains on Britain's housing, employment and transportation.

What Britain can and should do is seek firm reassurances from the Chinese that their commitments to economic and political freedom for Hong Kong will be honored.

Beyond that, Howe's offer to open its doors "if things did go catastrophically wrong" in the territory after 1997 — and to encourage other countries to do the same — is about the best that could reasonably be expected.

Rather than criticize Britain's reluctance to open her doors now, it would be preferable for the international community to work together to help out later, in a co-ordinated resettlement effort, should the understandable fears of Hong Kong residents be realized.

Newsday

New York City, New York, July 8, 1989

The marriage of the century — between Communist China and capitalist Hong Kong — now has all the romance of a shotgun wedding. The Chinese rulers who massacred pro-democracy demonstrators can hardly be trusted to respect civil and human rights in Hong Kong once the British colony goes behind the bamboo curtain in 1997.

This is hardly the ideal moment for Prime Minister Margaret Thatcher to pledge that despite her "utter revulsion and outrage at the indiscriminate firing on people," Britain would abide by its commitment to hand over the colony to China. That lends credibility to the notion that London values trade with Beijing over the rights of its Hong Kong subjects.

Instead, Thatcher should announce that since China has gone to war with its own people, her government intends to reassess the 1984 agreement by which London relinquishes the colony. Until Britain and the people of Hong Kong are confident that China will honor the treaty's terms preserving the territory for 50 years as a self-governing enclave, she should suspend negotiations with Beijing on the laws by which Hong Kong will be governed after it comes under Chinese rule.

Panicky Hong Kong residents deserve more than vague assurances from Britain and from China that their rights will be untrammeled. The sad fact is that London and Beijing have seen to it that those rights are severely limited. For most of 150 years, the whole wealthy, productive territory has been run by a governor general sent by the queen. Shamefully, direct elections for a chief executive and council aren't envisioned until 2011.

For their own protection and for a voice in their own future, the people of Hong Kong should have democratic institutions long before the Union Jack comes down for the last time. And if a haven for refugees ultimately is needed, Britain is obliged to provide one. It cannot simply abandon Hong Kong's population to the tender mercies of Beijing.

Bush Warns South Korea on Trade Protectionism

While in South Korea, during a tour of Pacific Rim nations, U.S. President George Bush Feb. 27, 1989 made a speech to the National Assembly in which he issued a stern warning to the nation's influential farmers to open South Korea's agricultural markets to American produce.

Bush had reportedly extended his stay beyond the airport visit originally planned and added the address to the assembly at the request of South Korea.

Bush referred to the "fool's gold" of trade protectionism, which he urged farmers to abandon.

"Nothing will stop the engine of Korea's economic growth faster than new barriers of international trade," he said.

Bush also lauded South Korean President Roh Tae Woo's efforts to improve relations with North Korea and said he would work closely with Roh to "draw the North toward practical, peaceful and productive dialogue."

Ten opposition lawmakers boycotted the speech.

In Seoul, Bush met with opposition leaders, including Kim Dae Jung. Opposition politicians and government officials told him of rising anti-American sentiment in South Korea, particularly with regard to U.S. trade pressure.

Students and others staged anti-U.S. protests Feb. 26-27. Riot police clashed with demonstrators protesting the Bush visit in Pusan and Inchon, and more than 500 people were arrested in the two-day period.

On his return to the U.S. Feb. 27, Bush commented that his trip to the Far East had been "productive and rewarding" and underscored "that America is and will remain a Pacific power." "Common ground was found."

In a related development, in his final week in office Reagan administration U.S. Trade Representative Clayton Yeutter, now the Bush administration's agriculture secretary, targeted the European Community and South Korea for market opening talks and potential retaliation on telecommunications, it was reported Jan. 25, 1989. The action complied with a provision of the 1988 Omnibus Trade and Competitiveness Act that forced the executive branch to formally identify trading partners that blocked U.S. telecommunications exports.

The Washington Post
Washington, D.C., March 1, 1989

SOUTH KOREA gave President Bush a conspicuously cool reception during his short visit. It became still cooler when he got onto the sensitive subjects of trade and protectionism. The Koreans' extraordinary rise in wealth is a matter of intense national pride, and any foreign criticism of their trade strategy is naturally met with hostility. Korea's output per person has more than doubled in the past decade, rising far faster than Japan's. While Koreans seem to take Mr. Bush's words as an attempt to deflect a potential competitor, that's a serious misunderstanding.

Mr. Bush told them bluntly that protectionism is a threat to their progress. His point goes beyond economic theory, and apparently it hasn't yet been fully grasped in Seoul.

Protectionism, some economists argue, can speed up the growth of a small and poor country's prosperity if—this condition is crucial—it has access to open markets abroad. Korea's export-led growth strategy has succeeded because the American market, despite some notorious exceptions, has remained relatively open. Mr. Bush was bearing the unwelcome message that Korea has now become sufficiently strong that its excursions into protectionism will no longer be ignored by other countries, including this

one. There has been a shift in American attitudes on trade in favor of demanding greater access to foreign markets for American exports.

Mr. Bush is accurately conveying the spirit that currently prevails here. Korea is now too large a force in world trade—too rich, too successful, too far advanced in its technology—to keep claiming poverty as grounds for special exceptions. Without fully realizing it, Korea has joined the small circle of major trading nations that share the responsibility for enforcing the rules of open markets.

For Americans, Mr. Bush's address to the Koreans raises another question: Will he say in Washington what he said in Seoul? "Protectionism may seem to be the easy way out," he declared, "but it is really the quickest way down." Right—but will Mr. Bush tell that to the steel industry, now lobbying frantically for extension of the restrictions on imported steel? Or the automobile industry, in regard to the similar restrictions on imports of Japanese cars? Or the semiconductor industry?

President Reagan always denounced protectionism roundly in his speeches, but his practice was another matter. The American economy was in fact much more highly protected when he left office than when he arrived. It's one Reagan habit that Mr. Bush needs to avoid.

The Honolulu Advertiser
Honolulu, Hawaii, January 29, 1989

Hopes for reduced tension and even eventual reunification are rising in Korea these days. The situation is heady, fragile, dangerous and intriguing.

Contacts between the democratic South and communist North are being made on a variety of fronts. Proposals include meetings of top leaders, a non-aggression pact, and joint business ventures. Trade has already begun.

This is heady because reunification of the peninsula divided at the end of World War II has strong appeal for Koreans, who were united for 1,600 years. For some it is now a bigger issue than further democratic reforms.

The situation is fragile because there have been false starts before, and the great unknown is the sincerity of North Korea's Kim Il Sung, a die-hard totalitarian leader.

That makes for dangers. South Korean President Roh Tae Woo and others who are riding the political tide are also warning that talks will be long and difficult at best and any progress gradual. Roh stresses the need for keeping defenses strong. Some feel the North's aim is to promote the withdrawal of U.S. troops.

But North Korea's economy is in grave trouble, and it may want help from the prosperous South. The North could also fear further isolation at a time when its Soviet and Chinese sponsors are making deals with the non-communist world.

In any event, the positive moves are worth encouraging, despite lingering doubts that a dangerous North Korea wants to follow world trends toward peace.

San Francisco Chronicle

San Francisco, California, February 3, 1989

THE MOST SIGNIFICANT indication yet that two old enemies may at last be ready to inter their fractious ways comes in the news that North and South Korea have agreed to a joint business project. This development marks the first such understanding to be achieved in 43 years of unremitting hostility between the two nations.

It is not surprising that this first step toward rapprochement comes in the field of business. The realities — and necessities — of human commerce are generally ahead of the doctrinaire moves of governments. Here there is the unspoken factor that negotiations could not have taken place without some kind of official sanction.

The chairman of South Korea's big Hyundai corporation, Chung Ju Yung, said he had signed an agreement in North Korea's capital, Pyongyang, with officials of that country's Taesong Bank to develop an area on North Korea's coast as a tourist site. Since the two countries are still technically at war and have no official relations, the project is being handled on a businessman-to-businessman basis, not as a government-to-government effort. But the implications are broad.

ANY RESORT SITE needs people in order to thrive. And nearby neighbors in prosperous Japan and South Korea are likely sources of patronage. The clear lesson here is that people, and their commerce, break down barriers more effectively than governments nursing deep-seated antipathies.

The Register-Guard

Eugene, Oregon, March 1, 1989

During his brief stopover in South Korea last week, President Bush spent some time talking about trade. That's understandable. South Korea and the United States are major mutual customers, and the trade balance last year favored Korea by about $9 billion.

Oregon benefits greatly from this commerce. And it's only fair to note that, through port activity, the state's economy gains regardless of whether the goods are going to or coming from South Korea.

In terms of goods that pass through Oregon ports — a definition that excludes most trade with Canada — South Korea has been Oregon's second best customer for a number of years. It is also the state's second most important source of imports. Japan is No. 1 in both cases.

According to the Institute for International Trade at Portland State University, exports moving through Oregon ports bound for South Korea during the first six months of 1988 totaled $301 million; imports from South Korea came to $386 million.

During 1987, the last full year for which figures have been compiled, Oregon exports to South Korea were $379 million and imports were $599 million.

Most of the exports are goods that actually originate in Oregon. The chief export commodities shipped during 1987 were grains ($289 million), hides and skins ($20 million); animal and vegetable oils ($17 million) and logs ($14 million).

By contrast, most of the South Korean goods passing through Oregon are headed elsewhere. The list is dominated by motor vehicles — $347 million worth in 1987 — followed by communications equipment ($66 million), foot and head wear ($51 million) and metals and metal products ($34 million). The Korean-made Hyundai autos account for much of the motor vehicle total.

In Seoul, the president issued this cautious warning: "For the American people and for the Korean people as well, reducing our bilateral trade imbalance will be both a challenge and an opportunity. The challenge will be to resist calls for protectionism; the opportunity will be to expand the prosperity of both our countries."

All Americans have reason to support the president's efforts to reduce the U.S. trade deficit. But especially in the case of South Korea and other Asian trading partners, Oregonians also have good reason to hope that pressures are applied gently and carefully enough to avoid provoking reactions that would reduce the overall flow of goods.

The Houston Post

Houston, Texas, January 16, 1989

NORTH AND SOUTH KOREA have now conducted their first direct trade ever. It was a comparatively small transaction, involving the importation into South Korea of a little more than $100,000 in art works. But no matter how insignificant it may have been monetarily, it represents an important psychological step.

This is additional evidence of willingness on the part of North Korea (under pressure from the U.S.S.R. and China) to open itself to the outside world. Moreover, officials in the south say they expect more trade. It is impossible for any bad to flow from this; a great deal of good might. With trade comes understanding and the dismantling of decades-long misperceptions and mistrust on both sides.

It may not portend peace in our time between the two Koreas, but if it only hints at a wary yet genuine truce, that's an improvement.

Birmingham Post-Herald

Birmingham, Alabama, February 5, 1989

Americans too young to remember the "police action" now known as the Korean War, which saw 54,246 Americans fighting under the United Nations banner killed, may find it difficult to justify this nation's continued mistrust of communist North Korea. Especially since North Korea, in the past year, has made overtures toward appeasement.

Despite the North's refusal to participate in the Seoul Olympics and the very real threat that it might try to sabotage the Games in South Korea, the communists have for the most part improved ties with the South. And in doing so they have cracked the door for improved relations with the United States. But it remains too early to put out the welcome mat.

We join those cheering two developments that occurred within the past week that show promise of greater cooperation between the two Koreas, if not the actual reunification that many Koreans pray for.

The first direct merchandise shipment from the North to the South since the Korean War began in 1950 occurred Friday when the *Conch*, a Panamanian-registered freighter, brought 20,900 tons of anthracite coal to the western port of Inchon.

And Thursday, Chung Ju-yung, honorary chairman of the automobile, electronics and construction conglomerate Hyundai, returned from a 10-day trip as the first South Korean business leader approved by both governments to visit the North Korean capital of Pyongyang since the division of the Korean peninsula in 1945. Chung signed an agreement that calls for Hyundai and a state-run North Korean corporation to jointly develop a tourist resort near Mount Kumgang.

But we must not forget that North Korean leader Kim Il Sung is considered by experts to be one of the most unpredictable rulers in the world. All this may simply be part of a propaganda ploy by yet another communist nation beset by debt. We cannot ignore recent reports that over the past two years the North has expanded its armed forces by 160,000 troops to more than 1 million soldiers.

There are 32,000 American service personnel in Korea. Their lives must be protected and our position in that part of Asia maintained. North Korea has not earned our trust. Until it does, we can continue to applaud progress made in improving its relationship with the South, but we must keep up our guard.

Part III:
Europe, Canada & Mexico

During his tenure as President of the United States, Ronald Reagan vowed to "get tough" with our trading partners. Diplomatic arm twisting and the threat of unilateral protectionism extracted from other nations "voluntary" agreements to hold back exports to the U.S. of steel and automobiles, among other products. All this pressure had an effect. In 1980, 20% of the goods produced in the U.S. were protected from foreign competition by barriers other than outright tariffs. Just four years later, over 35% of U.S. products were similarly sheltered. The dollar would eventually fall, but many of these impediments to commerce would remain.

But trade tensions mounted around the world. America's Western allies applauded the U.S. economic recovery in the 1980s from the recession of the 1970s, but they worried about the outflow of savings to the U.S. How were they to rebuild their older industries, they wondered, if their capital was going to pay America's bills? To preserve their capital and make themselves more attractive to international investors, they were forced to raise their own interest rates. But this tactic made it more expensive for Europeans to borrow money, which in turn threatened to slow down their economies.

The Europeans – troubled by double-digit unemployment and eager to export – were also riled by American protectionism. The European Economic Community threatened to retaliate against U.S. quotas on European steel and other products. Jacques Delors, the head of the Common Market Commission in 1985, summed up the state of transatlantic relations as "abysmal." Eu-

rope, he said, is the victim of an "increasingly aggressive and ideological American administration." Canada, the U.S.'s largest trading partner, was incensed when election-year pressures led to duties on certain timber products.

In 1986 more was spent on research and development in the U.S. than the combined research and development spending of Great Britain, West Germany and Japan.

The European Community was established in 1958 with the aim of promoting a harmonious development of economic activities, increased stability, an accelerated raising of the standard of living and closer relations among its member states.

On July 1, 1987 the European Community revised its original treaty with provisions aimed at creating a single Community market, "an area without economic frontiers in which the free movement of goods, persons, services and capital is ensured." Though the fall of communism in Eastern Europe has complicated the future of this process, there is no doubt that the face of the European Community has changed.

In the wake of the Persian Gulf crisis and President George Bush's rhetoric concerning what he dubs the "New World Order", international trade and cooperation has been subject to greater scrutiny.

Critics of Bush's vision of a "New World Order" question just what those words mean and how they will be implemented. They claim that, in essence, it is a calculated effort to reorganize the world's trading partners on a North-South axis through the General Agreement on Trade and Tariff's (GATT), the international body for regulating trade through a series of bilateral free-trade agreements, most immediately in the case of the United States with Canada and Mexico. The issue came to a head when the U.S. Congress conferred "fast track" authority on Bush, which forced yes-or-no votes on these international trade agreements.

GATT is just one of three international institutions set up by the Western developed nations during World War II to bring the existing colonies into line with the industrial world. The other two were the International Monetary Fund (IMF) and the World Bank. The job of the IMF was to peg currencies to the dollar or to gold, then dominated by the U.S. The World Bank set out to reconstruct wartorn Europe and then turned to the Third World, building an infrastructure to speed goods and export of raw materials. GATT was supposed to harmonize and liberalize trade – all the while making sure Third World governments did not make goods they could buy from the developed nations.

As the major economic satrapy of the U.S. on the North American continent, Canada is expected to provide a growing share of energy resources in the 21st Century. In recent times the U.S. has come to regard the place as a resource bin into which it dips as deeply as it needs.

Whether called, as it was originally, the "continental policy" or, more recently, "free trade policy," the U.S. stance regarding Canada has always been simple enough: As fuels were depleted in the U.S., driving prices up, the U.S. petroleum and mining concerns that dominate the Canadian resource economy would find it economically profitable to open up the Canadian North, just as railroads opened the Canadian West in the 19th Century.

U.S. hegemony in Canada dates back to the early part of the 20th Century, when direct American investment began to replace the indirect bond holdings of the British. By 1958, U.S. companies owned 50% of Canadian manufacturing and 40% of the mining business. By 1964, 80% of foreign investment came from the U.S. Canada depends on its exports, and at least 70% of them consist of raw material shipped to the U.S.

Following the implementation of the free-trade agreement in 1988, there were a rash of mergers with an attendant loss of jobs. Critics of the agreement point out that small Canadian companies either closed up or planned for closing in the face of competition from much larger American companies. Canadian branches of U.S. companies closed to rationalize their operations making it possible for U.S. companies to increase production, sell into Canada and close down their Canadian operations.

Meanwhile, the free-trade agreement did not guarantee Canadian producers access to U.S. markets. When American farmers protested the export of Canadian pork into their market, the U.S. put an eight cents per kilo tariff on Canadian pork, costing Canadian pork processing jobs. Ultimately, the Canadian Labor Congress calculated that instituting "free trade" with the U.S. cost Canada 105,000 jobs.

The U.S. is also attempting repeat the process in Mexico where the economy is 3.6% the size of the U.S.'s. Because of its small size, the overall impact would be small, although a reduction in Mexico's high tariffs might open new markets for U.S. goods. Labor costs account for two-thirds of the price of U.S. manufactured goods and cheap Mexican labor could cost jobs for unskilled U.S. workers.

Group of Seven Reaches Accords on Major Issues

Leaders of the Group of Seven (G-7) major industrial democracies met in Houston, Texas July 9-11, 1990 for their 16th annual summit on world economic issues. The leaders reached significant agreements on several major issues despite their differing approaches to a world economy rapidly changing because of the collapse of communism in Eastern Europe.

The Houston summit was the first since the opening of the Berlin Wall, and the impending reunification of Germany was reflected in heightened influence for West German Chancellor Helmut Kohl. The German leader took his place beside U.S. President George Bush and Japan's premier, Toshiki Kaifu – who was attending his first summit meeting – as a leading power at the summit.

Also attending the Houston meetings were Prime Minister Margaret Thatcher of Great Britain, Premier Giulio Andreotti of Italy, Prime Minister Brian Mulroney of Canada and President Francois Mitterrand of France. European Community Commission President Jacques Delors was also present.

Agreements were signed on Soviet aid, agriculture, trade and the environment. The accords were compromises among the policies advocated by the seven nations. While no single leader could claim a complete victory for a personal agenda, representatives of the seven governments said they were generally pleased with the summit's results. "There's no victory," said Delors, "only a good compromise."

Major accords were signed in the following areas:

■ *Aid to the Soviet Union.* The G-7 agreed to commission a study of the Soviet economy to decide if economic aid would perform a helpful function and what possible forms that aid could take. Although they postponed any unified action on aid, the leaders agreed that individual G-7 governments should be free to provide economic assistance to the Soviet Union as they saw fit.

■ *Farm Subsidies.* The U.S. won agreements from the European nations and Japan to pursue policies that would phase out agricultural trade barriers and domestic subsidies to farmers. But the agreements were signed with the understanding that policies would take into account "differences in the social and economic conditions of farming" in individual nations.

■ *Global Warming.* The U.S. achieved a victory in that environmental issues were de-emphasized and any definite commitment to cut back carbon dioxide emissions was postponed until 1992. But the G-7 statement contained an implicit rebuke of the U.S. reluctance to act on the global warming problem.

The economic communique pledged that the summit nations would work hard to reduce farm subsidies as part of the General Agreement on Tariffs and Trade talks aimed at reducing protectionism.

The pledge was seen as a limited victory for Bush, who had lobbied energetically for commitments from European nations to open their agricultural markets to cheaper products grown in the U.S. and the Third World.

The problem of agricultural subsidies had stymied the GATT Uruguay Round of multilateral trade negotiations that were scheduled to be completed by the end of 1990. The negotiations had as their goal the elimination of barriers to free trade worldwide.

The elimination of protection for Europe's farmers was a highly sensitive political issue especially in France and West Germany. Both nations currently maintained subsidies that supported internal prices and exports, as well as import barriers.

The economic communique said that the G-7 recognized the need "to make substantial, progressive reductions in support and protection of agriculture – covering internal regimes, market access and export subsidies…"

Chicago Tribune

Chicago, Illinois, July 11, 1990

In sweltering Houston, President Bush has turned up the heat on some of his colleagues at the seven-nation economic summit. He wants them to push for a successful conclusion to trade liberalization talks that began four years ago in Uruguay.

Getting an unequivocal pledge, especially from the Europeans, won't be easy. There are several contentious issues in the trade negotiations, but the most divisive is the agricultural subsidies that waste tax money and force up food prices around the world.

If no plan emerges to phase out farm subsidies, the United States and most of the developing countries that export food have threatened to walk away from the Uruguay talks.

In that case, an increasingly integrated world economy could fragment into competing interest groups. The goal of expanded markets and a greater flow of goods and services would collapse under fierce protectionism and gradual economic decline.

More than other modern presidents, Bush understands what's at risk. A multinational trading system dedicated to lowering tariffs has brought increased commerce and prosperity to many nations over the past 40 years. The jump in exports from this country has been especially dramatic in the past decade as barriers fell under the push for freer trade. U.S. merchandise exports have more than doubled since 1980, while service exports have jumped sixfold.

When the 97 member-nations of the General Agreement on Tariffs and Trade began talking in Uruguay in 1986, the aim was a treaty by the end of this year that toughens penalties for violators of international trade rules and broadens the rules to include uncovered areas in services, investments and textiles. But the talks are barely alive, despite the approaching December deadline. They need a strong prod from leaders of the seven economic powers.

The U.S., backed by Australia, Canada and even—to a limited extent—Japan, wants farm subsidies reduced sharply and eventually eliminated. The nations of the European Community, especially France and West Germany, support some modifications but don't want to set specific methods and timetables. Their leaders argue that they must protect their 10 million farmers who work mostly small, inefficient farms. Drastic cuts in subsidies, they say, would throw many farmers out of work and drive up food prices.

Of course there would be painful dislocations, as there are whenever businesses die. The death of a farm is especially sad; no one has epitomized grit and hard work and value to society more over the ages than the farm family. But Western Europe's inefficient, subsidized farms make no better economic sense than Eastern Europe's inefficient, subsidized factories. The general public is better off when open markets set prices and determine how many people can make a living in what fields.

France and Germany and the rest of the European Community are wrong: Ultimately, food prices will fall, not rise, with an end to subsidies. It's the short-term political consequences that scare Francois Mitterrand and Helmut Kohl, not the long-term economic results.

The world's 24 largest nations spend an estimated $240 billion a year protecting their farmers with price supports and other subsidies. In the European Community, this economic madness costs taxpayers and consumers nearly $100 billion a year. Export subsidies alone, which help farmers sell their products overseas, cost European taxpayers $11.5 billion a year. (Farm subsidies have been coming down in the U.S., but they still total about $10 billion a year—an area ripe for slicing in current budget negotiations.)

The Western leaders can't be expected to work out the details of a trade pact this week in Houston. But at a minimum, they should pledge that the Uruguay Round of trade talks will succeed. Several breakthroughs, especially a commitment to cut agricultural barriers and subsidies, will be needed for that to happen. The leaders in Houston must order their trade ministers to take whatever steps are necessary to preserve an effective multilateral trading system.

Houston Chronicle
Houston, Texas, July 11, 1990

What a pleasure it must have been for the leaders at the Economic Summit of Industrialized Nations to issue their political declaration Tuesday.

The declaration was a salute to democracy.

A few years ago, words such as "welcome" and "applaud" could never have been sprinkled so frequently in an assessment of developments in Europe, Africa, Latin America and Asia.

The political declaration smooths the way for the concluding statement today on thorny economic issues, such as aid to the Soviet Union. "Each of us stands ready to help in practical ways those countries that choose freedom, through the provision of constitutional, legal and economic know-how and through economic assistance, as appropriate," it says.

The democratic achievements well deserve the salute from the Group of 7. Glowing generalities such as "Europe is at the dawn of a new era" can be excused in light of the recent events.

Unification of Germany is applauded. Replacement of repressive regimes in Central and Eastern Europe is welcomed. Soviet moves toward a democratic political system and a market economy are welcomed. Positive developments in South Africa are welcomed. In Latin America, freedom in Chile and free elections in Nicaragua are applauded. The statement even goes so far as to "acknowledge some of the recent developments in China" without giving details.

Summit declarations set tone as well as a policy. For the leading industrialized democracies, the tone is decidedly upbeat.

THE DENVER POST
Denver, Colorado, July 13, 1990

THE HOUSTON "economic summit" featuring the leaders of the world's seven largest industrial nations received relatively little attention from a public becoming rather bored with the sight of world leaders having lunch amid the glare of the television cameras.

But despite its low profile and low drama, the meeting did mark continued progress toward freer world trade.

The U.S. pressed its partners to eliminate the massive agricultural subsidies that distort world trading patterns — and, not so incidentally, reduce the exports of America's ultra-efficient farmers. In the end, the most the summiters would do was pledge to work for "substantial and gradual reductions" in such subsidies.

For their part, Europeans tried to wrest a commitment from the U.S. to accept target ceilings on the emission of gases blamed for global warning. President Bush would only pledge to begin working on "appropriate implementing protocols."

Finally, the summiters agreed to go their separate ways on the question of how much aid — if any — to give to Eastern Europe, China and the Soviet Union. That only underscored the obvious fact that West Germany's intense interest in East Germany is different from — though not contrary to — the interests of France, Britain or America in encouraging Eastern Europe's migration to freer markets. And while neither America nor Europe seems interested in pouring money into China to buttress the blood-stained Deng dictatorship, Japan is eager to court the billion potential customers living at its doorstep.

In contrast to that "do-your-own-thing" approach on aid, all seven heads of state agreed to aggressively support freer trade in the ongoing Uruguay round of world trade talks in which some 100 nations participate. The seven leaders pledged "substantial, progressive reductions" in export subsidies, domestic price supports and barriers to imported goods.

The summit communique also called for the industrialized nations to pursue domestic policies that help promote world economic growth, reduce budget deficits, encourage savings and increase competitiveness. The summiters also announced further steps to reduce Third World debt burdens.

In a sense, the summit's lack of drama is a testimony to the underlying consensus of the seven nations. Nobody disrupted the summit by grandstanding for domestic political purposes, indicating that all seven at least recognize that their common interests outweigh their differences. The result is that the world will continue to move toward freer trade and away from the protectionist policies that caused disaster in the 1930s.

THE ANN ARBOR NEWS
Ann Arbor, Michigan, July 10, 1990

The western economic powers meeting at Houston are split on the question of $15 billion of economic aid to the Soviet Union. That divided opinion is as good a sign as any that aid to the Soviets is premature.

The leaders of France and West Germany strongly support aid, the latter's position based on her desire for Moscow's approval of reunification. President Bush and British Prime Minister Margaret Thatcher are opposed to Soviet aid.

The U.S. position was stated by Secretary of State James Baker III, who said, "The absence of real progress toward a market economy in the Soviet Union argues against the provision of assistance at this time."

The key words are, of course, "at this time." There will be ample opportunity in the future to bring the Soviets into the west's trade and economic orbit, but not before the Kremlin makes some major policy adjustments.

The Soviet government is still spending heavily on its own military machine, still underwriting client states in Cuba and Angola, and still a long way from the hard decisions that will move a giant country toward a market economy.

The communist state is not being dismantled. No-strings aid would be apt to disappear into the rat hole of the worker state bureaucracy and wasteful central planning schemes. There's no question the Soviet Union could use hard currency, but there are major questions over how much is needed and what impact it would have.

From a moral standpoint, it can be argued that other countries, legitimately struggling to establish democracies, have a stronger claim on our foreign aid dollars than the Soviet Union, so recently our implacable foe and around which there is so much unsettling speculation over what might happen if hardliners replaced Mikhail Gorbachev.

Change in eastern Europe has come too fast, its impact yet to be fully understood and carefully gauged, to warrant rushing in with dollops of foreign aid. American public opinion is not ready to support a politician — Gorbachev — who is vastly more popular abroad than he is at home.

Let's not make it easy for the Soviets to avoid the tough decisions; any aid we send could easily be diverted into maintaining and improving Soviet armed forces. America is interested in a Soviet Union which can stand on its own and whose people are free, but we're also interested in political justice for the Baltics and the shape that economic reforms will take in the Soviet Union.

Until some of these major issues sort out, there shouldn't be any question about western aid. The Soviets don't even have the institutions, such as a price system that reflects supply and demand, to ensure that foreign aid wouldn't be wasted. With little experience in matters of private property and western-style banking methods, the Soviets need to experiment with a market economy within the framework of perestroika. But not with our foreign aid dollars.

If the Soviets cut substantially from their military budget and phase out aid to Cuba and introduce a market economy that promises to get the most from agricultural resources while improving the standard of living, then western economic aid will be both timely and necessary. And with more of an economic apparatus in place, progress toward democracy will accelerate.

From its own debtor status, the U.S. is not so wealthy (or desperate for the affection of Gorbachev) that it needs to acquiesce to the views of France and West Germany on Soviet aid. They have their own reasons for wanting to feed the Bear.

President Bush's wariness is well taken. A line of credit and a certain level of technical assistance are what we ought to be prepared to give at this time. Let's wait and see how Gorbachev's unusual pledge — if life isn't better in two years, I'm outta here — stands up.

San Francisco Chronicle

San Francisco, California, July 13, 1990

THESE ANNUAL economic summit meetings between leaders of the world's seven major industrial nations are, to begin with, not supposed to pay off in dramatic decisions for definitive action. These are occasions for consensus, for collegiality; times when problems are weighed and general solutions brought into broad focus. Most of the work is done well ahead of time, anyway — by so-called bureaucratic "Sherpas" who shape the eventual scorecard.

The Houston meeting was no different. Those who fault it for lack of accomplishment just aren't being realistic about the nature of the process.

Besides, there was movement at Houston amidst the compromise. President Bush, who had pressed hard on the matter, won a pledge to try to end a longstanding trade deadlock. On agriculture, the seven leaders ordered negotiators in the stalled international trade talks to complete a draft resolving outstanding issues at a meeting two weeks from now in Geneva. So the word has gone out: There will be talks on farm subsidies — an issue, U.S. Trade Representative Carla Hills noted, that the Europeans "were not willing to touch with a 10-foot pole."

So score one, at least, for George Bush — particularly since the issue is volatile politically; cutting agricultural subsidies will involve sacrifice on the part of U.S. farmers, too.

As for the matter of economic aid to the Soviet Union, this was resolved pretty much on a do-your-own-thing basis. And the pronouncement on the environment was, of course, considered too wishy-washy by the conservationist crusaders.

THESE SUMMITS HAVE a special value in the subtle personal relationships that are fostered in face-to-face diplomacy. George Bush, being hostly — as he was — under the spacious skies of his home state, proved particularly good at that.

The State

Columbia, South Carolina, July 15, 1990

THE SUMMIT meeting of the West's seven leading industrial democracies was, as usual, a great photo opportunity, providing footage of our leaders cavorting with their peers and discussing the great issues of the day.

The gathering of the Group of Seven at Houston last week, while still heavy on the show biz, had a bit more substance than in recent years. This is not to say that a great deal of action was agreed to by the United States, Great Britain, France, West Germany, Japan, Italy and Canada.

President Bush and his high-level guests agreed on little that will be of help to the global environment, primarily because the Americans managed to block a European effort to specify how much each nation should reduce carbon dioxide emissions.

It is possible, however, that a last-minute compromise on the thorny issue of reducing agricultural subsidies could amount to something. Mr. Bush has been pushing for the elimination of farm supports, which is an even more politically sensitive subject in Europe than here. The agreement to "make substantial, progressive reductions" in all categories of farm subsidies is so short of specifics that it may lead to nowhere. But if carried out, it will brighten the world trade picture.

The chief accomplishment at Houston was the approach adopted to provide help to the Soviet Union and thus bolster the reform policies and political fortunes of President Mikhail Gorbachev.

West Germany and France came to Houston with proposals for a joint $15 billion in package in direct assistance for Moscow. With the backing of Britain and Japan, President Bush advanced a better idea. He argued that the Soviet economy is so feeble and so inefficient at this point that a blank check would be wasted.

Instead, he offered technical assistance (Western know-how) now. And the leaders agreed to ask the International Monetary Fund to head up a study of Soviet needs.

Importantly, they told Moscow that prospects for long-term aid would be greatly enhanced if Moscow reduces military spending substantially and eliminates aid to "states which create regional conflict," such as Cuba ($5 billion in Soviet aid a year), Vietnam ($2.5 billion) and Syria ($1.5 billion). It certainly makes no sense to give money to Moscow as long as it is sending money to such troublemakers.

Nothing in this agreement will keep West Germany, which wants to ensure Soviet blessing of reunification with East Germany, from unilaterally giving Mr. Gorbachev an immediate gift of $3.1 billion or Japan from reviving aid to China if they so choose. But the seven as a group will take the wiser course of going slow.

The very fact that the democracies discussed aid to the Soviet Union as a priority issue at their summit says a lot about the changing times. The collapse of communism in Eastern Europe has given the Group of Seven the freedom to disagree. And there was plenty of disagreement at Houston despite efforts to paper it over.

Newsday

New York City, New York, July 10, 1990

Amidst all the Houston hoopla this week, leaders of the Group of Seven industrial nations meeting to decide how to help the Soviet Union rebuild its economy are expected only to agree, politely enough, to disagree.

Germany wants to send money. Canada may provide commercial credits. The United States will supply only technicians. Each is responding in part to its own political objectives. And some critics say that President George Bush, bowing to his party's conservative wing, is passing up the last, best chance of keeping the Soviet Union from falling apart — with dire results for world stability.

But Bush is probably right. The limited help he is prepared to offer is likely all that the Soviet Union can absorb. However much the West would benefit from throwing Soviet

President Mikhail Gorbachev a rope, the Soviets are unprepared to pick up their end of it.

What Washington should do is come up with a large-scale program not only to send U.S. personnel to the Soviet Union but also to bring Soviets here — a potent means of effecting change. And it should find a way to use its technician-ambassadors to identify constructive projects worthy of western aid later on.

West Germany is seemingly the most forthcoming of the Big Seven nations: It will put up more than $3 billion — most likely long-term loans — and is pushing the others to sweeten the pot to $15 billion. But the Soviet economy is in such disarray, and its leaders so divided over economic reform, that an infusion of cash is more likely to be used to paper over problems than to fix them. To Bonn, though, eager

to soften Soviet resistance to German unification, it looks like a good investment.

Canada backed away from its early stance against aid and may provide commercial credits to help the Soviets buy imports. An infusion of consumer goods, financed with credits, might help Gorbachev buy time with the Soviet citizenry. But the Soviet Union's ability to distribute goods has decayed so badly that few are likely to reach stores anyway.

That doesn't leave much. The help Bush is offering won't transform the Soviet economy. But then, the West can't hold the Soviet Union together; only the Kremlin can. What the West *can* do is help the Soviets along the path to some form of market economy. Only when Soviet leaders know where they're going will large-scale financial aid make sense.

TO THE SUCCESSFUL CONCLUSION OF WORLD WAR II !

Omaha World-Herald
Omaha, Nebraska, July 13, 1990

The leaders of the world's major industrial nations who met in Houston this week were wise to suggest that Western aid to the Soviet Union be linked to continuing Soviet reforms. However, Moscow already seems more deserving of Western help than does China, contrary to what Japanese Prime Minister Toshiki Kaifu said.

The summit's communique said "meaningful and sustained economic assistance" to the Soviet Union would be more likely if the Soviets acted "to introduce more radical steps toward a market-oriented economy, to shift resources substantially away from the military sector" and cut support for such nations as Cuba.

Kaifu advised the leaders at the economic summit to go slow with help for the Soviet Union and to embrace China. A Kaifu associate compared direct financial aid to Moscow with "giving sugar to a diabetic" unless the Soviet Union undertook more economic and social change. Japan wanted the Western democracies to relax the sanctions they imposed against Beijing after its crackdown against a pro-democracy movement.

Kaifu, like President Bush, approved of technical assistance for the Soviets but not financial aid. West Germany and France are expected to proceed with assistance, including direct financial aid, to Moscow. The summit agreement essentially leaves each of the seven industrial democracies free to go its own way on economic policies toward Moscow and Beijing.

Soviet reforms have bogged down, but at least the Soviets are trying. China, while embracing limited capitalism, has not made significant social and human-rights reforms in recent years. Soviet President Mikhail Gorbachev, mean-

while, has been making what appear to be serious, good-faith efforts to accelerate economic reforms. Ethnic violence and secessionist movements have been met, with some notable exceptions, with measured, restrained responses. Similar movements in China have been crushed.

In what sounded like an apology for Beijing's brutality, a Japanese official said that introducing "such a Westernized notion as democracy" to a large country such as China, "which lacks a tradition of individualism," is difficult.

As if the same things haven't been difficult in the Soviet Union. As if the Soviets have a long history of individualism.

If Beijing is chafing under Western economic sanctions, it has itself to blame. Tokyo should not be surprised that Western leaders aren't eager to end their sanctions against Beijing.

The old Stalinists who run China like a fiefdom have dug in with a bunker mentality. Overtures from President Bush apparently have not brought any improvement in human rights or a slackening in the anti-democratic crackdown.

Beijing seems to like the economic benefits that result from a less regimented economy, yet it clings to political regimentation. China's leaders haven't learned that independent thinking can't be turned on and off like a light switch: on for business, off for politics.

The old men in Beijing are the managers. China is their company. The Chinese people are the workers. The managers have deluded themselves if they think mixing Adam Smith with Mao and Stalin will work. The workers don't seem happy.

How odd that the leaders of a nation as managerially astute as Japan would urge their allies to endorse, with their investments, this company called China.

St. Paul Pioneer Press & Dispatch
St. Paul, Minnesota, July 9, 1990

The annual economic summit of the world's fattest nations used to be a yawner to the non-economist. The most exciting thing going was to see once again that Prime Minister Margaret Thatcher of the United Kingdom was the only leader there carrying a tasteful handbag. But the action has picked up in the last couple of years, what with the geopolitical explosion and the greening of the economic mainstream.

By saying no to a development mindset that uses up tomorrows to pay for today

When the top bananas of Japan, Canada, France, Germany, Britain, the United States and Italy meet in Houston this week, the environment is bound to be hot — figuratively as well as what the shank of summer generates in southern Texas.

FOCUS '90

The location would be a perfect place for President Bush to jump aboard the train of thought that global warming needs much more attention from the big industrial countries.

Houston also provides an opportunity for this important group of resource-rich and high-consuming countries to undo major damage by withdrawing support for the Tropical Forestry Action Plan.

Stop support for an international program that sounds like a helpful package of economic incentives to manage the endangered rain forests? Yes.

The Tropical Forestry Action Plan shows alarming signs of making the monumental problem of deforestation worse. Since the mid-1980s, the plan has poured money from the World Bank and multilateral development banks into investments that clearly are geared toward projects that reward cutting timber rather than saving it.

A comprehensive forests program that involves support from the world's financial leaders is invaluable. The Tropical Forestry Action Plan could be a useful component of such a commitment, if it is reformed.

The leaders meeting in Houston could play an important part in that reform by stopping all World Bank funding to the Tropical Forestry Action Plan until it broadens its scope. That refocused plan should include conservation policy incentives by recipient countries and commitment to public participation in project planning, and it should provide thorough oversight.

By saying no to a development mindset that uses up tomorrows to pay for today, the economic summit can help offset the ecological losses. That's sound economics and good politics.

Eurotunnel Cost Estimate Rises;
Channel Tunnel Workers Meet

British Rail Corp. March 8, 1989 unveiled a revised plan to build a high-speed rail link between London and the planned tunnel under the English Channel.

State-owned BR's plan was revised from one outlined in July 1988 in order to allay concerns about the environmental impact of the high-speed link. However, considerable opposition to the proposal remained.

(The plan came amid growing concern over rail safety following a series of fatal crashes. Under the revised plan, train speeds would be limited to a maximum 140 miles per hour rather than the 187 miles per hour allowed under the preliminary plan. Furthermore, the train would run two-thirds of the 68-mile route from London to the Channel underground, and it would run primarily along existing rail and road routes.

Workers Oct. 30, 1990 drilled a small hole through 100 meters of chalk marl to connect the two sections of a tunnel being dug between Britain and France under the English Channel.

The breakthrough was made 57 yards under the English Channel seabed in what would become the service tube for the Channel tunnel. Two other tubes being dug would carry rail traffic.

The 32-mile tunnels from Folkestone, England to Coquelles, France would be the longest in the world after the Seikan Rail Tunnel, which connected the Japanese islands of Honshu and Hokkaido. The undersea sections of the tunnels were about 23.5 miles long. The rail tunnels, owned by the Anglo-French company Eurotunnel, were scheduled to begin operations in June 1993.

Construction workers from France and Great Britain Dec. 1 met in one of the three "Eurotunnels" being constructed under the English Channel.

The tunnel had been linked a month earlier by a 60-millimeter (2.5-inch) hole bored between the section being dug from France and the one being dug from England. But on Dec. 1 the construction workers, Englishman Graham Fagg, 42, and Frenchman Philippe Cozette, 37, shook hands through an opening, then used jackhammers to knock a hole big enough for each to climb through. The workers had earned the honor by winning a lottery.

The meeting, at about 11:15 a.m., came in the service tunnel that would be used to help maintain the two other railroad tunnels being dug under the channel. The men met at 13.9 miles from the English coast and 9.7 from the French coast. The meeting took place three years after digging began on the English side.

After the breakthrough, entourages from both sides climbed through the hole and boarded shuttle trains on the other side to complete their journeys under the channel from France to England, or from England to France.

The News and Observer
Raleigh, North Carolina,
December 12, 1990

Now that the English Channel tunnel project has the crude beginning of a service lane punched through, maybe some French entrepreneur will get busy planning a fast-food delivery service to save the English from their home cooking.

That's the good news. The bad is that the tunnel could also be used to speed home cuisine to the hordes of English who've never been able to stomach anything about France except their cherished annual vacations in its sunny South.

A three-hour tunnel trip couldn't do much damage to bangers and mash or fish and chips, and would save the English from the awful fate of having to go native eating bouillabaisse.

Sadly, the tunnel is unlikely to doom the English fried egg, which is left on the griddle until it has the consistency of double-strength Jell-O and then let cool thoroughly, its yellow eye glimmering balefully and greasily like a hung-over hobo's, before serving. What a pity the omelets and souffles of France won't travel.

In many ways the tunnel will be a mixed blessing. The French had a hard time holding down pollution of their language by English when they had a 25-mile water barrier to help. Now, all may be lost.

Channel train boats and auto ferries have been a memorable part of the European experience for tourists, especially those prone to mal-de-mer. There'll be precious little sense of history to gain from a high-speed plunge through an undersea tube.

But between now and the full tunnel's completion, transatlantic tourists may be scarcer anyway with U.S. economic indicators diving even as airfares ascend. Besides, Europe's eyes these days are on Europe. The tunnel is just one of many new things emerging in the Old World — and one that's bound to help some of the best from each side, along with the worst, find its way to the other. Vive le Chunnel. Or is it la Chunnel?

ST. LOUIS POST-DISPATCH
St. Louis, Missouri, November 19, 1990

Britain and France have drawn closer together with workers boring from opposite directions linking up underneath the English Channel. Giant boring machines digging holes that are three stories high have come close to each other on the way to completing the world's costliest tunnel. When finished, travelers will be able to cover the distance between Paris and London in three hours.

Of course, they already can do so in a lot less time — by air. But it is the bane of the late 20th century that by the time travel to and from airports on both ends of a journey is included, the time required to make the trip has jumped astronomically. On the London-Paris route, the real time by air is three hours, just what the tunnel will take. Presumably the reason for building the tunnel is that in the future, the total time required for air travel between the two capitals will actually increase. But the tunnel will also permit more trade between Britain and the European continent.

It has been said that the tunnel's completion will mark the end of Britain's status as an island. In fact, that began to occur when the first airplane was flown between Calais, France, and Dover, England, back in 1911. Perhaps the greatest irony of the tunnel joining the historically antagonistic peoples of Britain and France is that it is being dug by Japanese machines.

The Globe and Mail

Toronto, Ontario, November 3, 1990

AS the British argue about the merits of greater European unity, and Margaret Thatcher deals with Thursday's resignation of deputy prime minister Sir Geoffrey Howe over that issue, the Chunnel proceeds apace.

So far, only a five-centimetre-wide probe has linked the advancing British and French tunnel diggers. It is scarcely enough to admit a single rabid European fox to pollute the garden of England, but it added momentum on Tuesday to a growing sense of occasion as it spiralled through from the British tunnel to the French. After three years of digging under the English Channel, just 90 metres of chalk remains to be drilled to full dimension on this, the service tunnel that will lie between the two railway tunnels still to be built.

When the wall finally tumbles, and the boring machine with the eight-metre cutting head backs away from the rubble, will the subterranean air fill with cheers or just chalk dust? Will there be champagne for the French workers and beer for the British? Will 210 bank presidents and half a million Channel Tunnel shareholders hug each other with delight, or simply peer through the gloom, hoping to see light at the end of a long financial tunnel?

Surely there will be a historian. The meeting of these laser-guided tunnels is as heavy with significance as it is with debt. Here ends the blessed island isolation that has played so large a part in shaping Britain's destiny. It is the largest construction program Europe has ever known, and has been described as "the first great infrastructure project of the new Europe." Hardly poetry, but hardly far-fetched either.

The image of a new Europe, crisscrossed with gleaming railway tracks over which streamlined trains streak at speeds of around 300 kilometres an hour, is not one that excites all Britons with the dazzling prospect of 21st-century life. Many are audibly uneasy. Continentalism will not immediately come thundering through the sluice gate; it may well, for reasons that touch on such imponderables as tradition, pride and culture, as well as technical preparedness, flow no more easily through a full-sized operational tunnel than a five-centimetre probe.

For a time, at least, it may have great trouble getting any farther north than Folkestone. There is a segment of the British public that mourns the passing of island status, talks with deep nostalgia of the seafaring tradition and experiences dismay as the descendants of Napoleon's army creep toward the white cliffs.

The foot-dragging has assumed embarrassing proportions as French high technology waits impatiently at its end of the tunnel. No red carpet has been rolled out for the *train à grande vitesse* (TGV), which is capable of hurtling from Paris to the French tunnel entrance in 65 minutes. At the other end of that tunnel it will encounter track that obliges it to slow to about 70 kilometres an hour. The British do envisage a high-speed link to London, but it will not be completed until 1997 at the earliest — four years after the tunnel opens.

The main reason for the delay appears to have been the flat refusal of Prime Minister Margaret Thatcher to provide the cash for track upgrading. She insists that this be handled privately, and British Rail chairman Sir Robert Reid is experiencing some difficulty persuading a reluctant private sector that it is on to a good thing. Meanwhile, French Transportation Minister Michel Delebarre says he will spend $38-billion (U.S.) on 14 new TGV lines over the next 20 to 25 years.

The cost of the tunnel, cheerfully estimated in 1986 at $9-billion, appears to lie closer to $17-billion. Eurotunnel, the Anglo-French company managing the project, recently had to go back to the bank for more cash and met a chillier reception than it had on the first trip. It is technically in default on the first loan.

Perhaps it would have been unrealistic to expect an enterprise of this size to move smoothly forward, with no technical or financial hitches, no worker deaths (there have been nine) and no cries of alarm from those who are disturbed by the prospect of dramatic change.

But the fact is that it has gone ahead, sometimes like a battering ram, sometimes like a Cuisinart blade and sometimes like a condemned man to the gallows. Within a week or two, the service tunnel will link Britain to the continent. In three years, trains will be running and, by 2003, about 45 million passengers a year will be going back and forth under the Channel.

Less a few million claustrophobes, perhaps.

The Hartford Courant

Hartford, Connecticut, November 8, 1990

It is still only the size of a mouse hole, but the first direct link between Britain and the continent since the Ice Age 8,000 years ago has enormous symbolic value. Moreover, once it's finished, the Channel Tunnel may have as much impact on the United States as on Europe.

The $17 billion project is expected to open by June 1993. High-speed freight and passenger trains would move between Britain and France in two 32-mile-long tubes just six months after the European Community officially drops its remaining trade barriers.

The 12 members of the community constitute a market of 320 million people. With the collapse of the Iron Curtain, West European entrepreneurs have started pushing eastward and are likely to extend their reach to the Soviet Union.

Construction of the tunnel, which to many is the eighth wonder of the world, began in 1987. A French crew drilled through layers of chalk from a spot near Calais and British tunnelers drilled near Folkestone.

Using two Japanese-designed boring machines, crews stopped within 100 yards of each other last month. The two tunnels were only 20 inches out of perfect alignment.

The English Channel has been more than just a moat protecting the "scepter'd isle" from invasions. The island mind-set fueled the British feeling of superiority and of distrust and led to far-flung adventures that culminated in an empire.

Almost 200 years ago, a French engineer named Albert Malthieu tried to persuade Napoleon to build the tunnel under what the French call La Manche, but the English warned him off. Other attempts to link Britain with the continent failed.

Insular Britons continue to fear and distrust the emerging Europe. Prime Minister Margaret Thatcher has given the tunnel project and European unity in general only grudging support. But soon the trains will roll.

With a unified Europe, the United States may finds itself in not-so-splendid isolation. Much of the continent is preparing for monetary and even political union.

But Americans still cannot decide whether to convert to the metric system. Let's marvel at the Chunnel, as the British call it, but let's also prepare to bridge the gap.

THE CHRISTIAN SCIENCE MONITOR

Boston, Massachusetts, November 5, 1990

BOR-RING! No, not in the sense of ennui. In the sense of an 800-ton drill clawing and chawing its way through chalk marl beneath the English Channel. From both sides of the channel, a consortium of 10 British and French construction companies is engaged in the largest engineering project of the century: a 32-mile tunnel (actually three tunnels – two rail bores for carrying passengers and freight, and one for maintenance) connecting Britain and France.

The Channel Tunnel (or "Chunnel"), begun in 1987, won't be ready for service until 1993. A breakthrough occurred last week, though, when a two-inch-wide probe penetrated the remaining 100 yards of stone blocking the maintenance tube. That tube should be cleared before the month is out.

The tunnel has been at once an engineering marvel and a financial nightmare. The latest estimate lifted the projected cost, originally $9 billion, to $14 billion. The 210 banks and half-million shareholders financing the project (which receives no government funding) are getting edgy. Meanwhile, an American engineer was recently brought

in to resolve disputes between the project's owner, Eurotunnel, and the construction consortium.

But somehow the money and managerial problems will be resolved, and the drilling goes on.

The French, who have always loved *grands projets* (the Suez Canal), are enthusiastic. They readily perceive the trade and employment benefits that will flow when high-speed trains can whisk beneath the channel. Grand plans exist for the tunnel's French terminus, near Calais.

The English are more ambivalent. For them, the channel has never been a barrier so much as a protecting moat. The British terminal, near Dover, will be little more state-of-the-art than Waterloo Station. Critics have groused about a range of anticipated horrors. Beneath it all, however, lurks that special English dread of *foreignness*.

Britain's insularity, its "splendid isolation," has been, in a way, part of its charm. But Britain is ineluctably being drawn into Europe. As with many other steps toward European unity, Britain will, in the long run, benefit mightily from the Chunnel. As usual, though, it will be the last to know.

The News Journal

Wilmington, Delaware, November 1, 1990

All sorts of celebrations are being held. It is a wonderment. Two engineering parties, one British and one French, have bored their tunnels beneath the English Channel. Will that name now be outmoded? They managed to drill so accurately that they have met only 20 inches out of alignment.

A two-inch puncture in the wall between the probes was completed Tuesday, allowing air to pass between the sections for the first time since construction began late in 1987.

Whatever else it is, it is an outstanding display of international cooperation.

"It is an example of what Europe is about," British Prime Minister Margaret Thatcher said in London. She and French President Francois Mitterrand are expected to greet each other in the tunnel on Jan. 26.

It was a more than two-nation project; two Japanese-designed machines have been drilling the shafts.

The 31-mile Chunnel's cost originally was to be $9.4 billion. The estimate now is $16.7 billion. There have been seven British construction deaths and two French. That's the toll in time, money and lives for a great engineering feat that deserves to be saluted.

When travelers emerge from their respective trains in London and Paris after the whole project is finished in 1993, the two countries, which long faced each other as enemies, will be bonded more strongly.

We wait to see if travelers will detrain expecting to hear French spoken in London and English in Paris.

San Francisco Chronicle

San Francisco, California, December 4, 1990

WHEN WORKERS from France and England shook hands at the breakthrough of the English Channel tunnel, it represented not only one of the greatest engineering feats in history but it may also symbolize the future economic linkage of Britain to the continent.

The 31-mile-long tunnel is expected to open in June 1993, just six months after the 12-nation European Community is to remove its last trade barrier and set up a massive single market with more than 330 million consumers.

Digging for the tunnel began three years ago and has been marked by nine worker deaths, cost overruns and a financing crisis for the $15 billion project. Apathy on the English side has stalled construction of a high-speed rail line to connect the tunnel with London, and anti-Gallic sentiment has the British concerned with an invasion of rabid French foxes through the tube.

THE UNITED KINGDOM — at least while under the leadership of former Prime Minister Margaret Thatcher — has resisted a number of European Community proposals, most notably a common monetary authority and a single currency. Now that the island nation is rejoined to the mainland for the first time since the Ice Age, the miracle of a truly united Europe may be closer to reality.

Omaha World-Herald
Omaha, Nebraska, November 10, 1990

Peace and commerce are bringing about what centuries of war didn't come close to achieving. Britain and the European continent are figuratively moving closer together.

The movement is symbolized in the recent Chunnel breakthrough. Workers from Britain and France who are building the under-the-channel project recently linked their tunnels.

Napoleon dreamed in 1802 of a land route over which he could move armies. His goal of conquering England was thwarted by the restless waters of the English Channel. Hitler had the same goal 140 years later. His Wehrmacht rumbled over the European continent with barely a pause, then came to a halt at the rocky coast of France. The Luftwaffe pounded London, but the British remained free beyond the white cliffs of Dover.

Times change. It took almost 200 years of dreaming, discussion, planning and design work to make the Chunnel a reality. Soon, the 2-inch bore hole linking the tunnels will become six feet wide, then 50. Eventually the result will be a three-story-tall tunnel, ready for crews with rails and ties.

In a fundamental sense, Britain will seem less like an island. The French are building a system of superfast trains to link England, through the tunnel, with a multibillion-dollar bullet train system being developed across Europe. The movement of people and the movement of goods will be more efficient.

The continent has seen swift and radical changes in the past year — the reunification of Germany, the startling developments in the Soviet Union and its one-time client states, the surge of democracy. The physical linkage of France and England, Europe and the British Isles, seems to exemplify the new age of cooperation and commerce that is developing.

Post-Tribune
Gary, Indiana, December 5, 1990

Former British Prime Minister Margaret Thatcher lost her job in part due to her reluctance to link Great Britain's economy to other countries on the European continent.

There's a certain amount of irony to the fact that less than a week after Thatcher's departure, workers broke through to join two segments of a tunnel that will physically connect Great Britain to Europe for the first time in history. The so-call "chunnel" fulfills a nearly 500-year-old dream of linking Great Britain and Europe via a land route.

Although the United States isn't involved in the project, Chunnel builders appear to have taken a lesson from the American defense industry. Anticipated to cost $9.5 billion when construction began in late 1987, the cost since has increased to $14.8 billion.

TULSA WORLD
Tulsa, Oklahoma, November 5. 1990

INITIAL success of the "Chunnel" — the historic tunnel beneath the English Channel — comes at a time of growing economic unification in Europe, and it will in turn further the free trade of goods among the Common Market nations.

Workers from Great Britain and France, digging from either side of the Channel, last week poked a two-inch diameter hole that for the first time links the two countries underground. When the $15 billion tunnel — actually a service tube and two train tubes — is complete in 1993 it will speed passengers, cars and freight between London and Paris in three hours.

The Chunnel — its official name is Eurotunnel — is the world's largest civil engineering project as the world moves into the final decade of the 20th century. In some respects it is a throwback to the monumental engineering feats of the early years of the century — such as America's Grand Coulee Dam, Golden Gate Bridge and Lincoln Tunnel. Like those huge projects, the Chunnel will have profound cultural and economic impact.

That earlier era of the giant, expensive construction projects is over. Most of the attainable ones have been done. Nowadays the world's attention is turned toward complex medical and social problems, the environment and outer space.

The Chunnel, among other things, is an exciting reminder of the era of the monumental engineering achievements.

The TENNESSEAN
Nashville, Tennessee, November 18, 1990

WHERE diplomacy has failed for centuries, technology has triumphed in linking Great Britain with France across the English Channel.

At 31 miles and close to $17 billion in cost, the Channel tunnel or "Chunnel," as the historic link between the two nations is called, is rather more than just a hail-and-hardy hands across the sea gesture. The French and British, who've been grudging allies only in this century, wouldn't stand for that.

But both nations and their fellow members of the European Community will enjoy the economic bonanza promised by linking Britain with the rest of the continent by two rail tunnels. By the time the 12 nations of the European Community are officially linked in 1992, the tunnel builders are expected to be just months away from joining Britain and the continent by tunnel and rail.

In the first year, officials project that 28 million travelers will have "chunneled" from one nation to the other. The rail will cut the time from London to Paris by automobile/ferry by two-thirds.

This linkage has been a dream of the English and French for centuries. British monarchs tried to link their claims to French territory by marriage. Napoleon couldn't build a land passage in 1802 to mirror the Chunnel and add Britain to his conquests.

What the ancients couldn't join, technology has wrought. Europe's about to become one, physically as well as economically. ∎

The Hutchinson News
Hutchinson, Kansas, December 6, 1990

It has the cutest name — a chunnel — but the tunnel that now joins Britain with France is anything but cute. Deep beneath the waters of the English Channel, the tunnel is an engineering feat as well as a potential economic boon to the two nations.

In the future, the train trip between London and Paris will take about the same time as getting from Hutchinson to Kansas City — about 3.5 hours — a brief trip, but one that connects two of Europe's most sought-out tourist spots.

But more impressive was the engineering that went into the project. Just as naysayers wondered if the two halves of the St. Louis Arch would match when the final link was put into place, doubters wondered aloud whether the two tunnels would match up when the time came. They did, magnificently.

Whether the tunnel will improve relations between citizens of the two countries remains to be seen. Past relations between the French and the English have not exactly been a lovefest.

But England is no longer an isolated island in the classic sense. It now has an umbilical cord that ties it to the community of Europe, a most symbolic gesture for a new age.

GATT Talks Suspended; Largest Exporters Reported

The General Agreement on Tariffs and Trade (GATT) Uruguay Round of multilateral trade talks Dec. 7, 1990 was suspended after negotiators failed to agree on a plan to reduce farm subsidies.

The talks had broken down Dec. 6, when Latin American nations pulled their delegates from negotiating sessions after it became clear that the European Community would not alter its hard-line stance on agricultural protection.

The EC stood firm on its offer to reduce such direct farm subsidies as internal price supports by no more than 30% over 10 years, retroactive to 1986. In addition, it refused to firmly commit to reductions in export subsidies on farm sales, or in tariffs and quotas on agricultural imports.

The U.S., Latin America, Australia, Canada and other areas economically reliant on agricultural exports said subsidies gave EC farmers an unfair competitive advantage. The U.S. and the Cairns Group of farm exporting nations favored a 75% cut in tariffs and quotas and a 90% cut in export subsidies.

The talks foundered at the end of a week of around-the-clock efforts to break a deadlock on the agricultural question. Sweden's agricultural minister, Mats Helstrom, Dec. 6 put forward a proposal under which the EC nations would commit to 30% reductions in each of the three types of farm subsidies under negotiation. Although Britain and the Netherlands expressed some interest in the proposal, the EC rejected it, reportedly at the insistence of France.

The failure to make progress on the agriculture issue meant the suspension of GATT talks on trade liberalization in a variety of other areas. The Uruguay Round had been launched four years earlier with the hope of ushering in a new era of freedom in world trade. Intellectual property, investment and trade in services had been among the areas slated for reform.

The reluctance of the EC to pursue meaningful agricultural subsidy reforms had been due mostly to intransigence on the part of France and Germany. Both nations had been reluctant to eliminate trade subsidies that kept the nations' small farmers – a politically potent lobby in each country – in business.

Delegates said there remained some hope of a resumption of talks in January or February 1991. Arthur Dunkel, director general of GATT, planned a series of missions to various world leaders to urge them to seek compromise in the trade talks. But U.S. Trade Representative Carla A. Hills cautioned that the U.S. would not return to the negotiating table unless it had some assurance of definitive movement on the European side.

The stalled GATT multilateral trade talks received a boost Feb. 20, 1991 when the EC agreed to set specific targets in negotiating reductions of agricultural subsidies. The action amounted to an acceptance of a U.S. formula for negotiating subsidy cuts in three categories: domestic price supports, exports subsidies and import barriers. The GATT talks had been stalled since December 1990.

Federal Reserve Board Chairman Alan Greenspan Feb. 20 presented the Fed's semiannual monetary policy report to the Senate Banking Committee. Greenspan commented on a wide range of recent trends and developments in the U.S. economy, including the breakdown in the GATT Uruguay Round of multilateral trade negotiations. Greenspan said the U.S. and its trading partners would "pay a significant price" if the talks were not successfully revived.

In 1990, Germany regained its position as the world's largest exporter, according to figures from the GATT released March 25, 1991. Thanks to a 16.5% increase in the value of the mark relative to the dollar during the year, German merchandise exports for 1990 were valued at $421 billion, topping the U.S.'s $394 billion. All of eastern Germany's exports during the year ($22.5 billion), were counted for the united Germany. Japan ranked third with $286 billion.

The Phoenix Gazette
Phoenix, Arizona, December 1, 1990

It will soon be a year since Taiwan applied for membership in the General Agreement on Tariffs and Trade, the 100-nation agency that oversees global trade.

It is in the best interests of the United States and its trading partners to approve Taiwan's request.

The government of Taiwan has already done much to meet demands to reduce trade barriers and open its markets to U.S. goods and services. Having Taiwan accept the obligations of internationally agreed-upon trading rules would bring further progress.

Not only would the United States benefit from Taiwan's inclusion, so would less developed nations. Taiwan has promised to provide $1 billion in aid to developing nations if admitted to GATT.

The major obstacles to membership are the opposition of mainland China, not a GATT member, and the reluctance of the Bush administration to antagonize China at a time of negotiations about the Persian Gulf and other foreign policy issues.

The Taiwan government has demonstrated its sensitivity to Beijing's objections by applying for GATT membership as the "customs Territory of Taiwan, Penghu, Kinmen and Matsu," rather than as a sovereign nation.

As a brochure issued by Taipei says, membership in GATT is solely an economic issue. This small, free-market, economic dynamo is America's fifth largest trading partner. It generates the 12th largest volume of trade of any nation in the world and it needs the economic benefits that membership in the multilateral trade organization would offer.

The Chinese government should not dictate our policy toward Taiwan by linking GATT membership with the contested issue of Taiwan's sovereignty.

Unfortunately, although the GATT is scheduled to meet in Geneva this month, Taiwan's application is not on the agenda. The Bush administration should support the creation of a GATT task force to discuss Taiwan's membership and speed the approval process.

THE BUFFALO NEWS
Buffalo, New York, December 10, 1990

SEVEN ROUNDS of trade talks since the end of World War II have contributed to worldwide prosperity by lowering the barriers to trade. Now the eighth, the "Uruguay round," has been suspended amid acrimonious argument and doubts that anything can be salvaged from the wreckage.

One reason for the stalemate in the 107-nation talks is that the objective this time was more ambitious than in any previous round — to put agricultural products under international agreement for the first time. In the final showdown, the political will was lacking to attack the system of subsidies that distorts trade in farm products.

The world's major industrial nations spent $250 billion last year in subsidies to their farmers. Two-thirds of the budget of the European Community consists of farm subsidies. Such subsidies create tremendous burdens on other sectors of the economy, and they create farm surpluses that are then dumped on world markets.

The United States offered, in return for a reduction in the farm subsidies, to make concessions in other areas, such as manufactured goods, banking, telecommunications and textiles. But when the EC farm concessions proved inadequate, the entire package fell apart, and the talks were suspended. In the end, the political power of the 10 million EC farmers proved too much.

The hard negotiating line taken by the United States was better than yielding at the last moment and accepting a largely meaningless agreement. The interests of all the participants will best be served by hammering out a major new trade pact that includes farm products for the first time.

Fear of economic recession around the world contributed to the hesitancy of some nations in taking bold, new initiatives. But they should also fear the consequences of not taking such action. If the talks finally fail, increased protectionism and trade friction can be expected. It is frightening to recall that rampant protectionism in the 1930s helped to deepen the effects of the Great Depression.

Few expect outright trade wars, but the economic giants — the United States, the EC and Japan, could be expected to protect their own interests and retreat somewhat into their own trading blocs.

The United States has several trade complaints that it has been sitting on pending the outcome of the trade talks. If the talks fail, it would process these under existing international agreements.

Fortunately, there is still hope that the negotiations, which have been going on for four years, can be salvaged. The talks will continue in Geneva with lower-level officials, and, after a cooling-off period, there may be opportunities for new decisions at the highest level.

THE KANSAS CITY STAR
Kansas City, Missouri, December 3, 1990

This week the final round of international talks under the General Agreement on Tariffs and Trade will take place in Brussels. The prospect of success is slim. There is a good chance this round of negotiations, the eighth such effort under the GATT since World War II, will collapse. Key participants are far apart on several deal-killing issues, notably agriculture.

The United States, along with some other countries that export farm products, seeks deep reductions in agricultural subsidies. With unbelievable stubbornness, the European Community has resisted. Farm products comprise less than 5 percent of EC exports, yet the Community has offered a purported 30 percent subsidy cut that in reality works out to some 15 percent. As for export subsidies, the EC has made no clear commitment whatsoever.

It took weeks for the EC nations to agree on a position. That the effort was so difficult and the result so tepid does not suggest that the EC's position can change much. Barring significant movement, that indicates a collapse in the talks or at least a delay in their conclusion.

Agriculture is central because Third World countries have no incentive to open markets to Western high technology as long as Western countries restrict Third World commodities. Ditto for textiles, where many developing countries have a comparative advantage.

Washington deepened the overall muddle by attempting, at the last minute, to exempt from the talks several service categories, including aviation.

Perhaps the goal of the talks, begun four years ago, was too ambitious. Perhaps they attempted to clear up too many contradictions. Consider: The industrial world spends about $250 billion a year subsidizing farmers in relatively wealthy countries. That is about five times what taxpayers in those countries are spending on foreign aid — money that frequently is spent on dubious projects.

Would it not be more reasonable for Western countries to open their markets wider, and permit less-developed nations to have greater participation in the process of modern wealth-creation? "Trade, not aid" is no platitude. How can we expect poorer countries to reform their economies unless they can sell more of what they grow and manufacture?

Listen to the folly of our lawmakers. They allocate billions for export subsidies to enrich the farm sector, and in the process destroy the markets of Third World producers. They enact outrageously restrictive measures to bar certain Third World manufactured products, namely textiles, and then fill the air with piety over the plight of the world's poor.

"Trade liberalization" is an abstraction whose critical importance is difficult to convey. Its benefits are in the future and are less clearly defined than the problems to be faced by industries, and workers, that must adjust to changes in the rules.

But over time, lower trade barriers benefit everyone through lower prices and enhanced productivity. U.S. officials estimate that success in the talks would increase world output by $4 trillion over the next decade.

In most negotiations, the hardest bargaining takes place as the deadline grows near. It is time for all parties to recognize the tremendous stakes involved.

The Wichita
Eagle-Beacon
Wichita, Kansas, December 3, 1990

Americans consume only about half of the annual U.S. wheat harvest. Aviation and aerospace products are the United States' No. 1 export and overseas markets are vital to the future health of the industry. Are there any doubts that no state in the union has a greater stake in international trade than Kansas?

After four years of jawing, it's crunch time this month in talks on the General Agreement on Tariffs and Trade, the pact that regulates international commerce. Four U.S. cabinet officers, a dozen members of Congress, scores of administration and congressional spearcarriers and hundreds of advisors and lobbyists from the private sector are expected in Brussels, Belgium, today to hassle with 105 other nations on liberalizing world trade.

The primary issue for the United States and many other countries is agriculture, which in one of the least freely traded items in world commerce.

Over the past few years, the United States, Canada, Australia, Argentina and other producing countries have been bickering with the European Community on cutting agricultural subsidies and export incentives. The Europeans, who are the world champions in farm supports, have resisted change, largely because every time the EC cuts a farm subsidy several thousand tractors roar through Paris, Bonn and other European capitals in protest.

A key question in Brussels is whether the Europeans are willing to risk toppling the entire world trade structure to continue their huge farm payouts. The Bush administration and its foreign allies on the farm issue have made it clear that failure to reach agreement on agriculture would jeopardize freer trade in financial services, construction projects, computer software and world copyright protections.

The primary culprits are Germany, Ireland and France, which use farm subsidies as a social program to keep people away from big cities. Germany goes so far as to subsidize quaint farm operations as a tourist attraction.

While nostalgia for the rural life warms everyone's heart, agriculture must join the international economy. As the world's most efficient producers, American farmers need fair access to world markets if the United States is to have any hope of maintaining an equitable balance of trade.

Without a GATT agreement, the world could plunge into a depression reminiscent of the 1930s, when governments around the world erected trade barriers in a doomed effort to protect their own industries.

Moreover, world trade is a critical element in building a more peaceful world. It's much better for nations to fight over market share than territory or ideology.

The United States, however, can't blink in Brussels on the agricultural issue. If trade is to be free it must start on the farm.

Edmonton Journal

Edmonton, Alberta, December 16, 1990

With the world's leading agricultural producers unable to find a way to cut government supports, Canada is an unwilling player in a ruinous game: subsidizing exports in order to compete.

In the short term, there's little choice — we have to afford subsidies, no matter how costly.

We should be under no illusions that the world's trade wars will be quickly resolved. If the General Agreement on Tariffs and Trade fails to find a compromise on agricultural subsidies, there is every likelihood that the developed world will split into trade blocs: Europe, North America, and Japan and its economic satellites.

And being part of the North American trading bloc would be no panacea for our farmers. We could compete well in the continental economy, because the U.S.-Canada free-trade agreement prohibits export subsidies on bilateral trade. But Canada would still have to compete with United States export subsidies on sales to other markets. Canada has far less tax revenue with which to pay for exports.

There is little alternative to working through the GATT, hoping for the best, keeping up the effort to bring European and American subsidies to a reasonable level.

But in the meantime, we can look at changing the structure of subsidies paid to Canadian farmers, so that they are not a direct drain on tax dollars. The $275 million paid every year to dairy farmers, the $235 million paid for western grain stabilization, the $99 million spent on agricultural stabilization payments, might all be reduced if the subsidies were looked at differently.

They're considered payments to farmers, but a substantial amount of that money is really a subsidy for consumers.

Most of the money is destined to ensure that producers recover the costs of production, and get a fair price for their product.

But if consumers were willing to pay more for their milk and bread, those payments to producers could be reduced.

It makes little sense to shelter urban dwellers from the true cost of food, when farmers are unable to cover their costs by selling their crops.

The "world price" of wheat and other grains is really a price that's set by the export-driven subsidies of other countries. While we might have to compete with that price for our exports, there's no reason that price has to apply to domestic consumption.

This would effectively mean a two-tier price system: a domestic price that accurately reflects production costs, and an export price that reflects subsidy wars.

Since there has never been a free market (free of subsidy) price for wheat in Canada, it is difficult to say how much more food might cost, if consumers were asked to pay the full cost. Some claim that a loaf of bread might rise to $5 — but some farmers say that right now, they only get a nickel from the grain that goes into a loaf.

What might be best is a five-year transition to a market price for grain consumed domestically: at the end of the period, the price farmers received would cover production costs. That would at least end the imbalance on the domestic side.

A two-tier price system wouldn't eliminate subsidies, but it would make sure that we spent money only to compete on the world market, until GATT can get its act together. It's an alternative that deserves a serious look.

The Des Moines Register

Des Moines, Iowa, December 11, 1990

Four years of effort toward broadening the rules of world trade collapsed last weekend. A big opportunity was lost, at least temporarily.

The world could have used better news — what with major industrial countries slumping toward recession, with ex-communist countries needing a quick inclusion in the world trading system, with parts of the Third World showing glimmers of progress that won't last without nurturing.

A successful conclusion of the latest negotiations under the General Agreement on Tariffs and Trade could have brightened prospects in those areas, because expansions of trade lead to expansions of prosperity. The collapse doesn't mean imminent doom, but does mean that the world will be less prosperous in years ahead than it might have been.

The talks collapsed because the European Community refused to change the methods by which it subsidizes farmers — methods that amount to dumping on world markets. The United States and other agricultural-trading nations demanded that the Europeans find other ways to help their farmers, but European governments were held hostage by rioting French farmers and politically powerful German ones.

While agriculture was the cornerstone of the talks, much more than farm trade was lost in their collapse. Because no agreement was reached, American computer software will continue to have no protection against foreign piracy, American filmmakers face limits on their exports, the patents of American pharmaceutical companies can't be enforced abroad.

In all, some 15 areas of trade were involved. Besides agriculture, perhaps the most important involved services such as banking, insurance and accounting. Services are the fastest-growing areas of world trade, yet are not covered by GATT rules.

Thus, failure of the talks means that a large, growing segment of international trade will fall outside customary rules, that trade frictions could grow, that the world could evolve toward three huge, hostile trading blocs — Europe, Asia and North America — rather than into one unified economy.

The collapse is the first serious setback for the post-World War II American vision of a world bound together by trade and prosperity. GATT was an American invention under which barriers to trade have been lowered. As the barriers fell, trade soared, and so did prosperity among the trading nations.

One of the fondest hopes of the former communist-bloc nations is to be admitted to the trading community. Ironically, this comes just as the failure of the latest negotiations raises doubts about the future of the GATT trading system.

GATT could recover from the setback and go on to help fulfill the dream of creating one planetary community, one in which goods and services — and peace — flow freely among all nations.

Or this moment could be the start of the decline of the world trading system, the beginning of the division of the world into super blocs of economic — and perhaps military — rivals.

The original dream is far superior, which is why every effort should be made to get the GATT talks going again early next year.

THE DAILY OKLAHOMAN

Oklahoma City, Oklahoma, December 11, 1990

COLLAPSE of the world trade talks in Brussels is bad news for American producers, especially our farmers.

The talks, held under the General Agreeement on Tariffs and Trade, began in 1986 in Uruguay. The aim was to broaden and strengthen the rules that govern international commerce.

Chief cause for the breakdown was the European Community's refusal to cut internal farm price supports. Japan also balked on opening its closed rice market.

A successful GATT agreement could increase U.S. exports to developing countries alone by $200 billion over the next 10 years — a large portion of which would be agricultural goods. The United States needs more export sales to help the economy and lower the trade deficit.

Negotiators might get the talks back on track in January. If not, fallout may include increasing trade frictions, rising protectionism and possibly even a global trade war. Instead of a new era of free trade and prosperity, the world could split into regional trading blocs, each with its own barriers.

This at a time when world leaders should be striving for more, not less, cooperation.

Houston Chronicle

Houston, Texas, December 10, 1990

For General Agreement on Tariffs and Trade — GATT — substitute world trade. More to the point, make it: eliminating barriers to increased world trade. Better still, for GATT read: the general welfare of the Houston Ship Channel and thousands of Houston-area jobs.

That begins to bring some simple meaning to the complex and arcane negotiating process to set world trade rules known as the Uruguay Round of GATT. The further translation of GATT into specifically Houston terms begins to express the concern that the talks should have stalled for the moment. GATT is about jobs; some of them are Houston jobs.

The process of setting new international rules on matters ranging from banking to patent protection stumbled last week in Brussels on the issue of agricultural protection. U.S. negotiators, backed by most of the world's other large agricultural exporters, wanted to cut internal farm supports by 75 percent; the Europeans would agree to only a 30 percent cut.

In effect, the interests of a few heavily subsidized European farmers now threaten the trade structure that has brought increasing global prosperity since just after World War II. There's nothing arcane about that threat; it's plainly and simply wrong.

The stumble comes as there is talk of expanding the GATT framework to include the Soviet Union and other Eastern bloc countries emerging as market economies. That's a formidable task that will require a trading framework firmly in place.

The GATT ministers will meet in Geneva after the first of the year to try to break the deadlock. The subsidies of inefficient European farmers must be cut in the interests of freer global trade.

THE INDIANAPOLIS NEWS

Indianapolis, Indiana, December 6, 1990

Protectionism is a politician's delight because it delivers visible benefits to the protected parties while imposing the costs as a hidden tax on the public.

— Murray L. Weidenbaum, former chairman of the President's Council of Economic Advisers

For four years, leaders from more than 100 countries have been negotiating a trade agreement to relax protectionism worldwide. One item has kept them from making significant progress — farm subsidies.

Under the General Agreement on Tariffs and Trade, the United States has offered the boldest concessions for agriculture, following a period that marked record-high spending on its own farmers. The United States is calling for worldwide farm subsidy reductions of 75 percent to 90 percent in the next 10 years.

In response, the European Community has come up with a pathetic proposal of a 30 percent cutback on farm trade barriers over 10 years, with a 1986 starting date, which comes out to a 15 percent cut by 1996.

The gap between the two proposals threatens to shut down the entire GATT process and destroy progress on other trade considerations, such as banking, telecommunications and the protection of patents and trademarks.

If a GATT agreement is scrapped, every country involved in negotiations, and many that aren't, will suffer. Their consumers will continue to pay too much for food and for taxes to support farmers.

If barriers came down, U.S. Trade Representative Carla Hills says a GATT pact could increase world trade by as much as $4 trillion during the next 10 years. That should be enough to move the 107 countries involved in GATT closer to an agreement, but it hasn't been.

Trade barriers don't come down simply because that would make good economic sense. Quotas and subsidies are valuable political tools.

Germany's Chancellor Helmut Kohl needed farmers' votes for his reelection, but now that that is over, he may be able to put some pressure on the French, who have heavy protections for their wheat farmers.

If there is to be any significant movement in freeing trade in this round of GATT talks, the EC must make a credible offer. In the long run, the taxpayers and the consumers in the community and the rest of the world would be better off.

The losers, of course, will be politicians who have come to depend on farm subsidies almost as much as the farmers.

The Record

Hackensack, New Jersey, December 4, 1990

Every American concerned about our economy should hope that trade talks under way in Brussels don't collapse. A breakdown in negotiations is clearly possible, and that would be a disaster. American jobs depend on reaching new trade agreements. So does the access of American consumers to high-quality products at low prices. Without the agreements, a recession is likely to pinch even more severely.

The idea behind the talks is simple. Representatives of 107 countries are drafting a wide-ranging set of rules that will govern world trade for the coming years. An agreement could add $4 billion to world trade in the next decade, according to U.S. Trade Representative Carla Hills. Much of the benefit would be felt in America, where overseas trade — and trade agreements — have become more important as U.S. companies turn to foreign markets. Proposed new rules on "intellectual property," for example, would help prevent foreign manufacturers from ignoring copyrights and patents and copying U.S. products, ranging from music cassettes to sophisticated new drugs. New markets for American farmers could open in Europe. And U.S. trade barriers that help keep prices on textiles and sugar high in this country could come down.

Such agreements have been reached seven times since World War II. But stubborn obstacles stand in the way of efforts to arrive at a new version of what's known as the General Agreement on Tariffs on Trade. One of the problems is the insistence in Japan and in much of Europe on protecting farmers. Japan bans imports of rice. Governments in France and other nations subsidize farmers by buying their products for above market prices, then dumping them on the market at discount prices. Americans have been a smaller part of the problem in negotiations, through practices such as refusing to yield on policies that protect its own textile manufacturers and sugar producers.

Negotiators have worked for four years to resolve such problems. But the danger is that trade representatives in Brussels this week will be unable to reach a final agreement. Even if there is an accord, the agreement won't be binding on the United States unless it is approved by Congress. And members of Congress, worried by the threat of a recession and influenced by sugar producers and other special interests, may try to push through amendments that would require lengthy new negotiations.

Unless a general trade agreement is reached — and reached soon — more and more nations will begin responding to domestic political pressures with import barriers that help local manufacturers but punish consumers and manufacturers in other countries. That means economic hardship around the world, not just in America.

The trade talks in Brussels may not be one of the most glamorous issues in the world today, but they are one of the most important.

St. Paul Pioneer Press & Dispatch
St. Paul, Minnesota, December 3, 1990

Fasten your seat belts; the ride on a bumpy economic road will get rougher if there is no miraculous conclusion this week to the three-year talks toward the General Agreement on Tariffs and Trade.

As the Uruguay Round of international trade talks moves inconclusively toward the finish line in Brussels this week, the ever-present agricultural subsidies roadblock seems bigger than ever. Count in potholes on other matters, notably anti-dumping and trade-related investment measures. It seems unlikely that a fully formed GATT could emerge by the Thursday deadline.

> **No one can afford bitter trade wars in this uncertain world.**

The GATT must not fail. No one can afford bitter trade wars in this uncertain world. But, short of the political will in capitals up to their ears in all kinds of crises, the trade talks haven't received the momentum they need.

A small extension seems worth trying to rescue the process. Get all possible mileage this week, then send negotiators back to work quickly. The GATT has to stay on a fast track, most pointedly to come out cleanly in the United States, where a trade pact must reach Congress by March 1 to avoid death by political amendment.

But a little more time to deal creatively among the 15 sectors at stake could smooth the road. Either that, or expect nations or trading communities to build the roadblocks higher and wider, diverting history to a terribly wrong turn.

The London Free Press
London, Ontario, December 11, 1990

The collapse last week of GATT talks in Brussels is bad news for a major trading country like Canada, but could have even more devastating consequences for impoverished peoples in Eastern Europe and the Third World.

The current round of GATT discussions has been under way for four years and is still not definitively over. Representatives of the 107 nations involved have decided to meet in Geneva within a month or two for one last effort to reach agreement, but the chances for success will be slim, unless the European Community (EC) can come up with something better than its offer to cut agricultural subsidies by a meagre 15 per cent from existing levels.

Canadian negotiators were not in a strong position to criticize the EC because of the gross inconsistency in Canada's own trade policies. In the case of milk, eggs and poultry, for example, Canada has been seeking GATT permission for even tougher supply management import barriers than now exist, while insisting that Canadian agricultural exports like beef, pork and grains should be free from trade-distorting subsidies and import barriers imposed by the EC.

> **According to GATT estimates, trade protection in agriculture costs the industrialized countries alone an estimated $250 billion each year.**

On this basis, no agreement was possible. In the end, the EC simply refused to budge, despite strong pressure from more consistent free traders in the U.S. and Canada's partners in the Cairns group of agricultural exporting nations.

Some European and North American farmers who shelter behind import barriers will benefit from this deadlock, but it's bound to be costly for the great majority of consumers and taxpayers. According to GATT estimates, trade protection in agriculture costs the industrialized countries alone an estimated $250 billion in lost income each year.

Debt-ridden less-developed countries in Eastern Europe and elsewhere stand to lose out even more. Many have little hope of generating poverty-reducing economic growth without the increased access to industrialized markets which only a successful conclusion to the GATT round could provide.

With the bilateral trade agreement between Canada and the U.S. in place, Canadians are fortunate to have a secure foothold in one of the world's major markets. That deal might well be extended to Mexico, but a broader multilateral agreement through the GATT would be much preferable.

As it is, Western grain farmers are talking about the need for another $1.1 billion in extra subsidies this year to compensate for low international prices brought on largely by EC export subsidies. And that's just a small indication of the total cost to Canadians if the GATT round should end in total failure.

To stave off such a disaster, Canada and the U.S., as well as the EC, should be prepared to make some major additional concessions. A 15- or 20-per-cent cut in EC agricultural subsidies is not much; but it would be a lot better than no deal at all and the risk of a mutually damaging, all-out trade war.

RAPID CITY JOURNAL—
Rapid City, South Dakota, December 16, 1990

World history and current events tell us that economic conflict often leads to military conflict. War results from selfish interests as well as ideological differences.

We don't have to go far in space or time to realize this. Our own nation grew on the bones of the original inhabitants largely because of the lust to farm, mine or otherwise profit from land already occupied by another culture. Indians were exterminated and pushed into tiny pockets because they stood in the way of "progress" or "Manifest Destiny" — largely economic matters.

Taxes were a factor leading us into our Revolutionary War. One of the first international wars our new nation fought was against a band of pirates who hindered international trade. One of our first internal physical conflicts was the "Whiskey Rebellion" fought over fiscal policy. The cotton trade and differing economic concerns helped instigate our Civil War. Economic and energy concerns underlie our current Mideast stand.

This is why the breakdown of the world trade conference and the virtual collapse of the General Agreement on Tariffs and Trade (GATT) process earlier this month is so troubling. For four years, the nations of the world have met in attempts to lower trade barriers and reduce protectionism. The effort aimed to improve the economic condition of the world. Individual sacrifices would be necessary, but the resulting increase would have been the rising water that lifts all boats. The economic surge among western democracies that followed World War II is proof that cooperation is superior to factionalism.

Instead, Europe's refusal to compromise on the issue of agricultural protectionism sank the talks. The agreement is in peril. The consequences of failure are frightening.

Protectionist pressures mount in many quarters. If unchecked, there is little doubt — considering human nature and history — that this will result in increased factionalism and selfish provincialism. This leads to distrust, emotional nationalism, and a desire to return economic blow for economic blow. Economic, philosophical blows struck in such an atmosphere often turn into actual military conflict.

There is still a chance to save the situation — but after the failure of talks in Belgium last week, precious little chance. The United States fogged the issue by bringing up services it wanted to exempt from free trade at the eleventh hour, but dropped those demands when they proved counterproductive.

Unfortunately, many European nations refused to work in the common interest. Britain and Germany tried to break the deadlock and lead the European Community to sanity, but others — notably France and Ireland — would not yield on the question of agricultural subsidization.

If Europe doesn't come to its senses, and soon, its action is bound to touch off protectionist, reactionary and pro-subsidization agricultural policies around the globe. No one can predict the long-term effects of a return to factionalism, but history and human nature suggest consequences won't be limited to higher farm support prices for American taxpayers. Quite literally, the price of such selfishness may someday be counted in blood.

Winnipeg Free Press

Winnipeg, Manitoba, December 22, 1990

There is an obvious piece of advice for Trade Minister John Crosbie when he answers the call for GATT negotiators to return to Geneva on January 15 to determine whether anything can be salvaged from the Uruguay round of talks. It is to insist on some agreement on the reduction or elimination of agricultural subsidies before agreeing to any other changes in the world's trade rules.

The talks collapsed when no agreement could be reached on the question of agricultural subsidies. When they return to the talks, the Canadian negotiators may well discover that the representatives of the European Community are pressing to conclude negotiations on trading rules for services, for intellectual property and for textiles, where most members are in agreement. Canada should continue to press, with other like-minded nations, the need for an agreement on agriculture as a condition for any other changes to be made.

Representatives of the European Community are under considerable political pressure to make no changes at all in the subsidies they pay their farmers, which raise the prices those farmers receive to nearly triple what the EC charges for agricultural products on world markets. There is nothing the EC countries would like more than to be able to conclude negotiations on other matters and to quietly push agriculture into the distant future, regardless of consequences.

This is something neither Canada nor other western countries can accept. Because of the size of its own national treasury, the United States can help its farmers cope with the dumping practices of the European Community. Canada clearly cannot afford to do the same. Although the U.S. can afford to continue the food war for some time, it is not its intention to do so. American representatives have made it clear that an agreement on agricultural subsidies is necessary before agreements on other products and services can be changed. The European Community has sent just as clear a signal that it is not prepared to budge on its subsidies.

The new agreements on services and intellectual property are badly wanted by the European Community. The negotiators have produced packages in these areas which are attractive to other countries as well. As attractive as these proposals are, they must not be accepted without some change in agricultural subsidies.

Mr. Crosbie appeared well aware of the importance of reaching an agreement on agriculture during the last attempts by GATT negotiators to reach a settlement. He needs to take the same attitude with him when he attends the January talks which are aimed at reaching a successful conclusion to the Uruguay round.

San Francisco Chronicle

San Francisco, California, December 10, 1990

THE DOMINANT POWERS in the European Community hurt not only the United States, their best customer, but themselves in causing world trade talks to collapse. The four-year-long negotiations aimed at revising the General Agreement on Tariffs and Trade ended with the refusal of Germany, France and some other states to reduce agricultural trade barriers.

The results of the failure may prove tragic.

Ruinous tariffs that led to the Great Depression

The 12 members of the European Community now require their citizens to subsidize their nations' farmers by $100 billion a year. In the process, they not only increase the price their people must pay for food, but they also shut out farm products from the United States, Canada, Australia, Argentina and major agricultural exporters.

While selling their products with relative freedom in this country, the EC states are hampering American sales in their countries. Under these conditions, the U.S. trade deficit continues to grow — at the very time the United States bears the chief military and financial burden of defending the Mideast oil supply essential for European prosperity.

U.S. Trade Representative Carla Hills has already received petitions urging retaliatory action, not only against Europe but also against Japan, which continues to refuse to open its rice market to imports from abroad.

WHAT MAY OCCUR if the GATT agreement cannot be saved is a worldwide trade war similar to the ruinous tariff battles that led to the Great Depression of the 1930s. The United States is dedicated to free trade, but patience is running out.

ARGUS-LEADER

Sioux Falls, South Dakota, December 20, 1990

Before the talks collapsed, international negotiations in Belgium had been considered crucial to corporate America and the future of free world trade.

"Much is at stake," *The Wall Street Journal* reported in a front-page story. U.S. Trade Representative Carla Hills likened a potential agreement to a "locomotive that would drive world economic growth into the 21st century."

The talks were held under the lofty auspices of an international pact called the General Agreement on Tariffs and Trade. But negotiations broke down Dec. 7 unceremoniously over a lingering dispute over farm subsidies.

Editorial

Four years of talks involving more than 100 countries have been wasted, at least for now.

Negotiators should not give up, however. A new framework for world trade is in order.

While business interests in the United States look for reasons to be optimistic for future talks, some farm interests consider the failure of the talks a victory. The United States had wanted European Community nations to significantly reduce farm subsidies, which would have led to cuts in U.S. price supports.

But any victory for U.S. farmers in the collapse of the talks is shallow and short term.

U.S. farmers and ranchers are the most productive in the world. Potential long-term economic benefits of a freer world market stand to far outweigh short-term costs.

The United States should stick to its strong free-market position on agricultural trade when talks resume and not shy away from applying more pressure on European allies.

Gasps and cries of concern went up around the United States when, for example, a Japanese company announced its plans to buy the U.S. company that owns Universal Studios, a Hollywood movie studio. But there is hardly a word of protest about overly protective European trade policies.

The United States, as a world leader, should continue to take strong positions on trade and worry less about temporarily offending the European Community.

Obviously, cooperation will be needed to reach a new world trade agreement. But the global economy has become a reality. There is no denying that, and no turning back. The United States should act accordingly.

The Arizona Republic

Phoenix, Arizona, December 8, 1990

WE probably should be grateful today that two cataclysmic events predicted for the first week of December failed to materialize.

In New Madrid, Mo., the townsfolk no doubt will be slapping their knees for years to come over the Great Earthquake Scare. If nothing else, it put their Missouri Bootheel community on the world's video map, courtesy of those television news directors who didn't want to get scooped just in case the predictions of a New Mexico climatologist happened to come true.

In Brussels, where the member nations of the General Agreement on Tariffs and Trade were attempting to wrap up the so-called Uruguay Round of trade talks, the media confronted a case of the sky falling — a more difficult picture to bring into focus. At least the networks can be forgiven for not having more cameras on the scene.

New Madrid may yet have its catastrophe — a 19th-century shaker in that vicinity was a doozy, and earthquakes, like history, have a habit of repeating themselves — and the sky could still fall if the trade talks, which collapsed yesterday over the issue of the European Community's farm subsidies, don't get started again.

But let us keep our heads. Cutting the subsidies that the EC provides its tillers and toilers to keep them down on the farm might be an admirable goal. But it would be a fool's bet that it is going to happen anytime soon.

When it doesn't happen, life will go on pretty much the way it has since the end of World War II, which is to say that European, and especially French, farmers — today a pretty prosperous lot — will continue to work their fields, take their harvests to market, pocket their subsidies and raise Cain anytime some meddling bureaucrat proposes new rules to deny them their comfortable lives.

True, without a farm-trade agreement, consumers will pay more for food (unless they are buying it at fast-food burger joints, now engaged in cutthroat competition). And, true, American and other farmers will find it tougher (if not impossible) to sell their own government-subsidized products in European markets. But is this the apocalypse? Quite simply, no.

Until the Uruguay Round began, the agriculture sector was not even covered by GATT rules. Guess who insisted on such exclusion? The United States. But America is a different player these days. During the '80s attempts were made to wean farmers from their subsidies (wrecking the family farm, for all practical purposes, and underwriting big agribusiness conglomerates), to the point that U.S. negotiators were offering 75 percent cuts over 10 years in protection and internal supports.

But Europe refused to bite, and now the trade talks are on hold. Negotiators talk about a return to Geneva, but no one seems in a hurry to see whether something can be salvaged. Even as the inevitable was unfolding, however, the climatologists of world trade were revving up with predictions of Armageddon.

"If this conference fails," the president of the Federated Farms of New Zealand told *The New York Times*, "my message to New Zealand farmers is: 'Batten down the hatches. There are going to be trade wars, and we're going to get trampled.' "

That has the suspicious ring of a special interest looking out for No. 1, not the noble goal of free trade for all. Trade wars? In this day and age? Bet on New Madrid first.

The San Diego Union

San Diego, California, December 5, 1990

At stake in Brussels this week is an international trade agreement that could expand global commerce by $4 trillion during the 1990s.

Negotiators representing the 107 member nations of the General Agreement on Tariffs and Trade are working against a Friday deadline to reach an accord that, according to U.S. Trade Representative Carla Hills, "could become the locomotive that would drive world economic growth into the 21st century." To reach agreement, however, the GATT representatives must overcome a multitude of parochial interests and mounting protectionism in many nations.

The fate of the talks hinges on whether the trading partners are willing to make major concessions on agricultural subsidies, textiles and services.

American and European politicians long have resisted reductions in agricultural supports for fear of alienating powerful farm lobbies. But the European Community, which has many times more farmers than the United States, has rejected even modest GATT proposals for reform of agricultural payments. The opposition has been led by Germany and France.

Earlier this week, however, German Chancellor Helmut Kohl won a resounding electoral victory. This leaves him in a better position to stand up to the EC's farmers. He can break the impasse that threatens to sink a new GATT agreement by endorsing the gradual phasing out of subsidies. As Germany assumes an increasingly important role in European economic affairs, Kohl's leadership will become even more crucial to the rest of the world.

The United States and the 14-nation Cairns Group of farm exporters, including Argentina, Australia, Brazil and New Zealand, have staked out a reasonable position for Kohl to support. They have proposed a 75 percent reduction in farm subsidies and a 90 percent cut in export subsidies during the next 10 years. The EC's pallid response thus far has been a 30 percent reduction in overall support by 1996, with vague references to more open markets in the years to come.

The surest way to secure affordable food supplies is through an unfettered international exchange of agricultural products. This necessarily will entail taking the political risk of weaning farmers from support payments, which protect them from the competitive rigors of the market place.

The same free-market approach should be applied to textiles. It makes no sense for industrialized nations to prop up domestic clothing manufacturers when Third World exporters can supply the goods at a fraction of the cost to consumers.

There is also a move to broaden world trade in banking, insurance and other financial services. One progressive proposal, supported by Canada, Japan, Sweden and Switzerland, would enable foreign financial institutions to compete for business across international boundaries. This could open up all manner of investment opportunities in a rapidly expanding global economy.

At a time when Latin American and Eastern European countries are opening their economies to market forces, the entire global trading order needs to be liberalized. Freer markets would mean increased trade and prosperity for all nations. That is why the high-stakes talks in Brussels must succeed, even if the Friday deadline must be extended.

THE TAMPA TRIBUNE
Tampa, Florida, December 12, 1990

The failure of what was to have been the final session of the four-year Uruguay round of international trade negotiations shows this:

When the economic going gets tough, soft economies get tougher with protectionism.

The controversy between the European Community and world agriculture producers over reducing restrictions on trade in farm products held the spotlight and was acknowledged to be the keystone to eliminating barriers on imports of nonmanufactured products and services. In retrospect, though, the central problem was more basic: The session at Brussels was the first in the 43-year history of the General Agreement on Tariffs and Trade to be held in a time of worldwide economic doldrums.

So it was not just that the European Community feared that 2 million of its 12 members' 10 million farmers would be driven from the land by free trade in farm products. It was also that its governments deemed the short-term joblessness that restructuring of world trade would cause in some economic areas to be too high a price to pay for the long-term general prosperity free trade is expected to bring.

Germany's Chancellor Helmut Kohl and France's President Francois Mitterrand were not alone in the inconsistency of their positions. But their adamant resistance to relaxing the European Community's barriers against food from other producers illustrates the dilemma of world leaders.

Optimists hoped that Kohl would be more accommodating after the German election, but he stood fast — although Germany as the world's third largest exporter has much to gain in the long run. Faced with an outlay estimated from $600 billion up to restructure the economy of newly absorbed East Germany, Kohl was as unyielding after his sweeping election victory as before. And Mitterrand, who is long on rhetoric about the industrialized nations helping underdeveloped ones, stood equally firm — even though opening up the European Community market to Third World farmers would be worth twice as much to those struggling countries as they get in direct foreign aid.

The Europeans blamed President Bush for making agriculture the keystone, saying his stubbornness prevented agreements on other matters. Yet the United States did offer to yield in some service areas it was seeking to protect; the Europeans sloughed off even a slight compromise on farm products offered by Sweden.

Now the troubles begin. U.S. Trade Representative Carla Hills says her desk is covered with complaints from U.S. farmers demanding investigation of alleged unfair trade practices which, if proved, can bring retaliation under U.S. law. Early targets may be Japan for its outright ban on rice imports, and the Europeans for their barriers to U.S. pork and other meat products.

Nobody at Brussels would say that a trade war is in the offing, only that it is a distant threat. But the underdeveloped nations, which were the first to give up and walk out at Brussels, already are putting out feelers on bilateral agreements between free traders at the expense of nations with closed markets. And among industrialized nations, there is the likelihood of a rising tide of "voluntary restraint agreements." The United States now has them with foreign automobile and steel producers. Under the practice, a nation "voluntarily" accepts an export quota on its products in exchange for other concessions.

Nor does anybody see long-term economic advantage in retaliatory measures or voluntary restraints. But in a period of economic sluggishness they are attractive to those wooing the special interests they benefit. That myopic view, history reminds us, was how the world stumbled into the Great Depression.

The New York Times
New York City, New York, December 17, 1990

The Uruguay Round of international trade negotiations collapsed 10 days ago in Brussels when the European Community refused to cut back its protectionist food policy. Denied access to European markets, negotiators from third world food-exporting nations were left with no option other than to pack their bags.

The fallout from Brussels could turn ugly, and fast. Without rules to govern trade in agriculture, services and investment, countries will be free to accuse each other of unfair trade practices, and to unilaterally impose sanctions. Sanctions, in turn, invite retaliation.

The threat of escalating trade wars is no mere speculation: within days of the suspended talks in Brussels, the U.S. and several of its trading partners began saber rattling.

The U.S. is reportedly preparing to raise duties on European exports of food and beverages by 200 percent — in part to retaliate against a European ban on pork and beef imports from the U.S. The Administration is also drawing up plans to retaliate against countries deemed to discriminate against U.S. companies selling financial services; Japan, South Korea and Brazil are the likely targets.

And without international trade rules for intellectual property, Washington will be pressured to impose sanctions on countries like Thailand that tolerate massive pirating of copyrighted and patented materials.

The United States won't be the only country to engage in unilateral sanctions. That's why international rules are important, and why the trade talks must be salvaged.

All sides must give. But the Europeans must give the most. The European Community could break the logjam by agreeing to phase out export subsidies. These allow European farmers to dump surplus food at subsidized prices on international markets, devastating third world farmers. The E.C. could insulate the rest of the world from its internal food policies in another important way: helping its farmers with direct income payments rather than with production subsidies.

For their part, the U.S. and other food-exporting countries could back off from demands that would require the Europeans to cut food supports by 75 percent or more. The E.C. agriculture policy is deeply ingrained, politically and economically. It needs to be phased down over time, not dismantled all at once.

The White House could also emphasize to the Europeans that it, too, is prepared to take a political beating by pushing through Congress a trade agreement that would undo an elaborate U.S. system of quotas on peanuts, sugar and textiles.

In Brussels, the E.C. — at the insistence of President François Mitterrand of France and Chancellor Helmut Kohl of Germany — made an understandable but hardly noble political decision to protect its own farmers rather than protect world trade. If world trade is to flourish, the E.C. will have to find ways to do both.

THE ARIZONA REPUBLIC
Phoenix, Arizona, December 3, 1990

SHORTLY after the massacre of unarmed civilians in Tiananmen Square, which horrified the entire civilized world, Beijing's application for membership in the General Agreement on Tariffs and Trade was put on the shelf, where it has remained ever since.

Given the brutality of the provocation, this was a reasonable — indeed a moderate — response. One of the prices that ought to be exacted for butchery on such a scale is an end to normal commercial ties with governments that disdain to mow down their critics.

Unfortunately, the tiny but prosperous nation of Taiwan, no friend of the mainland's communist masters, is being penalized as well. Owing to GATT's "one China" policy, Taipei's membership application is being held up until Beijing's can be dealt with, even though Taipei, sensitive to such niceties, prudently applied as "the Customs Territory of Taiwan, Penghu, Kinmen and Matsu," not as a sovereign nation.

Even though punishing Taipei for the massacre in Beijing is altogether irrational, the U.S. State Department persists in opposing Taiwan's admission. This opposition stems in part from a forlorn hope that Beijing will support the U.S. position on the Persian Gulf. The kowtowing has not worked. When the U.N. Security Council on Thursday approved the American deadline for evacuation of Kuwait, Beijing abstained.

Neither diplomatically nor commercially does discrimination against a friendly government in Taipei serve the interests of the United States, which benefits from expanding GATT membership, not curtailing it. Taiwan ranks 13th among the world's trading nations, is this country's fifth largest trading partner and ranks just behind Japan in foreign reserves.

Nearly all member nations favor Taiwan's admission to GATT, as does Congress, and for good reason. GATT membership would fix 94 percent of Taiwan's tariffs at no more than 30 percent and by 1992 lower the effective rate to 3.5 percent, which is comparable to the tariff of other developed countries. Taiwan also would become a party to the six agreements signed at the GATT Tokyo Round negotiations — all in the interest of the United States and other member nations.

The only obstacle is political — a curious reluctance to give offense to the government in Beijing, even though admitting Taiwan as a separate "customs territory" is entirely consistent with the GATT charter and finesses the sticky "one China" question entirely.

Over the past 10 years Taiwan has liberalized its internal politics and its trade with other countries and, through steadily lowered tariffs, has allowed greater and greater access to its own domestic markets. It has eased import restrictions, lifted controls on foreign exchange and strengthened copyright protections. Mainland China, on the other hand, has become increasingly hostile to outsiders, including Americans, and increasingly reprehensible in its domestic affairs.

It is time Washington quit worrying about Beijing's "sensitivities" and looked to this country's national interests. This would entail, among other useful changes, expediting Taiwan's admission to GATT.

Chicago Tribune
Chicago, Illinois, February 2, 1991

Already involved in one war, the Bush administration is trying to head off another—this time over international trade. It soon will ask Congress for an extension of special authority to negotiate trade agreements on a so-called fast track.

This vital power allows the White House to work out trade pacts that Congress can approve or disapprove in their entirety but not kill through minor amendments. The current fast-track authority doesn't expire until June, but the administration must request a two-year extension by March 1. And some lawmakers have foolishly indicated they will oppose it.

President Bush wants the authority in order to negotiate a free-trade agreement with Mexico and, if need be, to salvage the Uruguay Round of global trade talks that ended in disarray in December. But some legislators, siding with organized labor, oppose any pact with Mexico for fear jobs in their district will head south. Others, angered by recession and the limited gulf war participation of some allies, want to protect domestic industries from competition. But throwing up barriers to commerce invites retaliation, and this isn't the time to start a harmful trade war.

With a growing budget deficit and continued dependence on foreign capital to finance it, Washington can't rely on the traditional tools of fiscal stimulus or monetary policy to pull the economy from recession. The gulf war itself won't boost production much because it is being fought from a well-stocked arsenal. But growth could be fed by increased exports and expanded trade of manufactured goods, services and farm products.

To accomplish that, Americans need determination, lower tariffs and access to markets. The latter two can be achieved through regional free-trade agreements like the one the Bush administration wants to negotiate with Mexico and Canada, and eventually with other countries in the Western Hemisphere. U.S. Trade Representative Carla Hills will ask Congress to extend the fast-track authority to complete an agreement for a continent-wide free-trade zone.

But she also may need it if a serious effort is made to restart the talks to expand and liberalize the General Agreement on Tariffs and Trade, the rules that govern most international commerce. Those talks broke off recently when the 12 nations of the European Community refused to make meaningful cuts in their agricultural programs, which pay farmers to overproduce and which subsidize farm exports to give them a competitive advantage. The U.S. and other agricultural exporters want those subsidies reduced substantially.

Support seems to be growing in Europe for a plan to cut price supports in favor of direct payments to farmers. Such a scheme could be less distorting to world trade and might break the deadlock in the Uruguay talks, but any successful conclusion still is many weeks away. Most experts believe negotiations can't be completed before March.

America needs stronger, more liberal trade rules that foster open markets. Without them, protectionism will increase and destructive trade wars could follow. Meantime, the administration should pursue agreements with any country that seeks open trade. And Congress should not stand in the way.

The Miami Herald
Miami, Florida, February 27, 1991

SINCE 1934, Presidents have been able to negotiate international-trade agreements without worrying that Congress might later pick them apart, approving some parts and rejecting others. Over the years Congress has agreed, within limits, to put trade pacts on a "fast track," voting Yea or Nay on the entire document.

The Bush Administration's current "fast track" authority is about to expire, and the timing couldn't be worse. Just as Canada, Mexico, and the United States begin work on a North American Free Trade Agreement, the global-trade talks that stalled last December have seemingly come back to life. The President's Enterprise for the Americas initiative — a trade-and-development pact covering the entire hemisphere — also depends on "fast-track" approval.

Except that Congress always hates to part with any power, the "fast-track" authority shouldn't be controversial. Congress must be consulted throughout any negotiation process, and it always can reject a treaty entirely if it chooses. Yet the list of broad, historic trade agreements now under discussion makes almost anything labeled "trade" more controversial than usual.

So when U.S. Trade Representative Carla Hills went before the House Ways and Means Subcommittee on Trade recently, temperatures were rising. The topic at hand was the North American pact, but the message was broader: The future of "fast track" authority is anything but certain.

The resuscitation of global-trade talks, known as the Uruguay Round after the country where they began, is the most promising trade news in months. It comes after intense, often-bitter, American negotiations with the European Community.

The resumption of those talks is a partial, yet remarkable, American victory. But without "fast track" authority, it's pointless. So are virtually any trade talks, anywhere. Few governments would take American negotiators seriously once they knew that Congress can start nit-picking the final agreement before the ink is dry.

President Bush will ask Congress for the fast-track extension this week, and Congress ought to grant it promptly. With U.S. exports finally expanding, this is no time to walk away from negotiations that will define world markets for the 21st Century.

THE ⬛ SUN
Baltimore, Maryland, February 7, 1991

Big business in the United States, Japan and the European Community is mounting one last try to save and broaden the international trading system before it founders over agriculture policy.

Unless the EC backs away from high farm support prices and export subsidies before the end of February, Congress may go on a protectionist binge — refusing to extend the president's negotiating authority under the General Agreement on Tariffs and Trade and renewing the "Super 301" provisions of 1988 legislation that would require automatic retaliation against certain countries, especially Japan, that engage in unfair practices.

If all that comes to pass, GATT would start to wither as regional trading blocs and special bilateral deals increasingly dominate the world trade scene. (Note the rapid development of a U.S.-Mexico-Canada combo to offset the 12-nation EC.) Hopes of widening the scope of GATT from manufactures to service industries, intellectual property rights and agricultural products would be a goner.

GATT has been under intensive care since a supposedly final session of the four-year Uruguay Round negotiation collapsed in bitterness Dec. 7. Efforts to revive it have produced only posturing and platitudes so far. President Bush has until March 1 to ask Congress to permit further bargaining, perhaps for only six months, but his special trade representative, Carla Hills, has said she won't even make such a request unless the Europeans start to deal. Chances are fading fast.

Even if the administration claims enough progress to move ahead, there is no assurance Congress will agree. Thirty-seven senators, including Maryland Democrats Paul Sarbanes and Barbara Mikulski, signed onto a protectionist resolution last fall that would hobble the administration and, in effect, kill any chance of a new GATT agreement. Free-trade groups hope to impress Senator Sarbanes with the adverse foreign-policy implications of a U.S. descent into protectionism — especially since our chief adversaries, Japan and the European states, are the very nations whose support is needed in the gulf war.

If there is ever to be a stable, peaceful "new world order" after the war, a free flow of commerce will be one of its key underpinnings. On this issue, the United States and most developing countries in the Third World are solidly on the same side. We hope our two senators reconsider.

Newsday

New York City, New York, March 11, 1991

Hills

Now that the administration is no longer preoccupied with the gulf war, it must revitalize stalled negotiations to modernize world trade rules. Those talks are just as important — maybe more important — to America's economic future as the outcome of the war.

And Congress must give the White House time to achieve that goal, by extending for two more years the deadline for a new trade agreement. No easy job; special interests who want to keep competition out will try to block it.

The so-called Uruguay round of talks to modernize the General Agreement on Tariffs and Trade broke down in December after European negotiators failed to come up with real reforms to their nations' farm programs. Both France and Germany lavish subsidies on their inefficient farms; that puts other countries' farmers at a disadvantage in world trade.

GATT talks have quietly resumed after Europe signaled it was ready to make genuine concessions. Whether it is remains to be seen. But now that Washington is free to disagree with its allies, it's time to twist arms.

Congress has its work cut out for it, too. Technically, U.S. trade negotiator Carla Hills is seeking a two-year extension for the GATT talks. But the White House also wants to start free-trade negotiations with Mexico, which would come under the same negotiating authority. The Mexico pact is far more controversial; labor and farm groups oppose it.

It's hard to hold out against determined special interests. But the promises of freer trade — new U.S. jobs, new opportunities for business, more choice for consumers — far outweigh the costs. It's those benefits Congress must keep in mind when the vote comes.

The Hartford Courant

Hartford, Connecticut, March 6, 1991

In December, negotiations to liberalize international trade collapsed over agricultural subsidies. Countries with heavy farm-support programs, such as Germany, Japan, France and South Korea, refused to remove key import barriers.

That deadlock has now been broken. The 12-member European Community has moved closer to the U.S. position by agreeing to negotiate commitments to reduce domestic price supports, export subsidies and import barriers.

Even though the negotiations have resumed in Paris, success is far from assured. The source of obstruction this time is the United States, where several industrial and labor groups are seeking protection from imports.

Under existing procedure, Congress cannot tinker with trade agreements negotiated by President Bush. Lawmakers can only vote yes or no on the entire package. The administration's so-called fast-track authority will expire in May, and Mr. Bush has asked for a two-year extension.

He needs the authority, he says, because international trade agreements are complex, tightly interwoven documents that would fall apart if amended by parochial-minded politicians.

The segments of labor and industry affected by imports oppose the two-year renewal. But without an extension, the current round of negotiations in Paris may fail.

Participants in the talks on the General Agreement on Tariffs and Trade insist that agreements negotiated with the president be binding; Mr. Bush must have the power to finalize deals. They have a point. What would be the use of making compromises to reach agreement that could then be amended by lawmakers anyway? Congress retains its constitutional power to reject the agreement, but it should not be able amend it to death.

Congress must not give in to narrow self-interests. Open international trade is vital to the economic growth of the United States and the rest of the world.

Minneapolis Star and Tribune

Minneapolis, Minnesota, March 9, 1991

After four years, world trade talks hardly seem on the fast track. But, after a standstill in December, prospects are picking up for a successful conclusion to this round of talks to strengthen and expand the General Agreement on Tariffs and Trade (GATT). To keep up, President Bush needs congressional approval for extending his fast-track negotiating authority. Lawmakers should speed him on his way.

The fast-track authority allows the president to negotiate trade agreements and then requires Congress to vote them up or down, without amendment, within 90 days after the president submits them for approval. The authority expires in June, and the president notified Congress March 1 of the need for an extension. A majority vote in either the House or Senate would deny the request.

The case for extending the negotiating authority is powerful: A successful GATT round will add $4 trillion to world trade over the next decade. And in the past couple of weeks, chances for success have improved. After nearly torpedoing the talks, the European Community is finally considering changes in its heavily subsidized agricultural system. The United States and other farm-exporting countries have a real chance to reduce subsidies and import barriers that hamper trade. And with a breakthrough on agriculture would come agreements on new rules governing services, finance and intellectual property.

But the extension faces strong resistance. Already groups that benefit from trade barriers — notably textile manufacturers and sugar producers — are fighting it. They are joined by labor unions opposed to plans to negotiate a U.S.-Mexican free-trade agreement, also under fast-track authority.

And after the Persian Gulf victory, some Democrats see trade protectionism as a blunt instrument with which to beat Bush in the 1992 presidential election. But the casualties would be widespread. Soybean, corn and wheat farmers, who already sell much of their crop overseas, would lose new markets. High-tech and financial-services industries would lose global opportunities. Consumers would be denied more products at less cost; workers would lose jobs in industries expanding to serve world markets. Congress should keep the United States on the fast track.

The Buffalo News

Buffalo, New York, March 11, 1991

THE MAJOR industrial nations spend $250 billion a year on various kinds of subsidies to agriculture with drastic consequences in distorting world trade. The European Community, the biggest offender, spends $100 billion a year in this way, artificially stimulating farm output and then dumping its products at low prices on the world's markets.

The trade negotiations sponsored by GATT, the General Agreement on Tariffs and Trade, are again grappling with this tough problem after a suspension of the talks last December. The EC, traditionally protective of its farmers, has now made a significant change by accepting the U.S. approach in the talks.

All that has been achieved, however, is an agreement to negotiate, and months of hard work lie ahead.

All trading nations of the world would benefit by the removal of these barriers to trade. U.S. Trade Representative Carla Hills said successful conclusion of the GATT talks "would be like writing a check for $17,000, payable over 10 years, to every family of four in the world."

Impoverished Third World nations are especially concerned by the dumping of food products that compete with their struggling agricultural exports. Until their concerns are met, these nations are resisting controls on the illegal trade in copyrighted or patented materials. The United States loses billions of dollars each year in the trade of pirated materials.

Another positive result of successful negotiations on farm trade would be modification of the blatant protectionism in U.S. sugar policy. To please a few U.S. sugar producers, the American consumer pays an extra $3 billion a year for sugar while mountains of sugar sell on the world market at one-third the U.S. price.

Many attempts have been made over the years to end this sweet deal, but sugar-state congressmen and the powerful sugar lobby always manage to prevail. Perhaps in the context of a worldwide trade agreement, this scandalous policy will at last be buried.

Bush Gains, Wins on 'Fast Track' Powers

President Bush's quest to obtain a free hand in international trade talks over the next two years won the approval of two key congressional committees May 14, 1991.

Legislation that would have curtailed Bush's so-called fast-track authority to negotiate agreements with minimal congressional input was defeated by the committees by unexpectedly large margins. The votes were 15 to 3 in the Senate Finance Committee and 27 to 9 in the House Ways and Means Committee.

If the full houses of Congress voted down the legislation as well, fast-track authority would automatically be extended June 1. The authority meant that Congress could vote on trade treaties only as a package, after the president had negotiated them.

Bush had been seeking fast-track extension for trade talks in two key areas. One was Mexico. Labor groups and environmentalists had sought to rally opposition to a Mexican free-trade agreement because of concerns about job losses and the possibility that U.S. companies would move to Mexico to take advantage of its less stringent environmental regulations.

The other area was the Uruguay Round of General Agreement on Tariffs and Trade multilateral trade talks. Those negotiations had been strongly supported by the Bush administration. But disputes with the European Community over agriculture had hampered the talks.

The Bush administration had worked in recent weeks to address lawmakers' concerns about the Mexico negotiations, the more sensitive of the two areas. Those efforts May 9 had won the support of House Majority Leader Richard A. Gephardt (D, Mo.), an influential critic of the administration on trade issues.

The administration later had antagonized Gephardt and others, however, by injecting a racial element into the free-trade debate. "Unfortunately, some of the opponents of free trade have resorted to slurs against our Mexican neighbors," Bush said May 12. Gephardt May 13 accused the president of "practicing racial division."

President Bush May 23-24 won votes in both houses of the U.S. Congress authorizing him to negotiate international trade agreements with a free hand.

In the House, 91 Democrats joined with 140 Republicans May 23 in a 231-192 vote to extend the president's so-called fast-track negotiating authority. The Senate May 24 passed the measure, 59-36.

The votes defeated measures that would have canceled the renewal of the administration's fast-track authority. The result meant that any trade pact would be considered by Congress in its entirety, as negotiated by the president. Fast-track opponents believed Congress should have greater input in negotiating such treaties.

Bush May 23 praised the House action, the closer of the two votes. "It's going to be good for the working man in this country and good for the environment," he said. The opponents of fast-track authority were mostly unions and environmental groups who said the costs of a free-trade agreement Bush was seeking with Mexico outweighed its benefits.

"The old days when the American worker earning $12 an hour could beat a guy on the other side of the world earning a dollar an hour, because he was 20 times as productive, are gone" said Rep. Don J. Pease (D, Ohio), a fast-track opponent May 23.

The lobbying campaign against fast track had been spearheaded by the United Auto Workers union and other labor groups that said a Mexican treaty would encourage U.S. corporations to move factories to Mexico, where labor was cheap. The failure to halt fast track was seen as a blow to the labor movement.

Many environmentalists said a Mexican trade pact would encourage American factories to relocate to Mexico to escape tough U.S. environmental regulations.

The trade vote had been the most contentious one in the area of economics in Congress so far in 1991. Its outcome was a major victory for President Bush, who had sought to address the concerns of labor and environmentalists to insure its passage.

In addition to allowing the U.S. to pursue the talks with Mexico, the vote meant the continuation of a set of talks on trade barriers with a wider group of nations. Those negotiations, the Uruguay Round of multilateral trade talks of the General Agreement on Tariffs and Trade, were currently stalled.

The Cincinnati Post

Cincinnati, Ohio, May 28, 1991

Congress handed George Bush a major victory last week by extending his authority to negotiate a free trade agreement with Mexico. It is a victory not only for the president but for our southern neighbor and the United States as well.

For the anti-free trade lobby, however, the news must appear grim. Some environmentalists teamed with big labor in a prodigious effort to deny the president his negotiating authority. It was, in truth, an unholy alliance, tainted with xenophobia, willful misrepresentation and economic mysticism.

Neither expense nor the truth was spared. A main thrust of labor's campaign was to discredit the "maquiladora" factories along the U.S.-Mexico border. In effect, these are mini-free trade zones to which Mexican workers have been flocking since they were established in 1965.

The AFL-CIO provided all congressmen with videotapes representing the areas as squalid cesspools — with the implication that the entire border would be so transformed under free trade. Newspaper advertisements conveyed the same impression. It was a particularly ugly lie, as those who retailed it may well have known it to be.

Environmentalists asserted that any free trade agreement would be an ecological disaster for both sides of the border. They conveniently overlooked that environmentalism is something only prosperous economies can afford. A prosperous Mexico will be a cleaner Mexico.

Opponents also brandished the scare scenario of massive U.S. layoffs — an assertion that was economically nonsensical. Almost every reputable economist envisages a net gain in U.S. job creation as a result of freer trade.

These arguments shared an underlying theme: That close association with Mexico would somehow sully the United States. There's no place in our political discourse for such unseemly insinuations. Congress and the president have done their country proud by rejecting them so decisively.

Detroit Free Press

Detroit, Michigan, May 29, 1991

The United States cannot credibly demand the dismantling of trade barriers abroad while it attempts to maintain them at home. Congress' vote to authorize President George Bush to pursue a "fast track" in negotiating trade agreements with other countries — particularly Mexico — was correct.

The vote allows the White House to make and sign trade treaties that still must be approved by Congress, but are not subject to last-minute, special-interest amendments that could weaken the bargaining position of U.S. negotiators.

Mr. Bush sought the fast-track extension primarily to facilitate trade talks with Mexico. A similar extension governs U.S. participation in the Uruguay Round of global negotiations within the General Agreement on Tariffs and Trade.

Protectionist-minded lawmakers huff that Washington should work to assure jobs domestically rather than in Mexico. That becomes an either/or proposition only when your definition of industrial policy is nothing more than beggar-thy-neighbor.

Proponents of a U.S.-Mexico free-trade agreement argue persuasively that both nations will benefit from the removal of restrictive tariffs and other barriers. New export markets would develop for both countries, creating jobs and relieving the pressure of illegal immigration from Mexico. Include Canada — which has a free-trade pact with the United States — in a North American trade zone and you have a formidable competitor to a unified European Economic Community and an Asian trade bloc headed by Japan.

Of course a free-trade agreement cannot become an excuse for tolerating economic exploitation or environmental degradation in Mexico. A substantial federal commitment to retraining and other help for U.S. workers whose jobs might be threatened must accompany any treaty.

But a carefully negotiated pact would leave Washington in a stronger position to challenge corporate abuses on both sides of the border. Congress remains empowered to reject the final product.

The best interests of the United States are served by free and fair trade that maximizes competition. Where the global playing field is tilted against U.S. autoworkers or farmers, the nation must move aggressively to right the balance. It will be in a better position to do so to the extent that it overcomes protectionist sentiments at home.

THE LINCOLN STAR

Lincoln, Nebraska, May 16, 1991

A free trade agreement with Mexico won't subject Americans to pesticide-laden citrus nor promote child labor.

It will cement the economic reforms of Mexican President Gotari de Salinas and further the Enterprise for the Americas Initiative, a plan for increased trade and better relations between the United States and all of Latin America.

Critics of the plan have raised valid concerns. But those have been answered by President Bush, who has pledged that a closer working relationship with Mexico will give the United States more leverage on issues of environmental protection and worker safety.

There's no getting around the loss of some manufacturing jobs to Mexico. But this is a trend already underway with very few impediments, because a significant amount of trade between the United States and Mexico is already duty free.

Nor will health and safety standards required of imports be abandoned simply because the tariffs on trade will be lifted on products from Mexico, which is our third largest trading partner.

THE UNITED STATES and Mexico share a 2,000-mile border.

Millions of Mexicans illegally pour across it every year, seeking jobs and better lives than they can find at home.

They will wash dishes, scrub floors and pick beans at wages most Americans — even unemployed Americans — reject. They risk assault, robbery, rape, even death to get here.

Bush's free trade pact with Mexico won't end this influx, and it will likely accelerate the migration of some manufacturing jobs south. But increased trade and the economic development it spurs will make living and working conditions in Mexico better, enticing more Mexicans to seek opportunity and employment in their homeland.

AND EXPANDED trade will also create jobs in the export industries in both countries.

This is a long-term process, but it begins with one step: reauthorizing the so-called fast-track procedure that allows the president to negotiate trade agreements while denying Congress the ability to add amendments. Two congressional committees have given it a green light, but it still faces strong opposition when debated by the full House and Senate.

To deny fast-track approval on this pivotal trade issue would send the wrong signal to Mexico — as it struggles toward a market economy — and to the emerging democracies of Latin America.

Mexico's problems are increasingly ours. U.S. labor and environmental groups may want to turn a cold shoulder to the agreement because Mexico's standards do not match ours, but our porous border won't allow us to ignore the human misery across the Rio Grande. Nor will environmental catastrophes respect any dividing line.

The Washington Post

Washington, D.C., May 22, 1991

WHEN CONGRESS votes on fast track, as it will in the next few days, the real question will be whether the United States should enter into trade agreements. Fast track is nothing more than a procedure to get these agreements enacted, along with the implementing legislation that they require. Either house of Congress can abolish fast track. The effect would be to cut off President Bush's authority to negotiate any trade agreements that require legislation, as all the major ones do. The people fighting fast track are not simply against this or that provision of a possible agreement. Fearing losses of jobs, they are against any foreign trade agreements at all.

If fast track is extended, two separate negotiations will go forward. One of them, to develop a free trade agreement with Mexico, has not yet begun. The other, the enormously complex worldwide talks known as the Uruguay Round, is stuck in a quarrel over agriculture. The time to make up your mind on them is in the future, when and if the terms of these deals get clearer.

The accusations brought against fast track deserve answers. The most common complaint is that it shuts Congress out of the process of developing the agreements and gives it only an up-or-down vote on the finished product. That's wrong, and the proof is the actual experience with all three of the previous agreements passed under fast track. In each case the congressional committees were deeply and actively involved while the negotiations were still underway. The president signed them only after Congress had been through every line of them. It played as large and influential a role in these agreements as in any other major legislation.

Fast track threatens American environmental standards, some of the opponents charge. But they can never quite show how or why. In fact, there's nothing in this procedure that weakens existing environmental protection or makes it easier for foreign governments to attack.

The prospect of a Mexican trade agreement in particular spooks a lot of people in Congress. It would certainly encourage more American companies to open factories in Mexico. Would that damage this country?

Consider a historical example. In the 1950s, low-wage industries like textiles were moving from New England to the South—over the bitter protests of the labor unions that are now fighting fast track. That southward migration certainly cost some New Englanders their jobs. But now, a generation later, New England is not only richer. It is richer in relation to the national average than it was 40 years ago, when the flight of the mills was beginning. Meanwhile southern prosperity has grown even faster. The disparities between the country's richest states and its poorest are significantly narrower than they were in 1950.

The process that has worked across state borders will also work across national borders. The choice on fast track and trade is a choice about economic growth. Congress won't have a better opportunity this year to vote for growth and a rising standard of living here in the United States.

THE CHRISTIAN SCIENCE MONITOR
Boston, Massachusetts, May 31, 1991

AFTER weeks of strenuous public debate over the effects of a proposed free-trade agreement with Mexico, Congress last week voted to preserve the president's "fast track" authority to negotiate trade pacts. Trade agreements placed on the fast track receive expedited review by Congress, which must vote on such agreements without amending them.

The fast-track approvals in both houses were victories for the Bush administration and free-trade advocates over organized labor and some environmentalists. But the fast-track fight was, in a sense, just talk about talks. Now come the hard, substantive trade negotiations themselves.

While public attention during the fast-track skirmish focused mainly on US trade with Mexico, the president's renewed authority also applies to other trade negotiations, notably ongoing global trade talks under the auspices of the 108-member General Agreement on Tariffs and Trade (GATT). As it gears up for talks with Mexico, the administration should also press vigorously for a satisfactory conclusion to GATT's Uruguay Round, begun in 1986.

The Uruguay Round has had an ambitious agenda. Besides continuing GATT's 40 years of progress in lowering tariffs, the current talks have aimed to achieve major liberalization in multilateral trade policies on agriculture, textiles, services like banking and insurance, intellectual-property rights such as patents and copyrights (services and intellectual property aren't presently covered by GATT), and dispute-resolution mechanisms.

The multilateral talks nearly collapsed late last year when European farmers resisted requested changes in their price supports and export subsidies. But enough progress has been made on those issues to breathe life back into the negotiations.

With the growing interest in regional trading blocs around the world, an overarching GATT accord is more important than ever to prevent such blocs from developing into protectionist alliances. Back on the fast track, the Bush administration should push the pedal to the metal on GATT.

The Times-Picayune
New Orleans, Louisiana, May 26, 1991

These days the phrase "free trade with Mexico" is bringing smiles to the faces of Louisiana businessmen who anticipate a new era of flourishing trade between the state and nearby Mexican markets.

Particularly appealing to Louisiana business interests is the prospect of an increase in export trade. A leading Southern state in Mexican trade, Louisiana exported $377,426,000 worth of goods to Mexico in 1987. By 1990, Louisiana's Mexican exports had grown to about $736 million a year.

Congress' approval of "fast-track" legislation giving President Bush the authority to negotiate a tariff-removing trade agreement with Mexico heightened Louisiana's hopes of broadening its trade ties with Mexican businesses and consumers.

The fast-track concept effectively bars Congress from changing a trade agreement once it is signed. Lawmakers have one take-it-or-leave-it vote on a treaty.

The favorable congressional vote was seen as a major spur to Mr. Bush's attempts to work out a free trade treaty with Mexico along the lines of one negotiated earlier with Canada.

While trade is already thriving between the United States and Mexico, some tariff barriers still exist on both sides, particularly in textiles, fruits and vegetables and steel products.

Some special interest groups, notably labor unions and environmentalists, have voiced concerns over loss of jobs and threats to the environment, but many of Louisiana's business and political leaders are supportive of the president's opening to Mexico.

Growing interest in new opportunities for commerce with Mexico was one of the main topics of discussion at the North American Free Trade Conference held Thursday in New Orleans. It was attended by 150 public officials, business people and economic development experts from throughout the United States and Puerto Rico, who listened to various sides of the issue.

Gov. Roemer, who hosted the conference, said the event is part of his Latin American initiative to expand Louisiana's relationships with Mexico and other Latin American countries.

While benefits of a new Mexican trade pact are expected to be more long-range than immediate, Louisiana is well positioned to cash in on the lifting of tariffs. The states that border Mexico — Texas, Arizona and California — should get the lion's share of new business, but Louisiana, because of its close proximity, also has a great advantage.

Eugene Schreiber, managing director of the World Trade Center of New Orleans, noted that Mexico, the United States' third-largest trading partner, has become an increasingly important market for U.S. exporters. He cited Commerce Department figures showing that Mexicans get around 70 percent of their total imports from the United States.

At a time when the economic borders of Europe are giving way to a united continent, the United States and its nearby trading partners, principally Mexico and Canada, need to look ahead to joining hands in a similar effort that will allow them to be more competitive.

The prospect of removing our remaining trade barriers with Mexico is exciting news, not only for the nation but for Louisiana as well.

Minneapolis Star and Tribune
Minneapolis, Minnesota, May 29, 1991

In a fit of good sense, Congress last week gave President Bush the authority he needs to negotiate trade agreements. This is a startling development. It runs counter to the can't-do vision of America's future, where a typical U.S. worker in a Chinese-made uniform serves Argentine hamburgers to Japanese computer executives. The ketchup is Mexican, the cookware German, the worker downcast. But now Congress has acknowledged that Americans are regaining the courage to compete.

The negotiating authority is overoptimistically called "fast track." It doesn't mean that trade officials rocket through deliberations; only that Congress, which in any case is consulted as trade talks proceed, has to vote a signed treaty up or down. Without that provision, Congress can rewrite an otherwise completed trade pact. Its approval of fast track was an act of statesmanship.

Critics who lament foreign competition want import protection for fear that otherwise the United States will sink into a service economy. If a service economy were a low-skill employment swamp, Americans would have reason to be concerned. But it isn't a swamp; service includes banking and law as well as hamburgers.

And the United States isn't sinking. As Fortune magazine points out, this country is regaining its competitive edge. Manufacturing's share of gross national product grew in the 1980s, as did productivity. According to a report Monday in the Star Tribune, not only did U.S. manufacturing productivity rise 3.5 percent a year, but by the end of the '80s it was higher than that of other leading industrial nations. With a weaker dollar, the drive for competitiveness strengthened exports in products ranging from refrigerators to semiconductors.

Behind that drive are people like those cited by Fortune, most but not all of them in business. We admit a provincial bias: Sandra Hale is among the 25 the magazine singled out. Hale's success as Rudy Perpich's administration commissioner was not simply in cutting costs and improving service. Her more enduring accomplishment was to create a can-do vision of the future, giving workers the incentives and the means to become more productive.

Congress' statement of confidence is similarly refreshing. As the United States gets its economy out of recession, it will have the fast-track negotiating authority the 1990s require.

The Phoenix Gazette
Phoenix, Arizona, May 30, 1991

Well into the next century, Americans will be enjoying the fruits — and vegetables — of Congress' well-considered decision to extend the fast-track process for the proposed U.S.-Mexico free trade agreement.

A vigorous lobbying campaign had opposed the so-called "fast track" negotiation, which requires the president to inform Congress on a strict timetable, but gives Congress a simple up-or-down vote, without amendments, once its provisions are drafted. Opponents include labor unions, fearing the loss of jobs to Mexico; farmers, worried about an influx of lower-priced fruits and vegetables from south of the border; and environmentalists, concerned about Mexico's less rigorous pollution controls.

They all argue that a treaty will cost Americans jobs; that U.S. firms will move to lower-wage Mexico and raise unemployment.

But standing with President Bush in support of a long-awaited trade agreement are virtually every economist, as well as executives and workers of most American high-tech and automobile firms, which can expand their already profitable business with Mexico, a developing nation that complements ours in a neat trade fit.

Many of the industries — textile firms, for example — that oppose the treaty, are among the least competitive American companies now. We cannot protect them from foreign competition forever. Besides, many of them are moving to Pacific Rim nations anyway. If these jobs are going to move, doesn't it make more sense to have them in Mexico, which is a heavy American trading partner already, than in far-off Asia, where they will likely buy their supplies from Japan?

Mexico buys more than 70 percent of her imports from the United States. If the trade agreement works to make more Mexicans better consumers, won't that mean more U.S. goods will be purchased? Of course, it does. That's why so many high-tech firms, the growth industries for the United States, are so eager for an agreement; because it will lower trade barriers that block their sales in Mexico.

A treaty that raises the standard of living in Mexico will lessen the intense economic pressure on Mexican workers to migrate to the United States, where they would compete for jobs in the low-wage sector anyway.

The essence of any negotiation is that both parties benefit. Yes, there will be some short-term economic dislocations. But those job losses might have occurred anyway. In the long term, the U.S.-Mexico treaty will expand the economies of both nations and improve the prospects of workers in both countries. And that's a future that deserves a place on the fast track.

The Spokesman-Review
Spokane, Washington, May 24, 1991

By the end of today, the Bush administration should have another two years of "fast track" authority for negotiating rade deals.

In a vote Thursday, the House declined to derail the extension; the Senate is expected to follow suit today.

Under fast track, which Congress first created in 1974, the administration presents any trade agreement it negotiates to Congress, which then has 150 days to accept or reject it — as is. No amendments.

Thus, as Bush seeks to strike a free trade agreement with Mexico and to reopen the Uruguay round of the General Agreement on Tariffs and Trade (GATT), he can reassure whoever sits across the table that any deal they come up with will be dealt with in a reasonable time frame and won't be mobbed by 435 different quasi-negotiators in Congress.

Having received Congress's go-ahead, however, the White House also has some serious obligations to honor.

In any deal that is reached with Mexico, U.S. negotiators must guard against Mexico's becoming merely a haven where U.S. manufacturers can escape stringent U.S. labor and environmental laws. Trade Representative Carla Hills, Environmental Protection Agency Administrator William K. Reilly and Bush himself all have given assurances that those concerns will be addressed.

The United States and Canada already have joined in one free-trade agreement. Talks with Mexico are aimed at broadening that pact to create a trilateral, North American trade alliance that would be the world's largest with 360 million consumers and a collective $6 trillion economy.

It will take more than a trade agreement to realize the full potential of the North American bloc but the numbers make this region a formidable player in the global economic game.

The European plan also makes GATT, the 107-nation trade-regulating forum, of vital importance, especially to agricultural states who would benefit from U.S. attacks on tariffs. Washington, known as the most trade-dependent state in the nation, has a specially keen interest.

Congress is wise to give Bush the tool he wants. Now it's up to the president and his administration to use the tool effectively.

The Buffalo News
Buffalo, New York, May 28, 1991

CONGRESS HAS granted President Bush excessive authority in approving his request for fast-track negotiations of a potential free-trade agreement between the United States and Mexico.

This authority will permit the president's negotiators to accelerate their trade talks with Mexico for the next two years. What is more necessary, however, is a hard look by the administration at the economic and environmental booby traps hidden in this trade partnership.

This is not to argue that such potential difficulties can never be avoided. But Bush is moving too hurriedly.

Legitimate fears loom that Mexico's impoverished and plentiful workers, many paid something like $1 an hour, will lure U.S. plants there and, in the transition, cost thousands of better-paid Americans their steady jobs. Buffalo workers, with the loss of plants to the U.S.-Mexican border, have experienced this unpleasant phenomenon first-hand.

"This U.S.-Mexico free trade agreement is really a jobs program for Mexico," Sen. Donald Riegle, D-Mich., said in debate. "What is clear is the United States needs a jobs program for this country."

Other potent doubts about this free-trade pact center in frightening environmental degradation soiling Mexico and a government there not fully free or democratic.

The president has pledged to consider environmental and worker concerns in the trade negotiations, and he surely must.

Beyond the merits of an accord is the process by which it is fashioned. Congress has now agreed that Bush can negotiate a pact, present it to Congress and insist that Congress vote it either all up or all down. No amendments would be allowed.

That cedes excessive latitude to the administration by Congress. It foreshadows a take-it-or-leave-it climate of debate when any proposed treaty is submitted. How different this is from the usual condition of compromise and accommodation.

Rightly, Bush has promised to keep Congress closely informed during negotiations. Even so, a flat yes-or-no choice leaves but narrow room for Congress' part in the deliberative process.

As for the reservations about working and environmental conditions, Bush assures that any trade pact "is going to be good for the working man in this country and good for the environment."

We're more than a little skeptical about that. But the House and Senate have now provided the president with a chance to deliver on that pledge. Everyone should read the fine print with care.

U.S. and EC Begin Trade War over Hormones in Meat

A long-threatened trade war between the U.S. and the European Community over meat from hormone-fed cattle began Jan. 1, 1989. The EC imposed a ban on all imports of beef from hormone-treated cattle, which affected $130 million of U.S. exports, and the U.S. retaliated by imposing 100% tariffs on $100 million of imported EC food products.

U.S. Trade Representative Clayton K. Yeutter in December 1988 had charged that the EC had consistently blocked U.S. efforts to bring the issue of the hormone ban before a scientific dispute-settlement panel at the General Agreement on Tariffs and Trade. The U.S. maintained that the EC decision to implement the ban constituted an unfair trade practice.

The European products affected by the punitive U.S. duties included boneless beef and pork from northern Europe, fruit juices, wine coolers and canned tomatoes from southern Europe, French cheeses, and instant coffee.

Although the amount involved was small compared with the overall $150-billion-a-year value of U.S.-EC trade, the dispute represented one of the most serious crises in U.S.-EC trade relations in years. With neither party inclined toward compromise, many officials feared that the dispute could escalate into a more bitter conflict involving retaliation and counter-retaliation that would affect transatlantic commerce more extensively.

Relations between the U.S. and the EC had worsened in December 1988 when the impasse between the two trading partners over world farm-trade reform caused the breakdown of a Montreal meeting of GATT.

Even before the standoff in Montreal at the midterm review of the Uruguay Round of GATT, trade relations between Washington and the EC had been characterized by increased apprehension and anxiety.

The U.S. on several occasions had expressed its fear that the planned establishment of a single internal market in 1992 by the 12-nation EC would lead to discrimination against U.S. goods and services, while the EC worried about possible export losses resulting from the U.S.-Canada free trade accord, which would create a free market between those nations by the year 2000.

In the hormone-treated meat dispute, the U.S. and the EC each charged the other with being the first to break GATT rules. Under Article 3 of GATT, no nation was allowed to treat foreign products less favorably than its own, which the EC was not doing. But all GATT members also agreed not to "use health-related arguments to restrict imports" and to leave consumers free to choose whether or not to buy a safe but politically controversial imported product.

The European demand for a ban on all growth hormones had originated in 1980 after calf producers in Italy had injected illegal synthetic hormones known as diethlstilbestrol (DES) into calves' breast muscles. The muscles had been made into baby food, allegedly causing babies to grow breasts and enlarged genitals and to menstruate.

In December 1985 the EC adopted a ban on all domestic and imported hormone-treated beef on consumer-safety grounds, giving all producers until the beginning of 1988 to comply. The EC granted the U.S. an extension until the start of 1989 after the U.S. contested the EC decision, insisting that scientific evidence proved that American meat was safe.

Despite the ban, many European farmers reportedly continued to use growth hormones illegally, injecting them more dangerously into the muscle of cattle rather than applying them as pellets implanted into the animals' ears, as in the U.S. According to the U.S. Department of Agriculture, traces of DES recently had been found in imported West German beef. A Belgian consumer magazine had found that 25% of Belgian hamburger meat sampled contained growth hormones.

EC ambassadors Jan. 5 approved a European proposal to impose 100% duties on $96.6 million of imported U.S. walnuts and dried fruits in response to U.S. punitive tariffs on EC goods.

The Chattanooga Times

Chattanooga, Tennessee, December 29, 1988

Unless United States or European community trade negotiators blink at the last minute, a stand-off over American meat exports is likely to escalate to tariff skirmishes on Jan. 1. That's when a European ban on hormone-treated meat goes into effect. In fact, it will take some extraordinary measure to prevent a trade blow-up. Negotiations have stalled, no further talks are scheduled, and both sides have announced retaliation and counterretaliation measures for each others' anticipated actions.

At issue is the U.S. refusal to certify that American meat exports are free of five specific growth hormones now widely used domestically to help fatten cattle. The European community announced in 1985 that it would ban hormone-tainted beef for health reasons beginning Jan. 1, 1988. The deadline was extended for further negotiations for one year, during which time Australia, New Zealand, Brazil and Argentina decided to export hormone-free beef.

U.S. officials have refused to budge, however, even though this country's beef sales to Europe, worth $150 million annually, presumably will slip to competitor nations. That is a fraction of total American sales and doesn't seem to bother the cattle industry, whose spokesmen agree with the Reagan administration contention that there is no scientific evidence the hormones pose a health threat. Both the administration and the industry contend that regulation would be costly and produce no real health benefit.

In anticipation of the European community's implementation of the ban, however, the administration has prepared a list of European foodstuffs on which it will double import duties in retaliation — a move that will double their wholesale costs and effectively price them out of the market. Europeans have warned they will counterretaliate, and Washington has counterwarned it will counter the counterretaliation. So now, Washington is considering a ban of all European meat imports, worth $450 million a year. If the tariff skirmish gets that far, it isn't likely to end there.

The whole exercise appears somewhat bull-headed. A more constructive effort would better serve our trade relationship and, quite possibly, American consumers. Given the government's delay in officially recognizing and regulating other health hazards, and the industry's vested interest in continuing to artificially fatten cattle, the American trade position is not surprising. But many American consumers might favor hormone-free beef products, and a voluntary hormone-free program, with random checks to catch cheaters, seems like a more useful approach to defuse the trade issue.

In view of the continuing trade deficit, the administration clearly needs to be looking for ways to enhance trade, not to undermine it. American products will face an increasingly competitive market in Europe as the 12-member European trading community nears its 1992 economic union. Now is not the time to begin building trade barriers; besides, the United States already has comparable bans on European products, such as the barrier against non-pasteurized milk products that keeps out selected European cheeses.

What is needed is a commitment to respect our trading partners' genuine health concerns and a desire to negotiate solutions, not to compile retaliatory measures. After all, our total trade relationship with the European community amounts to $150 billion a year. Avoiding friction that could damage that relationship for no sound reason is certainly to the advantage of the United States.

PORTLAND
EVENING EXPRESS
Portland, Maine, December 30, 1988

As any school cafeteria worker knows, hormones have a way of starting food fights, particularly among rambunctious young boys. But no cafeteria worker has seen anything like the international trade battle hormones could ignite Saturday at midnight.

With the start of the new year will come a change in import policy for the 12-nation European Community. As of Jan. 1, the European nations have agreed to ban all imported meat products which contain growth hormones such as those used in American cattle to increase bulk.

The looming ban has placed annual two-way trade totaling $150 billion between the United States and Europe in jeopardy.

In retaliation, the American government stands ready to impose $100 million worth of trade barriers on European products such as hams, wine coolers and canned tomatoes imported here. And if Europe ups the ante, U.S. Trade Representative Clayton Yeutter says, the American government will retaliate again.

That way lies acrimony and economic disruption, the sorry legacy of protectionism. It's a legacy that fails to serve either this country or the European Community, now committed to becoming a major trading bloc by 1992. Negotiations to resolve the conflict, starting immediately, ought to be welcome.

While no one questions the right of European nations to decide for themselves what they will — or will not — import, the argument that growth hormones in meat damage human consumers has not been made convincingly. Indeed, Yeutter, soon to become U.S. Secretary of Agriculture, says there is no scientific evidence to support it. And European countries have yet to refute him.

What then is the hurry? The ban should be put on hold while European and U.S. trade representatives talk.

Pittsburgh Post-Gazette
Pittsburgh, Pennsylvania, December 30, 1988

The European Community's worries about imported meat from U.S. cattle that have been fed growth hormones represents ham-handed protectionism.

Goaded by West Germany, the EC complains that U.S. meat products, whose growth has been hormonally stimulated, represent a danger to Europe's health. So, as of Jan. 1, U.S. meats will be blocked from the EC, and, in retaliation, the United States will impose 100 percent duties on imported European foods, totalling about $100 million in trade.

Considering the great appetite among Europeans for animal parts that most Americans wouldn't touch with a pole much less a fork, continental qualms over U.S. prime cuts of steak are apt to puzzle the public on this side of the Atlantic. Indeed, as far as health is concerned, the more important story is how lean American beef has become as U.S. cattle producers have sought to address genuine health concerns over cholesterol.

Yet the issue reflects less of a concern for protecting public health than a determination to close ranks behind a system of unwieldy and unyielding agricultural subsidies that no one in the community, except perhaps British Prime Minister Margaret Thatcher, seems to have the stomach to challenge. Perhaps the matter didn't begin precisely as a Machiavellian scheme to use the hormone issue as a way to establish a ban on imported meats in order to protect European farmers. Consumer activists, it seems, first began to press for the ban. Still, once consumers raised this dubious concern, the politics of European agricultural protectionism, which is recognizably adept at ways of disguising itself, greased the way for a ban. The underlying motive seemed even more evident when the U.S. insisted that scientific evidence for the hormone hysteria should be arbitrated under the General Agreement on Tariffs and Trade and the EC refused on the grounds that its arbitrary action was within the bounds of its sovereign power and authority under GATT.

Yet before the Europeans waste too much time in searching for a principle to rationalize a wrong-headed restriction on U.S. meat produced with hormones that are also widely used, if not officially recognized, by European farmers too, they might question the truly unproductive direction in which this is all leading. Presumably the United States could back down, accept the ban, as Argentina, Australia, Brazil and New Zealand have done, and thus avoid escalating the confrontation.

But there is more at stake than the beef. With Europe now flexing its muscle as it anticipates completing its economic union in the decade of the 1990s, its leaders would only be encouraged to rationalize additional schemes for keeping competitors out of the common market by novel methods of protectionism — particularly as in that most stubborn of area of trade disputes, agriculture.

The U.S. has pressed for arbitration of the scientific merits of the complaint. Europe has a responsibility to accept that recourse as a way of seeing that its badly argued case doesn't lead to a trade war that ranges across the entire frontier of agricultural imports.

The Wichita
Eagle-Beacon
Wichita, Kansas, December 29, 1988

THE U.S. Food and Drug Administration says hormones used in U.S.-raised cattle pose no threat to humans. The World Health Organization says the same thing, and so did an independent panel of European scientists.

Yet the European Economic Community, citing no persuasive scientific evidence, says hormones are a danger and, beginning Sunday, will ban U.S. meat from animals treated with the chemicals. Moreover, the EEC refuses to submit the hormone issue to an international group of scientists to evaluate health fears. And the Common Market allows some hormone-treated, European-raised meat to be sold to consumers.

So much for the intellectual honesty of the EEC on the beef hormone dispute. The controversy, which could spark a trans-Atlantic trade war, has little to do with human health, and much to do with economic protectionism.

The basic problem is that, because of its lavish farm subsidy program, the EEC has built a mountain of surplus beef. The EEC seized on the opposition from some consumers to growth hormones as an excuse to limit import competition for EEC meat from the United States.

This time, however, the United States is not willing to help the EEC clean up its economic mess. American trade officials this week released a $120 million hit list of EEC products that would be subjected to import restictions should the Europeans ban U.S. meat. If the Europeans counter-retaliate, as they say they will, the cycle could get out of control and rip up the entire world trading structure.

Although both sides seek compromise before Sunday's deadline, the beef issue should put additional pressure on U.S. and EEC negotiators to reach agreement on new farm trade rules. That effort, part of the talks over the General Agreement on Tariffs and Trade, is aimed at reducing agricultural trade barriers worldwide. The discussions, however, are stalled over what to do about farm subsidies that distort world markets.

Constantly fighting beef hormones and similar issues work against a stable farm trading system. But the root cause of such disputes is virtually always the same — the reluctance of governments to allow farmers to compete in open markets.

Chicago Tribune
Chicago, Illinois, December 16, 1988

Increasing tension between the United States and Europe over farm policy is threatening the maintenance and expansion of an open world trading system. The strain wrecked last week's 96-nation trade negotiations in Montreal, which had been on the verge of important agreements liberalizing trade in banking, insurance and other services.

Several Latin nations that have been stung by growing protectionism balked at any new accords until the dispute over agricultural trade is settled. After five days, frustrated negotiators put everything on hold until their April gathering in Geneva.

The Montreal meeting was supposed to give a political boost to the four-year round of trade talks that began in 1986. Previous rounds under the 40-year-old General Agreement on Tariffs and Trade resulted in lower tariffs and increased exchange of goods. This latest one, though, has been marred by warnings of imminent trade wars and threats of an increase in market-distorting subsidies.

The friction began in 1987 when President Reagan called for an end to all food subsidies among all trading partners by the year 2000. His administration recently modified its all-or-nothing stance by dropping that deadline; it still insists, however, on gradual cuts ending in elimination of payments to farmers.

World leaders agree that farm subsidies raise food prices, worsen budget deficits and make low-cost Third World producers less competitive. But they are timid about setting a specific date for ending them. Despite pleas from Western Europeans, U.S. Trade Representative Clayton Yeutter stuck to a hardline stance at Montreal in hopes of getting a solid commitment from them to abolish all farm subsidies. But they have four to five times more farmers to protect than does America, and their common agricultural policy is at the center of their drive to form a unified West European market in 1992. They say they are willing to reduce subsidies gradually but insist they cannot eliminate them completely for political reasons.

Now that Yeutter has been tapped to become agriculture secretary in the Bush administration, he is in a strong position to fight tooth and nail to wean American farmers from government payments. But even with his formidable negotiating skills and his expertise in farming, he's not likely to win agreement on a final phaseout date.

Agriculture is the most protected segment of international trade, a severe drain on governments and consumers around the world. The World Bank estimates that in the United States and Western Europe alone, the annual bill comes to $50 billion. With budget deficits and global trade imbalances threatening so many national economies, this is madness. It will be up to President-elect Bush and his newly named trade representative, Carla Hills, to take the lead in getting the Europeans to understand that multinational agreements to cut the subsidies are in everyone's best interests. And that includes the farmers, so long as they have time to adjust and plan for a more sound, reliable, rational future.

Like other imminent crises that Reagan is passing off to Bush, this one needs quick attention. Congress will consider a 1990 farm bill soon and it will be in no mood to reduce subsidies unilaterally, burdening American farmers with unfair competition. In Europe, the closer the Common Market countries get to their 1992 unification and its profound changes, the harder it will be for them to alter their agricultural policies.

Compromise is needed, and soon. If the United States continues its rigid insistence on a total phaseout, this round of trade talks may flop and a united Europe could become even more protectionist. The crusade to cut agricultural subsidies is a just one, but it won't succeed without flexibility—and compassion. A schedule of sizable annual cuts by the trading partners, leaving the final phaseout date open, is the best way to proceed and to open more world markets for American products.

THE DAILY OKLAHOMAN
Oklahoma City, Oklahoma, December 31, 1988

TRADE disputes often break out for the most petty reasons, and a good example is the current flap over U.S. meats sold in Europe.

The European Common Market's council of ministers took a totally unreasonable position in voting to ban imports of U.S. meat containing growth hormones. No scientific evidence has been produced to show the hormones, fed to cattle to increase their bulk, pose any threats to consumers.

Concerns among European officials about the health effects of the hormones on children are simply unfounded.

As the Senate Agriculture Committee chairman, Sen. Patrick Leahy, D-Vt., points out, farmers in Europe also use growth hormones in animals. The substances are out of the meat before slaughter takes place, so there is no basis for an issue.

Nevertheless, if the European Community makes good on its threat to institute the ban Jan. 1, the Reagan administration is prepared to retaliate by imposing $100 million worth of trade sanctions against such products as hams, canned Italian tomatoes and imported wine coolers. The Europeans have warned they will counter-retaliate with additional tariffs on U.S. honey, nuts, dried fruit and canned corn.

Two-way trade between the United States and the 12-nation European Community amounts to $150 billion annually. Jeopardizing trade relations over such a groundless complaint is an arrogant and childish act on the part of the EC.

Surely reason will prevail and an undesirable shift toward protectionism can be averted.

The Register-Guard
Eugene, Oregon, December 30, 1988

The United States and the 12 nations of the European Economic Community stand at the threshold of a costly trade war. The issue currently in dispute is minor in relation to the overall volume of trade, but the stakes could quickly escalate. Exporters and consumers on both sides of the Atlantic would suffer if the disagreement is not resolved soon.

Under pressure from West German consumer groups, Europe's farmers are prohibited from using hormones to promote the growth of livestock. The ban was supposed to be extended to imported meat a year ago, but the United States objected that the restriction constituted an unfair trade barrier. Efforts to negotiate an end to the argument have failed, and the ban is scheduled to go into effect Jan. 1.

The ban would block about $100 million a year worth of American meat exports to Europe. The United States has said it would retaliate with steep tariffs on such goods as cheeses and canned vegetables. The economic community has threatened to counter-retaliate, in which case the United States would have to consider still stronger sanctions. A continuing round of tariffs and bans would jeopardize a two-way trading relationship whose volume exceeds $150 billion a year.

The dispute over hormones is a thorny one. The Europeans claim to have banned hormones for health reasons. Such regulatory actions are permitted under the rules of the General Agreement on Tariffs and Trade. The United States argues that hormones pose no health hazard, and points out that the rules do not allow regulations that impose unfair limits on trade.

Other events magnify the importance of the current impasse. Policies to protect farmers from foreign competition are fairly common in Europe and are a major barrier to an expansion of trade. At the same time, the nations of the European Economic Community plan to erase internal trade barriers by 1992; many fear that Europe will turn inward as a result, closing its markets to goods produced outside the 12-nation group.

The dispute over hormones could indicate how successfully the United States and Europe are able to cope with larger agricultural trade problems. And it could be a sign of trouble to come as the European economic integration progresses. It's important for both sides to establish a pattern of success in resolving their differences.

One possible method of settling the dispute would be to submit the issue to arbitration by an impartial third party. Even if neither the United States nor the Europeans were wholly pleased with the result, a precedent for settling future disagreements would be established.

The Register

Santa Ana, California, December 28, 1988

Better stock up now on imports from Europe of Danish hams, Italian canned tomatoes, and several types of tomato sauce, alcoholic drinks, instant coffee, boneless beef, tomato sauce, fruit juices, pork, and pet food. Our government may hit these products with a 100 percent import duty, all but driving them from the market. The action is in retaliation against a threat by the European Economic Community to ban American meat treated with growth hormones. The Reagan administration's attitude is: However hard the Europeans hurt their consumers, we can hurt American consumers more.

The EEC claims that the hormones may cause health problems in humans. The facts are disputed by scientists; some American officials say the real factor is that the EEC is using the health issue as a way to restrict US imports. Yet for whatever reason, the EEC is wrong to impose the ban. If the European people want to eat hormone-injected American meat, that's their business. Let the people choose.

But whatever the EEC's action, that's no excuse for our government to retaliate by punishing Americans, who will be the first to suffer from the retaliation. European producers will be hurt, but they will be able to search for markets elsewhere. American consumers will be hit hard fast. The ban would also add to the national inflation rate, possibly sparking higher interest rates that could lead to a recession.

US retaliation would be the second shot fired in a trade skirmish. Just because the EEC fired the first shot is no excuse for us to fire back. If the trade skirmish turns into an all-out, no-prisoners-taken trade war, as happened in the 1930s, then what does it matter who fired the first shot if everyone's economy collapses?

And the United States isn't exactly an exemplar. Our Food and Drug Administration routinely bans European drugs for reasons more flimsy than what the EEC used to ban US meat. Beta-blockers, a heart drug, and AZT, the AIDS drug, were long produced and used in Europe but banned here. We'll never know how many lives such FDA paranoia has cost. It's pure hypocrisy for our government to complain about European actions that only mimic ours.

There are better ways to deal with trade problems. The General Agreement on Trade and Tariffs provides for ways to resolve such disputes. Certainly peoples so friendly and similar as those in America and Europe should be able to resolve this problem without resort to sanctions and retaliation. And even if it isn't resolved, there's no reason to hurt the American people, whom our government claims to serve.

The Wichita Eagle-Beacon

Wichita, Kansas, December 26, 1988

"I guess we have no choice but to retaliate," said Rep. Dan Glickman, D-Kan., when asked about the European Economic Community's plan to ban hormone-treated U.S. meat beginning Jan. 1.

Mr. Glickman, chairman of the House feed grains subcommittee, reflects the general attitude of U.S. agriculture officials. This is not the best time to fight over food quality, but the EEC leaves the United States no option other than to hit back if beef and other meat imports are cut.

The hormone issue is seen differently on the two sides of the Atlantic Ocean. The EEC, under pressure from some consumers and environmentalists, says hormone-treated meats pose a health risk and should be banned. The United States disputes any health problem, saying the EEC is using the matter as a smokescreen to protect European farmers.

At stake is the approximately $170 million in annual sales of U.S. meats to Western Europe. Faced with the potential loss of that market, U.S. officials say they will restrict a similar dollar amount of European goods from entering the United States. The American target list includes EEC hams, canned tomatoes, fruit juices and alcoholic beverages. If the United States follows through on its threat, the EEC says it will counterattack by limiting imports of other U.S. goods, including honey, fruit and other products.

The hormone issue is certain to aggravate already testy relations between the United States and the EEC on farm trade. Because of the disagreements, negotiations broke down in Montreal earlier this month on the General Agreement on Tariffs and Trade, which sets international trading rules. Unless the United States and the EEC reach agreement on farm issues by April, the GATT talks could be jeopardized and hopes for a more open world trading system could be dashed.

The primary sticking point is the huge subsidies offered American and European farmers. The United States has proposed ending subsidies that interfere with market mechanisms, such as price supports and export promotions. That would allow governments to assist farmers with income subsidies and other programs, so long as an open world market was the dominate factor in determining price. The EEC, however, has rejected the U.S. approach, setting the stage for what could be a showdown on farm issues this winter.

Price subsidies distort the agricultural economy. They give the largest checks to farmers who grow the most products, thus encouraging surpluses. If a trade war over meat hormones will help bring major reform to farm programs, let the battle begin.

The Dallas Morning News

Dallas, Texas, December 29, 1988

The dispute between the United States and Europe over a Common Market ban on U.S. meat containing growth hormones could escalate into a full-scale trade war if allowed to fester much longer. Neither side can afford to let that happen.

If the U.S. and Europe are unwilling to bend in their positions concerning the distribution of hormone-treated meat, then it would be beneficial to seek an outside arbiter to resolve the issue. Failure to do so will damage important trade relations between this nation and our European allies.

No one appears ready to budge yet. Europeans don't want U.S. beef that has been grown with the aid of so-called growth hormones because they assert that it is bad for children's health. U.S. officials have countered that this is nonsense, and Europeans have yet to present supporting evidence for that assertion.

Accordingly, U.S. trade representative Clayton Yeutter has announced retaliatory sanctions against European agricultural products totaling about $100 million. The Europeans say that is an act of trade warfare and they will soon retaliate. Since U.S. beef exports to the European Community are only about 1 percent of that industry's total exports, it is clearly the principle of the thing. But in this case that also may be true for the Europeans. Since the beef exports don't seem to pose any great threat to the continental beef producers, it may be that the old country really prefers to play it safe rather than discover later that there really are harmful side effects.

Taking stands on principle is fine, but the U.S. may well have picked a poor principle on which to take its stand. Just because a product represents a small dollar amount or percentage of overall trade does not mean unfair restrictions should be ignored. But even in the absence of clear-cut evidence of harmful effects, people have some right to be nervous about substances pumped into their food. After all, some hormones have been found bad for our health by U.S. experts.

There is surely room for compromise. A full-blown trade war could tilt the world economy into the abyss. More than half of all U.S. beef is fattened without using hormones. The U.S. simply doesn't want to build expensive testing facilities to do the sampling. Maybe there is a way the Europeans can share this cost.

The U.S. is well-advised to stop playing patsy on the trade front. It is well-advised to get tough on silly restrictions that are merely excuses to keep "Made in USA" products out. But the hormone issue seems to be more than that. This is the wrong reason to go to war.

THE CHRISTIAN
SCIENCE MONITOR
*Boston, Massachusetts,
January 5, 1989*

A HEADLINE writer called
the trade dispute between
the United States and the
European Community over the
12-nation group's ban on US
meat raised with growth hormones a "food fight."

The spat does have something
of the irrational in it. But this is
not just high-spirited trade diplomats misbehaving in the manner
of youths throwing food about a
school cafeteria. The issues are
serious, and not easily resolved.

For the US, the ban reeks of
covert protectionism. Over the
past decade or so, Washington
has seen farm exports from the
EC grab a larger share of the
world market. High domestic
prices safeguarded by high import barriers and rising farm productivity have resulted in European over-production. The surpluses are heavily subsidized to
make them sell on world markets.

American concern was heightened by the tough bargaining at
trade negotiations in Montreal
last month. The meeting deadlocked over agricultural issues,
postponing further action until
spring. The US wanted to set the
elimination of farm subsidies that
distort international trade as a
goal for these ongoing negotiations. The EC refused, saying this
was unrealistic.

For the EC, the presence of 12
million farmers makes changes in
its farm policy difficult, to say the
least. The beef issue becomes
even more troublesome because it
rouses consumers' concerns that
hormone remnants in meat can
be harmful. The issue has been
taken up by "Green" parties, notably in West Germany.

The hormones are adminis-
tered to supplement natural hormone production and direct more
feed into the growth of muscle.
The US finds no scientific evidence that its beef presents a
health threat.

But many people in Europe
don't believe this, and the European Parliament voted overwhelmingly in early 1985 to ban
meat produced with the use of
hormones. Later that year, the
community agricultural ministers
agreed to implement the ban, but
postponed imposing it against US
beef until now.

The US is retaliating with tariffs as high as 100 percent against
$100 million of EC goods, such as
Danish ham and Italian canned
tomatoes. In turn, the Europeans
have drawn up their own potential hit list that could include US
honey, dried fruit, shelled walnuts, and canned corn.

It's hard to tell how far such
tit-for-tat measures could eat into
the $165 billion of trade across
the Atlantic. But with emotions
high on both sides of the Atlantic
and with transition teams at work
in both Washington and Brussels,
the risks are substantial of a real
food fight developing. Both sides
must exercise caution.

The Washington Post

Washington, D.C., January 1, 1989

WITH FLAGS flying and drums beating,
the United States and the European
Common Market are celebrating New
Year's Day by marching into a trade war with
each other. It's a stupid idea, reflecting—on both
sides—a failure of common sense. Trade wars,
like the other kind of wars, are easier to start
than to stop.

The issue is a peculiar one. It concerns growth
hormones fed to cattle to produce beef with more
lean meat and less fat. The first thing to be said
about this dispute is that it is trivial compared
with the serious trade tensions between the
United States and the Europeans. It has nothing
to do with the multibillion-dollar agricultural subsidies over which the world trade conference in
Montreal deadlocked last month. Nor is it really
related to the rising American fears of European
protectionism, as the Common Market presses its
plans for greater internal trade by 1992. The only
connection is that, to the extent that the beef war
sours relations among the trade negotiators, larger quarrels with far more at stake will be harder
to manage sensibly.

Some years ago a baby-food manufacturer in
Italy was found to be loading his products with
hormones to make the babies cuter and chubbier.
That was a genuine scandal, but in the ensuing
uproar the Green parties—the back-to-nature
crowd—opened a strident attack on all hormone
additives anywhere in the food chain. They got a
surge of immediate public support although there
is no evidence that hormones fed to beef cattle
have any effect on human health.

The United States wants the Common Market
to put the health question to a board of scientists.
The Common Market refuses because the European politicians know perfectly well what the
verdict would be. Instead they argue that the
European prejudice may be irrational, but it's
genuine, and in democracies people have the right
to set their own rules. As long as the meat
standards are precisely the same for all producers, domestic and foreign, international law
permits them to impose whatever rules they
want.

The American response is that fake health
standards can easily be manipulated in ways that,
although legally nondiscriminatory, do in fact hit
foreign imports. That's also right.

The political reality is that the Greens'
strength has been rising in Europe, particularly in
Germany, and governments there are not anxious
to do anything that might give them more fuel. It
is equally true that the American negotiators are
being pushed hard by beef producers here who
are incensed by the suggestion that their meat is
less safe than the Europeans'.

The Europeans' case is, by the thinnest of
margins, better than the Americans'. The depressing thing is that this case could, with a
modest amount of good will, be quickly settled.
The Europeans could let in hormone-treated beef
with conspicuous labeling and allow the consumers to choose. Or the American producers, like
Europe's other foreign suppliers, could produce
hormone-free beef for that market.

Instead there's hysteria on one side and, on the
other, a bullying insistence that American health
practices have to be the world's standard. That's
not a very attractive beginning to an otherwise
pristine new year—or a happy send-off to the
Bush administration's trade diplomacy.

THE BLADE

Toledo, Ohio, January 2, 1989

THE United States and the European Economic Community are heading into a
trade confrontation in which there will be no
winners. It should be resolved, either by
negotiation or by arbitration, before matters
get completely out of hand to the detriment of
both sides.

As in most such issues, there are persuasive
arguments on both sides. This one centers on
U.S. beef exports to the countries of western
Europe. The EEC has imposed a ban on
American beef imports which have been
treated with growth hormones. They will take
beef free of hormones. These shipments are
worth around $100 million a year. The U. S.
government has countered by slapping sanctions on certain imports from Europe which
will also amount to $100 million.

On the European side EEC spokesmen say
that the hormones can be detrimental to
health and that is why four Common Market
countries have banned all hormones in cattle
breeding for years. They contend that they
are within their rights to protect the health of
their citizens. Moreover, other beef-exporting
nations — including Australia, New Zealand,
Argentina, and Brazil — have agreed to
export only hormone-free beef to Europe.

American officials counter by saying that
the hormones used in raising beef cattle are
harmless and administered in doses far less
than the average human would encounter
normally. About half the cattle in this country
are given hormones to stimulate growth.

As a practical matter, the EEC is responding to consumer interests which say they are
worried about the effect of hormones. For its
part, the United States has one eye on the
political clout of the cattlemen who produce
the beef for export. Both are shortsighted
responses in the light of the benefits of freer
international trade.

The tit-for-tat action and reaction could go
to ridiculous lengths. The Europeans warn
that U.S. retaliation for their import ban will
bring on a counter-retaliation by them; Washington has counter-warned that it will counter
the counter-retaliation, going as far as to
impose a ban on all European meat imports,
worth at least $450 million a year.

This kind of escalation is, to be blunt about
it, stupid. And all this is taking place at a time
when EEC members are looking toward 1992
when the community is to become virtually
barrier-free internally and when the United
States is worried about the impact of that on
trade relations.

Barring common-sense negotiations to resolve this controversy, the whole mess should
be referred to the General Agreement on
Tariffs and Trade organization which is in the
middle of a four-year round of trade talks.
GATT was established to handle just this kind
of problem, and it should be given the opportunity to end the impasse before irreparable
damage is done.

The News and Courier

Charleston, South Carolina, January 8, 1989

Trade wars can be hell.

The United States and Europe are at it hormone and tariff, with the European Economic Community banning all U.S. meat that has been treated with hormones and the United States responding with 100 percent tariffs on European foodstuffs.

The trouble began when the United States decided on an all-or-nothing approach to the problem of agricultural subsidies during the recent international trade talks in Montreal. The Europeans indicated their willingness to go along with a plan to eliminate farm subsidies in a series of gradual steps. The United States decided that intransigence was the best policy, despite the fact that subsidies on certain agricultural products, like dairy goods and tobacco, are as deep-rooted here as in Europe.

The consequence was that the EEC introduced a ban on all U.S. meat produced from animals that have been treated by hormones. As most U.S. meat comes from animals that have been given growth-inducing hormone injections, the ban was seen both as a serious threat to U.S. agricultural exports and as an alarming precedent.

Hormone-treated meat is banned in Europe, as a result of pressure from consumer organizations. There is no scientific evidence to suggest that such meat is harmful. The EEC could have solved the problem by introducing regulations to ensure that all hormone-treated meat is labeled as such, and allow consumers to make their own decision.

The U.S. decision to retaliate by imposing 100 percent tariffs on European foodstuffs imported into this country was clearly meant to send a message that America is going to be tough and that the Europeans should expect no concessions.

With the trade negotiators on both sides engaging in blitzkrieg tactics, each hoping for a quick victory, there promises to be no winners. But there will be hundreds of millions of losers: we, the consumers, on both sides of the Atlantic.

The Oregonian

Portland, Oregon, January 4, 1989

The trade war with Europe has barely begun, and already the battle lines are fuzzy. At the very time the United States brings out the heavy artillery of tariffs to keep European agricultural products from crossing the border, the Department of Agriculture proposes to end import restrictions on British pork.

But the point is not so much to open the American consumer market to foreign pork products as to use selected British swine and semen to improve domestic stock.

The development coincides with a historic agreement reached with China to import Chinese breeds. Again the purpose is primarily research.

Animal scientists expect cross-breeding experimentation with the British and Chinese hogs to enlarge litters, make American pigs more resistant to disease and parasites and increase size. At the same time the quality of American pork would be maintained.

The program may have limited application in Oregon. With the Hansell ranch at Hermiston a notable exception, hogs are not a large factor in the agricultural industry here. The state has fewer than 100,000 swine, compared with more than 1.5 million cattle and nearly 500,000 sheep.

The research is to be conducted at major institutions in the Midwest where hog volumes run into the millions in some states.

But improvement of the product is always in order. Moreover, if the profitability of pork can be enhanced by increased yields for the investment, the number of pigs on Oregon farms is likely to grow.

Wisconsin State Journal

Madison, Wisconsin, January 1, 1989

The United States is on the brink of a trade war with Europe over meat — and the bone of contention between the two sides is hollow.

The 12-nation European Community is set to block the importation of all meat cut from animals treated with hormones. European meat producers have been barred from using the growth-enhancing hormones since 1985. The EC says allowing other nations, including the United States, to ship hormone-enhanced meat into Europe gives those nations an unfair trade advantage, because hormone-treated animals get bigger faster. But the biggest issue, raised principally by the West Germans, is unfounded fears of health hazards posed by the hormones.

If the Europeans go ahead with the ban, U.S. trade officials, led by Secretary of Agriculture-designate Clayton Yeutter, have threatened to immediately impose 100-percent duties (effectively doubling the price) on $100 million worth of food brought into this country from Europe each year.

That's just a shot across the bow in terms of the $150 billion in two-way trade between Europe and the United States each year. The food categories subject to the immediate tariff include beef and pork products, canned tomatoes, instant coffee, wine coolers, fruit juices and pet food. Imported goodies like chocolate, beer, wine and cheese are not affected — yet.

It is hard to argue with the contention of European Commission President Jacques Delors that each country has the right "to decide what is good or not for the health of its citizens."

But in the case of hormones and meat, the EC is basing its right on a wrong-headed conclusion.

The hormones in question have been used in most meat-producing countries for more than 20 years. Despite rigorous testing, there is no scientific evidence of harm to humans who eat meat from animals treated with hormones, which are metabolized by the animals so completely it is virtually impossible to detect any residue at all after the animal is butchered.

That's the conclusion reached by the federal Food and Drug Administration in the United States — and by a special panel of scientists assembled by the EC to study the issue. But alarmist pseudo-consumer groups and animal-rights activists have been much more successful at fear-mongering in the EC nations — the United Kingdom, Ireland, France, Belgium, the Netherlands, West Germany, Italy, Greece, Spain, Portugal, Denmark and Luxembourg — than have their counterparts in the United States, where fully 95 percent of all meat animals are treated.

Philosophically, the EC objections to hormones in meat are hard to swallow, coming as they do from nations that do not routinely pasteurize milk. There have been no deaths directly attributable to hormones in meat, while untold numbers have died from tuberculosis, salmonella, undulant fever and other diseases contracted through consumption of unpasteurized dairy products.

The meat battle is but a skirmish in a larger trade war between the United States and the EC. America is pushing the EC to reduce protectionist trade barriers and crop subsidies, while the Europeans are struggling to preserve their agricultural economy.

Both are worthy goals that need to be reconciled at the negotiating table using facts — not fiction and fears — as weapons.

U.S.-Mexico Trade Pact Signed

Mexican President Carlos Salinas de Gortari Oct. 3, 1989 signed an agreement intended to expand bilateral trade and investment with the U.S. The signing was the highlight of a state visit by the Mexican leader to the U.S. Oct. 1-5.

The trade agreement was one of seven signed by Salinas and U.S. President Bush Oct. 3 at the White House. It was reported to be the broadest economic agreement ever between the two countries. The pact expanded a 1987 accord that had set up consultative talks on trade disputes.

Under the new pact, the two countries agreed to decide by November which specific industrial sectors would be targeted for lower import tariffs. A first round of talks on tariff provisions would be completed by July 1990.

(Trade between Mexico and the U.S. in 1988 totaled $44 billion. Mexico was the third-largest market for U.S. goods after Canada and Japan. Three-quarters of Mexican exports went to the U.S.)

The two presidents also signed an environmental accord Oct. 3. It called for the U.S. and Mexican governments to work to alleviate air and other pollution in Mexico City and in border areas between the two countries.

In addition, an agreement on steel limited Mexican shipments to the U.S. over the next two and a half years and eliminated trade-distorting practices in the steel sector. The level to which Mexican shipments was lowered was not disclosed.

An Oct. 3 textile pact committed the U.S. to "review and improve" an import restraint agreement between the two countries and provided for "continued expansion of trade in textiles and apparel."

On the issue of protection of patents and copyrights in Mexico, which had been a source of friction for years, the two nations declared that negotiators had found an "improved and constructive atmosphere on matters concerning the protection of intellectual property rights to promote technological innovation and investment in Mexico."

The two nations also agreed to increase cooperation on tourism.

Salinas arrived in the U.S. Oct. 1 and was a guest of President Bush at Camp David that day.

He told reporters Oct. 3 that the war on illegal drugs was a top priority of his government. Salinas said two-thirds of the Mexican attorney general's staff was involved in the drug war and that one-third of all army troops were assigned to eradicating drug crops. (As a prelude to Salinas's trip, Mexican authorities Sept. 29 burned six tons of pure cocaine and smaller amounts of marijuana, opium gum and heroin.)

Salinas talked with *Washington Post* journalists at a breakfast in Washington, D.C. Oct. 4. He said he wanted Mexicans to work at home, not in the U.S., and cited a target of one million new jobs in 1989, linking higher employment to the opening of Mexican markets.

In an address to the U.S. Congress later Oct. 4, he accused the U.S. of exploiting Mexican immigrant workers. He called for "new mechanisms" to "do away with the network of corruption and illegality" surrounding migrant workers.

Salinas also urged the U.S. to lower trade barriers. He said, "Our country is already practically free of barriers, but we continue confronting them in the United States."

In a later development, U.S. President Bush April 7, 1991 assured Mexican President Carlos Salinas de Gortari that he was committed to a proposed free-trade agreement between the U.S. and Mexico. The two leaders met in Houston as Salinas began a tour of the U.S. and Canada to promote trilateral trade.

A U.S.-Canadian free-trade pact had taken effect in 1989. Canadian participation in the free-trade talks between Mexico and the U.S. had been set in early 1991. The proposed U.S. free-trade accord with Mexico – and another between Mexico and Canada – would create the world's largest free-trade zone, reducing tariffs and restrictions on the movement of money, labor and goods across the borders of North America.

The Oregonian

Portland, Oregon, February 10, 1989

Combining the United States, Canada and Mexico into the world's largest common market is an exciting prospect. Putting it into effect, though, calls for attention to detail.

The United States and Mexico have been working publicly toward a free-trade agreement since last June. This week the three countries announced that Canada would be joining the negotiations.

Their aim will be to eliminate most of the barriers to trade and investment among them, along the lines of the free-trade agreement the United States and Canada reached two years ago.

The negotiations are an about-face for Mexico. It historically has protected its industries from foreign competition and has been suspicious of foreign economic domination. Americans who winced when a Japanese company bought Rockefeller Center might understand the feeling.

But Mexico's President Carlos Salinas de Gortari sees investment by foreigners as a way of making jobs for Mexicans. He wants to capture some of the money U.S. and Canadian manufacturers otherwise might put into factories in Asia and newly opened countries of Eastern Europe.

For the United States and Canada, a free-trade area offers the prospect of access to raw materials and to a market of 85 million Mexican consumers, likely to become 100 million by the end of this decade.

A mixed consequence is that it also would offer northern manufacturers a chance to move some of their plants to a nearby country where labor is abundant and cheap, and where fringe benefits and anti-pollution restrictions are much fewer and less costly than at home.

The threat of exporting jobs has to be taken seriously, although some argue that work that goes where labor is cheapest has left the United States for Asia already and might actually be coming back to Mexico.

This is a reason to question why the Bush administration is in a hurry to complete the free-trade agreement by next year. Within a few weeks it expects to ask the necessary committees of Congress to vote to allow the talks to proceed on a so-called "fast-track" basis — meaning that when the trade agreement is completed Congress cannot amend it, but can only accept or reject it.

The administration and Congress must take enough time to ensure that any losses to the United States in low-technology jobs are likely to be balanced by gains from the things the United States does best: design, management and high technology.

Another factor in the equation, though, is the benefits to all three countries that would come from strengthening Mexico's economy. The alternative to having some jobs move south of the Rio Grande is likely to be the continued flood of illegal and easily exploitable Mexican immigrants northward.

The Houston Post

Houston, Texas, October 18, 1991

THE CANADIAN decision to join the United States and Mexico in negotiations for what amounts to a continental free-trade zone offers the exciting prospect of an economic union involving 360 million people. It holds potential economic benefits of one kind or another for all of them.

But it also threatens some sectors, largely because of Mexico's substantially different technological development and labor costs. Any economic union should be agreed to only after thorough study of its effects and a transition period long enough to help mitigate some of the negative ones.

Canada and the United States already have agreed to eliminate trade barriers by the end of 1998. That treaty caused a fierce disagreement on national identity in Canada that brought about national elections.

Canada's decision to participate in U.S.-Mexico talks has occasioned concern in all three countries. Many Canadians (and Americans) are concerned that more jobs might find their way to Mexico. U.S. and Mexican officials are worried about Canadian participation slowing matters down, something Canada assures will not happen. Mexicans would not be likely to allow U.S. or Canadian participation in petroleum exploration or development.

On the positive side, many facets of business and industry in the three countries see great benefit in expanded markets, as well as prospects of being able to compete on a more even footing with a Europe that will be united economically after 1992.

U.S.-Canadian trade amounted to $173 billion last year, more than that between any other two countries. Mexico was the United States' third bilateral trading partner, at more than $51 billion. Canada and Mexico already compete for some U.S. markets, notably in auto parts, steel, textiles and shoes. Trade between Canada and Mexico was only $2.5 billion. Removal of barriers should increase trade.

Sen. Lloyd Bentsen, D-Texas, wants a study of the proposed U.S.-Mexico agreement. He rightly notes that it would have a substantial impact on many U.S. economic sectors, and that it is especially important to understand its impact on the U.S.-Mexico border region.

The potential benefits would seem to outweigh the drawbacks. Let's study the matter, carefully but promptly, to make sure they do. If the prospects look as bright after investigation as they seem now, we should go ahead with a will. The continent has become too small to let unnecessary artificial barriers interfere with the economic well-being of its people.

The Miami Herald

Miami, Florida, September 19, 1991

NEARLY three months after he first announced his "Enterprise for the Americas Initiative," President Bush has sent his refined proposal to Congress. It's his only major Latin American policy endeavor, and it could be, as he hopes that it will, a boost for developing Latin America's free-market economies.

The initiative has three principal elements, two of which can be implemented with only minor difficulty: Reduction of debt and interest owed the U.S. Treasury that could reach $7 billion for countries that meet specific criteria. The plan includes "debt for Nature" swaps of U.S. Export Import Bank loans to Latin American countries, and the creation of a $500-million multilateral investment fund in the Inter-American Development Bank that would be increased by contributions from Japan, Canada, and other industrial countries.

The initiative's third element — bilateral free-trade agreements with Latin countries, culminating in a "hemisphere-wide free-trade system" — will take years to negotiate. The President is keen on reaching such an agreement with Mexico. But in Latin America the goal of a "free trade zone" will meet obstinate resistance from countries wary of U.S. hegemony.

Congress must appropriate the money for the investment fund and also authorize reduction of Latin American debt to the Treasury. The initiative deserves passage during this session. The United States can provide other creditor countries a needed example by forgiving part of this debt, as Mr. Bush proposes to do.

Latin America desperately needs such help. The World Bank's annual report reiterates what the whole region already knows: Massive foreign debt and high inflation devastated most Latin American economies in the past decade. Foreign investment in the region dried up.

Ironically, democracy also swept the region during the '80s, so democratic governments have inherited the dire economic legacy of military dictatorships. Most of these democracies are doing their best to open up their economies. Mr. Bush's proposals recognize this. May they signal the beginning of more-concerted U.S. interest in Latin America's future.

THE SUN

Baltimore, Maryland, March 14, 1991

With a cease fire in the Persian Gulf, the Bush administration and Congress can start fighting over trade policy. At least three separate issues are converging that will pit free-traders against protectionists, multinational corporations against labor and Republicans against Democrats.

At stake is nothing less than the future of the world trading system, the fate of President Bush's call for a free trading zone embracing the U.S., Canada and Mexico and bilateral trade relations between the U.S. and its key trading partners.

On each question, the Bush administration presents the more persuasive case. It is seeking "fast-track" authority so it can negotiate trade agreements subject to quick up-or-down votes with no amendments allowed. And it is opposing efforts to renew and even toughen mandatory retaliatory measures against trading competitors who, by U.S. prescription, engage in unfair practices.

In coming weeks, Capitol Hill will ring with rhetoric about preserving congressional prerogatives to shape trade legislation. Despite its surface plausibility, don't believe this argument. The real issue is whether the executive branch is to have the credibility to negotiate complicated trade agreements. If foreign nations know Congress can nibble to death any pact offered to it, there won't be any. A new world trade pact under the General Agreement of Tariffs and Trade (GATT) won't materialize. A free trade zone from the Yukon to the Yucatan will remain a figment of President Bush's imagination.

Complicating the picture is a related effort to renew the "Super 301" provisions of the 1988 trade act which force the executive branch to penalize countries with "broadly restrictive" trade practices. While the provisions did put pressure on Japan, especially, the administration believes Super 301 has worn out its welcome. We would add it has hurt the U.S. negotiating position in GATT because Washington is seen as unilaterally imposing conditions that are supposed to be set by universal GATT rules. This is counter-productive. An expanded GATT that would make agriculture, service industries and patents subject to international rules is very much in the U.S. public interest.

At this stage, such influential Democrats as Sen. Lloyd Bentsen and Rep. Dan Rostenkowski, who chair committees with jurisdiction over trade, favor extending the fast-track authority. Other Democrats, including House majority leader Richard Gephardt and Maryland's two senators, want protectionist measures that run counter to the whole spirit of an open world trading system.

The situation suggests that Senator Bentsen would make a more acceptable Democratic presidential candidate than Representative Gephardt in 1992 because he would remove some of the partisanship that usually erupts over trade policy.

LURIE'S BUSINESS WORLD

D/55 Oct 1 '90

FREE TRADE AGREEMENT

MEXICO

"Gee whiz, Mulroney - - don't you have more important things to do in Ottawa?!"

The Toronto Star

Toronto, Ontario, November 28, 1989

The outcome of next year's free trade talks between the United States and Mexico will have profound implications for Canada's own trade deal with the U.S.

That's going to be true, regardless of whether Canada turns this two-way negotiation into a three-way deal.

During the Canada-U.S. bargaining, Canadians were told that the costs of a deal were more than justified by the unique access they would gain to the rich U.S. market.

That meant we would no longer have an economic border with the U.S. But the elimination of that border also meant that Canadian companies could shift their operations and supply Canadian markets from the U.S.

By and large, the closing of plants in Canada and their drift southward has been the most visible image of free trade so far.

While many Canadians blame Ottawa's high interest rate-high dollar policies for this distressing loss of jobs and businesses, the shift was facilitated by the effective elimination of the border under free trade.

Now, before Canadians have even had a chance to reap any benefit from their special access, U.S. President George Bush is effectively neutralizing the advantage.

With the proposed U.S.-Mexico deal, Canada will be forced to compete in the U.S. market on an equal footing with one of the lowest-cost producers in the world.

That's one example of how Canada's interest could be compromised in a U.S.-Mexico deal. Recognizing such risks, Ottawa has announced that it will try to forge a three-way, North American deal.

But in effect, that would mean wiping out another economic border, and freeing companies now located in Canada to supply the entire North American market from low-cost plants in Mexico, not just Tennessee.

In other words, a deal with Mexico would compound the pressures on Canadian workers and businesses that are already evident under Canada-U.S. free trade.

To make matters worse, both the U.S. and Mexico have made it clear that they don't want Canada's participation to complicate or slow down the talks.

"If the effort to broaden the process is not viable, because it produces unacceptable delays," Bush said this week, "then we will proceed bilaterally with Mexico."

So it's already clear that Canada is being treated as a third wheel that will be jettisoned the moment it squeaks.

While there may be advantages to a three-corner agreement, Ottawa has glossed over some potentially significant problems.

What, for example, would happen to Canada's auto industry if Mexico, with its cheap labor pool, became a full partner in the Canada-U.S. auto pact?

Also, Mexico says its oil will not be on the table. But what kind of a three-way deal would it be if Mexico didn't have to share its oil the way Canada is obliged to do?

The Mulroney government has been silent on these key issues.

Houston Chronicle

Houston, Texas, September 28, 1989

The idea of a free-trade zone extending from the Guatemalan border of Mexico to the far reaches of northern Canada has moved from the fantastic to the possible.

The United States and Canada already have a free-trade agreement, and Mexico and the United States are to begin talks next year on a similar pact. Canada is now asking to participate in the U.S.-Mexico negotiations for a three-way deal.

With the changes the world is undergoing today, the American nations may find it increasingly advantageous to forge closer trade ties. A continental free-trade zone would approximate the geographic size of the European Economic Community. It is certainly an idea worth exploring for all three nations.

The Register

Santa Ana, California, April 21, 1991

On June 1, President Bush's current authority for "fast-track" free-trade negotiations will expire. He has called for Congress to extend this authority because he is now engaged in crucial negotiations over the US-Mexico free-trade pact and the latest Uruguay Round of talks on worldwide free trade under the auspices of the General Agreement on Tariffs and Trade.

Our five Orange County congressmen support free trade, and so they should make passage of the "fast-track" authority their No. 1 priority in the next few weeks. Southern California is the country's top area for imports and exports, and our vital high-tech industries rely heavily on exports. If this "fast-track" authority is not extended, not just our county and nation, but all the world could experience a wave of protectionism that could lead to a deep recession, even a depression.

Even moderate protectionism hurts all Americans. It raises the cost of imported goods, costing families at the check-out counter. It raises parts and supply costs for businesses. It especially hurts poor families, since much of their incomes go to such protected items as food and clothing.

Union leaders once understood this, and endorsed the free-trade movements of the late 1940s and early 1960s that dismantled most US protectionism. Now, alas, most unions favor protectionism. On Thursday Lane Kirkland, president of the AFL-CIO, wrote an article in *The Wall Street Journal* entitled, "US-Mexico Trade Pact: A Disaster Worthy of Stalin's Worst." What? Stalin was one of the worst enemies of free markets (and free peoples) the world has ever seen.

Mr. Kirkland wrote that a free-trade pact would worsen "the rising hepatitis rate along rivers flowing from the *maquiladora* areas [where US firms are now permitted to build plants, mostly near the border] into the US." His solution: foreign aid. Although he didn't specify where the money would come from, you can bet it would be from taxes or fees paid by US companies and taxpayers. But the real solution to such problems is the free-trade pact itself. It would extend free trade from the borders to all of Mexico, encouraging companies to build plants deep inside Mexico.

And it is precisely economic development that brings the higher living standards necessary to ensure decent sanitation. Just 100 years ago many American cities suffered from ailments similar to those in the *maquiladora* cities. But then the free market spurred a century of economic development.

For most of the 20th century, Mexico's government has imposed a harsh socialism that denied the country the bounty of the free market. But recently Mexican President Carlos Salinas has been dismantling socialism. We should help him — not with foreign aid, but with free trade. The free-trade pact would help everyone: Mexican consumers and workers, and US consumers and workers — including those union workers Mr. Kirkland so mischievously claims to represent.

Birmingham Post-Herald

Birmingham, Alabama, April 25, 1991

Protectionists in Congress are pulling no punches in their attempts to scuttle President Bush's effort to enter this nation into a free trade agreement with Mexico.

A free-trade zone uniting the United States, Canada and Mexico would create the world's single largest market, with 360 million people and $6 trillion in annual output.

But labor unions and many congressional Democrats oppose such a pact, fearing many U.S. workers would be laid off by U.S. firms moving to Mexico in search of cheap labor.

Instead of making that argument directly, however, free trade opponents have instead gone the emotional route.

They have had congressional witnesses depict the worst cases of abuse under Mexico's lax job safety laws, saying such problems will increase if more U.S. companies move south.

A mother testified Tuesday that her 16-year-old son was killed by a grinder at a Ford Motor Co. glass factory operating in Mexico under the maquiladora system.

Maquiladora currently allows U.S. firms to locate in Mexican border areas under a limited free-trade zone.

Sen. Howard Metzenbaum, D-Ohio, said maquiladora has created an "abominable" situation along the Texas-Arizona border with Mexico.

Metzenbaum said U.S. companies employ 500,000 Mexicans, some as young as 12 years old. Workers are paid about $1.15 an hour, and on-the-job deaths run about four times higher than in the United States.

No one is arguing with Metzenbaum's assessment that such an "abominable" work environment needs to be cleaned up. But this country cannot dictate to Mexico what its labor laws should be.

Our government can use its influence to get U.S. companies operating in Mexico to treat workers better. Waiting for that, however, is no reason to block a free trade act.

Creating a U.S./Mexico/Canada common market would help the impoverished people of Mexico, not hurt them. And it would give the economies of each nation a needed boost. The protectionists should stand aside.

THE ☼ SUN

Baltimore, Maryland, April 22, 1991

The administration's bid for creditable authority to negotiate a free trade agreement with Mexico could be the most crucial long-range foreign policy issue on the 1991 congressional agenda. Yet with a June 1 deadline approaching for showdown votes on Capitol Hill, the White House has been losing ground in a running debate with environmentalists, unions and other special-interest groups.

What gives free trade foes an edge is the grain of truth found in their scare stories. The ecology-minded fear an industrial boom just south of Mexico's northern border that will increase already serious pollution problems. Labor bosses fear the loss of American jobs to factories in Mexico paying seven times less than comparable U.S.-based jobs.

There are powerful answers to these powerful arguments, and they need to be driven home in a hurry. A poor Mexico is a dirty Mexico. A poor Mexico is a low-wage Mexico. Unless our neighbor to the south can prosper, it will never have the resources to clean up its environment, improve its living standards and stop being a perennial source of massive illegal migration.

The AFL-CIO likes to talk about workers making only 60 cents to $2 an hour in the *maquiladora* industries that U.S., Japanese and European companies have set up just south of the border. What it does not like to talk about is the differential between the wages of *maquiladora* workers and the much poorer laborers in the rest of Mexico. They will continue to migrate northward in ever-increasing numbers unless the Mexican economy is transformed. So the issue is whether Mexico will export people or goods to the United States. If the answer is people, there will be a continuing drag on U.S. wage levels. If the answer is goods, their manufacture will require many parts and products from the United States. Labor leaders should think again.

Environmentalists are focused on the undoubted pollution and runaway growth seen in northern Mexican manufacturing centers. These factories, for all their faults, are a lot kinder to this planet than antiquated factories in Mexico's old, highly protected industries. Compare the atmosphere over Mexico City, for example, with that of Tijuana. President Carlos Salinas de Gortari has pushed through environmental protection laws that are as enlightened as his efforts to open up and liberalize the Mexican economy. What his government lacks is the financial wherewithal to enforce these laws. Environmentalists should think again.

As showdown votes approach, members of Congress and especially the pro-labor protectionists on the Maryland delegation should also think again. A prospering Mexico will be a cleaner Mexico. A prospering Mexico will be a higher-wage Mexico. A prospering Mexico linked in a free trade zone with the U.S. and Canada will give the North American continent the heft to compete effectively with European and Asian regional trading blocs.

Times-Colonist

Victoria, British Columbia, April 18, 1991

Chances of Canada and the United States including Mexico in a free trade agreement are slim to zero. There is, at present, too much fear in the two wealthy nations that adding Mexico would cost much more in jobs than it would produce in profitable trade.

The recession intensifies those fears but there are numerous other factors working against a deal. Part of the problem for Canadians is that the promised benefits from the Free Trade Agreement between Canada and the United States are simply not apparent.

The "overview" on the opening page of the FTA, which came into effect almost 2½ years ago, promised the agreement "will add significantly to economic growth, incomes and employment in Canada." Many Canadians see no proof of that claim being fulfilled. Some see evidence of the reverse, jobs lost to the U.S. through closing of branch plants in Canada.

In fact, it may be impossible to measure the effects of an agreement of this magnitude because national economies never stand still. Increasing populations generate new jobs to serve new numbers. Businesses rise and fall. Markets change. New products replace old. Boom times and recessions come and go. But Canadians, being Canadian, fear the worst. And many have a congenital unease about shrewd Yankee traders.

Considering Mexico, both Canadian and American critics note that a lack of environmental standards in the workplace and radically lower wages and standards of living in Mexico will work against North America. Who can argue? But that's part of what freeing trade is about, the part that is never talked about by politicians because it is too hard to sell.

While some consumers benefit, freer trade is always paid for by the wealthier partner, as wealth is redistributed, frequently at the expense of the better-paid worker. That may be what the authors were getting at when they wrote in the FTA preamble that both governments are resolved "to contribute to the harmonious development and expansion of world trade . . .".

After 2½ years, there's something to recall about our own Free Trade Agreement: it is basically an agreement to seek many sub-agreements on new trade rules. Unless negotiators are able to do this within five years (with the possibility of a two-year extension), there is no Free Trade Agreement. It dies.

Just how far Canada and the U.S. are still apart on trade matters is illustrated by the current dispute over the export of Canadian pork to the U.S. The Americans imposed a punitive duty on this $400 million trade, arguing that it was unfairly competing with their hog industry. When they lost a panel ruling, they appealed under the "extraordinary challenge" provision of the FTA, which is only supposed to be used when there is suspicion of misconduct or when the panel has exceeded its authority.

Somehow, it seems appropriate that a major FTA dispute involves pigs. That's how we must look to Mexicans and to many people in the Third World.

Fort Worth Star-Telegram

Fort Worth, Texas, April 9, 1991

President Bush and Mexico's President Carlos Salinas de Gortari want to remove trade barriers between the United States and Mexico. Including Canada, which already has a free-trade agreement with the United States, the eventual result could be a free-trade zone representing almost 400 million people.

In his last meeting with Salinas Sunday, Bush again praised the free-trade proposal but admitted there was opposition.

That opposition takes various forms. Some of the concerns expressed are legitimate and must be addressed — such as labor's fear that U.S. jobs will be exported to Mexico. Others are indirect — such as environmentalists' worry that businesses will go to Mexico to avoid pollution laws in the United States — or even specious — such as charges that free trade would increase illegal drug traffic.

But the underlying fact is that the direction of world trade is toward the formation of free-trade blocs, spurred by Europe's progress toward tearing down all of its economic borders by 1992.

Mexico already is the United States' No. 3 trading partner, trailing only Canada and Japan. Mexico is breaking with its own tradition by moving toward encouragement of foreign investment. A more vibrant, less-government-controlled Mexican economy will be a better market, one the United States will need. A workable North American free trade zone would provide a balance to Europe's Economic Community.

A bonus would be that a better Mexican economy would provide jobs at home for Mexican workers who otherwise seek jobs north of the border. Free trade is the correct path. The trick will be to strengthen Mexico as an economic partner without costing either the jobs or the domestic investment needed here in the United States.

THE INDIANAPOLIS NEWS
Indianapolis, Indiana, April 18, 1991

If the United States and Mexico sign a free trade pact, as they seem sure to do, not everyone will be a winner. There will be a few losers.

In the United States, some automobile workers may have to find different jobs. Some U.S. fruit and vegetable growers, mainly in California and Florida, may discover that they can make a better living doing something else.

In Mexico, the pharmaceutical industry stands to lose so much it has asked the government to exempt it from any trade pact. And many Mexican farmers of grain and other products probably won't be able to compete with their U.S. counterparts.

In general, Mexico's agricultural sector, which makes up about one-third of the population, will suffer. Its main trade protectionism has come from Mexico's poor transportation system, which hampers imports.

There also would be winners, which is why countries trade at all.

The winners come out so far ahead, in fact, that it may make sense in the long pull to compensate the losers to keep the trade going.

North of the border, the winners in a U.S.-Mexican trade pact would include U.S. grain farmers who have proven they can outproduce just about anyone in the world. In particular, Midwestern grain farmers who grow wheat, corn and soybeans stand to gain.

Further, judging from the impact of Mexico's entry into the General Agreement on Tariffs and Trade (GATT) in 1986, there will be lots of other winners.

Since that time, U.S. exports to Mexico have more than doubled to $28.4 billion in 1990. The increase created 320,000 U.S. jobs. The U.S. winners included the auto, telecommunications and steel industries. For a few companies, being able to shift some jobs to Mexico may protect domestic jobs that would be lost if the company could not cut costs in order to compete.

In return, Mexico can expect to attract new capital investments, which will enhance the economic reform already taking place there. Since 1987, Mexico has cut its budget deficit from 15 percent of gross domestic product to less than 3 percent. It also is struggling to control inflation and to manage its foreign debt.

Besides bringing in investments, Mexico is likely to export more textiles, fruits and vegetables and glassware.

Making these historic improvements will take time and patience on both sides, which means any trade agreement must be phased in over at least a 10-year period.

Overall, when trade is freer, Americans and Mexicans will be better off because both countries will use their resources more efficiently. More will be produced, and the peoples on both sides of the border will have a higher standard of living.

There will be a period of painful adjustment. But many experts say that the long-term benefits will more than ease the pain.

Planing an economic knock out

THE CHRISTIAN SCIENCE MONITOR
Boston, Massachusetts, April 17, 1991

The debate over the proposed U.S.-Mexico free trade agreement continues to degenerate. It was brought to its lowest point yet the other day by Lane Kirkland, president of the AFL-CIO.

Writing in the Wall Street Journal, Kirkland offers a vigorous rebuttal to the very idea of a free trade agreement. The Bush administration hopes to include both Canada and Mexico in such a treaty, establishing a zone for the free movement of goods and services "from the Yukon to the Yucatan."

As with many specious arguments, Kirkland begins by setting up a straw man and jeering at him. He paraphrases the proponents' argument like so: "If the tightly regulated economies of the Soviet Bloc and China produced vast degradation, then the opposite must also be true — free trade with Mexico will bring Heaven on Earth."

Pish posh. The argument for free trade is vastly more subtle, drawing on centuries of economic experience. The benefits of free trade are as close to axiomatic as anything can be in economics, but no one claims they bring Utopia.

Kirkland then grossly mischaracterizes the mini free-trade areas that have already been es-tablished along the U.S.-Mexican border. These arrangements have created new lives for thousands of Mexican workers, who flock to the relatively high-paying jobs offered there. But Kirkland says the areas "rival any of the well-publicized disasters of the worst Stalinist regimes." This moves beyond hyperbole into crass dishonesty.

It is also important to remember that Kirkland's "arguments" aren't being presented against the free trade agreement *per se*. The agreement hasn't even been negotiated yet. The bone of contention now is merely the president's authority to negotiate such an agreement. When a treaty is reached between the two countries' executive branches, Congress will still face its constitutional duty to debate and then approve or disapprove it.

But this point too is lost amid the opponents' dissembling. Lane Kirkland is an honorable man. During the cold war he did as much as any private citizen to aid and comfort the oppressed peoples of the Soviet empire. He does that hard-earned reputation great harm by retailing the lies and misjudgments of the frantic opponents of free trade.

The Cincinnati Post
Cincinnati, Ohio, April 24, 1991

IF some Democrats hope to trip up George Bush by linking the US-Mexico free trade proposal to unemployment and economic downturn at home, they could end up doing the stumbling. The free-trade pact will doubtless threaten a number of American jobs, but its long-term benefits will more than make up for that.

Unimpeded trade will sharply stimulate a Mexican economy that's starting to emerge from the doldrums of the '80s. President Carlos Salinas de Gortari has tied economic liberalization in Mexico to expanded trade with the US, and the resulting prosperity should provide both a larger market for American exports and better jobs and income for Mexicans.

The latter, of course, will do more than stronger border patrols ever could to stem illegal immigration into the US.

Some commentators, such as Rudiger Dornbusch of MIT, liken Mexico's outlook for growth under a free-trade pact to that of Spain after inclusion in the European Community. The expanded market benefited both Spain's less developed economy and neighboring powerhouses like Germany. Professor Dornbusch argues that increased Mexican imports have already produced 150,000 new jobs in the US over the past five years, with much more to come as trade grows.

Economic benefits on the northern side of the border, however, are comparatively small next to the pluses for Mexico. And these transcend the financial: Mexico's slow evolution away from corrupt, one-party rule could be speeded by the breakup of calcified, state-centered economic interests under a free-trade regimen.

And the drawbacks?

Parts of the US will suffer economic dislocation as some kinds of manufacturing work migrate southward. Industries particularly affected should get special attention in the pact, such as a longer phase-in period to allow time to retrain workers.

Mexico's traditionally lax environmental regulation presents a major hurdle to trade negotiators. But Mr. Salinas has been talking tough on this issue, and any final agreement should incorporate a realistic schedule for enforcing effective environmental regulations in Mexican plants. Likewise, an agreement should be reached on safe labor practices, including enforcement of child-labor laws.

Free trade won't happen overnight. It should be phased in with due concern for labor and environmental issues. But its benefits to both countries shouldn't be blocked by shortsighted politics. Congress should give President Bush the "fast track authority" he needs to move the pact with Mexico toward fulfillment.

Part IV: Education

"Our Nation is at risk. Our once un-challenged preeminence in commerce, industry, science, and technological innovation is being overtaken by competitors throughout the world. . .

If an unfriendly power had attempted to impose on America the mediocre educational performance that exists today, we might well have viewed it as an act of war. As it stands, we have allowed this to happen to ourselves."

—National Commission on Excellence in Education, "A Nation at Risk," April 1983

These alarming opening words, from the report of a national commission appointed in 1981 to assess the state of American education, set the stage for the school debate and educational challenges of the 1980s. The tone and findings of the commission's report and the spate of others which followed generated waves of controversy that came to encompass all the complexities of universal education.

The last ten years have seen renewed federal attention to education, focusing on improving the quality of the U.S. educational system in order to recoup a perceived decline in national scientific and industrial preeminence. In addition, the nation's schools have been called to account for the perceived deficiencies.

Public school administrators have defended themselves by pointing to shrinking budgets and suggesting that the government's commitment to the situation is, at best, superficial. But the current debate, as it has developed among educators, parents and legislators has gone beyond the pros and cons of the specific recommendations made by the national commission, to explore the more fundamental question of what is meant by "excellence in education."

Central to the 1980s reform movement was its emphasis upon traditional academic subjects, particularly math and science, and a corresponding deemphasis upon job training courses and other electives, in elementary and high school curriculums.

Functions that many have come to depend on public schools to provide — driving and typing instruction, physical exercise programs, cooking and shop courses — were increasingly viewed as distractions from the main goal of increasing academic course requirements and improving students' performances in these areas.

The relative importance of academic subjects themselves is also under debate. Some argue for the predominance of language skills, others for math and problem-solving skills. The inclusion of computer science in the commission's list of "new basics" is a reflection of the changing nature of curricular priorities.

However, U.S. educators argue that in the eight years since the federal panel reported that a "tide of mediocrity" had engulfed the nation's schools, the pace of reform has been glacial. Though the case is often made that the top 20 to 25 percent of American public schools are still the best in the world, proof that American children are learning more or learning better is very hard to find.

Despite President Bush's heartening pledge that U.S. schools will lead the world in science and mathematics by the year 2000, critics argue that the vast majority of American students currently achieve only a superficial grasp of essential subject matter. International comparisons tend to bear out that gloomy contention. On science and math tests, American high school seniors score well below their counterparts from almost every other nation in the industrialized world.

"U.S. educational policy over the past three decades has been a massive experiment that has tested whether spending more money. . .will result in better-educated students," wrote John E. Chubb of the Brookings Institution. "The results are in. The experiment has failed."

The difficulty for politicians, parents and taxpayers is knowing exactly what it is about the American public school system that is broken. The seven years following the blue-chip panel's report saw a variety of reform proposals, all of which were based on different and sometimes conflicting notions of where the problem lay.

The resulting muddle has prompted America's education leaders to point out that in a system that includes 40.7 million students, 15,500 school districts, 83,000 schools and more than 4 million professional and paraprofessional workers, there are simple solutions and there are good solutions — but there are no good, simple solutions.

U.S. Scores Low in Math, Science

U.S. students placed last in an international comparison of mathematics and science skills, according to a report released Jan. 31, 1989 in Washington, D.C.

The study, funded by the U.S. Department of Education and the National Science Foundation, had compared the abilities of a representative sampling of 13-year-old students from the U.S., South Korea, Great Britain, Ireland, Spain and the Canadian provinces of British Columbia, New Brunswick, Ontario and Quebec. The latter three provinces were divided in the study into English and French-speaking groups. The students had answered an identical series of 63 math questions and 60 science questions.

In math, South Korean students outperformed those in all other countries surveyed. Some 40% of Korean students had understood measurement and geography concepts, while 78% could use intermediate skills to solve two-step problems. The comparative figures for U.S. students were about 10% and 40%.

In science, students in South Korea and British Columbia were ranked at the top. More than 70% of them were able to use scientific procedures and analyze scientific data. By comparison, only 35% to 40% of students in the bottom-ranked countries and provinces – the U.S., Ireland and the French-speaking groups in New Brunswick and Ontario – could handle similar problems.

Ironically, 68% of U.S. students described themselves as "good at mathematics," while only 23% of South Korean students said the same.

The Record

Hackensack, New Jersey, February 7, 1989

The nation's education deficit continues to grow.

Last July, when young adults, ages 18 to 24, from nine countries were tested on their knowledge of geography, the United States came in last. Significant numbers of the Americans tested had difficulty locating the Pacific Ocean and the United States on a world map.

In December, the results of another survey gave U.S. high school students a failing grade in economics. Two-thirds of the 12th graders quizzed did not understand the concept of "profits."

Now, there's additional disturbing news. In a six-nation comparison of 13-year-old students, the United States finished last in math and near the bottom in science.

Obviously, the tests reflect serious deficiencies in U.S. education. The tests were no fluke. Each was given to thousands of students. And each was conducted on behalf of a credible group (the National Geographic Society, the Joint Council on Economic Education, and the Educational Testing Service) with no agenda other than discovering how American students were performing academically.

Besides doing poorly on the tests, the American students also fared poorly in relation to their counterparts from other countries. Students from South Korea placed first in math and shared first in science with students from the Canada. It's interesting to note that Korean students start school a year later than kids in the United States and attend classes with almost twice as many students.

Where has America gone wrong?

Clearly, the United States has become a victim of its own prosperity. In a society wealthy enough to put television in almost every home, it should come as no surprise that American kids have become television junkies. A survey conducted in conjunction with the math and science tests revealed that 31 percent of U.S. students watch five hours or more of television each day. Only 7 percent of the Korean students watch that much.

More and more, we are becoming a society of latchkey kids. With parents at work, many kids are free to make their own choices when they get home from school. In the absence of supervision, television almost always beats out homework — or even reading for pleasure. Parents have a responsibility to make sure their children's free time is used wisely.

The schools can also do more to provide children the skills they will need to compete. In Japan, all students must take at least a semester of economics to graduate from high school. In the United States, only 15 states require any economics. Students can't be expected to understand concepts they haven't been taught.

Consideration should also be given to extending the school year. With a calendar of 180 class days, the United States has one of the shortest school years of any industrialized nation.

In short, it's time teachers and parents demanded more from students.

Omaha World-Herald

Omaha, Nebraska, February 3, 1989

It is nothing new to read that American students compare unfavorably to students of other countries in tests of educational achievement. And it's getting tiresome to read the excuse that American schools, because they must educate all students and not just the elite, must be judged by different standards.

A recent study by the Educational Testing Service produced disturbing indications. Based on tests administered to 24,000 students from six countries, the study indicated that average Korean students have better math skills than average students in the United States. In science comprehension, U.S. students were among the lowest in the survey, while Koreans and Canadian students from the province of British Columbia did best.

The American students did so badly in math and science that Secretary of Education Lauro Cavazos called the situation a national tragedy. He wasn't the first to express alarm about educational deficiencies.

A presidential commission in 1983 said that American education was being pulled into a rising tide of mediocrity.

In 1986, a group of Southern governors said American students were becoming "international illiterates" because of deficiencies in knowledge of geography and foreign languages.

William Bennett, when he was secretary of education, stated more than once that the discipline, amount of homework, parental involvement and higher educational standards of the Japanese schools gave them a significant advantage over American schools.

James Fallows, the Washington editor of Atlantic magazine, alleged in 1987 that America's lowest levels in just about everything educational are much lower than Japan's lowest levels and that the gap was widening.

The need for a higher level of performance can't be wished away or excused. America can't maintain its competitive edge if it falls significantly behind other countries in the education of tomorrow's mathematicians, scientists and engineers, to say nothing of linguists, diplomats and managers. And it can't provide the opportunities that its citizens deserve if the education provided to students of middle and lower ability is inferior to what is available in other countries.

FORT WORTH STAR-TELEGRAM

Fort Worth, Texas, February 6, 1989

Three excellent points about U.S. education were made in the wake of test results comparing American 13-year-olds with those in several other countries.

The test showed that American teenagers are near the bottom in math and science. Korean teens scored highest in both categories.

Albert Shanker of the American Federation of Teachers made one discomforting statement when he pointed out that the next generation of elementary school teachers "has already been educated without math or science."

He calls it a "pipeline problem," meaning that the kids coming through the pipeline now are being taught by teachers who are not required to be up to snuff in math and science. It is a legitimate worry. We have to start now to correct the situation.

In defense of U.S. students, Archie LaPointe of the Educational Testing Service pointed out that we are educating our young people "on our own terms."

"We are," he said, "educating every child in America."

That is a valid point. In theory, at least, U.S. education attempts to educate everyone — those who will be tomorrow's scientists and those who will be tomorrow's fry cooks. This is as it should be in a democracy whose future depends on an educated citizenry. But it may also leave some of our most ambitious young people having to catch up in a hurry in high school and college when they become directed toward higher educational goals. While taking care not to leave anyone behind, we must also be careful not to slow others' progress.

The third point revealed something about cultural self-satisfaction, or perhaps cultural overconfidence.

Only 23 percent of the highest achievers, the Korean students, considered themselves "good at mathematics." Two-thirds of the low-achieving U.S. students considered themselves good at math.

That indicates that those Korean teenagers are being challenged to greater achievement than the American kids and consequently are more likely to work harder to learn even more in the future.

It is bad enough to be bringing up the rear in such important comparisons as math and science backgrounds. It is even worse to be sub-par and think we are doing well. America either must give its young people higher goals or risk falling further behind.

BUFFALO EVENING NEWS

Buffalo, New York, February 5, 1989

ACCORDING TO the latest international assessment of student knowledge, American youngsters spend more time watching television than any of their counterparts in five other countries, as well as less time in class or on homework than most of the other students.

That may help explain why the U.S. youngsters also scored last in math and close to last in science when matched against their foreign peers.

The results of the six-nation comparison released by the Educational Testing Service would seem to underscore a relationship between schoolwork, homework and achievement that most observers probably already took for granted but which the nation has nevertheless been slow to act on.

The educational deficiencies showed up in tests of 24,000 students from the United States, Britain, Ireland, South Korea, Spain and four Canadian provinces. The U.S. probably would have been still further behind had not Japan declined to participate in the study.

But what is is equally as worrisome as the poor performance itself is that the analysis involved eighth-graders. That means American students already are behind in these subjects before they ever set foot inside the high school that has the task of preparing them for college and beyond.

It also suggests that reforms initiated in the wake of the warning about a "rising tide of mediocrity" in 1983 may have not taken hold in time to help the next crop of high school students. Thus, without intensive remedial work to help those youngsters catch up, many of those who will be filling many of the nation's critical jobs in years to come are likely to be overmatched by their foreign counterparts.

Albert Shanker, president of the American Federation of Teachers, was not overstating the problem when he called the report "devastating" and noted that "the United States loses by the time we get to the eighth grade."

U.S Education Secretary Lauro F. Cavazos was similarly blunt when he asked: "How many times must this nation be reminded of its educational deficit?"

The report would seem to make clear that many American students — who have one of the shortest school years of any in the study — are not spending enough time learning, either in class or at home where parents are allowing TV to unduly shove homework into the background.

But in addition to spending more time on the task, students also must be taught better. The new report comes only days after the National Research Council concluded that American schools are failing in math education. That panel called for major reforms, including adoption of voluntary national standards to replace current piecemeal efforts that obviously are not working.

While the diversity of America's student population and the country's proper emphasis on local control of schools argue against an enforced national curriculum, a greater emphasis on voluntary national standards could do much to make sure that all schools are teaching at acceptable levels.

The alternative seems a continuation of the same policies that are failing to keep America in the forefront of educational excellence and to ensure a competitive workforce.

Chicago Tribune

Chicago, Illinois, February 2, 1989

The problem is as precise and indisputable as a series of algebra equations: Math education is seriously deficient in the United States. Most students are bored or psyched out of taking more than minimal math courses and leave school inadequately prepared for a technological society.

Because of biases in instruction, women and minorities do less well in math than white males and are handicapped in attaining many high-paying jobs. There is a serious shortage of good math teachers. American competitiveness suffers because other industrialized countries are better at math education.

This newest, well-documented blast at American education comes from the National Research Council, a consortium of educational organizations, scientists, mathematicians and researchers. Its findings echo all those sad statistics that show how consistently American students lag behind those in other nations. For example, American 13-year-olds scored lowest in math in a six-country study announced this week.

"Everybody Counts," the title of the new report, telegraphs its conclusions. It urges a focus on "a significant common core of mathematics for all students," not just a minimum for the majority and advanced math for a few. It calls for a major overhaul in the ways math is taught, beginning early in elementary school. It wants teachers to build on the natural interests children have in mathematical matters, avoid a boring emphasis on memorization and stress learn-by-doing techniques instead of lectures. It advocates the use of calculators, computers and new teaching methods at all levels and an emphasis on discovering patterns instead of learning formulas.

Most realistically, the report calls for a years-long process of serious discussion, consensus building, action and change involving not only teachers and universities, but also parents, public officials, business leaders and students themselves. It recognizes the futility of change imposed from the top like the disastrous "new math" two decades ago and the inappropriateness of imitating the educational methods of nations, like Japan, whose students achieve better than ours.

(Differences between males and females in math and science abilities have declined almost to zero and probably have little or no innate gender basis, according to new research reported at the American Association for the Advancement of Science's annual meeting. Cultural expectations, gender differences in education and biased assumptions built into teaching materials accounted, generally, for females' poorer showing in the past. Changes in such factors can almost totally eliminate differences in achievement.)

"No longer can we afford to sit idly by while our children move through school without receiving the mathematical preparation appropriate for the 21st Century," insists the National Research Council's study. Nor can we afford to toss the report on the shelf with all those other earnest studies about the alarming need for education reform. Somehow we must figure out how to move beyond commission-naming and report-writing and turn some of those nice-sounding recommendations into practical reality.

THE SACRAMENTO BEE
Sacramento, California, February 4, 1989

The most recent set of embarrassing test scores — those on which American 13-year-olds scored behind Korea, Spain and three other nations in math and science — should hardly be surprising. Those kinds of numbers have been reported periodically in a variety of academic fields for years.

Still, it may be that part of the real message of those tests is being missed. The predictable reaction to each documentation of U.S. academic shortcomings is a call for tougher standards. That's hardly wrong, but too often it devolves into a call for more "basics"; and basics — rote learning, drill, tables — is not at the heart of the failure. What U.S. kids lack are more sophisticated skills: the ability to solve problems and adequately comprehend mathematical concepts and logic. The latest survey, conducted by the Educational Testing Service, found, for example, that while 40 percent of the Korean 13-year-olds understood geometric concepts and could apply different strategies to complex mathematical problems, only 9 percent of their American counterparts could do so.

But that's only part of it. Significantly, when asked if what they learned in science

was important in their daily lives, 50 percent of American students said yes, while 82 percent of Koreans answered affirmatively. And though Americans scored lowest on the test, they rated their own abilities more highly than students of other nations.

The point, reinforced by quantities of data from other sources, is that American culture seems still not to value academic skills and achievement as highly as other cultures but, at the same time, smugly believes in its own superiority. And it's the entire culture — television, the demands and assumptions at home, the example set by national models — that creates the environment for learning. That doesn't mean that the schools shouldn't do better, but as long as the schools are expected to do it all, there will always be a problem.

ST. LOUIS POST-DISPATCH
St. Louis, Missouri, February 3, 1989

Here's a word problem that takes little mathematical skill: If each year after eighth grade, the number of students taking math is cut in half, what happens to the pool of graduates who can succeed in professions demanding math skills? The answer is that the number grows dangerously small; the challenge is to do something about it.

That and other bleak statistics come from a report titled, "Everybody Counts," issued by the National Research Council. Shirley Hill, a professor at the University of Missouri at Kansas City and chair of the panel that wrote the report, said schools must change the way they teach math, to keep it from increasingly excluding women and minorities as the subject matter becomes more sophisticated.

With math, as with other subjects, the problem is not only that the material is too

difficult but that the way it is taught is too dull. Students are natural problem solvers, but this inherent tendency to become mathematical detectives too often is short-circuited by a curriculum in which the teacher lectures and the students dutifully follow. Over a period of years, classes get smaller as the material gets more challenging.

A better approach, the report said, is to involve students in solving realistic problems requiring math concepts that get more and more complex. Students should be encouraged to work together and to use computers and calculators that can free them from sheer number drudgery and allow them to concentrate on ideas. Maybe not everyone can be a math whiz, but more students can go further in math than are doing so now — and if they don't, our scientific future may not count for much.

THE CHRISTIAN SCIENCE MONITOR
Boston, Massachusetts, February 3, 1989

AMERICANS pride themselves on being problem solvers. But according to recent studies, that's the very thing American students *don't* do well – solve problems. Not problems requiring mathematical skills, at any rate.

For too many Americans, education experts say, math simply means arithmetic – doing their sums and memorizing the multiplication table. They don't recognize mathematics as a language about concepts and a methodology for solving conceptual – but very real – problems.

This isn't just a theoretical distinction. Because of deficiencies in their math skills, many Americans are being left behind in the surge to a more technological workplace. Indeed, America itself may be at a growing disadvantage in world competition.

In a 1987 study of 12,000 students in 20 countries, US researchers found that American students were generally outperformed in mathematics by students in other industrialized countries. (Japan – surprise! – led the pack.) The study placed much of the blame on math curricula in US schools.

The grim findings of this and other studies – including one just released of 13-year-olds in six industrialized countries, in which US kids placed last in solving math and science problems – lie behind the National Academy of Sciences proposal last week to revamp math curricula in the US.

The thrust of the changes, the authors of an academy report said, must be to change the view of math as a method of calculation – which can be done by machines – to a means of using concepts to solve problems. The concepts include, for instance, change, probability, logic, and dimension, which have wide-ranging applications in work.

In fact, Americans are problem solvers. Many changes in US education have already begun to appear in response to the "Nation At Risk" study of a few years ago. It's time to put American ingenuity to work in overhauling math education.

Herald News
Fall River, Massachusetts, February 12, 1989

When experts deplore the state of American education, they love to cite statistics. No wonder students are more anxious about their marks than they are intrigued with the joy of learning anything.

Such a penchant for putting the cart before the horse will never raise SAT scores or produce competent adults for a world in which complex mental skills will be required.

For students, there's a simple recipe: become proficient in any field of learning, and the marks you're so worried about will take care of themselves.

In a multi-national test of objective math and science scores, U.S. students came out at the bottom of the ladder. Seventy-eight per cent of South Korean teenagers answered questions that only 40 per cent of their American peers could answer. Students from the USA were also outranked by students from Ireland, the United Kington, Spain and Canada.

These symptoms genererate a lot of heat — but not much light — on the educational and political scenes.

In a recent tv discussion, Charles Bierbauer drew a battery of conflicting comments from U.S. Secretary of Education Lauro Cavasos; Sen. Christopher Dodd, D-Conn., and author-educator Marva Collins, a pioneer in the private school concept of inner-city education.

Secretary Cavasos, benign and hopeful, expressed trust in the vision of George Bush as "the education president." He called for a mutual commitment of parents, teachers and government, and invoked traditional American enterprise. "We're proud of our work ethic; now we need a learning ethic," he declared. He also vowed to fight the horrors of the school drug scene, and stressed that teachers should be held, in popular bottom-line terms, "accountable."

Dodd was more alarmist, convinced that commitment should be measured in terms of money. He warned that American teenagers, in falling far behind, are "jeopardizing the position of the country." He insisted teachers should be paid more, and programmers should recognize the fact that two out of every three women in the workforce are sole providers for young children. In making education its top priority, the U.S. must "lay down the dollars between now and the year 2000," Dodd exhorted.

Ms. Collins, a freethinker caught between two true believers, recalled her disillusion with the public school system, and her development of a new methodology, in which deprived students from the poorest areas receive the best education: "the only way to break the self-perpetuating cycle of poverty."

"Money is not the answer to all problems," Collins said, underscoring the primary need of "dedicated, bright teachers" who help children "watch television analytically and critically." She did not expatiate on what specific methods bring about this ideal condition.

As the abstract sparring continued, the listener's mind wandered to the 13-year olds, subjected like guinea pigs to today's laboratory of standardized tests, all designed to program competitive achievement.

Why can't Johnny compute a percentage, or tell the difference between an amoeba and an anemone? There was no talk of student accountability, nor of equipping young minds with the tools of the trade, nor of inculcating skills of concentration and proper study habits.

DESERET NEWS
Salt Lake City, Utah, February 13, 1989

When it comes to teaching mathematics and science, America's schools are falling down on the job.

Just how badly they are failing can be seen from a new study the other day that found 13-year-olds from Korea, Ireland, the United Kingdom and several Canadian provinces are outperforming their American counterparts in math and science.

Since this is the fourth study in the past year to show shortcomings in math and science education in American schools, the evidence must be considered conclusive.

So is its potential impact on this nation's future.

Americans are becoming less competent in science at a time when the economy is relying more and more on technologically oriented industries. This nation's ability to compete is bound to suffer unless our schools start doing a better job of teaching science.

Likewise, mathematics is essential to a wide variety of essential tasks, ranging from keeping track of the AIDS epidemic and projecting the greenhouse effect on the atmosphere to studying the flow of traffic in an effort to ease traffic congestion.

Part of the problem is that the schools aren't recruiting enough science and mathematics teachers. Some teachers aren't able to get students excited in these subjects because the teachers themselves don't always find math and science interesting.

If the only way to get enough of the best science and math teachers is to start paying them more than other educators, so be it. As it is now, the U.S. Chamber of Commerce reports that American businesses are spending $40 billion a year on remedial training for new employees just to get them up to minimum levels of competency. That is a staggering amount of money, and much of it would be better spent on the schools.

More money, however, isn't the entire answer. Most school systems around the country put more emphasis on theory and fact than on practical applications. Many teachers, as the Boston Globe noted recently, "seem more interested in testing memorization than in giving students the basis for understanding math and science for everyday use."

The remedies, then, should be as clear. And the need for improvement is urgent. If the schools keep flunking when it comes to teaching math and science, eventually the rest of America will pay for this failure.

Report Faults U.S. Schools

An annual government assessment released May 3, 1989 concluded that educational progress had been "stagnant" despite increases in school spending. The report found nationwide student achievement "merely average."

"We are standing still," Education Secretary Lauro F. Cavazos said at a press conference in Washington, D.C. "The problem is that it's been this way for three years in a row. We cannot be satisfied with mediocrity, and so it's time to turn things around."

Among specific problems cited by Cavazos were the nation's graduation rate, which had fallen to 71.6%, and the school drop-out rate, which he called a "national tragedy."

Nationwide scores on the American College Test (ACT), a widely used admissions test, had improved by only 0.1% since 1987. Cavazos noted, however, that test scores for minority students had continued to improve.

Cavazos asserted that higher school spending was not the answer, and he offered a series of suggestions for improved performance, including more homework, higher parental expectations and greater emphasis by schools on raising graduation rates.

His conclusions were criticized by some education officials, who said that they reflected the Bush administration's desire to improve school performance without increasing federal spending on education. (Bush had already submitted an education budget for 1990 that did not allow for an inflation increase.)

"It is sad to hear the same rhetoric that 'money alone is not the answer,'" said Mary Hatwood Futrell, president of the National Education Association. "If we are calling for improved performance, then we are all going to have to accept the responsibility of identifying the fiscal and physical resources necessary to turn things around."

The Chattanooga Times

Chattanooga, Tennessee, May 10, 1989

On the campaign trail last year, George Bush proclaimed that he intended to be known as the "education president." In his inaugural address and other speeches, Mr. Bush has said that the nation has "more will than wallet." Maybe so, but if he intends to live up to his goal of becoming the education president, the president will have to find a thicker wallet.

He will also have to do better than use federal reports, such as the one released last week by Education Secretary Lauro Cavazos, to excuse lack of action at the federal level. Mr. Cavazos said the report showed that while education spending nationwide is up, progress toward better schools is at a standstill. The nation's students are, the report noted in a damning phrase, "merely average."

In and of itself, the president's education proposal on education has much to recommend it. The nation must seek out and reward outstanding schools; it has to attack the horrendous dropout rates and crime that afflict inner-city schools; it should help teachers and administrators improve their teaching and management skills.

Mr. Cavazos' report suggests that the nation's schools are heading rapidly toward disaster. Maybe, but many educators — among them California State Superintendent William Honig, himself a Republican — disagree. But even if, for the sake of argument, the Cavazos report's conclusions are deemed valid, how does the administration propose to deal with them? Mr. Cavazos offered mere panaceas: more homework, higher standards, more parental

involvement in children's education. Those are nice, safe, non-controversial suggestions, and there is nothing wrong with any of them, as far as they go. Trouble is, they don't go very far.

The administration, which argues adamantly that more money is not the answer, wants educators to do more even while it is in effect doing less. Its budget would cut the Education Department's budget by not allowing increases for inflation. Its legislative package would authorize 10 new programs for about $441 million, mostly to reward excellent schools and teachers.

A better course for the administration would be to restore some of the cuts that occurred during the Reagan administration's tenure — and which contributed to the problems that Congress, Mr. Bush and many others are trying to solve. A study by the National Education Association has outlined a serious reduction in federal support for such fundamental programs as adult education, remedial programs in math and science, college tuition grants and the like.

The goal of restoring federal funding in such areas is limited by budget constraints caused by the deficit, which means Mr. Bush has to set priorities. It also means that if he truly hopes to become known as the nation's "education president," he will have to decide the benefits of spending more to improve U.S. schools — and the short- and long-term consequences of not spending enough. So far, the president seems to be opting for short-term advantage, and that's tragic.

The Evening Gazette

Worcester, Massachusetts, May 9, 1989

The report card on the nation's educational performance is in, and it is discouraging.

The grade is S — for "stagnant."

Education Secretary Lauro Cavazos says education in the United States is characterized by mediocrity that threatens the country's role as a world power. "We must do better or perish as the nation we know today," he warned in unveiling the sixth annual State Education Performance Chart.

Cavazos blames "our education deficit" — and he does not mean a fiscal crisis. In fact, money is not the only solution to the problem, which includes a steady decline in high school graduation rates and falling scores on college entrance exams in half of the states. The problem is that "we are standing still."

Cavazos' observations are shared by many concerned educators, even though some charge that the secretary's information is based on flawed data. They pretty much coincide with the views of his predecessor, William Bennett, who often bemoaned the deficiencies of American public education.

Cavazos recommends some immediate goals: Improve classroom attendance; bring high school graduation rates up to 90 percent; reduce by half the number of students who fail a grade level; emphasize the importance of homework and reduce paperwork for teachers. He also recommends establishing high-quality vocational training for those not heading for college.

These are good suggestions. But Cavazos, like Bennett, can do little more than warn, recommend and try to inspire. In fact, there is a danger that frequent reminders of danger may sound like crying wolf. Yet these warnings must be taken seriously.

The responsibility of reducing the education deficit belongs to the states and local schools systems. Imaginative leaders on the local level need to set education improvement goals. While a budget pinch may force spending limitations, education must never be shortchanged if the United States is to remain a world leader.

But no one can do more to end the stagnation than teachers, parents and students. Good education has many ingredients, but three stand out: Skilled educators dedicated to quality teaching, students willing to work hard and parents determined to see that their children make the best use of education opportunities.

The Charlotte Observer

Charlotte, North Carolina, May 8, 1989

The good news is that the schools are not worse; the bad news is that we are not making progress.

— Lauro Cavazos
— U.S. Secretary of Education

Secretary Cavazos was glum last week in releasing his department's annual report on America education. As critics quickly noted, his statistics don't tell the full story. But nobody should argue for complacency.

Unfortunately, the secretary invited criticism. At times he sounded more like a guardian of the administration's political agenda than a steward of the nation's schools, arguing that "money alone is not the answer" and stressing the need for parental freedom to choose schools.

Money is only one factor in the nation's reform efforts. But *less* money isn't the answer: Look at the need for higher pay for teachers. Because resources are distributed unequally among the nation's schools, with their varying mixes of state and local funding, federal investment and leadership are vital. Education is the nation's first-line of defense for the long term. Washington's role must be more than scold and commentator.

The secretary is right about the need for greater parental say and choice about many things. But there is no magic. Colleges, often cited as models of choice, are typically selective in admission and have their own problems with dropouts, loan defaults and ill-educated graduates.

Measuring schools is difficult. The secretary's measures — ranging from College Board scores to graduation rates — are incomplete and subject to argument. While there is much in schools that is excellent — and much that is hopeful — even some simple measures yield alarming results.

More than a quarter of the nation's young people don't graduate from high school, for example. Too many of the rest get a diploma but not an education. Tests show American students rank discouragingly low in the world. That's not good enough.

There are explanations to be offered, including poverty and family breakdown. Schools can't be expected to make scholars of young people pulled away from learning by everything else around them. The educational measures that shock us so are verdicts on society as well as schools.

Schools cannot be expected to win this battle alone, but they are our best hope. What schools need from Washington's Bully Pulpit is not cheerleading or bullying, and not just exhortation. They need leadership, support and the key national investment that can help our system of local education succeed in an increasingly strenuous international competition.

THE ARIZONA REPUBLIC

Phoenix, Arizona, May 9, 1989

THE American education system is slowly sinking beneath a rising tide of mediocrity, and the nation's future is going down with it. Secretary of Education Lauro Cavazos last week released the government's annual report card on the state of the nation's public schools, and it was far from encouraging.

"We are standing still," Mr. Cavazos said, "and the problem is that it's been this way for three years in a row."

By virtually any standard of measurement, achievement standards are far below what they were in the 1960s and they have improved little in the last decade in spite of what is widely recognized, at least for purposes of paying it lip service, as a crisis in education.

Money is decidedly not the problem. The United States this year will spend almost $200 billion on elementary and secondary education. Spending across the board — from dollars per pupil to teachers' salaries — has gone up sharply in recent years to an all-time high.

We spend more on education than either Japan or West Germany, but fall behind them in student achievement. "As a nation," said Secretary Cavazos, "our educational performance is merely average." And average is not good enough in the increasingly competitive world economy.

Americans traditionally have held to the belief that almost any problem can be overcome if we just spend enough money on it. Even so challenging a task as putting men on the moon was accomplished through a single-minded commitment of national resources.

And so we have tried to meet the education crisis the traditional — and easy — way, by throwing money at the schools willy-nilly, when what is needed is a response commensurate to the gravity of the situation.

What we need is a fundamental restructuring of our educational system, innovative approaches and bold new strategies. In the past we have tended, and to a degree still do, to use as a standard of education success the amount of money put into it, rather than focusing in the quality of the products coming out.

And in Arizona the outlook is as grim as it is for the rest of the country. Only in the dropout rate does our state rise above the national average — 35 percent drop out in Arizona compared with a national average of 29 percent — a dubious distinction to be sure.

Sadly, the nation seems content to accept this stagnation with a ho-hum attitude. The education establishment, meanwhile, continues to resist fundamental reforms as it lobbies for ever-increasing budgets to fund more of the same. As a nation we simply have failed to treat the education deficit as the profound threat to our future it is.

The Honolulu Advertiser

Honolulu, Hawaii, May 4, 1989

No one can be happy with American education as portrayed by U.S. Education Secretary Lauro Cavazos' annual "wall chart" comparing the states. But mixed with all the indicators of stagnation are a couple of heartening items.

Hawaii is second in improvement in Scholastic Aptitude Test scores from 1982-88. As originally reported last fall, Cavazos' list pointed out that Hawaii's average on the SAT improved seven points from 1987 to 1988 while the U.S. average went down two.

Despite narrowing the gap, Hawaii remains well behind national SAT averages (888 here vs. 904), although some of the difference may be because a high percentage of students takes the test here. Math again was our college-bound students' very strong suit, and the verbal portion of the test was their Achilles' heel.

Hawaii students' 1988 performance ranked only 14th among the 22 states relying on the SAT. That leaves us down there with states that have the most improving to do.

Some of Cavazos' statistics are open to challenge. But year after year, the comparison draws attention to real weaknesses in Hawaii's education system.

The difference is that this year finds Hawaii firmly committed to some of the things Cavazos says are needed to turn education around — fundamental restructuring and more parental involvement in school.

It'll be a while before the effects, if any, of recent state spending increases and these reforms show up on the federal chart. But there is reason for hope. Superintendent of Education Charles Toguchi is leading impressive reform efforts within his department which complement moves urged by the governor, Legislature and business community.

We have the green light for converting schools to community-based management, and more funding that can be used to improve our kids' language skills. Now let's get to work.

FORT WORTH STAR-TELEGRAM

Fort Worth, Texas, May 5. 1989

The recently issued "federal report card" on public education in the United States offers little reason for encouragement. Perhaps the most disturbing element of that report is concerned with the staggering dropout rate.

In announcing the findings, Education Secretary Lauro Cavazos revealed that an average of 3,600 students drop out of school daily in the United States. A corresponding state report indicates that 87,000 Texas students in grades 7 through 12 dropped out during the 1987-88 school year.

Those are alarming figures.

The 1984 education reforms have begun to pay rich dividends in this state, but all the reform in the world will not accomplish anything if students do not remain in school to take advantage of them.

It is obvious from the numbers that too little attention has been paid to the dropout problem in the past, which makes it all the more imperative that workable solutions be put into effect as soon as possible to reverse a devastating trend.

Legislation adopted in 1987 requires school districts to institute a dropout-prevention program, and that represents at least a start in the right direction. Many districts have adopted "self-worth" programs to instill in students pride of accomplishment and the desire to remain in school. Statewide, schools are now trying to identify potential dropouts in first, second and third grades in order to establish counseling programs with the children and their parents.

But more must be done. Cooperation between public and private sectors will be essential in developing dropout-prevention programs of value to each. Businesses are already paying a heavy price to provide remedial training for employees who did not gain the necessary skills in schools. The money could be better spent at the front end, helping finance programs to keep kids in the classroom.

But the real key lies with parents. Students will never be persuaded to remain in school unless their parents can be convinced of the importance of education. America's school administrators, business leaders, civic officials and other concerned citizens must launch a cooperative effort toward that end, and soon.

Schools cannot turn the tide by themselves, no matter how effective their program might look on paper.

The Houston Post

Houston, Texas, May 5, 1989

IT SEEMS THAT THE big argument over America's inability to make advancements in education is centered around money. Some people are saying more funding is needed to provide the resources necessary to improve students' educations while others are saying that throwing money at the same old educational programs just won't cut it.

Texas, which fared poorly in just about all categories of the national report card issued by Secretary of Education Lauro Cavazos, is making strides toward improving education in the state. But it could use more financial support to achieve the hoped-for success of its newest programs. Certainly in Texas, more money is needed to equalize the educations provided by the state's many school districts. Legislators are already working on that, and there is no doubt it will cost us.

And the programs to test teachers and second-year college students will take a bite out of our overall education budget. Those are just two of the good and necessary programs that should help improve education in Texas.

Currently, about half of the entire state budget goes to education, and of that half, two-thirds goes to grades K through 12. Over the past few years Texas has made great progress in teachers' pay, graduation rate, pupil-teacher ratio and spending per pupil. But for all that running, Texas seems to be falling farther behind other states, which are doing even more.

But money is certainly not the entire answer. While education is expensive, and a lot of taxes are needed to run schools, we must use wisely what little money we do have. Indeed, there are many aspects of education and schooling that do not involve more spending.

Do we have the best curricula money can buy? Better curricula and innovative methods of teaching can replace what we now have for the same amount of funding.

Can money buy the much-needed classroom discipline that is so vital to a successful learning atmosphere? Without classroom discipline, schools are lost. Today, there is not much a teacher or school can do with an unruly student except suspend him — then that student doesn't learn anything because he's not in school, which makes him a prime candidate for joining the nation's 700,000 other dropouts.

Can money buy higher teacher/student standards of achievement? High achievement standards must be set — with visible rewards at the end of much hard work. The motivations of past years aren't working well today; consequently, students and teachers should be asked what motivates them to achieve higher standards. No one knows better than they.

Then there is the all-important parental concern. It costs nary a cent.

When we involve students in what they learn, and how they learn it, we might see a change in their attitude about the importance of education. Today, many students feel education is being stuffed down their throats, and they don't *really* see a reason for it.

Granted, students have always felt that way. But students today are much different from those of the 1960s and early '70s when achievement was higher. Many of today's students are not as disciplined, and not as hungry for success as students were in the past; consequently, we have to deal with them differently.

When we unify all the things money can't buy with the $199 billion we are spending on education each year, we just might see some improvements in our national report card.

THE SACRAMENTO BEE

Sacramento, California, May 5, 1989

You don't have to be a defender of the sad state of American education to understand that most of what Education Secretary Lauro Cavazos reported about it the other day wasn't very helpful.

Cavazos' state-by-state ranking of crude educational measures, such as graduation and dropout rates, reflected, as much as anything else, the general state of social and economic welfare in various areas of the country. It's not surprising that Iowa, Minnesota and Nebraska, states with relatively few immigrants and minorities and lots of middle-class, small-city residents, would score better than New York or California or Washington, D.C. And his discussion of the stagnation in SAT scores in the past year or two took no account of the fact that in places like California, the number of students taking the test has increased, a change that would almost certainly tend to hide real gains. That doesn't absolve schools, legislatures and parents of responsibility for performance, but it does demand something far less simplistic — both in analysis and recommendations — than what Cavazos delivered.

The effect, if not the purpose, of Cavazos' report is to reinforce arguments that more money isn't the answer for education's problems. But other than preaching at the schools about homework and parent involvement and lower dropout rates — hardly new discoveries — Cavazos had nothing to offer. Worse, he seemed not even to recognize that the changing demographics of American schools might be making their job ever more difficult. Thus just staying even, in the absence of significant new resources, may be a victory.

Of course, more money alone isn't the answer, but there's hardly any answer that will not require more money: for educational programs and for the many medical, nutritional and community services — support for all of which has been reduced in the past decade — that help create the conditions in the home and neighborhood that give students half a chance to succeed.

Cavazos is supposedly speaking on behalf of the man who says he wants to be the education president. So far, the most concrete manifestations of that desire have been a handful of useful but marginal initiatives to reward successful schools and teachers, a little preaching at schools and a reduction of real federal spending for education. By whatever measure, that's not enough.

THE SPOKESMAN-REVIEW
Spokane, Washington, May 6, 1989

The U.S. Department of Education's latest report card on the nation's schools is not encouraging for residents of Washington state.

And certainly not for state lawmakers who, although they appear almost ready to wrap up this year's business in Olympia, will have to respond eventually to the challenges the federal report portends.

Most alarming of the statistics released this week was the state's 46th-place ranking with regard to student-teacher ratios. According to the Department of Education, Washington state had 20.2 students per teacher in 1988 compared with a national average of 17.6.

Overcrowded classrooms make it substantially harder for teachers to deliver the individual attention it will take to overcome the "stagnation" which U.S. Education Secretary Lauro Cavazos says characterizes the nation's public schools. What's more, the fastest growing element of new enrollments in Washington's public schools is at-risk children whose backgrounds indicate they will require an even greater share of their teachers' attention if they are to receive a satisfactory education.

Demographic trends, legislative enactments and economic realities all loom as imposing barriers to meeting this challenge.

At present, school enrollments in Washington are on the rise, having climbed back to about the same level where they were 10 years ago. They will climb substantially higher as the so-called baby-boom echo works its way through the school-age years.

It will require adding hundreds of teachers a year just to maintain the present student-teacher ratio and even more new hires if we want to improve on it.

But it's not as simple as merely hiring more teachers. For one thing, the perennial budget pinch which haunts state legislators is expected to get tighter in the near future. For the first time in a decade, school enrollment and welfare caseloads — the two biggest influences on state spending — are rising at the same time. The state's economy, meanwhile, is expected to slacken from the relatively robust pace of late.

And to complicate matters further, the whole nation is headed into a widely recognized labor shortage which will make the competition for skilled workers and professionals, including good teachers, keener. That phenomenon will be particularly evident in Washington where the Legislature has decreed that beginning in 1992 teachers will have to attain master's degrees.

But even if the budgetary hurdles are overcome and money is found to put more teachers in the classroom, where will the classrooms come from?

Officials of School District 81 say that a class-size reduction of one student at the elementary school level would require 22 more classrooms in Spokane, roughly the equivalent of one school building.

State school-construction funds are so hard to come by in Washington now that the Legislature is about to use general fund money — traditionally reserved for operating expenses — to help relieve classroom overcrowding problems around the state.

Once those legislators have finished their work in Olympia and get back home for a vacation from lawmaking, they ought to spend a little time studying their newly released report card. It will give them some ideas of what they must study if they want to see improvement next year.

Minneapolis Star and Tribune
Minneapolis, Minnesota, May 9, 1989

The Bush administration made headlines last week by releasing the federal government's annual report card on education. As they have in previous years, federal officials used the report to pinpoint weaknesses in the nation's schools. The report serves a useful purpose by documenting trends in student performance. Its disturbing statistics on dropouts are enough to make even the staunchest defenders of public education cringe. But it is increasingly clear that simply identifying education's failings will not make things better.

Education Secretary Lauro Cavazos made front pages and newscasts by calling American education "stagnant." Cavazos exhorted educators to do better, saying "we cannot be satisfied with mediocrity." But many educators already know where they are failing, and in many cases they know why. Less clear to them, and to policy-makers, is what can be done to improve their success rate with kids. Education doesn't need more report cards. It needs a commitment to try innovative approaches in the search for more positive results.

Minnesota has done well in innovation, with its bold open-enrollment strategy and other experiments. But even Minnesota has been slow to warm to the innovation that research says holds the most promise for improving education — giving teachers a larger role in running their schools and in applying their own innovations to the tasks of teaching. One major barrier is a state law that keeps education policy issues out of the collective bargaining process. By law, bargaining is only supposed to be about money and work rules.

But teachers are not janitors, they are teaching professionals. They are trained in pedagogy, and they, more than anyone, know what barriers stand between their students and learning. Preventing them from playing a key role in developing education policy and introducing innovative teaching techniques is an unwise waste of talent and wisdom. The law should be changed.

SAT, ACT Scores Drop; Bush, Governors Hold Summit

The College Entrance Examination Board Sept. 11, 1989 released results of the Scholastic Aptitude Test and the American College Test. Scores on both tests declined from 1988.

Nationally, the average SAT score was 903 on a scale that ranged from 400 to 1,600. That average was down one point from the previous year.

President George Bush met with the nation's governors in Charlottesville, Va. Sept. 27-28 in an effort to devise a plan to improve the nation's schools. The meeting had been called by Bush, who had frequently stated during his campaign for the presidency that he wanted to be known as the "education president."

At the end of the conference, which was held at the University of Virginia, Bush and the governors issued a joint statement outlining their goals for the future. "We believe that the time has come, for the first time in U.S. history, to establish clear, national performance goals." the statement said. "This agreement represents the first step in a long-term commitment to re-orient the education system and to marshal widespread support for the needed reforms."

Specific details on how to achieve the goals were to be worked out jointly by the administration and the governors in time for the National Governors' Association meeting to be held in February 1990.

The joint statement called for progress in seven areas, among them:
■ The readiness of children to start school.
■ The performance of students on international achievement tests, particularly in mathematics and science.
■ A reduction in the drop-out rate and an improvement in academic performance.
■ Adult literacy.
■ An improvement in training levels in order to ensure a competitive work force.

In order to achieve those, the conferees gave their approval to several reform measures.

The Washington Post

Washington, D.C., September 16, 1989

IT'S ALWAYS a temptation to look to the annual scores on the Scholastic Aptitude Test, taken every year by about 1 million seniors applying to college, for a barometer on the quality of the schools. This year, with the scores down slightly, educators have rushed to condemn the slow progress of education reform. In fact, the SAT isn't a good indicator of either overall school quality or school reform. The test is taken only by those who choose to, the numbers' meaning fluctuates with the participation of different groups of students, and the skills it measures—math and "developed verbal ability"—are a poorly understood mix of long-term and short-term study, family background and the quality of schools. But there aren't many precise numbers of any kind out there on student achievement, and so the information the SAT does offer is grounds for interest and, this year, mild dismay.

Its clearest and most troublesome message is that fewer students took the SAT this year—4 percent fewer, although the overall number of high school seniors dropped only a single percentage point. The implication is that fewer students are aspiring to college, a not entirely unexpected fallout from the years of rising college costs and shrinking aid sources.

The score shifts themselves send a more complicated signal. They are no longer rising, as they seemed to be doing for a time in the early 1980s; the average math score is stuck at 476 on a 200-to-800 scale, and the average verbal score has actually gone down a point, to 427. This is happening despite years of agitation about improving the schools—and despite some concrete changes, such as the higher numbers of courses required for high school graduation, that the test-makers' own research suggests should help.

Increased participation by minority seniors, who still score lower as a group than whites, could be dragging down the overall average while individual minority groups continue to improve. In the past 10 years, for instance, average black scores have risen 21 points in verbal and 28 in math. Minority test-takers have also been reporting that they take greater numbers of academic courses. But even here the news is mixed. Black verbal scores dropped two points this year while black math scores rose the same amount.

The continuing score deficit in the face of more required high school courses should refocus attention on the quality of those courses. And the quality, it's no secret, still needs a lot of work. The present drive for better measurement of what students learn—at all points in school, not just when they apply to college—seems doubly urgent in view of this continuing pessimism and perplexity.

The State

Columbia, South Carolina, September 17, 1989

OFTEN, when South Carolina competes with the rest of the nation, it seems as though she has to run twice as fast just to stay in the same place. But that wasn't the case with the latest Scholastic Aptitude Test scores.

Palmetto State students had an average score of 838. That's the exact result achieved in 1988. Still, the state moved up one notch in national standings in 1989 and out of the national cellar. In the past, the state has made impressive gains but couldn't edge out of last place.

Confusing? If so, that's only one of the ambiguous aspects of SAT results.

Walter R. Jacobs Jr., director of Academic Services of the College Board Regional Office in Atlanta, pointed out one usually overlooked factor in gauging SAT scores: "The College Board has been consistent in its warnings that this ranking has always been unfair and simplistic," he said. "Nevertheless, it has been perceived by the public-at-large as a barometer of the academic performance of college-bound students at the state level.

"Consequently, South Carolina's last-place ranking in terms of state SAT score average has, on occasion, dampened public enthusiasm for the state's forward progress in SAT growth."

Educators have also maintained that where a high percentage of students takes the SAT test, as in South Carolina, it tends to lower the average results.

Nevertheless, South Carolina school watchers have a choice in grading what's happening in the classroom. They can rejoice that the state no longer clings to the bottom rung in one embarrassing statistic. And they can take pride that SAT test results have improved significantly over the past several years.

But they can justifiably lament that the average score didn't budge one iota during the past year.

Or, finally, after they pore over all the results, they can wistfully conclude, "After all, this was only a test."

THE ASHEVILLE CITIZEN
Asheville, North Carolina, September 24, 1989

This is where the excuses stop.

North Carolina's poor showing on the Scholastic Aptitude Test long has been explained by economic and social conditions. Our state has high rates of poverty and illiteracy. Many North Carolinians are school dropouts. Only two other states have a higher percentage of adults without high school educations.

Children from such families tend to do poorly in school, and they drag down average SAT scores in the state. North Carolina students usually rank about 49th in SAT scores. This year the state's SAT average fell five points — enough to drop North Carolina to 50th place, behind South Carolina.

The assumption has been that the general level of education in North Carolina compares to that in other states, that our schools perform about as well as those elsewhere, and that low SAT scores come entirely from the fact that poor achievers make up a larger percentage of school enrollment here than in most states.

How then do we explain that even our best students perform worse than their counterparts elsewhere?

SAT scores were compared among students of similar backgrounds and the results released along with average scores. High school seniors in North Carolina who rank in the top 10 percent of their classes scored 68 points below the top 10 percent of students nationally.

Students in North Carolina whose parents hold graduate degrees scored 61 points below similar students nationwide.

North Carolina students from families with incomes of more than $70,000 scored 54 points below the national average for their group.

Keep in mind that national averages themselves are low. American students on the whole perform lamentably compared to European, Canadian and Japanese students. The cream of U.S. schools — the top 5 percent of students — also do not measure up to similar students abroad.

The average score of all North Carolina students who took the SAT was 67 points below the national average. A similar gap in the scores of our brightest students shows that the problem does not owe entirely to demographics and to family income and education levels.

The conclusion is inescapable: Our schools simply are not educating students to the same degree as schools elsewhere.

The above findings apparently came as a surprise to educators also. Like most parents, North Carolina educators have assumed that low rankings come from poor students and that our better students leave high school as well-prepared as their counterparts nationally.

Suzanne Triplett, assistant state superintendent for research and development, urged schools to re-examine that comfortable belief. She told 134 school superintendents meeting in Raleigh: "We may be making the wrong assumptions."

She was being polite. Many educators clearly are making some wrong assumptions.

Parents and schools need to push students harder. We demand too little of all students, but especially our better students. Parents of children who do well in school should insist that they take advanced courses at the high school level. Too often such decisions are left to the students themselves, and they take only the minimum they need to qualify for college. Where schools do not yet offer advanced courses, parents should insist that they do — and pledge that their children will be in them.

American education must be strengthened at every stage. The nation has far to go before our schools are brought up to an adequate level — and North Carolina has even farther to go.

The Hartford Courant
Hartford, Connecticut, September 26, 1989

College entrance examination scores don't measure academic achievement broadly, but they show the direction of the educational winds. For many minority students, the test results are an encouraging sign.

The scores of black, Hispanic and Asian students on the Scholastic Aptitude Test last year continued to improve or hold steady, as they have done for the past decade. The gap between white and non-white students is narrowing.

For example, black students as a group have improved their scores on the verbal section of the SAT by 21 percent since 1979 while whites have improved their scores by 2 percent. Math scores among Puerto Ricans improved by 18 percent compared with the 9 percent improvement among whites over the same period.

However, the combined scores for white students are still much higher than for minority students. There's a lot of catching up to be done.

What explains the progress made by minority students? One answer is the effort to purge the tests of biased questions that favored whites, although that is still a point of contention. Another answer is that schools with predominantly minority enrollments schools are getting better. After all, SAT test scores reflect the quality of high school preparation.

Other, and perhaps more persuasive, answers have to do with the growth of the education-minded black and Hispanic middle classes and a rising popularity of college-level courses in city schools.

Still, we mustn't read too much into SAT scores. They don't give us the entire picture because not all students take the test. The SAT students are a self-selected group and therefore aren't representative of their respective racial or ethnic groups.

But seeing minority students' scores rise at double-digit rates is better that seeing them drop.

THE DENVER POST
Denver, Colorado, September 17, 1989

WHEN ROY Romer heads east for the "education summit" with President Bush and the other 49 governors later this month, he'd better bring along plenty of copies of the latest Denver Post/News 4 Poll. It shows with appalling clarity how badly our schools are failing.

The survey, based on telephone interviews with 303 high school students in the Denver metro area, revealed a shocking lack of basic knowledge in the subjects that form the core curriculum in virtually every school in the country, public or private.

In history, for example, fewer than half the respondents were able to name Abraham Lincoln as the man who was president of the United States during the Civil War, and in literature, only two out of three could identify Shakespeare as the playwright who authored the line, "To be or not to be: that is the question."

But it was in math that the students stumbled most astoundingly. Barely half knew that a room 10 feet long and 10 feet wide would contain 100 square feet, and just 43 percent calculated correctly that a 5 percent sales tax on a $2 purchase would amount to 10 cents.

These were currently enrolled high school students, remember — not grade-schoolers. And most were sophomores, juniors and seniors — not freshmen. Worse, almost all of them said their grades were average or above-average — and astonishingly, three-fourths said they planned to go on to college.

No wonder American businesses are complaining about their entry-level workers. Failure rates like these might be expected on questions dealing with the causes of the Civil War or the theme of "Othello." But on a simple multiplication test? No way.

The schools may be covering the basics, but what they are teaching obviously isn't being learned.

Romer and his colleagues had better get this message across to the nation's educators, or else American school children may just as well start taking nothing but Japanese — because that's all they'll be speaking in 20 years.

FORT WORTH STAR-TELEGRAM
Fort Worth, Texas,
September 30, 1989

This week's education summit laid the groundwork for improvement of the nation's public schools. That was the easy part; the tough job is yet to be done, and it will be a long, hard grind.

Prior to the summit, which provided a forum for the country's governors to discuss educational matters with President Bush, we urged the participants not to take the easy way out and merely issue a report on what's wrong with America's schools. We said that success could only be registered by production of a "tough, pragmatic agenda for improvement."

They appear to have batted about .500. They were not content merely to point out deficiencies in the current system, which is good, but some of the recommendations that emerged are too vague to inspire a great deal of confidence. "Providing for drug-free schools," for example, is a noble goal, but a step-by-step plan for accomplishing the goal would have been far more welcome.

Despite the shortcomings, the summit could have a positive effect on education if — and it's a very big if — the federal government acknowledges its responsibility to provide the necessary resources and the governors perform the tasks they have laid out for themselves.

Only adequate financing and a change in the public's attitude toward education can bring about genuine improvement. Instead of offering lessons in lip-reading, the president should pledge that sufficient money will be available to do the job. The governors, on the other hand, are ideally situated to bring about the attitude change by marshalling public support for the new agenda.

Improvement will not come overnight. It took the schools a long time to get sick, and it will take them a long time to get well. Meanwhile, Bush and the governors — who said repeatedly that they want to hold the schools "more accountable" — must themselves be held accountable for the recovery's progress. They cannot be permitted to merely get the program started. They must see it through to completion.

The Honolulu Advertiser
Honolulu, Hawaii, September 24, 1989

What's needed from President Bush's education summit with the nation's governors this week is not another report, but a strategy for applying what's already been learned in the ferment over "A Nation at Risk."

Many governors, educators and lawmakers have called for measurable performance goals for American schools — like the Europeans have. Bush already is a big fan of letting schools choose their own paths toward such goals.

The other loud call will be for more federal funding against social problems that hinder school performance — poverty, alcohol and drug abuse, poor infant and maternal health and too little child care.

Governor Waihee and Schools Superintendent Charles Toguchi will be among those at the summit this week. Waihee says the spirited leadership hoped for from our "education president" must be of the kind that mobilized the nation to put a man on the moon in the 1960s.

Democratic congressional leaders announced in advance their own "National Goals for Educational Excellence." They include lower dropout and illiteracy rates, early childhood education for all poor 4-year-olds by 1995, greater competence in math, science and languages, and more and better teachers.

The administration and financing of education are primarily local responsibilities. That won't change. But it's become clear the nation can't have a vigorous economy and a functioning democracy if educational attainment is wildly inconsistent across the land. There is a federal role.

Americans have repeatedly signaled a willingness to pay more taxes for education, if they can be assured of results. The governors will try to impress on Bush that changing education strategy is just a first step. He and Congress must make sure schools have the resources to meet new goals.

BUFFALO EVENING NEWS
Buffalo, New York, September 30, 1989

IN CALLING a meeting with governors to figure out how to improve the country's stagnant educational system, President Bush has succeeded again in doing what we hope will not become his administration's major accomplishment: focusing national attention on a vital problem.

The unprecedented two days of closed-door talks between Bush and the nation's governors unquestionably helped shape the discussion at a time when critical analyses and complaints from employers have made education a national issue.

The resulting consensus on the need for national standards and ways to measure progress toward them is a significant first step. The broadly worded goals laid out at the conference at least point the nation in the right direction at a time when some wayward districts like Buffalo are cutting staff and offerings and promising to turn out less prepared graduates. It is encouraging to see that a national effort may be developing.

But the real task lies ahead. Though using needlessly cynical language, former federal education secretary William Bennett did put the University of Virginia summit in perspective when he said after one session that everyone had agreed that "they like little children."

Vague goals need refining

The first real challenge will be transforming verbal commitment into concrete proposals. Some of the problems, based on experience, are easy to predict.

How, for example, to produce the annual "report cards" that hold schools accountable while not stigmatizing — and thus turning off — those who, for a variety of reasons, will inevitably fare poorly?

Or how to provide "real rewards" for teachers without falling prey to the opposition that proposals like merit pay automatically provoke from teacher unions?

Those will be the challenges for the National Governors' Association, which plans to have preliminary goals and timetables worked out by its February meeting.

As one participant noted, there undoubtedly is some school somewhere in the country dealing successfully with each of the ills afflicting American education. If the association can compile those solutions, it might be able to come up with a plan that gives schools the flexibility to use whatever works in exchange for accountability.

What about funding?

But moving from what Bennett called standard political "pap" to specific planning is still only part of the answer. Many of the solutions will cost money.

The last time Bush brought the symbolism of the presidency to bear on an issue — in that case drugs — the funding reality failed to live up to the rhetoric. This time, the promise is even less.

It would have been encouraging at least to hear the president make a general pledge of federal support for a comprehensive educational effort, as he eventually did in promising to expand on the invaluable Head Start program.

Still, with no specific proposals yet in hand, the president can for the time being get away with offering "more will than wallet." But for all the euphoria coming out of the University of Virginia, merely shining a spotlight on the schools will not bring them out of the dark.

It will take a commitment by educators to pursue new methods and to have schools challenged and measured. And, eventually, it will take an education president willing to find a way to pay for that.

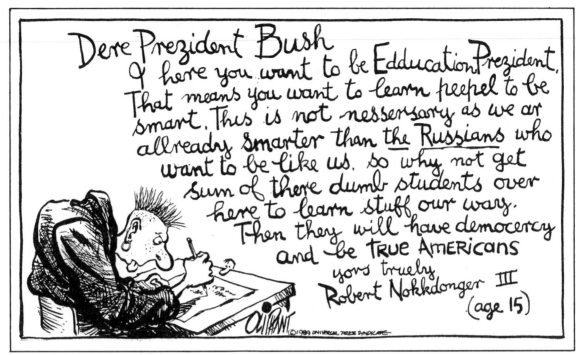

Dere Prezident Bush
I here you want to be Edducation Prezident.
That means you want to learn peepel to be
smart. This is not nessersary as we ar
allready smarter than the Russians who
want to be like us. so why not get
sum of there dumb students over
here to learn stuff our way.
Then they will have democercy
and be TRUE AMERICANS
yors truely
Robert Nokkdonger III
(age 15)

The Providence Journal

Providence, Rhode Island, September 26, 1989

President Bush and the governors of all 50 states will be holding an unprecedented national summit meeting on education this week at the University of Virginia. The 'education President' is determined to make a difference.

As it happens, some observers are already complaining that history will remember this event more for its symbolism than its concrete accomplishments. That may very well be true — but it underestimates the importance of symbolism in such matters. The very fact that the summit is being held is a healthy sign of widespread consensus and concern. The American system of primary and secondary education is not performing up to expectations: We spend a greater proportion of our Gross National Product on education than any other major industrial country, yet our students' relative performance on cross-national tests is embarrassingly weak in virtually every field of study.

It isn't just a matter of youngsters at the bottom half of the academic rankings pulling down the overall achievement levels, dropping out at unacceptably high rates, and performing below par *even* when they do stay in attendance long enough to be granted a high school diploma. That is part of the problem, and by itself would be cause enough for serious concern.

But equally disturbing is the fact that many of our better students — those going on to post-secondary education — are conspicuously ill-prepared for the challenges they face. A recent nationwide survey by the Carnegie Foundation for the Advancement of Teaching found that nearly three-quarters of college faculty members believe their students lack the skills to do college-level work; and two-thirds think their institutions are spending too much time and money trying to teach undergraduates what they should have learned before entering college.

Should our institutions of higher learning, including the very best, be engaged in what amounts to remedial instruction? Are America's secondary schools seeking to impart the fundamental knowledge and skills necessary for gainful employment or advanced education? Is it possible that bachelors degrees are now being granted to people whose meager academic skills might not have sufficed to get them through high school decades ago?

The defects in our educational system are real and complex, and it would be implausible to expect concrete solutions to emerge from a two-day summit. But this event can have a beneficial effect if it helps accelerate the reform movement that has been developing over the past decade. Yes, some governors may attend simply because it will be an irresistible photo opportunity; but most participants can be expected to recognize the summit's value in keeping the spotlight on a problem that is seriously affecting our nation's political, economic and cultural well-being.

The Birmingham News

Birmingham, Alabama, September 25, 1989

There should be no doubt that President Bush is serious about wanting to improve public education in this nation. His convening of every governor in the nation this week to discuss what must be done to improve our schools is no public relations ploy. He is seeking answers that will put the country back on track academically.

But anyone who expects the myriad problems facing our schools to wither away after one such summit is being unrealistic. As Education Secretary Lauro Cavazos put it, this is just the beginning.

Every governor is expected to attend the two-day meeting at the University of Virginia. They will form six working groups that will separately discuss the following topics: teaching, learning environment, governance, choice and restructuring, a competitive work force and lifelong learning, and post-secondary education.

Bush will participate in each of the six working group sessions with 16 or 17 governors and five or six Cabinet members. Each working group will be co-chaired by a Republican governor and a Democratic governor.

A report will be prepared that the president and the governors will consider in plenary sessions.

The only educator that we know will be in attendance is Cavazos, a former college professor. But he pointed out that each governor may bring one aide and some may bring the heads of their education departments. In addition, the president has met with a number of educators prior to the meeting to get their input.

What is hoped for are some solutions that do not require additional funding. While there are school systems that need more money, including virtually every one in Alabama, in general money is not the most critical problem facing America's public schools.

The nation already spends $353 billion a year on education at all levels, from kindergarten through graduate school, including an average of more than $5,200 for every public school pupil.

What the president wants is to generate ideas to get the most out of the money being spent on education now. Those ideas will undergo development in meetings among educators and public officials to be held after the education summit in Virginia. A good, hard look at the school choice concept is expected.

We pray that the governors and President Bush are successful in devising some strategy to improve the current state of public education.

Nothing dramatic is expected to come out of their two-day meeting, but it should set the stage for more important revelations down the line.

THE LINCOLN STAR

Lincoln, Nebraska, September 27, 1989

Of what value is education?

Americans tend to value education for its very practical and financial benefits.

As individuals, we finish high school and get more training in order to get good jobs with good pay.

Businesses often value education for the trained workers it can supply, for the increased productivity those workers provide.

But Americans in general do not view learning with reverence. We do not value the learning itself; we value more its promise.

And a sustained discussion about that reverence for learning (or lack of it) probably will not be a major part of President Bush's Education Summit for governors that begins today.

The nation's governors are expected to deal with broad national goals and the practical problems public schools face.

THEY WILL TALK about the high school dropout problem, a tragedy at the individual level. Americans without high school degrees have little to look forward to but unemployment and poverty.

In fact, the correlation between high school dropouts and inmates of the nation's prisons is a trifle higher than the correlation between smoking and lung cancer.

They will talk about boosting the scores of students on international math and science tests in order to assure that the nation will continue its technologically superior status.

They will talk about national goals and standards, and they will talk about a Bush favorite — school choice, the popular idea that parents should be able to choose which public schools their children will attend. Nebraska will begin allowing school choice next year.

They may even talk about details — the myriad theories on the particulars of educational reform: more homework, fewer students in each class, better discipline, better teacher pay.

There are a few other important issues that governors ought to be thinking about as they look at American education.

THEY SHOULD BE concerned about equal access to education. Some school systems are much better funded than others and provide students with much better opportunities. That inequity should not exist.

Governors should look for ways to balance competing educational needs — to maintain high expectations and high standards while providing opportunities for all students to have success.

They should make certain that there is adequate funding for Head Start programs and pre-school nutrition programs, which make an amazing difference in the lives of children.

And in the discussion this week, the governors might look at the way they value education.

A nation that honors education for its intrinsic worth is more likely to produce more children eager to learn.

THE ARIZONA REPUBLIC

Phoenix, Arizona, September 26, 1989

IT would be difficult for any knowledgeable observer to hold out much hope that President Bush's "education summit" with the nation's governors this week will result in real progress toward improving public schools.

If an optimist is a pessimist who lacks experience, ample pessimism is warranted. Experience instructs that such a gathering undoubtedly will focus more on political mischief than on education reform. Nearly everyone involved admits that America's schools are failing, yet few are willing to embrace the radical changes that could bring significant progress.

In fact, more than six years after the landmark report "A Nation at Risk" warned that the "educational foundations of our society are presently being eroded by a rising tide of mediocrity," efforts to shore up America's academic footing have been half-hearted at best. Despite the talk of education reform, the fact remains that Johnny still cannot read, add or subtract or find his country on a world map.

Yet some slight hope has emerged that the president and the governors may be willing to do more than moan about money at their two-day confab that opens Wednesday in Charlottesville, Va. If the agenda is an indicator, some positive steps already may have been taken.

The White House and the National Governors Association have agreed to formulate a set of national education goals focusing on improving classroom achievement. These are expected to include boosting math and science scores of U.S. students on international tests, reducing the dropout rate, increasing college attendance and strengthening preschool programs.

These are familiar goals, but there is evidence that some fresh thoughts have emerged about how to attain them. A few progressive governors armed with innovative programs in their states — from school "choice" to teacher accountability — have begun to stem the education malaise. These should become working models for rebuilding the nation's failing school systems.

Fiscal concerns, of course, will come up. Those in search of another excuse to reach deeper into the taxpayers' pockets will use the conference to further the notion that more money is what is needed. The facts, however, belie the fiction that America is uncommitted to education. We spend more on schooling than any other nation, one-third more in real dollars than just a decade ago. The problem is not money, but how it is spent. On that point, it is plain that our children are being shortchanged.

The Washington Post

Washington, D.C., September 16, 1989

PREPARATIONS for the upcoming "education summit" in Charlottesville have taken an unexpected turn. Suddenly it appears possible, even likely, that President Bush and the governors will emerge from their meeting with a call for national educational targets or goals—what American students should know and how many of them should know it. Short of that, some governors have let it be known that they support setting other, less controversial goals—a high school completion rate of 90 percent by the year 2000, say, or less illiteracy at that old favorite, full funding of Head Start and Chapter 1 federal aid programs to disadvantaged students. Schools, of course, don't need the president to tell them that dropout rates should be lower, but the new focus on national goals and measurements is significant nonetheless. It represents the weakening of a long-standing and rather peculiar orthodoxy among American educators—the sanctity of local control of schools.

The idea of a nationally imposed curriculum in the European mode has always made educators skittish—not least because the choice of what kids will learn in school has profound political resonances, and people don't like having it dictated from without. But a nationally *suggested* curriculum is something else. The willingness of educators to endorse one—to say that 16,000 school districts need not reinvent the wheel every time they try to improve their schools—comes partly from a recent Gallup poll that showed Americans much more amenable to this idea than previously thought. Some of the impetus also comes from business leaders who would like to see *somebody* specify, preferably with their help, what the American high school graduate should be expected to know and be able to do.

The focus on results is also a reaction to the discovery by would-be reformers that once you've decided to improve your schools, it's hard to find tests to measure how well you are doing. The government collects bales of statistics on education, but until recently it has concentrated on such things as budget, faculty salaries, class size and numbers of students on federal aid rather than on accomplishment. The few widely used standardized tests, such as the ones that test reading at grade level, are old, intended to diagnose individual students' problems and unsuited to comparing larger groups. The far more comprehensive, federally funded National Assessment of Educational Progress is better—but until recently it was forbidden by law to be used in state-by-state comparisons. That's a measure of how much the political climate has changed since the law was written in the mid-1960s.

Calling for more measurement is a lot simpler than actually deciding what and how to measure. It also leaves open the important question of how to treat the results. Should schools that make progress toward national goals be rewarded with recognition and funding? Should laggards be penalized? Or will the mere presence of data be ample incentive? These are the tricky areas into which the president and the governors are now edging. They will want to go slowly.

DESERET·NEWS
Salt Lake City, Utah, September 26, 1989

Even before this week's education summit opens, President Bush deserves high marks just for having summoned the nation's governors to what can be a historic session.

More than just a step toward redeeming Bush's campaign pledge to become "the education president," the Sept. 27-28 summit should focus national attention on school problems and show the governors how various states are solving them.

What's more, the summit can help set reasonable goals for schools and loosen sometimes artificial and arbitrary restrictions on the use of federal funds for education.

Unhappily, there's also the risk that the summit can raise expectations too high. Keep in mind that the federal deficit is still discouragingly big and persistent. That limits President Bush's ability to promise major resources .to carry out education initiatives.

Consequently, some Utah educators were not being entirely realistic this week in asking Gov. Bangerter to seek at the summit more federal funding and increased local control. By all means, if Washington is going to mandate school programs not always wanted by various states, it ought to provide funds to help operate them. But keep in mind that more federal funds and more federal requirements are generally accompanied by more federal controls, not less.

Meanwhile, there's certainly no shortage of challenges facing the education summit. As a nation, we are spending a third more in real dollars on education today than we did a decade ago. What's more, many reforms have been made. Yet American students still lag behind their counterparts in other industrialized nations on virtually every international study, particularly in mathematics and science. America's schools are beset with drug and dropout problems unheard of in Japan, which graduates nearly all of its teenagers from high school.

The problems, however, are anything but insurmountable. South Carolina, for example, has succeeded in boosting its students' average scores on college entrance examinations by 46 points, an amazing turnaround. Arkansas now has the lowest dropout rate in the South. Schools in various other states have made impressive gains in keeping drugs and crime out of the schools.

What's their secret? Often it's not just more money but more effective use of funds and a dogged commitment from the top down to keep improving their schools.

By convening the first national summit on education, President Bush is demonstrating a commitment that could be a vital factor in the needed reform of America's schools. But whatever comes out of this week's summit, the ultimate responsibility for the future of those schools still resides at the state and local level.

The Oregonian
Portland, Oregon, September 27, 1989

Something is seriously wrong with education in the United States today. Studies show it. Parents know it. The education summit beginning Wednesday offers an opportunity to talk about what ails American schooling.

Bringing together the president and governors in Charlottesville, Va., should put the national spotlight on our education in a way not done since the the 1983 publication of "A Nation at Risk." It still belongs there.

But President Bush and the governors would do best to talk about education rather than the tempting topic of education funding. The facts are that the United States is spending far more in real dollars on education than in 1983 and more teachers are teaching fewer students than in earlier decades. Our nation spends much more than almost all other developed nations do in producing students that outscore ours.

The summit might succeed if the assembled seriously debate the basics of U.S. education:

How should our system of education be organized? Do our schools need a fundamental restructuring? If so, should that restructuring also include programs to involve parents more actively in the education of their children? What are the advantages and disadvantages of expanding school-choice programs in education? Should we move to some kind of national curriculum to promote cultural literacy?

Perhaps such a high-voltage, political affair will accomplish little more than expanded news coverage for educational issues.

Still, the governors at least will able to talk to one another about programs that work and that don't. What about New Jersey's alternative teacher-certification program of mentor teachers who watch over prospective teachers who do not have teacher-education degrees? Does it really lead more minorities and better-qualified instructors into teaching? What about Minnesota's program to allow high-school juniors and seniors to attend college classes? What has that meant for high schools' college-prep programs?

The summit will also provide governors a chance to tell Bush how the rules and regulations of his Education Department are stifling creativity and diversity in their states. It should allow Bush to recommit his administration to stripping away the red tape.

The Boston Globe
Boston, Massachusetts, September 23, 1989

The nation's 50 governors are to meet for two days of closed-door discussions with President Bush next week. It will be only the third such national summit meeting in 80 years, a fact that raises — perhaps unduly — the expectations for what may be accomplished.

The first national summit was convened by President Theodore Roosevelt in 1908 and dealt with conservation and environmental issues. The second was called by President Franklin Roosevelt to deal with the Depression.

This third summit appears a less-focused undertaking. Its subject matter is education, and with less than a week remaining before the president and the governors meet at the University of Virginia, there is no clear sense of what can be accomplished.

There is an agenda, but it is predictably composed of items that have been thoroughly chewed over in the six years since the publication of "A Nation at Risk": teacher training, parental choice, dropout prevention, math and science, and school environment.

Many governors, and the education community, hope that money — in the form of increased federal funding — will also be on the agenda, but that is not likely except in the negative form of "You can't solve problems just by throwing money at them."

Since it is a national summit, presided over by the president, it is reasonable to expect discussion of the federal role in education. The summit's gubernatorial co-leader, Bill Clinton of Arkansas, has called for "a national set of performance goals."

That discussion might well focus on *whether* there is any federal role in education, for that is where the summit threatens to come apart before it begins.

From long tradition, education in the US is not a state matter, let alone a federal matter. It is local. The basic funding is locally raised, augmented by state and (a few) federal dollars. Governance is almost totally local, under various degrees of state control — but almost no federal control. The same holds for curriculum, even after the recent imposition of statewide assessment tests.

The imposition of statewide standards means little if the ability to meet those standards varies from community to community. The dropout rate will be higher in a poor community, and the test scores lower, and the poor community has fewer resources with which to address the problem.

The same is true of the national standards that will be on the agenda. Not only will poor states have less ability to meet them than rich states, but the governance mechanisms differ so widely from state to state (even more than from community to community within each state) that uniformity of approach is virtually impossible.

Unless Bush and the governors want to overturn 300 years of American history and restructure the education system into a national rather than a local one, the best they can do at Charlottesville is to imbibe some of the inquiring spirit of the University of Virginia's founder, Thomas Jefferson.

History, Civics
Report Issued

American students had only a limited grasp of history and civics, according to a report issued April 2, 1990 by the National Assessment of Educational Progress (NAEP).

The report was the latest in a series of studies conducted by the NAEP, which had been mandated by Congress to test student achievement across the U.S. The tests were administered by the Educational Testing Service of Princeton, N.J., under a contract from the Education Department. Previous NAEP studies had examined student achievement in reading, writing and geography.

The latest report examined the results of two tests – one on history and the other on civics – that had been given to fourth-, eighth- and 12th-grade students in 1988. About 16,000 students across the U.S. had taken the history test, and 11,000 had taken the civics exam.

The results showed that students were better with facts and figures than with analyzing the meaning behind them, according to the NAEP. "It seems students know snippets of information, isolated names and dates, but not the implications of history," said Christopher T. Cross, an assistant secretary at the Education Department. "They are generally familiar with the basic structure of our government, but many do not understand the interactions and underpinnings of key parts of our system."

THE BLADE
Toledo, Ohio, April 10, 1990

THROUGHOUT history the reading of it has been a bore to many people, and this is particularly the case in an era when history frequently is learned through the distorted medium of semifictional TV docudramas.

The National Assessment of Educational Progress continues to put out disturbing data on students' performances. A survey of fourth, eighth, and 12th graders showed, for example, that 56 per cent of fourth graders knew the names of Columbus' ships but only 36 per cent knew why he sailed west in 1492. Among eighth graders 84 per cent knew that Abraham Lincoln was assassinated, but only 25 per cent knew that his avowed goal in the Civil War was to preserve the Union.

It is encouraging that students in many cases recall the names, faces, and dates that are important in history, but disturbing to find that so many of them are weak on the concepts. Without a strong conceptual understanding history becomes at best a kind of educational quiz and at worst a supreme bore.

A citizen should understand the meaning of the Fifth Amendment to the U.S. Constitution, which affords protection against self-incrimination. The duties and relationships of the three branches of government both at the state and federal level should be clearly understood. It would be well if students had at least a basic understanding of the parliamentary system, both the federal type as in Canada and the unitary type as in Britain.

Recall of facts, figures, dates, and historical names and events is important — something like learning the multiplication table. However, many students fall short in connecting events and interpreting their meaning. One reason they cannot do that is that history — in fact, book learning in other subjects, too — has little relevance to a generation hooked on video games and programs and obsessed by the need for immediate gratification. The joy and usefulness of reading is not always immediately apparent.

Schools have contributed to the problem by referring to the study of history, civics, and sometimes geography under the oxymoronic term "social science." Textbooks have been "dumbed" down — watered down — to the point where few read them unless compelled to. This has been done in part to guarantee that no state board of education, no matter how narrow-minded, will reject the books.

The failure on the part of young people to link the past with the present and find relevance in the connection is hardly new; it is just that the situation today, thanks in part to the "innovators" in education who go about proclaiming that words are dead and that pictures are everything, may well be worse than it has ever been.

The Honolulu Advertiser
Honolulu, Hawaii, April 9, 1990

By this time, everyone should be shocked but not surprised by a report that American kids are hazy on history, dim on democracy. We've had similar depressing notices about student performance in reading and writing, math and science, foreign languages and geography.

The National Assessment of Educational Progress — known popularly as the Nation's Report Card — found students have a passing familiarity with the facts of history and civics, but cannot apply what they've learned or draw conclusions that show understanding.

Some may laugh off kids' (and adults') inability to identify names, faces or dates. They could look it up — in theory, anyway. But ideas about democracy, freedom and civic responsibility aren't so simple.

For example, three-fourths of 8th graders identified Martin Luther King Jr.'s "I Have a Dream" speech, but fewer than half knew King insisted on non-violence. That bit of ignorance could have chilling repercussions in the inner city.

Is there a remedy for these endless bad reports? As Chester Finn Jr., chairman of the National Assessment's governing board, says, "Kids tend to learn that which they study, and they tend to learn it in rough proportion to the amount of time they spend studying it."

Last year, the U.S. Education Department increased federal funding for the National Assessment to provide more state-by-state comparisons and analyses. Aside from guaranteeing more damage to our national self-esteem, what's the use of all this scrutiny?

We have to hope our efforts at school reform will mean better performance by our kids. And we couldn't be sure we are getting better if we didn't know where we began, which on average is not the honor roll.

THE DAILY OKLAHOMAN
Oklahoma City, Oklahoma, April 9, 1990

THE American public has a right to be upset by a new report showing a "dismaying" lack of knowledge among students about civics and U.S. history.

Coming as it does amid intense debate over the status of the nation's schools and how to improve them, the report provides additional ammunition for critics who have contended that the present education system shortchanges our children. It raises disturbing new questions about the quality of the teaching and the structure of the schools.

The report was compiled from civics and American history tests given to fourth-, eighth- and 12-graders in 1988 by the National Assessment of Educational Progress.

An NAEP board member commented the test results seem to show a "Trivial Pursuit sort of familiarity with some of the key figures and dramatic events of our past." If so, the reason may be that civics and history are taught in a sort of fast-food approach. One education expert said many school systems try to squeeze all of U.S. history into 45 minutes a day in the 11th grade.

Traditionally many children show an aversion to learning history because they consider it dull. Good teachers — and there are some — can make history a living, breathing thing that should fascinate even the less-motivated pupils. Especially now, with monumental changes going on in the world, students should be gaining a thorough knowledge about their country and its democratic tradition.

Perhaps there has been too much emphasis on science and mathematics and the social studies like history, civics and geography have been slighted. If so it's time to correct the balance.

DESERET NEWS
Salt Lake City, Utah, April 4, 1990

Is there any field of learning in which America's schools are not falling down on the job?

In recent months, a series of nationwide tests conducted for the U.S. Department of Education has shown that American students don't know nearly as much as they should about science, mathematics, and geography.

Now the results are in from the very latest in this same series of tests, and the new findings are just as embarrassing as the old.

They show that American students are woefully ignorant of many of the rudiments of U.S. history and government. For example:

— Barely half of 12th-graders know that presidential candidates are nominated by national conventions, or that the Constitution guarantees religious freedom.

— Among younger students, 62 percent of eighth-graders apparently did not know that Congress makes laws. Nearly a third could not identify such historical figures as Benjamin Franklin or Abraham Lincoln. Only a quarter knew that Lincoln's main goal in the Civil War was to preserve the union.

— Though more than half of fourth-graders knew the names of Columbus' three ships, only 36 percent knew why the explorer sailed to America in the first place.

It's bad enough that American students aren't as aware of their own nation's heritage and government as foreign students often are of theirs.

What's worse is that the American students are learning much less than they need to know in order to be informed voters and effective citizens.

For this unhappy situation, there's plenty of blame to go around. The schools are to blame for using boring textbooks and unimaginative teaching techniques that rely too much on rote memorization and too little on the writing of thoughtful, analytical essays.

For their part, this nation's homes can be faulted for failing to pry Johnny and Jane away from the TV tube and insist that the youngsters get at their homework. In this latest nationwide test, like the previous ones, the best scores were achieved by students who spent less time watching television and more time doing homework.

Finally, these tests raise some disturbing questions.

With so many students flunking the tests of the U.S. Department of Education, why is it that so few flunk in their neighborhood schools? Are the DOE tests too hard? Or could it be that local school tests are too easy? Or does mere attendance matter more than learning? And shouldn't there be some relationship between the pay raises that teachers keep seeking and how much their students are learning?

Arkansas Gazette
Little Rock, Arkansas, April 4, 1990

American students are flunking history, according to the U.S. Education Department, which tested a batch of fourth-, eighth- and 12th-graders last year for the "Nation's Report Card," a continuing educational accounting system established by Congress more than 20 years ago.

The report says a third of the eighth-graders didn't know who Ben Franklin, Abraham Lincoln and Martin Luther King Jr. were.

Are we disappointed? Certainly. Surprised? Not really.

If our recollection serves us right, students have generally never been excited by American history. Nor, for that matter, by its companions in that nebulous category called "social studies" — civics and geography. (The new report card shows poor test results in civics, too; a previous report on geography had similar results.)

It may be neither the students', the teachers' or the parents' fault. Perhaps the real culprit is the curriculum design, which points to textbook writers. Too often, history studies are a tedious and disjointed presentation ... a hodgepodge of dates and names to be memorized with no apparent connection and no salient relevance to the lives of youth with gleams of eternity in their eyes.

Then, too, as time goes on, there is simply more to learn, so the sheer volume of information may be overwhelming to many young minds, though there is no way to stop the clock (nor would we suggest it if there were).

What remains to be seen is whether the poor showing in social studies will be repeated in the test results for math and science, two critical areas given the president's goal to be the world's pacesetter in those disciplines, come the next century. Both subjects are immediately and appreciably convertible to everyday application and the value of mastering them is unchallenged. We are keeping our fingers crossed that the eventual report card for math and science will relieve fears that education in America is failing.

As for history, textbook editors may need to restructure their materials so that historical information is dispensed in a story-telling fashion rather than the commonly terse and sterile form that is nearly guaranteed to bore.

Meanwhile, we're inclined to give it time, trusting that students will hold the subject in higher regard as they grow older. Perhaps history is something we don't appreciate until we have some of our own.

■

The report card on civics says one fourth of the eighth-graders tested thought the president is allowed to break the law. Wonder if the history of recent administrations had anything to do with that.

Chicago Defender

Chicago, Illinois,
April 5, 1990

The newest "Nation's Report Card" showed that African Americans and Hispanics 12th graders are closing the gap between their history and civics scores and those scores by whites. The test results were released recently by the National Assessment of Educational Progress group in Washington D.C.

Some observers might say, "So what? Who cares if a youth knows whether or not Dr. King was born before Harriet Tubman? What does it matter if a teen doesn't know if the U.S. Congress, Supreme Court, United Nations or Joints Chiefs of Staff have the authority to declare war?"

History and civics matter greatly because it give a student a better understanding of self and the time in which he or she is living. The subjects help a person to better comprehend how past occurrences impact the present. They also aid an individual in learning exactly how our government works and the limits of the powers of its officials.

Knowing what your rights are and the limitations of your leaders can sometimes be a matter of life and death. For example, when former President Richard Nixon wanted to extend the Vietnam War into Cambodia, a large number of Americans swamped their congressmen, White House staff and news media with protesting phone calls and letters. Thousands demonstrated against the move. As a result, the war was not escalated. The concerned citizens knew they had a right to protest. As a result, many American and Cambodian lives were spared.

Using education to develop a proper understanding of the history and laws of the land can help people conduct themselves in ways which may help avoid being abused by authorities. In other words, people don't have to depend on lawyers, judges or the judicial system for total protection. Education and awareness can permit individuals to participate in their own protection.

The minorities who took the national report card examination also sent a good message about the learning ability and academic recall of minority students: history and civics are not subjects that Blacks and Hispanic students need fear. Such a message can be applied to chemistry and mathematics. In fact, with proper study and application, minorities don't have to take a back seat to anyone.

Las Vegas Review-Journal

Las Vegas, Nevada, April 4, 1990

While U.S. colleges are restricting First Amendment rights (often to the cheers of students and faculty), American high school seniors are demonstrating they know very little about the history of this country or the laws that govern it.

Yes, the latest Nation's Report Card compiled by the National Assessment of Educational Progress is in, and it's bad.

The report, released this week, involved a multiple-choice and essay test administered to 16,000 American 12th-graders in 1988, during the height of the presidential campaign. Among the results:

— Fewer than 40 percent of seniors knew presidential candidates are chosen in national conventions.

— Only 14.5 percent knew the Supreme Court majority can strike down laws.

— 40 percent couldn't identify any differences between the U.S. and U.S.S.R.

— 22 percent thought U.S. courts could declare war.

— 80 percent didn't have the foggiest idea what the Reconstruction was.

— 41 percent didn't know the United States interred Japanese-Americans during World War II.

— 58 percent didn't know who Teddy Roosevelt was.

We could go on, but it only becomes more depressing. (You might take heart in the fact that 97 percent of the high school seniors knew defendants have the right to a lawyer, until you realize the kids have seen so many cop shows on TV that this particular fact sank in via osmosis.)

The results of the multiple-choice test were dismal, but the performance on essay questions was appalling. Most seniors (94 percent) knew Ronald Reagan was president in 1988 but only 19 percent could write a brief, intelligible essay on the powers of the president.

The lousy performance on the civics and history test was not unexpected. Survey after survey has shown American students are also largely ignorant of geography, mathematics and science and have poor reading and writing skills.

The crisis in American education continues unabated. Until school districts and state legislatures find the political will to enact real education reform, this situation won't change.

WALT HANDELSMAN FOR THE TIMES-PICAYUNE

...KIDS TODAY DON'T EVEN HAVE A BASIC KNOWLEDGE OF AMERICAN GOVERNMENT...

...I HAVE HALF A MIND TO WRITE TO PRESIDENT WHAT'S-HIS-NAME!...

NEWS

REPORT— STUDENTS FAIL IN CIVICS

FORT WORTH STAR-TELEGRAM

Fort Worth, Texas, April 9, 1990

All American high school graduates, whatever their age, have been exposed to the basic tools needed for responsible citizenship in a system of representative democracy.

Many of them — us — learned about the Bill of Rights and the Emancipation Proclamation and the reasons for the American Revolution and the Civil War and so forth and remember some of it.

Not all of them — us — use those lessons on a daily basis or even refer to them when called upon to make the serious decisions for which citizens in a democracy are responsible and for which some knowledge and perspective are necessary.

But there is a difference between having the knowledge and not using it, and not having it at all.

The latest in a series of dismal reports on the achievement of American students reveals that most eighth graders, and far too many of today's high school students, just plain do not know the history and civics lessons — the nuts and bolts of appreciation of America's past and present — that should give them the means to make intelligent choices.

As the chairman of the National Assessment Governing Board, which issues these report cards, points out, peoples the world around are struggling to attain the freedoms and political rights that are the essence of U.S. democracy, while our own children are not learning to appreciate the heritage that soon will be theirs to defend, to maintain, to improve or to let slip away.

This threatens a continued erosion of the democratic process here in the land that has so long been a beacon of liberty for the world. It is not enough that America produce its share of Nobel Prize scientists and mathematicians. America must also have a citizenry steeped in the "why" of the American experience and the "how" of its survival. It is as important for a laborer to know how modern America emerged, and how its institutions work, as it is for a college professor or a lawyer.

As worrisome as the overall "test" performance of U.S. students is, the breakdown by sociological divisions is even more troublesome.

It is not enough that a white student reared in a suburban setting leave school knowing the rudiments of American history and government. The minority student reared in an urban *barrio* must have the same understanding of our nation's past triumphs and failures. Otherwise, the minority student's future is sacrificed. He or she must have the same opportunity to lead, or to follow with discrimination about *who* leads, as the suburban white.

It is not entirely the schools' fault, for instance, that only 21 percent of minority high school students are up to speed about American history. Students learn that which is important to them. History and civics are "taught" to everyone; what is needed is the sense of importance necessary for learning and retaining the information, and that begins at home and is bolstered at school.

Poverty is an obstacle to learning. An unstable home life or social circumstances can pose serious obstacles. A child to whom the presence of neighborhood drug dealers or a lack of shoes constitutes reality will not see the value in learning about Abraham Lincoln or the role of political parties in a democracy.

But reducing the numbers of Americans beset by poverty, removing the hold of drug use on Americans and creating a more stable, secure society will require the participation of those same students. Not only will African-American, Hispanic and other minority citizens increasingly populate the work force in the next decades, so must they be full partners in establishing public policy.

Education remains the key, not only to the nation's economic survival in the 21st century, but also to its political and social survival. Our children — all children — must learn the three R's, but at the same time they must be taught the importance of learning where America has been in order to direct where it is going.

Otherwise the experiment in democracy is in serious jeopardy.

The Record

Hackensack, New Jersey, April 4, 1990

If there had been a question on the tests about the Teenage Mutant Ninja Turtles, the scores would have been higher. But the latest tests in the Nation's Report Card series only asked questions about history and civics. The results are frightening.

One-third of the eighth-graders tested could not identify Benjamin Franklin, Abraham Lincoln, or Martin Luther King Jr. Almost one-quarter thought the president was permitted to break the law. One-third of the high school seniors tested did not know the reason for the Bill of Rights.

"It is no coincidence that American children spend less time learning things than anybody in the industrial world," said Chester Finn Jr., head of the federal board that released the scores. He called for a top-to-bottom overhaul of poorly focused social studies programs and the expansion of the class day and year.

The test-givers found few students who could go beyond multiple-choice questions to write thoughtfully on issues. They couldn't explain the reasons for things.

P.S. The more television watched by the eighth- and twelfth-graders tested, the lower their scores. Maybe it's time to turn off the Turtles and start cracking the books.

THE INDIANAPOLIS NEWS

Indianapolis, Indiana, April 11, 1990

"Education," wrote Edward Everett, "is a better safeguard of liberty than a standing army."

If so, Congress ought to reconsider its proposed military cuts.

The latest dismal news on the nation's education front comes in the form of a recent report from the National Assessment Governing Board indicating that American youngsters may know a few historical facts, names and dates, but they have little grasp of this nation's history.

Some of the findings, according to the survey of 27,000 students in 1,000 public and private schools, show:

• Only half of all eighth-graders tested know the United States is a representative democracy.

• Just over a third know that Congress enacts laws.

• Although more than half of all fourth-graders can name Columbus' three ships, fewer than a third know why he sailed to America in the first place.

• Fewer than half of the eighth-graders surveyed knew that Martin Luther King Jr. endorsed non-violence.

• Although most high school seniors know it is illegal not to pay taxes, fewer than two-thirds know it is legal to organize a recall election, take part in a boycott or hunger strike or impeach legislators.

• Less than 40 percent of high school seniors know that presidential candidates are chosen at national political conventions, even though the survey was taken during the height of the 1988 presidential race.

"Freedom," warned Christopher Cross, assistant secretary of education for research, "is not ours by accident. In the end, our children and every generation of Americans must themselves take up the rights, the privilege and the responsibility of self-governance."

He added, "At a time when people across Eastern Europe are embracing the principles of democracy, our own youngsters, who stand less than a year away from voting booths, have as a group a tenuous grasp of the institutions and ideals that make freedom possible."

According to Chester Finn, chairman of the National Assessment Governing Board, fewer than half of all high school seniors attained a score of 300 on the history or civics survey — considered the level of adequate functioning for a citizen of the United States.

Mary Frances Berry, president-elect of the Organization of American Historians, says, "If the national assessment report is accurate, our high school graduates, on the whole, lack the kind of understanding of the nation's heritage that is necessary to be an informed citizen in a democracy."

Or the knowledge to preserve this democracy.

SAT Verbal
Scores Drop

The College Entrance Examination Board Aug. 28, 1990 released results of the Scholastic Aptitude Test. Although scores on the mathematics section of the test remained level, scores on the verbal section declined from 1989.

The SAT included two sections – verbal and math – each of which was scored on a scale that averaged from 200 to 800.

Although the national average on the mathematics section of the test had remained level at 476, the average score on the verbal section had fallen to 424 from 427, the lowest level in a decade.

The average verbal score for women was 419 (down two points from 1989), and for men 429 (down five points). In math, the average score for women was 455 (up one point), and for men 499 (down one point). Black students averaged 352 on the verbal section (up one point from 1989) and 385 on the math section (down one point). That compared with 442 (down four points) and 491 (unchanged) for white students on the verbal and math sections, respectively.

THE BLADE

Toledo, Ohio, August 31, 1990

IT USED to be that going to school in the fall was an act that primarily affected individuals — young ones mostly, who traded the magic summer world of the outdoors for a classroom full of desks and smelling of blackboard chalk. Learning went on, but seemed to have no cosmic significance to our future as a nation.

That was then. Now, though, the kids are streaming back to classes amid a continuing and seemingly unresolvable national debate about why U.S. schools are failing our youth. In Princeton, N.J., the College Board issued another grim verdict. The verbal skills of college-bound high school seniors, as measured by the Scholastic Aptitude Test, declined to 424 out of a possible 800, the lowest such score in a decade.

A lot of things could be read into those scores, but at the very least they show that American high-school students' skill levels are not improving. College Board president Donald Stewart warned that "reading could become a "lost art" unless students "pay less attention to video games and music videos." He might have lumped in mainstream television as well; other critics have.

So what else is there to do? Ohio is spending $7 billion for elementary and secondary schools in the current two-year budget. Large amounts of money have been thrown at the problem, and although money is needed in many districts, lack of financing is not the basic cause of educational failure.

Other factors can be singled out — breakdown of family life, the flight of middle-class whites to the suburbs, the lack of respect for teachers (and often teachers' lack of respect for their own profession), the bureaucratization of school systems, and the feeling that universal public education has had its day.

To that last point, a word is in order. There is a lot of talk about the need for freedom of choice, new educational options, and so on, but a real problem is the extent to which tax dollars are spent to undergird private and sectarian schools. In Ohio and elsewhere this has speeded up the trend toward public schools becoming the repository of minorities and the poor generally. Alternative schooling options benefit a minority, but to the detriment of the majority.

Much can be done to improve all schools. Teachers should be given more responsibility and power. Good students must be encouraged to become teachers and rewarded when they do well. More policy should be decided at the building level, including questions of class size, curriculum, and class assignments.

The lock on teacher certification by colleges of education should be smashed so that specialists in other fields could switch to teaching if they desire and if they show an aptitude and eagerness to do so.

Every country with a high educational performance level places great emphasis on schooling. Students work hard to master skills, and parents become involved. To the extent that American families fall short of that standard, one can continue to expect pessimistic reports along with the ringing of school bells every fall.

FORT WORTH
STAR-TELEGRAM

Fort Worth, Texas, August 29, 1990

No one is exempt from responsibility for this state's dismal showing on the most recent entries in a growing list of educational shortcomings registered by students in the public schools — not educators, not lawmakers and definitely not parents.

First came results of the 1989-90 Scholastic Aptitude Test taken by college-bound students — of which Texas should be ashamed — followed by a report issued by a national parents' organization that gave this state an "F" on its feeble education efforts.

Nationwide, the scores that students posted on the SAT showed a troubling three-point decline on the verbal portion — from 427 to 424 — while the average math score remained static at 476.

Neither of those marks is anything to boast about, and Texas students fared considerably worse than the national average, with a mean score of 413 on the verbal portion — down from 415 in 1989 — and 461 in math — down from 462. Only six states and the District of Columbia registered lower verbal scores than Texas. Only three were worse in math, and one had the same score as Texas.

It is not fair to compare Texas with Iowa — the state with the best scores on both portions (511 in verbal and 577 in math) — because only 5 percent of eligible students took the test in Iowa while 42 percent took it in Texas. But it is fair to compare Texas with states that tested a comparable percentage of students, and the results are disheartening.

Four other states had a test turnout of between 40 and 50 percent, and all four posted higher scores on both portions of the exam than Texas students did. In light of that, the "F" assessed Texas by the American Association of Parents and Children should not have come as a surprise.

The AAPC, a non-profit, independent research group, based its findings on parental involvement, participation in the Head Start program, student-teacher ratios, per-student spending, graduation rates and standardized test scores. Unfortunately, Texas was found lacking on all counts. The fact that five other states joined Texas on the failure list is of little comfort.

People of good intention in this state have been hammering for years on those same factors, only to have their protests fall on deaf ears. Can it be that the people responsible for this shameful situation — and that includes lazy educators, pinch-penny lawmakers and irresponsible parents — do not mind being humiliated?

Millions of Texas schoolchildren deserve much better from their elders.

The Phoenix Gazette

Phoenix, Arizona, August 29, 1990

Education reform is beginning to take on the characteristics of a bad national joke, with schools increasingly becoming fodder for comedians and cartoonists.

However, the high rate of illiteracy and difficulty with basic math and reading demonstrated even by high school graduates is no laughing matter. The continuing slide in college entrance scores is further evidence of the failure of the school reform movement begun almost a decade ago.

Nationally, average verbal scores on the Scholastic Aptitude Test have dropped to their lowest level in 10 years while math scores remained stagnant. Verbal scores are now equal to the worst levels since national averages were first compiled in 1971. SAT scores totaled 900 for the 1989-90 school year — 476 on the math section, 424 on the verbal, according to the College Board, a non-profit organization that provides the tests. The highest possible score is 800 on each section, or a combined 1,600.

In Arizona, the news is increasingly dismal. Although state scores are above the national norm, they are declining even more rapidly. SAT verbal scores fell by three points nationally and by seven points in Arizona, from 452 in 1989 to 445 in 1990. Nationally, math scores were the same this year as last, but in Arizona they declined three points, from 500 in 1989 to 497 in 1990.

Arizona SAT score declines are especially disturbing because the students taking the SAT tend to be those with the strongest academic backgrounds, applying to the nation's most selective colleges and scholarship programs. The usual excuse of blaming disappointing results on poor and minority students won't work.

A testing official blamed the national slide on students watching music videos and playing video games instead of reading. No doubt youngsters spend too much time at the tube, but the explanation is incomplete.

The same official came closest to the truth when he blamed poor verbal scores on parents and schools. "The requirement to read through homework has been reduced. Students don't read as much because they don't have to read as much," said College Board president Donald M. Stewart.

Stewart's assessment is a sad comment on the so-called school reform movement. It indicates that high expectations, universally recognized as a prerequisite to improvement, are as lacking as the skills the test is supposed to measure.

Parents are remiss for not monitoring television and reading habits and perhaps for assuming that education is self-correcting. Experience indicates that schools respond to the same incentives that drive the rest of the economy. Until jobs and paychecks depend upon schools and children succeeding, improvement will remain elusive.

Sadly, there is growing evidence to suggest that increasing spending simply perpetuates the failed systems that created the problem.

Portland Press Herald

Portland, Maine, August 30, 1990

● SAT scores continue to decline both nationally and in Maine.

The news on the education front is not promising. Despite years of talk about making a fresh commitment to improving schooling in America, one of the standard measures of progress in that area suggests that there has been little progress at all. Indeed, we seem to be slipping backward.

For the third year in a row, Scholastic Aptitude Test scores, used for college entrance, show a decline, both nationally and here in Maine. In fact, Maine has again dropped below the national average on the student SAT scores.

Average scores on the verbal section of the test fell three points to 424 nationally, but they fell eight points to 423 in Maine. On the math side scores averaged 476 nationally — unchanged from last year — but dropped three points to 463 in Maine.

Donald M. Stewart, president of the College Board, which administers the SATs, places the blame for poor scores on both schools and parents. Neither, he says, demands enough from our kids.

"The requirement to read through homework has been reduced," he complains. "Students don't read as much because they don't have to read as much." And parents are careless about letting their children spend more time playing video games than reading books.

America has no more important obligation than providing kids with a solid education. But parents have to demand it if schools are to supply it. It may be that we have spent too much time just talking about it.

The Washington Post

Washington, D.C., August 31, 1990

THE PRESIDENT of the College Board, which sponsors the Scholastic Aptitude Test, was moved this year by the continuing fall in national verbal SAT scores to lament that "reading is in danger of becoming a lost art" among American students. The scores are becoming an all too dependably gloomy indicator within the narrow slice of the American educational scene that they reflect—college-bound seniors who take the optional test as part of college admissions requirements. The SAT measures only certain skills; it reflects changes in school quality only over many years; and, historically, it has also reflected income differences from locality to locality and from school to school, which, of course, also have a great impact on those schools' quality. That unfortunate pattern is borne out in this region, where the more affluent suburbs have higher average scores and the District's public schools tend to trail.

In the 1989-90 results, the District's scores went *up* for the second straight year. But for the second straight year, that increase came entirely from private schools, while the public school system saw declines despite concerted efforts to teach these skills—including special after-school sessions for the strongest students. (We note, again, that The Washington Post Co. owns a coaching service, Stanley Kaplan, which prepares students for the SAT.)

Nationally, the math score stayed static at an unimpressive 476 points on the 200-to-800 scale, and the verbal test dropped three points to 424. That combined score of 900 is still well above the District's 850—or the D.C. public schools' 707—but it is pretty low for a nation that has been talking about school reform, and loudly, since the current crop of test-takers was in sixth grade.

You can hear frustration at this continued slump in the statement released with the scores by College Board President Donald Stewart. He pointed to another, more broad-based study—done under auspices of the National Assessment of Educational Progress—that asked students how much time they spent on reading every day (more than half said 10 pages or fewer) and how much time they spent every day watching TV or music videos (more than half said at least three hours). "Maybe we ought to give a video SAT," a disgruntled Virginia schools official told a Post reporter.

You can hear the same frustration in the tendency of national spokesmen to abandon the slow, even imperceptible work being done system-by-system and school-by-school and to turn instead to grandiose schemes for overhauling the way education is structured. But broad issues of school governance aren't what show up on tests like the NAEP and the SAT. What shows up there is skills—ordinary, straightforward, old-fashioned—and if the more affluent schools are the ones that succeed at teaching those skills, this at least shows it can be done. Everyone has been saying since 1983 that it's going to be a long, slow process. The lack of results is no excuse for not following through now that the going's gotten tough.

LAS VEGAS REVIEW-JOURNAL

Las Vegas, Nevada, August 26, 1990

The sight, shown last week on TV, of Iraqi leader Saddam Hussein laughing and grinning as he exhibited Western hostages, including young children, was sickening. That Saddam has taken to hiding behind a human aegis is despicable.

Americans are justifiably angry at the contemptible behavior of the Iraqi president. What is not justified is the reaction of a small minority of Americans that has decided the conflict in the Middle East is license to harass and threaten Arabs, Arab-Americans and people of Middle Eastern descent in this country.

Consider these examples:

— According to Jack G. Shaheen, a professor at the University of Southern Illinois-Edwardsville, an American of Arab descent was interviewed by a newspaper about the situation in the Middle East and later received a letter threatening his life.

— A caller vowed to kill the editor of Arab-American newspaper in Detroit if Americans in Kuwait are harmed, according to Shaheen. The editor is an American citizen.

— Closer to home, an R-J editor watched a customer at a Las Vegas filling station berate the Arabic-looking attendant over the Middle East conflict.

These instances of bigotry, while isolated, are as deplorable as Saddam's treatment of Western citizens stranded in Iraq and Kuwait. Americans must resist the irrational urge to take out their anger on the 2.5 million Arab-Americans and the thousands of Arab students studying in this country. To do so is to embrace an ugly notion of collective guilt.

Americans of Arabic descent are individuals and U.S. citizens and deserve to be treated as such, not lumped in with the likes of Saddam. And Arab nationals in the U.S. should be treated with respect and hospitality.

Anything less and Americans will have stooped to Saddam's level.

The Clarion-Ledger

Jackson, Mississippi, August 29, 1990

Two reports in the news regarding education should serve as a "wake up" call for parents.

The first shows Scholastic Aptitude Test scores nationwide sank for a third year in a row, spurring fears that reading may become "a lost art."

The second is a report card by the American Association of Parents and Children prepared after an earlier study found nine out of 10 teachers think parents don't care about education. Mississippi got a "D."

The group graded states in six broad areas: parental apathy, Head Start participation, student-teacher ratios, per-student spending, graduation rates and standardized test scores. But it concluded that the key to improving scores was parental involvement.

"It's a disastrous message to create the impression with parents that when you look at the national education crisis, the only people who need to be concerned are teachers and school administrators and state lawmakers," said the group's executive director, Scott Stapf.

"Unless you create a picture that includes parents in the equation as well, you're really missing a big part," he said.

The falling SAT scores should underscore that. Sure, there are more single parents than a decade before, more families where both parents work, and more diversions to keep children from reading, like video games and movies.

But if we want a nation that is literate and able to compete in the world of ideas with other nations, our children must read. Parents must enforce at home what children are taught at school. Learning is a full-time job.

The Mississippi's BEST education reform plan passed by the Legislature but left unfunded would have addressed some of the concerns raised by the report card. But without parents taking an active role in supporting education at home, only half the battle against ignorance is waged.

IF YOU'RE EIGHTEEN AND CAN READ THIS YOU MUST BE JAPANESE.

THE INDIANAPOLIS NEWS

Indianapolis, Indiana, August 29, 1990

Despite a huge influx of money and a rash of educational reforms across the nation, dismal Scholastic Aptitude Test scores, both nationally and in Indiana, suggest that the tide of mediocrity is still on the rise.

Nationwide, SAT scores earned by high school students who are considering going to college declined to their lowest level in a decade on verbal examinations and remained steady for the third straight year on the math portion of the test.

Indiana SAT scores generally followed that pattern, with a four-point drop in verbal test scores and unchanged math results. The state's combined math and verbal score of 867 is substantially below the national average combined SAT score of 900. Indiana's combined math and verbal score is also lower than the score in every other state tested, except Georgia, North Carolina and South Carolina.

Since the percentage of students who take the test varies from school to school and from year to year, the SAT examination is an imperfect indicator of educational achievement. Other tests and educational surveys, however, tend to confirm its general pattern of declining student achievement.

In fairness, it also must be said that current educational reforms aren't necessarily reflected on these tests of upper-level high school students. It will take more time to see if recent efforts, such as Indiana's Operation Prime Time or its A-Plus program, will bear fruit.

It may be a case of passing the buck, but educators see a lack of concern among students and parents about educational achievement as a major stumbling block to improvement.

"Students must pay less attention to video games and music videos and begin to read more," warns College Board President Donald M. Stewart, who added that reading could soon become a "lost art."

Frank L. Tout, principal of Howe High School, also notes that high school students are spending too much time working. He said a survey of Howe seniors taken a couple of months ago indicates that three-fourths of all Howe seniors are working an average of 23 hours or more a week.

"That just boggles our minds," he said. "That's just that much less time spent on studying."

The rising tide of educational mediocrity threatens to drown this nation over the next generation if something isn't done to stop it.

This country is in danger of becoming a nation of Bart Simpsons — and not being ashamed of it.

The Hutchinson News

Hutchinson, Kansas, August 29, 1990

The growing illiteracy among the nation's young people didn't just happens in the sort of vacuum that exists in too many young brains these days.

It happened because those who should be stretching the kids' minds have given up the fight.

The national College Board reported the year's Scholastic Aptitude Test scores the other day. The results were dismal.

They have been dismal for years, but the record now shows that the latest batch of American students has reached the lowest level in a decade, equal to the worst levels since national averages were first taken nearly 20 years ago.

The experts said the kids are watching music video and playing video games instead of reading. What the experts didn't say, and should be said, is that if anybody really cares, nobody is doing much about it.

The decline occurred in all categories, among all types of students, and in a way that is not only appalling, but a far greater threat to the American way of life than Saddam Hussein ever will be.

There is no easy fix in fighting illiteracy and ignorance, no matter how much an educational establishment or an indifferent home life may suggest. The fight against illiteracy and ignorance is a lifelong event, and it takes more than a share of mental pain and anguish.

After all these years, and all the national studies about an educational system that has failed, and fails now to suppress the natural forces of ignorance by replacing ignorance with knowledge, why are illiteracy and ignorance winning?

The answer lies partly in an educational system that has failed to restructure itself to correct its problems, but also in homes where the suppression of ignorance and illiteracy has taken a back seat to entertainment.

The year's SAT scores should sound the alarm, once again, about the failures both at home and in the classroom. But can anyone hear the alarms when the music is so loud on the tube in the living room?

The Providence Journal

Providence, Rhode Island, August 31, 1990

School test scores don't tell everything about student academic performance but they tell a lot. The latest news is disappointing: Verbal skills of American high-school seniors taking the Scholastic Aptitude Test have slipped for the fourth straight year, to their lowest level in a decade. Rhode Island scores are even gloomier, with a combined average SAT score (verbal and mathematics) 17 points lower than the national average.

This decline is worrisome. It suggests that students and schools alike are putting less emphasis on reading and other basic language skills. Since 1967, national scores on the SAT verbal test have slid 42 points, from 466 (out of a possible 800) to this year's 424.

For several years, declining SAT scores could be partly explained by noting that more seniors, including some of lesser ability, were taking the test. But this reason no longer applies: The share of seniors taking the Scholastic Aptitude Test has held nearly constant at 40 percent.

Verbal scores have slipped, many education experts agree, because reading and vocabulary-building are receiving less stress than in previous years, and because many textbooks and high school curricula are being watered down. Electronic distractions don't help: Donald Stewart, president of the College Board, which administers the SAT, blames declining test scores partly on a preoccupation with television and video games.

To be sure, the SAT results are not all bleak. Mathematics scores, at least, did not decline; women and minority students showed improvement in both the verbal and math tests. On the math test, in fact, women registered their highest average in 14 years.

Even so, the verbal decline hurts. If American students continue to weaken in their ability to read and write, their own futures will be the poorer. The goal of an educated nation, capable of understanding its rich heritage and attuned to the challenges of its future, will be weakened. Our schools are not doing their job unless they work harder at teaching the basics of reading and writing, and exposing pupils to literature. Our curriculum planners and textbook editors are doing no one a service by diluting their products. And parents do no one a favor, least of all their children, by letting evening television shut out homework.

America is alive with talk of school reform, which is encouraging; but the rhetoric will do little good unless pupils begin to show improved abilities by the time they graduate. Results count. More than ever, reading and writing are fundamental.

THE ASHEVILLE CITIZEN
Asheville, North Carolina, August 29, 1990

Educators warn against reading too much into average scores on the Scholastic Aptitude Test, and their warnings hold substance. Incremental changes in SAT scores from one year to the next tell us as much about education and the performance of particular schools and groups of students as daily fluctuations in the Dow Jones average tell us about the economy and the strength of specific companies.

But SAT scores do serve as a general index to how schools are doing. The long-term trend is what matters, and the trend isn't good. With few exceptions, it got no better in the school year that ended three months ago.

Average scores nationally were down; average scores in North Carolina were up.

To speak of a "national" average in the context of SAT scores is misleading. Only 22 states use the SAT predominantly. The other 28 mostly use a similar exam, the American College Test. Some students take both.

Not every student graduating from high school in those 22 states takes the SAT. Only students with an interest in going to college take it, and the percentage varies widely from state to state. The percentage of students taking it has much bearing on average scores in a state, and on small changes in average scores from year to year.

> Our education system may need structural reform ... but that is not the fundamental problem. In the absence of rigor, neither will it help much.

Take all that into account, and the news still isn't good. Except for a brief rise in the early 1980s, national scores have been going down for 20 years. Scores this year fell another 3 points, with all of the loss coming on the verbal portion of the test. Math scores remained unchanged.

Within that overall grim picture, you can pick out a few points of light. Women students make slow but steady gains. American Indians and blacks have improved their scores dramatically over the past decade, although they still lag other students.

Educators can make whatever excuses they will, but that is not the picture of an education system on the mend. The state of American education grows steadily worse.

North Carolina remains at the bottom of the worst. For years average scores in our state have ranked 49th. Last year they slipped just enough (and South Carolina's gained just enough) to drop us to 50th. This year the seesaw tipped the other way, and we edged ahead of South Carolina to regain 49th.

Average scores in North Carolina gained 5 points. Some of that represents real improvement. Some of it comes from coaching and "teaching the test." North Carolina scores remain about 60 points below the national average, which itself is abysmal.

It is our better students who do poorly on the SAT, in comparison to their peers in other states. North Carolina students from deprived and modest backgrounds score about as well as similar students nationally. North Carolina students from well-educated and high-income families score about 60 points below comparable students nationally.

Parents and schools simply do not push students enough. That is true nationwide; it is especially true in North Carolina. We demand too little of all students. Most of all, we demand too little of our best and brightest.

In North Carolina, fewer college-bound students take physics, pre-calculus, advanced English and the other courses that enable students to do well. American parents and schools let students slack off. In North Carolina, we let them slack off even more.

Our education system may need structural reform — changes in the way it is organized and managed — but that is not the fundamental problem. In the absence of rigor, neither will it help much.

Schools simply have to get tougher: strengthen the curriculum at every level, from first grade on; bring students along at a faster pace; and demand more work from them.

Why is it that most European students go to school 210 days a year, while American students gripe about being in school 180 days? Why is it that the average European student does three hours of homework a night, while the average American student does hardly any? Why is it that European students take advanced geometry and algebra in the seventh and eighth grades, while American students get them in the 11th and 12th grades, if at all?

It's because we're lazy.

And our schools will not get much better unless we become less lazy.

Omaha World-Herald
Omaha, Nebraska, August 29, 1990

What a downer. The country has spent much of the past seven years in debate about improving learning in the schools. Now the 1990 results of the Scholastic Aptitude Test suggest that some students are learning less instead of more.

The overall SAT score was down for the third year in a row. It was pulled down by verbal marks that ranked with those of 1980 and 1981, the worst on record. Donald M. Stewart, who heads the organization that conducts the test, said the problem is too little reading.

"The requirement to read through homework has been reduced," he said. "Students don't read as much because they don't have to read as much."

That might come as a surprise to the public. Haven't officials and educators been saying that the schools raised standards after a 1983 presidential commission warned of a rising tide of mediocrity in American education?

If Stewart's views of reading and homework are accurate, momentum has been lost.

A few bright spots need to be acknowledged. Nationwide, the scores of black and American Indian students continued to improve. Women's math scores reached their highest level in 16 years.

But the overall picture is alarming. The SAT is required for admission to some of the nation's more academically rigorous colleges and universities. If reading ability is declining among the students who are applying to those colleges and universities, what must be happening in the middle and the bottom of the student body?

In the past, some people have attempted to make excuses. More students beneath the top academic ranks are taking the test, they said, which makes it inevitable that average scores would drop.

But this year the number of test-takers was stable. Lynn Cheney, chairman of the National Endowment for the Humanities, said: "We can no longer get away with saying scores are going down because the number of kids taking the SAT is going up." She blames "textbooks that are still dumbed-down, teachers that are not as prepared as they should be and curricula that are not as demanding as they should be."

It isn't only the SAT that raises concern. Stewart said the new scores are the second recent indication that "the verbal skills of many American students are weak enough to seriously hamper their future opportunities, in school and college and the world of work." An earlier National Assessment of Educational Progress study suggested that students at all grade levels spend less time reading and writing and that few students can analyze or understand the full meaning of what they read.

Another study has indicated that fewer than two-thirds of the white students, and a lower percentage of Hispanics and blacks, are proficient readers by the age of 13.

Stewart blamed television and video games. Research for the U.S. Department of Education indicated that kids who watch more than six hours of television a week scored 10 percent lower on a writing test than kids whose TV-watching didn't exceed two hours a week.

The ability to read, and the importance of reading, appears to be taken for granted in some schools — and, even more tragically, in some households. Some parents not only don't read to their kids — they don't even talk to them. Syndicated columnist George Will, in a Newsweek column last spring, wrote about young mothers who are too self-absorbed to talk with their infants and toddlers, thereby withholding the stimulation that is essential to verbal and intellectual development.

Once those intellectually underdeveloped kids reach school, a clinical psychiatrist told Will, it is too late to catch up.

How sad it is to contemplate a family where the joys of a bedtime story, or the excitement of reading together, are unknown. How much sadder to know that young men and women are being sent every day into the world unprepared to compete, never realizing how much they are missing.

THE DENVER POST

Denver, Colorado, August 29, 1990

CRITICS OF the nation's educational system like to cite the results of the annual Scholastic Aptitude Test as evidence that the public schools just aren't measuring up.

In truth, however, it's risky to argue that the latest decline in the average verbal score — or, for that matter, the lack of improvement in the math portion of the SAT — indicates that anything is basically wrong with the schools.

For one thing, the proportion of high school seniors taking the SAT and the other major college-entrance test, the American College Testing exam, has been going up in recent years. This has naturally caused the average scores to drop, as the high achievers have been offset by the less well-prepared.

What's more, the tests aren't really designed to measure how well students are learning what the schools are teaching. They were created primarily to predict how well individual students will perform in college — and along with high school grades, they still appear to fulfill this function pretty well.

If it's important to know how well students in general are prepared for life as citizens and productive members of society, as the reformers often argue, surely a standardized test could be developed to measure these skills. It might even be designed to gauge common sense, perceptual abilities and other areas of competence that are largely ignored on academic exams.

But it's unwise and unfair to expect the SAT and its counterparts to serve as intellectual yardsticks for the entire younger generation. The population of test-takers is too limited, and too variable from year to year, to justify such all-encompassing judgments.

Birmingham Post-Herald

Birmingham, Alabama, August 31, 1990

Schools' most elementary task is teaching language — reading, writing and speaking.

So the news that the average verbal SAT score has declined again, for the fourth straight year, and is now as low as it has ever been (424 out of 800) should be lighting a fire under parents and principals across America.

Granted, the SAT — a standardized test taken by many college-bound high school students — is only one indicator of verbal skills.

But others confirm the dismal state of affairs: Employers and college teachers loudly complain that young people coming out of our high schools write and speak without clarity and never read books.

Please note, too: The usual excuses for lower SAT scores do not explain away the current decline.

Neither the weaker performance of minorities nor an increasing number of high school students aspiring to college and, thus, taking the test accounts for this embarrassment.

White students' mean SAT scores declined nine points from 1976 to 1990 — while blacks' and Mexican Americans' rose, by 20 points and 9 points respectively. The share of seniors taking the SAT nationwide was stable this year, about 40 percent.

In Alabama, the percentage of students taking the SAT is much smaller — 8 percent in 1990 — because a second test for college-bound students, the ACT, is preferred by more colleges and universities in this region.

The group of students taking the SAT in Alabama tends to be composed of the state's better students because they are the ones most likely to be considering a university outside the region that requires the SAT. As a result Alabama's average SAT scores are usually above the national averages.

But not even this group resisted the downward trend in SAT scores. The average verbal score in Alabama in 1989 was 482; it dropped to 470 this year.

Adults interested in their young people's future — starting with the ability to make a favorable impression in job interviews and on college applications — should not waste their energy denying that this educational deficit exists. They should take action. There are simple steps every willing parent can take.

At home, parents — even weary single parents — must make conscious efforts to talk to their children and listen to them. This matters enormously, from infancy on.

Adults must read to children — all the better if it means turning off the television and the video games. The government's National Assessment of Educational Progress reports that students spend three hours a day watching TV — but do little reading and writing.

Parents' next job is to march down to their children's school and ask the principal what the school plans to do to give language the priority it deserves.

Principals must be put on the spot. Will children write every day, from first grade on? Will they be taught grammar? Will their papers be corrected? Will they have written homework every night? Reading? Summer reading?

If not, why on earth not?

Roanoke Times & World-News

Roanoke, Virginia, August 31, 1990

NATIONAL scores on the Scholastic Aptitude Test are becoming a surer bet than stocks. They keep falling — three years in a row now.

When you play the stock market, you try to buy low in hopes values will rise. Taxpayers spend more billions on education every year. When does this investment begin to appreciate?

If one looks only at the mathematics score, there's some small consolation. These averaged 476 nationally, unchanged for the fourth consecutive year.

The overall score was dragged down by a continuing decline on the verbal part of the test. Those averages fell during the 1989-90 school year to 424, the lowest since 1980 and equal to the lowest levels since annual averages first were compiled in 1971.

Each test is scored on a scale of 200 to 800. Virginia students did worse than the national average on math, 470, and better on verbal, 425. But on both, their scores declined from the preceding year.

In Virginia, 58 percent of high-school seniors were tested; the national average is 40 percent. The College Board, which administers the SATs, says scores drop when more students take the tests.

Educators may take whatever comfort they can from that; parents and taxpayers will not find much.

Noting the slide in verbal scores, College Board President Donald M. Stewart says: "Reading is in danger of becoming a lost art . . . and that would be a national tragedy." The art won't be lost. But already, tens of millions of Americans are functionally illiterate. If trends continue, proportionately fewer of our youth will be able to read on more than a rudimentary level.

That means fewer will have the skills to seek and apply for jobs, let alone fill them. It means shrunken opportunities for economic advancement and improvement in quality of life. A labor force that lacks elementary abilities such as reading is unqualified to fill the kind of positions most in demand in a technologically oriented society. That affects everyone else.

Poverty in reading ability also inhibits ability to understand and debate public issues. It means an electorate more readily led by appeals to emotion and by arguments reduced to simplistic terms and television ads. It means a severe setback to the functioning of democratic institutions.

Americans have always prized education, especially as a ladder up from low-level jobs. We still put much faith in education's ability to increase useful knowledge, consciousness and ability to cope. We undergird that faith, as we should, with our tax dollars. We are entitled to ask why those dollars are not buying a better level of education for everyone.

Bennett Issues School Critique

Secretary of Education William J. Bennett declared in a report released to the press April 24, 1988 that the U.S. educational system was "still at risk" despite five years of improvement.

The report, officially presented to President Ronald Reagan April 26, was intended as an evaluation of the nation's schools on the fifth anniversary of "A Nation at Risk," the landmark 1983 report published by the government's National Commission on Excellence in Education. That report had painted a bleak picture of the state of the American educational system and had spurred a national reform movement.

Bennett's report, titled "American Education: Making It Work," asserted that "undeniable progress" had been made over the previous five years to boost academic standards and student achievement. "We are doing better than we were in 1983," the report said. "But we are certainly not doing well enough, and we are not doing well enough fast enough. We are still at risk."

St. Petersburg Times

St. Petersburg, Florida, September 12, 1990

In 1983 the National Commission on Excellence in Education sparked controversy with the report, "A Nation at Risk." That September the Carnegie Foundation for the Advancement of Teaching released its critical assessment, "High School: A Report on Secondary Education in America." Since then, parents, teachers and policy-makers have been treated to a torrent of critiques, assessments and recommendations about public schools.

Where do we stand now? Mixed results emerged from a 1988 follow-up survey by the Carnegie Foundation, "Report Card on School Reform: The Teachers Speak." A majority of teachers said their schools had successfully implemented certain Carnegie recommendations, such as defining school goals and setting higher expectations for students. Two-thirds of the 13,500 teachers surveyed said their students had improved in mathematics, reading and writing. The original Carnegie study had recommended that language skills be given reform priority.

In the rush to raise standards, however, some schools may have unwittingly shifted the emphasis from quality to quantity. While 45 states have overhauled high school graduation requirements over the last five years, the Carnegie follow-up survey included this caution:

"These are impressive gains, but rejoicing should be muted. Curriculum reform has been more quantitative than creative, and there has been a disturbing tendency to focus on course labels, rather than on content. In most schools, the K-12 curriculum still lacks clarity and coherence."

And further:

"Raising course requirements, without providing support, is especially harmful to disadvantaged students. Indeed, despite the reforms of the past half-decade, high dropout rates persist in most inner-city schools."

Sixty-three percent of teachers reported an increased emphasis on testing, but again, more is not always better.

The Carnegie survey noted "a good beginning" for efforts to make school schedules and calendars more flexible, and to reach more students by improving programs for the gifted, the disadvantaged, preschoolers and latchkey children.

At the same time: "Today's young people often have few positive relationships with adults, and many students, especially those in urban schools, drop out because no one noticed that they had, in fact, enrolled."

Nationwide, teacher salaries have increased by roughly 40 percent since 1983. The increase has been particularly dramatic in Florida. Florida teachers ranked 34th on the national pay scale during the 1982-83 academic year, earning an average of $18,353. Last year Florida teachers earned an average of $25,198, 29th on the scale.

Yet according to the Carnegie report, working conditions have deteriorated in some schools. Significant percentages of the teachers reported larger classes, less preparation time and/or less time to spend with colleagues than five years ago. "On these issues," the report concludes, "we believe the reform movement deserves a failing grade." The 13,500 teachers gave school reform a "C."

President Reagan was pushing to dismantle the Education Department in the early 1980s, claiming that federal involvement in public education had lowered school standards. Most observers found that logic hard to swallow, particularly after "A Nation at Risk" was published. Yet while state governments began appropriating more dollars for local schools, the Reagan administration slowly but systematically withdrew federal support. Over the last eight years, the federal share of school support has fallen from more than 9 percent to 6 percent.

A 1988 Gallup poll for the National Education Association found that voters regard quality education as the No. 1 election-year issue, more urgent than the drug problem, the federal deficit or economic competition from overseas. Apparently, most voters have not been fooled by the halfhearted, superficial reform proposals touted by outgoing Education Secretary William Bennett.

Americans want an education system they can be proud of. They want schools that can be trusted to prepare all children for a 21st-century world, regardless of an individual child's social or economic background. That task will require a cold, hard look at today's curriculum, expanded social programs for students and, of course, additional money. State and local governments have struggled for five years to meet the challenge alone.

Come November, voters will select new federal partners in the effort to craft meaningful educational reforms. Without strong allies in Washington, our schools will remain "at risk."

THE INDIANAPOLIS NEWS
Indianapolis, Indiana, April 7, 1990

A high-ranking government official recently excoriated the country's public school system. It is underfinanced, he said, and has become a bureaucratic nightmare that is failing to provide a proper foundation for the pursuit of higher education.

The latest Carnegie Foundation report, perhaps, or "A Nation at Risk, Part II"?

Nyet.

The speaker was Yegor K. Ligachev, the number-two man in the Soviet Union's Communist Party, and the school system he was lamenting was the U.S.S.R.'s, not that of the United States.

On opposite sides of the world with ideologies to match, the Soviets and the Americans are nonetheless struggling with many of the same problems in educating the next generations.

Ligachev, known in the past for his resistance to social and economic change, advocated greater support and reorganization of Soviet schools in a speech before the party's Central Committee. He criticized the Soviet Union's practice of forcing every school to teach the same material on the same day and called for more local control of schools. To illustrate sagging competency at the university level, he cited an engineering school where 70 percent of the students could not pass a mathematics test.

Although Ligachev recognized that the Soviet Union was reversing the steady decline in the percentage of the national budget allocated to education, he predicted that even more would be needed to correct the abysmal physical conditions of the country's schools. About 40 percent lack indoor toilets; 30 percent, running water; and 21 percent, central heating.

Ironically, a Carnegie report issued last week on U.S. urban schools echoed Ligachev's criticisms. Many of these inner-city districts have become stifling bureaucracies, the report charged, where unmotivated students languish in crumbling schools. Among other changes, the report urged greater autonomy for teachers and principals and the upgrading of facilities.

Not all aspects of educational reform in the two nations are parallel, of course. While U.S. reformers are seeking to better prepare students to become thoughtful participants in the democratic process, the Soviets — Ligachev included — insist that the Communist ideology remain at the heart of Russian education.

Still, as each successive report paints a grimmer portrait of U.S. public education, there's some small comfort in knowing Americans are not struggling alone.

THE DAILY OKLAHOMAN

Oklahoma City, Oklahoma, May 1, 1990

THE knee-jerk reaction of the education establishment to the five-year update of the controversial school assessment, "A Nation at Risk," helps explain why the report finds problems still existing.

The establishment, of course, is made up of people who run the nation's public schools — superintendents, other administrators, principals and teachers. One of the chief representatives is the National Education Association, which seldom manages to see anything good about the Reagan approach to improving schools and always manages to find excuses for spending more federal dollars on the problem.

The immediate reaction from the NEA was expressed in the rally near the White House about the time Secretary of Education William J. Bennett was releasing the update.

The NEA president, Mary Hatwood Futrell, complained the report reads as if the federal government's role in education doesn't exist. Read that as meaning: The federal education budget should be vastly expanded. But Bennett asserted the education establishment wants a whitewash of the problem and a blank check.

Efforts have been made in Oklahoma to improve the schools; to wit, a 1981 law requiring upgraded teacher training and stricter certification procedures. Dr. John Folks, superintendent of public instructions, has pushed a number of reforms.

But Oklahoma, along with the rest of the nation, is still plagued with a high rate of high school dropouts. This was one of the five areas cited by Bennett where work is needed.

The others are: varying quality in school curricula, the rarity of schools for the disadvantaged, hiring and promotion of teachers and administrators in ways that make excellence a matter of chance and the absence of an "ethos of success."

If more money were all it took, these and other problems would have disappeared long ago. The Cato Institute points out total U.S. spending on education has risen from $24.7 billion in 1967 to $165.6 billion in 1980 to $308 billion in 1988. Adjusted for inflation, that's 218 percent in 28 years. Yet, Scholastic Achievement Test scores declined for most of that period.

More public support for education is vital. But the public must be convinced educators are sincerely interested in improving schools, not just their paychecks, before it will increase its support with tax dollars.

The Virginian-Pilot

Norfolk, Virgina, June 3, 1990

In September 1983, just four months after the National Commission on Excellence in Education ("A Nation at Risk") jolted the American people with its claim of a pervasive classroom mediocrity "that threatens our very future as a nation," the Carnegie Foundation for the Advancement of Teaching issued "High School: A Report on Secondary Education in America."

The Carnegie study was highly acclaimed. And the timing of its release — while "A Nation at Risk" was still fresh in the public mind — proved fortuitous: The two reports acted in tandem to increase the national impetus for classroom reform.

Now, as politicians, educators and others assess the impact five years later, the Carnegie group has published a follow-up study titled "Report Card on School Reform: The Teachers Speak."

This study, based on an exhaustive survey, tabulates and interprets responses from more than 13,500 teachers on 55 different issues. The issues range from the highly specific — salaries, in-service education, core requirements for graduation, etc. — to subjective concerns such as community respect for teachers.

The teachers' assessments are not unlike those others have made: Public education has taken measurable strides since 1983, but a long journey remains. Two percent of the teachers gave classroom reform an A, 29 percent a B, 50 percent a C, 13 percent a D, 6 percent an F.

Some of the teachers' perceptions are overwhelmingly positive: 74 percent feel academic expectations for students are higher today; almost two-thirds rate math, reading and writing skills as improved; 74 percent say use of technology for teaching is better; 59 percent cite progress in salary scales.

By contrast, in a whole series of questions on working conditions — class size, non-teaching duties, preparation time, teaching load, etc. — as few as 15 percent to 20 percent cite improvement. Which may account for 49 percent responding that teacher morale is worse and only 23 percent saying morale is better.

The report noted: "The past five years have been special, perhaps unique, in the history of American education. There has been a growing consensus about school goals; the leadership role of the principal has been strengthened; achievement levels of many students have improved. . . ."

But the report focused on a teacher skepticism that persists despite gains in pay and other areas. "Almost forgotten is the fact that, when the renewal movement first began . . . there was a clear signal that teachers were the problem, rather than the solution, and the focus was on failure, not success.

"Further, the reform movement has been driven largely by legislative and administrative intervention. The push has been concerned more with regulation than renewal. Reforms typically have focused on graduation requirements, student achievement, teacher preparation and testing. . . . But in all of these matters, as important as they are, teachers have been largely uninvolved."

So, the report calls for recognition that "whatever is wrong with America's public schools cannot be fixed without the help of those already in the classroom. . . . The challenge now is to move beyond regulations, focus on renewal and make teachers full participants in the process."

This statement makes so much sense it ought to be accepted on its face. But if any skeptic should demand supporting evidence, "Report Card on School Reform: The Teachers Speak" is filled with it.

The Boston Globe

Boston, Massachusetts, July 14, 1990

In the five years since "A Nation At Risk," the report calling for an overhaul of US education, was issued, Americans have heard much about the need to improve schools. The reaction of the educational bureaucracies — officials, superintendents and the leadership of teachers unions — has been simple: give us infusions of cash but do not ask us to change.

This attachment to the status quo is exemplified in the phalanx of educational bureaucracies allied against a pilot program offering open enrollment in suburban schools for students in Boston and Worcester. The plan, sponsored by Senate President William Bulger, is part of a budget package facing Governor Dukakis. The governor should sign the bill.

When the educational bureaucrats define "the system," they usually mean themselves — principals, teachers, school boards, unions, lobbyists, contractors — a permanent interest group. They seldom define the system as the students, whose welfare is the presumed concern of the system but whose tenure in it is short. Because schooling is a once-in-a-lifetime opportunity, students should be given the widest choice available and not imprisoned by geography.

"Clearly, the buildings of many of our suburban neighbors are much more attractive. The milieu of many of our metropolitan-area school systems is much more conducive to teaching and learning," Boston School Superintendent Laval Wilson wrote to Dukakis. That statement sounds like support for the students who would benefit by open enrollment, but Wilson says such a choice "would not be a positive public policy decision."

The governor, who has already shown an admirable willingness to ignore special interests, has a chance to put his pragmatism to work. The educational bureaucracies feel threatened. They do not see open enrollment as a chance to improve all schools through competition. They have budget priorities to advance and political turf to defend.

In this battle, students are innocent bystanders. Dukakis should rescue the students by signing the open enrollment bill.

Bennett Offers Elementary Curriculum

Secretary of Education William J. Bennett, at a Washington, D.C. news conference, Aug. 30, 1988 outlined what he called a model curriculum for the nation's elementary schools.

Bennett's proposal, which covered grades kindergarten through eight, was issued for a fictional James Madison Elementary School. It was considered a sequel to the model curriculum for the nation's high schools that Bennett had offered in 1987.

At the news conference, Bennett asserted that U.S. elementary school students lagged behind their counterparts in other major countries.

"Despite recent advances, the absolute level of American school achievement is still too low," he said.

The centerpiece of the education secretary's latest plan was a rigorous core curriculum of literature, mathematics, science, history, geography, foreign languages, art, music and health.

According to Bennett, grade-school students should be exposed to classic fiction and nonfiction literature as early as possible. Among the book titles he suggested were *The Tales of Pippi Longstocking*, *The Red Badge of Courage* and *Alice's Adventures in Wonderland*.

Math instruction should move away from boring and repetitive lessons toward more interesting and challenging problems, Bennett said. He maintained that students should be taking pre-algebra and algebra by the time they reached the junior high-school level.

In science, the education secretary suggested that fifth-grade students study life sciences, while sixth-, seventh- and eighth-graders should be taught physical science, biology, chemistry and physics.

In social studies, fourth- and fifth-grade students should study American history, sixth- and seventh-graders should study world history, and students in the eighth grade should study U.S. constitutional government and world geography, Bennett proposed.

The Register

Santa Ana, California, August 25, 1988

Five years ago the President's Commission on Excellence in Education issued its famous report, *A Nation at Risk*. It alerted Americans to a "rising tide of mediocrity" spreading through the government (i.e., "public") schools. Crash programs were introduced at many schools to stiffen standards and increase the quality of education. How have these programs fared?

Test scores have inched up a bit. But, as economist Warren Brookes recently noted, the scores have "stalled 74 points below their 1963 levels," and high schools still suffer a 30 percent dropout rate.

Despite this calamitous performance, one area has risen during the past five years: spending of taxpayers' dollars on schooling. The US Department of Education announced that spending per pupil in America has risen to $4,810 in government elementary and secondary schools, up more than $2,000 since 1980. If the spending increase had merely followed the inflation level, school spending would now be only $3,462.

California spending rose slightly less, to $4,319 per pupil, up from $2,918 in 1982-83. Orange County spent $3,255 per pupil in 1986-87, the most recent figures, up from $2,106 in 1980-81.

Spending keeps going up but school achievement remains low. The "tide of mediocrity" has not receded, though it has swallowed billions more in taxpayers' dollars. No surprise. The decline in standards coincides precisely with the involvement of the federal government in schooling, which began in massive amounts in the late 1950s and early 1960s. State involvement in school-

ing has also burgeoned since then, largely responding to the need to administer all those federal bucks.

As a result, local control of government schools has declined sharply. In California today, 75 percent of government school money is doled out by Sacramento; only 25 percent, by local school boards. The result is that parental and community involvement in government schools has withered. It still exists, of course. But, because local school boards are accountable for little, and nowadays don't do much more than administer the edicts of distant state school bureaucrats, no one can be held responsible for the decline in standards. And when no one is responsible, there's no reason to improve things.

And it's going to get worse. Both Michael Dukakis and George Bush promise to spend more billions of dollars on the same old failed federal school programs, which means the "tide of mediocrity" will not ebb. State school bureaucracies will become even more ossified, local school officials even more timid, in the face of the new federal assault.

Perhaps only when the school system decays further will drastic corrective steps be taken to free American education from the strangling grip of government control. A strong impetus to real reform will be the increasing inability of an uneducated populace to compete economically with well-educated Japanese and Europeans. It's obvious what the diagnosis is: American education is sick. Now we need to convince the patient of the cure: freedom from government.

Chicago Tribune

Chicago, Illinois, September 16, 1988

Chicago Democrats are threatening to kill the Chicago school reform bill because they don't like the changes inserted by Gov. Thompson. They're particularly upset by his amendment making the governor an equal partner with the mayor of Chicago in appointing a reform oversight body.

"It is important that Chicagoans run Chicago schools," said State Sen. Richard Newhouse, speaking for the legislature's black caucus.

"The problem is that we have a governor who is not committed to education," said Hank Rubin, former director of the Citizens Schools Committee.

Men from Mars could not come up with two more out-of-touch observations.

Chicagoans run Chicago schools. They will continue to run them if the governor's changes are ratified by the legislature. More specifically, the Chicago Teachers Union and the mayor of Chicago, who has sole authority to appoint the Board of Education, which in turn has sole authority to hire the school superintendent, will continue to run Chicago schools. That is a statement of fact; it is not meant to be reassuring. The same combination of powers has presided over the Chicago school system while it sank to what is arguably the worst in the nation.

And Gov. Thompson gets blamed as the "problem."

Who was ready to pass a tax increase to help public schools, particularly those in Chicago? The Republican governor, grudgingly supported by the Republican leadership from the suburbs. Who killed the tax increase? It was Speaker Michael Madigan, a Democrat from Chicago, and his obedient flock of House Democrats—including all 31 from Chicago.

Who watered down the school reform bill crafted over many months by Chicago parents, civic groups and business leaders? Not Gov. Thompson, not Downstate Republicans, not even those hard-hearted suburbanites. It was the Democratic Speaker of the House from Chicago, the Democratic black caucus from Chicago and the leadership of the Chicago Teachers Union, all fighting for the status quo that has given Chicago children such a miserable education.

This same group delayed action on the bill to postpone its start-up date to July, 1989. And now they would rather see the entire reform effort die than accept the governor's amended version, which does no more than restore the parent-civic coalition's language.

The stand-pat forces know they won't get the supermajority of votes needed to knock out the governor's changes, but they do have enough votes to make it impossible for the pro-reform faction to ratify the amended bill. In that case, the entire bill dies.

A quicker way to kill it has been hatched by Speaker Madigan and his obedient House Democrats. It's described in the letter by Rep. Thomas McCracken in the adjacent column: Madigan's flock will give him the right to rule the bill out of order—preventing the House from voting on it—on the grounds that the governor exceeded his authority with his amendments.

With that brazen power play, the Little Dictator of Springfield will defy the Illinois Constitution, which gives the governor amendatory veto powers, the Illinois Supreme Court, which upheld those powers, and the coalition that worked for a year on school reform.

Awful, isn't it, what those nasty Downstaters and Republicans are doing to Chicago's schools.

THE DAILY OKLAHOMAN
Oklahoma City, Oklahoma, August 27, 1988

EDUCATION shapes up as a big issue in this year's presidential election.

The Republican candidate, Vice President George Bush, has already staked out a position on education. The Democrats scoff that he has come late to this issue and is not really sincere about it.

In the Democrats' view, you can't be sincere about improving education unless you're ready to support a greatly increased federal share in the cost.

Their candidate, Gov. Michael Dukakis, can be counted on to follow this line, which will win him the support of the National Education Association.

Most Americans, judging by the opinion polls, believe the nation's schools can and should be improved. Yet it is not written in stone that the only way to achieve this is to boost federal spending.

Indeed, money alone is not the answer to education reform. In 1988, a Republican task force reports, the nation will spend about 4.1 percent of its gross national product on elementary and secondary education, or $185 billion. More than $56 billion of that has been added since 1982.

The task force, acknowledging the reform movement has brought many improvements, urges "reinvigoration" of the education debate. Attention should be focused, it asserts, on greater accountability by educators, with greater rewards for successful schooling and greater penalties for failures. Along with that should be a strengthening of content and curriculum.

Voters will decide in November which course they prefer.

AKRON BEACON JOURNAL
Akron, Ohio, December 18, 1988

BY NOW, virtually everyone associated with education has been given some share of the blame for children not learning enough in school. Indeed, when public education fails, many are at fault: classroom teachers for not doing their jobs well enough; education professors for not preparing teachers well enough; public officials for not funding schools well enough; school administrators for not setting standards high enough.

Parents, too, are at fault for putting too much of the burden of their children's education on schools and not enough on themselves. Last week, in a new report by the Carnegie Foundation for the Advancement of Teaching, parents got their lashes from teachers. And if what the teachers perceive is correct, then the state of the American home is in more trouble than many of us can imagine.

Teachers in the survey describe students as "emotionally needy" and "starved for attention." A large majority found poverty, poor health, undernourishment and neglect to be problems at their schools.

And a full 90 percent named lack of parental involvement as a problem in their schools.

As Ernest Boyer, the Carnegie Foundation president, pointed out, the teachers' responses suggest America has "not just a school problem, but a youth problem."

Five years ago, the now-famous *A Nation at Risk* report shocked the nation with its grim assessment of public education. This new Carnegie report, based on a survey of 22,000 public school teachers — the most comprehensive study of teacher attitudes to date — is shocking as well.

Of course, efforts to reform the schools should continue. Academic standards should be higher, for example, and pupils should not advance from the primary grades without a solid foundation in reading and mathematics.

But change from within, as much as that is needed, will not be enough to solve education's problems. Children cannot help but take their personal troubles to school, where the teacher must deal with them.

Indeed, the nation faces a "youth problem." Poverty, drug use, homelessness and hunger are aspects of that problem. School reform will have limited success while those problems persist for so many.

Arkansas Gazette
Little Rock, Arkansas, August 27, 1988

Educational reform is a phrase always in search of definition. Ideas are not reform unless they actually work, actually increase learning.

We are learning which among the innovations of the Arkansas school movement at mid-decade have worked, although final judgments will have to wait years more. A three-year study commissioned by the Winthrop Rockefeller Foundation and directed by the Carnegie Foundation for the Advancement of Teaching analyzed the major elements of Gov. Clinton's school program of 1983-84.

Scores on standardized tests were the basis of part of the evaluation, but more convincing were surveys and interviews with thousands of teachers and administrators. There was an overwhelming consensus on only one change: the reduction in class sizes. Other elements of the accreditation standards adopted in 1984 — broadened secondary courses, tougher graduation requirements, performance testing of students, programs for gifted and talented students, course content guides, longer school days and school years — were thought by most to have helped but there was substantial disagreement.

Opinions changed from the adoption of the standards and other new programs until their final implementation in 1987. In 1984, the test of teachers' basic skills was considered an important reform, not only among community leaders but with a high percentage of teachers and administrators as well. Reduced class sizes, which were mandated by the standards, was not ranked highly.

By last year, almost no one thought the teacher test had improved education. Ninety-nine percent of the teachers thought the smaller class sizes had improved teaching and learning. Even in cases where classes were reduced by only one or two students, teachers said it made a difference in how they were able to teach and the time spent organizing and disciplining classes.

The standards required schools to have no more than 20 in kindergarten classes with progressively higher limits for higher grades. At that, classes are still well above those where research has shown that dramatic improvement in learning occurs in the critical years, kindergarten and the primary grades. It is particularly vital where many students reach school deprived and needing the attention that can only be given in small groups.

There is a message here on how the state should spend its money and its energy on the next round of educational reform.

The Duluth News-Tribune
Duluth, Minnesota, May 21, 1988

Speaking of school reform — and lots of people, including us, have been lately — we'll offer a few more thoughts on the topic:

☐ The operation of our public schools is so important and so imperfect that reform is a logical and necessary topic.

☐ We mustn't let our collective guilt over school failures end in ill-conceived reforms that do more harm than good.

☐ Reform shouldn't be trivialized by becoming one of 1988's fad issues (the omnipresent war on drugs is clearly one already).

Columnist Joan Beck has some thoughts elsewhere on this page on a business approach to the school reform topic, an approach that sounds good, at least in principle.

Gov. Rudy Perpich, who laudably wants to make Minnesota the Brain State, has other ideas — many of which have great appeal and some of which have already become law.

The governor Thursday urged a study of more reforms for consideration in the 1989 legislative session — including the ticklish one of using tests to make local districts more accountable to taxpayers, parents and, presumably, state government.

Friday's News-Tribune told of a Chicago class that will have to go to summer school because, school officials say, their teacher can't teach or maintain discipline, and four principals have been unable to fire her.

Our general comments today won't allow conclusions on these or other school reform issues. But we'll plead for serious thinking on the topic and that top priority goes to the key elements: the students who must learn and the teachers who must help them.

We mustn't let such things as accountability, testing, vouchers, early childhood education, open enrollment, and other concepts become set in concrete in ways that imprison the young minds in our schools.

Census Pegs Adult Illiteracy at 13%; NEA Report Faults Reading Skills

Studies over the years have indicated that the number of years of education positively correlates with skill levels and with earnings but only indirectly measures occupational skills. Some high school dropouts may have the same reading and math skills as high school graduates. The illiteracy rate is a reasonable measure of skill levels: individuals who fail to meet minimal competency levels generally lack skills. Because most jobs require workers with basic reading, writing and math proficiency, basic competency is essential to function effectively in today's labor market, even in most entry-level jobs. Low competency usually correlates with low earnings and low educational attainment.

A U.S. Census Bureau study had found a 13% illiteracy rate among adults living in the U.S., the *New York Times* reported April 21, 1986. The bureau said the study provided the most accurate measure yet of U.S. illiteracy. The Census Bureau's last estimate of adult illiteracy, in 1979, had placed the rate at just 0.5% for those over age 14. That figure was based simply on how many of those surveyed reported fewer than six years of education. The new estimate derived from a 26-question multiple-choice test given to 3,400 adults in 1982. The sample did not include prisoners or hospital patients. A score of fewer than 20 correct answers was taken to show illiteracy.

Critics contended that many of the questions were framed in bureaucratic language difficult even for literate citizens to understand. But they disagreed on whether the survey's estimate of the illiteracy rate was too high or too low.

According to the Census Bureau, the test results showed an illiteracy rate of 9% among U.S. adults whose native language was English. But that figure rose to 48% among adults for whom English was a second language.

Of all adult illiterates, 51% were found to live in small towns and suburbs and 41% in metropolitan areas. 41% were found to be English-speaking whites, 22% black and 22% Spanish-speaking. A plurality, 40%, were aged 20 to 39. These results were reported in the May 5, 1986 issue of *Time* magazine. About 60% of native English speakers who had graduated from high school answered every question correctly; 70% of those who had failed had not finished high school; and 42% had been without work for a year before taking the test.

Most U.S. students were "unable to write adequately except in response to the simplest of tasks," according to a report released Dec. 3, 1986 by the National Assessment of Educational Progress. The study, entitled "Writing Report Card," found among other things, that fewer than 25% of the high school students surveyed had performed adequately on tests of the writing skills needed for success in business, the professions or academic study. Fewer than 33% of all the students surveyed had been able to adequately back up a point with evidence, and students at all levels were found "deficient in higher-order thinking skills." The study drew on writing samples from 55,000 public and private school students in the fourth, eighth and 11th grades.

Richmond Times-Dispatch
Richmond, Virginia, September 1, 1988

The National Assessment of Educational Progress has found that almost 40 percent of 13-year-olds lack such "intermediate" reading skills as the ability to locate information within a paragraph or to draw logical conclusions based on what they have read. Non-readers who try to land good jobs in this Information Age will be severely handicapped; moreover, they will miss the pure enjoyment of great literature.

Government-sponsored tomes do not always help in the struggle against illiteracy; in fact, they may be so ponderous as to make readers want to renounce the pastime. A notable exception is a slim, easy-to-read booklet entitled "Becoming a Nation of Readers: What Parents Can Do." Published by D. C. Heath and Co. in cooperation with the Office of Educational Research and Improvement, this publication goes beyond the usual advice.

Yes, parents should read aloud to their preschoolers, and often. That is the "single most important activity" for building a knowledge base for eventual success in reading. But the "what" and "how" of reading to children are important, too. This booklet offers many possible sources of reading material and techniques for making reading-time a family "social event" and jumping-off point for lively discussions. And in the process of reading to tots, parents can begin acquainting their children with written language and the association between sounds and letters. Something like the "M" shape of McDonald's golden arches can be a starting place. Having children dictate journals or stories, or make letter scrapbooks are some good ways for child and parent to enjoy language together.

The publication also provides tips for supporting children's continued growth as readers. "Parents of children who become successful readers," it states, "monitor their children's progress in school, become involved in school programs, support homework, buy their children books or take them to libraries, encourage reading as a free-time activity, and place reasonable limits on such activities as TV viewing." (Ten hours a week is suggested as a prudent upper limit; research has shown that more TV time than that impedes children's learning.)

"Becoming a Nation of Readers: What Parents Can Do" is 26 pages of good ideas priced at just 50 cents per copy. Contact the Consumer Information Center, Pueblo, Colo. 81009.

PORTLAND
EVENING EXPRESS
Portland, Maine, July 31, 1988

Both in Maine and across the nation it's estimated one in five citizens cannot read well enough to order dinner off a simple menu tonight or figure out from printed listings what they want to watch on TV.

Functional illiteracy forces between 23 million and 27 million Americans into lives without choice, lives where "Have it your way" means nothing because they don't know how many ways there can be.

It's a crippling disability both at home and in the work place. And it can only get worse.

Technological change paired with global competition is remaking the marketplace, leaving little room for Americans who can't read. As of now, 40 percent of all jobs can be held by persons who failed to finish high school. By the end of the century, however, that number is expected to plummet to just 14 percent.

Sen. George J. Mitchell explains why. "We are moving from a manufacturing economy to a service economy. We will rely more on brains than on muscle," Mitchell warns. Without improvement in their literacy, many people will be left behind.

To forestall that, Mitchell, together with Sen. Paul Simon, D-Ill., and 10 other senators, has introduced legislation designed to boost existing literacy programs. The measure would allocate $225 million in 1990 to expanding programs such as the Vista Literacy Corps, the Library Literacy Program and adult education.

The bill would also support public-private efforts to improve adult literacy and funnel money into literacy programs conducted in the workplace.

Essentially, the point is to make it as easy as possible for Americans to confront their inability to read and do something about it.

All in service of a single word: F-u-t-u-r-e.

THE ROANOKE TIMES
Roanoke, Virginia, July 20, 1988

ONLY IN AMERICA? No, the British, too, aren't teaching English the way they should. That's the complaint of none less than Prince Charles; his own staff, he says, can't speak or write the language properly.

"All the letters sent from my office I have to correct myself," he said, "and that is because English is taught so bloody badly." Strong talk: In Great Britain, "bloody" borders on obscenity.

But the prince evidently feels strongly. He was criticizing a new national curriculum, to go into effect this fall for Brits 5 to 7 years old, that would further weaken educational levels. A study committee that recommended the new curriculum said that standard English is just one dialect of many and "should not be confused with 'proper,' 'good' or 'correct English.' "

A bit of class conflict is involved here. In Britain's "public" (actually private) schools, the upper classes get more stringent instruction in standard English, and in their circles, the rules of the language's use are more strictly observed. But those who educate the masses contend that while standard English should be taught, children ought not be barred from speaking their own dialects "where appropriate." Irregular forms such as "he ain't" and "done good" do not hinder real communication, they say, but are only "social irritants."

Social or not, the prince is royally irritated. He's right to be.

Granted, the English language was not handed down, engraved on stone tablets, from some mountaintop. It is a dynamic thing, changing and growing. What's accepted now in everyday use was once subnormal, and sometimes vice versa.

But from this, it follows that there is, at any given time, a form of standard, accepted speech and (usually stricter) written English. This form is not, as some may think, fancified and complex; at its best, it clarifies and strengthens expression. It improves communication. Others, if taught and skilled in standard English, understand it better. And unless one uses good English from habit, one needs to know grammatical terms and rules in order to find and correct one's own errors.

Various groups may have their own patois that they use among themselves, but for common ground with other groups they need standard English. They vary from it at their peril. Whenever a listener or reader begins to pay more attention to the way another speaks or writes than what is being said or written, the message gets garbled or lost. That is what we hear the prince saying. If educators cannot understand him, they are victims of their own methods.

The Atlanta Journal
AND
THE ATLANTA CONSTITUTION
Atlanta, Georgia, April 30, 1988

While it is tempting to think of illiteracy as a significant problem only in backwater countries where schooling is neither free nor mandatory, nothing could be further from the truth.

In Georgia alone, a staggering 1.7 million people are unable to decipher the instructions on a medicine bottle — or read these words.

Even more shocking is what happened to a 52-year-old north Fulton County man who grew weary of hiding his handicap and having to rely on others.

Horse-breeder Sonny Johnson has made the rounds of local literacy programs in recent years, attending, he guesses, 60 classes in his search for a program that can teach him to read. He has not found one, to his exasperation — and the distress of some of those trying to reach him.

He has wound up in literacy programs designed for Hispanics, who already read and write in their native language; in programs that relied on poorly trained volunteers who didn't always show up for their appointed sessions, and in programs that met, embarrassingly, in fast-food restaurants or other public places where a grown man trying to sound out the vowels and consonants in a third-grade primer might have stood out and been subjected to ridicule.

His illiteracy was itself a barrier to hooking up with the right program, since he couldn't read a telephone directory or public service announcement. The most promising programs were too far away.

And if the handful of Georgians trickling into celebrated downtown programs like Literacy Action Inc. are any indication, few exhibit Mr. Johnson's perseverance.

Something's got to give, if the Sunbelt Institute is right in predicting a collision course between between two demographic trends: a shrinking pool of workers and a rising demand for those with at least two years of education beyond high school.

Some of the answers are fairly obvious. Programs must be overhauled and satellite learning centers opened in rural and inner-city areas and workplaces.

Some solutions are not. Failures issue not so much from lack of resources, program operators complain, as from a lack of students, a problem not adequately addressed by either the federal government or the private sector.

Television and radio, the keys to reaching the functionally illiterate, are not being used — or generating their own public-service announcements — nearly enough.

Businesses have been slow to follow the example of a Columbus firm, now working with local schools to start basic skills classes for 300 of its employees and to assure employees that those who seek help won't be dismissed if they are found out.

If, as is sometimes said, identifying the problem is half the battle, the way is clear. Georgia has an illiteracy problem of staggering proportions — and no time to lose.

INDEX

C